Untapped Power

Contributor List

Carla Koppell, Editor, has worked in over thirty countries to resolve conflict and promote development. Her work in conflict affected and fragile states encompasses efforts to advance peace negotiations and mediation; to oversee the provision of humanitarian relief, and to enhance civilian protection and reconstruction. She has also fostered global development, particularly through advancing women's empowerment and gender equality; combatting climate change and promoting alternative energy sources; and by improving housing and urban development.

Currently, Koppell is senior advisor for diversity, equity and inclusion and teaches at the Edmund A. Walsh School of Foreign Service at Georgetown University. She is also a distinguished fellow with the Georgetown Institute for Women, Peace and Security. Her work encompasses collaborating with deans of graduate schools of international affairs and public policy nationwide to better address diversity, equity and inclusion. Previously, she was a vice president with the U.S. Institute for Peace, as well as chief strategy officer and senior coordinator for gender equality and women's empowerment for USAID. Koppell has also served as Deputy Assistant Secretary for International Affairs with the U.S. Department of Housing and Urban Development, and directed the Institute for Inclusion Security. Her career began with the Food and Agriculture Organization of the United Nations. Koppell received a Bachelor of Science degree from Cornell University, and a Master of Public Policy degree from the Harvard Kennedy School.

Sayed Ikram Afzali is the Executive Director of Integrity Watch. He served as the Chief Information Commissioner of Afghanistan (2015–2018) and was the architect behind Afghanistan's Access to Information Law. Afzali plays a leading role in many transparency and accountability initiatives, including the Construction Sector Transparency Initiative, the Extractive Sector Transparency Initiative, and the Open Government Partnership. He has also been involved in anti-corruption institution-building, including in the establishment of the Access to Information Commission and Transparency Afghanistan. Afzali has degrees from the London School of Economics and Political Science and the American University of Afghanistan.

Sabina Anne Espinoza advises the World Bank on social inclusion, equality, poverty reduction, and human rights. She leads research and provides project support on issues around the exclusion of vulnerable and discriminated groups. Previously, she was an advisor for the UN Global Compact and the European Parliament on human rights and social issues, and worked for the Platform for International Cooperation on Undocumented Migrants (PICUM), a network of nongovernmental organizations supporting migrants' rights. She also taught courses on research methods and international human rights standards and institutions for the master's degree program at the School of Public Policy at University College London. Sabina holds a PhD in political science and a master's degree in human rights from University College London, as well as a bachelor's degree in philosophy, politics, and economics from the University of Oxford.

Michael Ashley Stein cofounded and is Executive Director of the Harvard Law School Project on Disability and Visiting Professor of Law at the Harvard Law School. Considered one of the world's leading experts on disability law and policy, Dr. Stein served as legal counsel to Rehabilitation International, Disabled Peoples' International, and Special Olympics International throughout the drafting of the Convention on the Rights of Persons with Disabilities, and has subsequently worked on implementing disability rights projects in forty-three countries He holds a JD from Harvard Law School and a PhD from Cambridge University.

Teuta Avdimetaj is a Researcher at the Kosovar Centre for Security Studies, where she focuses on several topics: preventing and countering violent extremism, gender and security, democratization, and the intersection between technology and security. She holds a master's degree in security studies from Georgetown University. Teuta previously served as a Policy Advisor to the fourth President of the Republic of Kosovo and as an External Advisor in the Ministry for European Integration in Kosovo. She has also consulted for international organizations, including the International Organization for Migration, the Commission for International Justice and Accountability US, the Tony Blair Institute for Global Change, and the Center for Research on Extremism (C-REX).

Daniel Baer is a senior fellow at the Carnegie Endowment for International Peace. . Previously, Baer was US ambassador to the Organization for Security and Cooperation in Europe (OSCE) and a Deputy Assistant Secretary of State for Democracy, Human Rights, and Labor. He was assistant professor at Georgetown's McDonough School of Business, Faculty Fellow at Harvard's Safra Center for Ethics, and project leader at the Boston Consulting Group. Baer holds a doctorate from Oxford and a degree in social studies and African American studies from Harvard. He lives in Colorado with his husband, Brian.

Gary Barker is CEO and founder of Promundo, which has worked for twenty years in more than forty countries. Beginning in low-income areas of Rio de Janeiro, Brazil, Promundo's approaches have been incorporated into ministries of health and education around the world. Gary is cofounder of MenCare, a global campaign working in forty-five countries to promote men's involvement as caregivers, and cofounder of MenEngage, a global alliance of more than 700 NGOs. He created and leads the International Men and Gender Equality Survey (IMAGES), the largest-ever survey of men's attitudes and behaviors related to violence, fatherhood, and gender equality. He holds a PhD in developmental psychology.

Michelle Barsa specializes in models of inclusion for peace and security processes, with an emphasis on women and civil society. She currently serves as the Program Director for Democracy and Social Identity at Beyond Conflict and recently held senior advisory positions on countering violent extremism at USAID, the US Department of Homeland Security, and Equal Access International. Previously, as a director at the Washington, D.C.–based Inclusive Security, she advised on US foreign policy related to women, peace, and security, in addition to leading initiatives in Syria, Afghanistan, Pakistan, Palestine, Sudan, Libya, and Nigeria. She also regularly advises the US Departments of Defense and State, the United Nations, and NATO on how to improve the effectiveness of security assistance provided to partner nations. She holds a master's degree from the Fletcher School of Law and Diplomacy at Tufts University and a bachelor's degree in finance and philosophy from Boston College.

Shaazka Beyerle is a researcher, writer, and educator in nonviolent action. She is a Senior Fellow at the Terrorism, Transnational Crime and Corruption Center (TraCCC), Schar School of Policy and Government, George Mason University, and former Senior Research Advisor with the Program on Nonviolent Action at the United States Institute of Peace. From December 2015 to June 2017 she was lead researcher for a World Bank–Nordic Trust Fund project and coauthor of *Citizens as Drivers of Change: Practicing Human Rights to Engage with the State and Promote Transparency and Accountability*. In 2016, she was visiting professor at the University for Peace (Costa Rica). She is author of *Curtailing Corruption: People Power for Accountability and Justice* and *Freedom from Corruption: A Curriculum for People Power Movements, Campaigns and Civic Initiatives*. Beyerle holds a master's degree in international relations from George Washington University and a bachelor's degree in psychology and women's studies from the University of Toronto.

Elis Borde is Assistant Professor at the Faculty of Medicine of the Federal University of Minas Gerais (UFMG) in Belo Horizonte, Brazil. She holds a doctorate in public health from the National University of Colombia and a master's degree in public health from the Brazilian National School of Public Health. Her research focuses on urban violence, social determinants of health and health inequities. Recent publications include "Masculinities and Nonviolence in Contexts of Chronic Urban Violence," in *International Development Planning Review* (January 2020), and "Revisiting the Social Determinants of Health Agenda from the Global South," in *Global Public Health* (June–July 2019).

Maitreyi Bordia Das is Practice Manager in the Urban, Resilience and Land Global Practice of the World Bank. Previously, she was the Bank's first Global Lead on Social Inclusion. She has long-standing research and policy experience in social protection and social development, gender, urban issues, water and sanitation, demography and health. She is the lead author of the World Bank's flagship report on social inclusion, "Inclusion Matters: The Foundation for Shared Prosperity," among other noteworthy publications. She started her career as a lecturer in St. Stephen's College, University of Delhi. She has also been a MacArthur Fellow at the Harvard Center of Population and Development Studies and an advisor to the United Nations Development Program. She has a PhD in sociology (demography) from the University of Maryland. Before joining the World Bank, Dr. Das was in the Indian Administrative Service (IAS).

Yvette Burton, PhD, is an Adjunct Professor at New York University's School of Professional Studies, and Chief People Innovation Officer for a publicly traded fintech company. Burton's current business research examines the structure of work-based teams and disruptive innovation. She is a Professor of Practice Emeritus at Columbia University's School of Professional Studies, and served in a variety of roles for the Clinton and Obama administrations. She was awarded the Crown Prince of Dubai's 2019 Business Innovation Award, and is listed in the Crain NY Business list of Top 40 LGBT Executives. She has held senior executive leadership roles in the public and private sectors, including previous leadership roles at Ernst and Young LLP, Lockheed Martin, Deloitte Consulting LLP, IBM, and the New York City Department of Health. She currently serves as Board President of Pride Live's Stonewall Day, a global social media campaign for LGBT equity and civil rights.

Joshua Castellino is Executive Director of Minority Rights Group International and Professor of Law at Middlesex University, London. He was founding Dean of the School of Law at Middlesex, and holds visiting professorial positions in the United Kingdom, Ireland, Hungary, Poland, and Italy. He worked as a journalist in Mumbai, India, was awarded a Chevening Scholarship, and completed his PhD in International Law in the United Kingdom (1998). He has authored and edited eight books in international law, on self-determination, title to territory, minorities, and indigenous peoples' rights, and several articles on a range of these and other legal subtopics.

Amelia Cotton Corl is an expert in international development, strategy, and program management. Her most recent work has focused on improving program management and monitoring and evaluation practices in conflict and post-conflict environments. Additional projects have focused on using framing theory and discourse analysis to examine violations of human rights, including female genital cutting and conscription of child combatants. She spent nearly a decade working at the US Agency for International Development and the US Institute of Peace. Amelia received her BA from Macalester College and completed graduate work in sociology and human rights at the University of Minnesota.

Charlie Damon has more than fifteen years' experience in the nongovernmental organization sector, predominantly in the area of gender and disaster management. Charlie is currently the CARE Australia Pacific Humanitarian Capacity Coordinator responsible for supporting local partners in Fiji, Solomon Islands, and Tonga in implementing their disaster management programs with a gender and social inclusion lens. Charlie has lived and worked in Vanuatu, Timor Leste, and Mali managing gender, disaster management, and youth programs and has deployed to support or manage disaster preparedness and response programs in Solomon Islands, Tonga, Laos, Cambodia, Indonesia, and Myanmar.

Hugo van der Merwe has worked as a civil society activist and scholar for the last twenty-five years, evaluating South African and other African transitional justice processes, developing interventions, and advocating for ways that these programs can better serve victims, promote sustainable peace, and fight impunity. As Research Director at the Centre for the Study of Violence and Reconciliation, and Founding Editor in Chief of the *International Journal of Transitional Justice*, he has participated in promoting this critical policy engagement and empirical evaluation of peacebuilding processes across African and the globe. He holds a PhD in conflict analysis and resolution from George Mason University.

Lara Domínguez, is Acting Head of Litigation at Minority Rights Group (MRG). She oversees MRG's strategic litigation on behalf of minorities and indigenous communities around the world. Prior to joining MRG, Lara worked at Three Crowns LLP and specialized in international arbitration. She received her JD from Yale Law School, where she was student director of the Immigration Legal Services Clinic, a member of the Allard K. Lowenstein International Human Rights Clinic, and a Herbert J. Hansell student fellow at the Center for Global and Legal Challenges. She has published white papers and academic articles on various topics of international and human rights law.

Maksym Eristavi is a prominent Eastern European writer and journalist. A self-described "bridge-builder," he amplifies and explains stories from global front lines for equal human rights. His works sits at the nexus of disinformation, foreign policy, and identity politics. Eristavi is one of the few openly queer journalists in the region and has been outspoken in raising regional civil rights issues abroad. He has contributed to news outlets globally and has testified before national officials in the United States and in Europe. Eristavi is a senior fellow with the Center for European Policy Analysis.

Claudia Escobar Mejía is a former magistrate of the Court of Appeals of Guatemala and is recognized internationally as a corruption fighter. She is a visiting professor and researcher at the Terrorism, Transnational Crime and Corruption Center at George Mason University and the executive director of Be Just. She obtained her PhD at the Universidad Autónoma de Barcelona, and her law degree at the Universidad Francisco Marroquín in Guatemala. Georgetown University's Walsh School of Foreign Service elected her as a Centennial Fellow. Previously, she was a fellow at Harvard University–Radcliffe Institute for Advanced Study. She was honored by the National Endowment for Democracy in 2016 with the Democracy Award.

Sarah Federman came to the University of Baltimore as an assistant professor in the School of Public and International Affairs after completing her doctorate at George Mason University's School for Conflict Analysis and Resolution as a Presidential Scholar. Federman is also a Fulbright Specialist in Peace and Conflict, and a regular guest instructor at the Foreign Service Institute at the US Department of State. Federman's coauthored textbook *Introduction to Conflict Resolution Discourses and Dynamics* offers a genealogical overview of the field. She has taught at SciencesPo and Grinnell College and given invited talks at Harvard University, Johns Hopkins University, McGill University, and elsewhere.

Wazhma Frogh, an International Woman of Courage, is an activist and civil society leader. She was a member of Afghanistan's High Peace Council in 2017 and 2018, appointed by the President of Afghanistan to mediate with the Taliban. Frogh founded the Women and Peace Studies Organization and mediated inter-community disputes around land, water and other resources.

From 2016 to 2018, she served as elected cochair of the Afghan Women, Peace and Security Working Group for implementation of the National Action Plan on UN Security Council Resolution 1325. Previously, Frogh worked for several international civil society organizations and donor country governments in Afghanistan and Pakistan. She received a master's degree in law and human rights from the University of Warwick.

Leymah Gbowee is a Liberian Peace Activist, trained Social Worker and women's rights advocate. A 2011 Nobel Peace Prize winner, she established and is the current President of the Gbowee Peace Foundation Africa, which provides educational and leadership opportunities to women and young people in West Africa and around the world. She also currently serves as the Executive Director of the Women, Peace and Security Program at Columbia University's Earth Institute. She cofounded and is a former Executive Director of the Women Peace and Security Network Africa (WIPSEN-A). She is also a founding member and former Liberia Coordinator of Women in Peacebuilding Network (WIPNET).

Anne Marie Goetz is a global leader in the field of women, peace and security. As a professor with the New York University Center for Global Affairs, she is analyzing how development efforts in fragile states advance the interests of marginalized groups. Previously, Goetz was Policy Director of Governance, Peace and Security with UN Women. Earlier in her career, she worked for the Institute of Development Studies at the University of Sussex and with the United Nations Development Programme in Chad and Guinea. She has authored seven books on gender, politics, and policy in developing countries and on accountability reforms. She has a PhD from the University of Cambridge.

Eduardo González is a Peruvian sociologist who served on the managerial team of Peru's Truth and Reconciliation Commission. He went on to serve at the International Center for Transitional Justice, where he supported the work of about twenty truth commissions and similar initiatives worldwide. Since 2015, as an independent consultant, he has continued to support transitional justice processes across the globe, including local truth commissions in the United States. He holds a master's degree in sociology from the New School for Social Research.

Zuhra Halimova has more than twenty years of experience working on post-conflict transitions. She was an observer with the Inter-Tajik Dialogue, a Track II diplomacy effort that brought together factions from the Tajik Civil War until the signing of the 1997 peace treaty. She was previously Executive Director of the Open Society Institute Assistance Foundation (OSF) in Tajikistan. Currently, Halimova is a member of the Transition Assistance Practice Group of the Institute for Integrated Transitions and the Asian Women in International Affairs Initiative. She has a master's degree in international relations from the Fletcher School of Law and Diplomacy, Tufts University, and a master's degree from the Department of Oriental Studies of Tajik State University.

Pip Henty is passionate about enhancing the effectiveness, efficiency, and appropriateness of humanitarian action, with a focus on diversity, inclusion, equity and equality. She currently leads Humanitarian Action Group's multiyear research exploring diverse and inclusive humanitarian leadership. Over the past eight years, she has worked in operational and technical roles in the not-for-profit and private sectors, including in the areas of international development and humanitarian action across the Asia and Pacific regions, including in Fiji, Vanuatu, Tonga, Indonesia, and Thailand. Recently, she developed and piloted a framework to measure women's leadership in COVID-19 response in the Asia-Pacific; conducted research on humanitarian civil-military coordination; developed strategies for gender equality in the emergency management sector across the Pacific; and worked with humanitarian organizations to strengthen and embed approaches to localization. She holds a master's degree in international development from La Trobe University and is currently Deputy Chair and Lead of the Access and Inclusion committee for Minus18.

Lisa Hilbink's work centers on the judicial role in democracy and democratization, with a particular focus on Latin America and Iberia. She is an Associate Professor of Political Science at the University of Minnesota, Twin Cities. Dr. Hilbink is a two-time Fulbright grantee to Chile and Spain, and before joining the faculty at Minnesota was a postdoctoral fellow in the Society of Fellows at Princeton University and lecturer in the Princeton School of Public and International Affairs. She currently leads research examining the origins of public perceptions of judicial institutions and their consequences for access to justice in the Americas.

Atifete Jahjaga served as the fourth President of the Republic of Kosovo, the first woman to hold that post. She was Kosovo's first nonpartisan presidential candidate, the first female head of state in the modern Balkans, and the youngest woman to be elected to a country's highest office. She worked diligently to bring women to the forefront of Kosovo's political, economic, and social life. In 2012, she hosted an international women's summit, "Partnership for Change—Empowering Women," which brought together about 200 women leaders from around the world. In 2014, Jahjaga established the National Council for Survivors of Sexual Violence During the War in Kosovo. She is a member of the Council of Women World Leaders and is a recipient of numerous honors and awards, including an honorary doctorate from the University of Durham (2013), the Leadership in Public Service Award from the Clinton Global Initiative (2014), and an honorary doctorate of laws from the University of Leicester (2015). In March 2018, she established the Jahjaga Foundation, which focuses on empowering youth and women for social change in Kosovo.

Janet E. Lord is an international human rights lawyer and inclusive development expert. She served as legal counsel to Disabled Peoples International and several lead governments throughout the drafting of the Convention on the Rights of Persons with Disabilities. She brings more than fifteen years of practice in designing, implementing, monitoring, and evaluating disability rights and inclusive development programming in more than forty countries. She holds an LLM in international and comparative law with highest honors from the George Washington University Law School and an LLB and LLM from the University of Edinburgh in Scotland. She sits on the Board of Directors for Amnesty International USA.

Nomathamsanqa Masiko-Mpaka is a feminist peace advocate and human rights activist. She has extensive experience in women's rights programming, research, policy analysis, and advocacy, with a particular focus on gender-based violence and women, peace, and security. She is the Gender, Human Rights and Human Security Programme Manager at the Embassy of Ireland in Pretoria. Previously, she was a Senior Advocacy Officer at the Centre for the Study of Violence and Reconciliation in Cape Town. She has worked for the Institute for Security Studies, the Centre for Conflict Resolution, the African Leadership Centre, and the Institute of African Studies at the University of Ghana. She holds a bachelor's degree in political science and public policy administration from the University of Cape Town, a master's degrees in international relations from Stellenbosch University, and a master's degree in security, leadership, and society from King's College, London.

Tatiana Moura is a Senior Researcher at the Centre for Social Studies at the University of Coimbra (Portugal), where she coordinates European projects and programs focusing on masculinities, gender equality, fatherhood, and caregiving. She is also Coordinator of Promundo Portugal. Between 2011 and 2019 she was the Executive Director of Instituto Promundo (Rio de Janeiro, Brazil), and led several projects on masculinities, violence, and nonviolent trajectories in urban peripheries, particularly in Latin America. Her research interests include feminism and international relations, masculinities, new wars, and urban violence. She holds a doctoral degree in peace, conflicts, and democracy.

Katia Papagianni directs Policy and Mediation Support for the Geneva-based HD Centre. Her work focuses on the design of peace processes. She has supported peace processes in Liberia, Nigeria, Libya, Syria, Myanmar, Thailand, the Philippines, and Ukraine. She was seconded to the United Nations to support the national dialogue in Yemen in 2012–2013. Previously, she worked for the National Democratic Institute, the OSCE, the UN Office of the High Commissioner on Human Rights, and UNDP in Russia, Bosnia and Herzegovina, and Iraq. She holds a PhD from Columbia University and has taught at Geneva's Graduate Institute for International and Development Studies and at Columbia University.

Colette Rausch is a research professor at George Mason University's Mary Hoch Center for Reconciliation. Previously, she was a senior advisor with the United States Institute of Peace. She has more than twenty years' experience in more than two dozen countries across the globe. Her work and publications focus on justice, security and rule of law, transitional justice, reconciliation, and post-conflict transitions. Rausch previously held positions with the Organization for Security and Cooperation in Europe in Kosovo; the US Department of Justice in Bosnia and Hungary; the Nevada US Attorney's Office; the Nevada Attorney General's Office; and the Nevada Federal Public Defender's Office. She received degrees from the University of Nevada, Reno and Santa Clara University School of Law.

Lakshitha Saji Prelis has more than twenty years' experience working with youth movements in conflict and transition environments in more than thirty-five countries. He has advised governments about ways to engage young people. As the cochair of the Global Coalition on Youth, Peace and Security, he co-led successful advocacy for the UN Security Council Resolution 2250 (2015), Resolution 2419 (2018), and Resolution 2535 (2020). Prelis is also the director of children and youth programs at Search for Common Ground (SFCG). Prior to joining SFCG, he was the founding director of the Peacebuilding and Development Institute at American University (AU) in Washington, D.C. Over eleven years at AU resulted in him co-developing more than a hundred training curricula exploring the nexus of peacebuilding with development from a human-centered perspective. Saji received the distinguished Luxembourg Peace Prize for Outstanding Achievements in Peace Support and obtained his master's degree in international peace and conflict resolution from American University in Washington, D.C.

Madison Schramm is an Assistant Professor in the Department of National Security and Strategy at the US Army War College. Prior to joining the War College, she was a postdoctoral fellow at the Institute for Politics and Strategy at Carnegie Mellon University (2020–2021), the Postdoctoral Fellow in Innovative Approaches to Grand Strategy at the International Security Center at the University of Notre Dame (2019–2020), and the Hillary Rodham Clinton Research Fellow at the Georgetown Institute for Women, Peace, and Security (2018–2019). She received her PhD from Georgetown University in Government. Her dissertation, "Making Meaning and Making Monsters: Democracies, Personalist Regimes, and International Conflict," received the 2020 Kenneth N. Waltz Best Dissertation Award from the American Political Science Association's International Security Section.

Meaghan Shoemaker holds a PhD in international relations and military and defense studies from Queen's University, Kingston, Ontario. Her work and research focus on diversity and the integration of women into international organizations and national militaries, as well as the transition of military personnel to civilian life. She has worked with Canada's Department of National Defence and conducted research with NATO and the Danish armed forces.

Henny Slegh is a Dutch-trained psychotherapist and medical anthropologist specializing in mental health, gender, and culture in conflict areas. She is director of international programs for Living Peace Institute DRC and senior fellow for Promundo US. She is based in Mali and has lived and worked in African countries for more than fifteen years. She coordinated IMAGES studies in Rwanda, DRC, Mali, and Mozambique for Promundo, and she is coauthor of the Living Peace methodology in DRC, a gender-specific mental health and psychosocial support model that she has adapted for youth in DRC and the far north of Cameroon, for Syrian refugees in Lebanon, and for former combatants in DRC. Currently, she is coordinating a study to develop a contextualized violence prevention program for adolescents in Mali.

Kate Sutton is a leading contributor to the humanitarian sector in Australia and the region. She has spent more than twenty years in operational and leadership roles in international organizations, including eight years field-based in humanitarian contexts. Kate has a specialist interest in humanitarian protection and displacement, and technical expertise in research, evaluations, training, and facilitation. Kate's recent work includes undertaking evaluations of Australia's humanitarian assistance in Syria, Vanuatu, and Myanmar, and coauthoring The Sphere Handbook chapter on Protection Principles. Kate was selected as one of Australia's top 100 Women of Influence in 2015 and has also recently published work on women in humanitarian leadership.

Valmaine Toki was the first New Zealander appointed by the President of the UN Economic and Social Council as an Expert Member on the UN Permanent Forum on Indigenous Issues, where she served two terms. Professor Toki is of Ngatiwai, Ngapuhi descent and holds a BA, LLB (Hons), MBA, LLM, and PhD in law from Te Piringa, Faculty of Law, University of Waikato, New Zealand. Her research, writing, and teaching are in the area of Indigenous peoples' rights. She provides international keynotes on Indigenous rights within many jurisdictions and also to UN agencies including the World Intellectual Property Organization. As a solicitor and barrister, she also represents Indigenous peoples in matters, including environmental issues.

Ann Towns is Professor in Political Science at the University of Gothenburg and a Wallenberg Academy Fellow. She is currently conducting a large research project on the intersection of gender and international hierarchies in diplomacy with generous funding from the Knut and Alice Wallenberg Foundation and the Swedish Research Council, and she was awarded a Bertha Lutz Prize from the International Studies Association in 2018. She is the author of *Women and States: Norms and Hierarchies in International Society* (Cambridge University Press, 2010) and of articles in *International Organization, European Journal of International Relations, Millennium, Party Politics*, and many other venues.

Acronyms

AAP	accountability to affected populations
ACHPR	African Commission on Human and People's Rights
ACTUP	AIDS Coalition to Unleash Power
AI/AN	American Indian/Alaskan Native
AIM	American Indian Movement
AU	African Union
AWID	Association for Women's Rights in Development
BAME	Black and minority ethnic
BBBEE	broad-based Black economic empowerment
BLM	Black Lives Matter
BRAC	Building Resources Across Communities
CANZUS	Canada, Australia, the United States, and New Zealand
CBM	community-based monitoring
CDCCC	Community Disaster and Climate Change Committee
CEDAW	Convention on the Elimination of Discrimination Against Women
CESCR	Covenant on Economic, Social and Cultural Rights
CHT	Chittagong Hill Tracts
COVID-19	coronavirus disease
CRPD	United Nations Convention on the Rights of People with Disabilities
CSO	civil society organization
CSSR	Civil Society Support Room
CVE	countering violent extremism
DAWN	Development Alternatives with Women for a New Era
DDR	disarmament, demobilization, and reintegration
DFID	Department for International Development
DPOs	disabled people's organization
DPPA	United Nations Department of Political and Peacebuilding Affairs
DRR	disaster risk reduction
E-SUD	National E-Justice System
EAC	East African Community
EBIT	earnings before interest and taxes
ECOSOC	United Nations Economic and Social Council
ECOWAS	Economic Community of West African States
ELA	Empowerment and Livelihood for Adolescents
EMRIP	Expert Mechanism on the Rights of Indigenous Peoples
EU	European Union
FAS	Femmes Africa Solidarité
FAWE	Forum for African Women Educationalists
FGC	female genital cutting
Findex	Global Financial Inclusion Database

FMI	Feminist Mobilization Index
FMLN	Farabundo Marti National Liberation
GAD	gender and development
GBV	gender-based violence
GCC	Gulf Cooperation Council
GDP	gross domestic product
GIWPS	Georgetown Institute for Women, Peace and Security
GNP	gross national product
GNWP	Global Network of Women Peacebuilders
HD	Centre for Humanitarian Dialogue
HLRF	High Level Revitalization Forum
HPG	Humanitarian Policy Group
HRC	Human Rights Campaign
IACHR	Inter-American Commission on Human Rights
ICC	International Criminal Court
ICCPR	International Covenant on Civil and Political Rights
ICCPR	International Covenant on Civil and Political Rights
ICRC	International Committee of the Red Cross
IDAHO-T	International Day Against Homophobia and Transphobia
IDC	International Disability Caucus
IFRC	International Federation of the Red Cross
IHRL	International Human Rights Law
IITC	International Indian Treaty Council
ILO	International Labor Organization
IMAGES	Men and Gender Equality Survey
IMAGES-UV	Men and Gender Equality Survey—Urban Violence
IMF	International Monetary Fund
IRL	international refugee law
ISIL	Islamic State of Iraq and the Levant
ISIS	Islamic State of Iraq and Syria
ITD	Inter-Tajik Dialogue
IUCN	International Union for Conservation and Nature
KSF	Kosovo Security Force
LGBTQI	lesbian, gay, bisexual, transgender, queer/questioning, intersex, asexual, and others of the community
LPA	Libyan Political Agreement
LPDF	Libyan Political Dialogue Forum
LRA	Lord's Resistance Army
LSN	Landmine Survivors Network
LTR	land tenure regularization
LTTE	Liberation Tigers of Tamil Eelam
MPC	Myanmar Peace Centre
MDGs	Millennium Development Goals
MRG	Minority Rights Group International
NATO	North Atlantic Treaty Organization
NDC	National Dialogue Conference
NDI	National Democratic Institute
NGO	nongovernmental organization

NOREF	Norwegian Centre for Conflict Resolution
OAS	Organization of American States
OECD	Organization for Economic Co-operation and Development
OHCHR	Office of the High Commissioner for Human Rights
OPDs	Organizations of Persons with Disabilities
OSCE	Organization for Security and Cooperation in Europe
OSE	Office of the Special Envoy
PEPFAR	President's Emergency Plan for AIDS Relief
PRIO	Peace Research Institute Oslo
PTSD	post-traumatic stress disorder
RCT	randomized control trial
RRS	Regional Roma Survey
SDGs	Sustainable Development Goals
SGBV	sexual and gender-based violence
SGM	sexual or gender minority
SIGI	Social Institutions and Gender Index
SOFEPADI	Female Solidarity for Integrated Peace and Development
SOGI	sexual orientation and gender identit
SRRIP	United Nations Special Rapporteur on the Rights of Indigenous Peoples
SRSG	United Nations Special Representative of the Secretary General
SSN	social safety net
SSR	security sector reform
SWAY	Survey of War-Affected Youth
SWIPD	Syrian Women's Initiative for Peace and Democracy
TC	truth commissions
TDC	Truth and Dignity Commission
TIRI	Making Integrity Work
TJ	transitional justice
TRC	Truth and Reconciliation Commission
UCDP	Uppsala Conflict Data Program
UDHR	Universal Declaration of Human Rights
UN	United Nations
UNDP	United Nations Development Programme
UNDRIP	United Nations Declaration on the Rights of Indigenous Peoples
UNESCO	United Nations Educational, Scientific and Cultural Organization
UNFPA	United Nations Population Fund
UNFPII	United Nations Permanent Forum on Indigenous Issues
UNGA	United Nations General Assembly
UNHCR	United Nations High Commissioner for Refugees
UNIBAM	United Belize Advocacy Movement
UNICEF	United Nations Children's Fund
UNIFEM	United Nations Development Fund for Women
UNOY	United Network of Young Peacebuilders
UNPFII	United Nations Permanent Forum on Indigenous Issues
UNRWA	United Nations Relief and Works Agency
UNSC	United Nations Security Council
UNSMIL	United Nations Special Envoy in Libya
UNSCR	United Nations Security Council Resolution

UNWGIP	United Nations Working Group on Indigenous Populations
UPP	Unidade de Polícia Pacificadora
URNG	Guatemalan National Revolutionary Unity
US	United States
USAID	United States Agency for International Development
USD	United States dollar
USIP	United States Institute of Peace
VET	vocational and education training
WAB	Women's Advisory Board
WASH	water, sanitation, and hygiene
WCIP	World Council on Indigenous Peoples
WDR	World Development Report
WGDD	Women, Gender and Development Directorate (African Union)
WHO	World Health Organization
WILPF	Women's International League for Peace and Freedom
WIPNET	Women in Peacebuilding Network
WOMEN	Women Organized for a Morally Enlightened Nation
WPSO-A	Women and Peace Studies Organization—Afghanistan
YYC	Yes Youth Can!

Introduction

Why This Book? Why Now?

The need to attend to diversity and to foster equity and inclusion stand out among myriad international challenges calling for greater global attention. This is because the diversity of countries and communities has critical implications for prosperity and stability. It is also because the world remains rife with unjust marginalization and inequities.

While societies have always been heterogeneous, today the mix of people and ideas is greater and more evident around the world. People are migrating in record numbers and with greater ease, whether in search of economic opportunity or looking for greater physical security.

At the same time, technological advancement has augmented awareness of diverse perspectives and views, increasing the flow of ideas. The prominent voices in the world, both inside and outside governments, are growing more varied. As a result, the rich mix of people and ideas is felt with greater intensity. At the same time, separatist, discriminatory narratives have also become more prominent.

The controversy is puzzling. The global community has dedicated decades to putting in place substantial legal commitments to equity and inclusion. An entire regime of laws, resolutions, and organizations exists to protect and advance human rights. Specific efforts focus on the rights of women; youth; indigenous communities; ethnic, religious, and linguistic minorities; people of different races; people with disabilities; older people, and members of LGBTQI communities. International regimes have been adapted for different regions and countries around the world.

Additionally, the evidence of the substantial benefits that accrue from diversity and inclusion has become clear. From a purely demographic perspective, workforce mobility can provide nations with aging populations the labor force they need to continue thriving economically, even as it provides economic opportunities for people from countries unable to provide all their residents with jobs. Equally significant, greater diversity brings a wealth of expertise, perspectives, and skills not found in homogeneous environments. A substantial and growing body of research underlines the value of and potential benefits to be accrued from a diverse workforce and a heterogeneous society. When harnessed, those benefits can deliver quantifiably for the economic, social, and political well-being of countries and communities.

Failing to embrace and capitalize on diversity also brings substantial risk. Not fostering inclusion, particularly when faced with greater diversity of people and ideas, risks compromising efforts to foster peace and prosperity. Exclusion can breed grievance and fray social cohesion, undermining stability. Marginalization compromises economic and social development and leaves vast inequalities within societies. The inability to cultivate and leverage the talents and perspectives of all groups and individuals fundamentally undermines efforts to promote durable development and end poverty.

In conflict zones and in fragile states, embracing diversity is particularly critical. Social exclusion, yawning inequalities, and economic stagnation undermine stability and impede the path to peace.[1] Efforts to negotiate an end to conflicts are often hampered and undermined by a failure to engage potential spoilers, or to foster broad popular investment in accords.[2] Post-conflict recovery and reconstruction are frequently impeded because segments of society aren't harvesting a "peace dividend"—that is, seeing the benefits of an end to conflict.[3]

The increasing diversity within societies has important implications for the conduct of diplomacy as well as efforts to resolve conflict and promote development. Experts need to attend to a wider range of stakeholders who influence public perceptions and outcomes. Professionals need to heed a growing number of international laws that reinforce the need to foster inclusion. Fundamentally, foreign affairs leaders need to embrace the importance of diversity and inclusion to global affairs, and respond to the changing global environment. Without greater awareness and a broader skill set, efforts to eliminate extreme poverty and prevent conflict are profoundly hampered.

Fortunately, there are strategies and tools to enhance the focus on inclusion in diplomacy and development. Some of the approaches have promoted inclusion of a specific marginalized group. Elsewhere, the tactics have advanced inclusion generally in a specific sector. Taken together, these demonstrate that a range of options exists for strengthening conflict resolution and development efforts for a twenty-first-century world.

Defining Terms and Clarifying Concepts

Diversity, Equity, and Inclusion

The words "diversity," "equity," and "inclusion" risk becoming jargon or a collective catchphrase today. Yet a shared understanding of these terms is essential to productive discussion, especially as "diversity" and "inclusion" are often conflated, though they are distinct concepts.

Diversity is the composition or mix of people in a community or country. Greater heterogeneity in a specific place means more diversity. For the purpose of this volume, "diversity" is broadly defined. It encompasses people and groups of different ability status, ethnicity, gender identity, linguistic community, national origin, political perspective, race, religion, sex, sexual orientation, social or socio-economic status, and more.[4]

Increasing the complexity in explorations of diversity is the reality that every individual has multiple identities that influence their position within society. For example, a woman from a minority ethnic group who has a disability will face different attitudes and challenges than will a man without any disability from the dominant ethnic group; each piece of their identity will impact their position in society. That "intersectional" analysis of identity enables deeper understanding of an individual's rights, roles, and status.[5]

Inclusion relates to the strategies and tactics that enable diverse individuals and communities to fully engage in society.[6] Advancing inclusion encompasses efforts to ensure that laws, norms, systems, and services in a society are available and accessible to everyone. Fostering inclusion means enabling universal access, influence, and a welcoming climate using approaches that communicate respect, provide protection, and harness and bring together differences to reap the greatest possible value for individuals and for societies. A culture of inclusion makes it possible for people to apply their varied perspectives and talents in pursuit of common goals.[7]

There are multiple dimensions to inclusion: social, political, economic, and cultural. Inclusiveness can progress (or regress) in one or multiple areas. Additionally, inclusiveness can be measured along a spectrum; it is not an all-or-nothing proposition. A nation or a community can be more or less inclusive in a range of ways for different people and groups. For example, a society may provide everyone access to services, without providing them the opportunity to influence or control the delivery of those services. Alternatively, a society can provide some individuals or groups both access and influence, while leaving others excluded or limited in the extent to which they are served or engaged. The world must strive for communities and societies in which all groups and individuals have economic, social, and political access, influence, and opportunity.

Fundamentally, inclusion is a tactic, whereas equity and belonging are desired outcomes. Equity within societies means there is fairness and justice. Belonging results from feeling accepted and "at home" (see Chapter 2). The authors in this book believe that by recognizing and valuing diversity and enabling inclusion, equity is fostered and facilitated, allowing more equitable societies to emerge. Further, ensuring inclusion facilitates belonging, creating the potential for everyone to feel valued and appreciated. That said, as becomes clear from discussions throughout the volume, fostering inclusion does not automatically result in equity or belonging; rather, it helps pave the way.

Similarly, advancing a focus on diversity, equity, and inclusion does not guarantee *equality* or *justice*, though it increases the potential for people to attain equal status, or to receive redress for historical injustices.[8] In a world where disparities are large and growing, equality will be achieved only if there is a concerted effort to close the many gaps in wealth, status, rights, and opportunity that currently exist, and to intentionally enable those who are disadvantaged to close those gaps. Further, where marginalization and inequality have profoundly impeded progress for particular groups, explicit recognition and indemnification may be important; equality and justice may become possible only if harm is acknowledged and affirmative efforts are made to compensate for the past.

Related Terminology

While centuries of discussion have focused on how different individuals and groups within societies relate and interact, scholar and practitioner explorations have blossomed over the last thirty years, particularly regarding social capital and social exclusion.[9]

These concepts are central in thinking about the implications of diversity. While some simple definitions of relevant terminology are provided here, a more detailed discussion of concepts is provided in Chapter 2.

Social capital. While capital is generally considered a measure of economic assets like money, social capital represents "an accumulation of various types of social, psychological, cognitive, institutional and related assets that increase the amount or probability of mutually beneficial cooperative behaviors that are beneficial for others, not just one's self."[10] Essentially social capital encompasses nonmonetary assets, such as personal and professional networks. (See Chapter 2 for a more extensive discussion.)

Social exclusion (and social inclusion). If inclusion is a strategy for advancing equity, then, "broadly defined, social exclusion refers to the societal and institutional processes that exclude certain groups from full participation in the social, economic, cultural and political life of societies."[11] Conversely, social inclusion is "the process of improving the ability, opportunity and dignity of people, disadvantaged on the basis of the identity, to take part in society."[12]

Social cohesion. As the reader will hear throughout this book, inclusion is a vehicle for enhancing relationships across communities, which in turn increases social cohesion with benefits for equity, peace, and prosperity. That said, "social cohesion refers to two broader intertwined features of society which may be described as: (1) the absence of latent social conflict—whether in the form of income/wealth inequality; racial/ethnic tensions; disparities in political participation; or other forms of polarization and (2) the presence of strong social bonds, measured by levels of trust and norms of reciprocity (i.e., social capital); the abundance of organizations that bridge social divisions ('civil society'); and the presence of institutions of conflict management (e.g., a responsive democracy, an independent judiciary, and so forth)."[13]

Social trust. Underlying discussions around equity and inclusion are efforts to enhance social trust within and across increasingly diverse societies. To that end, we consider social trust to be "the expectation that arises within a community of regular, honest, and cooperative behavior, based on commonly shared norms, on the part of other members of that community . . . Social capital is a capability that arises from the prevalence of trust in a society or in certain parts of it. It can be embodied in the smallest and most basic social group, the family, as well as the largest of all groups, the nation, and in all the other groups in between."[14]

Purpose and Goals of This Text

This book was created to frame and contextualize the opportunities and challenges that diversity presents for the field of international affairs. Further, it arms practitioners and experts with knowledge and tools for working in diverse communities, and for fostering equity and inclusion in diplomacy and development.

The text paints an extensive portrait. It details how movements for inclusion have advanced and laid the groundwork for a more effective approach to international affairs. The book also discusses concrete, field-tested tactics for engaging with diversity and fostering inclusion. Further, it considers the road forward, discussing how research, policymaking, and field practice can further evolve to meet the need for change.

Specifically, the book is structured to:

- Enable a general understanding of why attention to diversity and inclusion is increasingly important, both by providing an overview of global trends and by presenting the most up-to-date research and data regarding the implications of exclusion for underdevelopment and conflict, as well as the dividends offered by fostering inclusion.
- Provide an overview of a range of movements for inclusion with an eye toward understanding how progress has been achieved and where there are enduring challenges.
- Provide specific guidance regarding strategies that would foster inclusion and leverage diversity at different stages and in various ways through conflict resolution and development efforts.

For some, the text won't go far enough. There are those who believe that inclusion, equity, and justice are not achievable simply by working within and through existing institutions, which frequently bear discriminatory legacies and sometimes continue to perpetuate inequities and injustices.[15] For them, this book may feel insufficient. While it touches on that important perspective, particularly in the Conclusion, the narrative focuses on how practitioners and policymakers can make critical gains through existing organizations and systems. It predominantly discusses transformation from within. To ensure advancement, we must have conversations about the need for both incremental change *and* systemic transformation. But progress is needed immediately, even if it is incremental; it cannot wait for fundamental shifts that may never be realized.

How the Book Is Structured

Structured as mutually reinforcing sections, this book provides an in-depth overview of why a focus on diversity and inclusion is essential internationally and how to advance that agenda during critical stages of conflict resolution and global development processes. Woven into many of the chapters are rich case studies and examples that apply theory to practice and reflect on the lessons that emerge from around the world, including in diverse places including Afghanistan, the Congo Basin, Guatemala, Kosovo, Liberia, Papua New Guinea, Peru, and Sierra Leone.

The book begins with a section that frames the overarching case for inclusion. Chapter 1 discusses contemporary trends that mean inclusion and equity concerns are increasing in import. Chapter 2 starts with a review of the philosophical, analytical, and legal bases for thinking about diversity and inclusivity, then turns to examining how empirical research and data strongly indicate that fostering inclusion is essential to advancing durable development and to preventing and resolving conflict. The section aspires to convince even skeptics that a focus on related issues is overdue.

Section II focuses on examining the status of movements for inclusion of a variety of disempowered and marginalized groups, including women and girls, youth, indigenous peoples, minority groups, LGBTQI community members, and people with disabilities. Each chapter makes the case for inclusion based on cutting-edge academic and practitioner research. The chapters overview movements for inclusion, discussing how they have evolved and progressed. Finally, each chapter talks about the road ahead: what is needed to make inclusion and equity realities for that specific group, and how best to approach the challenges. The chapters as a whole provide fascinating insights into how the push for inclusion has evolved in different ways for various groups, and they illuminate the lessons that emerge from a study of movements.

The third section focuses on the process of conflict mediation and resolution, exploring issues of diversity and inclusion at moments and stages when attention to diversity and a focus on inclusion are particularly important. The section looks at how to mediate and negotiate inclusively as well as how to implement peace accords in ways that involve and engage a wide range of stakeholders. The section includes chapters focused on the transitional justice process and on efforts to reform security sectors, recognizing that those efforts offer opportunities to enhance the focus on equity and inclusivity in the post-conflict transition to peace. Additionally, the section includes chapters examining issues of exclusion in humanitarian assistance and in addressing societal violence, as these are domains where exclusion and inequity are particularly pronounced.

Section IV focuses on how diversity and inclusion are relevant in efforts to promote development. Chapters look at the relevance of equity and inclusion issues in economic and social development, in justice sector development, and in the promotion of inclusive governance and rule of law. Additionally, the chapter looks at strategies for strengthening and engaging civil society in development efforts, an effective means for broadening stakeholder engagement in the development process and fostering inclusion. Similarly, a chapter on the role of norms in influencing the equity and inclusiveness of development efforts offers important insights into how communities can pave the way toward inclusive development that successfully navigates local beliefs and traditions.

The book concludes by offering lessons from across the volume for research as well as for practice. Building on the research and observations of scholars and practitioners from around the world, the final chapter enables the reader to understand the universality of the call to better involve a wider range of stakeholders and better serve a larger set of beneficiaries in global efforts to foster peace and prosperity.

Why the Authors Matter, a Lot

Forty exceptional authors from around the world have come together to write this book. They represent the broad, global movement for equity and inclusion that cuts across regions, areas of specialization, generations, and backgrounds. These experts bring extraordinary passion, experience, and expertise to their analysis.

Included among them are world leaders, including a Nobel Peace Prize recipient, Leymah Gbowee of Liberia; former president of the Republic of Kosovo Atifete Jahjaga; former Afghanistan High Peace Council member Wazhma Frogh; and former Guatemalan judge Claudia Escobar. Also featured are the leaders of diverse movements for inclusion, such as Lakshitha Saji Prelis, who is among those spearheading the charge for youth inclusion in peace and security processes; Valmaine Toki, a scholar and activist descendant of Ngatiwai, Ngapuhi iwi, who is a member of the United Nations Permanent Forum on Indigenous Issues; and Maksym Eristavi, a journalist and leader of the LGBTQI equality movement in Eastern Europe.

Leading scholars in their fields are represented as well, among them Michael Ashley Stein, executive director of the Harvard Law School Project on Disability; Anne Towns, from the University of Gothenburg; Lisa Hilbink, from the University of Minnesota; and Elis Borde, of the Federal University of Minas Gerais. They are joined by scholar practitioners including Joshua Castellino, former dean of Middlesex University, London and head of Minority Rights Group International; Maitreyi Bordia Das, of the World Bank's Urban, Resilience and Land Global Practice; Anne Marie Goetz, of New York University; and Hugo van der Merwe, of the Centre for the Study of Violence and Reconciliation in South Africa.

Exceptional practitioners lend their expert voices, among them Sayed Ikram Afzali, executive director of Afghanistan Integrity Watch; Gary Barker, CEO of Promundo; Dan Baer, former US ambassador to the OSCE; Katia Papagianni, director of policy and mediation support for HD Centre; Eduardo González, who assisted the Peruvian Truth and Reconciliation Commission; and Zuhra Halimova, who was involved in the Inter-Tajik Dialogue. Emerging scholars and experts such as Lara Dominguez, Teuta Avdimetaj, Nomathamsanqa Masiko-Mpaka, Madison Schramm, and Meghan Shoemaker are also represented. Though the contributors are too numerous and accomplished to individually discuss here, their short biographies at the front of this volume are well worth reviewing; these authors represent more than twenty countries on six continents, and they are emblematic of the wonderful global mosaic of brilliant experts around the world striving for equality and inclusion.

Notes

1. World Bank 2018.
2. Council on Foreign Relations 2018. Data from International Interactions and International Peace Institute.
3. O'Hearn 2000.
4. For an in-depth definition and discussion of diversity, see Gardenswartz and Rowe 2003.
5. For an extensive exploration of intersectionality, see Crenshaw 2017.
6. For an in-depth discussion of the distinction between diversity and inclusion, see Roberson 2006.
7. World Bank 2013.
8. For a discussion of debates around conceptions of "justice" in the international sphere, see Dietzel 2018.
9. Social Capital Research and Training 2018.
10. Uphoff 2000.
11. Narayan-Parker 1999.
12. World Bank 2013, 22.
13. Kawachi and Berkman 2000.
14. Fukuyama 1996, 26.
15. See, for example, Andrews 2021; Klein 2008; Robinson 2019.

Bibliography

Andrews, Kehinde. 2021. *The New Age of Empire: How Racism and Colonialism Still Rule the World*. New York: Bold Type Books.

Council on Foreign Relations. 2018. "Women's Participation in Peace Processes." July 31. https://www.cfr.org/interactive/womens-participation-in-peace-processes.

Crenshaw, Kimberlé. 2017. *On Intersectionality: Essential Writings*. New York: New Press.

Dietzel, Alix. 2018. "Introducing Global Justice in International Relations Theory." E-International Relations. January 2. https://www.e-ir.info/2018/01/02/global-justice-in-international-relations-theory/.

Fukuyama, Francis. 1996. *Trust: Social Virtues and the Creation of Prosperity*. New York: Simon and Schuster.

Gardenswartz, Lee, and Anita Rowe. 2003. *Diverse Teams at Work: Capitalizing on the Power of Diversity*. Alpharetta, GA: Society for Human Resource Management.

Kawachi, I., and L. Berkman. 2000. "Social Cohesion, Social Capital, and Health." In *Social Epidemiology*, edited by L. F. Berkman and I. Kawachi, 174–190. New York: Oxford University Press.

Klein, Naomi. 2008. *The Shock Doctrine: The Rise of Disaster Capitalism*. New York: Metropolitan Books.

Narayan-Parker, Deepa. 1999. *Bonds and Bridges: Social Capital and Poverty*. Washington, DC: World Bank.

O'Hearn, Denis. 2000. "Peace Dividend, Foreign Investment, and Economic Regeneration: The Northern Irish Case." *Social Problems* 47, no. 2: 180–200.

Roberson, Quinetta M. 2006. "Disentangling the Meanings of Diversity and Inclusion in Organizations." *Group and Organization Management* 31, no. 2: 212–236.

Robinson, Cedric J. 2019. *Cedric J. Robinson: On Racial Capitalism, Black Internationalism, and Cultures of Resistance*. Edited by H. L. T. Quan. London: Pluto Press.

Social Capital Research and Training. 2018. "Evolution of Social Capital." https://www.socialcapitalresearch.com/literature/evolution/.

Uphoff, Norman. 2000. "Understanding Social Capital: Learning from the Analysis and Experience of Participation." In *Social Capital: A Multifaceted Perspective*, edited by Partha Dasgupta and Ismail Serageldin, 215–252. Washington, DC: World Bank, 2000.

World Bank. 2013. *Inclusion Matters: The Foundation for Shared Prosperity*. Washington, DC: World Bank.

World Bank. 2018. "Pathways for Peace: Inclusive Approaches to Preventing Violent Conflict." https://openknowledge.worldbank.org/handle/10986/28337.

SECTION I
THE INCLUSION IMPERATIVE

1

Growing Urgency

Why Today's Global Landscape Demands a Focus on Diversity, Equity, and Inclusion

Carla Koppell

Issues of exclusion and inclusion are assuming new significance for both developed and developing countries. . . . Countries that used to be referred to as developed are grappling with issues of exclusion and inclusion perhaps more intensely today than they did a decade ago. And countries previously called developing are grappling with both old issues and new forms of exclusion thrown up by growth. . . . These changes make social inclusion more urgent than it was even a decade ago.

—World Bank[1]

Nationalist, isolationist movements have arisen in many corners of the world, embroiling nations in struggles framed as defining their identity. Today, India, Germany, and the United States, for example, each confront substantial countervailing social movements regarding the need to embrace diversity and promote equity and inclusion.

In the United States, nationwide Black Lives Matter protests exploded in 2020 following the deaths of Black Americans, including George Floyd, Breonna Taylor, and Ahmaud Arbery, at the hands of police.[2] Revelations of vast differences in the treatment of White and Black people (as well as other people of color) by law enforcement and the justice system mobilized millions calling for equal treatment.[3] Those demonstrators were met by counterprotesters seeking to deny, explain, or justify the disparities.[4] Domestic white supremacist organizations, growing in prominence, were deemed by the US Department of Homeland Security "the most persistent and lethal threat" in the United States.[5] At the same time, protests for racial justice spread abroad, with minorities calling attention to incidents of bias.[6] The protests help shine a spotlight on how poorly structured laws and regulations, and their uneven application, can open the door to unequal treatment of minorities. The pushback exposed deeply embedded pockets of bias and racism.[7] Continuing for over a hundred days in cities across the country, the protests resulted in violent

clashes, lost lives, billions of dollars in property damage, and deepened polarization.[8] They also resulted in legal reforms, changes in the approach to policing,
and more frequent investigations into police misconduct, in an effort to root out
inequalities.[9]

As civil rights protests continued, the global COVID-19 pandemic similarly revealed dimensions of the disturbing inequity and exclusion that persist across the
world. First emerging in China in 2019, COVID-19 spread rapidly, carried by world
travelers to virtually every country in the world in just a few months. The virus affected developed and developing nations alike, with millions of new cases per day
and over three million deaths recorded in less than a year and a half.[10] (The actual death toll in that period was likely almost seven million, as COVID-19 deaths
were underreported around the world.)[11] Information flow was instantaneous, with
numbers of cases and deaths tracked globally and continually updated on a vast
number of digital platforms.[12]

Underlying the overall statistics were stark disaggregated data that poor and
minority groups were disproportionately represented among the infected and
dead in most countries.[13] In the United States, Native American and African
American communities faced hospitalization rates 3.5 times and 2.8 times
higher, respectively, than those for White populations; Latino populations
faced rates that were three times higher than for Whites.[14] COVID-19–related
death rates were also significantly elevated for African Americans and Hispanic/
Latino populations, as well as for American Indian, Alaskan Native, and Pacific
Islander peoples."[15] Their vulnerability was greater because of inadequate access
to healthcare before and during the crisis; disproportionate exposure to the disease as a result of jobs and living conditions; and systemic bias that reduced
the responsiveness of the healthcare and governing systems to their needs. The
pandemic also revealed different vulnerabilities for subgroups in societies. For
example, rates of domestic violence and violence against women soared around
the world, as people were confined at home with abusive family members for extended periods of time.[16]

Marginalized groups face greater challenges to recovery as well. Their sources
of income and their businesses were at greater risk. They were less likely to have
accumulated intergenerational wealth to fall back on, and their jobs were often less
secure even before the pandemic. They returned to school at lower rates, setting
back families and communities for the long term. At the same time, budget cuts
reduced services for the neediest.

Slower recuperation by the poor and vulnerable impeded recovery. Continued
illness in disadvantaged communities extended the spread of disease. Persistent
economic dislocation among minority groups and women slowed the pace of return to prosperity. Vaccination rates in minority and low-income communities
lagged.[17] Whole societies suffered for longer because countries and communities
failed to appreciate that they are stronger when everyone is protected and resilient to upheaval.

The combined crises of 2020 were revelatory. They showed how questions of diversity, equity, and inclusion loom ever larger. Additionally, they revealed structural and attitudinal barriers to progress. Protest movements against diversity exposed fundamental discomfort with growing societal heterogeneity. At times, they also underscored dominant groups' resistance and active opposition to ceding power and control to nondominant groups. Simultaneously, protests against unequal treatment provided contemporary evidence of the anger, pain, and polarization that result from exclusion and inequality. The rapid global spread of COVID-19 illustrated our global interdependence, interconnectedness, and inequality, and it drove home the need for global intentionality in advancing equity and inclusion.

The Challenge the World Faces Today

The premise of this volume is clear. Communities and countries should strive for equity and inclusion across their societies. Inclusive governance is more effective. A more equal society is more just. Inclusion and equality pay dividends. They offer pathways to economic, social, and political stability and progress when pursued with intention and vigor. Further, inadequate attention to diversity and the need for inclusion creates growing risks and vulnerabilities, with clear, increasingly evident costs for stability and prosperity. All of that said, there are strategies for leveraging diversity and fostering inclusion in addressing conflict and pursuing development. Similarly, there are robust lessons regarding what works (and what does not).

This chapter examines how and why a focus on diversity, equity, and inclusion is growing in importance. The analysis highlights key trends that were identified through data analysis and field work in developing and fragile states around the world; the research supports the conclusion that these trends translate into an increasingly urgent need to better address gaps in the rights, opportunities, and status of people, and among groups within societies. Specifically:

- *Shifting demographics* are altering the contours of the diversity within many societies, with evident implications for economic well-being and social cohesion around the world.
- *Advances in communications technology and digital media* are bringing communities into greater contact, both directly and virtually, increasing awareness of diversity and of disparities in access, power, and wealth. Those disparities have implications for grievance and dissatisfaction, and they augment the need to address exclusion, inequity, and marginalization.
- *Dramatic economic inequality* is revealing the need to focus on vulnerable, marginalized subpopulations as part of strategies to eliminate extreme poverty and to ensure continued stability and prosperity.
- *A growing overlap of fragile states and developing countries* renders inclusion increasingly essential to economic, political, and social progress. We now know

that instability and underdevelopment feed each other, and exclusion and inequity drive both.

- *Changes in the dynamics, combatants, and tactics of war* reveal how economic stagnation, grievance, and marginalization are root causes of violence and conflict. Simultaneously, the stakeholders in conflict are evolving, signaling the necessity of engaging a wider range of people in peacebuilding and development efforts.

- *Underlying all the trends, climate change and environmental degradation* are creating increasing dislocation and disruption that undermine development and stability writ large, with disproportionate impacts on the vulnerable and marginalized.

Why These Trends?

These six trends loom particularly large in discussions of diversity and inclusion. They interrelate and intertwine, but they have differing implications. Demographic, technological, and economic trends signal that questions of diversity and exclusion loom ever larger globally; we continue to ignore them at our peril. The changing landscape of developing, fragile, and conflict-affected countries signals that changes in practice are needed to better address and engage with issues of diversity, inequity, and exclusion; the global community undermines progress by treating societies as homogeneous and limiting the stakeholders involved in decision-making and leadership. Finally, the specter of climate change—with its dramatic, potentially devastating implications for countries and communities, and especially for the vulnerable and marginalized in those places—adds further urgency; support must be provided to build resilience and help adaptation by communities already facing extreme vulnerability.

Critical Trendlines: How Diversity and Disparity Loom Ever Larger, Reshaping Societies

Shifting Demographics

Beyond naturally occurring heterogeneity, the composition of countries and communities is evolving dramatically. In many countries, the age distribution of the population is changing (see Figure 1.1). As of 2013, the population was shrinking in eighty-three countries, including Russia, Japan, Germany, and Italy; fertility rates dipped below two births for every woman.[18] Elsewhere, in nations such as Pakistan, Kenya, and Nigeria, youth constitute a substantial majority of the population.[19] Even as many countries age, the number of young people is the largest in history, with many born in poor, unstable countries (see Figure 1.2).[20]

PERCENT OF POPULATION AGES 65 AND OLDER

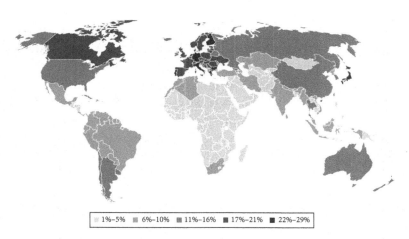

1%–5%   6%–10%   11%–16%   17%–21%   22%–29%

Figure 1.1 Percent of Population Ages 65 and Older

Credit line: Population Reference Bureau, International Data: Percent of Population Ages 65 and Older, www.prb.org/international.

PERCENT OF POPULATION UNDER AGE 15

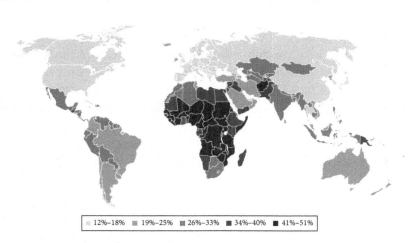

12%–18%   19%–25%   26%–33%   34%–40%   41%–51%

Figure 1.2 Percent of Population Under Age 15

Credit line: Population Reference Bureau, International Data: Percent of Population Under Age 15, www.prb.org/international.

For countries where the youth population is growing, there are opportunities and threats. Some refer to the share of young people as a "demographic dividend," providing labor, new ideas, energy, and vibrancy. Others refer to the growth as a "youth bulge," increasing the burden on societies and economies as well as the risks posed by potential growth in unemployment and associated grievance born of marginalization.[21] Political scientist Henrik Urdal analyzes youth groups extensively in conjunction with unemployment, fertility, and expansion of higher education; he concludes that larger youth populations do correspond with violence, but the correlation is weaker when young people have greater voice and opportunity, among several variables.[22] Whatever the frame for assessing the impact of a growing youth population for economies and societies, the emergence of an important interest group is undeniable (see Chapter 4).

Countries with aging populations face their own challenges. These nations are facing labor shortages. At the same time, pensions, social security assistance, and healthcare costs are soaring. To maintain economic growth and vibrancy, such countries need to ensure they can maintain industries and services.

Partly as a result of these demographic shifts (and the related opportunities and needs), a record number of people are on the move globally. The number of economic migrants, people moving in search of employment and opportunity, is substantial. In 1990, 2.89 percent of the world's population were migrants; by 2017, that had risen to 3.43 percent.[23] Young people are migrating in particularly large numbers from countries with surplus labor in search of work. In 2013, 27 million young people migrated to find economic opportunities abroad.[24] They often resettle in countries where the population is aging and workers are needed, shifting the age distribution as well as the ethnic, racial, and religious composition of states.

At the same time, a growing share of migrants have been forced from their homes. The United Nations estimated that by the end of 2018, over 70 million people had been displaced by war or natural disaster. More than 40 million people moved within their home country.[25] Over 25 million crossed international borders as refugees, and the number continues to rise.[26] Those displaced by conflict are also away from home for longer; today, refugee displacement averages twenty years.[27] And, more often, displaced people live in cities and towns, alongside locals, rather than being isolated in camps far from permanent residents.[28] This increases the likelihood of their permanence and brings them into greater contact with longer-term residents.

The impact of population movements on the demographic composition of countries is significant (see Figure 1.3). In 2013, for example, 95 percent of the 1.7-million-person population increase in the European Union resulted from net migration.[29] Moreover, according to the Pew Research Center, "as of mid-2016, the Muslim population of Europe was estimated at 25.8 million (4.9% of the overall population)—up from 19.5 million (3.8%) in 2010. Even if all migration into

% foreign born, 2017

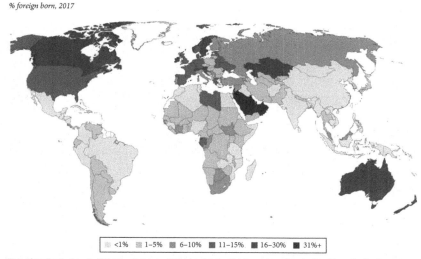

<1%   1–5%   6–10%   11–15%   16–30%   31%+

Note: Share foreign born in U.S. is for 50 states and District of Columbia. Countries and territories without shading have populations less than 1 million and are not included.
Source: Pew Research Center analysis of United Nations and U.S. Census Bureau data.
PEW RESEARCH CENTER

Figure 1.3 Percent Foreign-Born Population

Credit line: Immigrant share in U.S. is lower than in many other countries, in "Immigrant share in U.S. nears record high but remains below that of many other countries." Pew Research Center, Washington, D.C. (2019) https://www.pewresearch.org/fact-tank/2019/01/30/immigrant-share-in-u-s-nears-record-high-but-remains-below-that-of-many-other-countries/.

Europe were to immediately and permanently stop—a 'zero migration' scenario—the Muslim population of Europe still would be expected to rise from the current level of 4.9 percent to 7.4 percent by the year 2050."[30] This trend is changing the contours in countries that were previously fairly homogeneous; population diversity is growing, and it is increasingly felt.

The changes in demographics create the potential to stoke competition and spark resentment. Whether justified or not, there are concerns that immigrants are taking resources and jobs away from those who are citizens by birth, and more specifically from those who have traditionally constituted the dominant demographic in those countries. In Germany, for example, negative sentiments toward immigrants and multiculturalism, particularly in the East, have altered the political landscape, increasing the prominence of right-wing, populist political parties and leaders.[31]

Advances in Communications Technology and Digital Media

Even as populations are on the move, technology is decreasing the distance, both physical and virtual, between groups. Travel is easier and less expensive; this is facilitating movement, both international and local. It is also creating proximity where previously there was none. For example, increased rural-urban migration is resulting in coexistence among groups that previously would have had limited interaction.

Greater interconnectedness is also increasing awareness of diversity within societies, enabling greater interaction among people of different backgrounds and perspectives, whether face-to-face or virtual. Internet usage and access to smartphones are increasing significantly, particularly in emerging economies.[32] In 2016, for instance, "89% of South Africans owned a mobile phone. Today, the share who own a mobile phone of some kind has ticked up to 94%, while smartphone ownership has grown from just over a third (37%) to a majority of the population (60%)."[33]

Communications technologies are also facilitating information dissemination and collaboration, making it easier and less expensive to cross geographic divides and to connect different subgroups within societies and abroad. For example, technology is allowing nongovernmental and civil society organizations to connect with their members and advocate across borders.[34] It is also facilitating the flow of information and financial resources, and bringing diverse groups within societies into greater contact. These trends are increasing "felt" diversity—the extent to which people perceive there are others with different perspectives, experiences, and cultures.[35]

Communications technology is also enabling the mobilization of people in ways that can foster bias, divisions, and conflict. The Islamic State of Iraq and Syria (ISIS) uses sophisticated digital media and communications to recruit fighters, foster violence, and cultivate support internationally.[36] In Myanmar, "Facebook has been a useful instrument for those seeking to spread hate, in a context where, for most users, Facebook is the Internet."[37] Online hate speech, much of it emanating from outside the country, has spurred interethnic violence in South Sudan, where digital hate speech correlated with attacks on civilians of specific ethnic groups and where false information, "fake news," and rumors have been spread digitally by clan-based kinship groups.[38] Governments and businesses around the world, too, are using digital media and surveillance technology in ways that may, whether intentionally or not, promote inclusion and equity or foster marginalization, vulnerability, and further societal divides.[39]

Communications technology and digital media are creating a global community; they have vast potential to build bridges and create understanding. At the same time, there is substantial evidence of how they are sowing distrust and misinformation, promulgating narratives about grievance, spreading misinformation, or providing a platform for hate speech aimed at communities of diverse ethnic, racial, or cultural background.[40] Further, there is growing evidence of the ways technology risks extending marginalization, polarization, suppression of ideas and movements, or the subjugation of groups within societies.

Dramatic Economic Inequality

Increasing the need to focus on equity and inclusion are data revealing the extreme disparities in wealth and income that characterize economies around the world. In-depth analyses of economies globally today reveal stark differences in wealth and well-being, whether the country in question is peaceful or conflict-riven, less developed or more. Oxfam has found that "in 2019, the world's billionaires, only 2,153 people, had more wealth than 4.6 billion people."[41] Among the most extreme examples is South Africa; in 2015, the top 10 percent of the population held about 71 percent of net wealth and the bottom 60 percent held only 7 percent. South Africa's Gini coefficient is one of the highest in the world, reflecting this income inequality.[42]

Unfortunately, making the picture even more disturbing is that in many countries differences in income and wealth are growing; the rich are getting richer in absolute and relative terms. Wealthy individuals and families are increasing their control over and their share of resources, both financial and tangible. While income inequality increased in forty-nine countries and decreased in fifty-eight countries between 1990 and 2016, over 70 percent of the world's population lives in countries where income inequality increased.[43]

Not surprisingly, vulnerable and marginalized populations within societies, as well as minority groups, are most often among the most disadvantaged. That is, their income is growing most slowly, and their share of resources is declining despite overall increases in societal wealth and well-being. India's fast-growing economy has led to an overall reduction in poverty, but horizontal inequalities among different subgroups remain.[44] Marginalized groups like the Scheduled Castes and Scheduled Tribes have suffered exclusion for centuries, despite efforts to constitutionally redress disparities. For example, in 2015, 38.7 percent of men and 30.4 percent of women in India had twelve or more years of education. Yet only 17.5 percent of men in the Scheduled Tribes and 23.2 percent of men in the Scheduled Castes had twelve or more years of education. Women members fared even worse; only 10.6 percent of women from Scheduled Tribes and 15.7 percent of women from Scheduled Castes completed twelve or more years of school.[45] The COVID-19 pandemic risks leaving the vulnerable and marginalized worse off; already, the return to school has been lower among minorities and the disadvantaged in the United States and elsewhere.[46]

Inequalities are being perpetuated and exacerbated by structural and attitudinal barriers.[47] Fiscal and expenditure policies can advance equality and equity or they can foster disparities.[48] Regulations can impose rules that introduce or mitigate bias and unequal treatment. Tax systems can enable redistribution of resources to tackle inequalities or they can place a relatively greater burden on lower-income groups. Similarly, public expenditures can provide services such as education, public transportation, and healthcare in ways that reduce or accentuate inequality. In recent decades, ballooning disparities have been driven by the failure to leverage taxation of the rich to redistribute wealth; stagnant wages for lower-income people; and reduced access to quality education, healthcare, and well-paid employment.[49] Some argue that deeply embedded biases are integral to capitalist economies, which routinely ascribe greater market value to the contributions of dominant groups within societies (such as men or Whites) and to certain productive activities (such as, for example, investment banking rather than childcare).[50]

The growth in inequality has significant implications for stability and for development. Though inequality doesn't inevitably lead to violent conflict, certain types of inequality increase the propensity for conflict.[51] For example, horizontal inequalities—differences in the wealth or opportunities among different subgroups within societies—are more likely to spark violence (see Chapter 2). Inequalities also create fertile ground for conflict when coupled with calls to address injustice or to blame another group within society for inequity.[52] Moreover, inequality increases the likelihood that conflict recurs.[53] Extensive study has looked at the impact of different types of inequality on violent conflict, finding that the intersections of identity, exclusion, and inequality have critical implications.[54]

Inequality also has significant negative consequences for development. Looking at an average across countries, some 25–35 percent of gross domestic product (GDP) is estimated to be lost as a result of inequalities among individuals and households, while up to 32 percent of GDP is sacrificed in some countries as a result of income inequalities among ethnic groups.[55] A three-point reduction in the Gini coefficient has increased the predicted duration of a period of economic growth by 50 percent. And a one-point increase in the Gini coefficient has been correlated with a 3 percent greater infant mortality rate.[56]

Sadly, many trends are invisible because data analysis generally isn't disaggregated to reveal how overall developmental progress is or is not resulting in shared prosperity or collective advancement. Further, structural impediments to equality, including discriminatory laws and institutions, impede universal progress, yet they remain in place.[57] Increases in wealth or income at a national or societal level mask maldistribution of the growth and benefits from development. Though GDP per capita has been rising in countries around the world and is "widely used as a reference point for the health of national and global economies," it doesn't capture unpaid labor (such as household work, including childcare) and it masks extreme disparities and persistent pockets of extreme poverty.[58] Looking only at aggregated data doesn't enable societies to manage for inclusive growth or comprehensive societal well-being. Additionally, structural barriers continue to fundamentally undermine progress toward equity; concerted, intentional efforts are needed to ensure that the benefits of development and progress accrue to all subgroups within societies.

A Changing Global Landscape

This section explores how inequality and exclusion alter the environment for promoting security and development.

The Growing Overlap of Less Developed Nations and Fragile States

In the past, there existed a large set of fairly peaceful, developing countries.[59] Economic, political, and social development could be promoted in relatively stable nations that were home to many of the poorest people in the world. Violent conflict could often be resolved by militaries and diplomats in nations of varied developmental status, often far from nations striving to improve governance, infrastructure, healthcare, and education, among other systems and services.

That is no longer the case.[60] "Armed conflicts today are overwhelmingly concentrated in poor, developing countries with illiberal and corrupt political regimes."[61] Additionally, a growing share of low-income, least-developed nations are fragile— that is, unstable or conflict-affected.[62] "The share of global poor living in fragile and conflict-affected countries increased from 14 percent in 2008 to 23 percent in 2015," and it is predicted that by 2030, two-thirds of the world's extreme poor will live in countries affected by conflict, violence, and fragility.[63] According to the World Bank, "Half of the people living in extreme poverty in 2015 can be found in just five countries. The most populous countries in South Asia (Bangladesh and India) and Sub-Saharan Africa (Democratic Republic of Congo, Ethiopia, and Nigeria) are the five topping the list."[64]

There are multiple interconnections between poverty and stability. Underdevelopment correlates with a greater propensity to violent conflict, and conflict undermines the path to prosperity. Underlying underdevelopment and fragility are often inequities and grievances born of marginalization. In fact, according to the 2019 Fragile States Index, each of the five countries with the largest number of extreme poor faces trends relating to diversity, equity, and inclusion that reduce stability.[65] For example, demographic pressures in all five are negatively impacting the population by straining natural resources or public services, and India, Bangladesh, and Ethiopia are all facing increases in social polarization as signaled by a worsening of group grievances.

Conflict Impact on National Economic Well-Being

At the most basic level, stable nations are more prosperous. In the 2011 *World Development Report*, the World Bank found that "a country that experienced major violence during the period 1981–2005 had a poverty rate that was, on average, 21 percentage points higher than a country without violence."[66] Similarly, the 2018 Global Peace Index found that "in the last 70 years, per capita growth [was] three times higher in highly peaceful countries when compared to countries with low levels of peace." The report also found that "per capita GDP growth [was] seven times higher over the last decade in countries that improved in peacefulness versus those that deteriorated."[67] The absence of violence similarly led to lower and more stable interest rates, lower inflation, and greater foreign direct investment. Overall, "if the least peaceful countries had grown at the same rate as highly peaceful countries, the global economy would be almost 14 trillion dollars larger."[68]

That said, any calculation of the prosperity lost to conflict and underdevelopment would need to recognize and consider how the prosperity of peaceful, advanced economies has been (and sometimes continues to be) bolstered at the expense of poorer countries. Colonization and its legacies impede countries' progress and may reduce well-being, income, and stability in some nations, while economically benefiting trading partners. Trade deals and resource extraction practices continue to benefit wealthy nations over resource-rich poorer countries.[69] For example, wealthy nations produce 34 percent of the solid waste in the world even though they are home to only 16 percent of the population, and they export solid waste to developing nations, avoiding the consequences of local consumption and despoiling environments abroad.[70] Countries can also economically benefit from conflict. A conservative estimate of the global value of the arms trade in 2017 neared $100 billion.[71] Greater peace and stability threaten weapons sales, with economic consequences for arms producers and dealers. Improving prosperity and stability in some places will reduce wealth elsewhere.

Notwithstanding those mitigating factors, it is clear that countries not facing conflict progress along a more predictable developmental path. According to the United Nations, peaceful and stable countries steadily reduce poverty, while the poverty rates of conflict-affected nations stagnate or rise. "On average, poverty reduction in conflict-affected countries is nearly one percentage point slower per annum than in other countries, and over time, the cumulative gap between those two groups has expanded significantly."[72] Conflict-affected countries continue to falter.

Various other developmental indicators also stagnate in conflict-affected and fragile states. Health issues and conflict are often related. In a 2007 study on sub-Saharan African countries, 27 percent of children under five were undernourished in conflict-affected countries, compared with 22 percent in countries without recent conflicts. Further, "median under-5 mortality in countries with recent conflict is 197/1000 live births, versus 137/1000 live births in countries without recent conflict."[73]

Violent conflict and instability result in setbacks for development. For example, in Afghanistan, rapid gains in health and educational achievement following the expulsion of the Taliban in 2001 have eroded, while insecurity has persisted. The World Bank's biannual *Afghanistan Development Update* noted that the proportion of Afghans living below the national poverty line increased from 38 percent to 55 percent between 2011/12 and 2016/17.[74] A multidimensional analysis further revealed that "the poorest of the poor are those residing in rural areas, from minority ethnic groups, women and persons with disabilities of all ages, women disabled at birth or due to an unknown cause, and elderly age groups."[75] In particular, women and people with disabilities faced the greatest deprivation.[76]

Not surprisingly, conflict takes the greatest toll on the poorest countries. For example, nations with low health service capacity pre-conflict and the most diminished capacity post-conflict have the highest civilian mortality rates.[77] In Yemen, for example, conflict exacerbated existing health sector vulnerabilities, such as access to functioning facilities, medication, and clean water. A Health Resources and Services Availability Mapping System (HeRAMS) survey conducted by the WHO in 2016 showed that 17 percent of health facilities in the country were "nonfunctional," meaning no services were offered due to infrastructure damage and lack of resources.[78] An additional 38 percent were "partially functional," as only some services were being offered.[79] As a result, 2016 saw an increase in mortality in children under five years and in maternal mortality.[80]

Intractable, long-enduring conflict has particularly devastating effects on development.[81] In 2010, Syria's GDP was over $60 billion, but for the five years from 2012 through 2016, Syria had a negative GDP growth rate, resulting in a 70 percent drop by 2017.[82] Compounding the loss of wealth and income are the casualties, demographic movements, and lower returns on investment."[83] Syrian life expectancy decreased by five years since the start of the war, reversing years of steady progress among men, women, and children.[84]

Conflict also affects countries' developmental trajectories in other ways. For example, conflict-driven migration alters the progress of neighboring nations. In 2017, over 60 million people globally had been displaced in the long term by violence; an estimated 85 percent of those who were displaced now reside in developing regions, with the "least developed countries providing asylum to a growing proportion, some one-third, of the global total of 6.7 million refugees."[85] Often, refugees' host countries are fragile, developing nations themselves, and the influx affects host nations' well-being. It can also impact host countries' respect for human rights.[86]

In 2017, Lebanon hosted the largest number of refugees as a share of its population in the world; some one in six residents was a refugee.[87] Jordan hosted the second-largest number of refugees as a share of its population (one in fourteen residents).[88] When Palestinian refugees under the mandate of the United Nations Relief and Works Agency for Palestine Refugees in the Near East (UNRWA) are included, the figures rise to one in four for Lebanon and one in three for Jordan.[89] In addition to increasing the diversity within the country, the refugees in Lebanon and Jordan put immense strain on the countries' healthcare system, education system, housing, and economic infrastructure. For example, some Jordanian schools were forced to provide two half-day shifts at school to accommodate all of the children.[90]

Similar challenges are being felt in other parts of the world. The influx of Rohingya refugees in Bangladesh has presented various economic, developmental, and social challenges. Rohingya refugees work as day laborers at lower wage rates relative to host country workers, and a United Nations Development Programme (UNDP) household survey in 2018 showed that poverty in Teknaf and Ukhiya increased by over 2.5 percentage points as a result of declining wages for agricultural and other unskilled workers. The arrival of Rohingya refugees has also affected public health services such as solid waste management, sanitation, and hygiene. With an increase of about 10,000 tons of solid waste produced per month, water resource contamination is a growing concern. Contaminants spread waterborne diseases to refugees and host communities, as a majority of the population relies on water from wells, ponds, and canals for daily use.[91]

The Impact of Underdevelopment on Stability

At the same time that conflict undermines development, underdevelopment correlates with an increased propensity to conflict. Today, a country at the 50th percentile for income has a 7–11 percent risk of civil conflict within five years, while a country in the 10th percentile has a 15–18 percent risk.[92]

There are a number of reasons why this may be the case. Interestingly, many of them derive from grievances fed by inequality. Inequality sets the scene for tension between groups in power and groups at the margins of society. "In the absence of incentives to avoid violence or address grievances, group leaders may mobilize their cohort to violence. Emotions, collective memories, frustration over unmet expectations, and a narrative that rouses a group to violence can all play a role in this mobilization."[93]

Systemic weaknesses are often perpetuated by poor governance, which has been correlated with an increased risk of armed conflict.[94] When governments are unable or unwilling to deliver services equally well across societies, it undermines economic progress and can drive polarization. Similarly, when corruption undermines faith in government, it reduces investment, undermining economic progress and stability (see Chapter 18). In Kenya, for example, poverty is more saturated in areas where minority groups tend to live.[95] This type of concentrated poverty may lead to violence and conflict, as it further entrenches inequalities.

All of this means that efforts to foster development and work to create stability must go hand in hand. There used to be substantial scope to promote development without focusing on drivers of instability, but that is no longer true. Investments in development must actively strive to reduce fragility, as the parts of the world that remain poor are, with increasing frequency, the ones that are also unstable; that poverty is often driven in large part by inequities.

The Changing Nature of Warfare and Conflict

Even as the connections between poverty, fragility, and conflict become clearer, the nature of violent conflict has evolved substantially. Since the end of the Cold War in the early 1990s, there has been a dramatic evolution in the nature of wars and the types of conflict that predominate globally. The combatants and tactics of war have shifted. Today, a more diverse set of players have the power to propel or prevent conflict.[96] Additionally, the impacts of violent conflict are felt directly by a greater variety of people, and particularly by civilians. This has critical implications; efforts to reduce instability and to prevent, resolve, and recover from violent conflicts must involve a wider range of stakeholders. That is, they must be more inclusive.

Changing Definitions of War and Violent Conflict

After the end of the Cold War, it seemed that war was abating globally. When conflict is narrowly defined, that still appears to be the case. According to the Peace Research Institute Oslo (PRIO) and the Uppsala Conflict Data Program (UCDP), there were fifty-two state-based violent conflicts in the world in 2018.[97] At the same time, the number of "conflict casualties" decreased in 2017; 22 percent fewer people died as a direct result of conflict.[98] Yet today's reality of conflict is much more complex, and narrow definitions mask evolving realities.

The share of civilian, noncombatant victims of conflict has risen substantially even as the number of direct combat-related deaths has fallen. Though data collection is inconsistent and definitions vary, it is clear that the majority of casualties of war today are civilian noncombatants.[99] For example, it is estimated that over 43,000 civilians had died violent deaths in the war in Afghanistan as of October 2019, whereas coalition forces lost 3,635 soldiers between 2001 and 2019.[100] In Iraq, of some 109,000 violent deaths between 2004 and 2009, about 66,000 were civilians, while approximately 15,000 were members of the Iraqi security forces, and 3,771 were US and allied soldiers.[101] Compounding the impact on civilians, the war in Afghanistan continues to exacerbate poverty, malnutrition, healthcare accessibility, and sanitation.[102] Families and communities affected by conflict have always been stakeholders in conflict; today, they are the vast majority of those directly affected by wars and violence.

At the same time, the number of recurrent conflicts has increased. In the early 2000s (the most recent period for which data is available), some 60 percent of conflicts relapsed, with countries returning to war following accords.[103] Many of those extended conflicts are driving a substantial share of forced displacement. Over two-thirds of the displaced people globally are fleeing one of five conflicts: those in Afghanistan, Myanmar, Syria, Somalia, and South Sudan, all long-enduring wars or situations of extended instability.[104] The displacement has implications for the diversity of societies around the world (with related consequences for social cohesion). Among the root causes of these conflicts are grievances born, in part, of perceptions of inequity and exclusion.

Increasing the complexity today is that the highest levels of violence are often experienced outside the context of war (see Chapter 14). "Criminal activity causes many more deaths than conflicts and terrorism combined. The 464,000 victims of homicide surpassed by far the 89,000 killed in armed conflicts and the 26,000 fatal victims of terrorist violence in 2017."[105] According to studies conducted by the US government and the UN, two dominant gangs—MS-13 and M-18—operating in El Salvador, Guatemala, and Honduras have some 54,000 members.[106] Beyond the civilian casualties, rule of law and broader economic growth are stunted in those nations. Sadly, criminality born of marginalization and exclusion undermines socioeconomic stability, terrorizes communities, and creates conditions of exclusion that limit citizens' access to economic opportunity. The violence and lawlessness also impact neighboring countries' socioeconomic stability, as "unprecedented levels of violence outside a war zone" drive large-scale migration.[107] Approximately 500,000 people migrate to Mexico annually, "the majority from El Salvador, Honduras, and Guatemala."[108] One survey found that 39 percent of migrants credited "direct attacks or threats to themselves or their families, extortion or gang-forced recruitment as the main reason for leaving home."[109]

The wars and violent conflicts of today underline the ways in which diversity and inclusion issues are central to peacebuilding. Grievances born, in part, of marginalization and exclusion are driving and sustaining long-running conflicts and brutal violence. Those intractable situations are spurring displacement and driving further marginalization and grievance in many places globally.

Changing Tactics of Warfare

Digital media, online technology, and the use of drones have also broadened the effects of conflict. Today, cyberwarfare, "the use of computer technology to disrupt the activities of a state or organization, especially the deliberate attacking of information systems for strategic or military purposes," can have a catastrophic impact on national sovereignty and rule of law, notwithstanding the limited number of casualties of combat.[110] Russian hacking in the 2016 US presidential election, as well as Russian interference in the domestic elections of Ukraine and other Balkans states, are examples of this new form of battle.[111]

Social media is frequently used by the same actors involved in cyber attacks, as was the case in the 2016 US election; sophisticated Russian hacking attacks were paired with disinformation campaigns to exacerbate social tensions around sensitive domestic issues.[112] Often, the online campaigns involve sowing grievance and advancing exclusionary narratives to weaken social cohesion, as they did in the United States, where online disinformation campaigns stoked divides by race and political ideology.[113] These international campaigns often involve and touch individual citizens across societies, broadening those targeted and affected by these newer weapons and tactics of war.

Digital technology is also being used to foster narratives of grievance to radicalize populations and to facilitate recruitment into violent movements. For instance, at its peak in 2015, ISIS recruitment saw between 1,500 and 2,000 foreign fighters crossing into Iraq and Syria per month.[114] By the end of the year, representatives of eighty-six countries had joined ISIS and other violent extremist groups in the region.[115] This widespread recruitment relied on aggressive digital propaganda highlighting the caliphate "brand" to create ideological and political appeal for recruits. A study conducted by Quillium in 2015 found that ISIS disseminated an average of 38.2 unique propaganda pieces per day, including videos, audio statements, news bulletins, posters, and theological essays.[116]

The prioritization of combating cyberwar lies in the catastrophic impact it can have on national sovereignty and rule of law, notwithstanding the limited number of direct casualties of related combat. Consequently, cyberwar became one of the US Army's top priorities in 2017–2018, and the Department of Defense outlined a cybersecurity plan to protect the validity of the 2020 presidential elections.[117] The European Union has also taken several steps to prioritize information security and fight cybercrime. In 2013, a directive on attacks against information systems was created to tackle large-scale cyberattacks and required implementation by member states by September 2015.[118] This directive strengthened national cybercrime laws, increased cooperation between member states, and toughened criminal sanctions.[119]

Further adding complexity and increasing the exposure of the general population to violent conflict is the use of uncrewed drones, especially to target suspected terrorists. Few countries have drones, and even fewer have conducted drone strikes, but they remain ethically, strategically, and politically controversial.[120] Over the past decade, for example, the United States has undertaken over 14,000 drone attacks, especially in Pakistan, Afghanistan, Yemen, and Somalia. It is estimated that 8,000–17,000 people have been killed, including some 900–2,000 civilians.[121] Scholars debate the place drones should have in conflict. Daniel Byman concludes that "drone strikes remain a necessary instrument of counterterrorism," while Michael Walzer warns they may easily bleed into the ethical gray area of targeted killing, and Audrey Cronin questions their efficacy.[122] Regardless, they further enmesh civilians in violent conflicts and engage soldiers in remote warfare.

Broadening the Range of Stakeholders in Violent Conflict

The importance of a focus on inclusiveness also emerges in analyses of the changing stakeholders in wars. Today, a wider range of players need to be engaged in combating violence, including those who are currently promulgating violence and those who are currently pushing nonviolently for change.[123] Terrorist actors, citizen movements, and even individuals financing activism are stoking and leveraging grievance from afar. These groups and individuals represent the wider range of interests that need to be addressed in efforts to promote stability, prosperity, and inclusion.

Terrorists and Extremists

Even as the number of state-based conflicts continued to decline, the number of nonstate conflicts increased from sixty-two in 2016 to seventy-six in 2018.[124] These nonstate conflicts involving forces outside of government take place around the world, and they are often among the most destructive. Extremists and terrorists feature prominently in Iraq, Syria, Afghanistan, and Nigeria. In some cases, their territorial control and their military might approach that of nation-states. For example, the US military estimates that ISIS/ISIL had as many as 30,000 combatants in its ranks as of 2016, rivaling the active-duty forces of small countries such as Portugal.[125]

Yet despite their import in global peace and conflict today, there is no structured or organized global forum for engaging with or confronting the challenges posed by radicalized, violent nonstate actors. As a result, unresolved grievances remain, perpetuating feelings of marginalization and impeding resolution of critical issues related to extremists and terrorists globally. For example, in 2020, some 70,000 former ISIS combatants and their family members remained in Syria, housed in festering ungoverned camps. They were unable to depart, and no organized process existed for maintaining their health and well-being, adjudicating their crimes, or managing their repatriation.[126] The regeneration and expansion of extremist sentiment in these informal settlements perpetuates and feeds grievances.

Civil Society Movements

Local civil society movements and organizations today also have greater influence on violent conflict, increasing the importance of engaging them in conflict transformation efforts (see Chapter 18). The influences are multifaceted. Civil society movements can be essential partners in resolving conflicts. This was the case in Liberia, where a coalition of Catholic and Muslim women successfully pushed peace negotiators to reach an accord ending the three-year Second Liberian Civil War and over twenty years of civil strife.[127]

Movements can also foster nonviolent conflict transformation and government accountability. For example, the Black Monday Movement in Uganda started in 2012 to protest corruption in the government.[128] Protestors took to the streets of Kampala, and countries such as Ireland, Britain, Norway, and Denmark all suspended financial aid to Uganda as a result. The protests led Ugandan authorities to investigate corruption and dismiss government officials who were involved. The movement generated media coverage and debate, influencing government action and Uganda's public sphere. Since then, Black Monday activists have continued their campaign, relaunching the effort in 2019.[129]

At times, movements that begin peacefully can culminate in violence or oppression. Sadly, rather than ushering in peaceful transitions to democracy, many of the street protests and popular movements for inclusion that launched in 2010 and spread across the Middle East and North Africa as part of the Arab Spring ultimately resulted in violent conflict, vacuums in governance, and a new generation of autocratic leaders.

Nonetheless, it is important to recognize that nonviolent civil society movements are almost twice as likely as violent efforts to successfully foster more inclusive societies.[130] In places ranging from Timor-Leste to Burma, civil resistance has led to government that is more representative and inclusive. These nonviolent stakeholders are often allies in efforts to foster equity and inclusion. For example, the ousting of Philippine dictator Ferdinand Marcos from power in 1986 relied on a broad, nonviolent coalition of various groups, including religious leaders, students, and workers.[131] Utilizing mass demonstrations, the movement attracted widespread media coverage that challenged the regime. It placed pressure on Marcos and motivated diverse grassroots groups to get involved.

Diaspora Communities

Communities of people from conflict zones living abroad, as well as descendants of people from countries at war, are also increasing their influence over violent conflicts. People living outside conflict can foment division using social media. They can also lobby politically, provide financial support to armed groups and governments, and physically return to participate in armed conflict.[132] This involvement can escalate conflict and undermine efforts to achieve peace. A 2004 World Bank study found that the involvement of a "large diaspora considerably increases the risk of repeat conflict," primarily as a result of the financial support they provide to parties to conflict.[133]

When they were forced to leave their home areas because of violence or trauma, members of a diaspora are particularly likely to support radical positions and encourage conflict over peaceful resolution of disputes.[134] The case of the Sri Lankan diaspora is particularly illustrative. Conflict between Tamil separatists and Sri Lankan state forces hardened ethnic divisions in the country, leading to over 20 years of violence.[135] In the 1980s and 1990s, over 700,000 Tamils fled the country. The Tamil diaspora distributed propaganda and raised funds for the separatists, the Liberation Tigers of Tamil Eelam (LTTE). It is estimated that by the mid-1990s, 80–90 percent of the LTTE military budget was raised by the diaspora; the Sri Lankan government estimated that approximately $80 million/year was flowing in from abroad.[136]

That said, diaspora communities can be assets to their home communities, providing money and human capital for entrepreneurial and development efforts. They also play important roles in drawing attention to and generating support for human rights.[137] Recently, for example, members of the Rohingya and Uyghur diasporas have focused attention on the plight of their peoples in China and Myanmar.[138]

More generally, diaspora communities' influence over countries' development, even in the absence of instability, is growing. As migration accelerates, the importance of remittances—transfers of money back home from people employed abroad—are huge and growing. Globally, remittances represented the largest financial flow into many countries, totaling $406 billion in 2012 alone.[139] In the Philippines in 2019, for example, total remittances increased by 3.3 percent from 2018 to $33.5 billion, or 9.3 percent of GDP.[140] That capital increased national income substantially, but it also represented a loss of human capital and undercut domestic development, reducing domestic investment and production.[141] In the case of the Philippines, one in ten citizens now lives abroad.

As the conflict and fragility landscape evolves, many more stakeholders are affected by conflict. Additionally, a wider range of players can influence conflict dynamics. Efforts to prevent and resolve conflict must adapt to successfully involve a wider range of players, to increase the resilience of societies to conflict, to resolve grievances, and to ensure that peace, once brokered, is durable.

The Threat of Climate Change and Environmental Degradation

Increasing the urgent need to focus on marginalization and vulnerability are environmental threats. Climate change is already affecting countries and communities around the world, with consequences for stability and prosperity. The trend is toward a generally warmer planet with more frequent and severe weather events and altered microclimates. The implications for the global environment and human well-being are vast and include altered fresh water availability, changes in plant and animal habitats, higher sea levels, increased water salinity, and increased average temperatures.

Economies and societies around the world will be significantly affected. Agriculture, animal husbandry, and tourism need to adapt. Food security, economic well-being, and global health are all placed at risk by increased volatility. Droughts have become more frequent in Africa, and flooding has become more common in Asia.[142] Wildfires in North America and Australia are becoming more severe and widespread.[143]

Climate change is also causing more severe and more frequent El Niño events, cyclical changes in climate that raise water temperatures and affect marine life and weather patterns.[144] For example, from September 2018 to April 2019, the El Niño event in the Horn of Africa, East Africa, and southern Africa triggered drought cycles for the second time in three years.[145] Farmers and other agricultural workers struggled to produce enough food for the region, exacerbating food insecurity, particularly among the most vulnerable populations.

Of equal significance are the secondary implications for stability and prosperity, particularly in the face of insufficient action to stop the growth in greenhouse gas emissions or to reduce vulnerability and adapt to the changing environment. More severe and increasingly frequent severe weather events such as hurricanes, earthquakes, cyclones, and tornadoes have caused economic devastation in places ranging from Haiti and Nepal.[146] Losses from natural disasters have been trending upward (see Figure 1.4).[147]

The impacts are disproportionately felt by the poor and marginalized. In the Asia-Pacific region, "losses due to disasters will undermine the ability of economic growth to reduce poverty and inequality by 2030, by widening inequalities in outcomes and opportunities and disempowering at-risk communities. Disasters could include more frequent and more severe cyclones, floods, dust storms, heatwaves, tsunamis, earthquakes, droughts, storm surges, and severe thunderstorms. . . . [A] 1 percentage point increase in exposure to climate events increases the Gini coefficient by 0.24, increases under-five mortality rates by 0.3, and decreases education rates by 0.26 percentage points, respectively."[148] Decreases in the availability of water are also already believed to be contributing to tensions in Sudan, the Lake Chad Basin, and Syria, often because they exacerbate conflict among groups over unequal resource distribution and access.

Environmental degradation, especially in developing economies, is taking a toll on communities, particularly those that rely on natural resources for their well-being.

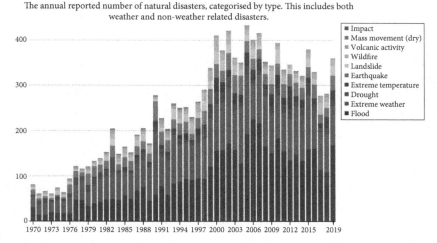

The annual reported number of natural disasters, categorised by type. This includes both weather and non-weather related disasters.

Legend:
- Impact
- Mass movement (dry)
- Volcanic activity
- Wildfire
- Landslide
- Earthquake
- Extreme temperature
- Drought
- Extreme weather
- Flood

Figure 1.4 Global Reported Natural Disasters by Type, 1970–2019

Credit line:

Source: EMDAT (2020): OFDA/CRED International Disaster Database, Université catholique de Louvain – Brussels – Belgium. OurWorldInData.org/natural-disasters.

This work is licensed under Creative Commons Attribution 4.0 International License (CC BY).

In Indonesia, large-scale deforestation has threatened the well-being of indigenous communities. The country lost 24 million hectares of forest cover between 2001 to 2017 due to a lack of government oversight of forest clearing for oil palm plantations.[149] A study by Human Rights Watch found that violations by oil palm companies have adversely affected indigenous peoples' livelihoods, food and water access, and culture in Bengkayang regency, West Kalimantan, and Sarolangun regency, Jambi.[150]

Though everyone is affected by climate change, the impact on the poor and vulnerable is already proving disproportionate. Between 2008 and 2014, an annual average of 22.5 million people were displaced due to weather and climate-related hazards.[151] By the end of 2019, it was estimated that 5.1 million "climate migrants"— people who have moved because of environmental stressors—were living in ninety-five countries.[152] Of those, the majority are women, who often survive on more marginal land, frequently without land tenure and with fewer inputs such as drought-resistant seed varieties, to help them ride through turbulent periods.

This increased global vulnerability, particularly for certain segments of the population, once again demands a greater focus on inclusion.

The Bottom Line: Increasingly Intertwined Goals—Prosperity, Stability, Inclusion

Taken together, these trends point to the need for substantial changes in the approach to preventing and resolving conflict, and to fostering global development. There are several overarching implications.

Efforts to foster stability and development at local, national, and global levels must authentically engage a wider range of stakeholders. Whether it's the wider range of parties to violent conflict around the world or the ways migrants and refugees are altering the composition of countries, a growing body of evidence clearly demonstrates that broader engagement with diverse interest groups is necessary for steady economic, political, and social progress, and for continued stability globally (see Chapter 2).

Even as we recognize that inclusion is fundamental to success, the heterogeneity of interested and influential parties is growing. The diversity within communities and countries is increasing, and the influence of diverse stakeholders is growing as well. Technology is bringing us closer and altering the power dynamics among us. Navigating the ever-evolving mix of influencers necessitates appreciation for the promise of engagement and the risks associated with marginalization.

Underlying those shifts are a series of trends that augment the urgency. Interdependence is growing; we thrive or fail as a global community in seeking to address collective challenges like climate change or health pandemics. From a purely pragmatic standpoint, we are only as strong as our weakest links. We can only contain pandemics if we halt the spread of the disease writ large. We can only reduce changes in the climate if we lower net emissions worldwide.

The dynamics of prosperity and stability are changing as well. To foster the development of nations today, we must better reduce fragility and resolve conflicts. The convergence of underdeveloped nations with conflict-affected and fragile states demands it. Underlying that effort must be greater commitment to equity and inclusion as well. Conflict is both a cause and a consequence of marginalization. Poverty is a driver and a result of exclusion. Unless we address growing disparities, we undermine our efforts to promote development and to enhance stability.

Enhancing inclusion in less-developed and fragile states is opportunistic and essential. From a moral standpoint, we must recognize and address the disparities that are growing as a result of inattention to inequality and exclusion, and as a result of trends that disproportionately impact those who are vulnerable by virtue of their exposure to risk or their historical disadvantage. At the same time, taking full advantage of the diversity within societies offers the potential for enormous social, economic, and political benefits. Failing to engage everyone within societies undermines peace and prosperity in countries and communities around the world. Globally, fostering equity and inclusion in increasingly diverse countries and communities is a defining challenge of the twenty-first century.

Notes

1. Das, Fisiy, and Kyte 2013.
2. Hoofnagle et al. 2020.
3. Edwards, Lee, and Esposito 2019.

4. Bella 2020.
5. Rodríguez 2020; US Department of Homeland Security 2020.
6. Kirby 2020.
7. See, for example, Lavin 2020.
8. Taylor 2020.
9. Dave 2020.
10. World Health Organization 2020; Institute for Health Metrics and Evaluation n.d.; World Health Organization n.d.
11. Institute for Health Metrics and Evaluation 2021.
12. For example, see World Health Organization 2019.
13. Ro 2020.
14. CDC 2021.
15. Wilder 2021. For incidence data, see Artiga et al. 2020. For mortality rates, see APM Research Lab 2020.
16. Bettinger-Lopez and Bo 2020.
17. CDC n.d.
18. UNDESA 2015.
19. Pew Research Center 2014.
20. Leckman, Panter-Brick, and Salah 2014. See also Das Gupta et al. 2014.
21. For the African context, see Sommers 2011. See also Lin 2012.
22. Urdal 2006.
23. OECD 2019; World Bank n.d. a.
24. DSPD/UNESDA and ILO 2013.
25. UNHCR 2019.
26. Edwards 2018.
27. European Commission n.d.
28. UNHCR 2019.
29. European Commission 2015, 5.
30. Pew Research Center 2017.
31. Dowling et al. 2019.
32. Taylor and Silver 2019; Silver 2019.
33. Silver 2019.
34. Hall, Schmitz, and Dedmon 2020.
35. Sawyer 2011.
36. Zeitzoff 2017. See also Koerner 2016.
37. Human Rights Council 2018.
38. IRIN 2017; Peace Tech Lab 2017; Reeves 2017.
39. Matamoros-Fernández and Farkas 2021.
40. For more information on the use of technology in conflict, see Gohdes 2018.
41. Revollo 2020.
42. World Bank 2019. The Gini coefficient measures "the extent to which the distribution of income [or, in some cases, consumption expenditures] among individuals or households within an economy deviates from a perfectly equal distribution. A Gini index of zero represents perfect equality and 100, perfect inequality" (OECD 2006).
43. United Nations 2020, 26. For a detailed exploration of how income inequality is evolving between and within nations, and over time, see Milanovic 2016; Piketty and Goldhammer 2015.
44. Horizontal inequalities refer to "inequalities among groups with a shared identity." They are composed of a wide range of racial, political, economic, and cultural dimensions, among other categories (Stewart 2016).
45. UNDP 2019, 56.

46. OECD 2020; Vazquez-Martinez, Hansen, and Quintero 2020.

47. Piff, Kraus, and Keltner 2018.

48. Stewart, Brown, and Cobham 2009.

49. PIIE 2020.

50. See, for example, Thomas 1999.

51. Cramer 2003.

52. World Bank 2018b.

53. Hegre and Nygard 2012.

54. For a detailed revision of the literature, see World Bank 2018b.

55. Gross domestic product (GDP) "measures the monetary value of final goods and services—
that is, those that are bought by the final user—produced in a country in a given period of
time (say a quarter or a year). It counts all of the output generated within the borders of a
country. GDP is composed of goods and services produced for sale in the market and also
includes some nonmarket production, such as defense or education services provided by
the government" (Callen 2020).

56. Pathfinders 2019.

57. World Bank n.d. b; PIIE 2020.

58. Callen 2020.

59. "Developing countries" are generally characterized by low per capita GDP, low GNI, a relatively less developed industrial base, and a lower HDI. That said, it is worth noting that organizations such as the World Bank are phasing the term out because of its imprecision and
the heterogeneity of nations to which it is applied. See Khokhar and Serajuddin 2015.

60. Ingram and Lord 2019.

61. Scheffran et al. 2012, 43.

62. "Fragile states are commonly described as incapable of assuring basic security, maintaining
rule of law and justice, or providing basic services and economic opportunities for their citizens" (Mcgloughlin 2012).

63. Madden 2019; International Development Association n.d.

64. Jolliffe, Lugo, et al., 2018, 29.

65. Fund for Peace n.d.

66. UNDP 2015, 3.

67. Institute for Economics and Peace 2018.

68. Institute for Economics and Peace 2018.

69. United Nations 2013. For more information on resource-driven economies, see Dobbs
et al. 2013.

70. Kaza et al. 2018.

71. Stockholm International Peace Research Institute n.d. For more information on the
military-industrial complex, see Turley 2014.

72. Hong 2015.

73. O'Hare and Southall 2007. See also Urdal and Chi 2013.

74. World Bank 2018a, 10.

75. Trani et al. 2016.

76. Trani et al. 2016.

77. Haar and Rubenstein 2012, 2–3. See also Levy and Sidel 2016, 206: "War and other forms
of armed conflict cause extensive morbidity and mortality among military personnel and
noncombatant civilians. Morbidity includes a wide range of disorders, from disabling
injuries to adverse effects on mental health, some of which continue for long periods and
even impair future generations. Populations suffer much morbidity during, and in the aftermath of, armed conflict because of damage to the health-supporting infrastructure of

society, including systems to provide safe food and water, medical care and public health services, sanitation and hygiene, transportation, communication, and electrical power."

78. Qirbi and Ismail 2017, 916.
79. Qirbi and Ismail 2017, 916.
80. El Bcheraoui et al. 2018.
81. World Bank 2017b, i.
82. Statista n.d.; Trading Economics n.d.; Central Intelligence Agency n.d.
83. World Bank 2017b, viii–ix, i.
84. Mokdad, Farouzanfar, and Daoud 2016.
85. UNHCR 2018, 2.
86. Chu 2020.
87. For more information about the impact of refugee influx in Lebanon, see Ghosn, Braithwaite, and Chu 2019.
88. UNHCR 2020.
89. Mansour-Ille et al. 2018.
90. Karasapan and Shah 2018.
91. UNDP 2018, 22–25.
92. Rice, Graff, and Lewis 2006, 5.
93. Leckman, Panter-Brick, and Salah 2014, 109.
94. Thian Hee et al. 2016.
95. Young 2012.
96. Kaldor 2012.
97. Uppsala Conflict Data Program n.d. UCDP defines state-based armed conflict as "a contested incompatibility that concerns government and/or territory where the use of armed force between two parties, of which at least one is the government of a state, results in at least 25 battle-related deaths in one calendar year" (Uppsala Universitet n.d.).
98. Dupuy and Ruustad 2018.
99. Epps 2013.
100. Watson Institute 2020; Statista 2020.
101. Leigh 2010.
102. Epps 2013.
103. Von Einsiedel 2014.
104. UNHCR 2019; Specia 2018.
105. UNODC 2019, 12. See also Applebaum and Mawby 2018; Mc Evoy and Hideg 2017.
106. Leggett et al. 2012, 29.
107. Medecins Sans Frontières 2017.
108. Medecins Sans Frontières 2017, 4.
109. Medecins Sans Frontières 2017, 5.
110. Lexico n.d.
111. US Senate 2019a; Stronski and Himes 2019; Polyakova and Boyer 2018.
112. Brattberg and Maurer 2018, 3; see also US Senate 2019b.
113. DiResta et al. 2018.
114. Wilson Center 2017.
115. Benmelech and Klor 2016, 1.
116. Winter 2015.
117. RAND Corporation 2018; Cronk 2020.
118. European Union 2013.
119. European Commission 2017.
120. Bergen, Salyk-Virk, and Sterman 2019.
121. Bureau of Investigative Journalism n.d.

122. Byman 2013, 32; Walzer 2013; Cronin 2013.
123. Pettersson and Eck 2018.
124. Rudolfsen 2019. Nonstate conflicts are defined as "the use of armed force between two organised armed groups, neither of which is the government of a state, which results in at least 25 battle-related deaths in a year" (Uppsala Universitet n.d.).
125. Stanford University 2017; International Institute for Strategic Studies 2018.
126. International Crisis Group 2020.
127. Global Nonviolent Action Database n.d.
128. Essoungou 2013.
129. Independent Uganda 2019.
130. Chenoweth and Stephan 2013, 32.
131. Chenoweth and Stephan 2013, 32.
132. Chenoweth and Stephan 2013, 32.
133. Collier and Hoeffler 2004, 575.
134. Democratic Progress Institute 2014, 8–9.
135. Democratic Progress Institute 2014, 11–12.
136. Cochrane, Baser, and Swain 2009, 690.
137. Brinkerhoff 2011.
138. Petersen 2006; Leider 2018.
139. USAID 2016.
140. Xinhua 2020.
141. Vargas-Lundius et al. 2008.
142. Dutta and Hearth 2004.
143. Williams et al. 2019; Yu et al. 2020.
144. Wang et al. 2019.
145. Food and Agriculture Organization 2019.
146. World Bank 2017a; Regmi 2016, 8.
147. Insurance Information Institute 2020.
148. Alisjahbana, Zahedi, and Bonapace 2019.
149. Global Forest Watch 2018.
150. Human Rights Watch 2019.
151. Nansen Initiative 2015.
152. Migration Data Portal 2020. For more information, see Institute for Environment and Human Security 2015.

Bibliography

Alisjahbana, Armida Salsiah, Kaveh Zahedi, and Tiziana Bonapace. 2019. "Executive Summary." In *The Disaster Riskscape Across Asia-Pacific: Pathways for Resilience, Inclusion and Empowerment*. Bangkok: ESCAP. https://www.unescap.org/sites/default/files/APDR%202019%20Executive%20summary.pdf.

Amnesty International. 2020. "Uyghurs Tell of China-Led Intimidation Campaign Abroad." https://www.amnesty.org/en/latest/research/2020/02/china-uyghurs-abroad-living-in-fear/.

APM Research Lab. 2020. "The Color of Coronavirus: Covid-19 deaths Analyzed by Race and Ethnicity in the U.S." May 20. https://www.apmresearchlab.org/covid/deaths-by-race.

Applebaum, Anna, and Briana Mawby. 2018. "Gang Violence as Armed Conflict." Georgetown Institute for Women, Peace and Security. November. https://giwps.georgetown.edu/wp-content/uploads/2018/12/Gang-Violence-as-Armed-Conflict.pdf.

Artiga, Samantha, Kendal Orgera, Olivia Pham, and Bradley Corallo. 2020. "Growing Data Underscore That Communities of Color are Being Harder Hit by COVID-19." Kaiser Family

Foundation. April 21. https://www.kff.org/coronavirus-policy-watch/growing-data-undersc ore-communities-color-harder-hit-covid-19/.

Bella, Timothy. 2020. "White Men Mocked George Floyd's Death at a Protest. Now a Corrections Officer in the Group Has Been Suspended." *The Washington Post*. June 10. https://www.was hingtonpost.com/nation/2020/06/10/george-floyd-new-jersey-protest/.

Benmelech, Efraim, and Esteban Klor. 2016. "What Explains the Flow of Foreign Fighters to ISIS?" NBER Working Paper 22190. National Bureau of Economic Research, Cambridge, MA. https://doi.org/10.3386/w22190.

Bergen, Peter, Melissa Salyk-Virk, and David Sterman. 2019. "World of Drones." New America. November 22. https://www.newamerica.org/international-security/reports/world-drones/.

Bettinger-Lopez, Caroline, and Alexandra Bo. 2020. "A Double Pandemic: Domestic Violence in the Age of COVID-19." Council on Foreign Relations. May 13. https://www.cfr.org/in-brief/ double-pandemic-domestic-violence-age-covid-19.

Brattberg, Erik, and Tim Maurer. 2018. *Russian Election Interference: Europe's Counter to Fake News and Cyber Attacks*. Washington, DC: Carnegie Endowment for International Peace, 2018. https://carnegieendowment.org/files/CP_333_BrattbergMaurer_Russia_Elections_Int erference_FINAL.pdf.

Brinkerhoff, Jennifer M. 2011. "Diasporas and Conflict Societies: Conflict Entrepreneurs, Competing Interests or Contributors to Stability and Development?" *Conflict, Security and Development* 11, no. 2: 115–143. doi: 10.1080/14678802.2011.572453.

Buchanan, Larry, Quoctrung Bui, and Jugal K. Patel. 2020. "Black Lives Matter May Be the Largest Movement in U.S. History." *The New York Times*. July 3. https://www.nytimes.com/interactive/ 2020/07/03/us/george-floyd-protests-crowd-size.html.

Bureau of Investigative Journalism. n.d. "Drone Warfare." The Bureau of Investigative Journalism. https://www.thebureauinvestigates.com/projects/drone-war

Byman, Daniel. 2013. "Why Drones Work: The Case for Washington's Weapon of Choice." *Foreign Affairs* 92, no. 4 (July/August): 32–43.

Callen, Tim. 2020. "Gross Domestic Product: An Economy's All." International Monetary Fund, February. https://www.imf.org/external/pubs/ft/fandd/basics/gdp.htm.

CDC. 2020. "Cases, Data, and Surveillance." Centers for Disease Control and Prevention. February 11. https://www.cdc.gov/coronavirus/2019-ncov/covid-data/investigations-discov ery/hospitalization-death-by-race-ethnicity.html.

CDC. n.d. "COVID Data Tracker." Centers for Disease Control and Prevention. Accessed March 28, 2020. https://covid.cdc.gov/covid-data-tracker.

Central Intelligence Agency. n.d. "The World Factbook: Syria." https://www.cia.gov/library/publi cations/the-world-factbook/geos/sy.html.

Chenoweth, Erica, and Maria J. Stephan. 2013. *Why Civil Resistance Works: The Strategic Logic of Nonviolent Conflict*. New York: Columbia University Press.

Chu, Tiffany S. 2020. "Hosting Your Enemy: Accepting Refugees from a Rival State and Respect for Human Rights." *Journal of Global Security Studies* 5, no. 1: 4–24. https://doi.org/10.1093/ jogss/ogz043.

Cochrane, F., B. Baser, and A. Swain. 2009. "Home Thoughts From Abroad: Diasporas and Peace-Building in Northern Ireland and Sri Lanka." *Studies in Conflict and Terrorism* 32, no. 8: 681–704.

Collier, Paul, and Anke Hoeffler. 2004. "Greed and Grievance in Civil War." *Oxford Economic Papers* 56: 563–595.

Cramer, Christopher. 2003. "Does Inequality Cause Conflict?" *Journal of International Development* 15 (2003): 397–412. http://www4.fe.uc.pt/mapsd/christophercramer_africa_2 004.pdf.

Cronin, Audrey. 2013. "Why Drones Fail: When Tactics Drive Strategy." *Foreign Affairs* 92, no. 4 (July/August).

Cronk, Terri Moon. 2020. "DOD's Cyber Strategy of Past Year Outlined Before Congress." DOD News, US Department of Defense. March 6, 2020. https://www.defense.gov/Explore/News/ Article/Article/2103843/dods-cyber-strategy-of-past-year-outlined-before-congress.

Das, Maitreyi Bordia, Cyprian F. Fisiy, and Rachel Kyte. 2013. "Inclusion Matters: The Foundation for Shared Prosperity." World Bank, Washington, DC. 2013. http://documents. worldbank.org/curated/en/114561468154469371/Inclusion-matters-the-foundation-for-shared-prosperity.

Das Gupta, Monica, Robert Engelman, Jessica Levy, Gretchen Luchsinger, Tom Merrick, and James E. Rosen. 2014. "The Power of 1.8 Billion: Adolescents, Youth, and the Transformation of the Future." United Nations Population Fund, New York.

Dave, Paresh. 2020. "Factbox: What Changes Are Governments Making in Response to George Floyd Protests?" Reuters. June 12. https://www.reuters.com/article/us-minneapolis-police-protests-response/factbox-what-changes-are-governments-making-in-response-to-george-floyd-protests-idUSKBN23J36O.

Democratic Progress Institute. 2014. "Makers or Breakers of Peace: The Role of Diasporas in Conflict Resolution." Democratic Progress Institute, London. http://www.democraticprogress. org/wp-content/uploads/2014/08/Makers-or-Breakers-of-Peace-The-Role-of-Diasporas-in-Conflict-Resolution.pdf.

Dev Regmi, Kapil. 2016. "The Political Economy of 2015 Nepal Earthquake: Some Critical Reflections." *Asian Geographer* 33, no. 2 (September 28). https://doi.org/10.1080/10225 706.2016.1235053.

DiResta, Renee, Kris Shaffer, Becky Ruppel, David Sullivan, Robert Matney, Ryan Fox, Dr. Jonathan Albright, and Ben Johnson. 2018. *The Tactics and Tropes of the Internet Research Agency.* Austin, TX: New Knowledge. https://int.nyt.com/data/documenthelper/533-read-rep ort-internet-research-agency/7871ea6d5b7bedafbf19/optimized/full.pdf#page=1.

Dobbs, Richard, Jeremy Oppenheim, Adam Kendall, Fraser Thompson, Martin Bratt, and Fransje van der Marel. 2013. *Reverse the Curse: Maximizing the Potential of Resource-Driven Economies.* New York: McKinsey Global Institute. https://www.mckinsey.com/~/media/McKinsey/Ind ustries/Metals%20and%20Mining/Our%20Insights/Reverse%20the%20curse%20Maximiz ing%20the%20potential%20of%20resource%20driven%20economies/MGI_Reverse_the_cu rse_Full_report.ashx.

Dowling, Siobhán, Bettina Vestring, Derek Scally, and Ronja Scheler. 2019. "Politics of Resentment." *Berlin Policy Journal.* September 5. https://berlinpolicyjournal.com/politics-of-resentment/.

DSPD/UNESDA and ILO. 2013. "Youth and Labor Migration: Summary of Week 5 Online Discussions." 2013 UN World Youth Report: Youth Migration and Development. UN Department of Economic and Social Affairs. https://www.ilo.org/wcmsp5/groups/public/---ed_emp/documents/genericdocument/wcms_209613.pdf.

Dupuy, Kendra, and Siri Aas Ruustad. 2018. "Trends in Armed Conflict: 1946–2017." Peace Research Institute Oslo. https://www.prio.org/Publications/Publication/?x=11181.

Dutta, Dushmanta, and Srikantha Hearth. 2004. "Trend of Floods in Asia and Flood Risk Management with Integrated River Basin Approach." Unpublished paper. https://pdfs.sema nticscholar.org/20ea/6f5a25f7857f5ba34563b5ae7719fcdf9a40.pdf?_ga=2.75781905.585585 171.1593725763-339835723.1591143880.

Edwards, Adrian. 2018. "Forced Displacement at Record 68.5 Million." UN Refugee Agency. June 19.   http://www.unhcr.org/en-us/news/stories/2018/6/5b222c494/forced-displacement-rec ord-685-million.html.

Edwards, Frank, Hedwig Lee, and Michael Esposito. 2019. "Risk of Being Killed by Police Use of Force in the United States by Age, Race-Ethnicity, and Sex." *Proceedings of the National Academy of Sciences* 116, no. 34: 16793–16798. https://doi.org/10.1073/pnas.1821204116.

El Bcheraoui, Charbel, Aisha O. Jumaan, Michael L. Collison, Farah Daoud, and Ali H. Mokdad. 2018. "Health in Yemen: Losing Ground in a Time of Crisis." *Global Health* 14:42. https://www. ncbi.nlm.nih.gov/pmc/articles/PMC5918919/.

Epps, Valerie. 2013. "Civilian Casualties in Modern Warfare: The Death of the Collateral Damage Rule." *Georgia Journal of International and Comparative Law* 41: 309–353. https://digitalcomm ons.law.uga.edu/cgi/viewcontent.cgi?article=1036&context=gjicl.

Espinoza Revollo, P. 2020. "Time to Care: Unpaid and Underpaid Care Work and the Global Inequality Crisis: Methodology Note." Oxfam. https://dx.doi.org/10.21201/2020.5419.

Essoungou, André-Michel. 2013. "The Rise of Civil Society Groups in Africa." Africa Renewal, United Nations. December. https://www.un.org/africarenewal/magazine/december-2013/rise-civil-society-groups-africa.

European Commission. 2017. "EU Cybersecurity Initiatives." https://ec.europa.eu/information_society/newsroom/image/document/2017-3/factsheet_cybersecurity_update_january_2017_41543.pdf.

European Commission. 2015. "Short Analytical Web Note—Demography Report." Employment, Social Affairs and Inclusion, European Commission. https://ec.europa.eu/eurostat/documents/3217494/6917833/KE-BM-15-003-EN-N.pdf/76dac490-9176-47bc-80d9-029e1d967af6.

European Commission. n.d. "Forced Displacement: Refugees, Asylum-Seekers and Internally Displaced People (IDPs)." European Civil Protection and Humanitarian Aid Operations, European Commission. https://ec.europa.eu/echo/what-we-do/humanitarian-aid/refugees-and-internally-displaced-persons_en#:~:text=Forced%20displacement%20is%20no%20longer,years%20for%2090%25%20of%20IDPs.

European Union. 2013. "Directive 2013/40/EU of the European Parliament and of the Council." August 12. https://eur-lex.europa.eu/LexUriServ/LexUriServ.do?uri=OJ:L:2013:218:0008:0014:EN:PDF.

Food and Agriculture Organization. 2019. "El Niño." February 11. http://www.fao.org/emergencies/crisis/elnino-lanina/intro/en/.

Fund for Peace. n.d. "Fragile States Index: Country Dashboard." https://fragilestatesindex.org/country-data/.

Ghosn, Faten, Alex Braithwaite, and Tiffany S Chu. 2019. "Violence, Displacement, Contact, and Attitudes Toward Hosting Refugees." Journal of Peace Research 56, no. 1: 118–133. https://journals.sagepub.com/doi/full/10.1177/0022343318804581.

Global Forest Watch. 2018. "Tree Cover Loss in Indonesia 2018." https://www.globalforestwatch.org/dashboards/country/IDN?category=summary&economicImpact=eyJ5ZWFyIjoyMDA1fQ%3D%3D.

Global Nonviolent Action Database. n.d. "Liberian Women Act to End Civil War, 2003." Swarthmore College. https://nvdatabase.swarthmore.edu/content/liberian-women-act-end-civil-war-2003.

Gohdes, Anita R. 2018. "Studying the Internet and Violent Conflict." Conflict Management and Peace Science 35, no. 1: 89–106. doi:10.1177/0738894217733878.

Hall, Nina, Hans Peter Schmitz, and J. Michael Dedmon. 2020. "Transnational Advocacy and NGOs in the Digital Era: New Forms of Networked Power." International Studies Quarterly 64, no. 1: 159–167. https://doi.org/10.1093/isq/sqz052.

Hegre, Havard, and Havard Mokleiv Nygard. 2012. "Governance and Conflict Relapse." University of Oslo. July 12. http://folk.uio.no/hahegre/Papers/GovernanceandConflictRelapse2012.pdf.

Hong, Pingfan. 2015. "Peace and Stability as Enablers for and Outcome of Development: Background Paper for World Economic and Social Survey 2014/2015: MDG Lessons for Post-2015." United Nations. February 13. http://www.un.org/en/development/desa/policy/wess/wess_bg_papers/bp_wess2015_hong1.pdf.

Hoofnagle, Mark H., Ronnie N. Mubang, D'Andrea K. Joseph, Bellal A. Joseph, Ashley Britton Christmas, and Tanya L. Zakrison. 2020. "Eastern Association for the Surgery of Trauma Statement on Structural Racism, and the Deaths of George Floyd, Ahmaud Arbery, and Breonna Taylor." Annals of Surgery 272, no. 6: 911–914. https://doi.org/10.1097/SLA.0000000000004430.

Human Rights Council. 2018. "Report of the Independent Fact-Finding Mission on Myanmar." A/HRC/39/64. September 12. https://www.ohchr.org/Documents/HRBodies/HRCouncil/FFM-Myanmar/A_HRC_39_64.pdf.

Human Rights Watch. 2019. "Indonesia: Indigenous Peoples Losing Their Forests." October 7. https://www.hrw.org/news/2019/09/22/indonesia-indigenous-peoples-losing-their-forests.

Independent Uganda. 2019. "CSO's Re-Ignite Black Monday Campaign." *The Independent Uganda.* December 16. https://www.independent.co.ug/csos-re-ignite-black-monday-campaign/.

Ingram, George, and Kristin M. Lord. 2019. "Global Development Disrupted: Findings from a Survey of 93 Leaders." Brookings Institution, Washington, DC. https://www.brookings.edu/wp-content/uploads/2019/03/Global-Development-Disrupted.pdf.

Institute for Economics and Peace. 2018. "2018 Global Peace Index." http://visionofhumanity.org/app/uploads/2018/06/Global-Peace-Index-2018-2.pdf.

Institute for Environment and Human Security. 2015. "5 Facts on Climate Migrants." United Nations University. November 26. https://ehs.unu.edu/news/news/5-facts-on-climate-migrants.html.

Institute for Health Metrics and Evaluation. 2021. "COVID-19 Has Caused 6.9 Million Deaths Globally, More than Double What Official Reports Show," May 6, 2021. http://www.healthdata.org/news-release/covid-19-has-caused-69-million-deaths-globally-more-double-what-official-reports-show.

Institute for Health Metrics and Evaluation. n.d. "COVID-19 Deaths." Accessed May 13, 2021. https://covid19.healthdata.org/.

Insurance Information Institute. 2020. "Facts Statistics: Global Catastrophes." January. https://www.iii.org/fact-statistic/facts-statistics-global-catastrophes.

International Crisis Group. 2020. "Virus Fears Spread at Camps for ISIS Families in Syria's North East." April 7. https://www.crisisgroup.org/middle-east-north-africa/eastern-mediterranean/syria/virus-fears-spread-camps-isis-families-syrias-north-east.

International Development Association. n.d. "Conflict and Fragility." World Bank Group. http://ida.worldbank.org/theme/conflict-and-fragility.

International Institute for Strategic Studies. 2018. *The Military Balance 2018.* New York: Routledge.

IRIN. 2017. *Words Matter: Hate Speech and South Sudan.* September 5. https://www.refworld.org/docid/59b8eb654.html.

Jolliffe, Dean, María Ana Lugo, et al. 2018. *Piecing Together the Poverty Puzzle: Poverty and Shared Prosperity 2018.* Washington, DC: World Bank Group. https://openknowledge.worldbank.org/bitstream/handle/10986/30418/9781464813306.pdf.

Jonnalagadda Haar, Rohini, and Leonard S. Rubenstein. 2012. "United States Institute of Peace Special Report: Health in Postconflict and Fragile States." United States Institute of Peace, Washington, DC.

Kaldor, Mary. 2012. *New and Old Wars: Organized Violence in a Global Era.* Cambridge: Polity.

Karasapan, Omer, and Sajjad Shah. 2018. "Syrian Refugees and the Schooling Challenge." Brookings Institute, Washington, DC. October 23. https://www.brookings.edu/blog/future-development/2018/10/23/syrian-refugees-and-the-schooling-challenge/.

Kaza, Silpa, Lisa Yao, Perinaz Bhata-Tata, and Frank Van Woerden. 2018. *What a Waste 2.0: A Global Snapshot of Solid Waste Management Until 2050.* Washington, DC: World Bank Group. https://openknowledge.worldbank.org/handle/10986/30317.

Khokhar, Tariq, and Omar Serajuddin. 2015. "Should We Continue to Use the Term 'Developing World'?" World Bank. November 16. https://blogs.worldbank.org/opendata/should-we-continue-use-term-developing-world.

Kirby, Jen. 2020. "'Black Lives Matter' Has Become a Global Rallying Cry Against Racism and Police Brutality." Vox Media. June 12. https://www.vox.com/2020/6/12/21285244/black-lives-matter-global-protests-george-floyd-uk-belgium.

Koerner, Brendan I. 2016. "Why ISIS Is Winning the Social Media War." Wired. March. https://www.wired.com/2016/03/isis-winning-social-media-war-heres-beat/.

Lavin, Talia. 2020. *Culture Warlords: My Journey into the Dark Web of White Supremacy.* New York: Hachette Books.

Leckman, James F., Catherine Panter-Brick, and Rima Salah. 2014. *Pathways to Peace: The Transformative Power of Children and Families.* Cambridge, MA: MIT Press.

Leggett, Ted, et al. 2020. *Transnational Organized Crime in Central America and the Caribbean: A Threat Assessment.* Vienna: United Nations Office on Drugs and Crime.

Leigh, David. 2010. "Iraq War Logs Reveal 15,000 Previously Unlisted Civilian Deaths." *The Guardian*. October 22. https://www.theguardian.com/world/2010/oct/22/true-civil ian-body-count-iraq.

Levy, Barry S., and Victor W. Sidel. 2016. "Documenting the Effects of Armed Conflict on Population Health." *Annual Review of Public Health* 37: 205–218. https://www.annualreviews. org/doi/pdf/10.1146/annurev-publhealth-032315-021913.

Lexico. n.d. "Cyberwar." Accessed May 12, 2020. https://en.oxforddictionaries.com/definition/ cyberwar.

Madden, Payce. 2019. "Figures of the Week: Fragility and Extreme Poverty." Brookings Institution, Washington, DC. January 24. https://www.brookings.edu/blog/africa-in-focus/2019/01/24/ figures-of-the-week-fragility-and-extreme-poverty/.

Mansour-Ille, Dina, Simone Haysom, Sebastian Ille, and Jessica Hagen-Zanker. 2018. "Jordan: Between the Making of a Nation and the Politics of Living." Overseas Development Institute. https://www.odi.org/sites/odi.org.uk/files/resource-documents/12541.pdf.

Matamoros-Fernández, Ariadna, and Johan Farkas. 2021. "Racism, Hate Speech, and Social Media: A Systematic Review and Critique." *Television and New Media* 22, no. 2: 205–224. https://doi.org/10.1177/1527476420982230.

McEvoy, Claire, and Gergely Hideg. 2017. "Global Violent Deaths 2017." Small Arms Survey. November. http://www.smallarmssurvey.org/fileadmin/docs/M-files/Armed_violence/Glo bal-Violent-Deaths-2017-ExSum.pdf.

Mcgloughlin, Claire. 2012. "Topic Guide on Fragile States." Governance and Social Development Resource Center, University of Birmingham. http://www.gsdrc.org/docs/open/con86.pdf.

Medecins Sans Frontières. 2017. *Forced to Flee Central America's Northern Triangle: A Neglected Humanitarian Crisis*. New York: Medecins Sans Frontières. https://www.msf.org/sites/msf. org/files/msf_forced-to-flee-central-americas-northern-triangle_e.pdf.

Migration Data Portal. 2020. "Environmental Migration." May 8. https://migrationdataportal. org/themes/environmental_migration.

Milanovic, Branko. 2016. *Global Inequality: A New Approach for the Age of Globalization*. Cambridge, MA: Harvard University Press, 2016. http://www.jstor.org/stable/j.ctvjghwk4.

Mokdad, Ali H., Mohammad Hossein Farouzanfar, and Farah Daoud. 2016. "Health in Times of Uncertainty in the Eastern Mediterranean Region, 1990–2013: A Systematic Analysis for the Global Burden of Disease Study 2013." *The Lancet Global Health* 4: E704–E713. https://www. thelancet.com/journals/langlo/article/PIIS2214-109X(16)30168-1/fulltext.

Nansen Initiative. 2015. *Agenda for the Protection of Cross-Border Displaced Persons in the Context of Disasters and Climate Change Volume 1*. Geneva: Nansen Initiative. https://environment almigration.iom.int/agenda-protection-cross-border-displaced-persons-context-disasters- and-climate-change.

O'Hare, Bernadette A. M., and David P. Southall. 2007. "First Do No Harm: The Impact of Recent Armed Conflict on Maternal and Child Health in Sub-Saharan Africa." *Journal of the Royal Society of Medicine* 100, no. 12: 564–570.

OECD. 2020. "The Impact of COVID-19 on Student Equity and Inclusion: Supporting Vulnerable Students During School Closures and School Re-Openings," November 19. https://www.oecd. org/coronavirus/policy-responses/the-impact-of-covid-19-on-student-equity-and-inclus ion-supporting-vulnerable-students-during-school-closures-and-school-re-openings- d593b5c8/.

OECD. 2019. "Permanent Immigrant Flows." https://data.oecd.org/migration/permanent- immigrant-inflows.htm.

OECD. 2006. "Gini Index." Glossary of Statistical Terms. February 16. https://stats.oecd.org/gloss ary/detail.asp?ID=4842.

Pathfinders. 2019. "Inequality and Exclusion." Pathfinders for Peaceful, Just, and Inclusive Societies, NYU Center on International Cooperation. September. https://cic.nyu.edu/sites/ default/files/pathfinders-inequality-challenge-paper-updated-october.pdf.

Peace Tech Lab. 2017. "Hate Speech Monitoring and Conflict Analysis in South Sudan: Report #5." October 12.

Pettersson, Therese, and Kristine Eck. 2018. "Organized Violence, 1989–2017." *Journal of Peace Research* 55, no. 4. https://journals.sagepub.com/doi/full/10.1177/0022343318784101.

Pew Research Center. 2017. "Europe's Growing Muslim Population." November 29. https://www.pewforum.org/2017/11/29/europes-growing-muslim-population/.

Pew Research Center. 2014. "Attitudes About Aging: A Global Perspective." January 30. https://www.pewresearch.org/global/2014/01/30/attitudes-about-aging-a-global-perspective/.

Piff, Paul K., Michael W. Kraus, and Dacher Keltner. 2018. "Unpacking the Inequality Paradox: The Psychological Roots of Inequality and Social Class." *Advances in Experimental Social Psychology* 57: 53–124. https://doi.org/10.1016/bs.aesp.2017.10.002.

PIIE. 2020. "How to Fix Economic Inequality." Peterson Institute for International Economics. November 17. https://www.piie.com/microsites/how-fix-economic-inequality.

Piketty, Thomas, and Arthur Goldhammer. 2015. *The Economics of Inequality*. Cambridge, MA: Harvard University Press.

Polyakova, Alina, and Spencer P. Boyer. 2018. "The Future of Political Warfare: Russia, the West, and the Coming Age of Global Digital Competition." Brookings Institution, Washington, DC. March. https://www.brookings.edu/wp-content/uploads/2018/03/the-future-of-political-warfare.pdf.

Qirbi, Naseeb, and Sharif A. Ismail. 2017. "Health System Functionality in a Low-Income Country in the Midst of Conflict: the Case of Yemen." *Health Policy and Planning* 32, no. 6: 911–922. https://doi.org/10.1093/heapol/czx031.

Quinley, John. 2019. "The Rohingya Diaspora Is Crucial to Achieving Justice." *Time*. February 14. https://time.com/5529321/rohingya-myanmar-genocide-fortify-rights-diaspora/.

RAND Corporation. 2018. "RAND Arroyo Center Annual Report 2017–2018." RAND Corporation, Santa Monica, CA. https://www.rand.org/pubs/corporate_pubs/CP708-2017-2018.html.

Reeves, Benjamin. 2017. "Online Fake News and Hate Speech Are Fueling Tribal 'Genocide' in South Sudan." Public Radio International. April 25. https://www.pri.org/stories/2017-04-25/online-fake-news-and-hate-speech-are-fueling-tribal-genocide-south-sudan.

Rice, Susan E., Corinne Graff, and Janet Lewis. 2006. "Poverty and Civil War: What Policymakers Need to Know." Brookings Institution, Washington, DC. https://www.brookings.edu/wp-content/uploads/2016/06/poverty_civilwar.pdf.

Richards, Joanne. 2014. "An Institutional History of the Liberation Tigers of Tamil Eelam (LTTE)." Centre on Conflict, Development and Peacebuilding, Graduate Institute Geneva. https://www.graduateinstitute.ch/library/publications-institute/institutional-history-liberation-tigers-tamil-eelam-ltte.

Ro, Christine. 2020. "Coronavirus: Why Some Racial Groups Are More Vulnerable." BBC. April 20. https://www.bbc.com/future/article/20200420-coronavirus-why-some-racial-groups-are-more-vulnerable.

Rodríguez, Dylan. 2020. *White Reconstruction: Domestic Warfare and the Logics of Genocide*. New York: Fordham University Press.

Rudolfsen, Ida. 2019. "Non-State Conflicts: Trends from 1989 to 2018." Peace Research Institute Oslo. https://www.prio.org/utility/DownloadFile.ashx?id=1859&type=publicationfile.

Sawyer, Rebecca. 2011. "The Impact of New Social Media on Intercultural Adaptation." Senior Honors Project, University of Rhode Island. http://digitalcommons.uri.edu/srhonorsprog/242http://digitalcommons.uri.edu/srhonorsprog/242.

Scheffran, Jürgen, Michael Brzoska, Hans Günter Brauch, Peter Michael Link, and Janpeter Schilling, eds. 2012. *Climate Change, Human Security and Violent Conflict Challenges for Societal Stability*. Berlin: Springer-Verlag.

Silver, Laura. 2019. "Digital Connectivity Growing Rapidly in Emerging Economies." Pew Research Center. February 5. https://www.pewresearch.org/global/2019/02/05/digital-connectivity-growing-rapidly-in-emerging-economies/.

Sommers, Marc. 2011. "Governance, Security, and Culture: Assessing Africa's Youth Bulge." *International Journal of Conflict and Violence* 5, no. 2: 292–303.

Specia, Megan. 2018. "The Five Conflicts Driving the Bulk of the World's Refugee Crisis." *New York Times*. June 19. https://www.nytimes.com/2018/06/19/world/five-conflicts-driving-refugees.html.

Stanford University. 2017. "The Islamic State." Center for International Security and Cooperation. October 23. http://web.stanford.edu/group/mappingmilitants/cgi-bin/groups/view/1.

Statista. 2020. "Soldiers Killed in Action in Afghanistan 2001–2019." January 31. https://www.statista.com/statistics/262894/western-coalition-soldiers-killed-in-afghanistan/.

Statista. n.d. "Syria: Gross Domestic Product (GDP) in Current Prices from 1984 to 2010." https://www.statista.com/statistics/326864/gross-domestic-product-gdp-in-syria/.

Stewart, Frances. 2016. "Horizontal Inequalities." In *World Social Science Report 2016*. UNESCO. https://en.unesco.org/inclusivepolicylab/sites/default/files/analytics/document/2018/9/wssr_2016_chap_07.pdf.

Stewart, Frances, Graham Brown, and Alex Cobham. 2009. "The Implications of Horizontal and Vertical Inequalities for Tax and Expenditure Policies." CRISE Working Paper No. 65. February. Centre for Research on Inequality, Human Security and Ethnicity, UK Department of International Development. https://assets.publishing.service.gov.uk/media/57a08b7ae5274a31e0000ba0/wp65.pdf.

Stockholm International Peace Research Institute. n.d. "Financial Value of the Global Arms Trade." https://www.sipri.org/databases/financial-value-global-arms-trade.

Stronski, Paul, and Annie Himes. 2019. "Russia's Game in the Balkans." Carnegie Endowment for International Peace. January. https://carnegieendowment.org/2019/02/06/russia-s-game-in-balkans-pub-78235.

Taylor, Derrick Bryson. 2020. "George Floyd Protests: A Timeline." *The New York Times*. July 10. https://www.nytimes.com/article/george-floyd-protests-timeline.html.

Taylor, Kyle, and Laura Silver. 2019. "Smartphone Ownership Is Growing Rapidly Around the World, but Not Always Equally." Pew Research Center. February 5.

Thian Hee, Yiew, M. S. Habibullah, Siong Hook Law, and W. N. W. Azman-Saini. 2016. "Does bad governance cause armed conflict?." *Indian Journal of Applied Business and Economic Research* 14, no. 6: 3741–3755.

Thomas, Chantal. 1999. "Causes of Inequality in the International Economic Order: Critical Race Theory and Postcolonial Development." *Transnational Law and Contemporary Problems* 9: 1–15.

Trading Economics. n.d. "Syria GDP Annual Growth Rate." https://tradingeconomics.com/syria/gdp-growth-annual.

Trani, Jean-François, Jill Kuhlberg, Timothy Cannings, and Dilbal Chakkal. 2016. "Multidimensional Poverty in Afghanistan: Who Are the Poorest of the Poor?" *Oxford Development Studies* 44, no. 2: 220–245. https://doi.org/10.1080/13600818.2016.1160042.

Turley, Jonathan. 2014. "Big Money Behind War: The Military-Industrial Complex." Al-Jazeera. January 11. https://www.aljazeera.com/indepth/opinion/2014/01/big-money-behind-war-military-industrial-complex-20141473026736533.html.

UNDESA. 2015. "World Fertility Report." United Nations Department of Economic and Social Affairs. https://www.un.org/en/development/desa/population/publications/pdf/fertility/wfr2015/worldFertilityReport2015.pdf.

UNDESA. n.d. "Youth and Migration." UN Department of Economic and Social Affairs. https://www.un.org/esa/socdev/documents/youth/fact-sheets/youth-migration.pdf.

UNDP. 2019. *Human Development Report 2019: Beyond Income, Beyond Averages, Beyond Today—Inequalities in Human Development in the 21st Century*. New York: United Nations. https://doi.org/10.18356/838f78fd-en.

UNDP. 2018. "Impacts of the Rohingya Refugee Influx on Host Communities." United Nations Development Programme. November. undp.org/content/dam/bangladesh/docs/Publications/Pub-2019/Impacts of the Rohingya Refigee Influx on Host Communities.pdf.

UNDP. 2015. "TST Issues Brief: Conflict Prevention, Post-Conflict Peacebuilding and the Promotion of Durable Peace, Rule of Law and Governance." United Nations Development

Programme. November 21. https://sustainabledevelopment.un.org/content/documents/263 9Issues%20Brief%20on%20Peace%20etc_FINAL_21_Nov.pdf.

UNHCR. 2019. "Global Trends: Forced Displacement in 2018." UN Refugee Agency. June 20. https://www.unhcr.org/5d08d7ee7.pdf

UNHCR. 2020. "Situation Syria Regional Refugee Response." Refugee Situations Operational Portal. UN Refugee Agency. https://data2.unhcr.org/en/situations/syria.

UNHCR. 2018. "Global Trends: Forced Displacement in 2017." UN Refugee Agency. https://www.unhcr.org/en-us/statistics/unhcrstats/5b27be547/unhcr-global-trends-2017.html.

United Nations. 2013. "Natural Resource Wealth Fails to Translate into 'Equivalent' Benefits for People, Fuelling Conflict, Instability, Deputy Secretary-General Tells Security Council." Meetings coverage and press releases, June 19. https://www.un.org/press/en/2013/sc11037.doc.htm.

United Nations. 2020. "Where We Stand Today." Chapter 1 of *World Social Report 2020*. New York: United Nations. https://www.un.org/development/desa/dspd/wp-content/uploads/sites/22/2020/02/World-Social-Report-2020-Chapter-1.pdf.

United Nations Economic and Social Council. 2019. *Special Edition: Progress Towards the Sustainable Development Goals: Report of the Secretary-General E/2019/68*. May 8 . https://undocs.org/E/2019/68.

UNODC. 2019. *Global Study on Homicide 2019*. Vienna: United Nations Office on Drugs and Crime.

Uppsala Conflict Data Program. n.d. "Number of Conflicts 1975–2018." https://ucdp.uu.se/#/.

Uppsala Universitet. n.d. "Definitions." Department of Peace and Conflict Research. https://www.pcr.uu.se/research/ucdp/definitions/.

Urdal, Henrik. 2006. "A Clash of Generations? Youth Bulges and Political Violence." *International Studies Quarterly* 50, no. 3: 607–629. www.jstor.org/stable/4092795.

Urdal, Henrik, and Primus Che Chi. 2013. "War and Gender Inequalities in Health: The Impact of Armed Conflict on Fertility and Maternal Mortality." *International Interactions* 39, no. 4: 489–510.

US Department of Homeland Security. 2020. "Homeland Threat Assessment." October. https://www.dhs.gov/sites/default/files/publications/2020_10_06_homeland-threat-assessment.pdf.

US Senate. 2019a. *Russian Active Measures Campaigns And Interference in the 2016 U.S. Election Volume 1: Russian Efforts Against Election Infrastructure with Additional Views*. Select Committee on Intelligence. Washington, DC: Government Printing Office. https://www.intelligence.senate.gov/sites/default/files/documents/Report_Volume1.pdf.

US Senate. 2019b. *Russian Active Measures Campaigns and Interference in the 2016 U.S. Election Volume 2: Russia's Use of Social Media with Additional Views*. Select Committee on Intelligence. Washington, DC: Government Printing Office. https://www.intelligence.senate.gov/sites/default/files/documents/Report_Volume2.pdf.

USAID. 2016. "Smarter Remittances Supporting Smarter Students in the Philippines: Development Innovation Ventures (DIV) Portfolio." US Agency for International Development. May 27. https://www.usaid.gov/div/portfolio/remittances.

Vargas-Lundius, Rosemary, Guillaume Lanly, Marcela Villarreal, and Martha Osorio. 2008. "International Migration, Remittances and Rural Development." Food and Agriculture Organization and International Fund for Agricultural Development. http://www.fao.org/3/a-ak405e.pdf.

Vazquez-Martinez, Alejandro, Michael Hansen, and Diana Quintero. 2020. "Unsafe School Facilities Reinforce Educational Inequities Among Marginalized Students." Brookings Institution, September 1. https://www.brookings.edu/blog/brown-center-chalkboard/2020/09/01/unsafe-school-facilities-reinforce-educational-inequities-among-marginalized-students/.

Von Einsiedel, Sebastian. 2014. "Major Recent Trends in Violent Conflict." Occasional Paper. United Nations University Centre for Policy Research. https://i.unu.edu/media/cpr.unu.edu/attachment/1558/OC_01-MajorRecentTrendsinViolentConflict.pdf.

Walzer, Michael. 2013. "Targeted Killing and Drone Warfare." *Dissent*. January 11. https://www.dissentmagazine.org/online_articles/targeted-killing-and-drone-warfare.

Wang, Bin, Xiao Luo, Young-Min Yang, Weiyi Sun, Mark A. Cane, Wenju Cai, Sang-Wook Yeh, and Jian Liu. 2019. "Historical Change of El Niño Properties Sheds Light on Future Changes of Extreme El Niño." *Proceedings of the National Academy of Sciences* 116, no. 45: 22512–22517. https://doi.org/10.1073/pnas.1911130116.

Watson Institute. 2020. "Afghan Civilians." Watson Institute for International and Public Affairs, Brown University. January. https://watson.brown.edu/costsofwar/costs/human/civilians/afghan.

Wilder, Julius M. "The Disproportionate Impact of COVID-19 on Racial and Ethnic Minorities in the United States." 2021. *Clinical Infectious Diseases* 72, no. 4: 707–709. https://doi.org/10.1093/cid/ciaa959.

Williams, A. P., J. T. Abatzoglou, A. Gershunov, J. Guzman-Morales, D. A. Bishop, J. K. Balch, and D. P. Lettenmaier. 2019. "Observed Impacts of Anthropogenic Climate Change on Wildfire in California." *Earth's Future* 7: 892–910. https://doi.org/10.1029/2019EF001210.

Wilson Center. 2017. "ISIS After the Caliphate." November 28. https://www.wilsoncenter.org/article/isis-after-the-caliphate-0.

Winter, Charlie. 2015. "The Virtual 'Caliphate': Understanding Islamic State's Propaganda Strategy." Quillium. July. https://www.stratcomcoe.org/charlie-winter-virtual-caliphate-understanding-islamic-states-propaganda-strategy.

World Bank. 2019. "Overview." The World Bank in South Africa. October 10, 2019. https://www.worldbank.org/en/country/southafrica/overview#1.

World Bank. 2018a. "Afghanistan Development Update—August 2018." World Bank. https://openknowledge.worldbank.org/bitstream/handle/10986/30293/129163-REVISED-AFG-Development-Update-Aug-2018-FINAL.pdf?sequence=1&isAllowed=y.

World Bank. 2018b. "Why People Fight: Inequality, Exclusion, and a Sense of Injustice." In United Nations and World Bank, *Pathways for Peace*. Washington, DC: World Bank, 2018. https://www.pathwaysforpeace.org/#download-center.

World Bank. 2017a. "Rapidly Assessing the Impact of Hurricane Matthew in Haiti." October 20. https://www.worldbank.org/en/results/2017/10/20/rapidly-assessing-the-impact-of-hurricane-matthew-in-haiti.

World Bank. 2017b. "The Toll of War: The Economic and Social Consequences of the Conflict in Syria." July 10. http://hdl.handle.net/10986/27541.

World Bank. n.d. a. "Population, Total." https://data.worldbank.org/indicator/SP.POP.TOTL?view=chart.

World Bank. n.d. b. "Women, Business and the Law." Accessed 2021. https://wbl.worldbank.org/en/wbl.

World Health Organization. 2020. "Coronavirus Disease (COVID-19)—Situation Report 122." May 21. https://www.who.int/docs/default-source/coronaviruse/situation-reports/20200521-covid-19-sitrep-122.pdf?sfvrsn=24f20e05_2.

World Health Organization. 2019. "Global Research on Coronavirus Disease (Covid-19)." https://www.who.int/emergencies/diseases/novel-coronavirus-2019/global-research-on-novel-coronavirus-2019-ncov.

World Health Organization. n.d. "WHO Coronavirus (COVID-19) Dashboard." Accessed May 13, 2021. https://covid19.who.int.

Xinhua. 2020. "Philippine Remittances Hit 33.5 Bln USD in 2019." February 17. http://www.xinhuanet.com/english/2020-02/17/c_138792402.htm.

Yifu Lin, Justin. 2012. "Youth Bulge: A Demographic Dividend or a Demographic Bomb in Developing Countries?" *Development Talk* (blog), World Bank. January 5. https://blogs.worldbank.org/developmenttalk/youth-bulge-a-demographic-dividend-or-a-demographic-bomb-in-developing-countries.

Young, Laura A. 2012. "Challenges at the Intersection of Gender and Ethnic Identity in Kenya." Minority Rights Group International. https://minorityrights.org/wp-content/uploads/old-site-downloads/download-1164-Challenges-at-the-intersection-of-gender-and-ethnic-identity-in-Kenya.pdf.

Yu, Pei, Rongbin Xu, Michael J. Abramson, Shanshan Li, and Yuming Guo. 2020. "Bushfires in Australia: A Serious Health Emergency Under Climate Change." *The Lancet Planetary Health* 4, no. 1: E7–E8. https://www.thelancet.com/journals/lanplh/article/PIIS2542-5196(19)30267-0/fulltext#seccestitle10.

Zeitzoff, Thomas. 2017. "How Social Media Is Changing Conflict." Journal of Conflict Resolution 61, no. 9. https://journals.sagepub.com/doi/10.1177/0022002717721392.

2

Making the Case

The Opportunity and Need to Address Diversity in Conflict Resolution and Development

Carla Koppell

The future of peace and prosperity that we seek for all the world's peoples needs a foundation of tolerance, security, equality and justice.

—Kofi Annan

Countries and communities have always featured rich mixes of people. Nations and neighborhoods include men, women, and nonbinary people as well as people of various ages and ability statuses, families with differing levels of education and wealth, and those with different sexual orientations. The mix of individuals and groups also varies by race, ethnicity, religion, and linguistic background. While the extent and dimensions of diversity vary from place to place, variety is a constant feature.

Though diversity is always present, equity and inclusion are not. People of different backgrounds vastly vary in status and in rights. Individuals and groups differ in their influence and their access to opportunities and services; many face exclusion and marginalization. Over generations, wealth accumulates, further exacerbating and entrenching injustice. In the absence of affirmative measures to address the causes of inequalities, the result is wide disparities and asymmetries in resources and influence around the world.

Inequalities have always existed among individuals and groups, often as a result of unequal status and rights under law or custom. Those controlling assets and power determine who is granted privileges and opportunities; too often they favor those from within their identity groups to the detriment of others. Colonialism, slavery, and genocide all reveal efforts by a dominant group to use exclusion and marginalization to maintain power and wealth. Less visible are inequalities embedded in laws and norms that pervade all societies, condemning some groups to perpetual disadvantage.

That said, for as long as there has been inequity there have also been calls for equality between people of different backgrounds. Over time, the case for inclusion and equity has become increasingly multifaceted and has gained strength.

This chapter considers the multiple rationales for advancing equity and inclusion. First, it considers how the moral and ethical justifications for equality have evolved and grown over time. Next, the text offers an overview of how the international legal framework has expanded to shape and reinforce the case for equity and inclusion. It then turns to discuss the pragmatic rationale for examining and advancing diversity. It first discusses seminal scholarly theories that conceptualize how and why equitable and inclusive communities and societies are more likely to progress and thrive. Then, in greatest depth, the chapter discusses the growing body of empirical data and evidence demonstrating that inclusion delivers concrete benefits. Fundamentally, the chapter methodically demonstrates how and why insufficient attention to disparities in well-being and power has costs for individuals and communities, as well as for stability and well-being around the world.

The Moral and Ethical Imperative

Philosophical Foundations

Philosophers and political theorists have long discussed whether there exist moral and ethical responsibilities to advance inclusion and equality, and how far those obligations might extend. The debate stretches back centuries. In the fourth and third centuries BCE, Greek philosophers Socrates, Plato, and Aristotle, among others, debated the responsibilities of individuals to society, as well as the nature of and obligations to equality within societies. In the *Laws*, for example, Plato explicitly reasoned that the good and wise, not the wealthy, should have greater power.[1]

Ancient debates even explored the relative rights of different subgroups within society. In the *Republic*, Plato argues for women's rights, particularly in education and employment. And though there are debates about the extent of Plato's commitment to gender equality given his inconsistent statements about women's merit relative to men's, Socrates and Aristotle are definitively more equivocal.[2] Aristotle decries economic inequality as politically unwise but references natural inequalities among men and women, and among "natural slaves" and free men.[3] Socrates speaks to theoretical equality but references the differentiated natural inclinations of men and women and discusses how these influence their roles in society.[4]

Similar discussions around the morality and efficacy of inequitable societies are found in Eastern philosophy. For example, Mohism, a Chinese school of philosophy put forth by Mozi in the fifth and fourth centuries BCE, promotes the fundamental equality of all individuals and the need for egalitarian society as a means for ending war and poverty and fostering prosperity.[5] During the Han Dynasty, which began in the second century BCE, Ban Gu discusses the importance of inclusion, at least within the ruling class, stating that "if the emperor cannot involve and tolerate his ministers, it will be difficult for him to maintain his dominance."[6]

In religious theory as well, there are reflections on human rights over the centuries. The world's major religions, including those in the Judeo-Christian tradition, Hinduism, and Islam, all consider issues of inclusion and equality. Their foundational texts speak to the equality of all souls and provide religious bases for the modern international human rights regime.[7] For example, the Koran notes, "Men are equals like the teeth of a comb."[8] Buddhist ethics reinforce contemporary protections of human rights, with the Dalai Lama, a Buddhist spiritual leader, calling adamantly for followers to advance their realization in order to foster peace and harmony.[9] That said, most religions often also foster and enable hierarchy, rather than equality, in daily life. Many reinforce men's empowerment over women's.[10] And Eastern belief systems including Hinduism and Confucianism reinforce rank order among adherents, though they encourage equality within ranks.

Political philosophers have also long debated and discussed equity and inclusion.[11] The concept of a "social contract" postulates that individuals are all naturally free and equal, surrendering some liberties to live together peacefully and prosperously within societies.[12] In the 1600s, Thomas Hobbes theorized the "inherent and inalienable principle of equality" among people and postulated that equality results in a propensity for competition and conflict. In the late 1600s, John Locke asserted the need for governing systems to maintain the justice and equality present in nature, protecting life, liberty, and property as preeminent rights. In the 1700s, Jean-Jacques Rousseau explored how the social contract must be shaped by societies to better address inequities. At the end of the 1700s, Immanuel Kant advanced the concept of moral equality, declaring, "All human beings are equal to one another, and only he who is morally good has an inner worth superior to the rest."[13] Sadly, however, many Enlightenment philosophers separate and subordinate women and people of other races and ethnicities. Kant defends the superiority of Whites, and Hobbes deliberates extensively around the relative worth and rights of women and the enslaved.[14]

Other philosophers extend the debates to make the case for equality of specific groups within society. Mary Wollstonecraft argued against slavery and for women's equality and empowerment in the 1700s.[15] In France, Olympe de Gouges was convicted of treason and executed after arguing for the rights of slaves and for women's equality in France in 1792.[16] And John Locke's views regarding the slave trade, which thrived during his life, influenced his philosophical perspective.[17] In the United States, Frederick Douglass wrote extensively against slavery; he reasoned that since Black people are human and have free will, natural law—the moral principles providing a foundation for human conduct—as detailed in the Declaration of Independence and Constitution should also apply to them.[18] In the 1970s, John Rawls advanced social contract discourse in *A Theory of Justice,* examining the just allocation of goods in society.[19] He explored how to balance liberty with equality, concluding that fair governing systems must be organized to reduce political, social, and economic inequality, at least to the extent that reduced disparities advance the common good.[20] More recently, Jamaican philosopher Charles Mills has examined what he terms the "racial contract," which posits that governing systems are structured to and continue to explicitly and implicitly subordinate nonwhite peoples to White peoples.[21]

Alongside discussions of the social contract is the emergence of the concept of "egalitarianism," the principle that all people are worthy of equality and equal treatment.[22] While egalitarianism first emphasizes the need to eliminate economic inequality (material egalitarianism), particularly as framed by Karl Marx, Locke interprets it to encompass equal political rights and civil liberties.[23] More recently for some, equality of opportunity has been placed alongside other egalitarian rights. Rawls, for example, speaks to the right to "equal participation" in government and governance; in the lexicon of this volume, Rawls would be calling for "inclusion" as a fundamental component of egalitarianism.

Complicating—or adding texture—to discussions of egalitarianism is analysis of "luck egalitarianism" by Elizabeth Anderson. She argues that inequalities born of natural differences in potential or voluntary choices are permissible, whereas those resulting from differences in circumstance such as wealth are unjust. Adjacent to the discussion of egalitarianism are considerations of "positive" and "negative" freedom.[24] Berlin distinguishes freedom from interference, or "negative liberty," from the freedom to actually pursue goals and desires, or "positive liberty." She argues that both types of liberty are required for true freedom.

Amartya Sen and Martha Nussbaum have also advanced the "capability approach," arguing that societies are obligated to provide the "freedom to achieve well-being."[25] Essentially, individuals must have access to the tools they need to fully enjoy and exercise their rights (such as education).[26] Sen has further extended contemplation of this approach to posit the need for global development to deliver political freedom, freedom from poverty, and opportunity as goals that are intertwined.[27]

Strengthening the philosophical case for equity and inclusion is utilitarianism, which argues that the best course of action is the one that brings the "greatest amount of good for the greatest number."[28] Implicit in utilitarianism is the idea that every individual is equally valuable in the overall calculation. John Stuart Mill and Jeremy Bentham, prominent utilitarians in the early 1800s, both advocated for women's rights.[29] Bentham, particularly, also advocated explicitly for gay rights and for an end to slavery.[30] More recently, Peter Singer has made the utilitarian case for a redistribution of wealth to address extreme poverty.[31]

Democracies have emerged around the world, founded on many of the principles of egalitarianism and the social contract. The thirteenth-century Magna Carta first laid out in the English-speaking world the concept of consultative government and equal rights under law, though commitments to women's equality and egalitarianism were lacking.[32] Antecedent democratic practices exist in many parts of the world among indigenous societies.[33] For example, African roots for participatory systems of governance are found in Egypt and in the precolonial African kingdoms of Mossi, Ghana, Mali, and Songhai, though hierarchy existed in those societies as well.[34] Today, English, French, and American democracies enshrine aspirations of equality for all people in their most important political treatises, often following revolutionary responses to the structural inequality of monarchic governing structures in Europe.[35] In Asia, Africa, and Latin America, democracies espousing values of equality have emerged, often following extended periods of domination under Western colonization or spheres of influence. Pan-Africanism, for example, united people of African origin in the push for equality and decolonization.[36] W. E. B. Du Bois, a leader of the modern movement, noted, "Africans themselves were consistently involved in activities leading to freedom from colonialism."[37]

Discussions of the societal obligation to inclusion and equality have become far more specialized over time. Feminist philosophy and feminist philosophers, including Simone de Beauvoir, make the case for women's equality and inclusion.[38] Supplementing the general arguments are applications of feminist philosophy to international relations by Cynthia Enloe and Anne Tickner, among others.[39] Philosophical explorations of race, particularly in connection with movements to abolish slavery and advance civil rights, have expanded, led by thinkers such as W. E. B. Du Bois and Kwame Anthony Appiah.[40] Here too, application is made to international affairs by scholars including Tilden J. Le Melle and Errol Henderson.[41] Similarly, movements shaping arguments for the inclusion of people with disabilities, members of LGBTQI communities, indigenous communities, and others who have been marginalized have expanded.[42] Scholars have also explored the unique impact of multiple identities on inclusion.[43] For example, Kimberlé Crenshaw examines the intersection of race and sex.[44] Still others explore intersecting identities, such as sexual orientation, class, religion, ethnicity, and gender identity, in seeking to explain privilege and oppression for individuals and communities. The expansions often focus on groups that have been undervalued and underserved, and feature increased visibility and recognition of critical thinkers from those communities and from different parts of the world. A common thread in the narratives argues that debates over equality arise because rights are always measured against a baseline, and that baseline is of able-bodied, cisgender White men.

Layered on top of philosophical explorations of the rights of different groups are discussions teasing out the nature of marginalization. For example, Iris Young has sought to characterize what she terms different forms of "oppression" faced by nondominant groups: exploitation, marginalization, powerlessness, cultural imperialism, and violence.[45]

Today, philosophical debates particularly focus on the extent to which societies must ensure they fulfill the social contract for all and the extent to which they are doing so given the numerous existing disparities in wealth, influence, and status. Amartya Sen, for example, decries the extreme material inequality that persists, connecting the disparities to ethical failures and social choices.[46] Joseph Stiglitz extends and expands the arguments against inequality, connecting disparities to polarization and environmental degradation.[47] Fundamentally, these debates are over whether or not commitments to equality encompass legal, political, economic, and social dimensions.

Also vigorously contested is the question of whether contemporary global systems and institutions—which bear legacies of colonialism, sexism, racism, and other forms of bias—are capable of transforming (and driving transformation) to advance inclusion and equality. For example, critical race theorists, such as Derrick Bell and Richard Delgado, question how to advance racial equity, inclusion, and justice given embedded biases in laws and institutions.[48] Their frame of analysis has been extended by Sara Ahmed to the realm of education and by Chantal Thomas to the international economic system.[49] Similarly, Nancy Fraser considers the need to reimagine global political space to advance justice in a globalized world. Each considers how systems need to be disassembled and reimagined to enable justice and equity.

All of that said, the expectations of society and international institutions with regard to equity and inclusion have dramatically shifted. Today, as Scheffler notes,

> the prevailing political morality holds that intentional discrimination based on largely unchosen factors such as race, religion, sex, and ethnicity is unjust, and that distributive inequalities resulting from such discrimination are unjust as well. It also holds that people of equal talent from different social classes should have equal access to the social positions for which their talents qualify them, and that it is unjust if inequalities result from a society's failure to provide this kind of equal opportunity.[50]

The Legal Imperative

As political morality has evolved to embrace ideals of equality and inclusion, the philosophical case has been buttressed by a growing international legal mandate for equal status and rights. An expanding international legal framework codifies the obligation to deliver for all the world's citizens. It creates an architecture for progress.

The modern human rights movement can trace its roots to the period following World War II. Spurred to action after witnessing genocide and the murder of over 11 million people simply on the basis of their identities, Eleanor Roosevelt, the US ambassador to the newly formed United Nations, led the charge for passage of the Universal Declaration of Human Rights (UDHR). Powerful in its call to recognize the fundamental equality of all people, the UDHR, adopted by the United Nations General Assembly in 1948, declares that protecting the rights of all citizens and residents of a nation is fundamental to fulfilling international obligations to guarantee human rights.[51]

The UDHR is criticized for reinforcing state sovereignty at a severe cost to international accountability.[52] Nonetheless, it has provided the foundation for an extensive international framework to protect and advance the rights of different subpopulations globally. That vast web of laws, resolutions, and guidance includes the Declaration on the Rights of Disabled Persons, the Declaration on the Right to Development, the Declaration on Cultural Diversity, the Declaration on the Rights of Indigenous Peoples, and the UN Resolution on Human Rights, Sexual Orientation, and Gender Identity.[53] Further, a number of conventions codify and solidify those rights, including the Convention on the Elimination of All Forms of Discrimination Against Women and the Convention on the Rights of Persons with Disabilities.[54] Often these are complemented by Security Council resolutions that apply the rights to different sectors; for example, a suite of resolutions on women, peace, and security pursues attention to women's priorities and needs in conflict resolution and peacebuilding.[55] Similar resolutions regarding youth, peace, and security have also passed.[56] The international mandates translate differently across regions and countries, and enforcement of protections ebbs and flows. Nonetheless, safeguards continue to expand. Today, over eighty nations have put in place national action plans for advancing attention to women, peace, and security as a result of the Security Council resolutions (and extensive advocacy by civil society and leaders, especially women, worldwide).[57]

Supplementing the drive to create legal definitions and protections for different subcommunities are movements for different groups' empowerment and inclusion. The goal is to ensure diverse communities equal voice, rights, access, and opportunities. Often these drives to enable equal influence are coupled with calls to protect vulnerable and marginalized groups. For example, the women, peace, and security movement links efforts to increase the presence and power of women in peace negotiations and post-conflict governance with a push to end impunity for sexual violence in conflict. Chapter 3 provides an in-depth examination of the movement to advance gender equality and women's empowerment, exploring its multifaceted nature.

Though the international legal mandate for inclusion continues to expand, widespread inequalities in rights persist. Unequal treatment under the law is common. Equally significant, compliance with the robust international legal framework is uneven. Countries frequently lack the capacity or the will to enforce mandates. Section II of this book explores movements for inclusion, reflecting on both the progress and the unfulfilled promise of a range of movements for equality and inclusion.

The "Business Case": Pragmatic Analyses

Centuries of debate have shaped the normative discourse and the legal framework conveying the need for inclusion. Today, those theoretical and philosophical arguments are complemented and buttressed by scholarly analysis and reflection, as well as extensive, concrete evidence that equity and inclusion are critical to continued progress advancing stability and prosperity globally.

Key Theories

Work relating to diversity, equity, and inclusion is fundamental in many fields including anthropology, economics, political science, sociology, and conflict and peace studies, among others. Particularly germane are social capital theory, social exclusion theory, and explorations of greed versus grievance as drivers of instability and conflict.

Social Capital Theory

Social capital theory provides an important foundation for discussing the import of diversity and inclusion to economies and societies. Social capital is "an accumulation of various types of social, psychological, cognitive, institutional and related assets that increase the amount or probability of mutually beneficial cooperative behaviors that are beneficial for others, not just one's self."[58] Implicit is the belief that interpersonal and interorganizational connections have value and impact within societies.[59]

Associational activities, interconnectedness, and relationships of trust within and across communities have long been discussed in economic and sociological analyses of communities and societies. The term "social capital" is relatively recent, but the idea of relationships, norms, and networks as important to societal well-being dates back centuries. Among philosophers and economists during the eighteenth century, Adam Smith, whom many view as the father of modern capitalism, touches on the importance of networks and associations to trade and economies in *The Wealth of Nations*.[60] Alexis de Tocqueville deems societal connections and organizations to be a fundamental strength of the American society and economy in the nineteenth century. More recently, three social scientists have been prominent among many in shaping development of "social capital" as a concept: Pierre Bourdieu, James Coleman, and Robert Putnam.[61]

The particular relevance of diversity and inclusion issues to analyses of social capital becomes apparent when different forms and types of social capital are examined. "Bonding" social capital comprises the connections among individuals and groups that are similar demographically, attitudinally, and in their access to information and resources. "Bridging," or horizontal, social capital encompasses "connections that link people across a cleavage that typically divides society (such as race, or class, or religion)."[62] "Linking," or vertical, social capital is further differentiated by some as "relations between individuals and groups in different social strata in a hierarchy where power, social status and wealth are accessed by different groups."[63] Fundamentally, social capital theory holds that the optimal balance of bonding, bridging, and linking social capital creates a foundation for prosperous communities (and individuals within communities) by contributing to social cohesion.[64]

Bridging social capital can grow communities' networks, reach, and access, leveraging diverse individuals' and groups' varied expertise and associations for greater collective prosperity. Linking social capital—viewed by some as most important to global development—creates opportunity and access to resources and opportunities for a broader cross section of the population, with benefits for the society as a whole.[65] Strong bridging and linking social capital are important to prosperity and peacefulness. Myriad analyses, theoretical and empirical, have concluded that a combination of types of social capital is fundamental to poverty alleviation, community resilience, and well-being because, in synchrony, they reduce asymmetries in power, wealth, and access, and reduce exclusion as well as perceived exclusion.[66]

While in a general sense, more social capital is preferable, social capital can have negative implications. For example, bonding social capital provides important networks of support within communities, but in isolation it can breed polarization, bias, and exclusion by cultivating a sense that outsiders are "Others," or by reinforcing norms that restrict access to opportunities.[67] For example, communities bonded by norms subjugating women or discriminating against people of different races or ethnicities can promulgate behaviors that undermine equality and inclusion.

The implications of increasing societal diversity for social capital are robustly debated. Putnam has hypothesized that increased diversity erodes social capital, at least when the diversity is new.[68] Contact and conflict theories contrastingly argue that greater diversity either fosters tolerance or sows distrust.[69] Further research indicates that the situation is more complex: the implications of diversity for social cohesion are dependent on many variables, including the stability of the society, the level of interaction among different groups within communities, and even the age of the population.[70]

The influence of social capital on violence and conflict has also been investigated. It becomes clear from empirical research that there are numerous intersections. According to Colletta and Cullen, "Social cohesion is the key intervening variable between social capital and violent conflict. The greater the degree to which vertical linking and horizontal bridging social capital integrate, the more likely it is that society will be cohesive, and will thus possess the inclusive mechanisms necessary for mediating or managing conflict before it turns violent." At the same time they note, "Social capital can be readily perverted to undermine social cohesion and fragment society for individual and group gain, and this manipulation has the potential to lead to violent conflict."[71] Ethnic, social, religious, or economic cleavages are often exploited and amplified to create polarization and reduce social cohesion in an effort to consolidate power over a group or to dominate others within societies. That fragmentation then has implications for stability and social cohesion.[72] Sisk and Cox explore how social cohesion strengthens and weakens in fragile, conflict-affected, and deeply fractured societies, finding that social, economic, and political factors can profoundly influence the extent to which multicultural countries and communities cohere.[73]

Social Exclusion Theory

Theories addressing social exclusion recognize that advancing prosperity depends on more than purely economic interventions; in essence, there are problems economic growth cannot solve.[74] Shrivastava and Yadav put it well: "Social exclusion is a form of discrimination. It occurs when people are wholly or partially excluded from participating in the economic, social and political life of their community, based on their belonging to a certain social class, category or group. In India, social exclusion occurs on the basis of identities including caste, ethnicity, religion, gender and disability."[75]

More formally, the Social Exclusion Knowledge Network of the World Health Organization (WHO) has said, "Exclusion consists of dynamic, multi-dimensional processes driven by unequal power relationships interacting across four main dimensions—economic, political, social, and cultural—and at different levels including individual, household, group, community, country, and global levels. It results in a continuum of inclusion/exclusion characterised by unequal access to resources, capabilities, and rights, which leads to health inequalities."[76] WHO focuses principally on how social exclusion results in disparities in healthcare, but in other contexts it leads to disparities in education, housing, and other resources.

Western discourse around social exclusion emerged in Europe in the 1960s and 1970s as part of discussions of social policy. But there are antecedents and related concepts that pre-date this elsewhere in the world.[77] In Africa, the humanist philosophical concept of ubuntu (humanity toward others) is used to advance inclusionary agendas.[78] The Confucian concept of a "harmonious society" (social harmony) has been invoked as part of recent efforts to reduce inequality in China.[79]

As a counterpoint to the concept of exclusion is social inclusion, which is defined as a means for fostering prosperity and stability, and a goal unto itself. According to the World Bank, "Social inclusion is the process of improving the terms on which individuals and groups take part in society—improving the ability, opportunity, and dignity of those disadvantaged on the basis of their identity."[80] Today, the goal of social inclusion has been woven into government policies in countries including India, Tanzania, Tunisia, and the European Union. That said, socially inclusive societies remain elusive. The promise of social inclusion hasn't been fully achieved anywhere, and a concerted focus on realization of the goal of social inclusion must be a central priority to prevent conflict and to promote shared prosperity.

Theories of Belonging

Underlying considerations of the value of social capital and inclusion are questions of belonging. The fields of psychology and sociology extensively study and analyze individuals' need to feel connected to family members and to larger social groups and communities as part of their social identity.[81] Garbutt has termed belonging the relational component of social inclusion.[82] Complementing general investigations of belonging are reflections on efforts to construct communities and shared identities to advance political or social agendas, which Yuval-Davis, among others, has termed the politics of belonging.[83]

More recent investigations have expanded on the idea of individuals' multiple identities, such as their sexual identity, race or ethnicity, religion, or citizenship, and how those impact individuals' affinity with varied groups. These explorations of intersectionality are influencing our understanding of belonging with implications for politics and social cohesion.[84] Analysis has further examined how demographic shifts driven by migration impact the sense of belonging, as well as the politics of belonging in countries around the world.[85] Antonsich has said it well: "The open question is whether increasing cultural and ethnic diversification of contemporary societies can lead to the creation of communities of belonging beyond communities of identity."[86]

Further, the analysis of belonging and how to cultivate a sense of it has been extensive within specific communities, such as educational institutions and private businesses.[87] Fundamentally, research and program development are focused on creating climates of inclusion that leverage diversity. While driven in part by the desire to create a welcoming environment, research is increasingly revealing the substantial links between belonging and inclusion, and between productivity and employee retention.[88]

Groupthink Theory

The value of diversity and inclusion for decision-making is highlighted by the psychological theory of "groupthink," which holds that when people are similar and think similarly, there is the substantial risk that differences in perspective and thought are diminished and subordinated, risking poor outcomes.[89] Irving Janis used this theory to explain suboptimal US foreign policy decision-making.[90] He concludes that constructing groups with people of diverse backgrounds and perspectives is likely to improve outcomes.

Since Janis coined the term "groupthink" in the 1970s, the benefits of diversity of thought and perspective have been extensively explored and debated.[91] Investigations have looked at various dimensions of diversity, including gender diversity, and the conditions under which diversity reduces the likelihood of groupthink.[92] Additionally, exploration has considered the impact of groupthink in different sectors, such as education and healthcare.[93] Research has also investigated the benefits of diversity for decision-making in general, because it introduces diversity of thought.[94] Most recently, research has focused on the value of diversity of thought and background within specific contexts, like corporate boardrooms, reflecting on the implications for profitability.[95]

Greed Versus Grievance Theory

Long debate and analysis have characterized the discussions of whether and how poverty, exclusion, and inequality drive conflict. Østby has noted that different theoretical approaches include "Marxist theory of class struggle and revolution, relative deprivation theory, and theories of ethnic conflict and structural inequality. What these theories have in common is the hypothesis that conflict is a result of widely felt grievances among the relatively disadvantaged in society."[96]

Greed versus grievance theory considers whether a desire for material resources fosters conflict (termed "greed"), or whether conflict is driven by identity-based disputes (termed "grievance"). In 2000, Paul Collier and Anke Hoeffler made the case for economic drivers of intrastate conflict, finding a stronger correlation of civil war with variables associated with income as opposed to grievances relating to inequality, political rights, or identity.[97] Conversely, Frances Stewart, among others, emphasized that it is grievances between groups within societies that affect stability.[98]

Underlying the examinations of greed and grievance are different types of inequality. Collier focuses on inequality between individuals and families, known as vertical inequality. While Stewart considers "horizontal inequalities (i.e. inequalities between culturally formed groups)," she finds that "groups' relative performance in economic, social and political dimensions is an important source of individual welfare and can cause serious political instability."[99] In essence, she examines how inequality and social cohesion interact to foster instability and violent conflict (or not). Østby posits that it is the distinction between types of inequality that explains the different conclusions reached.[100]

Over time, the discourse has evolved to consider the intersections of greed and grievance in driving violent conflict. For example, Walter analyzes how different types of grievances do (or do not) drive conflict in Central Africa.[101] There has also been increased examination of the different types of horizontal inequality—economic, political, and social—and how they precipitate and sustain conflict. While scholars debate types of grievances, the reasons for greed, and the extent to which grievance and greed explain persistent conflict, especially civil war, it is clear that widespread inequality and deprivation are linked to conflict.

Empirical Data and Research

Further strengthening calls for inclusion is a growing body of empirical research and data demonstrating that inclusion and equity offer enormous potential to strengthen economies and societies. Conversely, the failure to successfully foster inclusion is a binding constraint to development, a contributor to fragility, and an impediment to conflict prevention and resolution. The remainder of this chapter outlines the practical, business case, presenting data and evidence supporting the theories above and expanding on their relevance today.

The Vast Potential for an Inclusion Dividend

Tremendous dividends can accrue if societies leverage the skills, expertise, economic potential, and voices of everyone within. Similarly, inclusion offers the potential to help stabilize countries, and to enable societies to prevent and recover from violent conflict.

Untapped Economic Potential

From an economic standpoint, attention to diversity and the promotion of inclusion are essential to maximal increases in prosperity.

Societies forgo a great deal of potential economic productivity and wealth because groups within those societies lack equal rights and equal access to technical assistance and education, capital, and equipment, among other inputs. For example, the GDP of nations that are members of the Organization for Economic Co-operation and Development (OECD) would increase by 12 percent over two decades if men's and women's workforce participation were equalized by 2030.[102] That increase could be even greater—20 percent or more—in emerging economies.[103] Furthermore, the McKinsey Global Institute estimated in 2015 that "if all countries were to match the progress toward gender parity of the best performer in their region, it could produce a boost to annual global GDP of as much as $12 trillion in 2025."[104]

On a sectoral level, the gaps in productivity due to inequity become even clearer. While data is not available for every marginalized group, research indicates that "if women had the same access to productive resources as men, they could increase their farm yields by 20–30 percent, feeding an additional 150 million people."[105] Similarly, if gaps in educational access were closed, women's earnings would increase; every additional year of secondary school increases a woman's earnings by 10–20 percent, with a measurable impact on nations' GDP.[106]

There would be gains from inclusion at an organizational level as well. A growing body of research demonstrates that private firms with more diverse boards of directors are, on average, more profitable.[107] It is not difficult to imagine this might be the case. Directors of different backgrounds relate to different demographic groups; they are more likely to understand and successfully navigate varied markets and trends in a diversifying world. Research shows that the benefits extend even further: as diversity on corporate boards increases the range of perspectives and viewpoints that are expressed, it also widens the networks and reach of directors.[108]

Enhanced Governance and Rule of Law

Policies and programs that promote equality and inclusion also offer important, concrete benefits for countries' social and political well-being. The more that different subgroups within societies are afforded equal protection under the law and equal access to public services, the more they contribute to and foster the rule of law. In Iraq, for instance, political theorist Yasir Kuoti has causally linked political unrest to the exclusion of Sunnis from the constitution-drafting process.[109]

Relatedly, when a society, its laws, and its institutions serve all citizens equally, the sense of social cohesion increases. For example, countries that have policies facilitating equitable resource sharing, like Sweden and Norway, tend to have higher levels of social trust and cohesion. Conversely, where rampant, endemic corruption is pervasive, faith in government and governance is undermined, with consequences for social cohesion.[110]

The perception of equal treatment and equal service is important as well. When segments of society perceive a difference in status, it impacts confidence in government. Greater confidence increases faith in—and support for—government institutions, enhancing stability.[111] Similarly, visible efforts to advance realization of commitments to equality and equal protection increase support for governments and the sense of inclusion. As the 2017 World Bank–United Nations report *Pathways to Peace* noted, "Experience shows that more inclusive and representative power-sharing arrangements increase the likelihood of peaceful pathways. . . . The service delivery arena is critical because state legitimacy hinges, in part, on whether the population deems that the processes of service delivery are fair. In this arena, again, inclusiveness and perceptions of fairness matter as much—perhaps more— than the quality of services."[112]

Interestingly, when diverse voices within society are given space to share their perspectives, even negatively, stability is greater. The freedom to nonviolently voice criticism or support for policies or political positions without fear of retribution increases overall stability. It can also create a virtuous cycle: enhanced public accountability fosters improvements in the rule of law by, for example, helping reduce corruption, even as it increases citizen confidence in government and governance.[113] Similarly, increasing the number of women in government has been correlated with decreases in corruption and reduced perception of corruption.[114] Chapter 16 discusses the implications for governance of more women in government.

Reduced Risk of Violent Conflict
Societies and governments that more successfully foster inclusion are also able to lower the threat of violence and war. *Pathways to Peace* found that "the best way to prevent societies from descending into crisis—including but not limited to conflict—is to ensure they are resilient through investment in inclusive and sustainable development. For all countries, addressing inequalities and exclusion, making institutions more inclusive, and ensuring that development strategies are risk-informed are central to preventing the fraying of the social fabric that could erupt into crisis."[115]

There are also indirect ways in which greater collective well-being reduces the propensity for violent conflict. According to Collier, 80 percent of countries with the lowest gross national product (GNP) had civil wars in the late 1990s and/or 2000s.[116] That said, the connections are not so simple and direct. More recent research has focused on inequalities as drivers of violent conflict, particularly horizontal inequalities, as discussed earlier in this chapter. "Ethnopolitical exclusion is found to have a statistically significant and substantive risk inducing effect."[117] Additionally, differences in income among subgroups within communities can be compensated for (to some extent) by efforts at equity and inclusion in service provision.

Enhanced Conflict Resolution and Reconstruction

Attending to diversity and fostering inclusion are equally important when resolving violent conflict. For example, peace negotiations are more likely to result in an accord if there is broad participation by a range of conflict-affected stakeholders. When civil society groups are included in negotiations, peace accords are 64 percent less likely to fail. The accords are also 35 percent more likely to endure.[118] In Tunisia and Burkina Faso, for example, including political leaders of varied perspectives in the peace process helped ensure a successful conclusion to talks.[119] (See Chapter 9 for an in-depth look at the value of inclusion in peace talks.)

Participatory process is likely to increase the quality and durability of the accord for a number of reasons. The agreement is more likely to reflect a wider range of views. The sense of broad ownership is likely to be enhanced. The warring parties' public accountability to implement the accord increases. And the agreement itself is more likely to address issues and concerns of importance to a larger share of the affected population.

Wider engagement in peace talks also often broadens popular awareness of negotiations, augmenting support for accords. Female participants and civil society participants often publicize the status of negotiations in their communities and, in turn, funnel local perspectives back into talks.[120] Such linkages also frequently broaden the content of agreements, as broader participation often leads to more provisions in accords focused on sociopolitical issues.[121] This was the case for talks in Northern Ireland, for example, where the Northern Ireland Women's Coalition used their direct involvement in the peace talks to ensure provisions mandating attention to victims' rights, reconciliation, and unified education.[122]

The nature and quality of stakeholder participation will, of course, affect the extent to which negotiations are strengthened by the diversity of the participants and the inclusiveness of the process. Participation and inclusion can take many forms. The timing of and approach to fostering inclusion will dramatically affect its impact, as will the representativeness and credibility of the groups and individuals whose participation is enabled (see Chapter 9).

The inclusiveness of accord implementation will similarly affect whether agreements are likely to stick. Though more participatory negotiations improve the likelihood of successful accord implementation, it is no guarantee that peace endures and prosperity prevails. The implementation must itself be participatory. Chapter 10 of this book explores inclusion in the implementation of peace deals.

Implementation is strengthened by drawing on the skills and expertise of diverse groups within society to advance components of accords. Additionally, efforts to promote reconciliation, reintegrate former combatants, and advance transitional justice must engage a wide range of interest groups and stakeholders to reweave a post-conflict society. In Guatemala, successful, broadly participatory peace negotiations were weakened by noninclusive accord implementation. The extensive civil society assembly put together for the talks withered after the agreement was signed, weakening the peace.[123]

The Perils of Exclusion

As substantial as the benefits of inclusion can be, there are equally significant risks in allowing persistent marginalization and exclusion. The vulnerabilities posed to economic, political, and social well-being as well as to stability can be substantial. The drain on resources; the loss of potential economic, political, and social gains; the reduction in satisfaction and well-being; and the consequences for stability are all tremendous and quantifiable.

Marginalization and exclusion are both causes of and consequences of developmental stagnation and instability. That is, less developed or fragile countries and communities are more likely to perpetuate marginalization and exclusion because resources are limited and governance is weak. Moreover, marginalization and exclusion undermine well-being and stability within societies because individual and group access to social networks and opportunities is limited, constraining socioeconomic mobility and development of social capital.[124]

Forgone Productivity and Income, Economic Losses

The failure to economically empower all groups within societies has enormous costs. The first goal of the Agenda for Sustainable Development adopted by the United Nations in 2015 (also known as the Sustainable Development Goals, or SDGs) is ending extreme poverty by 2030. Yet in the absence of policies and programs to support inclusive economic advancement, achieving that objective will simply be impossible. Pockets of poverty will persist.

Today, over 700 million people live in extreme poverty, earning well below the international poverty line of $1.90 per day.[125] Though global poverty continues to decrease, certain regions of the world are struggling to make progress; sub-Saharan Africa now hosts many of the poorest parts of the world, a shift from when the preponderance of such areas was in Southeast Asia.

Within countries and communities, marginalized segments of society are often disproportionately represented among the extremely poor. While data for demographic subgroups like these are often unavailable, we do know that the global rural poverty rate is 17.2 percent, compared with the urban poverty rate of 5.2 percent.[126] In the United States in 2013, the poverty rate for working-age people with disabilities was 28.4 percent, compared to 12.4 percent for those without disabilities.[127] Similarly, White households in the United States have substantially greater wealth, on average, than Black and Latine households.[128] And "Saudi Arabia's Shia minority suffer disproportionately from poverty compared to their Sunni counterparts."[129] In France, Muslim immigrants are poorer than Christian immigrants.[130]

The core principle of the SDGs is to "leave no one behind," and the agenda makes specific commitments to children, youth, people with disabilities, people living with HIV/AIDS, older persons, indigenous people, refugees, internally displaced people, and migrants. Yet pockets of extreme poverty disproportionately feature these typically marginalized groups. That exclusion has dramatic global consequences for everyone. The losses to the formal global economy from women's underemployment, for example, are estimated to be approximately $12 trillion.[131] And in India alone, the economic cost of LGBTQI discrimination is estimated to be $32 billion as a result of lost labor and productivity, underinvestment in human capital, and inefficient allocation of human resources because of discrimination in education and hiring.[132]

The status of marginalized groups is often masked by macro-level data pointing to the overall well-being of economies without referencing disparities in income or breaking down data by demographic subgroups, which would reveal vast differences in well-being. For example, over the last two decades, the poverty gap between indigenous and nonindigenous people increased by 32 percent in Bolivia, by 13 percent in Ecuador, and by 99 percent in Brazil—yet macro-level data for those societies as a whole showed increasing prosperity (see Figure 2.1). Indigenous people were left behind, but that wasn't always visible because disaggregated data often isn't collected or provided.[133]

Reduced Education, Health, and Broader Social Well-Being
The costs of marginalization and exclusion for segments of societies become particularly clear when indicators of well-being are compared. This is true at both the individual and community levels.

Health offers particularly stark evidence of how inattention to diversity and inclusion has developmental costs for individuals and specific communities. In the United States, American Indians and Alaska Natives (AI/AN) face a 26 percent poverty rate, compared to an 11 percent poverty rate among non-Hispanic Whites.[134] Their health status and access to health care are severely constrained by cultural barriers, geographic isolation, inadequate sewage disposal, and low income.[135] Some 36 percent of AI/AN homes (145,000 in total) lack adequate sanitation, and some 6.5 percent (26,000) lack access to safe water and/or waste disposal, compared to less than 1 percent of homes for the US population as a whole.[136] The infant death rate in their community is 60 percent higher than the rate for Whites, and they are twice as likely to have diabetes as Whites.[137]

Disparities in access to education similarly plague marginalized groups, inhibiting their advancement and creating a drag on society as a whole. One particularly stark example is that of Roma communities in Europe, which face limited access to housing, medical care, electoral processes, and employment. Social marginalization is perpetuated through the exclusion of Roma children from quality

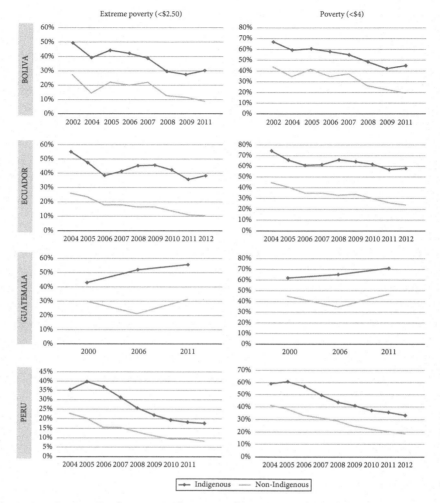

Figure 2.1 Poverty Evolution in Bolivia, Ecuador, Guatemala, and Peru

Credit line: World Bank Group. 2015. *Indigenous Latin America in the Twenty-First Century: The First Decade.* © World Bank. *https://openknowledge.worldbank.org/handle/10986/23751* License: CC BY 3.0 IGO.

education.[138] In Slovakia in 2016, over 50 percent of Roma schoolchildren were taught in Roma-only classes or attended classes in separate schools.[139] The poor quality of education available to them makes it unlikely that Roma students will continue school beyond the age of sixteen, and it often constrains youth to attend vocational schools without the possibility of university education later.[140] A 2010 UNDP study confirmed that "almost one in five Roma did not finish primary education (18.4%) and only 17% continued into secondary education, 15.2% of whom entered vocational training. Only 0.3% of Roma entered tertiary education."[141]

Differentials in public and private service provision and access also demonstrate how subgroups within societies can be disadvantaged vis-à-vis the general population. This is true around the world.[142] In Sweden and Germany, significant differences are found in the treatment of people of foreign backgrounds in educa-tion and in social service benefits registration, respectively.[143] In the United States, pronounced differences are found in the treatment of voter registration inquiries based upon ethnicity.[144] In South Africa, "whites [report] about eight times the av-erage per capita income and expenditure levels of [Black South] Africans"; addition-ally, almost one-third of Black South Africans live in "informal dwellings," and they are less likely to have piped water in their home, or to own refrigerators, televisions, and radios.[145] In India, poverty persists as a result of systematic exclusion based on the caste system, despite legal progress to move away from that system. Dalits, the lowest caste, continue to face repercussions through lack of access to resources and pervasive poverty.[146] And in the United States, a 2018 Economic Policy Institute report found that "Blacks are 2.5 times more likely than Whites to be living in pov-erty, their infant mortality rate is 2.3 times that of Whites, their unemployment rate is more than double that for Whites, they typically earn only 82.5 cents for every dollar earned by a White counterpart, and their household earnings are on average well under two thirds of those of their White equivalents."[147]

Even further disadvantaged are people and communities that face multiple dis-crimination, or those who risk marginalization for more than one reason. The impact is particularly acute in conflict zones. For example, when ISIS invaded northern territories in Iraq, fighters singled out Yazidi women for enslavement be-cause of their religion and their sex. Some 3,500 Yazidi women were raped, forced to marry ISIS fighters, and forced to convert to Islam. They were subsequently sold and traded during years of enslavement. An estimated 2,000 women remain in ISIS captivity.[148] Those who have managed to reunite with their families face daunting physical and mental health needs and stigma.[149] Traditional laws pre-vent many Yazidi women and girls from accessing care and moving forward in their communities.[150]

Weakened Rule of Law and Governance

Marginalization and exclusion erode governance and rule of law for individuals and for societies as a whole. Most directly, individuals who lack physical access to gov-ernment facilities such as voting sites, public utility offices, and schools simply do not enjoy equal rights within their societies and communities. For example, Haiti's former secretary of state for the integration of people with disabilities, Gerald Oriol, who uses a wheelchair, has discussed needing to be carried up flights of stairs to visit government officials.[151] Impediments to people with disabilities abound; for example, in Vietnam, 97 percent of those ages fifteen to twenty-nine without a disa-bility attended school, while only 44 percent of those with a disability have received education. Similar gaps exist in Egypt (89 percent vs. 43 percent) and in Indonesia (98 percent vs. 53 percent) as of 2018.[152]

Access to public services and the civic participation of certain ethnic groups and racial minorities can also be hindered when health clinics, schools, and polling sites are inconveniently located. In India, research has shown that "unequal access to government-provided goods and services [such as public schools, healthcare, utilities (water, electricity, gas), identity cards (voter ID, aadhar), issuance of driving license, and registration of land or property] reinforces, reproduces, and exacerbates the unequal social and economic structure."[153] And in East Jerusalem, restrictions on the movement of Palestinians impede access to healthcare.[154]

Legal barriers can be equally daunting. Laws restricting inheritance, property rights, and banking can be significant barriers to full socioeconomic participation. An inability to claim an individual national identity card, for example, can prevent community members from accessing services and registering to vote. Over 2.7 billion women globally are legally restricted from having the same access to employment as men; their access is constrained by laws such as those restricting their ability to work at night or to work in certain industries.[155]

Ethiopia, however, provides a case in point of how to make progress. A sweeping revision of the family code in 2000 stopped husbands from legally blocking their wives from particular trades and professions; eliminated husbands' sole control over property administration; enabled wives to divorce their husbands without the husband's consent; and raised the marriage age for women from fifteen to eighteen, providing a legal framework to prevent child marriage.[156]

Laws also restrict the rights of other groups. For example, same-sex marriage is legal in only thirty countries worldwide, with implications for the rights of same-sex partners to jointly own and inherit property, cohabit, raise children, and live openly within their societies.[157] Migrants and refugees face a range of restrictions on their work eligibility and reduced protections in the workplace.[158] For example, Syrian refugees in Jordan continue to face barriers and limitations on their employment, even after years of displacement due to conflict back home.[159]

Concrete restrictions can be compounded by attitudes and norms (see Chapter 19). For example, despite equality under law, Dalits in India face substantial discrimination and disadvantages.[160] In Europe, the Roma face bias despite a raft of policies to promote their advancement.[161] In some communities, women are unable to vote as they prefer because of the informal practice of "family voting," through which the husband or patriarch decides how every family member votes. In Macedonia's October 2017 municipal elections, Organization for Security and Cooperation in Europe (OSCE) observers reported family voting to be the largest category of observed irregularities.[162]

Women and girls are often impeded in their efforts to attend school or to work, due to limitations on their mobility, particularly after reaching puberty. In a number of countries worldwide, girls' enrollment in school has been correlated with the distance from home to school.[163] In parts of sub-Saharan Africa, girls sometimes drop out as teenagers because they risk falling victim to the traditional practice of "bride kidnapping" on the way to school; families don't want to risk their daughters' exposure, so girls are pulled out of school.[164] In Kenya, female enrollment has been linked to the availability of sanitary products and sanitation.[165]

Disparities in service delivery can also signal ways marginalization and exclusion undermine governance, particularly where discrimination or unequal treatment is illegal. In northern Ghana, for example, about a quarter of the poorest 20 percent of the population lack malaria-preventing insecticide-treated nets, compared to only 15 percent of the richest 20 percent. Similarly, families who live in cities are more likely to own bed nets than those in rural communities.[166] Banks do at times treat potential borrowers of different sexes, races, and ethnicities differently. The same is often true of real estate brokers seeking to maintain ethnically homogeneous neighborhoods, and of police officers who have different perceptions of people of different races and ethnic backgrounds.[167] The failure to hold public and private service providers accountable for disparities signals weaknesses in governance and rule of law.

Reduced Stability and Resilience to Conflict

Exclusion and marginalization have multifaceted implications for the stability of countries and communities. The implications will depend upon a wide range of factors, including the degree of exclusion (and perceived exclusion), the types of marginalization (and their duration, severity, and the implications for the affected groups), and the nature of the group(s) facing disadvantage.

At their most extreme, marginalization and exclusion can foster violence and spawn extremism. But the connection is not a clear one. Economic marginalization (or wealth and income) do not correlate closely with extremist ideology at the individual level; that is, poor people are not necessarily particularly prone to extremism or terrorism.[168] They may be drawn to extremist movements or terrorist groups by the promise of income, but they are not necessarily devoted to the cause espoused by leadership.

That said, marginalization and exclusion certainly result in disaffection and disillusionment that do, at times, lead to profound instability. For example, in 2010–2011, protests began to sweep across the Middle East. Many of the countries that faced broad-based popular mobilization as part of the Arab Spring had steadily progressed economically, but protesters nonetheless called for social and economic justice, less corruption, improved public sector governance, reduced inequality, and greater economic opportunity. In some countries, those protests precipitated violent conflict. Several of the countries—Syria, Libya, and Yemen among them—have not yet returned to political stability, and the ensuing conflict has resulted in enormous loss of human life, as well as loss of economic, social, and political well-being.[169]

Relatedly, migration spurred by exclusion and marginalization has implications for stability. Rohingya fleeing persecution in Myanmar have become refugees in Bangladesh, straining the host country economically and socially.[170] Syrian refugees have strained Lebanon's and Jordan's governments and institutions, particularly as refugees' displacement has lasted for years.[171]

Pervasive societal violence resulting, in part, from inequity and exclusion can persist (or grow) even in the absence of war. More than one-third of violent deaths in 2015 were in Latin America, a region that is home to less than 15 percent of the world's population.[172] The region's homicide rates in particular are disproportionately high, qualifying as an epidemic according to WHO standards.[173] The region also contains more than half of the twenty-five countries that have "high" and "very high" femicide rates.[174] In 2016, the Inter-American Commission on Human Rights (IACHR) linked the widespread violence to social inequality and exclusion, arguing that a "detailed analysis of the distribution of wealth, access to basic quality services on equal terms, and the enjoyment of rights shows profound differences and inequalities among segments of the population. Inequality, low social mobility, uncertainty of employment, and the intergenerational transmission of poverty are major obstacles" to social cohesion in Latin America.[175] The commission connects ongoing social exclusion to broader security and human rights concerns in the region, calling exclusion a source of "social conflicts, violence and insecurity" as well as a trigger for "repressive responses by States and practices that violate human rights."[176]

The Bottom Line: Enormous Lost Potential

There is tremendous untapped potential in the diverse communities that are not fully empowered and engaged in society and the economy. Though general global well-being continues to improve, it is an incomplete story. Those broad numbers hide vast inequities, and they obscure the many millions who are underutilized or left behind. The general numbers also mask the risks exclusion poses for stability and continued prosperity.

Marginalization and exclusion vary by country and within countries. The gaps in well-being, as well as the causes and consequences of exclusion, will also differ. That said, no country takes full advantage of the rich diversity within its borders. Exclusion and isolation undermine the well-being and stability of nations around the world. A focus on fostering inclusion offers tremendous promise for advancing well-being globally.

Notes

1. Rowe 2018.
2. Calvert 1975. See also Forde 1997.
3. Web Solutions n.d.
4. Carver 2003.
5. Fraser 2011.
6. Tang et al. 2015.
7. Patel 2005.

8. Marlow 1997.
9. Bagde 2014; Gyatso n.d.
10. Klingorová and Havlíček 2015.
11. See the Introduction for relevant terminological definitions for "equity," "inclusion," and related vocabulary.
12. Neidleman 2012.
13. Kant 1997, LE 27:462.
14. Kleingeld 2007; Lott 2002.
15. Wollstonecraft 1792.
16. De Gouges 2016.
17. Welchman 1995.
18. Sundstrom 2017.
19. Rawls 1971.
20. Ekmekci and Arda 2015.
21. Mills 1997.
22. Kenton 2019.
23. Arneson 2013.
24. Berlin 1969.
25. Alexander 2010.
26. Nussbaum 2013.
27. Sen 1999.
28. Driver 2014.
29. Ball 1980.
30. Bentham 1978; Schultz and Varouxakis 2005.
31. Singer 2010.
32. Stefanovska 2015; see, e.g., Scutt 2016.
33. Bentzen, Hariri, and Robinson 2015.
34. Tiky 2011.
35. For a compilation of sources and references, see Laqueur and Rubin 1989.
36. Chigozie 2018.
37. Romero 1976.
38. De Beauvoir 2011.
39. Harel-Shalev 2020; Enloe 2014; Tickner 1988, 1992.
40. Du Bois 1897; Appiah 2005.
41. Le Melle 2009; Henderson 2013.
42. Danforth and Rhodes 1997; Blackburn and Smith 2010. See also Powell and Foglia 2014.
43. Chaplin, Twigg, and Lovell 2019.
44. Crenshaw 1989.
45. Young 2014.
46. Sen 1992.
47. Stiglitz 2014.
48. See Crenshaw 1995; Delgado and Stefancic 2013.
49. Ahmed 2012; Thomas 1999.
50. Scheffler 2003, 5–6.
51. UN General Assembly 1948.
52. Glendon 2004.
53. UN General Assembly 1975, 1986, 2007, 2011; UNESCO 2001.
54. UN General Assembly 1981.
55. See UN Security Council n.d. a.

56. See UN Security Council n.d. b.
57. Peace Women n.d.
58. Uphoff 2000.
59. Adriani 2013.
60. Brennan 2012.
61. See Bourdieu 1984, 1986; Bourdieu and Wacquant 1992; Coleman 1986, 1987a, 1987b, 1988, 1990; Putnam, Leonardi, and Nanetti 1993; Putnam 2000; Adriani 2013.
62. Claridge 2018.
63. Claridge 2018. See also Healy and Cote 2001, 42.
64. Kawachi and Berkman (2014) define social cohesion as "the extent of connectedness and solidarity among groups in society."
65. Jordan 2015.
66. Narayan 1999; Onyx, Edwards, and Bullen 2007.
67. Narayan 1999.
68. Putnam 2007.
69. Hooghe, Lancee, and Dronkers 2011.
70. Semenas 2014.
71. Colletta and Cullen 2000, 13, 15.
72. Colletta and Cullen 2000.
73. Cox and Sisk 2017.
74. Das, Fisiy, and Kyte 2013.
75. Shrivastava and Yadav, n.d.
76. Popay et al. 2008.
77. Saloojee and Saloojee 2011.
78. Shanyanana-Amaambo and Waghid 2016.
79. Zhuang 2008.
80. World Bank n.d.
81. Yuval-Davis 2006.
82. Garbutt 2009.
83. Yuval-Davis 2011.
84. Bennett and Yuval-Davis 2007.
85. For example, see Croucher 2004; O'Neill and Spybey 2003; Chowdhury 2018.
86. Antonsich 2010, 644.
87. See, for example, Allen and Bowles 2012.
88. Carr et al. 2019.
89. Janis 1991, 3.
90. Schmidt 2013.
91. Esser 1998.
92. Kamalnath 2017.
93. Cleary, Lees, and Sayers 2019; Rose 2011.
94. Johansson 2017.
95. Rock and Grant 2016.
96. Østby 2013, 126. See also Marx 1967, 71–76, 146–154; Davies 1962; Feierabend and Feierabend 1966; see Gurr 1993, 2000, 2010; Galtung 1964; Hechter 1975; Horowitz 1985.
97. Collier and Hoeffler 2004.
98. Stewart 2002, 2000.
99. Stewart 2002, 1.
100. Østby 2013.
101. Walter 2020.
102. OECD 2012, 58.

103. Crebo-Rediker et al. 2015, 12.
104. Woetzel et al. 2015.
105. USAID n.d. a.
106. USAID n.d. b.
107. Hunt, Layton, and Prince 2014.
108. Creary et al. 2019.
109. Kuoti 2016.
110. Rothstein and Uslaner 2006.
111. Rothstein and Uslaner 2006.
112. Marc and Salmon 2017, 141.
113. Beyerle 2014.
114. Bauhr, Charron, and Wängnerud 2018; Watson and Moreland 2014.
115. Marc and Salmon 2017, xviii.
116. Collier 2000, 2004.
117. Scheffran, Brauch, and Schilling 2012, 49 (citing Cederman and Girardin 2007; Wimmer, Cederman, and Min 2009; Buhuang 2010).
118. Council on Foreign Relations 2018. Data from International Interactions and International Peace Institute.
119. World Bank 2018a.
120. Wanis-St. John and Kew 2008.
121. Lund and Mitchell 2017; Krause, Krause, and Branfors 2018.
122. Fearon 2002.
123. De Torres and Talbot 2009.
124. Burton and Welsh 2015, 3.
125. World Bank 2018b, 5.
126. World Bank 2017b.
127. Vallas and Fremstad 2014.
128. Tippett et al. 2014.
129. ADHRB *2017*.
130. Adida, Laitin, and Valfort 2010.
131. Ferrant and Kolev 2016, 2; Woetzel et al. 2015.
132. Badgett 2014; Badgett et al. 2014, 5.
133. Cruz-Saco and Cummings 2018.
134. US Department of Health and Human Services 2018.
135. US Department of Health and Human Services 2018.
136. Indian Health Service 2016.
137. US Department of Health and Human Services 2018.
138. Kóczé 2000.
139. UNCRC 2016, para. 44(a).
140. Amnesty International and European Roma Rights Centre 2017.
141. UNDP 2012, 92–93.
142. Van Acker 2020.
143. Hinnerich, Höglin, and Johannesson 2015. Hemker and Rink 2017.
144. White, Nathan, and Faller 2015.
145. Gradín 2012, 2.
146. Kurian and Singh 2017. Galtung 1969 discusses structural violence at length.
147. Economic Policy Institute 2018.
148. Wheeler 2016.
149. Wheeler 2016.
150. George 2015.

151. OAS 2013.
152. UNESCO 2018.
153. Demirguc-Kunt, Klapper, and Prasad 2018. Aadhar is a unique personal identification number issued to each resident of India.
154. World Health Organization n.d.
155. World Bank 2018c.
156. Hallward-Driemeier and Gajigo 2013, 12–14.
157. Pew Research Center 2018.
158. ILO 2004.
159. Sahin Mencutek and Nashwan 2020.
160. Narula 2008.
161. Rosenfield 2010.
162. OSCE 2018, 26; International Knowledge Network of Women in Politics. n.d.
163. Sperling and Winthrop, 2016.
164. Nkosi 2014.
165. Jewitt and Ryley 2014.
166. Kanmik et al. 2019.
167. Van Wyk 2015.
168. Ianchovichina 2018. See also Ghanem 2015.
169. Bunton 2016.
170. UNDP 2017.
171. Yahya 2018.
172. IACHR 2015, 27 (quoting United Nations Office on Drugs and Crime).
173. IACHR 2015, 28 (quoting Secretariat of the Geneva Declaration on Armed Violence and Development).
174. Four of those twenty-five countries are in the Caribbean, four are in Central America, and six are in South America (Nowak 2012). The definition of femicide, initially "the gender-based killing of women by men," has been expanded "to refer to any killing of a woman" (Nowak 2012, 1).
175. IAHCR 2016, 26.
176. IAHCR 2016, 26.

Bibliography

Acker, Wouter Van. 2020. "Combatting Racism and Discrimination in the Public Sector." Governance for Development, World Bank Group. July. https://blogs.worldbank.org/governa nce/combatting-racism-and-discrimination-public-sector.

ADHRB. 2017. "Overview: Poverty in Saudi Arabia." Americans for Democracy and Human Rights in Bahrain. https://www.adhrb.org/wp-content/uploads/2017/01/2017.1.06_SR-Povert y_Saudi-briefing_final-1.pdf.

Adida, Claire L., David D. Laitin, and Marie-Anne Valfort. 2010. "Identifying Barriers to Muslim Integration in France." PNAS 107, no. 52: 22384–22390. https://www.pnas.org/content/107/ 52/22384.

Adriani, Luca. 2013. "Social Capital: A Road Map of Theoretical Frameworks and Empirical Limitations." Birkbeck University of London. http://www.bbk.ac.uk/management/docs/ workingpapers/WP1.pdf.

Alexander, John M. 2010. Capabilities and Social Justice: The Political Philosophy of Amartya Sen and Martha Nussbaum. Farnham: Ashgate.

Allen, Kelly A., and Terence Bowles. 2012. "Belonging as a Guiding Principle in the Education of Adolescents." Australian Journal of Educational and Developmental Psychology 12: 108–119. https://files.eric.ed.gov/fulltext/EJ1002251.pdf.

Amnesty International and European Roma Rights Centre. 2017. "A Lesson in Discrimination: Segregation of Romani Children in Primary Education in Slovakia." http://www.amnesty.eu/content/assets/Slovakia_Discrimination_Report_FINAL.pdf.

Antonsich, Marco. 2010. "Searching for Belonging—An Analytical Framework." In *Geography Compass* 4, no. 6: 644–659. http://scholar.google.com/scholar_url?url=https://repository.lboro.ac.uk/articles/In_search_of_belonging_an_analytical_framework/9481013/files/17106191.pdf&hl=en&sa=X&scisig=AAGBfm0W32WepgXRfFNS_WNKWSWAs1Aa1w&nossl=1&oi=scholarr.

Appiah, Kwame Anthony. 2005. *The Ethics of Identity*. Princeton, NJ: Princeton University Press.

Arneson, Richard. 2013. "Egalitarianism." *Stanford Encyclopedia of Philosophy*, ed. Edward Zalta. https://plato.stanford.edu/entries/egalitarianism/.

Badgett, M. V. Lee. 2014. "The Economic Cost of Stigma and the Exclusion of LGBT People: A Case Study of India." World Bank Group. http://documents.worldbank.org/curated/en/527261468035379692/pdf/940400WP0Box380usion0of0LGBT0People.pdf.

Badgett, M. V. Lee, et al. 2014. "The Relationship Between LGBT Inclusion and Economic Development: An Analysis of Emerging Economies." USAID and the Williams Institute. http://williamsinstitute.law.ucla.edu/wp-content/uploads/lgbt-inclusion-and-development-november-2014.pdf.

Bagde, Uttamkumars. 2014. "Essential Elements of Human Rights in Buddhism." *Journal of Law and Conflict Resolution* 6, no. 2: 32–38. https://academicjournals.org/article/article1398693675_Bagde.pdf.

Ball, Terence. 1980. "Utilitarianism, Feminism, and the Franchise: James Mill and His Critics." *History of Political Thought* 1, no. 1 (1980): 91–115. www.jstor.org/stable/26211839.

Bauhr, Monika, Nicholas Charron, and Lena Wängnerud. 2018. "Exclusion or Interests? Why Females in Elected Office Reduce Petty and Grand Corruption." *European Journal of Political Research* 58, no. 4: 1043–1065. https://ejpr.onlinelibrary.wiley.com/doi/full/10.1111/1475-6765.12300.

Bennett, Jennifer, and Nira Yuval-Davis. 2007. "Intersectionality, Citizenship and Contemporary Politics of Belonging." In *Scratching the Surface: Democracy, Traditions, Gender*, edited by Jennifer Bennett, 7–22. Lahore: Heinrich Böll Foundation, 2007.

Bentham, Jeremy. 1978. "Offences Against One's Self." Edited by Louis Crompton. *Journal of Homosexuality* 3, no. 4: 389–405. http://www.columbia.edu/cu/lweb/eresources/exhibitions/sw25/bentham/.

Bentzen, Jeanet, Jacob Gerner Hariri, and James A. Robinson. 2015. "The Indigenous Roots of Representative Democracy." NBER Working Paper No. 21193. https://www.nber.org/papers/w21193.

Berlin, I. 1969. "Two Concepts of Liberty." In *Four Essays on Liberty*. London: Oxford University Press.

Beyerle, Shaazka. 2014. *Curtailing Corruption: People Power for Accountability and Justice*. Boulder, CO: Lynne Rienner.

Blackburn, Molly V., and Jill M. Smith. 2010. "Moving Beyond the Inclusion of LGBT-Themed Literature in English Language Arts Classrooms: Interrogating Heteronormativity and Exploring Intersectionality." *Journal of Adolescent and Adult Literacy* 53, no. 8: 625–634. https://search.proquest.com/openview/391b6b2703d524706c4f5c08cf8f3792/1?pq-origsite=gscholar&cbl=42001.

Bourdieu, Pierre. 1986. "The Forms of Capital." In *Handbook of Theory and Research for the Sociology of Education*, edited by J. G. Richardson, 241–258. New York: Greenwood Press.

Bourdieu, Pierre. 1984. *Distinction: A Social Critique of the Judgement of Taste*. Harvard: Routledge and Kegan Paul.

Bourdieu, Pierre, and L. P. D. Wacquant. 1992. *An Invitation to Reflexive Sociology*. Chicago: University of Chicago Press.

Brennan, Michael. 2012. "Virtues and Economic Relationships in Adam Smith and Antonio Genovesi." Working Paper, May 21. https://www.academia.edu/1622341/Virtues_and_Economic_Relationships_in_Adam_Smith_and_Antonio_Genovesi?auto=download.

Buhuang, Halvard. 2010. "Climate Not to Blame for African Civil Wars." *PNAS* 107, no. 38: 16477–16482. https://doi.org/10.1073/pnas.1005739107.

Bunton, Martin. 2016. "Arab Spring." Oxford Bibliographies. August 30. https://www.oxfordbibliographies.com/view/document/obo-9780195390155/obo-9780195390155-0131.xml.

Burton, Linda M., and Whitney Welsh. 2015. "Inequality and Opportunity: The Role of Exclusion, Social Capital, and Generic Social Processes in Upward Mobility." William T. Grant Foundation. https://wtgrantfoundation.org/library/uploads/2016/01/Inequality-and-Opportunity-Burton-and-Welsh-William-T.-Grant-Foundation.pdf.

Calvert, Brian. 1975. "Plato and the Equality of Women." *Phoenix* 29, no. 3: 231–243. doi: 10.2307/1087616.

Carr, Evan W., Andrew Reece, Gabriella Rosen Kellerman, and Alexi Robichaux. 2019. "The Value of Belonging at Work." *Harvard Business Review*, December. https://hbr.org/2019/12/the-value-of-belonging-at-work.

Carver, Terrell. 2003. "Gender." In *Political Concepts*, edited by Bellamy Richard and Mason Andrew, 169–181. Manchester: Manchester University Press. www.jstor.org/stable/j.ctt155jbcx.18.

Cederman, Lars-Erik, and Luc Girardin. 2007. "Beyond Fractionalization: Mapping Ethnicity onto Nationalist Insurgencies." *American Political Science Review* 101, no. 1: 173–185. doi: 10.1017/S0003055407070086.

Chaplin, Daniel, John Twigg, and Emma Lovell. 2019. "Intersectional Approaches to Vulnerability Reduction and Resilience-Building." Overseas Development Institute. April. https://odi.org/en/publications/intersectional-approaches-to-vulnerability-reduction-and-resilience-building/.

Chigozie, Nnuriam Paul. 2018. "The Influence of Pan Africanism on Africa's International Relations, 1945–1965." *Equatorial Journal of History and International Relations* 1, no. 1: 13–21. https://ssrn.com/abstract=3130717.

Chowdhory, Nasreen. 2018. "The Idea of 'Belonging' and Citizenship Among Refugees: Some Theoretical Considerations." In *Refugees, Citizenship and Belonging in South Asia*. Singapore: Springer.

Claridge, Tristan. 2018. "What Is Bridging Social Capital?" *Social Capital Research*. January 7. https://www.socialcapitalresearch.com/what-is-bridging-social-capital/.

Coleman, James S. 1990. *Foundations of Social Theory*. Cambridge, MA: Harvard University Press.

Coleman, James S. 1988. "Social Capital in the Creation of Human Capital." *The American Journal of Sociology* 94: S95.

Coleman, James S. 1987a. "The Creation and Destruction of Social Capital: Implications for the Law." *Notre Dame Journal of Law, Ethics and Public Policy* 3, no. 3: art. 3.

Coleman, James S. 1987b. "Norms as Social Capital." In *Economic Imperialism: The Economic Approach Applied Outside the Field of Economics*, edited by G. Radnitzky and P. Bernholz, 135–155. New York: Paragon House, 1987.

Coleman, James S. 1986. "Social Theory, Social Research, and a Theory of Action." *The American Journal of Sociology* 91, no. 6: 1309–1335. http://www.jstor.org/stable/2779798.

Colletta, Nat J., and Michelle L. Cullen. 2000. *Violent Conflict and the Transformation of Social Capital: Lessons from Cambodia, Rwanda, Guatemala, and Somalia*. Kyiv: World Bank.

Collier, Paul. 2004. "Development and Conflict." Centre for the Study of African Economics, Oxford University. https://www.un.org/esa/documents/Development.and.Conflict2.pdf.

Collier, Paul. 2000. "Crisis Prevention: Tackling Horizontal Inequalities." *Oxford Development Studies* 28, no. 3: 245–262.

Collier, Paul, and Anke Hoeffler. 2004. "Greed and Grievance in Civil War." *Oxford Economic Papers* 56: 563–595. https://www.econ.nyu.edu/user/debraj/Courses/Readings/CollierHoeffler.pdf.

Council on Foreign Relations. 2018. "Women's Participation in Peace Processes." July 31. https://www.cfr.org/interactive/womens-participation-in-peace-processes.

Cox, Fletcher D., and Timothy D. Sisk. 2017. *Peacebuilding in Deeply Divided Societies: Toward Social Cohesion?* Rethinking Political Violence. London: Palgrave Macmillan.

Creary, Stephanie J., Mary-Hunter McDonnell, Sakshi Ghai, and Jared Scruggs. 2019. "When and Why Diversity Improves Your Board's Performance." *Harvard Business Review*, March. https://hbr.org/2019/03/when-and-why-diversity-improves-your-boards-performance.

Crebo-Rediker, Heidi, Tina M. Fordham, Willem Buiter, and Ebrahim Rahbari. 2015. "Women in the Economy." Citi GPS: Global Perspectives and Solutions. https://www.citivelocity.com/citigps/women-in-the-economy/.

Crenshaw, Kimberlé, ed. 1995. *Critical Race Theory: The Key Writings That Formed the Movement.* New York: New Press.

Crenhaw, Kimberlé. 1989. "Demarginalizing the Intersection of Race and Sex: A Black Feminist Critique of Antidiscrimination Doctrine, Feminist Theories, and Antiracist Politics." *University of Chicago Legal Forum* 1: art. 8. https://chicagounbound.uchicago.edu/cgi/viewcontent.cgi?referer=&httpsredir=1&article=1052&context=uclf.

Croucher, Sheila L. 2004. *Globalization and Belonging: The Politics of Identity in a Changing World.* Lanham, MD: Rowman and Littlefield.

Cruz-Saco, Maria Amparo, and Joanne Toor Cummings. 2018. "Indigenous Communities and Social Inclusion in Latin America." United Nations Department of Economic and Social Affairs. https://www.un.org/development/desa/family/wp-content/uploads/sites/23/2018/05/2-1.pdf.

Danforth, Scot, and William C. Rhodes. 1997. "Deconstructing Disability: A Philosophy for Inclusion." *Remedial and Special Education* 18, no. 6: 357–366. https://deepblue.lib.umich.edu/bitstream/handle/2027.42/68721/10.1177_074193259701800605.pdf?sequence=2.

Das, Maitreyi Bordia, Cyprian Fisiy, and Rachel Kyte. 2013. *Inclusion Matters: The Foundation for Shared Prosperity.* Washington, DC: World Bank. https://openknowledge.worldbank.org/bitstream/handle/10986/16195/9781464800108.pdf?sequence=1&isAllowed=y.

Davies, James C. 1962. "Toward a Theory of Revolution." *American Sociological Review* 27, no. 1: 5–19.

De Beauvoir, Simone. 2011. *The Second Sex.* Translated by Constance Borde and Sheila Malovany-Chevallier. New York: Vintage.

De Gouges, Olympe. 2016. "Declaration of the Rights of Woman and the Female Citizen, 1791." In *Tolerance: The Beacon of the Enlightenment,* edited by Caroline Warman, 49–51. Cambridge: Open Book.

De Torres, Daniel, and Jonathan Talbot, eds. 2009. "Strategies for Policymakers: Bringing Women into Peace Negotiations." Institute for Inclusive Security. October. https://www.inclusivesecurity.org/wp-content/uploads/2013/05/Negotiations_FINAL.pdf.

Delgado, Richard, and Jean Stefancic, eds. 2013. *Critical Race Theory: The Cutting Edge.* 3rd ed. Philadelphia: Temple University Press.

Demirguc-Kunt, Asli, Leora Klapper, and Neeraj Prasad. 2018. "How Unequal Access to Public Goods Reinforces Horizontal Inequality in India." World Bank. http://pubdocs.worldbank.org/en/489761528721159930/Demirguc-Kunt-et-al-31st-May.pdf.

Driver, Julia. 2014. "The History of Utilitarianism." In *Stanford Encyclopedia of Philosophy*, ed. Edward Zalta. https://plato.stanford.edu/entries/utilitarianism-history/.

Du Bois, W. E. B. 1897. "The Conservation of Races." https://www.gutenberg.org/files/31254/31254-h/31254-h.htm.

Economic Policy Institute. 2018. "50 Years After the Kerner Commission." February 26.

Ekmekci, Perihan Elif, and Berna Arda. 2015. "Enhancing John Rawls's Theory of Justice to Cover Health and Social Determinants of Health." *Acta Bioethica* 21, no. 2: 227–236. doi:10.4067/S1726-569X2015000200009.

Enloe, C. 2014. *Bananas, Beaches and Bases: Making Feminist Sense of International Politics.* 2nd ed. Berkeley: University of California Press.

Esser, J. K. 1998. "Alive and Well After 25 Years: A Review of Groupthink Research." *Organizational Behavior and Human Decision Processes* 73, nos. 2–3: 116–141. https://doi.org/10.1006/obhd.1998.2758.

Fearon, Kate. 2002. "Northern Ireland's Women's Coalition: Institutionalising a Political Voice and Ensuring Representation." In *Public Participation* 13 (December): 78–81. https://

www.c-r.org/accord/public-participation/northern-irelands-womens-coalition-institution
alising-political-voice.

Feierabend, Ivo K., and Rosalind L. Feierabend. 1966. "Aggressive Behaviors Within Polities,
1948–1962: A Cross-National Study 1." *Journal of Conflict Resolution* 10, no. 3: 249–271.
https://econpapers.repec.org/article/saejocore/v_3a10_3ay_3a1966_3ai_3a3_3ap_3a249-
271.htm.

Ferrant, Gaelle, and Alexandre Kolev. 2016. "The Economic Cost of Gender-Based Discrimination
in Social Institutions." OECD Development Centre. June. http://www.oecd.org/development/
development-gender/SIGI_cost_final.pdf.

Forde, Steven. 1997. "Gender and Justice in Plato." *The American Political Science Review* 91, no.
3: 657–670. www.jstor.org/stable/2952081.

Fraser, Chris. 2011. "Mohism and Motivation." In *Ethics in Early China: An Anthology*, edited by
Chris Fraser, Dan Robins, and Timothy O'Leary, 83–104. Hong Kong: Hong Kong University
Press. www.jstor.org/stable/j.ctt1xwdxp.10.

Galtung, Johan. 1969. "Violence, Peace, and Peace Research." *Journal of Peace Research* 6, no.
3: 167–191.

Galtung, Johan. 1964. *A Structural Theory of Aggression*. Oslo: Peace Research Institute.

Garbutt, Rob. 2009. "Social Inclusion and Local Practices of Belonging." *Cosmopolitan Civil
Societies: An International Journal* 1, no. 3: 84–108. https://doi.org/10.5130/ccs.v1i3.1080.

George, Susannah. 2015. "Yazidi Women Welcomed Back to the Faith." UNHCR. June 15. http://
www.unhcr.org/en-us/news/stories/2015/6/56ec1e9611/yazidi-women-welcomed-back-
to-the-faith.htmlhttp://documents.worldbank.org/curated/en/145891467991974540/pdf/
98544-REVISED-WP-P148348-Box394854B-PUBLIC-Indigenous-Latin-America.pdf.

Ghanem, Hafez. 2015. "Roots of the Arab Spring." In *The Arab Spring Five Years Later: Toward
Greater Inclusiveness*, ed. Hafez Ghanem, 39–64. Washington, DC: Brookings Institution Press,
2015. https://www.jstor.org/stable/pdf/10.7864/j.ctt1657tv8.6.pdf?ab_segments=0%252Fdefa
ult-2%252Fcontrol&refreqid=excelsior%3Ab568930a295c19753d1c222c84bc6f67.

Gradín, Carlos. 2012. "Race, Poverty and Deprivation in South Africa." *Journal of African
Economies* 22, no. 2: 187–238.

Gurr, Ted Robert. 2000. *Peoples Versus States: Minorities at Risk in the New Century*. Washington,
DC: US Institute of Peace Press.

Gurr, Ted Robert. 1993. "Why Minorities Rebel: A Global Analysis of Communal Mobilization
and Conflict Since 1945." *International Political Science Review* 14, no. 2: 161–201.

Gurr, Ted Robert. 2010. *Why Men Rebel*. Rev. ed. Boulder, CO: Paradigm.

Gyatso, Tenzin. n.d. "Human Rights, Democracy and Freedom." Office of the Dalai Lama. https://
www.dalailama.com/messages/world-peace/human-rights-democracy-and-freedom.

Hallward-Driemeier, Mary, and Ousman Gajigo. 2013. "Strengthening Economic Rights and
Women's Occupational Choice: The Impact of Reforming Ethiopia's Family Law." World Bank
Development Research Group. http://documents.worldbank.org/curated/en/25986146802
1600567/pdf/WPS6695.pdf.

Harel-Shalev, Ayelet. 2020. "Feminist International Relations (IR) Theory." In *The Palgrave
Encyclopedia of Global Security Studies*. London: Palgrave, 2020. https://www.researchgate.net/
publication/333668170_Feminist_International_Relations_IR_Theory.

Healy, Tom, and Sylvain Cote. 2001. *The Well-Being of Nations: The Role of Human and Social
Capital*. Paris: Organisation for Economic Co-operation and Development.

Hechter, Michael. 1975. *Internal Colonialism: The Celtic Fringe in British National Development,
1536–1966*. Berkeley: University of California Press.

Hemker, Johannes, and Anselm Rink. 2017. "Multiple Dimensions of Bureaucratic
Discrimination: Evidence from German Welfare Offices." *American Journal of Political Science*
61, no. 4: 786–803. https://doi.org/https://doi.org/10.1111/ajps.12312.

Henderson, Errol A. 2013. "Hidden in Plain Sight: Racism in International Relations Theory."
Cambridge Review of International Affairs 26: 71–92. https://www.researchgate.net/publicat
ion/263150874_Hidden_in_Plain_Sight_Racism_in_International_Relations_Theory.

Hinnerich, Bjorn Tyrefors, Erik Höglin, and Magnus Johannesson. 2015. "Discrimination Against Students with Foreign Backgrounds: Evidence from Grading in Swedish Public High Schools." *Education Economics* 23, no. 6: 660–676. https://doi.org/10.1080/09645292.2014.899562.

Hooghe, Marc, Bram Lancee, and Jaap Dronkers. 2011. "Ethnic Diversity in the Neighborhood and Social Trust of Immigrants and Natives. A Replication of the Putnam (2007) Study in a West-European Country." In *Social Cohesion: Contemporary Theoretical Perspectives on the Study of Social Cohesion and Social Capital*, edited by Marc Hooghe, 77–103. Brussels: KVAB.

Horowitz, Donald L. 1985. *Ethnic Groups in Conflict*. Berkeley: University of California Press.

Hunt, Vivian, Dennis Layton, and Sara Prince. 2014. "Diversity Matters." McKinsey & Company, New York. November 24. https://www.insurance.ca.gov/diversity/41-ISDGBD/GBDExternal/upload/McKinseyDivmatters201411.pdf.

IACHR. 2015. "Violence, Children and Organized Crime." Inter-American Commission on Human Rights and OAS. http://www.oas.org/en/iachr/reports/pdfs/ViolenceChildren2016.pdf.

Ianchovichina, Elena. 2018. *Eruptions of Popular Anger The Economics of the Arab Spring and Its Aftermath*. Washington, DC: World Bank. http://documents.worldbank.org/curated/en/251971512654536291/pdf/121942-REVISED-Eruptions-of-Popular-Anger-preliminary-rev.pdf.

ILO. 2004. "Towards a Fair Deal for Migrant Workers in the Global Economy." International Labour Organization, Geneva. https://www.ilo.org/public/english/standards/relm/ilc/ilc92/pdf/rep-vi.pdf.

Indian Health Service. 2016. "Safe Water and Waste Disposal Facilities." September. https://www.ihs.gov/newsroom/factsheets/safewater/.

International Knowledge Network of Women in Politics. n.d. "Consolidated Response on the Prevention of Family Voting." https://www.ndi.org/sites/default/files/Consolidated%20Response_Prevention%20of%20Family%20Voting.pdf.

Janis, Irving. 1991. "Groupthink." In *A First Look at Communication Theory*, ed. E. Griffin, 235–246. New York: McGraw-Hill. http://williamwolff.org/wp-content/uploads/2016/01/griffin-groupthink-challenger.pdf.

Jewitt, Sarah, and Harriet Ryley. 2014. "It's a Girl Thing: Menstruation, School Attendance, Spatial Mobility and Wider Gender Inequalities in Kenya." *Geoforum* 56: 137–147. https://www.sciencedirect.com/science/article/pii/S0016718514001638.

Johansson, Anna. 2017. "Why Workplace Diversity Diminishes Groupthink and How Millennials Are Helping." *Forbes*. July 20. https://www.forbes.com/sites/annajohansson/2017/07/20/how-workplace-diversity-diminishes-groupthink-and-how-millennials-are-helping/#ab5e6b24b741.

Jordan, Julie Burress. 2015. "A Study in How Linking Social Capital Functions in Community Development." PhD dissertation, University of Southern Mississippi. https://aquila.usm.edu/cgi/viewcontent.cgi?article=1015&context=dissertations.

Kamalnath, Akshaya. 2017. "Gender Diversity as the Antidote to 'Groupthink' on Corporate Boards." *Deakin Law Review* 22: 85–106. https://ojs.deakin.edu.au/index.php/dlr/article/viewFile/723/668.

Kant, Immanuel. 1997. "Moral Philosophy: Collins's Lecture Notes." In *Lectures on Ethics*. Cambridge: Cambridge University Press.

Kawachi, Ichiro, and Lisa Berman. 2014. "Social Cohesion, Social Capital and Health." In *Social Epidemiology*, edited by Lisa F. Berkman, Ichiro Kawachi, and M. Maria Glymour, 174–190. Oxford University Press.

Kenton, Will. 2019. "Egalitarianism." *Investopedia*. May 8. https://www.investopedia.com/terms/e/egalitarianism.asp.

Kleingeld, Pauline. 2007. "Kant's Second Thoughts on Race." *The Philosophical Quarterly* 57, no. 229: 573–592. www.jstor.org/stable/4543266.

Klingorová, Kamila, and Tomáš Havlíček. 2015. "Religion and Gender Inequality: The Status of Women in the Societies of World Religions." *Moravian Geographical Reports* 23, no. 2: 2–11. doi: 10.1515/mgr-2015-0006.

Kóczé, Angéla. 2000. "Romani Children and the Right to Education in Central and Eastern Europe." European Roma Rights Centre. October 3. http://www.errc.org/roma-rights-journal/romani-children-and-the-right-to-education-in-central-and-eastern-europe.

Krause, Jana, Werner Krause, and Piia Branfors. 2018. "Women's Participation in Peace Negotiations and the Durability of Peace." *International Interactions: Empirical and Theoretical Research in International Relations* 44, no. 6: 985–1016.

Kuoti, Yasir. 2016. "Exclusion and Violence in Post-2003 Iraq." *Journal of International Affairs* 69, no. 2: 19–28. https://www.jstor.org/stable/10.2307/26494336.

Kurian, Rachel, and Deepak Singh. 2017. "Politics of Caste-Based Exclusion and Poverty Alleviation Schemes in Rural India." Paper presented at the Politics of Inclusion International workshop, Paris, July 6–7. https://repub.eur.nl/pub/114952.

Laqueur, Walter, and Barry Rubin, eds. 1989. *The Human Rights Reader*. New York: Meridian.

Le Melle, Tilden J. 2009. "Race in International Relations." *International Studies Perspectives* 10, no. 1: 77–83. https://academic.oup.com/isp/article-abstract/10/1/77/1842816?redirectedFrom=PDF.

Lott, Tommy L. 2002. "Patriarchy and Slavery in Hobbes' Political Philosophy." In *Philosophers on Race*, edited by Julie K. Ward and Tommy L. Lott, 63–80. Oxford: Blackwell.

Lund, Kristin, and Laura Mitchell. 2017. "Preventing Crisis and Conflict: Women's Role in Ongoing Peace Processes." *UN Chronicle*. October. https://unchronicle.un.org/article/preventing-crisis-and-conflict-women-s-role-ongoing-peace-processes.

Marc, Alexandre, and Jago Salmon. 2017. *Pathways to Peace*. Washington, DC: World Bank. https://openknowledge.worldbank.org/handle/10986/28337.

Marlow, Louise. 1997. *Hierarchy and Egalitarianism in Islamic thought*. New York: Cambridge University Press.

Marx, Karl. 1967. *Capital: A Critique of Political Economy*, vol. 1. New York: International Publishers. https://carlos.public.iastate.edu/607/readings/header_marx.pdf.

Mills, Charles W. 1997. *The Racial Contract*. Ithaca, NY: Cornell University Press.

Narayan, Deepa. 1999. "Bonds and Bridges: Social Capital and Poverty." Poverty Group, World Bank. http://documents.vsemirnyjbank.org/curated/ru/989601468766526606/107507322_20041117172515/additional/multi-page.pdf.

Narula, Smita. 2008. "Equal by Law, Unequal by Caste: The 'Untouchable' Condition in Critical Race Perspective." *Wisconsin International Law Journal* 26: 255–343. https://digitalcommons.pace.edu/cgi/viewcontent.cgi?article=2125&context=lawfaculty.

Neidleman, Jason. 2012. "The Social Contract Theory in a Global Context." E-International Relations. October 9. https://www.e-ir.info/2012/10/09/the-social-contract-theory-in-a-global-context/.

Nkosi, Makho. 2014. "Ukuthwala 'Bride Abduction' and Education: Critical Challenges and Opportunities Faced by School Principals in Rural Kwazulu-Natal." *Journal of Social Sciences* 41, no. 3: 441–454. https://pdfs.semanticscholar.org/a4e0/2b9b84d13ed28b1d40e569a93d9d7ed887f4.pdf.

Nowak, Matthias. 2012. "Femicide: A Global Problem." *Small Arms Survey*. February. http://www.smallarmssurvey.org/fileadmin/docs/H-Research_Notes/SAS-Research-Note-14.pdf.

Nussbaum, Martha C. 2013. *Creating Capabilities: The Human Development Approach*. Cambridge, MA: Belknap Press of Harvard University Press.

O'Neill, Maggie, and Tony Spybey. 2003. "Global Refugees, Exile, Displacement and Belonging." *Sociology* 37, no. 1: 7–12. doi: 10.1177/0038038503037001385.

OAS. 2013. "Member States Move Forward at the OAS in Dialogue on Social Inclusion." Organization of American States. February 26. https://www.oas.org/en/media_center/press_release.asp?sCodigo=E-069/13.

OECD. 2012. "Closing the Gender Gap: Act Now." Organization for Economic Co-Operation and Development. https://www.oecd-ilibrary.org/docserver/9789264179370-en.pdf?expires=1565212267&id=id&accname=ocid177385&checksum=AF9CF7FDF2AB96DF525864247BEAEB14.

Onyx, Jenny, Melissa Edwards, and Paul Bullen. 2007. "The Intersection of Social Capital and Power: An Application to Rural Communities." *Rural Society* 17, no. 3: 215–230. http://dx.doi.org/10.5172/rsj.351.17.3.215.

OSCE. 2018. "The Former Yugoslav Republic of Macedonia Municipal Elections: OSCE/ODIHR Election Observation Mission Final Report." https://www.osce.org/odihr/elections/fyrom/367246.

Østby, G. 2013. "Inequality and Political Violence: A Review of the Literature." *International Area Studies Review* 16, no. 2: 206–231. https://doi.org/10.1177/2233865913490937.

Patel, Dipti. 2005. "The Religious Foundations of Human Rights: A Perspective from the Judeo-Christian Tradition and Hinduism." University of Nottingham. https://www.nottingham.ac.uk/hrlc/documents/publications/hrlcommentary2005/religiousfoundationshumanrights.pdf.

Peace Women. n.d. "Member States." https://www.peacewomen.org/member-states.

Pew Research Center. 2018. "Same-Sex Marriage Around the World." October 28. https://www.pewforum.org/fact-sheet/gay-marriage-around-the-world/.

Popay, Jennie, Sarah Escorel, Mario Hernández, Heidi Johnston, Jane Mathieson, and Laetitia Rispel. 2008. "Final Report to the WHO Commission on Social Determinants of Health from the Social Exclusion Knowledge Network." https://www.who.int/social_determinants/knowledge_networks/final_reports/sekn_final%20report_042008.pdf.

Powell, Tia, and Mary Beth Foglia. 2014. "The Time Is Now: Bioethics and LGBT Issues." *Hastings Center Report* 44, no. 5: S2–S3. https://onlinelibrary.wiley.com/doi/epdf/10.1002/hast.361.

Putnam, Robert. 2000. *Bowling Alone*. New York: Simon and Schuster.

Putnam, Robert D. 2007. "E Pluribus Unum: Diversity and Community in the Twenty-First Century The 2006 Johan Skytte Prize Lecture." *Scandinavian Political Studies* 30, no. 2: 137–174. https://doi.org/10.1111/j.1467-9477.2007.00176.x.

Putnam, Robert D., Robert Leonardi, and Raffaella Y. Nanetti. 1993. *Making Democracy Work: Civic Traditions in Modern Italy*. Princeton, NJ: Princeton University Press.

Rawls, John. 1971. *A Theory of Justice*. Cambridge, MA: Harvard University Press.

Rock, David, and Heidi Grant. 2016. "Why Diverse Teams Are Smarter." *Harvard Business Review*. November. https://hbr.org/2016/11/why-diverse-teams-are-smarter.

Romero, Patricia W. 1976. "W. E. B. Du Bois, Pan-Africanists, and Africa 1963–1973." *Journal of Black Studies* 6, no. 4: 321–336. www.jstor.org/stable/2783765.

Rose, James D. 2011. "Diverse Perspectives on the Groupthink Theory—A Literary Review." *Emerging Leadership Journeys* 4, no. 1: 37–57.

Rosenfield, Erica. 2010. "Combating Discrimination Against the Roma in Europe: Why Current Strategies Aren't Working and What Can Be Done." *Human Rights and Human Welfare: Topical Research Digest: Minority Rights*. https://www.du.edu/korbel/hrhw/researchdigest/minority/Roma.pdf.

Rothstein, Bo, and Eric M. Uslaner. 2006. "All for All: Equality, Corruption and Social Trust." QOG Working Paper Series 2006:4. Quality of Government Institute, Göteborg University. https://gupea.ub.gu.se/bitstream/2077/39174/1/gupea_2077_39174_1.pdf.

Rowe, C. J. 2018. "Plato on Equality and Democracy." In *Democracy, Justice, and Equality in Ancient Greece*, edited by G. Anagnostopoulos and G. Santas. Philosophical Studies Series, vol. 132, 63–82. Cham: Springer.

Sahin Mencutek, Zeynep, and Ayat J. Nashwan. 2020. "Perceptions About the Labor Market Integration of Refugees: Evidences from Syrian Refugees in Jordan." *Journal of International Migration and Integration* 22: 615–633. https://link.springer.com/article/10.1007/s12134-020-00756-3.

Saloojee, A., and N. Saloojee. 2011. "From Social Exclusion to Social Inclusion: Theory and Practice over Two Continents." *African Journal of Public Affairs* 4, no. 2: 1–17. https://repository.up.ac.za/bitstream/handle/2263/57703/Saloojee_Social_2011.pdf?sequence=1&isAllowed=y.

Scheffler, Samuel. 2003. "What Is Egalitarianism?" *Philosophy and Public Affairs* 31, no. 1: 5–39. https://www-jstor-org.proxy.library.georgetown.edu/stable/pdf/3558033.pdf.

Scheffran, Jürgen, Hans Günter Brauch, and Janpeter Schilling, eds. 2012. *Climate Change, Human Security, and Violent Conflict: Challenges for Societal Stability.* New York: Springer.

Schmidt, Anna. 2013. "Groupthink." *Britannica.* https://www.britannica.com/science/groupthink.

Schultz, Bart, and Georgios Varouxakis, eds. 2005. *Utilitarianism and Empire.* Lanham, MD: Rowman and Littlefield.

Scutt, Jocelynne A. 2016. "Introduction—Magna Carta: Women's Rights or Wrongs?" In *Women and Magna Carta: A Treaty for Rights or Wrongs?*, 1–12. London: Palgrave Macmillan.

Semenas, Vilius. 2014. "Ethnic Diversity and Social Capital at the Community Level: Effects and Implications for Policymakers." *Inquiries Journal* 6, no. 4: 1–2. http://www.inquiriesjournal.com/a?id=888.

Sen, Amartya. 1999. *Development as Freedom.* Oxford: Oxford University Press.

Sen, Amartya. 1982. *Inequality Reexamined.* Cambridge, MA: Harvard University Press.

Shanyanana-Amaambo, Rachel, and Y. Waghid. 2016. "Reconceptualizing Ubuntu as Inclusion in African Higher Education: Towards Equalization of Voice." *Knowledge Cultures* 4: 104–120.

Shrivastava, Akhil and A. Yadav. n.d. "Poverty and Social Exclusion." Legal Services India E-journal. https://www.legalserviceindia.com/legal/article-4191-poverty-and-social-exclusion.html.

Singer, Peter. 2010. *The Life You Can Save: How to Do Your Part to End World Poverty.* New York: Random House.

Sperling, Gene B. and Winthrop, Rebecca. 2016. *What Works in Girls Education: Evidence for the World's Best Investment.* Washington DC: Brookings Institution. https://www.brookings.edu/wp-content/uploads/2016/07/whatworksingirlseducation1.pdf.

Stefanovska, Vesna. 2015. "The Legacy of Magna Carta and the Rule of Law in the Republic of Macedonia." *SEEU Review* 11, no. 1: 197–205. doi: 10.1515/seeur-2015-0023.

Stewart, Frances. 2002. "Horizontal Inequalities: A Neglected Dimension of Development." QEH Working Paper Series 81. Queen Elizabeth House, University of Oxford. https://www.researchgate.net/profile/Frances_Stewart2/publication/237370588_QEH_Working_Paper_Series_-_QEHWPS81_Page_1_Working_Paper_Number_81_Horizontal_Inequalities_A_Neglected_Dimension_of_Development/links/54297cae0cf2e4ce940ee469.pdf.

Stiglitz, Joseph E. 2014. "The Price of Inequality: How Today's Divided Society Endangers Our Future." In *Sustainable Humanity, Sustainable Nature: Our Responsibility.* Vatican City: Pontifical Academy of Sciences. http://www.pas.va/content/dam/accademia/pdf/es41/es41-stiglitz.pdf.

Sundstrom, Ronald. 2017. "Frederick Douglass." *Stanford Encyclopedia of Philosophy*, ed. Edward Zalta. https://plato.stanford.edu/entries/frederick-douglass/.

Tang, Ningyu, Yuan Jiang, Chiyin Chen, Zucheng Zhou, Chao C. Chen, and Zexuan Yu. 2015. "Inclusion and Inclusion Management in the Chinese Context: An Exploratory Study." *International Journal of Human Resource Management* 26, no. 6: 856–874. doi: 10.1080/09585192.2014.985326.

Tickner, J. A. 1992. *Gender in International Relations: Feminist Perspectives on Achieving Global Security.* New York: Columbia University Press.

Tickner, J. A. 1988. "Hans Morgenthau's Principles of Political Realism: A Feminist Reformulation." *Millennium—Journal of International Studies* 17, no. 3: 429–440.

Tiky, Narcisse. 2011. "The African Origins of the Athenian Democracy." October 28. https://poseidon01.ssrn.com/delivery.php?ID=904114091001093024065090005065023112112117009040087024023014000094108095088074006126117124123020032031057028102067085073094121079109033095005041121092065080026092031067042082017120018095080097114086118066116127115112005015124097074101085030023125115117017&EXT=pdf.

Tippett, Rebecca, Avis Jones-DeWeever, Maya Rockeymoore, Darrick Hamilton, and William Darity Jr. 2014. "Beyond Broke: Why Closing the Racial Gap Is a Priority for National Economic Security." Center for Global Policy Solutions and Duke Research Network on Racial and Ethnic Inequality at the Social Science Research Institute. http://globalpolicysolutions.org/wp-content/uploads/2014/04/Beyond_Broke_FINAL.pdf.

UN General Assembly. 2011. "Human Rights, Sexual Orientation and Gender Identity." A/HRC/RES/17/19. July 14. http://ap.ohchr.org/documents/dpage_e.aspx?si=A/HRC/RES/17/19.

UN General Assembly. 2007. "Declaration of the Rights of Indigenous Peoples." A/RES/61/295. September 13. https://www.un.org/development/desa/indigenouspeoples/declaration-on-the-rights-of-indigenous-peoples.html.

UN General Assembly. 1986. "Declaration on the Right to Development." A/RES/41/128. December 4. https://www.ohchr.org/EN/ProfessionalInterest/Pages/RightToDevelopment.aspx.

UN General Assembly. 1981. "Convention on the Elimination of All Forms of Discrimination Against Women." September 3. https://www.ohchr.org/en/professionalinterest/pages/cedaw.aspx.

UN General Assembly. 1975. "Declaration on the Rights of Disabled Persons." A/RES/3447. December 9. https://www.ohchr.org/EN/ProfessionalInterest/Pages/RightsOfDisabledPersons.aspx.

UN General Assembly. 1948. "Universal Declaration of Human Rights." Res 217 A (III). December 10. https://www.un.org/en/universal-declaration-human-rights/.

UN Security Council. n.d. a. "UN Documents for Women, Peace and Security." Security Council Report. https://www.securitycouncilreport.org/un-documents/women-peace-and-security/.

UN Security Council. n.d. b. "UN Documents for Youth, Peace and Security." Security Council Report. https://www.securitycouncilreport.org/un-documents/youth-peace-and-security/.

UNCRC. 2016. "Concluding Observations on the Combined Third to Fifth Periodic Reports of Slovakia." CRC/C/SVK/CO/3-5. United Nations Committee on the Rights of the Child. http://docstore.ohchr.org/SelfServices/FilesHandler.ashx?enc=6QkG1d%2FPPRiCAqhKb7yhskJo1IBhMr5sq%2BdAoPX0B%2Fun6w3GuJfElvddW5%2Beyns8cxWentbxSJJ7%2FfP14Xd9%2B6pn8%2B%2BWQVtosf1bQZFaWc1J4wKvAphaNDY%2FMJ%2FI8xue.

UNDP. 2017. "Social Impact Assessment of the Rohingya Refugee Crisis into Bangladesh: Key Findings and Recommendations." United Nations Development Programme and UN Women. December 6. https://www.humanitarianresponse.info/sites/www.humanitarianresponse.info/files/assessments/171207_social_impact_assessment_and_rapid_host_community_impact_assessment_summary.pdf.

UNDP. 2012. "Report on the Living Conditions of Roma Households in Slovakia in 2010." United Nations Development Programme.

UNESCO. 2018. "Education and Disability: Analysis of Data from 49 Countries." March 28. http://uis.unesco.org/en/news/education-and-disability-analysis-data-49-countries.

UNESCO. 2001. "Universal Declaration on Cultural Diversity." UN Educational, Scientific and Cultural Organization. November 2. http://portal.unesco.org/en/ev.php-URL_ID=13179&URL_DO=DO_TOPIC&URL_SECTION=201.html.

Uphoff, Norman. 2000. "Understanding Social Capital: Learning from the Analysis and Experience of Participation." In *Social Capital: A Multifaceted Perspective*, edited by P. Dasgupta and I. Serageldin, 215–252. Washington, DC: World Bank.

US Department of Health and Human Services. 2018. "Profile: American Indian/Alaska Native." Office of Minority Health. March. https://minorityhealth.hhs.gov/omh/browse.aspx?lvl=3&lvlid=62.

USAID. n.d. a. "Achieving Gender Equality in Agriculture." https://www.usaid.gov/what-we-do/gender-equality-and-womens-empowerment/addressing-gender-programming/agriculture.

USAID. n.d. "Promoting Gender Equality and Access to Education." US Agency for International Development. https://www.usaid.gov/what-we-do/gender-equality-and-womens-empowerment/addressing-gender-programming/promoting-gender.

Vallas, Rebecca, and Shawn Fremstad. 2014. "Disability Is a Cause and Consequence of Poverty." Talk Poverty. September 19. https://talkpoverty.org/2014/09/19/disability-cause-consequence-poverty.

Van Wyk, Jeannie. 2015. "Can Legislative Intervention Achieve Spatial Justice?" *The Comparative and International Law Journal of Southern Africa* 48, no. 3: 381–400. www.jstor.org/stable/26203991.

Walter, J. D. 2020. "Predicting and Mitigating Civil Conflict: Vertical Grievances and Conflict in Central Africa." PhD dissertation, Walden University. https://scholarworks.waldenu.edu/dissertations/7961.

Wanis-St. John, Anthony, and Darren Kew. 2008. "Civil Society and Peace Negotiations: Confronting Exclusion." *International Negotiations* 13: 11–36. https://www.american.edu/sis/faculty/upload/wanis-kew-civil-society-and-peace-negotiations.pdf.

Watson, David, and Amy Moreland. 2014. "Perceptions of Corruption and the Dynamics of Women's Representation." *Politics and Gender* 10, no. 3: 392–412. http://dx.doi.org/10.1017/S1743923X14000233.

Web Solutions. n.d. "Equality: Overview—Ancient Views of Equality." Accessed August 21, 2021. https://science.jrank.org/pages/9186/Equality-Overview-Ancient-Views-Equality.html.

Wedam Kanmik, Edmund, et al. 2019. "Socio-Economic and Demographic Disparities in Ownership and Use of Insecticide-Treated Bed Nets for Preventing Malaria Among Rural Reproductive-Aged Women in Northern Ghana." *PLoS ONE.* January 29. https://journals.plos.org/plosone/article/file?id=10.1371/journal.pone.0211365&type=printable.

Welchman, Jennifer. 1995. "Locke on Slavery and Inalienable Rights." *Canadian Journal of Philosophy* 25, no. 1: 67–81.

Wheeler, Skye. 2016. "Yezidi Women After Slavery: Trauma." Human Rights Watch. April 18. https://www.hrw.org/news/2016/04/18/yezidi-women-after-slavery-trauma.

White, Ariel R., Noah L. Nathan, and Julie K. Faller. 2015. "What Do I Need to Vote? Bureaucratic Discretion and Discrimination by Local Election Officials." *American Political Science Review* 109, no. 1: 129–142. doi: 10.1017/S0003055414000562.

Wimmer, Andreas, Lars-Erik Cederman, and Brian Min. 2009. "Ethnic Politics and Armed Conflict: A Configurational Analysis of a New Global Data Set." *American Sociological Review* 74, no. 2: 316–337. doi: 10.1177/000312240907400208.

Woetzel, Jonathan, et al. 2015. "How Advancing Women's Equality Can Add $12 trillion to Global Growth." McKinsey Global Institute, New York. https://www.mckinsey.com/featured-insights/employment-and-growth/how-advancing-womens-equality-can-add-12-trillion-to-global-growth.

Wollstonecraft, Mary. 1792. *A Vindication of the Rights of Woman.* https://www.bl.uk/collection-items/mary-wollstonecraft-a-vindication-of-the-rights-of-woman.

World Bank. 2018a. "Pathways for Peace: Insuring Inclusive Approaches to Preventing Violent Conflict." https://openknowledge.worldbank.org/handle/10986/28337.

World Bank. 2018b. "Poverty and Shared Prosperity 2018: Piecing Together the Poverty Puzzle." World Bank Group. https://openknowledge.worldbank.org/bitstream/handle/10986/30418/9781464813306.pdf.

World Bank. 2018c. *Women, Business and the Law 2018.* Washington, DC: World Bank. http://pubdocs.worldbank.org/en/999211524236982958/WBL-Key-Findings-Web-FINAL-2.pdf.

World Bank. 2016. "Poverty and Shared Prosperity 2016: Taking on Inequality." World Bank Group. https://openknowledge.worldbank.org/bitstream/handle/10986/25078/210958KeyFindings.pdf.

World Bank. n.d. "Social Inclusion." https://www.worldbank.org/en/topic/social-inclusion.

World Health Organization. n.d. "Occupied Palestinian Territory." http://www.emro.who.int/pse/palestine-infocus/seam-zone-access-health-services.html.

Yahya, Maha. 2018. "Policy Framework for Refugees in Lebanon and Jordan—Unheard Voices: What Syrian Refugees Need to Return Home." Carnegie Middle East Center. April 16. https://carnegie-mec.org/2018/04/16/policy-framework-for-refugees-in-lebanon-and-jordan-pub-76058.

Young, Iris Marion. 2014. "Five Faces of Oppression." In *Diversity, Social Justice, and Inclusive Excellence*, edited by Seth N. Asumah and Mechthild Nagel, 1–22. Albany: State University of New York Press.

Yuval-Davis, Nira. 2011. "Belonging and the Politics of Belonging." In *Contesting Recognition: Culture, Identity, and Citizenship*, edited by Janice McLaughlin, Peter Phillimore, and Diane Richardson, 20–35. London: Palgrave Macmillan.

Yuval-Davis, Nira. 2006. "Boundaries, Identities and Borders: Exploring the Cultural Production of Belonging." *Patterns of Prejudice* 40, no. 3: 197–214.

Zhuang, Juzhong. 2008. "Inclusive Growth Toward a Harmonious Society in the People's Republic of China: Policy Implications." *Asian Development Review* 25, nos. 1–2: 22–33. https://www. researchgate.net/profile/Juzhong_Zhuang/publication/241453908_Inclusive_Growth_to- ward_a_Harmonious_Society_in_the_People's_Republic_of_China_Policy_Implications/ links/54279e450cf238c6ea7ac8a6/Inclusive-Growth-toward-a-Harmonious-Society-in-the- Peoples-Republic-of-China-Policy-Implications.pdf.

SECTION II

MOVEMENTS TOWARD MORE INCLUSIVE PEACEBUILDING AND DEVELOPMENT

All human beings are born free and equal in dignity and rights. . . . Everyone is entitled to all the rights and freedoms set forth in this Declaration, without distinction of any kind, such as race, colour, sex, language, religion, political or other opinion, national or social origin, property, birth or other status.

—The Universal Declaration of Human Rights

Vibrant, far-reaching social movements buttress, codify, and advance the rights of different groups. They build on centuries of activism, and they involve actors in civil society, governments, and multilateral organizations. Many advance the cause of specific subgroups such as women and girls, youth, older people, indigenous peoples, or ethnic minorities. Others demand a focus on equity for non-identity-based groups, such as laborers and workers, or as part of broader causes, such as the environmental justice movement.[1] Local movements address vulnerability or marginalization in a given place, even as international activism seeks the empowerment of an entire class of global citizens.

Seen from afar, substantial progress has been made, both in recognizing the rights of diverse groups and in acknowledging the need for intentionality to achieve inclusion and equality. For example, the United Nations Sustainable Development Goals (SDGs), a global agenda for peace and prosperity that was adopted by UN member states in 2015, are more focused on addressing exclusion and inequality than their predecessors, the Millennium Development Goals (MDGs). They were developed through a more inclusive international negotiation, resulting in a universal, shared agenda. Additionally, the SDGs themselves underline the need to advance equality, justice, and inclusion. Two of the seventeen goals call for reduced inequality and gender equality. Five other goals explicitly call for a focus on inclusion in education, economic growth, urban development, industrialization, and infrastructure development, as well as in efforts to promote justice and rule of law. Further, targets for many of the goals specifically refer to people with disabilities, vulnerable people, and the need to address and eliminate discrimination.

This section overviews a range of global identity-based movements for the equality and inclusion of specific communities that are frequently marginalized and vulnerable. Each chapter considers a specific movement that is part of the broader push for greater equity and inclusion. The narratives discuss why progress for the specific marginalized group is so important, highlight tactics that have helped the movement advance, and relate best practices and lessons learned. The chapters conclude with reflections on critical next steps for progress.

Movements for inclusion and equity vary widely in their strategies and tactics, as well as in their path toward progress. A decades-long effort has increased women's inclusion in peacebuilding and advanced gender equality globally; Nobel laureate Leymah Gbowee joins Dr. Anne-Marie Goetz in discussing how that mobilization has evolved, expanded, and progressed. Newer efforts focus on expanding the role and voice of youth and pushing for international recognition of LGBTQI rights. Former ambassador Dan Baer and well-known Ukrainian activist journalist Maksym Eristavi consider advancement of LGBTQI rights globally. Lakshitha Saji Prelis tracks the progress of the youth, peace, and security movement, of which he is a leader. The movement for the rights of people with disabilities is explored by Dr. Michael Ashley Stein, who directs the Harvard Law School Project on Disability, and Janet Lord, a leading practitioner and activist in the field. Valmaine Toki, an indigenous rights scholar and activist, along with Lara Domínguez, offers an overview of the indigenous rights movement, and Dr. Joshua Castellino examines progress ensuring rights for minority groups.

As evident in the chapters, some movements, such as those for disability inclusion and indigenous peoples' rights, have focused particularly on strengthening the international legal framework and seeking its application and enforcement around the world. Other campaigns, such as the push for women's and girls' equality, have emphasized accumulation of data about the importance of inclusion and equality for progress. Still others, such as the movement for LGBTQI rights, have sought to use mass mobilization by civil society and shifting norms to spur advancement. In all cases, multifaceted, sustained international campaigns have gradually achieved progress over decades, codifying rights and advancing their realization.

In every case, there continues to be a vast need for sustained advocacy. While many rights and aspirations have been codified in law, gaps remain. Even more glaring are the vast disparities between rhetoric and reality. The discussion of the movement for the rights of indigenous peoples provides a particularly clear picture of the continuing struggle and the costs to people around the world. The overall picture that emerges is one of mass mobilization for equity and inclusion, with a great deal of progress needed for equality and inclusion to be universally shared.

Note

1. Sandler and Pezzullo 2007.

Bibliography

Sandler, Ronald, and Phaedra C. Pezzullo, eds. 2007. *Environmental Justice and Environmentalism: The Social Justice Challenge to the Environmental Movement*. Cambridge, MA: MIT Press.

3

The Global Movement Advancing Gender Equality and Women's Empowerment

Anne Marie Goetz and Leymah Gbowee

Our ministry is the outcome of the streets, the long-standing women's rights struggle. There have been more than 30 years of national women's *encuentros*, massive national protests at violence against women (Ni Una Menos), a national women's strike (Nosotros Paramos) where we showed that if we don't work the world stops, the abortion movement (La Marea Verde), which was massive in the streets. Our ministry is a political response to a rooted political movement.

—Edurne Cardenas, general director of public affairs, Ministry of Women, Genders, and Diversity, Argentina[1]

Introduction: The Case for Gender Equality in Development, Democracy, and Peace

It is well established that gender equality is essential to development, democracy, and peace, so much so that gender equality and women's empowerment are together a stand-alone goal of the Sustainable Development Goals (Goal 5) and the subject of targets and indicators across most of the other SDGs. Girls' education is foundational to national development efforts almost everywhere, because of its known contributions to overall life expectancy, family and community well-being, and fertility management. World Bank data suggest that secondary education for a girl generates a 25 percent increase in wages later in life, and educated girls have fewer and healthier children.[2] Women's engagement in paid work is an expected and desirable part of efforts to advance the productivity and economic growth of economies; indeed, if as many women were in paid employment as men, it would contribute as much as $12 trillion to global wealth.[3] While no country has achieved gender equality, in those countries where the gap between women and men in access to resources, physical security, economic opportunity, and political leadership is small, levels of human development (defined not just as income but as well-being in terms of education and health) are higher.[4] Peace and stability are also reliably associated with higher levels of gender equality.[5] And gender equality is associated with resilient liberal democratic institutions, lower corruption, and effective accountability systems.[6] Gender equality is a necessity for prosperity, peace, and stability.

Though it is a rational choice for countries seeking social and economic progress, advancement toward gender equality is profoundly hampered by discriminatory attitudes and gender-biased laws that can deny women the opportunity to profit from their own labor, to own property, or to enjoy physical safety even within their own homes. In 2018, 104 countries still had laws prohibiting women from specific types of employment.[7] This contributed to the fact that globally, women's participation in the formal labor force in 2018 was 63 percent (for those ages twenty-five to fifty-four), compared to 74 percent for men.[8] Women are still paid less than men—the global gender wage gap is at least 23 percent on average.[9] Women are less likely to have stayed in school as long as men, so their skill levels are lower. Most devastating is the fact that violence against women is common in many societies—with on average 35 percent of women (up to 70 percent in some countries) experiencing physical violence in their lifetimes from an intimate partner.[10] In spite of the prevalence of this human rights abuse, domestic violence is poorly policed and prosecuted, producing a sense of impunity for perpetrators. Social tolerance of violence against women deepens the constraints on women's efforts to improve their lives—82 percent of women parliamentarians in thirty-nine countries, for instance, report being the target of physical and psychological violence, bullying, and intimidation.[11]

While all of society benefits from gender equality, the fight for women's rights has tended to be initiated and sustained by women. The social force that has been the most effective in promoting gender equality is women's collective action. Women's movements—and particularly those with strong and autonomous feminist organizations that specifically challenge women's subordination to men—have changed the way people think about, for instance, gender-based violence, reframing it so that it is seen not as an individual misfortune but as a crime, as an expression of violent masculinity and patriarchal dominance.[12] Where women's movements and feminist organizations have politicized gender-based injustice as a public policy matter, states have been pressed to end male impunity for abuse of women. Women's movements have also pushed public authorities to mitigate the price that women pay for childbearing and child-rearing (such as career setbacks or lack of pensions) and to challenge cultures that demean women and devalue their labor.

The power of women's mobilization and activism can be measured and monitored. A significant recent cross-national study of the economic, political, and social conditions for the generation of gender equality policies in 120 countries between 1975 and 2015 shows that the most powerful predictor of change in relation to gender equality, particularly in policies designed to stop violence against women, is the size and strength of the autonomous women's movement—or feminist mobilization (people, mostly women, taking action to promote gender equality)—nationally and internationally.[13] Other global research shows that the strongest predictor of any country's propensity to engage in armed violence against its own citizens or others is the level of violence against women domestically.[14] If strong and autonomous women's movements are the most powerful agents triggering action to stop violence against women, and if violence against women is strongly associated with national belligerence, then by extension, women's movements are powerful peacebuilding agents. Women's movements have also demanded equal pay for equal work, secure livelihoods for women, and women's financial autonomy. Women's access to and control of property and income are strongly associated with economic equality more generally in societies.[15]

Autonomous women's movements are essential for democratization. Democracy alone does not ensure women's participation in legislatures.[16] Many countries have instituted gender quotas to ensure significant numbers of women in representative politics, and more gender-balanced legislatures and executives have generated improved policies to advance gender equality. Today, some countries even claim to have feminist governments (Sweden, Canada) and feminist foreign policies. But women's presence in legislatures, at its highest level ever in mid 2021 at 25.7 percent, does not necessarily produce gender equality policy.[17] That said, women have achieved success through demanding greater gender parity in male-dominated institutions, forming alliances with leaders in other social movements, and taking political actions such as advocacy and lobbying.

Women's and feminist movements have achieved a sweeping revolution in social relations in the last 200 years. But as important as women's participation has been for social justice reforms, poverty reduction, and economic development, as well as conflict resolution, women tend to be excluded from leadership, or so heavily burdened with unpaid care work that they are unable to participate in public decision-making. This has contributed to women's secondary economic and social status, relative invisibility in politics, and subjection to routine, often uncontested gender-based violence. While gender equality remains vital, women's access to livelihoods and resources is threatened by climate change, men's stubbornly low engagement in unpaid domestic care work, and the profound threatening of women's sexual autonomy and reproductive rights by conservative political and religious leaders (see Box 3.1).

Box 3.1 COVID-19 and the Movement for Gender Equality

The struggle to promote gender equality cannot be postponed or neglected, even—or perhaps most especially—in the context of recovery from the COVID-19 pandemic. The COVID-19 pandemic threatens to reverse the important gains women have made in the labor market (in most contexts, women were the first to lose their jobs and to remain unemployed) and in social relations (lockdowns saw child marriage, early pregnancy, and domestic violence increase).[18] Even before the pandemic, the project of advancing women's rights saw setbacks in the form of a slowdown in the pace of progress in women's economic empowerment (particularly in asset ownership, pay equality, and business leadership), and in efforts to achieve gender parity in public decision-making.[19] Other areas of women's rights remain poorly addressed or even under threat.

Feminist pro-democracy activism also saw a pause because of COVID-19, though it picked up in late 2020. Women's and feminist movements were highly visible in the year before the pandemic in Sudan, Lebanon, Hong Kong, Algeria, Puerto Rico, Belarus, and other contexts.[20] Women were leading opposition to immiserating neoliberal economic policies, corruption, market populism, irresponsible environmental policies, white supremacy, and misogyny. This signaled the emergence of new mass movements, new opportunities for engagement across borders, and alliances with other social movements. Much of that was put on hold by social distancing measures responding to the 2020 COVID-19 crisis, though this did not ultimately deter mass street protests in the United States supporting the Black Lives Matter movement, nor mass protests of the February 2021 military coup in Myanmar.

Many of the economic, political, and social processes that were the subject of these protests were at the root of developments that exacerbated the COVID-19 crisis, making health systems so underfunded and fragile, politics so volatile, and many states so incapable of an effective response. Women national leaders around the world, such as Jacinda Ardern of New Zealand and Tsai Ing-Wen of Taiwan, responded to the pandemic with striking effectiveness, communicating honestly with their populations and acting early and decisively to prevent runaway infection rates. This was in such marked contrast to the catastrophic mismanagement of the pandemic by right-wing populist leaders such as Trump in the United States and Bolsonaro in Brazil that it has become obvious to many that feminist leadership and gender equality in public policy is essential for effective recovery from the crisis.

The next section of this chapter clarifies what is meant by "women's movement" and "feminist mobilization" and reviews histories of efforts around the world since the late 1800s to contest male domination and imperialism, as well as the cultural and environmental destruction that accompanies it. Following that, the chapter discusses women's movements' contributions to economic and social development; analyses women's contributions to good governance and in particular conflict resolution and peace; and discusses key strategies and tactics of women's movements, reviewing the way feminists have sought to recast narratives about women's secondary status, how they have sought allies to institutionalize or "mainstream" gender equality mandates in development and peace institutions, and how they collaborate with "femocrat" insiders. It also addresses the anti-gender-equality backlash that is a part of the "illiberal drift" found in some advanced democracies as well as important emerging powers.[21]

The movement to advance gender equality is an ethical imperative and an integral part of achieving widespread political stability and economic prosperity across the globe. As the COVID-19 pandemic, climate change, increasing migration, political extremism, and other pressing global issues all threaten women's rights and livelihoods more severely than men's, there is a pressing need to center gender equality in any effort to address today's problems.

History of Women's Movements for Development and Peace

The nature and the priority concerns of women's movements everywhere have been shaped by the contexts in which they emerged. Women have mobilized to protect shared interests and advance social change projects throughout recorded history, but the degree to which they have been able to contest narrow gender roles for women and men, restrictions on women's liberties, and gender-based injustices (such as domestic violence, unpaid care work, and female genital mutilation) has depended on the contestability of patriarchal cultures and values (including the extent of women's segregation, isolation, and lack of resources such as education or income) and the extent of civil and political space open to mobilization to advance equal rights. Indeed, before women achieved the basic political right to vote and the putative status of equal citizens, they were highly constrained in their ability to politicize gender-based injustices and to make their concerns matters of public policy, causing them to focus on social welfare matters considered more in keeping with their dependent social status and family roles.

There are many types of women's organizations, and not all are focused on challenging gender-based injustices; indeed, conservative and traditional women's organizations may support patriarchal families and systems that privilege men, but offer women some security.[22] McBride and Mazur offer a careful definition of women's movements as being grounded in women's identity distinct from men, and oriented to representing women as a specific group in public life.[23] But this does not imply that they are dedicated to altering the gendered division of labor or protesting gender-based injustices. McBride and Mazur go on to note that specifically feminist movements are a subcategory of women's movements; they are characterized by "the belief that there is something wrong with the treatment and status of women" and they promote views that "challenge gender hierarchies and forms of women's subordination."[24]

This chapter is on the whole focused on the contributions of feminist movements to development and peace, and notes that female gender identity is not a requirement for holding feminist perspectives; men can participate in feminist movements too.

The question of what constitutes "feminist perspectives" or "women's interests," however, remains contested. As many scholars have pointed out, the project of defining "women's interests" a priori is problematic, as women are not a homogeneous group; their interests are shaped by class, caste, ethnicity, religion, disability, race, and other identities.[25] There is a tendency to adopt a biological reading of what concerns women (for instance, children's rights, reproductive health), as opposed to a more social reading of gender-related concerns (for instance, challenging male privilege in sexual, economic, and political relations). In addition, in the fields of development and peace, interventions to support women's rights are often instrumentalized on the grounds of women's supposedly inherent capacities such as thriftiness, fair-mindedness, and peacefulness. However, there are many intersecting types of disprivilege that affect women's lives and well-being, and gender is just one of them. Kimberlé Crenshaw introduced the concept of "intersectionality" in 1990 to explain how overlapping aspects of identity compound the discrimination women may experience because of their gender. Her particular focus was on race and nationality (particularly developing country origins) as a significant vector of power differences between women.[26] But other axes of social cleavage built around ableism and sexuality are also salient in determining how gender is experienced.[27]

Three major "waves" or periods in the development of women's movements—particularly in the transnational women's movements of the modern era—have been identified by feminist historians. Aili Mari Tripp (2006) identifies a first wave between 1880 and 1930, a second wave starting from the end of World War II up to 1975, and a third from 1985 onward. "First wave" local and transnational women's organizing often focused on improving elements of women's lives within their traditional roles—for instance, focusing on education, stopping child labor, supporting poor mothers, or preventing male alcoholism (an issue that continues to have massive mobilizational potential even today among rural women in Uganda and India, for instance). By the beginning of the twentieth century, growing transnational connections enabled solidarity and collaboration across borders in the demand for women's suffrage, and for peace after the outbreak of World War I. The International Congress of Women (founded in 1888) held a peace conference in the Hague in April 1915 attended by 1,500 women from Europe and North America, many of whom were seen as unpatriotic for their efforts to stop the war. They also argued forcefully for the need for institutions of global governance, supporting what eventually became the League of Nations as a mechanism for conflict resolution as well as for generating global agreement on women's rights. While many early transnational women's rights organizations were based in Europe and North America (such as the Young Women's Christian Association, founded in 1894, and the International Women's Suffrage Alliance, established in 1904), they often set up chapters around the world. For instance, the Women's Christian Temperance Union (founded in 1883) had branches in China, Japan, India, Korea, and Burma, and these eventually became the local headquarters for suffrage struggles in these countries.[28] Tripp's research identifies significant women's rights groups in the world over this period, multiplying in tandem with early anti-colonial struggles.

The second wave of women's mobilizing (1945–1975) was striking for the emergence of women's activism in national liberation struggles, independently and sometimes in direct opposition to Western women's movements, which had sometimes been associated with colonial governments and Christian "civilizing" missions that had stripped women of some of their traditional status and entrenched legal and financial dependence on men.[29] The 1950s and 1960s saw Latin American, African, and Asian women energized by achieving the vote and participating in nation-building projects, often experimenting with mechanisms to end dependence on former colonial powers through import substitution and socialist economies. There was growing recognition of the merits of working transnationally via the UN's Commission on the Status of Women (established in 1946), which lobbied for the UN's International Women's Year in 1975, organized four World Conferences on Women, and supported the Convention on the Elimination of Discrimination Against Women (CEDAW), launched in 1979.

According to Tripp, it was not until the "third wave" of women's development mobilization that the critique of development frameworks by women of the global South—or the developing world—fully emerged, strikingly evident by the 1985 Third World Conference on Women in Nairobi.[30] A revived feminist peace movement, critical of conventional international security approaches, emerged slightly later in the 1990s, benefiting from the room for maneuver opened by the end of the Cold War, as well as by the possibility of principled human-rights-based and democratically inclusive approaches to conflict resolution.

Research on women's rights activism has recently benefited greatly from a project led by political scientist Laurel Weldon at Simon Fraser University to calibrate the size and strength of feminist mobilization using consistent measures for 126 countries (covering 95 percent of the world's population) across every region of the world between 1975 and 2015.[31] The resulting Feminist Mobilization Index (FMI) recognizes that not all women's movements are concerned with gender equality. "Feminist movement" is defined as "collective action coordinated by the idea of making it a priority to improve women's status (or the status of some sub-group of women) and/or challenge patriarchal values, practices, systems, and power relations that maintain structures of male domination on the basis of gender."[32] The FMI measures whether a feminist movement exists at all, its relative strength (measured as policy influence and impact), and its relative autonomy or independence from the state, political parties, and other associations that do not have the status of women as their main concern.[33] The FMI is currently being tested to see how well it helps to explain feminist policy advances—it correlates very strongly, for instance, with progress in passing laws against violence against women and laws to promote women's economic empowerment.

Gender Equality and Development

Women's contribution to economic development and their needs for education, health care, access to resources, property rights, and physical security were barely acknowledged in post–World War II developmental frameworks. At best, women were a policy concern in relation to their reproductive functions, as the subjects of population control efforts. Data on the well-being and status of women compared to men in low-income countries was not consistently collected in the early decades of development after the war, and data remains scarce even now for significant indicators of women's status, such as women's personal income levels, women's asset ownership, and women's experience of domestic and other forms of violence.

Feminist critiques of development emerged in the 1970s with observations that not only were the benefits of economic growth often inaccessible to women in low-income countries, but many other forms of disadvantage and discrimination, including gender-based violence, were being ignored. In 1970, Ester Boserup, a Danish economist, published an eye-opening study, *Woman's Role in Economic Development*, which detailed the extent to which women's unpaid care work and underpaid work in the informal sector in developing economies contributed to development. She made a strong case for investment in girls' education as a crucial driver of population control and women's entry into the formal labor force.[34] In 1979, the UN Commission on the Status of Women produced the Convention on the Elimination of Discrimination Against Women (CEDAW), which was a global benchmark or agreement on women's rights (and has subsequently been expanded via over thirty General Recommendations). Initially it was largely women staff of bilateral aid agencies of industrialized countries that argued for dedicating resources to support women-in-development efforts. In 1982 a professional organization, the Association of Women in Development (AWID), was founded to support international networking among gender experts to encourage development donors and developing countries to invest in girls' education, women's health, and women's skills development. (It pivoted to become a global South activist-based organization after 2000 and was renamed the Association of Women's Rights in Development.)

Developing world networks of scholars and policy-makers formulated a strong critique of the additive women-in-development (WID) approach. This critique was most sharply voiced by a network formed in 1984, Development Alternatives with Women for a New Era (DAWN). Members of DAWN and other networks argued that women's inclusion in existing capitalist developmental approaches (particularly those based on primary commodity exports and extractive industries) would simply intensify their exploitation. This powerful critique suggested that WID policies simply made women's employment an instrument for capitalist expansion, and that WID approaches problematized models of development fixated on economic growth rather than human well-being or environmental sustainability. They significantly broadened the repertoire of women's movement concerns, linking women's poverty to militarization, malingering colonial-era dependencies, and corruption.

This critique was articulated at the 1985 Third UN Conference on Women in Nairobi, and expanded by the Fourth UN Conference on Women in Beijing in 1995 to include a critique of the structural adjustment policies that were seen to plunge states into debt, weaken their capacity to invest in social services on which women depend, and weaken women's power to organize collectively to demand labor rights.[35] This analysis became known as the gender-and-development (GAD) approach, foregrounding an anti-imperialist politics that highlighted the intersections between policies that benefit former colonial powers and advanced industrialized economies, on one hand, and racist and sexist institutions that exploit and oppress women, on the other. The neoliberal orthodoxy that has prevailed since then, which privileges elites through tax breaks and imposes austerity policies to cut state spending, has also been attacked by feminists for the way this ignores women's unpaid care work and undermines funding for public sector institutions (such as childcare or social protection) that can mitigate the time and labor costs women bear for having children and caring for families.[36] Studies show that women do at least two and a half times the amount of unpaid care work that men do, and that this sexual division and burden of work has changed relatively little over time.[37]

Women's associations at regional and subregional levels formed in the 1990s not only to advocate for policy attention and resources to gender equality issues but also to develop innovative programming. In Africa for instance, five women ministers of education created the Forum for African Women Educationalists (FAWE) in 1992, which expanded over the years to work with the World Bank and other aid donors to significantly accelerate girls' rate of primary school enrollment to near parity in sub-Saharan Africa.[38] All over the world, variations on women's saving circles inspired what has become one of the most important poverty reduction strategies: microfinance, expanded by organizations such as Women's World Banking and the Grameen Bank, to ensure women's access to bank accounts and the capitalization of their enterprises. The Grameen Bank and its founder, Mohammed Yunus, were awarded the Nobel Peace Prize in 2006 "for their efforts through microcredit to create economic and social development from below."[39]

Beyond economic development concerns, women's movements around the world were politicizing gender-based violence in the second and third waves of women's mobilization. However, the fact that this issue emerged explicitly only in the mid-1970s shows how deeply normalized violence against women used to be, and how firmly it was established as a male prerogative. It was not mentioned at the 1975 Mexico City UN Conference on Women. The 1979 global Convention on the Elimination of Discrimination Against Women, also did not mention it; this had to be added later via several General Recommendations. Eventually a Global Campaign on Women's Human Rights was formed at the Nairobi 1985 conference, and by 1993, the Vienna UN conference on women's rights firmly established that women's rights—and the struggle against gender-based oppression and violence—was a major human rights challenge. As Tripp points out, violence against women had become, by the turn of the century "the most important international women's issue and the most dynamic human rights concern globally."[40]

Gender Equality and Peace

Violence against women intensifies during war, and sexual violence in particular can be used as a combat tactic, either commanded or condoned by military leaders, used to terrorize populations, trigger displacement, or destroy the social fabric of communities, inhibiting recovery. As with domestic violence, focused advocacy to stop sexual violence during conflict emerged relatively late as part of gender equality policy work. This is in part because of the phenomenal stigma attached to victims of this crime, and in part because international humanitarian and human rights law—the laws of war—and international peace and security institutions have been slow to define this as a war crime and slow to establish effective frameworks for prosecution and protection of victims. But this is also because the focus of women's peace activism that has reached global attention has only partly been about the protection of women. Its major focus has been on conflict prevention and building peaceful societies; its major demand has been women's inclusion in peacemaking and peacebuilding institutions.

Women's peace activism has deeper roots than women's development activism. Women have mobilized for centuries against war, and the world's oldest continuously functioning women's organization is the Geneva-based Women's International League for Peace and Freedom (WILPF), established in 1915. Women's peace movements often invoke essentialist assumptions about women's preference for nonviolent approaches to conflict resolution and often take a principled pacifist stance. This nonviolent approach has also played an important role in liberation movements. India's independence leader Mohandas K. Gandhi, for instance, often included women wearing white saris at the front of marches and demonstrations, using their gender as a means of amplifying social disgust about the violence with which they were met by police. A form of pacifist response to war is the vigils held by Women in Black—peaceful anti-war protests that originated in Israel/Palestine in 1988.[41] They are not directed by any organizational structure, but they have expressed spontaneous opposition to violence from Palestine to Bosnia, from Turkey to South Africa.

Women's peace movements often emerge from community-level conflict resolution efforts managed by women around the world, sometimes linked to religious institutions. In spite of the proliferation of such organizations and their effectiveness in preventing or resolving conflict, women are rarely involved in formal conflict resolution processes. Women's participation is even rarer in key roles, such as mediators and signatories: for peace processes from 1992 until 2018, 13 percent of negotiators were women, 4 percent of signatories were women, and 3 percent of mediators were women.[42] Peace and security institutions—the military, mediation services, the diplomats who engage internationally to support peace processes—are male-dominated; indeed, women were historically barred in many countries from joining combat forces until relatively recently. Women, or at least married women, were excluded from foreign service institutions in many countries up until the mid-1970s and are still relatively rare at the highest ranks. The practices of women's peace movements—from exercises that reinforce the ideas of sisterhood and solidarity to discourses connecting peacebuilding and domestic violence along a continuum of violence—are rarely incorporated in mainstream peace and security debates and practices.

This makes it all the more remarkable that in 2000 the UN Security Council passed a resolution to include women in all aspects of its peace and security activity (Resolution 1325).[43] Resolution 1325 was the result of sustained lobbying by feminist peace organizations, working in alliance with the few women found at senior levels in the UN's peace and security institutions, such as the Department of Peacekeeping Operations, as well as with diplomats from countries such as Bangladesh and Namibia.[44] The text of the resolution reflects the social roles in which these activists worked: there is significant attention to the role of humanitarian workers, particularly in supporting refugee populations; there is a request that peacekeepers and mediators be trained to advance a gender perspective in their work; and there is considerable emphasis on the need to include women peace activists in peace negotiations.

Although Resolution 1325 has been followed by a number of additional women, peace, and security resolutions that greatly expand the UN's and national responsibilities to include women in peacemaking and to address gender issues in peacekeeping work, in efforts to counter violent extremism, and in long-term peacebuilding, implementation has been weak. Women are still very rarely involved in peace talks because they are not usually leaders of fighting forces, and peace negotiations are usually closed to social groups advocating accountability and justice, which are concerns that imply costs (such as convictions) for belligerents.[45]

Sexual violence and other types of violence against women and girls in conflict have not diminished in frequency, and more evidence is emerging not just of the extent to which such violence is organized but of the fact that men and boys are also its victims. Sexual exploitation and abuse by UN peacekeepers have not been effectively addressed, with extreme abuses emerging in contexts such as South Sudan during its revived civil war after 2013 and Central African Republic (2012–present). Women's capacities to support peacebuilding efforts after conflict are often undermined both by the perception that women do not have relevant skills and knowledge and by the poverty caused by displacement and destruction. Peacebuilding frameworks neglect women's capacity for analysis and leadership, as well as their needs for livelihood security, justice and reparations, and immediate health care (including reproductive health needs).

Tackling the gender biases embedded in approaches to conflict resolution and recovery is a major preoccupation of a range of women's organizations that engage with regional and multilateral security institutions. Femmes Africa Solidarité (FAS) is a pan-African organization that builds women's skills in conflict resolution at grassroots, national, and international levels and engages with the African Union to ensure that its conflict prevention work includes women.[46] Réseau Paix et Sécurité pour les Femmes de l'Espace CEDEAO supports women peacemakers in the ECOWAS subregion, using feminist lawyers in the region to lobby governments to ensure women's engagement in peace talks, as well as the prosecution of conflict-related crimes against women, as they did in Mali after the Islamist extremist incursions in the north of the country in 2012.[47] The Global Network of Women Peacebuilders supports women at the local community level in conflict-affected states to develop locality-specific action plans to implement Resolution 1325.[48]

Some of the most effective women's peace activism, however, has grown out of national grassroots efforts to work across lines of conflict—a key tactic to generate women's coalitions whose demands for peace are given credibility because of women's success in overcoming their differences. In Liberia, a group of Christian and Muslim women formed Women of Liberia Mass Action for Peace, led by Leymah Gbowee, co-author of this chapter. In 2003, with scant resources, and despite being denied direct access to the peace talks in neighboring Ghana, its members worked with the mediator, Nigerian general Abdulsalami Abubakar, to encourage delegates to reach an agreement to end the conflict, ushering in the period of peace that Liberia is still enjoying. (This experience is described in Box 3.2.) In Northern Ireland, Catholic and Protestant women created a political party (the Women's Coalition) in 1996 to participate in the election for seats in the Stormont talks. Once there, they provided a backchannel and informal mediation facility to support both sides in coming to an agreement in 1998.[49] In Democratic Republic of Congo, Female Solidarity for Integrated Peace and Development (SOFEPADI) has been supporting survivors of sexual violence and ensuring that global policy debates about peace, conflict, and sexual violence take into consideration the lived experience of women building peace (see Box 3.2).[50]

Box 3.2 Women Leading Peace in Liberia—Observations of Leymah Gbowee

The interventions of the women's peace movement in Liberia in 2003, known as the Mass Action for Peace, became widely recognized as an example of the significant influence of women organizing for peace. As a leader of the Mass Action for Peace, I was determined that our movement would be women-led, inclusive across religions and ethnic groups, and nonviolent. The women of Liberia had been sidelined from the fifteen unsuccessful peace agreements that were signed between 1989 and 1997. We did everything in our power to build the political will for the signing and implementation of the Accra Peace Agreement. We were tired of war and determined that for the sake of our families and our country, women would bring peace to Liberia.

The Mass Action for Peace is a defining example in Liberian politics of the influence of women mobilizing as a group. We staged a sex strike as a way to encourage interest in women's stories of peace rather than the mainstream narrative of the war, which had focused on drugged-up child soldiers. To push the warring parties to the peace table, we used strategies of marches and daily non-violent sit-ins, which resulted in President Charles Taylor agreeing to attend UN-backed peace talks in Accra. We used backchannel mediation to influence peace negotiations because we knew space at the peace talks would not be offered to us. We united as women across religion, ethnicity, and county by focusing on our shared experience of womanhood, claiming our moral authority by describing ourselves as the mothers of Liberia, and insisting that our experience of violence and war connected us more than our differences kept us apart. We knew that we needed to change the narrative about the Liberian war if we were to succeed in creating a different outcome, so we focused on the human toll of the conflict to put pressure on the warring parties. During the peace talks in Accra, we wrote daily letters to the chief mediator to report on the death toll and atrocities against civilians. We built alliances with members of foreign delegations and spoke with foreign media outlets. We built solidarity within West Africa, as women from northern Ghana joined us at the Ghana peace talks and women in Nigeria held a solidarity protest in support of our movement. We famously surrounded the conference hall at the peace talks, blocking entries and exits, demanding that the delegates stop stalling and drawing out the conflict. After three months of intense and consistent advocacy, a peace agreement was finally signed, and our movement's actions were credited with ensuring that the peace talks occurred and the peace agreement was signed and successfully implemented.

Activism requires financial resources to sustain the work. However, our movement was never well-resourced. The Mass Action for Peace was started with $10 of personal money from a founding member. NGOs working on conflict in the region were skeptical of our movement, fearing that we were subversive. Small amounts of funding were available for the training of women, but women's activism and organizing were not seen as a safe bet, and our work was critiqued as not strategic and not adequately credentialed. We sold ribbons and T-shirts as a local fundraising strategy. Small grants became the lifeblood of our movement, with the Lutheran Church in Denmark providing $5,000 and Oxfam providing a small grant as a result of existing funding relationships with our partner organization, WIPNET (the Women in Peacebuilding Network). When we followed the peace talks to Ghana, we had no idea how long the process would take. Once the funds from the Lutheran Church and Oxfam were exhausted, we contemplated pulling out of the peace talks. However, the African Women's Development Fund connected with us and offered a solidarity grant that allowed us to continue our activism to the point of breakthrough.

Ensuring that women are accepted as political actors is difficult. The perception of the role of women did have a limiting impact on what we were able to achieve. The chief mediator welcomed our participation and the public pressure we created to move the peace process along. However, he discouraged us from pushing for too much social change through the peace agreement. We missed the opportunity to use the 2003 Accra Peace Agreement to go beyond ending the war to address human security needs and fundamentally change gender relationships in Liberia. While the 2005 presidential election resulted in Ellen Johnson Sirleaf being elected president, it also represents the high-water mark in women's political participation and leadership in Liberia, with each subsequent election seeing fewer female candidates and lower rates of women turning out to vote. When I look to Rwanda and the increase in women's political participation there due to the inclusion of a quota in the 2003 constitution, I see we missed the opportunity to explore mechanisms that focus on the role and leadership of women at the household, community, and national levels.

Women peace activists such as Leymah Gbowee have been awarded the Nobel Peace Prize for their achievements, but peace and security institutions continue to resist the inclusion of women peace activists in all but the most gender-stereotyped aspects of peacebuilding work, such as community reconciliation and peace education. Studies of the impact of civil society engagement on making and sustaining peace have shown that the involvement of women's groups and women leaders significantly improves the durability of a peace agreement, increasing the chances that a country will not fall back into conflict.[51] Ignoring these findings and failing to address the entrenched gender bias in peace and security institutions are obstacles to effective peacemaking.

Institutionalizing Feminist Activism

A major project of women's rights activists everywhere has been to ensure that public institutions implement gender equality policies. This has involved engaging with organizations that are often highly male-dominated to promote new institutional mandates, gender parity in staffing and leadership, and gender equality in operational work—all in the interests of making gender equality a routine focus. Feminist movements around the world have shared some strategic approaches in this task. First, feminist movements often seek to "flip the narrative," or reframe the accepted definition of the policy problem. It is common to hear "culture" invoked as the reason gender inequality is more extreme in some contexts than others. Yet "culture" is a human construct that varies considerably even within the same region, among people of the same ethnicity, among those practicing the same religion, and among those adhering to similar traditions. Women's movements have successfully demonstrated that "culture" is not a historical constant; it exists in the eyes of its makers, and its makers have been elites and often men, seeking to establish women's subordination as a timeless fact, not a social construct. The best example of conceptual reconfiguration is the feminist slogan "The personal is political"—by which feminists insist that personal miseries (such as experiencing domestic violence) actually reflect structural, politically endorsed inequalities, such as the privileging of male perspectives and social tolerance of violence. A vital tactic in reconceptualizing injustices has been the feminist method of "consciousness-raising": reflection on the structural causes of abuses of women's rights.[52] Another example of this type of strategic conceptual shift is described in Box 3.3, in the discussion of the shift from understanding sexual violence in conflict as a form of collateral damage to framing it as a matter of command responsibility.

Another key strategy has been cultivating allies in other social movements and among feminist policymakers (see Box 3.3).[53] This strategy has been vital in combatting co-optation of feminist activists and objectives by mainstream public institutions. Co-optation, or the instrumentalization of feminist agendas for other goals, has been a perennial problem. For instance, some feminist scholars have alleged that the championing of women's employment as a new mechanism to advance economic growth by institutions such as the World Bank and the International Monetary Fund, private firms like McKinsey, and private sector apex groups like the World Economic Forum is a way of using women's labor to extend corporate globalization, ignoring the need for structural change in economies and societies to alter gendered divisions of labor and power.[54]

Box 3.3 Changing the Security Council's Approach to Sexual Violence in Conflict—Observations of
Anne Marie Goetz

As late as 2007, UN Security Council ambassadors sometimes said that sexual violence was one of the unfortunate forms of collateral damage in wartime about which little could be done. "Boys will be boys" was an expression some of them used, as if to imply that men—soldiers and civilians—cannot keep themselves from opportunistic rape in the fog of war. But a year later, the Security Council passed Resolution 1820, which recognized that sexual violence in conflict can be a tactic of warfare, so there could be command responsibility for organizing it or failing to prevent it. This represented a paradigm shift in the understanding of this crime—no longer an unfortunate but unavoidable feature of fighting, but rather something that can be prevented, or prosecuted through judicial mechanisms.

Generating this significant shift was work by feminist activists, lawyers, and human rights organizations working with a coalition of femocrats across UN entities. I was part of this process after joining UNIFEM in 2005, where I served as Chief Advisor on Governance, Peace and Security. I was assigned the "stop rape in war" brief and initially encountered a skeptical reception from many feminists in organizations struggling to generate effective responses to sexual violence in conflict. Activists from groups that had supported the 2000 Rome Statute such as Physicians for Human Rights, Amnesty International, Human Rights Watch, Women's Refugee Commission, International Rescue Committee, International Women's Health Coalition, and the Women's Caucus on Gender Justice, were skeptical about the UN's capabilities; UN peacekeepers enjoyed relative impunity for sexual exploitation and abuse, and humanitarian and peacekeeping responses to abuse of civilians in war were male-dominated and had historically ignored harms to women.

Working closely with the NGO Working Group on Women, Peace and Security, a coalition of peace-supporting organizations, we explored means of encouraging Security Council members to acknowledge that sexual violence was a humanitarian problem and a strategic component of the military projects of some armed actors. This conceptual reframing had to take place in the UN's intergovernmental arena (such as the Security Council) and within its operational agencies. At the time, no UN entity was responsible for addressing sexual violence in conflict. So thirteen UN entities joined forces in creating UN Action Against Sexual Violence in Conflict to bridge gaps in knowledge and approach among developmental, humanitarian, and peace and security organizations.

Insiders like me created policy justifications, drafted language for what would eventually become Security Council Resolution 1820, and assembled the leaders of UN agencies to fundraise and support coordinated field-level responses to sexual violence. External activist collaborators brought a sharp awareness of victims' suffering to the attention of Security Council members and UN leaders. At several meetings with Security Council permanent representatives, feminist activists working with sexual violence victims on the ground conveyed the horrors that victims experience, compounded by ostracization within their own communities. In fact, in one of these meetings (at Wilton House, Sussex, UK, May 2008), Leymah Gbowee participated, and I predicted that one day leaders in this effort would be awarded a Nobel Peace Prize; that did indeed happen, with Leymah receiving the award in 2011, and Nadia Mourad and Dr. Denis Mukwege receiving the prize in 2018. It is unlikely that Resolution 1820 would have been passed, or that efforts to stop conflict-related sexual violence would have attracted funding and institutional support, had it not been for the sustained pressure of feminist movement activists.

Institutionalizing feminist goals has involved sustained advocacy, lobbying, and monitoring by independent groups of mainstream national and international institutions supporting development, human rights, and peace. In addition, activists have been recruited to these institutions and charged with implementing gender equality mandates. A creative tension has emerged between activists and a growing number of feminist insiders—sometimes called "femocrats"—in mainstream institutions. Sometimes described as working "in and against" mainstream institutions, this tension has helped to keep insiders accountable to broader feminist goals and also to sustain external demand for the efforts of insiders, legitimizing their work even when they face concerted resistance from colleagues uninterested in changing the status quo.

Feminist organizations working with the growing number of feminist policymakers inside states and multilateral institutions have constituted what have been labeled "velvet triangles" of informal insider-outsider policy change collaborations.[55] An example of this type of collaboration is the 2007–2008 initiative by feminist civil society groups to work with UNIFEM and other UN agencies to support the first UN Security Council resolution on conflict-related sexual violence (discussed in Box 3.3).

Writing in 2006, Aili Mari Tripp noted, "In the past two decades we have witnessed the evolution of an international consensus around particular norms regarding women's rights," which has made a range of international institutions "intent on changing women's status and removing key impediments to women's advancement in almost every arena."[56] The 2010 creation of UN Women, which merged four marginal UN entities and expanded the mandate to support gender equality across the multilateral system, signaled a recognition by the UN of the imperative of ensuring adequate voice for women's rights representatives in all international matters.

Backlash

Women's movements the world over have successfully demonstrated that women's subordination to men and the deprivation, discrimination, exclusion, and violence that flow from this are socially constructed, "man-made," and can be contested and changed. They have also shown that gender inequality is costly for development, democracy, and peace. For example, in 2018, the World Bank estimated that states have lost more than $160 trillion through income inequality alone.[57] Discrimination against women in the workplace, the exploitation of women's unpaid care work, and violence all deplete women's capacities and diminish resources available for economies to prosper. In addition, the cultivation of ideologies of male superiority and the hegemonic masculinity embedded in governance institutions (particularly security and foreign policy institutions) distort decision-making in ways that have been shown to exacerbate risk-taking and encourage aggressive propensities.[58]

The depth of inequality within post-industrial countries and the pockets of extreme poverty in the North and extreme wealth in the South are dramatically changing approaches to and even the meanings of development and peace. Some of these dynamics are weakening women's movements. Membership and mobilization capacity are eroded when women are working two jobs in addition to domestic care work in order to make ends meet in a globalized economy. Neoliberal approaches to growth have sidelined labor rights movements and encouraged a shrinking of state social provision, all of which affects women's welfare more than men's.

These trends are of particular relevance in the context of the current "illiberal drift," in which autocratic leaders and right-wing populist parties have been coming to power even in some of the world's largest democracies, such as the United States, Brazil, India, the Philippines, and Turkey.[59] These leaders often deploy markedly misogynist rhetoric and have in some cases set about dismantling protections on women's rights, such as equal pay mandates and access to abortion and contraception.[60] In some contexts, women human rights defenders and women's organizations have come under attack, including for professing feminist principles, a development that suggests that gender equality is being framed as a threat to the state.

Gender equality and women's rights to work collectively to achieve it are becoming something over which there is deepening global polarization. Some governments, in contrast to right-wing populist contexts, have adopted feminist governance principles. Uruguay's Integrated National Care System, designed by feminist academics, seeks to ensure that women do not bear the cost of unpaid and unrecognized childcare and has made care a public responsibility.[61] Swedish prime minister Stefan Lofven declared in 2017 that his was a feminist government.[62] Canada's Justin Trudeau did the same in 2015. Sweden, France, Canada, Spain, Luxembourg, and Mexico have declared that they practice feminist foreign policy.[63]

Deepening polarization between countries on the matter of women's rights poses problems for women's movements because it makes multilateral forums nonviable as contexts for negotiating normative advances in gender equality. At the UN, for instance, annual meetings of the Commission on the Status of Women have become increasingly contested, with hostile states blocking efforts to expand women's reproductive and sexual rights and even challenging the legitimacy of efforts to promote gender equality.[64] The UN mechanism that proved so fruitful for the expansion of the global women's rights struggle, the periodic UN Conferences on Women, has not been used since 1995, for fear that the conservative shift among UN member states (significantly supported by the Vatican) will undermine previous normative advances.[65]

In this context, and with destabilizing forces such as climate change, sudden and rapid immigration, sudden changes in economic security caused by globalization, and global public health threats such as the COVID-19 pandemic, there are significant threats to women's rights achievements. However, domestically, regionally, and internationally, the variety and capacity of women's rights movements are vast, and they are holding the line against efforts to erode achievements. New alliances have been built with other social movements, as is evident from the effectiveness of women's groups in leading street protests that toppled President Omar al-Bashir in Sudan in April 2019 and Governor Ricardo Rosselló in Puerto Rico in July 2019. New tactics have been made possible through use of social media, as is clear from the speed and spontaneity of mobilizations such as the Women's March in the United States and the #MeToo movement in various contexts. There is evidence that in some contexts, even where traditional authorities are powerful, women's mass action has led to women's rights being socially normalized—for instance, in the referendum resulting in a decision to legalize abortion in Ireland in 2018, or in women's successful mass action to pressure the government of Argentina to legalize abortion in December 2020.

Conclusion

Women have engaged in collective action to protest gender-based injustices in their own countries and internationally at various points in history. Since the mid-twentieth-century anti-colonial independence movement, the sustained struggle by women in developing countries against the gender biases embedded in impe-rialist and development practice has become the basis of a global women's rights and gender equality movement that has dramatically challenged—and sometimes changed—economic and political liberalization and approaches to peacebuilding. Transnational feminist movements have worked since the 1970s across geopolit-ical barriers to advance a significant global consensus on women's rights; in part they have used the global convening platform of the UN and late twentieth-cen-tury advances in human rights frameworks to challenge male bias and gender-based injustices in the family, communities, markets, states, and the international community.

To truly understand the role that women's movements have played in conflict resolution and development, we must push back against a perception of feminism as a Western notion that has completed its work in the global North and now must be implemented in the global South. Indigenous concepts of change, development, and feminism must be forefronted to unshackle development, democracy, and peacebuilding from racism, paternalism, and a colonial mindset that views women as having neither the skills nor the knowledge to be legitimate actors and leaders.

Building gender equality as part of development processes helps to promote socially sustainable change to eradicate discrimination, injustice, and inequality. Engaging women in conflict resolution and peacebuilding ensures broad social buy-in to justice projects in poor, authoritarian, and conflict-torn societies, building a broader political settlement with a stronger chance of lasting. Women's engage-ment in development and peacebuilding supports attention to social, community, and family concerns that can be neglected in economic and security planning. This can ensure that development policy is not predicated on the unsustainable—and unjust—exploitation of women or any other social group. It can ensure that peace processes and long-term peacebuilding address the root causes of conflict and do not limit peacemaking to the dividing of spoils between belligerents.

The lurch away from democracy in some contexts shows that no gains supporting human equality can be taken for granted. Women's activism continues to be essential to preserving gains, and support for women's rights organizations is a crucial investment in social justice and democracy.

Gender equality, unfortunately, is never a done deal. Women's rights do not come automatically with economic development, or with peace, or with democracy. They must be negotiated and defended indefinitely. Without vigilant defense of women's rights, humanitarian and political leaders may sideline them and postpone gender equality concerns as a luxury for better times, without realizing that prospects for effective recovery will thereby diminish.

Notes

1. Interview with one of the authors, November 27, 2020.
2. UNESCO 2014.
3. McKinsey Global Institute 2015.
4. Kabeer 2005.
5. Hudson et al. 2012.
6. Sung 2003.
7. International Monetary Fund 2018.
8. UN Women 2018.
9. UN Women 2018.
10. WHO 2017.
11. IPU 2016, 3.
12. Weldon 2002.
13. Htun and Weldon 2018; Forester et al. 2019.
14. Hudson et al. 2012.
15. Calkin 2015.
16. Walsh 2010.
17. IPU 2020.
18. OECD 2020; United Nations 2020.
19. World Economic Forum 2020.
20. Gupta 2020.
21. Posen 2018.
22. Kandiyoti 1991.
23. Mazur and McBride 2006, 226.
24. Mazur and McBride 2006, 226.
25. Molyneux 1985.
26. Naples and Desai 2004.
27. Garland-Thomson 2005.
28. Tripp 2006, 56.

29. Tripp 2006, 59.
30. Tripp 2006, 60.
31. Forester et al. 2019.
32. Forester et al. 2019, 7.
33. Forester et al. 2019, 10.
34. Boserup 1970.
35. Sen and Grown 1987.
36. Hozic and True 2012; Moeller 2018.
37. ILO 2017.
38. World Bank 2019.
39. Nobel Media 2006.
40. Tripp 2006; Keck and Sikkink 1998.
41. On Women in Black, see http://womeninblack.org/about-women-in-black/.
42. Council on Foreign Relations 2019.
43. UN Security Council 2000.
44. Cohn, Kinsella, and Gibbings 2004.
45. O'Reilly, Ó Súilleabháin, and Paffenholz 2015.
46. The organization's website is http://www.fasngo.org/.
47. For information on REPSFECO (Réseau Paix et Sécurité pour les Femmes de l'Espace CEDEAO), see http://womencount4peace.org/fr/repertoire/institutions/organisation_sous-r%C3%A9gionale/repsfeco.
48. The organization's website is https://gnwp.org/.
49. Ford 2012.
50. Zawadi 2018.
51. Zawadi 2018.
52. Boles 1991.
53. See Beckwith 2007.
54. Hozic and True 2009.
55. Woodward 2003.
56. Tripp 2006, 51; Keck and Sikkink 1998.
57. Wodon and de la Brière 2018.
58. Bjarnegård 2013.
59. Posen 2020.
60. Goetz and Jenkins 2020.
61. Harman and Ivins 2016.
62. Government Offices of Sweden 2018.
63. Ridge et al. 2019; Government of Mexico 2020.
64. Goetz 2020.
65. Goetz and Sandler 2017.

Bibliography

Batliwala, Srilatha. 1994. "The Meaning of Women's Empowerment: New Concepts from Action." In *Population Policies Reconsidered: Health, Empowerment, and Rights*, edited by Gita Sen, Adrienne Germain, and Lincoln C. Chen, 127–138. Cambridge, MA: Harvard University Press.

Beckwith, K. 2007. "Mapping Strategic Engagements: Women's Movements and the State." *International Feminist Journal of Politics* 9, no. 3: 312–338.

Bjarnegård, Elin. 2013. *Gender, Informal Institutions and Political Recruitment: Explaining Male Dominance in Parliamentary Representation*. Basingstoke: Palgrave Macmillan.

Boles, J. K. 1991. "Form Follows Function: The Evolution of Feminist Strategies." *The Annals of the American Academy of Political and Social Science* 515, no. 1: 38–49.

Boserup, Ester. 1970. *Woman's Role in Economic Development*. London: George Allen & Unwin.

Bunch, Charlotte. 1995. "The Global Campaign for Women's Human Rights: Where Next After Vienna?" *St. John's Law Review* 69, nos. 1–2: art. 7.

Calkin, Sydney. 2017. "Disrupting Disempowerment: Feminism, Co-optations, and the Privatized Governance of Gender and Development." *New Formations* 91: 69.

Cohn, Carol, Helen Kinsella, and Sheri Gibbings. 2004. "Women, Peace and Security Resolution 1325." *International Feminist Journal of Politics* 6, no. 1: 130–140.

Council on Foreign Relations. 2019. "Women's Participation in Peace Processes." January 30. https://www.cfr.org/interactive/womens-participation-in-peace-processes.

Crenshaw, Kimberlé. 1990. "Mapping the Margins: Intersectionality, Identity Politics, and Violence Against Women of Color." *Stanford Law Review* 43: 1241.

Engle, Karen, Vasuki Nesiah, and Dianne Otto. 2022. "Feminist Approaches to International Law." In *International Legal Theory: Foundations and Frontiers*, edited by Jeffrey Dunoff and Mark Pollack. Cambridge: Cambridge University Press.

Ford, Maryann. 2012. "Women's Role in the Resolution of Northern Ireland Conflict." University of Massachusetts Lowell. https://www.uml.edu/docs/Ford_Paper_tcm18-91394.pdf.

Forester, Summer, Kaitlin Kelly-Thompson, Amber Lusvardi, and Laurel Weldon. 2019. "A Global, Comparative Map of Feminist Movements, 1975–2015: An Intersectional, Mixed-Methods Approach." Paper prepared for the Vancouver Workshop on Movements, Markets and Transnational Networks: Feminist Mobilization and Women's Economic Empowerment Worldwide, September. Available from laurel_weldon@sfu.ca.

Fraser, Nancy. 2009. "Feminism, Capitalism and the Cunning of History." *New Left Review* 56: 97–117.

Garland-Thomson, R. 2005. "Feminist Disability Studies." *Signs: Journal of Women in Culture and Society* 30, no. 2: 1557–1587.

Global Partnership for Education. 2014. "Why Educating Girls Makes Economic Sense." https://www.globalpartnership.org/blog/why-educating-girls-makes-economic-sense.

Goetz, Anne Marie. 2020. "The New Competition in Multilateral Norm-Setting: Transnational Feminists and the Illiberal Backlash." *Daedelus* 149, no. 1: 160–179. https://www.amacad.org/daedalus/women-equality.

Goetz, Anne Marie, and Paige Arthur. 2019. "The UN's Gender Parity Goals: The Backlash Begins." Passblue. January 23. https://www.passblue.com/2019/01/23/the-uns-gender-parity-goals-the-backlash-begins/.

Goetz, Anne Marie, and Shireen Hassim. 2003. *No Shortcuts to Power: African Women in Politics and Policy-Making*. London: Zed Press.

Goetz, Anne Marie, and Rob Jenkins. 2020. " Gender and Peacebuilding", Chapter 3 In *Gender and Security: Strategies for the Twenty-first Century*, edited by Chantal de Jonge Oudraat and Michael Brown, 47–71. New York: Routledge.

Goetz, Anne Marie, and Joanne Sandler. 2017. "Time for a Fifth World Conference on Women?" Open Democracy. March 8. https://www.opendemocracy.net/en/5050/time-for-fifth-world-conference-on-women/.

Government of Mexico. 2020. "Mexico Adopts Feminist Foreign Policy." Press release. January 9. https://www.gob.mx/sre/prensa/mexico-adopts-feminist-foreign-policy?idiom=en.

Government Offices of Sweden. 2018. "A Feminist Government." https://www.government.se/government-policy/a-feminist-government/.

Gupta, Alisha Haridasani. 2020. "In Her Words." *The New York Times*, January 28. https://www.nytimes.com/series/in-her-words?te=1&nl=in-her%20words&emc=edit_gn_20200128&campaign_id=10&instance_id=15530&segment_id=20742&user_id=712d8a9f0dd45d3905efd540729e94f0&regi_id=6465006920200128.

Harman, Til Johannes, and Courtney Price Ivins. 2016. "Uruguay's Award-Winning Innovations for Social Protection." *Governance for Development* (blog), World Bank. http://blogs.worldbank.org/governance/uruguay-s-award-winning-innovations-social-protection.

Hozic, A., and J. True. 2012. *Scandalous Economics: The Politics of Gender and Financial Crises.* New York: Oxford University Press.

Hudson, Valerie, Bonnie Ballif-Spanvill, Mary Caprioli, and Chad F. Emmett. 2012. *Sex and World Peace.* New York: Columbia University Press.

Htun, Mala, and S. Laurel Weldon. 2018. *The Logics of Gender Justice: State Action on Women's Rights Around the World.* Cambridge: Cambridge University Press.

ILO. 2017. "World Employment and Social Outlook: Trends for Women 2017." International Labour Organization, Geneva. http://www.ilo.org/global/research/global-reports/weso/tre nds-for-women2017/lang--en/index.htm.

International Monetary Fund. 2018. "Pursuing Women's Economic Empowerment." May 31. https://www.imf.org/en/Publications/Policy-Papers/Issues/2018/05/31/pp053118pursuing-womens-economic-empowerment.

IPU. 2016. "Sexism, Harassment and Violence Against Women Parliamentarians." Inter-Parliamentary Union Issues Brief, October. http://archive.ipu.org/pdf/publications/issuesbr ief-e.pdf.

IPU. 2020. "Gender Equality." Inter-Parliamentary Union. https://www.ipu.org/our-impact/gen der-equality.

Kabeer, Naila. 2005. "Gender Equality and Human Development: The Instrumental Rationale." Human Development Report Office, United Nations Development Programme. http://hdr. undp.org/sites/default/files/hdr2005_kabeer_naila_31.pdf.

Kandiyoti, Deniz. 1991. "Identity and Its Discontents: Women and the Nation." *Millennium* 20, no. 3: 429–443. https://doi.org/10.1177/03058298910200031501.

Keck, Margaret, and Kathryn Sikkink. 1998. *Activists Beyond Borders: Advocacy Networks in International Politics.* Ithaca, NY: Cornell University Press.

Mazur, Amy G., and Dorothy E. McBride. 2006. "The RNGS Data Set: Women's Policy Agencies, Women's Movements and Policy Debates in Western Post-Industrial Democracies." *French Politics* 4, no. 2: 209–236. https://doi.org/10.1057/palgrave.fp.8200101.

McKinsey Global Institute. 2015. "How Advancing Women's Equality Can Add $12 Trillion to Global Growth." https://www.mckinsey.com/featured-insights/employment-and-growth/ how-advancing-womens-equality-can-add-12-trillion-to-global-growth.

Moeller, Kathryn. 2018. *The Gender Effect: Capitalism, Feminism, and the Corporate Politics of Development.* Oakland: University of California Press.

Molyneux, Maxine. 1985. "Mobilization Without Emancipation? Women's Interests, the State, and Revolution in Nicaragua." *Feminist Studies* 11, no. 2: 227–254. doi:10.2307/3177922.

Naples, N. A., and M. Desai, eds. 2004. *Women's Activism and Globalization: Linking Local Struggles and Global Politics.* London: Routledge.

Nilsson, Desiree. 2009. "Anchoring the Peace: Civil Society Actors in Peace Accords and Durable Peace." *International Interactions* 38, no. 2: 243–266.

Nobel Media. 2006. "The Nobel Peace Prize for 2006." https://www.nobelprize.org/prizes/peace/ 2006/press-release/.

OECD. 2020. "Women at the Core of the Fight Against COVID-19 Crisis." April. https://www. oecd.org/coronavirus/policy-responses/women-at-the-core-of-the-fight-against-covid-19-crisis-553a8269/.

O'Reilly, Marie, Andrea Ó Súilleabháin, and Thania Paffenholz. 2015. "Reimagining Peacemaking: Women's Roles in Peace Processes." International Peace Institute, New York.

Paffenholz, Thania, Nick Ross, Steven Dixon, Anna-Lena Schluchter, and Jacquie True. 2016. "Making Women Count, Not Just Counting Women: Assessing Women's Inclusion and Influence on Peace Negotiations." Inclusive Peace. http://www.inclusivepeace.org/sites/defa ult/files/IPTI-UN-Women-Report-Making-Women-Count-60-Pages.pdf.

Parpart, Jane, and Kathleen Staudt. 1989. *Women and the State in Africa.* Boulder, CO: Lynne Rienner.

Posen, Barry R. 2018. "The Rise of Illiberal Hegemony." *Foreign Affairs.* February 13. https://www. foreignaffairs.com/articles/2018-02-13/rise-illiberal-hegemony.

Ridge, Alice, Caroline Lambert, Joanne Crawford, Rachel Clement, Lyric Thompson, Anne Marie Goetz, and Sarah Gammage. 2019. "Feminist Foreign Policy: Key Principles and Accountability Mechanisms, A Discussion Summary." Report of a CSW Workshop. International Center for Research on Women, International Women's Development Agency, Center for Global Affairs, New York.

Sen, Gita, and Caren Grown. 1987. *Development, Crises, and Alternative Visions: Third World Women's Perspectives.* New York: Monthly Review Press

Stone, Laurel. 2014. "Women Transforming Conflict: A Quantitative Analysis of Female Peacemaking." Seton Hall University. http://dx.doi.org/10.2139/ssrn.2485242.

Sung, Hung-En. 2003. "Fairer Sex or Fairer System? Gender and Corruption Revisited." *Social Forces* 82, no. 2: 703–723. http://muse.jhu.edu/journals/social_forces/v082/82.2sung.html.

Tripp, Aili Mari. 2006. "Challenges in Transnational Feminist Mobilization." In *Global Feminism: Transnational Women's Activism, Organizing and Human Rights*, edited by Myra Marx Ferree and Aili Mari Tripp, chapter 12. New York: New York University Press.

UN Security Council. 2000. "Resolution 1325 (2000), Adopted by the Security Council at its 4213th Meeting, on 31 October 2000." S/RES/1325.

UN Women. 2018. *Turning Promises into Action: Gender Equality in the 2030 Agenda for Sustainable Development.* New York: United Nations. https://www.unwomen.org/en/digital-library/publications/2018/2/gender-equality-in-the-2030-agenda-for-sustainable-development-2018.

UNESCO. 2014. "Teaching and Learning: Achieving Quality for All." EFA Global Monitoring Report.

United Nations. 2020. "Policy Brief: The Impact of COVID-19 on Women." April. https://www.un.org/sexualviolenceinconflict/wp-content/uploads/2020/06/report/policy-brief-the-impact-of-covid-19-on-women/policy-brief-the-impact-of-covid-19-on-women-en-1.pdf.

Walsh, Denise. 2010. *Women's Rights in Democratizing States: Just Debate and Gender Justice in the Public Sphere.* Cambridge: Cambridge University Press.

Weldon, Laurel. 2002. *Protest, Policy and the Problem of Violence Against Women: A Cross-National Comparison.* Pittsburgh: University of Pittsburgh Press.

WHO. 2017. "Violence Against Women." World Health Organization. https://www.who.int/news-room/fact-sheets/detail/violence-against-women.

WHO. 2020. "COVID-19 and Violence Against Women." World Health Organization. https://www.who.int/reproductivehealth/publications/vaw-covid-19/en/.

Wodon, Quentin T., and Bénédicte de la Brière. 2018. "Unrealized Potential: The High Cost of Gender Inequality in Earnings." World Bank Group. https://openknowledge.worldbank.org/bitstream/handle/10986/29865/126579-Public-on-5-30-18-WorldBank-GenderInequality-Brief-v13.pdf?sequence=1&isAllowed=y.

Woodward, Alison E. 2003. "Building Velvet Triangles: Gender and Informal Governance." In *Informal Governance in the European Union*, edited by Thomas Christiansen and Simona Piattoni, 76–93. Northampton, MA: Edward Elgar.

World Bank. 2019. "School Enrollment, Primary and Secondary (Gross), Gender Parity Index (GPI)." https://data.worldbank.org/indicator/SE.ENR.PRSC.FM.ZS.

World Economic Forum. 2019. "The Global Gender Gap Report 2020." https://www.weforum.org/reports/global-gender-gap-report-2020.

World Economic Forum. 2020. "Annual Report 2019–2020." November. https://www.weforum.org/reports/annual-report-2019-2020/.

Zawadi, Mambo. 2018. "Turning Victims into Survivors: SOFEDAI's Fight Against Sexual Violence in the DRC." The Fund for Global Human Rights. https://globalhumanrights.org/blogs/turning-victims-into-survivors-sofepadis-fight-against-sexual-violence-in-the-drc-chloe-gilot/.

4

The Critical Movement for Youth Inclusion

Lakshitha Saji Prelis

> If youth can be such a powerful force that can destroy a nation, why do
> people overlook our resources when we are working for peace?
> —Rwandan youth movement leader[1]

Introduction

From the U.S. civil rights movement to the Arab Spring, from the Revolution of Our Time in Hong Kong to the people's revolution in Sudan, young people have shaped free and open societies. There is a popular misperception that young people are violent, unstable, or merely passive victims without power. A fear of "angry young black/brown men" has driven a lot of Western policymaking and programming around young people, peace, and security in recent decades. This has reinforced structural violence against young people around the world, and has overlooked young people's positive contributions to preventing violence and building resilience.

There are over 1.8 billion young people in the world today, and between 408 and 600 million are affected by armed conflict and violence. While a very small group of youth use violence to deal with differences, the vast majority do not. Through creative means and actions, most are shattering myths that identify them as lazy, apathetic, victims, or perpetrators. Young people are constantly struggling with existing norms, power structures, and circumstances. It's important to recognize that they are proving to be one of the best untapped resources for bridging divided communities and creating lasting peace and stability (see Box 4.1).[2]

This chapter describes how young people today are affected by violent conflict, and it considers the incorrect yet influential myths and stereotypes about young people's contributions to violence. It then goes on to discuss the violence of exclusion experienced by young people and provides counterexamples of young people taking action for positive change. Finally, the chapter describes new positive policy developments that are essential for understanding foreign policy and development in the modern interconnected world.

Box 4.1 Young People Affected by Violent Conflict

Defining "Youth"

There are many definitions of what constitutes "youth," yet there is no consensus. For example, the United Nations defines youth as people between the ages of fifteen and twenty-four. The UN Security Council Resolution on Youth, Peace, and Security defines youth as those between ages eighteen and twenty-nine. The African Youth Charter and the Association of Southeast Asian Nations defines youth as all those between fifteen and thirty-five years of age. This chapter will use the term "young people" broadly to include children, adolescents, and youth, but it will focus more on the age cohort between fifteen and thirty. The transition from child to adolescent to youth and then adulthood varies depending on culture, ethnicity, age, gender, economics, and conflict dislocation. Young people in many parts of the world feel paralyzed and struggle to become adults when conflict, fragility, and violence make them feel trapped between youthhood and adulthood. The sense of being stuck[3] is further defined as "waithood" ("involuntary . . . suspension between childhood and adulthood"), a critical in-between period that many young people experience, according to social scientist Alcinda Hanwana.[4]

The 2007 World Development Report described five stages of the transitions young people go through from childhood to adulthood. These five transitions include (1) acquiring knowledge through education, (2) starting to work, (3) attaining a new lifestyle, (4) establishing families, and (5) taking an active role in citizenship.[5] However, conflict and/or policies and governance models frequently stand in the way of a smooth transition. The consequences of this for both individuals and society are high—for example, when young people's education is disrupted, when young people have long periods of unemployment due to conflict, or when young people choose risky health practices. It is also important to note that today, young people start playing an active role in citizenship at a very young age, even while they are in school.

Some staggering statistics show the impact fragility, conflict, and violence have on youth, in ways that contribute to this waithood:

- One in four young people today is living in or is affected by armed conflict and violence.[6]
- Over 90 percent of conflict-related deaths are young men below the age of thirty.[7]
- Gun deaths of school-age children in the United States have increased at an alarming rate, with 38,942 fatalities among five- to eighteen-year-olds from

1999 to 2017. To put this in context: in 2017, 144 police officers died in the line of duty; about 1,000 active-duty U.S. military personnel throughout the world died that same year; and a staggering 2,462 school-age children were killed by firearms.[8]

Young people are inextricably linked to conflict in their communities, where they play a variety of roles: rejectionists of the peace process; activists; criminals and vigilantes; negotiators and mediators; human rights defenders; security and justice actors; and peacemakers.[9] Youth also experience a range of less visible short- and long-term effects of violence and exclusion, such as repeat victimization, psychological trauma, identity-based discrimination, and social and economic exclusion. The first global report on shrinking civic space for youth, *If I Disappear Global Report on Protecting Young People in Civic Space,* identified the following interconnected barriers young people face. The include, in order of importance as highlighted by young people: sociocultural; political; financial; legal; digital; physical; and the impact of the global COVID-19 pandemic.[10]

Some of the earliest quantitative studies about the impact of violent conflict on young people originated from the Survey of War-Affected Youth (SWAY) regarding former child soldiers in Uganda.[11] During the war in northern Uganda between government forces and the Lord's Resistance Army (LRA), at least 66,000 young people between ages thirteen and thirty were abducted by the rebel LRA.[12] Adolescents were disproportionately targeted for recruitment because they were a very large population demographic in Uganda at the time, they were more effective guerrillas than younger children, and they were more easily indoctrinated and disoriented than young adults.[13] Forced recruitment of youth between fourteen and thirty-five years of age contributed to lower rates of employment and educational attainment after reintegration back into their communities.[14] The psychological impact on the Ugandan youth was far-reaching according to mental health, trauma, and psychosocial behavior experts who reviewed forty epidemiological trauma studies and found problems including post-traumatic stress disorder (PTSD), depression, anxiety, and psychosis, suicidal ideation, alcohol abuse, partner violence, child abuse, and feelings of guilt and revenge.[15]

Other visible and invisible identity markers that impact young people's lives influence the five stages of transition and are relevant to policy and practice. "Before I am a girl, I am black. Before I face sexism, I face racism. Before anyone takes note of my gender expression, their eyes focus on the color of my skin, a brown appearing golden in the sunlight," Eva Lewis, co-founder of Black Lives Youth, writes in *Teen Vogue.*[16] She goes on to describe these as her "intersections, social constructs that cross paths with each other to create my identity, and ironically, the things for which I am oppressed." Intersectionality, a term coined by UCLA professor Kimberlé Crenshaw, recognizes that individuals have multiple, intersecting, and overlapping social identities that affect their experiences, including experiences of structural discrimination and oppression.[17] In countries where political division, fear, and anxiety are high, and people's trust in institutions is low, intersectional understanding is critical in shaping policy and program implementations. As a result, as Eva Lewis argues, it is critical to understand the diverse identities young people carry throughout their lives. The following are just a handful of important identities to keep in mind, noting that they all might be equally important in conflict settings.

For young women, conflict and violence are exacerbated by their age and gender, coupled with societal norms, traditions, patriarchy, and culture.[18] When conflict erupts, the risks for adolescent boys increase, and multiply even more for girls.[19] For example, young women who were abducted by the LRA were forcibly given as wives to commanders, and they experienced physical and sexual violence, including verbal and physical abuse from extended family members and intimate partners while in the bush.[20] Sexual violence continues as part of a broader strategy of conflict that has significant impact on the lives of women and girls. The UN Secretary General's 2019 report on conflict-related sexual violence highlights how armed groups, local militias, and gangs, as well as national armed forces such as police and military troops, have committed sexual violence against women and girls in Democratic Republic of the Congo, Myanmar, Somalia, South Sudan, Syria, and many more.[21]

Sexual and gender-based violence (SGBV) against men and boys is also widespread during conflict.[22] The World Health Organization has identified sexual violence against men and boys as a problem that has been ignored.[23] The violations include rape, gang rape, sexual slavery, enforced nudity, and being forced to perform sexual acts with others. Studies have shown this pattern in contexts such as Chile, El Salvador, Libya, Sri Lanka, Syria, the United States, and the former Yugoslavia.[24]

Beyond the binary definition of sex and gender, research conducted in Bosnia and Herzegovina, Colombia, Lebanon, and Nepal outlines how being identified by others as belonging to a sexual or gender minority (SGM) brings additional vulnerability.[25] While threats are common during times of peace, violent conflict exacerbates them. "SGM individuals, couples and communities are likely to face exclusion, discrimination and violence not only from armed conflict actors but also from civilians, including close family members. Neither the end of a violent conflict nor an escape from a conflict zone automatically guarantees an end to these dynamics or the multiple dangers that SGM persons face."[26]

The sheer magnitude of conflict-related sexual violence against young women, young men, and sexual and gender minorities is difficult to ascertain because of a range of challenges, including underreporting because of the way survivors are intimidated and stigmatized.[27] On the other hand, understanding SGBV against young people requires a critical understanding of the harmful patriarchal attitudes that affect the rights, dignity, and agency of young people. The international community should focus on inclusion as a way to address these harmful practices. In doing so, it is critical to invest in nonviolent, gender-equitable masculine identities that challenge social norms too.[28]

It is estimated that between 180 and 200 million young people between the ages of ten and twenty-four are currently living with a disability.[29] This often has a profound impact on the smooth transition from childhood to adulthood in the five categories described earlier. The type of disability a young person experiences can bring negative attitudes and social stigma that can lead to denial of their rights. Using an intersectional lens, we can see that young persons with disabilities may face additional discriminatory attitudes because they are young women, members of the LGBTQI community, or part of racial or ethnic minorities, and hence they may be more vulnerable to violence.[30] Children with disabilities also experience sexual violence about three times more often than children without disabilities, and girls are at higher risk.[31] Poverty and risks associated with conflict settings and humanitarian contexts make it even more difficult for young people with disabilities to access or exercise their rights.[32] The United Nations Convention on the Rights of Persons with Disabilities (CRPD), adopted in 2006, insists on the rights of persons with disabilities of all ages to the full enjoyment of all human rights, including the right to equal participation in society and the right to live a life with dignity. The 2030 Agenda for Sustainable Development that all UN member countries have committed to also recognizes the rights of persons with disabilities and supports their equal access to employment and education. See Box 4.2 for youth demographics.

Box 4.2 Youth: A Demographic Reality

- In 2016, 1.8 billion people or 24 percent of the world's population were living in fragile contexts. This number is projected to grow to 2.3 billion by 2030 or 28 percent of the total world population.
- In many of these most fragile contexts around the world, the average median age is twenty years. A majority of these fragile contexts are in sub-Saharan Africa.[33]
- There were 1.85 billion young people in the world between ages ten and twenty-four in 2019.[34]
- This group of young people is the largest demographic on this planet.
- Nine in ten young people live in developing countries.[35]
- As of April 2017, over 50 percent of the global population was below eighteen years of age in seventeen countries; sixteen of those countries are in Africa.[36]
- One in every four young people ages fifteen to twenty-nine is affected by violent conflict.[37]

Stereotypes and Myths

A study entitled "The Missing Peace" provides an important framework that identifies and explores the most prevalent stereotypes and myths about youth that have shaped policy decisions. This section summarizes these myths and stereotypes.

Young people are associated with violence and viewed as a threat. Specifically, young men are seen as aggressive and violent, while young women are seen as victims of violence. While it is true that some young men are violent and many young women are victims, it is a myth that this is the reality for all young men and young women. Yet the myths have created a sense of urgency for many governments to address the threats.

Myth #1: "Bulging" Youth Populations Produce an Increased Risk of Violent Conflict

Many decision-makers around the world perceive that countries with large youth populations are at risk of violence and instability. This is known as the "youth bulge" theory.[38] Proponents of this theory believe there is a positive correlation between high proportions of youth and an increased risk of criminal and political violence.[39] Decision-makers base policies on these myths, creating barriers for young people wishing to make meaningful contributions to their societies. For example, the urgency that governments experience to respond to the rising threats of terrorism or violent extremism has led to widespread generalizations about young people being viewed as at risk of being recruited.

One argument against this theory is that it is missing a strong gender analysis. Newer research argues that the youth bulge theory, at least in the form in which it is dominant in mainstream international relations, is using a biological essentialist approach; therefore, it is based on a flawed theoretical assumption, because it is missing research and perspectives of feminist international relations scholars.[40] Pruitt argues that this bias has led to less effective policymaking and asserts that a gender analysis would help decision-makers gain a better understanding of young people in general and young men in situations of conflict in particular.

Another argument against the youth bulge theory is that it ignores the role of power. Based on their research, Nordås and Davenport write that "a statistical analysis of the relationship between youth bulges and state repression from 1976 to 2000 confirms [that] . . . controlling for factors known to be associated with coercive state action, we find that governments facing youth bulge are more repressive than other states."[41] Therefore, it is clear that repression by the state is one of the leading causes of violence, as is a sense of exclusion.[42] The fact that a population includes large numbers of youth is not a leading cause.

Myth #2: Young Refugees or Migrants Present New Threats of Terrorism and Violent Crime

Young people around the world leave their homes due to persecution, conflict, violence, or human rights violations. Over 70 million people have been forcibly displaced worldwide, and many more migrate for economic reasons.[43] The UN High Commissioner for Refugees estimates that at the end of 2018, those under eighteen years of age constituted roughly 51 percent of the global refugee population.[44] The number of people displaced due to conflict was equivalent to an average of 37,000 people being forced to flee their homes every day in 2018.[45]

Police and other officials frequently treat these young migrants, refugees, and internally displaced people as threats, rather than as people fleeing violence, conflict, or economic hardship. "Youth bulge" rhetoric shapes immigration policies and fuels racism and xenophobia. It has contributed to racial profiling, sometimes with gender dimensions, where "young migrant men [are] seen as praying on local women or as sexual deviants."[46]

Despite these stereotypes, as the *Pathways for Peace* report produced by the United Nations and the World Bank points out, "well-managed migration can offer many benefits and is an alternative to enduring the constraints felt by demographic transitions. Migrants contribute to their host countries by filling critical labor shortages, paying taxes and social security contributions, and creating jobs as entrepreneurs."[47]

Myth #3: Most Young People Are Susceptible to Recruitment into Violent Extremist Groups

A common assumption is that young people are susceptible to recruitment into violent groups. Some young people join violent extremist groups to pursue exclusionary ideologies, to rectify real and perceived injustice, or to feel part of something larger than themselves. Some feel coerced to use violence because of manipulation or fear.[48] In many instances, security responses aggravate tensions and trigger support for extremist ideologies.[49] This approach fails to engage youth as key allies in building resilience against violent extremism.[50]

For example, in some of the countries dealing with violent extremist groups, such as Libya, Mali, Nigeria, Somalia, and Tunisia, community members report they are more fearful of their government's violent actions than those of violent extremist groups.[51] Evidence confirms that this has become one of the most powerful motivating factors for young people to join violent extremist groups in Africa.[52] This shows that it is not the lure of violence per se that frames how or when young people are drawn to groups (see Box 4.3).

Box 4.3 Generalizing Large Portions of the Population as Terrorist Sympathizers is Misleading and Dangerous

---

In West Africa and especially the Lake Chad Basin, a violent terror group known as Boko Haram has recruited many children and youth into its ranks. People supporting this group or those sympathetic to this group are lumped into one category as active supporters of Boko Haram. It is widely known that young people join the group for a variety of reasons: ideological, to seek revenge, for economic gain, to flee physical abuse from family members, to escape boredom, out of fear of reprisal. Characterizing all cadres as "hardcore followers" excludes many who could be meaningfully disengaged, rehabilitated, and reintegrated back into their communities. Using such broad brushstrokes is counterproductive and leads to the unnecessary death of innocent victims.

Myth # 4: Young People Are Drawn to Violence Because of a Lack of Employment or Education

It is widely acknowledged that education and jobs provide a clear path for young people to succeed and to contribute to their societies. Yet there is thought-provoking evidence about the relationships between youth unemployment, education, and violence. In Afghanistan, Mercy Corps found through their vocational training and livelihood programming research that although 84 percent of participants found jobs and improved their economic standing, there was no measurable drop in their support for armed groups.[53] And in Somalia, the Mercy Corps Youth Leaders Initiative found that a change in employment status for graduates of the initiative had no effect on their willingness to engage in political violence.[54]

Economic marginalization and the lack of opportunities are certainly prevalent around the world, and young people are faced with the reality of a challenging future as they grow up. In Niger, the zones affected by rebel group violence are largely rural and often remote. These are also the zones where recruitment into violent extremist groups and support for these groups are greatest—for example, in Diffa and Tillaberi, Niger. Focus group discussions with young people from these rural zones of Niger in 2017 identify the following key recommendations to aid in their well-being:[55]

- Increased youth representatives in decision-making positions
- Revised security measures in cooperation with youth
- Support for youth initiatives
- Increased economic security
- Increased capacity development initiatives for youth

There is a growing body of evidence, including from the Mercy Corps research, the Progress Study on Youth, Peace and Security, and Search for Common Ground, that there is no strong relationship between joblessness and a young person's willingness to engage in or support political violence. Where young people pick up a gun, it is not because they are poor, but because they are angry at a system that is failing them.

In the United States, as in many places around the world, schools, workplaces, and the justice system are key pillars of society. Unfortunately, studies have shown that the structural barriers young men and women of color experience put them at greater disadvantage in school, in the workplace, and in the justice system. For example, graduation rates from the US public education system were around 59 percent for Black male students, 65 percent for Latino males, and 80 percent for White males; these disparities in graduation rates stem from disparities in school discipline and inequitable school supports.[56] Beyond graduation rates, data from the Department of Education's 2011–2012 report reveal that Black males were suspended from school three times as often as their White counterparts, while Black girls were suspended six times as often, and only 2 percent of White females were subjected to exclusionary suspensions, compared with 12 percent for Black girls.[57]

The unfair system negatively impacts young men and women of color in the United States and creates a cycle of incarceration and punitive justice. In 2019, approximately 48,000 youth in the United States were confined in correctional facilities away from their homes. The data show a striking difference based on race. As of December 2019, 42 percent of the boys and 35 percent of the girls in US juvenile facilities were Black, when only about 14 percent of youth under the age of eighteen are Black nationwide.[58] Studies have found that Americans' support for harsh criminal justice and policing correlates positively with the number of Black people in prison.[59] Additionally, the rate at which Black Americans are killed by police is more than twice the rate for White Americans, and young men of color are at greatest risk.[60]

The data just cited don't indicate that young Black men and women are committing more crimes than young White people. Rather, they are carrying the burden of "presumption of guilt and dangerous [and it] makes people of color vulnerable to unjustified violence, wrongful conviction, and unfair treatment."[61] This legacy of racism targets young people of color in the United States with "disparately frequent stops, searches, and violence and leads to higher rates of childhood suspension, expulsion, and arrest at school; disproportionate contact with the juvenile justice system; harsher charging decisions and disadvantaged plea negotiations; a greater likelihood of being denied bail and diversion; an increased risk of wrongful convictions and unfair sentences; and higher rates of probation and parole revocation."[62]

Myths and stereotypes combine with structural violence to put young people of color in the United States at greater disadvantage, hurting their chances in each of the stages of their life transitions.

Structural Violence Against Young People

The myths outlined earlier have created what some scholars are calling a "policy panic."[63] Policy panic has led to a greater emphasis on security approaches to address the problem of violence instead of investing in violence prevention or addressing the root causes of conflict.[64] For example, policies and practice are too often based on a fear of the "Other," which prompts the use of securitized approaches to address short-term problems rather than sustainable responses to long-term grievances.[65] Simpson argues that these policy panics have entrenched a form of structural violence that results in violence against and further exclusion of young people.

In the United States, widespread systemic racism in the criminal justice system, for example, means that "68 percent of [African American] men born since the mid-1970s have prison records."[66] People of color in the United States have experienced structural barriers to securing quality housing, healthcare, employment, and education for many decades, and these barriers permeate public policies, institutional practices, and cultural narratives, including within the criminal justice system, perpetuating racial inequalities.

Many young people in both urban and rural areas feel excluded from equitable access to decision-making structures and opportunities. The "Missing Peace" study describes this as a "form of structural and psychological violence that is indivisible from their political, social, cultural and economic disempowerment."[67] This is known as the violence of exclusion, and it causes young people to lose trust in the state. The types of exclusion young people experience can be grouped into six main categories: exclusion from political participation, exclusion from peace processes, exclusion from transitional justice processes, exclusion from economic prosperity, exclusion from cultural and civic spaces, and exclusion related to the COVID-19 pandemic.

Exclusion from Political Participation

Trust in governments has been declining among young and older citizens alike.[68] Political corruption alienates young people in two ways. First, young people under eighteen cannot vote or shape legislation, even though policies enacted today are inherited by young people as they grow up. Second, young people continue to name corruption as the biggest challenge they face, according to a survey carried out by the Accountability Lab and the World Economic Forum.[69] The vast majority of those surveyed believe corruption is holding their country back and depriving their generation of opportunity; corruption is also a key problem in elections and voting, obtaining legal documents and permits, workplace advancement, and avoiding problems with the police.[70] Therefore today there are many signs of political apathy, as young people tend to be less engaged in traditional political issues such as voting and political party membership (see Box 4.4 and Figure 4.1).[71] It is not due to a lack of interest in the political process; rather, it is the result of a "combination of contextual and psychosocial factors, including the real as well as perceived inadequacy of the existing political offer."[72]

Box 4.4 Youth Political Engagement at a Glance

- Globally, less than 6 percent of parliamentarians are under thirty-five years old, and less than 2.1 percent of parliamentarians are under thirty years old.[73]
- The gender imbalance is less pronounced among younger parliamentarians, where the male/female ratio is 60:40.[74]
- Voter turnout among those eighteen to twenty-five years old.[75]
- Two-thirds of countries do not consult young people in preparing poverty reduction strategies or national development plans.[76]

Many people view youth engagement in politics through a "youth deficit" lens.[77] In this model, young people (broadly defined as those between fifteen and thirty) are not considered smart enough to have political opinions; only adults are capable enough to socialize young people politically. Others argue, in contrast, that young people are already politically active through protests and other forms of social movement.[78]

Throughout history, young people have been at the forefront of democratic movements.[79] The pro-democracy movements in recent years, from the Arab Spring and Hong Kong to Sudan, Nigeria, and Myanmar, are clear signs that young people actively promote free and open societies. In the first two quarters of 2019, the world witnessed mass nationwide protests and strikes in Algeria and Sudan that led to the departure of two authoritarian leaders who had used brute force to stay in power; young people played prominent roles.[80] And in Myanmar, young people are risking their lives to mediate their country's future by protesting nonviolently against the illegal military takeover of power on February 1, 2021.[81] Research on nonviolent movements highlights that when the movements take an active and very public role to fight for the freedom and dignity of all people and deliberately choose not to use violence as a tactic, regimes that use violence lose credibility, eventually giving more confidence to the people.[82] Unfortunately, often the very youth who open the space in the first place lose their advantage after the movement has succeeded in its push for change, with older, more "knowledgeable" or better-connected and better-resourced actors " who maneuver in to steal the election, revolution or peace."[83] As a result, young people often occupy political spaces only temporarily; to survive within this difficult political space, they can turn to music or protests.[84]

Policymaking and practice must be attentive to diverse experiences and forms of inclusion in order to ensure equal protection of and participation by youth in the political sphere.

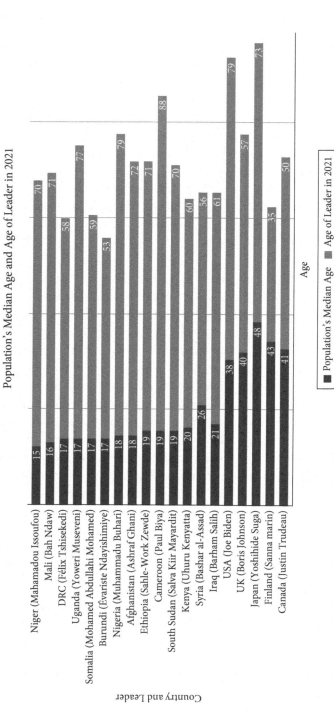

Figure 4.1 Median Age of a Country's Population vs. Age of the Country's Leader, 2021

Credit line: Image designed by Khushboo Shah.

Exclusion from Peace Processes

Though it is estimated that over 1,000 peace agreements have been signed in the last two decades, accords are traditionally negotiated by government leadership.[85] Thus young people often feel underrepresented, perceive the process as corrupt, and see themselves as primarily represented by nonstate actors.[86] Recent research on the topic of youth engagement in formal peace processes points out the importance of working with young people as critical partners for peace, as opposed to "inviting youth as an add-on or to tick the box of participation."[87] While scholars have argued that young people should be engaged in the implementation phases of a peace process, very little research exists about the roles of young people in shaping peace agreements themselves.[88]

The authors of the study *We Are Here* argue that young people as a group have a bridging effect across the three main conceptual frameworks of a peace process—elite dialogues (Track I), dialogue among those with influence on these elites (Track II), and grassroots dialogue (Track III)—and organically build relationships with influencers across all these tracks.[89] Using a three-layered integrated model (see Figure 4.2) provides a new way to understand youth engagement and contributions

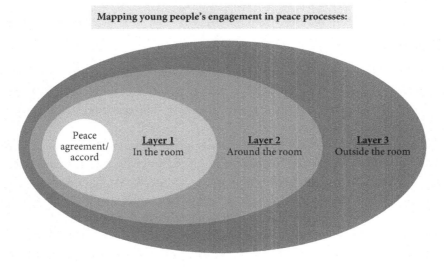

Mapping young people's engagement in peace processes:

Peace agreement/ accord

Layer 1
In the room

Layer 2
Around the room

Layer 3
Outside the room

Layer 1 -
In the room:

Youth participation within formal peace architecture and structures, inside the room during negotiations and political dialogues.

Layer 2 -
Around the room:

Young people not directly in the room, but close to the peace agreement and connected (able to get in the room) thorough formal or informal mechanisms.

Layer 3 -
Outside the room:

Young people who engage and participate through informal and alternative approaches.

Figure 4.2 Mapping Young People's Engagement in Peace Processes

Credit line: Altiok, Ali, and Irena Grizelj. "We Are Here: An Integrated Approach to Youth-Inclusive Peace Processes." UN Office of the Secretary General's Envoy on Youth, July 17, 2019. https://www.un.org/youthen voy/wp-content/uploads/2019/07/Global-Policy-Paper-Youth-Participation-in-Peace-Processes.pdf.

to peace processes, recognizing the interconnected nature of power and influence that exists today among young people.

Exclusion from Transitional Justice Processes

Breaking intergenerational cycles of violence and impunity is critical for transitioning nations. Children and youth need to be seen and treated as a special category of victims of violence, to help ensure that violations are addressed and that children in a recovering society grow up understanding that impunity is not acceptable. Sustainable peace therefore depends "on whether the next generations accepts or rejects it, how they are socialized during the peace process and their perception of what that peace has achieved."[90] If youth are generally sidelined from political and structured transitional justice processes, they are more likely to feel robbed of their ability to bring about change and resentful of what they have experienced, which may lead them to disengage.

Exclusion from Economic Prosperity

The economic conditions that affect young people are multilayered, and too frequently inhibit their contributions to their communities. Globally, youth unemployment and underemployment are high. The Global Financial Inclusion Database (Findex) released by the World Bank shows that young people ages fifteen to twenty-four are 33 percent less likely to own a bank account than an adult is.[91] Globally, over 40 percent of those fifteen to twenty-four years old lack a bank account or financial saving account.[92]

There is a gender disparity, too: in developing economies, 46 percent of men (males above the age of fifteen) report having an account with a financial institution (online or physical account), while only 37 percent of women (females age fifteen and above) do.[93] For young women, it goes beyond simply having a bank account, as they are expected to undertake unpaid domestic work, usually at the cost of their education. "Adolescent girls' enrolment in school often declines sharply due to the need for their help at home. Often, their education is considered less important than the education of their brothers or male peers."[94]

Investing in youth is considered smart economics.[95] According to the International Labour Organization (ILO), an increase in youth employment has a multiplier effect throughout the economy, boosting consumer demand and adding tax revenue. Asian high-growth economies (Hong Kong, South Korea, Singapore, and Taiwan) demonstrate this: capitalizing on the energy and dynamism of young populations was responsible for one-third of their economic growth from the 1960s to the 1990s.[96] On the other hand, not investing in young people leads to early school drop-out, stagnation in unskilled and low-paid jobs, high levels of underemployment, prolonged unemployment, substance abuse, and in some cases crime and violence.[97]

One important space for investing in young people is in education, as it has the potential to promote tolerance, diversity, and understanding. For example, research from Latin America, the Arab states, sub-Saharan Africa, and Central and Eastern Europe has shown that people with secondary education are more likely than those with only a primary education to express greater tolerance for people of different races or religions or toward immigrants.[98] It is estimated that doubling the percentage of youth with secondary education from 30 percent to 60 percent could reduce conflict by half.[99] Education also helps women have a voice in the family and society. In India, for example, "young women with at least a secondary education are 30 percent more likely to have a say over their choice of spouse than women with no education." More education also helps prevent child marriage and early pregnancy.[100] That said, poor-quality education does not accomplish as much, and it may not elicit the much-needed sense of hope for a better future. In fact, "young men may be more likely to join violent movements if education is not aligned with local employment opportunities."[101]

The evidence from the Survey on War-Affected Youth in Uganda suggests that the "main impact of war appears to be substantially lower education, diminished productivity, and increased poverty and inequality, largely due to time away rather than psychological distress. The impacts are greatest for children, who are more likely to have had schooling interrupted."[102] In a later report, the authors note that each year a young person is a child soldier, that young person sees a 55 percent reduction in wages in comparison to peers not abducted during the war.[103]

Exclusion from Cultural and Civic Spaces

Young people around the world talk about how difficult it is to be a civic activist. Activism is often met with violence, arrest, and suppression of speech. The *Freedom in the World 2019 Report* states that over the previous thirteen years, sixty-eight countries had a net decline in freedoms.[104] The Civicus Monitor, which rates the conditions for civil society or civic space in 196 countries, argues that only 3.4 percent of the world's population lives in countries with open civic space. The top ten violations to civic freedoms they identify include detaining protesters, harassment, censorship, intimidation, attacks on journalists, disruption of protests, restrictive laws, detaining journalists, use of excessive force, and detention of human rights defenders.[105] This shrinking civic space affects young people physically and psychologically. As governments and policies view young people as threats, public spaces such as town squares or online platforms are increasingly regulated and shut down. Congregating in these spaces provides a sense of community and a healthy outlet; shrinking space for young people poses a threat to democracy, the rule of law, and human rights.

Further compounding this shrinking civic space was the COVID-19 pandemic, which pushed many youth activists who relied on street protests and in-person activism to find other ways to organize. The number of public protests around the world dropped considerably in 2020. According to the Armed Conflict Location and Event Data Project, the number of protests between the first and second quarters of 2019 and the first two quarters of 2020 ending in May 2020 decreased by 38 percent around the world.[106]

Before the COVID-19 pandemic, it was not just physical civic space that was shrinking; digital spaces were also being restricted. In recent years social media has infiltrated every aspect of life, especially in digitally connected societies and especially for youth. Because of the internet and social media, young people can instantly see what is happening both in their backyards and in faraway places. They are immediate witnesses to the tragic problems of other young people: poverty, human rights abuses, gender and ethnic discrimination, shrinking civic space, and rapid climate change, to name but a few. As a result, they suffer from psychological stress.[107] Additionally, they can join movements virtually; the Arab Spring and the #MeToo movements have gone global. Borders no longer restrict connections across the world, and the realities of the world reshape expectations and aspirations. Youth activists, traversing local to global spaces online, could be broadly called "organic globalizers," insofar as "everyday life is a local/global space" for youth."[108]

Partly as a result of this, online platforms such as Facebook and WhatsApp are scrutinized by the state, security, and intelligence institutions.[109] They have also been used to facilitate increased violence and hate crimes.[110] Young people who disproportionately rely on new forms of media are the focus of much of the control, misinformation, and surveillance being newly imposed by oppressive regimes.

Young people with disabilities are particularly excluded from civic space. They seem to be underrepresented in mainstream youth-led organizations. Furthermore, young people are underrepresented in disability advocacy organizations and networks. Similarly, young women and young people who are sexual and gender minorities of varying sociocultural and economic backgrounds are particularly vulnerable.[111]

Exclusion and the COVID-19 Pandemic

In 2020, the COVID-19 global pandemic shocked the world, disrupting young people worldwide at least as much as older people. Traditional rituals of going to school, graduating, going to places of employment, and visiting places of worship all stopped as countries locked down to stop the spread of a virus that didn't discriminate based on religion or nationality, but has had a devastating impact on the poor globally. It quickly became a defining cultural and political moment for young people globally, while exposing the deep cracks in our social, political, economic, and health systems. Socioeconomic inequalities caused already marginalized populations to suffer disproportionately from the pandemic.[112] Many young people faced acute risks because of their economic and employment situations. As global unemployment rose because of restrictions on mobility and commerce, young people were particularly vulnerable; they were already three times more likely to be unemployed compared to an adult, up to 77 percent of working youth worldwide held jobs in the informal sector, and 126 million were classified as "extreme or moderate working poor."[113] The focus on COVID-19 also meant fewer resources dedicated to other diseases affecting children and youth, especially when the healthcare systems of conflict-affected areas were already devastated. For instance, twenty-three countries suspended measles vaccinations, potentially leaving up to 80 million children at risk.[114]

Existing social norms often made young women, LGBTQI, and disabled young people face added marginalization in healthcare access; for example, adolescents are the only age group for whom HIV/AIDS-related deaths have increased over the last fifteen years.[115] Young migrants and refugees faced additional challenges. In some cases, there is rising concern that xenophobic sentiments from host communities may make access to healthcare, food, and other services even more difficult.[116] For 2020 alone, the pandemic could double the number of people facing acute hunger, up to 265 million people globally, while those facing chronic hunger could also increase from the current 815 million people globally.[117] While COVID-19 has created novel challenges for youth, the exclusionary structures that created vulnerabilities among young people long preceded the crisis. Transforming those structures is critical in a post-pandemic world, so that the global community will be better prepared to manage the next crisis.

Policy Takeaways

Policies and programming based on problematic assumptions and misconceptions not only limit the positive contributions of young people but also result in ineffective use of taxpayer money for violence containment.[118] Global concerns over terrorism, organized transnational crime, and violent extremism perpetuate negative and inaccurate stereotypes and result in preemptive, hard security and law enforcement approaches that are not cost-effective and are even counterproductive.[119] These approaches further stigmatize youth, deepen their sense of injustice, and limit and repress avenues for peaceful expression and action.

Young People in Action

This section outlines how young people are organized and in what ways they are constructively influencing the world around them. Much youth-led peacebuilding work is local, small-scale, and peer-to-peer, but it can also extend community-wide and even to a national and international scale through youth clubs and national and international-level networking and programming.

Despite the enormous impact of youth, 64 percent of youth-led organizations around the world operate with budgets of less than $10,000 per year and rely on volunteers (who make up 97 percent of their members).[120] Unlike their adult counterparts, the youth groups surveyed exhibit much more horizontal leadership and are often gender balanced in leadership as well as in their membership.

How Young People Are Influencing and Addressing Conflict and Violence

In conflict-affected settings, youth-led groups struggle to operate safely under government repression.[121] Yet despite the exclusion young people experience, they are engaged in all stages of peace and conflict cycles. Youth populations have long been at the forefront of building peace in their communities, creating youth-led movements, organizations, and networks to mitigate adverse effects of conflict, prevent cycles of violence, and foster grassroots community development.[122]

Preventing Outbreaks of Conflict

Youth often work during times of relative peace to prevent violence before it breaks out. They employ diverse approaches, from education and after-school programming to peace debates and dialogues, civic and voter education, and community radio and festivals. For example, with support from the National Democratic Institute in 2010, youth-led, cross-tribal youth councils in Yemen successfully resolved at least twelve tribal conflicts through peer mediation teams they introduced in twenty local schools.[123] In Morocco, youth mediators reduced social tensions in Casablanca and Tetouan through conflict mediation and community dialogue facilitation, according to youth and community leaders surveyed.[124]

Tackling Violent Extremism and Criminal Violence

Young people around the world work to prevent and reduce extremist violence through efforts that celebrate diversity and constructive alternatives to violence. For example, several youth-led initiatives prevent recruitment by violent extremist and armed groups in the Lake Chad Basin region across Niger, Nigeria, Cameroon, and Chad.[125] Young people in the Netherlands target online polarization through their "Dare to Be Grey" platform, creating a "gray" middle ground for sharing and listening to different views and perspectives.[126] A network of twenty-three youth groups in Pakistan and Afghanistan, the Youth Peace Network, sends teams to schools and villages to prevent at-risk young people from joining militant groups through peer-to-peer engagement and training. They have reached 219 youth through their program, in addition to their influential school campaigns highlighting the negative impacts of militant groups and promoting the values of peace and nonviolence. Youth often lead this valuable work within repressive and dangerous policy environments that label broad populations of youth as threats to national security.[127] Around the world, young peacebuilders have highlighted how counterterrorism strategies frequently violate human rights and suppress peaceful protest and legitimate political expression and organization.

Young people involved in gangs and organized crime in places such as El Salvador, Guatemala, Honduras, Colombia, and Nigeria are manipulated and mobilized by elders and political elites to join gangs and criminal groups.[128] Despite the risks, many youth undertake courageous and creative initiatives to reduce organized crime and youth participation in violent gangs.

In the United States, Cure Violence's Safe Streets program in Baltimore worked with former members of gangs and violent groups to mediate conflicts and serve as role models for young people at risk for involvement in gun violence; participants were less likely to support the use of guns for settling disputes than those who did not experience Safe Streets programming.[129]

Preventing Election-Related Violence

A three-year youth-owned and -led initiative in Kenya called Yes Youth Can! showed promising results.[130] The initiative was set up to better engage young people impacted by the post-election violence of 2007 and 2008. Young people organized themselves into youth parliaments, called *bunges,* active in approximately 20,000 villages. In preparation for the 2013 national election in the country, youth helped 40,000 young people obtain the national ID cards required for them to vote. A complementary peace caravan carried messages of nonviolence, and peace pledges by major presidential candidates contributed significantly to reducing violence during and after the elections.[131]

Building Social Cohesion During Ongoing Violent Conflict

Youth also intervene to mitigate the impact of violent conflict. In Myanmar in 2015, for example, in response to increasing interethnic tension, violence, and discrimination against the country's Rohingya population, young people launched a social media campaign. Using the hashtags #myfriend or #friendshiphasnoboundaries, the campaign built a Facebook following of more than 30,000 in two years, encouraging people to post photos of themselves with friends of other ethnicities.[132] In another example, the Elman Peace and Human Rights Center, a youth-led organization in Somalia, has supported disengagement and reintegration of young combatants since the 1990s through their "Drop the Gun, Pick Up the Pen" initiative; over 3,500 individuals have participated in their program, which connects newly disengaged youth with reintegrated combatants who serve as mentors and help sensitize communities to reintegration. This center has also collaborated with the Ministry of Security on the national action plan for combating violent extremism.[133] In Liberia, a local organization led by reformed combatants and other formerly high-risk youth developed a short-term cognitive-behavioral therapy program for young people who have engaged in crime, drugs, or violence, including former members of armed groups. A randomized evaluation carried out between 2009 and 2012 found that those who received therapy were 55 percent less likely to carry a weapon in the short term, and recipients reported a long-term reduction in the impulse to use weapons to deal with needs or grievances.[134]

Shaping and Influencing Formal Peace Processes

Young people have been playing a multitude of roles, both formal and informal, during peace processes. For example, in South Sudan's High-Level Revitalization Forum, youth representatives outlined the important role of young people in the disarmament, demobilization, and reintegration (DDR) efforts in the country. It resulted in a more youth-sensitive approach to the DDR programs. A quota system by age in political parties was introduced, and a provision was included stating that that the minister of youth should be younger than forty. Strategic engagement between youth and women's groups helped ensure refugee populations were included in the negotiations, which led to better understanding of resettlement issues.[135]

Young people have also influenced peace processes in supportive roles. For example, tech-savvy young people played key roles in Myanmar via the former Myanmar Peace Centre (MPC), which provided technical support to the negotiations; approximately 60 percent of MPC personnel were under thirty-five, and 40 percent were young women.[136]

Responding to the COVID-19 Pandemic

Young people are finding innovative means to mitigate the effects of the COVID-19 pandemic, particularly in youthful countries, where the burden of containing the pandemic, preventing unrest, and rebuilding communities mostly falls on their shoulders.[137] They are stepping in as active citizens, utilizing the power of their numbers and their technological skills to contain the pandemic and help the most vulnerable in hard-to-reach places.[138]

Investing in young people as critical partners has long-term benefits. Young people who have received peace and conflict resolution training are more likely to prevent gender-based violence, disrupt bullying and discrimination, and become positively involved in their communities over time. There is evidence from Colombia, Democratic Republic of Congo, and Nepal showing that when young people participated in peace and conflict resolution opportunities as children, they were better able to understand what bullying and domestic violence meant, and had better tools to address them as they got older.[139] Building on how young people are shaping their communities and countries, the international community, in particular the United Nations, is starting to pay attention to how young people can be critical stakeholders in peace and security.

Transforming the Violence of Exclusion: The Beginning of a New Field in Foreign Policy

In December 2015, the United Nations Security Council unanimously adopted Resolution 2250, which for the first time recognized young women and men as essential partners and critical actors in peace and security.[140] This historic resolution established a normative framework for seeing young people as partners in peace and security.

The Untold Story of a New Normative Framework

Inspired by the historic UN Security Council Resolution 1325 on women, peace and security (passed in 2000), a handful of leaders in the United Nations, civil society, and international youth networks (co-led by the author of this chapter) started to lay the foundations for a movement that recognized young women and young men as political actors who play a critical role in conflict prevention and resolution.[141] This core group of people decided to focus on youth because while children below the age of eighteen had a robust ecosystem of support, older youth were missing from policy discourse and lacked dedicated institutions, policy frameworks, or other key support mechanisms.[142]

Initially the idea of young people as partners received minimal attention or support in the Security Council. When youth and civil society actors made a case for youth, they realized they could not do it alone. They had to work with multiple stakeholders within and outside the United Nations, forming an interagency working group to collaborate.[143]

In 2014, the working group launched the Guiding Principles on Young People's Participation in Peacebuilding to overcome the reality that the UN, international NGOs, youth-led groups, donors, and governments all speak different languages.[144] The Guiding Principles laid out the common language that had emerged through the working group. The coalition of partners successfully advocated for a Security Council resolution; Resolution 2250, which urges states to increase youth representation in decision-making at all levels, was unanimously adopted in December 2015.[145] The resolution established a normative framework on the positive roles of young people in conflict and crisis settings. The draft resolution, submitted by eleven member states, was unanimously adopted during a solemn eight-minute proceeding in the Security Council chamber at UN headquarters. The excitement was palpable, as attested to by the applause of young people and youth practitioners. It was a fantastic day for those who had worked for years toward adoption of the resolution (see Figure 4.3).

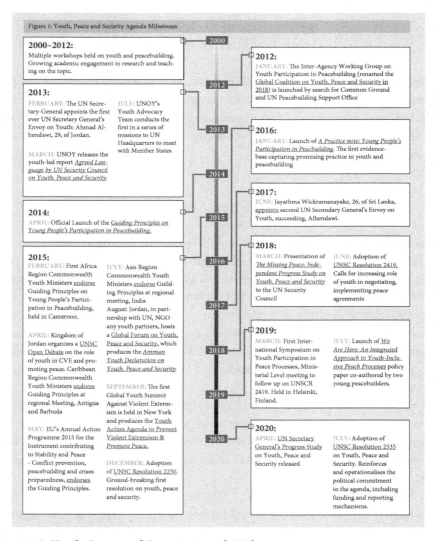

Figure 4.3 Youth, Peace, and Security Agenda Milestones

Credit line: Report: *More than a Milestone: The Road to UN Security Council Resolution 2250 on Youth, Peace and Security*. Authors: Helen Berents and Saji Prelis. Publisher: Global Coalition on Youth, Peace & Security. Page 7. https://www.youth4peace.info/topic/more-milestone-road-unscr-2250-yps.

Young women and men saw the resolution as a tool for advocacy to their governments, for partnership with state institutions and the UN, and for collaboration within their communities. Then, in June 2018, the UN Security Council unanimously adopted Resolution 2149, which reaffirmed the need to implement Resolution 2250 and focused more on youth as political actors, including mandating member states to engage young people in formal peace processes.[146] In July 2020, a third resolution was unanimously adopted, further strengthening the normative frameworks that encourage governments to see, listen to, and engage young people as partners. Resolution 2535 specifically recognized the increasing threats young people experience and urged states "to foster an enabling and safe environment for youth working on peace and security, including by protecting civic and political space and condemning hate speech and incitement to violence."[147]

A number of ingredients contributed to the movement's success. Specifically:

- *Long-term perspective.* Leaders in the effort took time to build the foundation necessary, without leaving people behind.
- *Partnerships and trust.* Working on this agenda required actors from across dividing lines to come together. Each set of actions brought more partners into the Global Coalition on Youth, Peace, and Security.[148]
- *Common language.* As partners came together, a common language was needed to ensure that institutional stakeholders built on each other's experiences and strengths without competition. Developing the Guiding Principles required stakeholders to collaborate and put the cause above self-interest.
- *Collaboration for collective impact.* Every stakeholder embraced the idea of collaborating to secure a global policy framework on youth, an achievement bigger than anything that could be accomplished individually.
- *Horizontal leadership model.* Traditional top-down models were eschewed and a more horizontal model was embraced, allowing everyone to feel like a leader and a collaborator.
- *Useful content and events.* Social media promotion was key to success. Events included the launch of the Guiding Principles, the Commonwealth Secretariat's ministerial meetings, an open debate at the United Nations Security Council on youth and countering violent extremism, and the First Global Forum on Youth, Peace, and Security in Amman, Jordan. Events made stakeholders feel progress was being made.[149]
- *Low cost.* Many results were accomplished without grants or new funds.
- *Youth-driven with broad coalition support.* Resolution 2250 came about because of youth activists. Over 11,000 young people from 109 countries helped advocate for the resolution, giving young women and men around the world a sense of ownership. The process of developing this resolution validated grassroots work, showing that international organizations had started to listen to youth movements and take their requests seriously.

- *Vision of youth as partners and positive contributors to society.* There was tremendous pressure to talk about youth within the traditional counterterrorism narratives and frameworks between 2015 and 2018. At the same time, the word "peacebuilding" was facing tremendous pushback from those who thought it was too weak, a Western agenda imposed on the global South, a violation of sovereignty, or all of those. Regardless, the core value of youth as partners was not changed to satisfy a temporary political agenda.

Using the foundation of UN Security Council Resolution 2250, a new set of norms regarding people-centered peace and security must be established (see Box 4.5). At the core of this is the need to carefully think through incentives for governments and multilateral organizations to support youth-inclusive systems and accountability mechanisms.[150]

Box 4.5 Transforming Violence of Exclusion

Building and sustaining peace in partnership with young women, men and sexual gender minorities requires a shift from reactive security responses to a comprehensive violence prevention approach. Transforming the violence of exclusion is the best means to transform violence (including extremist violence).

Looking Ahead

We are left with a question: why are most youth peaceful? Youth can explain this mystery. However, first, they must be asked.[151]

The youth, peace, and security movement has made significant progress. Now it is critical to translate this recognition into support for young people as partners in peace, security, and development. In the future, the youth, peace, and security movement must shift to foster a comprehensive ecosystem of policies and programmatic approaches across local, national, and international levels. Regional bodies and national governments must adopt and contextualize policies that build on UN Security Council Resolutions 2250 and 2419. International and national NGOs must adopt new approaches to engaging young people. To accomplish this, three mutually reinforcing strategies will harness young people's innovative contributions to peace. These complementary strategies are inclusion, partnerships, and investments.[152]

- *Inclusion.* Governments, regional bodies (such as the African Union, regional economic communities [RECs], and regional mechanisms [RMs]), the European Union, and UN agencies must create policies that prioritize young people as partners, not beneficiaries. The policies must build on young people's visions to transform peace and security processes from exclusion towards inclusion. Political transition processes, including peace processes, are particularly important. Specific efforts must include developing young people's participatory national assessments followed by comprehensive audits of existing laws and policies to target reforms.

- *Partnerships.* The global youth, peace, and security movement was developed through a partnership between youth and non-youth actors, civil society organizations, and multilateral agencies. This approach has been successful and deserves replication through the creation of coalitions at the regional, national, and local levels. The spirit and intent of these coalitions should be collaborative actions so that collective-level impact is experienced.

- *Investments.* To ensure that young people can realize their potential for leadership, increased investments in their capacity, agency, and leadership are required. The progress study *The Missing Peace* set a target of investing $1.8 billion in young people's leadership by 2025—in other words, $1 per young person. To target investments, coalitions of donors should work with young people to determine how resources are allocated, thereby moving from a transactional relationship to a real partnership model.

Building and sustaining peace in partnership with young women and men requires a shift from reactive security responses to comprehensive violence prevention efforts. Transforming the violence of exclusion is the best means to transform violence, including extremist violence.

The young environmental activist Greta Thunberg summarized the urgency around climate change in her speech at the World Economic Forum's annual meeting in Davos, Switzerland, in January 2019.[153] She concluded by saying to policymakers and world leaders, "I want you to act as you would in a crisis. I want you to act as if your house is on fire." A similar argument can be made in preventing violence and sustaining peace. The international community must radically change how young women and men are seen and supported in communities. It is up to all of us to act urgently. Young people are not just a demographic reality; they offer an urgent democratic opportunity that needs to be seized, so that this generation of young people has better alternatives to violence in coming years.

Notes

1. Quoted in SFCG 2009a, 3.
2. See also Search for Common Ground toolkits for children and youth, https://www.sfcg.org/tag/children-youth-toolkits/; for youth-led research guidance. https://www.sfcg.org/youth-led-research//.
3. Sommers 2012b.
4. Hanwana 2012.

5. World Bank 2006, 5.
6. Hagerty 2018.
7. UNFPA 2015a.
8. Rubenstein et al. 2019.
9. McEvoy-Levy 2001b.
10. United Nations, 2021. "If I Disappear Global Report on Protecting Young People in Civic Space." https://globalvirtual.solutions/youthprotection/.
11. Blattman 2005–2008.
12. Annan and Blattman 2006.
13. Annan and Blattman 2010.
14. Annan et al. 2008.
15. Dokkedahl et al. 2015.
16. Lewis 2016.
17. Crenshaw 1991.
18. See Grau and Prelis 2014.
19. UNFPA 2002.
20. Annan and Brier 2010.
21. United Nations 2019.
22. Sivakumaran 2010; United Nations 2019.
23. Kapur and Muddell 2016.
24. Kapur and Muddell 2016.
25. Myrttinen and Daigle 2017.
26. Myrttinen and Daigle 2017, 6.
27. United Nations 2019.
28. Simpson 2018.
29. UNFPA 2018.
30. UNDESA 2015; UNFPA 2018.
31. UNFPA 2018.
32. UNFPA 2018.
33. OECD 2018, 7.
34. UN Security Council 2020.
35. "Young People Urged to Speak Out: The World Is Listening." UNFPA, 23 August 2010. https://www.unfpa.org/news/young-people-urged-speak-out-world-listening.
36. Simpson 2018.
37. Hagerty 2018.
38. World Bank 2011a.
39. Goldstone 1991; Huntington 1997; Urdal 2006.
40. Pruitt 2021.
41. Nordås and Davenport 2013.
42. World Bank 2018.
43. UNHCR 2019.
44. IOM 2018.
45. UNHCR 2019.
46. Simpson 2018, 22.
47. World Bank 2018, 63.
48. Prelis 2018.
49. Simpson 2018.
50. This Youth Action Agenda was the first youth-led document produced by close to 100 young people living in the front lines of countries experiencing violent extremism's consequences. They produced it as part of the US State Department Summit on Youth and Violent

Extremism. The action agenda defines what violent extremism is to young people, what they are doing to address it, and the ways key stakeholders can partner with them in strengthening their role as key actors in preventing violent extremism in their communities. The UN Security Council further recognized this Youth Action Agenda by citing it in UN Security Council Resolution 2250 on Youth, Peace and Security. See also Youth Transforming Violent Extremism. Peacebuilding Approaches to Working with Young People by Lakshitha Saji Prelis, Michael Shipler, Rachel Walsh Taza, and Lena Slachmuijlder in the Ecology of Violent Extremism. Perspectives on Peacebuilding and Human Security. Edited by Lisa Schirch. Roman & Littlefield 2018, 278.

51. Simpson 2018, 26.
52. UNDP 2019, 73.
53. Mercy Corps 2015.
54. Mercy Corps 2013.
55. Tibi 2017.
56. Schott Foundation 2015.
57. Crenshaw, Ocen, and Nanda 2015.
58. Sawyer 2019.
59. Hetey and Eberhardt 2014; Eberhardt et al. 2004.
60. Edwards, Lee, and Esposito 2019.
61. Equal Justice Initiative n.d. "The Presumption of Guilt."
62. Equal Justice Initiative 2017.
63. Simpson 2018; Mutisi, Olonisakin, and Ismail 2017.
64. Simpson 2018; Novelli 2017; Wortley et al. 2008.
65. Wortley et al. 2008.
66. Western and Pettit 2010.
67. Simpson 2018, 61.
68. Edelman 2017.
69. World Economic Forum 2015.
70. World Economic Forum 2015.
71. IPU 2016.
72. Cammaerts et al. 2013.
73. Office of the Secretary-General's Envoy on Youth n.d.; IPU 2018.
74. IPU 2018.
75. Office of the Secretary-General's Envoy on Youth n.d.
76. These results emerged from over 1.3 million young people of a total number of approximately 2.1 million respondents who participated in the MyWorld2015 survey undertaken by the Office of the UN Secretary-General's Envoy on Youth to ensure the Post-2015 Development agenda reflects the aspirations of people around the world. This agenda led to the Sustainable Development Goals that the world community agreed to in 2015.
77. Damon 2004.
78. Earl, Maher, and Elliott 2017.
79. IPU 2016, 4.
80. According to the CIA World Factbook (CIA n.d.), it's estimated that 45 percent of the Algerian population is below twenty-four; the median age is twenty-eight. For Sudan, the same source estimates that 63 percent of the population is below twenty-four, and the median age is 17.9 years.
81. USIP 2021.
82. Stephan and Chenoweth 2008.
83. Berents and McEvoy-Levy 2015, 20.
84. Berents and McEvoy-Levy 2015.

85. Online databases that store peace agreements vary in their count of signed agreements in the last two decades. For example, the UN Peacemaker site lists 457 peace agreements; the PA-X from the Political Settlements Program lists 1,518 agreements; the Language of Peace lists around 1000 peace agreements. Altiok and Grizelj 2019, 9.

86. Taylor 2018.

87. Altiok and Grizelj 2019.

88. Schwartz 2010; Berents and McEvoy-Levy 2015.

89. Grizelj and Mubashir 2018.

90. McEvoy-Levy 2001b, 5.

91. Demargic-Kunt and Klapper 2012.

92. Demargic-Kunt et al. 2017.

93. Demargic-Kunt et al. 2017, 5.

94. UNDP 2006.

95. World Bank 2011a.

96. Paasonen and Urdal 2016.

97. World Bank 2011a.

98. Ehmer et al. 2017; UNESCO 2014, 13.

99. UNESCO 2014, 13.

100. UNESCO 2014, 6.

101. Burde et al. 2011, 20.

102. Annan and Blattman 2009.

103. Annan and Blattman 2010.

104. Freedom House 2019.

105. CIVICUS 2020.

106. ACLED 2020.

107. Hampton et al. 2015.

108. Berents and McEvoy-Levy 2015, 14.

109. Chakrabarti 2018.

110. Birnbaum 2019; Satariano 2019; Isaac and Roose 2019; Hatzipanagos 2018.

111. Meyers 2017.

112. In the United States, Black, Latino, and Native American populations face higher rates of infection and death. Its impact on poor and fragile countries could have long-term consequences. In Kenya, the poor are facing violent suppression in their efforts to access basic humanitarian aid. In India, where over 80 percent of people work in the informal sector, the headlines read a lockdown as an order to starve. See Odula and Juma 2020; USIP 2020; Godoy 2020.

113. ILO 2020.

114. See United Nations 2020.

115. Columbia University 2014.

116. See Žagar 2015.

117. Kretchmer 2020.

118. See Stimson Center 2018; US State Department 2019.

119. Aliaga and O'Farrell 2017; Attree 2017; Civicus 2017; Jennings 2017; Muggah 2012; Neumann 2017, 25; Nordås and Davenport 2013.

120. SFCG and UNOY 2017b.

121. SFCG and UNOY 2017b.

122. Schwartz 2010; Simpson 2018; McGill et al. 2015; McEvoy-Levy 2001b; Del Felice and Wisler 2007; SFCG and UNOY 2017b.

123. National Democratic Institute 2012.

124. SFCG 2009b.

125. Ekpon 2017.

126. This report was supported by the US State Department and is the culmination of online consultations and in-person interviews with youth, youth-led organizations, and government officials engaged in preventing and countering violent extremism (P/CVE) efforts in fourteen countries across three continents. In total, 122 individuals from Bangladesh, Cameroon, Indonesia, Jordan, Kazakhstan, Kyrgyzstan, Morocco, the Netherlands, Niger, Nigeria, Pakistan, Somalia, Tunisia, and Sri Lanka took part in these conversations. In addition to the consultations, over 300 youth responded to an online poll as part of the consultation process. Williams, Walsh-Taza, and Prelis 2015.

127. Williams, Walsh-Taza, and Prelis 2015.

128. OAS 2016; InterPeace 2017; Shepler 2012.

129. Webster et al. 2012.

130. NORC 2016.

131. NORC 2016.

132. Rigby 2015.

133. UNDP 2019, 33.

134. Blattman et al. 2017.

135. Altiok and Grizelj 2019, 18.

136. Altiok and Grizelj 2019, 22.

137. The UN Secretary General's Envoy on Youth has been capturing the creative ways young people are impacting their communities.

138. In consultations with over 400 peacebuilders from over sixty countries, a study by Peace Direct concluded, "Youth have creative ideas of how to overcome the challenges of lockdown, are skilled with technology and social media, and can strengthen the online capacity of the population" (Youth, Peace, and Security 2020). COVID-19 and the impact on local peacebuilding—Conducive Space for Peace, Humanity United and Peace Direct https://www.conducivespace.org/covid-19-and-the-impact-on-local-peacebuilding/.

139. McGill et al. 2015.

140. UN Security Council 2015.

141. The author of this chapter was intimately involved in shaping this new field, and therefore this section is written to provide a firsthand experience of the evolution of this field.

142. This includes dedicated UN agencies and international nongovernmental organizations providing protection and social services focused on child well-being, international norms and policies (such as the Convention on the Rights of the Child) that provide legal protection for children, funding instruments dedicated to ensure children have the necessary services, to mention just some of the key support mechanisms.

143. Berents and Prelis 2020.

144. Search for Common Ground (SCFG) n.d. At first the group was called the Sub–Working Group on Youth and Peacebuilding; later it became the Global Coalition on Youth, Peace, and Security.

145. The partners included United Nations agencies; international organizations such as World Vision, Mercy Corps, and Search for Common Ground; youth-led organizations supported by the United Network of Young Peacebuilders; intergovernmental bodies like the Commonwealth Secretariat; and several scholars.

146. UN Security Council 2018.

147. UN Security Council 2020.

148. The Global Coalition is co-chaired by the UN Peacebuilding Support Office, part of the UN Department of Political and Peacebuilding Affairs, United Network of Young Peacebuilders (youth-led group), and Search for Common Ground, an international peacebuilding organization. The Global Coalition's webpage is at https://www.youth4peace.info/about_GCYPS.

149. Global Forum on Youth, Peace and Security, 2015.
150. For resources regarding including youth in programming, see: Translating youth, peace and security policy into practice https://www.youth4peace.info/book-page/translating-youth-peace-security-policy-practice-guide-building-coalitions; Practice Note: Young People's Participation in Peacebuilding. https://www.youth4peace.info/search/all/Practice%20Note; Mapping Youth Leaders for Peacebuilding. https://www.sfcg.org/wp-content/uploads/2014/09/Mapping-Youth-Leaders-for-Peacebuilding.pdf; and Children, Youth, & Conflict: An Introductory Toolkit for Engaging Children & Youth in Conflict Transformation. https://www.sfcg.org/wp-content/uploads/2014/10/cyc-toolkit1.pdf.
151. Sommers 2015.
152. Simpson 2018 outlines more details of these three strategies, while this section attempts to summarize them.
153. Workman 2019.

Bibliography

Acker, J. 1990. "Hierarchies, Jobs, Bodies: A Theory of Gendered Organizations." *Gender and Society 4*, no. 2: 139–158. https://www.jstor.org/stable/189609.

ACLED. 2020. "Year in Review." Armed Conflict Location and Event Data Project. https://reliefweb.int/sites/reliefweb.int/files/resources/ACLED_AnnualReport2019_WebVersion.pdf.

Adegoke, Y. 2017. "The World's Youngest Continent Will Keep Being Run by Its Oldest Leaders." Quartz Africa, December 18. https://qz.com/africa/1162490/the-youngest-continent-keeps-on-being-run-by-the-oldest-leaders/.

Aliaga, L., and K. T. O'Farrell. 2017. "Counter-terror in Tunisia: Job Done or Mission Misunderstood?" Safeworld. March 2. https://www.saferworld.org.uk/resources/news-and-analysis/post/216-counter-terror-in-tunisia-job-done-or-mission-misunderstood.

Altiok, A., and I. Grizelj. 2019. "We Are Here: An Integrated Approach to Youth Inclusive Peace Processes." Office of the UN Secretary General's Envoy on Youth. https://www.un.org/youthenvoy/wp-content/uploads/2019/07/Global-Policy-Paper-Youth-Participation-in-Peace-Processes.pdf.

Amnesty International. 2018. *The Amnesty International Report 2017/18: The State of the World's Human Rights*. Amnesty International. https://www.amnesty.org/en/documents/pol10/6700/2018/en/.

Anderlini, S. 2011. "World Development Report, Gender Background Paper." World Bank, Washington, DC. https://openknowledge.worldbank.org/handle/10986/9250.

Annan, J., and C. Blattman. 2010. "The Consequences of Child Soldiering." *Review of Economics and Statistics* 92, no. 4: 882–898. https://www.chrisblattman.com/documents/research/2010.Consequences.RESTAT.pdf.

Annan, J., and C. Blattman. 2009. "Child Combatants in Northern Uganda: Reintegration Myths and Realities." In *Security and Post-Conflict Reconstruction: Dealing with Fighters in the Aftermath of War*, edited by R. Muggah, 103–126). London: Routledge. https://chrisblattman.com/documents/research/2012.ChildrenAndWar.PoPs.pdf.

Annan, J., and C. Blattman. 2006. "The Abduction and Return Experience of Youth." SWAY Research Brief 1. https://chrisblattman.com/documents/policy/sway/SWAY.RB1.pdf.

Annan, J., C. Blattman, K. Carlson, and D. Mazurana. 2008. "The State of Female Youth in Northern Uganda: Findings from the Survey of War-Affected Youth (SWAY) Phase II." Feinstein International Center, Tufts University. https://fic.tufts.edu/wp-content/uploads/SWAYIIreporthighres.pdf.

Annan, J., and M. Brier. 2010. "The Risk of Return: Intimate Partner Violence in Northern Uganda's Armed Conflict." *Social Science and Medicine* 70, no. 1: 152–159. https://doi.org/10.1016/j.socscimed.2009.09.027.

Anti-Defamation League. 2019. "Murder and Extremism in the United States in 2018." https://www.adl.org/murder-and-extremism-2018

Ashar, S. M. 2002. "Immigration Enforcement and Subordination: The Consequences of Racial Profiling After September 11." *Connecticut Law Review* 34: 1185.

Attree, L. 2017. "Shouldn't YOU Be Countering Violent Extremism?" Safeworld. March 14. https://www.saferworld.org.uk/resources/news-and-analysis/post/706-shouldnt-you-be-countering-violent-extremism.

Bauer, M., A. Cassar, J. Chytilova, and J. Henrich. 2011. "Warfare During Ontogeny Increases Egalitarian and Parochial Motivations." Working paper. https://editorialexpress.com/cgi-bin/conference/download.cgi?db_name=res2012&paper_id=240.

Beckett, L. 2019. "Parkland One Year On: What Victories Have Gun Control Advocates Seen?" *The Guardian*, February 19. https://www.theguardian.com/us-news/2019/feb/14/parkland-school-shooting-anniversasry-gun-control-victories.

Bellows, J., and E. Miguel. 2009. "War and Local Collective Action in Sierra Leone." *Journal of Public Economics* 93: 1144–1157. http://emiguel.econ.berkeley.edu/assets/miguel_research/24/_Paper__War_and_Local_Collective_Action.pdf.

Berancourt, T. S., R. McBain, and E. A. Newnham. 2012. "Trajectories of Internalizing Problems in War-Affected Sierra Leonean Youth: Examining Conflict and Post-Conflict Factors." *Child Development* 84 (2) (September 24): 455–470.

Berents, H., and S. McEvoy-Levy. 2015. "Theorising Youth and Everyday Peace(building)." *Peacebuilding* 3, no. 2: 115–125. doi: 10.1080/21647259.2015.1052627.

Berkman, H. 2007. "Social Exclusion and Violence in Latin America and the Caribbean." Working Paper No. 613, Inter-American Development Bank, Research Department, Washington, DC. https://publications.iadb.org/en/publication/social-exclusion-and-violence-latin-america-and-caribbean.

Birnbaum, E. 2019. "Facebook Unveils Plans for Preventing Spread of Misinformation Ahead of Elections Worldwide." *The Hill*, January 28. https://thehill.com/policy/technology/427296-facebook-unveils-new-plans-for-punishing-fake-news-ahead-of-european.

Blattman, C. 2009. "From Violence to Voting: War and Political Participation in Uganda." *American Political Science Review* 103, no. 2: 231–247. doi: 10.1017/S0003055409090212.

Blattman, C. 2005–2008. "Survey of War-Affected Youth." http://sway-uganda.org/.

Blattman, C., and J. Annan. 2010. "On the Nature and Causes of LRA Abduction: What the Abductees Say." In *The Lord's Resistance Army: Myth and Reality*, edited by Tim Allen and Koen Vlassenroot, 132–155. London: Zen Books. https://chrisblattman.com/documents/research/2009.Nature&Causes.LRAbook.pdf.

Blattman, C., J. Jamison, T. Koroknay-Palicz, K. Rodrigues, and M. Sheridan. 2017. "Sustainable Transformation for Youth in Liberia." Innovations for Poverty Action Dataverse. https://doi.org/10.7910/DVN/CORNOC.

Bohn, L. 2018. "The 28-Year-Old Woman Reshaping Afghanistan's Politics." CNN, October 17. https://edition.cnn.com/2018/10/17/opinions/afghan-parliamentary-election-women-outcome-bohn/index.html.

Brooks, A., D. Gatare, and R. Wolfe. 2017. "Reformed Warriors: A Case Study from Uganda." Mercy Corps. https://www.youth4peace.info/system/files/2018-04/13.%20CFR_Uganda%20-%20Reformed%20Warriors%20in%20Uganda_Mercycorps_0.pdf.

Burde, D., Kapit-Spitalny, A., Wahl, R., and Guven, O. 2011. *Education and Conflict Mitigation*. American Institutes for Research. Washington, DC: USAID.

Cammaerts, B., M. Bruter, S. Banaji, S. Harrison, and N. Anstead. 2013. "The Myth of Youth Apathy: Young Europeans' Critical Attitudes Towards Democratic Life." *American Behavioral Scientist and LSE Research* 58, no. 5: 645–664. doi: 10.1177/0002764213515992.

Caskey, M, and V. A. Anfara Jr. 2014. "Developmental Characteristics of Young Adolescents: Research Summary." Association for Middle Level Education. October. https://www.amle.org/BrowsebyTopic/WhatsNew/WNDet/TabId/270/ArtMID/888/ArticleID/455/Developmental-Characteristics-of-Young-Adolescents.aspx.

Chakrabarti, S. 2018. "Hard Questions: What Effect Does Social Media Have on Democracy?" Facebook. January 22. https://newsroom.fb.com/news/2018/01/effect-social-media-democracy/.

CIA. n.d. CIA World Factbook. https://www.cia.gov/the-world-factbook/.

Civicus. 2018. "People Power Under Attack 2018." https://monitor.civicus.org/PeoplePowerUnderAttack2018/.

Civicus. 2017. "State of Civil Society Report 2016." https://www.civicus.org/index.php/socs2016.

Civicus. 2016. "Year in Review: Civic Space." https://www.civicus.org/documents/reports-and-publications/SOCS/2016/summaries/YIR_Civic-Space.pdf.

Copland, S. 2019. "BBC Future Now." BBC. May 1. http://www.bbc.com/future/story/20190501-how-do-you-prevent-extremism.

Crenshaw, K. 1991. "Mapping the Margins: Intersectionality, Identity Politics, and Violence Against Women of Color." *Stanford Law Review* 43, no. 6: 1241–1299. doi:10.2307/1229039.

Crenshaw, K., P. Ocen, and J. Nanda. 2015. "Black Girls Matter: Pushed Out, Overpoliced and Underprotected." African American Policy Forum and Center for Intersectionality and Social Policy Studies. https://www.aapf.org/blackgirlsmatter.

Damon, W. 2004. "What Is Positive Youth Development?" *Annals of the American Academy of Political and Social Science* 591: 13–24. doi: 10.1177/0002716203260092.

Del Felice, C., and A. Wisler. 2007. "The Unexplored Power and Potential of Youth as Peacebuilders." *Journal of Peace Conflict and Development* 11.

Demargic-Kunt, A., and L. Klapper. 2012. "Measuring Financial Inclusion: The Global Findex." World Bank, Washington, DC.

Demirgüç-Kunt, A., L. Klapper, D. Singer, S. Ansar, and J. Hess. 2017. "The Global Findex Database 2017." World Bank, Washington, DC. https://globalfindex.worldbank.org/basic-page-overview.

Dokkedahl, S., H. Oboke, E. Ovuga, and A. Elklit. 2015. "The Psychological Impact of War and Abduction on Children in Northern Uganda: A Review." *International Journal of Mental Health and Psychiatry* 1, no. 3. doi: 10.4172/ 2471-4372.1000109.

Earl, J., T. V. Maher, and T. Elliott. 2017. "Youth, Activism, and Social Movements." *Sociology Compass* 11, no. 4: art. e12465. doi: 10.1111/soc4.12465.

Eberhardt, J. L., P. A. Goff, V. J. Purdie, and P. G. Davies. 2004. "Seeing Black: Race, Crime, and Visual Processing." *Journal of Personality and Social Psychology* 87, no. 6: 876–893.

Edelman. 2018a. "2018 Edelman Trust Barometer." https://www.edelman.com/research/2018-edelman-trust-barometer.

Edelman. 2018b. "Edelman Trust Barometer Global Report." https://www.edelman.com/sites/g/files/aatuss191/files/2018-10/2018_Edelman_Trust_Barometer_Global_Report_FEB.pdf.

Edelman. 2017. "2017 Edelman Trust Barometer." https://www.edelman.com/news-awards/2017-edelman-trust-barometer-reveals-global-implosion.

Edström, J., A. Hassinik, T. Shahrokh, and E. Stern, eds. 2015. *Engendering Men: A Collaborative Review of Evidence on Men and Boys in Social Change and Gender Equality.* London: Institute of Development Studies, Promundo-US, and Sonke Gender Justice.

Edwards, F., H. Lee, and M. Esposito. 2019. "Risk of Being Killed by Police Use of Force in the United States by Age, Race–Ethnicity, and Sex." *Proceedings of the National Academy of Sciences* 116, no. 34: 16793–16798. https://doi.org/10.1073/pnas.1821204116.

Ehmer, A. 2017. "Accommodating Religious Identity in Youth Peacebuilding Programs." Search for Common Ground. May. https://www.sfcg.org/wp-content/uploads/2017/05/Accomodating-Religious-Identity-in-Youth-Peacebuilding-Programs-050917-dr3.pdf.

Ekpon, T. 2017. "The Role of Young People in Preventing Violent Extremism in the Lake Chad Basin." Civil Society Platform for Peacebuilding and Statebuilding. https://www.youth4peace.info/system/files/2018-04/12.%20TP_The%20Role%20of%20Young%20People%20in%20Preventing%20Violent%20Extremism%20in%20the%20Lake%20Chad%20Basin_CSPPS.pdf.

Elbein, S. 2017. "The Youth Group That Launched a Movement at Standing Rock." *New York Times Magazine*, January 31. https://www.nytimes.com/2017/01/31/magazine/the-youth-group-that-launched-a-movement-at-standing-rock.html.

Equal Justice Initiative. 2017. "Black Children Five Times More Likely than White Youth to Be Incarcerated." September 14. https://eji.org/news/Black-children-five-times-more-likely-than-whites-to-be-incarcerated/.

Equal Justice Initiative. n.d. "The Presumption of Guilt." https://eji.org/issues/presumption-of-guilt/.

Fisher, M. 2011. "In Tunisia, Act of One Fruit Vendor Sparks Wave of Revolution Through Arab World." *Washington Post*, March 26. https://www.washingtonpost.com/world/in-tunisia-act-of-one-fruit-vendor-sparks-wave-of-revolution-through-arab-world/2011/03/16/AFjfsueB_story.html.

Freedom House. 2019. "Freedom in the World 2018: Democracy in Retreat." https://freedomhouse.org/report/freedom-world/freedom-world/2019/democracy-retreat.

Freedom House. 2016. "Freedom in the World 2016: Anxious Dictators, Wavering Democracies: Global Freedom Under Pressure." https://freedomhouse.org/report/freedom-world/freedom-world-2016.

Geneva Declaration. 2015. "Global Burden of Armed Violence 2015: Every Body Counts." http://www.genevadeclaration.org/measurability/global-burden-of-armed-violence/global-burden-of-armed-violence-2015.html.

Global Coalition on Youth, Peace and Security. 2014. "Guiding Principles on Young People's Participation in Peacebuilding." https://www.youth4peace.info/node/60.

Global Forum on Youth, Peace and Security: Final Report. 2015. August 21-22. https://www.un.org/peacebuilding/sites/www.un.org.peacebuilding/files/documents/final_report_-_global_forum_on_youth_peace_security_11.11.2015.pdf

Godoy, M. 2020. "What Do Coronavirus Disparities Look Like State by State?" NPR, May 30. https://www.npr.org/sections/health-shots/2020/05/30/865413079/what-do-coronavirus-racial-disparities-look-like-state-by-state.

Goldstone, J. A. 1991. *Revolution and Rebellion in the Early Modern World*. Berkeley: University of California Press.

GPY. 2015. "The Global Youth Call: Prioritizing Youth in the Post-2015 Development Agenda." Global Partnership for Youth in the Post-2015 Agenda. http://bit.ly/1HeSd9S.

Grau, A., and L. S. Prelis. 2014. "Engaging and Recruiting Girls in Peacebuilding Programs." Search for Common Ground. https://www.sfcg.org/wp-content/uploads/2014/09/Engaging-and-Recruiting-Girls-in-Peacebuilding-Programs.pdf.

Grizelj, I., and M. Mubashir. 2018. "The Youth Space of Dialogue and Mediation." Berghof Foundation Operations GmbH, Berlin. https://www.youth4peace.info/system/files/2018-10/Mir%20Grizelj%20Youth%20Space%20of%20Dialogue%20and%20Mediation_0.pdf.

Haberman, C. 2014. "When Youth Violence Spurred 'Superpredator' Fear." *New York Times*, April 6. https://www.nytimes.com/2014/04/07/us/politics/killing-on-bus-recalls-superpredator-threat-of-90s.html.

Hagerty, T. 2018. "Data for Youth, Peace and Security: A Summary of Research." Progress Study, Youth, Peace, and Security. https://www.youth4peace.info/system/files/2018-04/16.%20TP_Youth%20affected%20by%20violent%20conflict_IEP.pdf.

Hampton, K., L. Rainie, W. Lu, I. Shin, and K. Purcell. 2015. "Psychological Stress and Social Media Use." Pew Research Center. January 15. https://www.pewinternet.org/2015/01/15/psychological-stress-and-social-media-use-2/.

Hanwana, A. 2015. "Enough! Will Youth Protests Drive Social Change in Africa?" In *Collective Mobilisations in Africa / Mobilisations collectives en Afrique*, edited by M.-E. P. Kadya Tall, 43–66). Leiden: Brill.

Hanwana, A. 2012. *The Time of Youth: Work, Social Change and Politics in Africa*. Sterling, VA: Kumarian.

Hatzipanagos, R. 2018. "How Online Hate Turns into Real-Life Violence." *The Washington Post*, November 30. https://www.washingtonpost.com/nation/2018/11/30/how-online-hate-speech-is-fueling-real-life-violence/.

Haynes, S. 2019. "Next Generation Leaders: 'Now I Am Speaking to the Whole World': How Teen Climate Activist Greta Thunberg Got Everyone to Listen." *Time*, May 16. http://time.com/collection-post/5584902/greta-thunberg-next-generation-leaders/.

He, R. 2014. *Tiananmen Exiles: Voices of the Struggle for Democracy in China*. Basingstoke: Palgrave Macmillan.

Hendrixson, A. 2012. "The New 'Population Bomb' Is a Dud." *Different Takes* 75. https://www.scribd.com/document/109113722/The-New-Population-Bomb-is-a-Dud.

Hetey, R. C., and J. L. Eberhardt. 2014. "Racial Disparities in Incarceration Increase Acceptance of Punitive Policies." *Psychological Science* 25, no. 10: 1949–1954.

Honwana, A. 2019. "Youth Struggles: From the Arab Spring to Black Lives Matter and Beyond." *African Studies Review* 62, no. 1: 8–21.

Honwana, A. 2015. "Enough! Will Youth Protests Drive Social Change in Africa?" African Arguments. December 7. https://africanarguments.org/2015/12/07/enough-will-youth-protests-drive-social-change-in-africa/.

Honwana, A. 2005. *Makers and Breakers: Children and Youth in Postcolonial Africa*. Trenton, NJ: Africa World Press.

Horse, C. A. 2018. "Standing Rock Is Everywhere: One Year Later." *The Guardian*, February 18. https://www.theguardian.com/environment/climate-consensus-97-per-cent/2018/feb/22/standing-rock-is-everywhere-one-year-later.

Huntington, S. P. 1997. *The Clash of Civilizations and the Remaking of World Order*. New Delhi: Penguin Books.

ILO. 2017. *Global Employment Trends for Youth 2017*. International Labour Organization. http://www.ilo.org/global/publications/books/global-employment-trends/WCMS_598669/lang--en/index.htm.

Imbrie-Moore, W. 2018. "Harvard Youth Poll: Millennials Blame Government over Individuals." Harvard Political Review, October 11. https://harvardpolitics.com/united-states/harvard-youth-poll-millennials-blame-government-over-individuals/.

InterPeace. 2017. "Youth, Peace and Security in the Northern Triangle of Central America." https://www.youth4peace.info/system/files/2018-04/10.%20CFR_Northern%20Triangle_Interpeace.pdf.

IOM. 2018. "World Migration Report 2018." International Organisation for Migration, Grand-Saconnex, Switzerland.

IPU. 2018. "Youth Participation in National Parliaments: 2018." Inter-Parliamentary Union, Geneva. https://www.ipu.org/resources/publications/reports/2018-12/youth-participation-in-national-parliaments-2018.

IPU. 2016. "Youth Participation in National Parliaments." Inter-Parliamentary Union, Geneva. http://archive.ipu.org/pdf/publications/youthrep-e.pdf.

Isaac, M., and K. Roose. 2018. "Disinformation Spreads on WhatsApp Ahead of Brazilian Election." *The New York Times*, October 19. https://www.nytimes.com/2018/10/19/technology/whatsapp-brazil-presidential-election.html.

Jennings, P. 2017. "Young People on the Move and Their Engagement in Peace and Security: Case Study from the North of Central America and South Sudan." United Nations High Commissioner for Refugees. https://www.youth4peace.info/system/files/2018-04/7.%20T.

Kaplan, S., and M. Freeman. 2015. "Inclusive Transitions Framework." Institute for Integrated Transitions, Barcelona. https://gsdrc.org/document-library/inclusive-transitions-framework/.

Kapur, A., and K. Muddell. 2016. "When No One Calls It Rape Addressing Sexual Violence Against Men and Boys in Transitional Contexts." International Center for Transitional Justice, New York.

Kellough, R. D. 2008. *Teaching Young Adolescents: Methods and Resources for Middle Grades Teaching*. 5th ed. Upper Saddle River, NJ: Pearson Merrill Prentice Hall.

Kemp, S. 2019. "Digital 2019: Essential Insights into How People Around the World Use the Internet, Mobile Devices, Social Media, and e-commerce." We Are Social. https://p.widencdn.net/kqy7ii/Digital2019-Report-en.

Khosla, S. 2014. "These Maps Show Where the World's Youngest and Oldest People Live." Public Radio International, September 8. https://www.pri.org/stories/2014-09-08/these-maps-show-where-world-s-youngest-and-oldest-people-live.

Khurana, N. 2015. "The Impact of Social Networking Sites on the Youth." *Journal of Mass Communication and Journalism* 5, no. 12: 1000285. doi: 10.4172/2165-7912.1000285.

Klass, P. 2019. "When Social Media Is Really Problematic for Adolescents." *The New York Times*, June 3. https://www.nytimes.com/2019/06/03/well/family/teenagers-social-media.html.

Koser, K. 2011. "When Is Migration a Security Issue?" Brookings Institution, March 31. https://www.brookings.edu/opinions/when-is-migration-a-security-issue/.

Kretchmer, H. 2020. "Coronavirus Could Trigger a Hunger Pandemic—Unless Urgent Action Is Taken," World Economic Forum. https://www.weforum.org/agenda/2020/04/covid-19-coronavirus-could-double-acute-hunger-un-warns/.

Lee, K. S., et al. 2018. "Advanced Daily Prediction Model for National Suicide Numbers with Social Media Data." *Psychiatry Investigation* 15, no. 4: 344–354. doi: 10.30773/pi.2017.10.15.

Lewis, E. 2016. "Why I Am Passionate About Intersectionality." *Teen Vogue*, October. https://www.teenvogue.com/story/why-i-am-passionate-about-intersectionality-eva-lewis.

Luby, J., and S. Kertz. 2019. "Increasing Suicide Rates in Early Adolescent Girls in the United States and the Equalization of Sex Disparity in Suicide: The Need to Investigate the Role of Social Media." JAMA Network. May 17. https://jamanetwork.com/journals/jamanetworkopen/fullarticle/2733419.

McAlexander, R. J. 2019. "Terrorism Does Increase with Immigration—but Only Homegrown, Right-Wing Terrorism." *The Washington Post*, July 19. https://www.washingtonpost.com/politics/2019/07/19/immigration-does-lead-more-terrorism-by-far-right-killers-who-oppose-immigration/.

McEvoy-Levy, S. 2001a. "Youth as Social and Political Agents: Issues in Post-Settlement Peace Building." Kroc Institute Occasional Paper, University of Notre Dame.

McEvoy-Levy, S. 2001b. "Youth, Violence and Conflict Transformation." *Peace Review* 13, no. 1: 89–96. doi: 10.1080/10402650120038198.

McGill, M., C. O'Kane, B. Bista, N. Meslaoui, and S. Zingg. 2015. "Evaluation of Children and Youth Participation in Peacebuilding: Nepal, Eastern Democratic Republic of Congo, Colombia." European Partnership for Children and Youth in Peacebuilding, Brussels. https://www.sfcg.org/wp-content/uploads/2014/11/2015July_Eval-of-ChildYouth-Peacebuilding-Colombia-Nepal-DRC.pdf.

Mercy Corps. 2015. "Youth and Consequences: Unemployment, Injustice and Violence." Mercy Corps, Portland, Oregon. https://www.mercycorps.org/research-resources/youth-consequences-unemployment-injustice-and-violence.

Mercy Corps. 2013. "Examining the Links Between Youth Economic Opportunity, Civic Engagement, and Conflict: Evidence from Mercy Corps' Somali Youth leaders Initiative." Mercy Corps, Portland, Oregon. http://www.mercycorps.org/sites/default/files/somaliabrief_2_13_13.pdf.

Meyers, S. 2017. "Youth with Disabilities in Law and Civil Society: Exclusion and Inclusion in Public Policy and NGO Networks in Cambodia and Indonesia." January 25. http://repositoriocdpd.net:8080/handle/123456789/1563.

Miller, K. E., and A. Rasmussen. 2010. "War Exposure, Daily Stressors, and Mental Health in Conflict and Post-Conflict Settings: Bridging the Divide Between Trauma-Focused and Psychosocial Frameworks." *Journal of Social Science Medicine* 70, no. 1: 7–16.

Mottaghi, L. 2016. "MENA's Forced Displacement Crisis." World Bank MENA Knowledge and Learning Initiative. https://openknowledge.worldbank.org/bitstream/handle/10986/24383/MENA0s0forced0displacement0crisis.pdf.

Muggah, R. 2012. "Researching the Urban Dilemma: Urbanization, Poverty and Violence." International Development Research Centre. https://www.idrc.ca/sites/default/files/sp/Images/Researching-the-Urban-Dilemma-Baseline-study.pdf.

Mulderig, M. C. 2013. "An Uncertain Future: Youth Frustration and the Arab Spring." Pardee Papers, no. 16. Pardee Center for the Study of the Longer-Range Future. Boston University. http://www.bu.edu/pardee/files/2013/04/Pardee-Paper-16.pdf.

Murray, J. 2019. "Rebel Alliance." April 25. Business Green. https://www.businessgreen.com/bg/blog-post/3074582/rebel-alliance.

Mutisi, M., F. Olonisakin, and O. Ismail. 2017. "Youth, Economic Vulnerability, Socio-Political Exclusion, and Violence in Africa." International Development Research Center. https://au.int/sites/default/files/documents/39150-doc-continental_framework_on_youth_peace_and_security_-_english.pdf

Myrttinen, H., and M. Daigle. 2017. "When Merely Existing Is a Risk: Sexual and Gender Minorities in Conflict, Displacement and Peacebuilding." International Alert, London. https://www.international-alert.org/sites/default/files/Gender_SexualGenderMinorities_2017.pdf.

National Democratic Institute. 2012. "Youth Conflict Resolution Program Yields Results in Yemen." National Democratic Institute, April 9. https://www.ndi.org/Yemen-Cross-Tribal-Youth-Council-Program.

Neiwert, D. 2019. "A Deluge of 'Red-Pilled' Rage: Young White Men Are Being Radicalized Online and Acting Out Violently." *Daily Kos*, January 29. https://www.dailykos.com/stories/2019/1/29/1830633/-A-deluge-of-red-pilled-rage-Young-white-men-are-being-radicalized-online-and-acting-out-violently.

Neumann, P. R. 2017. "Countering Violent Extremism and Radicalisation That Lead to Terrorism: Ideas, Recommendations, and Good Practices from the OSCE Region." Organization for Security and Co-operation in Europe, and International Centre for the Study of Radicalization. https://www.osce.org/chairmanship/346841?download=true.

NORC. 2016. "Yes Youth Can! Impact Evaluation Final Report." National Opinion Research Center and USAID. https://www.youthpower.org/resources/yes-youth-can-impact-evaluation-final-report.

Nordås, R., and C. Davenport. 2013. "Fight the Youth: Youth Bulges and State Oppression." *American Journal of Political Science* 57, no. 4: 926–940. doi: 10.1111/ajps.12025.

Novelli, M. 2017. "Education and Countering Violent Extremism: Western Logics from South to North?" *Compare: A Journal of Comparative and International Education* 47, no. 6: 835–851. https://doi.org/10.1080/03057925.2017.1341301.

OAS. 2016. "The Consequences of Social Exclusion and Inequality: Youth, Peace and Security in the Americas, Colombia as a Case Study." Organization of American States, Washington, DC. https://www.youth4peace.info/system/files/2018-04/16.%20CFR_Colombia-Social%20Exclusion%20in%20the%20Americas-Catatumbo%20Region_OAS_0.pdf.

Odula, T., and I. A. Juma. 2020. "Coronavirus: Food Distribution Sparks Stampede in Kenya." Mercury News, April 10. https://www.mercurynews.com/2020/04/10/coronavirus-food-distribution-sparks-stampede-in-kenya/.

OECD. 2018. "States of Fragility Reports Highlights." OECD Directorate. https://www.oecd.org/dac/conflict-fragility-resilience/listofstateoffragilityreports.htm.

OECD. 2016. "Agents of Peace: Young People and Violent Conflict." In *Global Youth Development Index and Report 2016*, London: Commonwealth Secretariat. https://read.oecd-ilibrary.org/commonwealth/development/global-youth-development-index-and-report-2016_95429842-en#page1.

Office of the Secretary-General's Envoy on Youth. n.d. "#YouthStats: Public and Civic Participation." United Nations. https://www.un.org/youthenvoy/political-participation/.

Paasonen, K., and H. Urdal. 2016. "Youth Bulges, Exclusion and Instability: The Role of Youth in the Arab Spring." Peace Research Institute Oslo. https://www.prio.org/Publications/Publication/?x=9105.

Pettersson, T., and P. Wallensteen. 2015. "Armed Conflicts, 1946–2014." *Journal of Peace Research* 52, no. 4: 536–550. https://doi.org/10.1177/0022343315595927.

Pew Research Center. 2019. "Publics in Emerging Economies Worry Social Media Sow Division, Even as They Offer New Chances for Political Engagement." May 13. https://www.pewinternet.org/2019/05/13/publics-in-emerging-economies-worry-social-media-sow-division-even-as-they-offer-new-chances-for-political-engagement/.

Politiets Sikkerhetstjeneste. 2019. "What Is the Background of Right-wing Extremists in Norway." https://www.pst.no/globalassets/artikler/utgivelser/theme-report_-what-is-the-background-of-rightwing-extremists-in-norway.pdf.

Prelis, L. S. 2018. "Peacebuilding Approaches to Working with Young People." In *The Ecology of Violent Extremism: Perspectives on Peacebuilding and Human Security*, edited by L. Schirch, 277–283). Lanham, MD: Rowman and Littlefield.

Prelis, L. S. 2016. "Youth and Peacebuilding: Evidence and Guiding Principles." In *Global Youth Development Index and Report 2016*, 102. London: Commonwealth Secretariat. https://doi.org/10.14217/global_youth-2016-en.

Prelis, L. S. 2015. "Youth Engagement in Peacebuilding." In *World Youth Report: Youth Civic Engagement*, 129–137. United Nations Department of Economic and Social Affairs. https://www.un.org/development/desa/youth/world-youth-report/2015-2.html.

Pruitt, L. 2021. "Corrigendum 1: Rethinking Youth Bulge Theory in Policy and Scholarship: Incorporating Critical Gender Analysis." *International Affairs* 97, no. 2: xix. https://doi.org/10.1093/ia/iiab002.

Rigby, J. 2015. "Students in Myanmar Start Selfie Campaign to Promote Tolerance." Mashable, November 7. https://mashable.com/2015/11/06/myanmars-my-friend-campaign/#1ArEw PFAc8q6.

Roberts, D. 2004. "The Social and Moral Cost of Mass Incarceration in African American Communities." *Stanford Law Review* 56, no. 5: 1271–1305.

Roberts, F. L. 2018. "How Black Lives Matter Changed the Way Americans Fight for Freedom." American Civil Liberties Union, July 13. https://www.aclu.org/blog/racial-justice/race-and-criminal-justice/how-black-lives-matter-changed-way-americans-fight.

Romm, T., E. Dwoskin, and C. Timberg. 2019. "Sri Lanka's Social Media Shutdown Illustrates Global Discontent with Silicon Valley." *The Washington Post*, April 22. https://www.washing tonpost.com/technology/2019/04/22/sri-lankas-social-media-shutdown-illustrates-global-discontent-with-silicon-valley/.

Rosas, G. 2011. "A Lost Generation of Unemployed People." Presentation at the UNESCO Youth Forum. YouTube, posted October 19. https://www.youtube.com/watch?v=kM5OTfFO1cI.

Ross, M., and N. Holmes. 2019. "Meet the Millions of Young Adults Who Are Out of Work." Brookings Institution. April 9. https://www.brookings.edu/research/young-adults-who-are-out-of-work/.

Rubenstein, A., S. K. Wood, R. S. Levine, and C. H. Hennekens. 2019. "Alarming Trends in Mortality from Firearms Among United States Schoolchildren." *American Journal of Medicine* 132, no. 8: 992–994. https://doi.org/10.1016/j.amjmed.2019.02.012.

Ruch, D. A., A. H. Sheftall, P. Schlagbaum, J. Rausch, J. V. Campo, and J. A. Bridge. 2019. "Trends in Suicide Among Youth Aged 10 to 19 Years in the United States, 1975 to 2016." JAMA Network. https://jamanetwork.com/journals/jamanetworkopen/fullarticle/2733430.

Salazar-Xirinachs, J. M. 2012. "Generation Ni/Ni: Latin America's Lost Youth." *Americas Quarterly*, Spring. https://www.americasquarterly.org/salazar.

Satariano, A. 2019. "Facebook Identifies Russia-Linked Misinformation Campaign." *The New York Times*, January 17. https://www.nytimes.com/2019/01/17/business/facebook-misinformat ion-russia.html.

Sawyer, W. 2019. "Youth Confinement: The Whole Pie 2019." Prison Policy Initiative press release. https://www.prisonpolicy.org/reports/youth2019.html.

Scheper-Hughes, N. 2010. "Dangerous and Endangered Youth: Social Structures and Determinants of Violence." *Annals of the New York Academy of Sciences* 1036, no. 1: 13–46. https://doi.org/10.1196/annals.1330.002.

Schirch, L., ed. 2018. *The Ecology of Violent Extremism: Perspectives on Peacebuilding and Human Security*. Lanham, MD: Rowman and Littlefield.

Schott Foundation. 2015. "Black Lives Matter: The Schott 50 State Report on Public Education and Black Males." Schott Foundation for Public Education. April 27. http://schottfoundation.org/resources/black-lives-matter-schott-50-state-report-public-education-and-black-males.

Schroeder, J., and J. L. Risen. 2018. "Befriending the Enemy: Outgroup Friendship Longitudinally Predicts Intergroup Attitudes in a Coexistence Program for Israelis and Palestinians." *Group Processes and Intergroup Relations* 19, no. 1: 72–93. doi: 10.1177/1368430214542257.

Schwartz, S. 2010. *Youth and Post-conflict Reconstruction: Agents of Change.* Washington, DC.: US Institute of Peace. https://bookstore.usip.org/browse/book/9781601270498/ Youth%20and%20Post-Conflict%20Reconstruction.

Séraphin, A., D. Frau-Meigs, and G. Hassan. 2018. "Youth and Violent Extremism on Social Media: Mapping the Research." UNESCO. https://milunesco.unaoc.org/mil-resources/youth-and-violent-extremism-on-social-media-mapping-the-research/.

SFCG. 2017. "Youth, Peace and Security: Insights from Engaged and Disengaged Young Women and Men in Burundi, Nepal, Niger, Nigeria and Tunisia." Search for Common Ground, Washington, DC. https://www.youth4peace.info/system/files/2018-04/UNSCR%202 250%20Hard%20to%20Reach%20Consultations%20-%20Comparative%20Report%20S FCG%20final.pdf.

SFCG. 2015. "Global Youth Summit Against Violent Extremism." Search for Common Ground.

SFCG. 2009a. "Children, Youth, and Conflict: An Introductory Toolkit for Engaging Children and Youth in Conflict Transformation." Search for Common Ground, Washington, DC. https://www.sfcg.org/programmes/childrenandyouth/pdf/toolkit.pdf.

SFCG. 2009b. "Final Evaluation Report: Youth Community and Mediation Centers Project, Morocco." Search for Common Ground, Rabat https://www.sfcg.org/wp-content/uploads/ 2014/07/MAR_EV_Sep09_Mitigating-Communal-Conflict-by-Engaging-Youth.pdf.

SFCG and UNOY. 2017a. "Mapping a Sector: Bridging the Evidence Gap on Youth-Driven Peacebuilding." Search for Common Ground and UNOY Peacebuilders, Washington, DC. https://www.sfcg.org/mapping-a-sector-unscr-2250/.

SFCG and UNOY. 2017b. "Translating Youth, Peace and Security Policy into Practice: Guide to Kick-Starting UNSCR 2250 Locally and Nationally." Search for Common Ground and UNOY Peacebuilders. Global Coalition on Youth, Peace and Security. https://www.youth4peace.info/ node/117.

Shahrokh, J. H. 2015. "Public and Political Participation." In *Engendering Men: A Collaborative Review of Evidence on Men and Boys in Social Change and Gender Equality,* edited by J. Edström, A. Hassink, T. Shahrokh, and E. Stern, 151–162. London: Institute of Development Studies, Promundo-US and Sonke Gender Justice.

Shepler, S. 2012." Analysis of the Situation of Children Affected by Armed Conflict in the Niger Delta and Northern Region of Nigeria." UNICEF Nigeria and Search for Common Ground. https://www.academia.edu/4475007/Analysis_of_the_Situation_of_Children_Affected_by_ Armed_Conflict_in_the_Niger_Delta_and_Northern_Region_of_Nigeria.

Simpson, G. 2018. "The Missing Peace: Independent Progress Study on Youth, Peace and Security." UNFPA and PBSO, New York. https://www.youth4peace.info/system/files/2018-03/ Progress%20Study%20on%20Youth%2C%20Peace%20%26%20Security_A-72-761_S-2018-86_ENGLISH_0.pdf.

Sivakumaran, S. 2010. "Lost in Translation: UN Responses to Sexual Violence Against Men and Boys in Situations of Armed Conflict." International Committee of the Red Cross. https:// www.icrc.org/en/international-review/article/lost-translation-un-responses-sexual-violence-against-men-and-boys.

Sivakumaran, S. 2007. "Sexual Violence Against Men in Armed Conflict." *European Journal of International Law* 18, no. 2: 253–276. https://doi.org/10.1093/ejil/chm013.

Slachmuijlder, L. 2012. "Youth in the Great Lakes Region: The Making of a New Generation." *New Routes: A Journal of Peace Research and Action* 17: 34. https://www.sfcg.org/articles/GGL%20 for%20LPI%20NR%204p.pdf.

Sommers, M. 2019. "Youth and the Field of Countering Violent Extremism." Promundo-US, Washington, DC.

Sommers, M. 2015. *The Outcast Majority: War, Development, and Youth in Africa.* Athens: University of Georgia Press.

Sommers, M. 2012a. "Striving for Adulthood." In *Stuck: Rwandan Youth and the Struggle for Adulthood,* edited by M. Sommers, 115–140. Athens: University of Georgia Press.

Sommers, M., ed. 2012b. *Stuck: Rwandan Youth and the Struggle for Adulthood.* Athens: University of Georgia Press.

Stephan, M., and E. Chenoweth. 2008. "Why Civil Resistance Works: The Strategic Logic of Nonviolent Conflict." *International Security* 33, no. 1: 7–44. https://www.nonviolent-conflict. org/resource/why-civil-resistance-works-the-strategic-logic-of-nonviolent-conflict-article/.

Stimson Center. 2018. "Counterterrorism Spending: Protecting America While Promoting Efficiencies and Accountability." Stimson Study Group on Counterterrorism Spending, Stimson Center, Washington, DC.

Swisher, K. 2019. "Sri Lanka Shut Down Social Media. My First Thought Was 'Good.'" *The New York Times*, April 22. https://www.nytimes.com/2019/04/22/opinion/sri-lanka-facebook-bombings.html.

Taylor, S. 2018. "Five Frequently Asked Questions on the Inclusion of Women in Peace Processes." International Peace Institute, Global Observatory. https://theglobalobservatory.org/2018/08/five-questions-inclusion-women-peace-processes/.

Taza, R. 2017. "Four Tips from Peacebuilders on Working with Young People to Transform Violent Extremism." Euractiv, August 11. https://www.euractiv.com/section/justice-home-affa irs/opinion/four-tips-from-peacebuilders-on-working-with-young-people-to-transform-viol ent-extremism/.

Tew, R. 2017. "Counting Pennies: A Review of Official Development Assistance to End Violence Against Children." ChildFund Alliance, Save the Children, SOS Children's Villages, and World Vision International, The Global Partnership to End Violence Against Children, the Office of the SRSG on Violence against Children, and UNICEF.

Tibi, I. 2017. "Youth Consultations on Peace and Security: Findings from Focus Group Discussions and Individual Interviews Including Hard to Reach Youth in Niger." Search for Common Ground, PeaceNexus Foundation. https://www.youth4peace.info/system/files/2018-04/7.%20FGD_Niger_SFCG%20%28FINAL%29_0.pdf.

UN Security Council. 2020. "Resolution 2535 (2020)." S/RES/2535 (2020). https://undocs.org/en/S/RES/2535(2020).

UN Security Council. 2018. "UNSCR 2419." June 6. https://undocs.org/S/RES/2419(2018).

UN Security Council. 2015. "UN Security Council Resolution 2250 (2015)." December 9. https://undocs.org/S/RES/2250(2015).

UNDESA. 2015. "Youth with Disabilities." June 8. UN Department of Economic and Social Affairs. https://www.un.org/development/desa/youth/youth-with-disabilities.html/.

UNDP. 2019. "Frontlines: Young People at the Forefront of Preventing and Responding to Violent Extremism." UN Development Programme.

UNDP. 2017. "Journey to Extremism in Africa: Drivers, Incentives and the Tipping Point for Recruitment." UN Development Programme. http://journey-to-extremism.undp.org/content/downloads/UNDP-JourneyToExtremism-report-2017-english.pdf.

UNDP. 2014. "Fast Facts: Civic Engagement and Participation of Youth in Politics and Public Institutions." UN Development Programme. https://www.google.com/url?client=internal-uds-cse&cx=016364595556873131513:lg-p43v3tam&q=http://www.undp.org/content/dam/undp/library/corporate/fast-facts/english/FF-Civic-Engagement-and-Participation-of-Youth-in-Politics-and-Public-Institutions.pdf&sa=U.

UNDP. 2011. "Community Peace Recovery and Reconciliation: A Handbook for Generating Leadership for Sustainable Peace and Recovery Among Divided Communities." UN Development Programme. http://www.acordinternational.org/silo/files/community-peace-recovery-and-reconciliation-handbook.pdf.

UNDP. 2006. "Youth and Violent Conflict." UN Development Programme. http://reliefweb.int/sites/reliefweb.int/files/resources/810B078967D17D1AC12571920052088C-UNDP%20yo uth.pdf.

UNESCO. 2014. "Sustainable Development Begins with Education: How Education Can Contribute to the Proposed Post-2015 Goals." http://unesdoc.unesco.org/images/0023/002 305/230508e.pdf.

UNFPA. 2018. "Young Persons with Disabilities: Global Study on Ending Gender-Based Violence, and Realising Sexual and Reproductive Health and Rights." https://www.unfpa.org/sites/defa ult/files/resource-pdf/Final_Global_Study_Summary_English_3_Oct.pdf.

UNFPA. 2015a. "For People, Planet and Prosperity." https://www.unfpa.org/sites/default/files/pub-pdf/UNFPA_2015_Annual_Report.pdf.

UNFPA. 2015b. "State of the World Population 2015: Shelter from the Storm: A Transformative Agenda for Women and Girls in a Crisis-Prone World." UN Population Fund. https://pacific.unfpa.org/en/publications/shelter-storm-transformative-agenda-women-and-girls-crisis-prone-world.

UNFPA. 2014. "The State of World Population 2014: The Power of 1.8 Billion: Adolescents, Youth and the Transformation of the Future." https://www.unfpa.org/sites/default/files/pub-pdf/EN-SWOP14-Report_FINAL-web.pdf.

UNFPA. 2002. "The Impact of Conflict on Women and Girls: A UNFPA Strategy for Gender Mainstreaming in Areas of Conflict and Reconstruction." UN Population Fund. https://www.unfpa.org/sites/default/files/pub-pdf/impact_conflict_women.pdf.

UNHCR. 2019. "Global Trends: Forced Displacement in 2018 Refugee Statistics." UN Office of the High Commissioner for Refugees. https://www.unhcr.org/globaltrends2018/.

United Nations. 2020. "UN Chief Calls for Greater Protection for Children Caught Up in COVID-19 Crisis." UN News. April 16. https://news.un.org/en/story/2020/04/1061892.

United Nations. 2019. "Conflict Related Sexual Violence." Office of the Special Representative of the Secretary-General on Sexual Violence in Conflict. https://www.un.org/sexualviolenceinconflict/wp-content/uploads/2019/04/report/s-2019-280/Annual-report-2018.pdf.

United Nations. 2015. "State of Crime and Criminal Justice Worldwide: Report of the Secretary General." Thirteenth United Nations Congress on Crime Prevention and Criminal Justice." https://www.unodc.org/documents/data-and-analysis/statistics/crime/ACONF222_4_e_V1500369.pdf.

United Nations. 2005. "Gender Dimensions of Youth Affected by Armed Conflict." In *World Youth Report 2005*, 144–183. https://www.un.org/development/desa/youth/world-youth-report/world-youth-report-2005.html.

UNOY. 2017. "Beyond Dividing Lines: The reality of youth-led peacebuilding in Afghanistan, Colombia, Libya and Sierra Leone." UNOY Peacebuilder, The Hague.

Urdal, H. 2006. "A Clash of Generations? Youth Bulges and Political Violence." *International Studies Quarterly* 50, no. 3: 607–629.

US State Department. 2019. "Audit of the Department of State Implementation of Policies Intended to Counter Violent Extremism." Office of Audits, Middle East Regional Operations, Office of Inspector General, United States Department of State. June.

USIP. 2021. "Myanmar in the Streets: A Nonviolent Movement Shows Staying Power." United States Institute of Peace. https://www.usip.org/publications/2021/03/myanmar-streets-nonviolent-movement-shows-staying-power.

Velpillay, S., and P. Woodrow. 2019. "Collective Impact in Peacebuilding: Lessons from Networking Efforts in Multiple Locations." CDA Collaborative Learning Projects, Boston. https://www.cdacollaborative.org/wp-content/uploads/2019/03/CDA_Collective-Peace_Report_Final.pdf.

Virtual Exchange Coalition. n.d. "MIT Saxelab Research Partnership." http://virtualexchangecoalition.org/wp-content/uploads/2015/09/VirtualExchange_saxelab.pdf.

Webster, D., J. M. Whitehill, J. S. Vernick, and E. M. Parker. 2012. "Evaluation of Baltimore's Safe Streets Program: Effects on Attitudes, Participants' Experiences, and Gun Violence." Johns Hopkins Center for the Prevention of Youth Violence and Cure Violence. http://cureviolence.org/wp-content/uploads/2017/09/Safe-Streets-full-evaluation.pdf.

Western, B., and B. Pettit. 2010. "Incarceration and Social Inequality." American Academy of Arts and Sciences. https://www.amacad.org/publication/incarceration-social-inequality.

Williams, M., R. Walsh-Taza, and S. Prelis. 2015. "Working Together to Address Violent Extremism: A Strategy for Youth-Government Partnerships." Search for Common Ground, Washington, DC. https://www.sfcg.org/wp-content/uploads/2016/12/YouthGovtCVE_StrategyDocument_122116.pdf.

Workman, J. 2019. "'Our House Is on Fire': 16-Year-Old Greta Thunberg Wants Action." World Economic Forum, January 25. https://www.weforum.org/agenda/2019/01/our-house-is-on-fire-16-year-old-greta-thunberg-speaks-truth-to-power.

World Bank. 2018. *Pathways for Peace: Inclusive Approaches to Preventing Violent Conflict.* Washington, DC: United Nations and World Bank.

World Bank. 2011a. "Fact Sheet: Youth as a Smart Investment." UN Inter-Agency Network for Youth Development, New York.

World Bank. 2011b. *World Development Report 2011: Conflict, Security, and Development - Overview.* Washington, DC: World Bank. http://documents.worldbank.org/curated/en/806531468161369474/World-development-report-2011-conflict-security-and-development-overview.

World Bank. 2006. *World Development Report 2007: Development and the Next Generation.* Washington, DC: World Bank.

World Economic Forum. 2015. "The Impact of Corruption: Perspectives from Millennial Voices." http://widgets.weforum.org/partnering-against-corruption-initiative/.

World Health Organization. 2015. *Preventing Youth Violence: An Overview of the Evidence.* Geneva: WHO. http://apps.who.int/iris/bitstream/10665/181008/1/9789241509251_eng.pdf.

Worldometer. n.d. "Southern Asian Population." Accessed 2019. https://www.worldometers.info/world-population/southern-asia-population/.

Wortley, S., et al. 2008. *The Root Causes of Youth Violence: A Review of Major Theoretical Perspectives: A Report Prepared for the Review of the Roots of Youth Violence.* Toronto, ON: Ministry of Children, Community and Social Services. http://www.children.gov.on.ca/htdocs/English/professionals/oyap/roots/volume5/index.aspx.

Youth, Peace, and Security. 2020. "5th Anniversary of UN Security Council Resolution 2250." December. https://www.sparkblue.org/system/files/2020-12/5th%20Anniversary%20of%20UN%20Security%20Council%20Resolution%202250%20%281%29.pdf.

Youth Policy. 2007. "Middle East and North Africa: Fact Sheets." http://www.youthpolicy.org/mappings/regionalyouthscenes/mena/facts/.

Žagar, Danela. 2015. "Racially Motivated Crime Increases Across the EU." Civil Liberties Union for Europe. June 12. https://www.liberties.eu/en/stories/enar-shadow-report/4183.

5

Recognizing the Rights of LGBTQI People

Maksym Eristavi and Daniel Baer

> Expressing grave concern at acts of violence and discrimination, in all regions of the world, committed against individuals because of their sexual orientation and gender identity...
>
> —UN Human Rights Council, from the first-ever resolution about the human rights of LGBTQI people, June 2011

The Human Rights of LGBTQI Individuals in Context

It is difficult—particularly for those lucky enough to live in rights-respecting democracies—to appreciate the tremendous historical importance of the movement to recognize universal human rights. Eleanor Roosevelt led the charge at the nascent United Nations in the late 1940s, seizing a moment of opportunity following the tragedies of World War II to focus the world on recognizing certain universal moral truths.[1] The push was premised on the reality that we are, as the Universal Declaration of Human Rights puts it, "born free and equal in dignity and rights."[2]

Looking around the world in recent decades, it might seem strange to say that Eleanor Roosevelt and those she worked with internationally were successful. Hundreds of millions of people are still denied fundamental freedoms. But, in less than eight decades, dozens of countries have incorporated aspects of international human rights law into domestic law. Many nations have created institutions charged with monitoring domestic realization of internationally recognized human rights.[3] The language of human rights is routinely used to assess government failures and to defend the work of activists and advocates. Even governments that routinely violate human rights defend themselves using the language of human rights, implicitly conceding the legitimacy of those rights. Today, there are national and international courts that prosecute human rights violations and abuses. Only three generations ago none of this existed. The political project of human rights has come a long way in a short time. Though violations remain too widespread, too frequent, and too devastatingly sad to describe fully, Eleanor Roosevelt and her collaborators bequeathed us a project with the potential to have a lasting positive impact on the world.

Practically speaking, a commitment to universal human rights necessarily entails calling attention to gaps and seeking remedies for failings. This is some of the hardest work, because most often those who have been marginalized, the most vulnerable people in societies, aren't marginalized by accident—they are marginalized on purpose; they are vulnerable because social structures keep them vulnerable. Popular opinion among dominant groups often reinforces that marginalization and discrimination with prejudice and stigma. Whether talking about protecting members of a religious minority or a minority ethnic group, women, or LGBTQI persons, it's not just the building up of protections through laws and institutions that is needed; often it's necessary to counter the public perception that these individuals count less, or are less deserving of universal human rights. Reinforcing the universality of human rights protections—that you can't pick and choose who gets them and still call them universal—is central to political and practical human rights work. In this chapter, a diplomat and scholar joins with a journalist and writer to examine why and how the human rights of LGBTQI people have become a more prominent part of some governments' foreign policy, and of the work of local and transnational civil society groups (see Box 5.1).

Box 5.1 What's in a Name?

We use the terms "LGBTQI" and "queer" interchangeably to include the same people. But while Dan Baer is more likely to use "LGBTQI" (or "LGBTQ") in political discussions, Maksym Eristavi notes that "queer"—reclaimed in recent decades as an inclusive term—is more effective and less likely to draw negative attention in countries where anti-LGBTQI sentiment has been fomented, or where LGBTQI reads as "foreign" or "Western" to local audiences.

The Nature of the Problem: Discrimination and Violence Against LGBTQI People

In some countries in the global North, it has become common to marvel at the speed with which law and society have evolved to respect the equal dignity of LGBTQI persons. Yet the situation remains dire, and is even worsening, in many parts of the world. The trends may be correlated: LGBTQI activists on the front lines observe that the reinforcement of homophobic and misogynistic policies has coincided with the recent expansion of queer rights in the global North. The fact that progress happened relatively quickly in some places may reflect how far the pendulum needed to swing toward justice. In other places, the situation of LGBTQI people remains stuck; it will remain there until the pull of activism and justice dislodges it (see Box 5.2).

Box 5.2 Debunking the Claim of "Special Rights"

As with other historically marginalized groups, those resisting recognition of the human rights of LGBTQI persons often argue that recognition entails according "special rights" to members of a particular group. Members of certain minorities may, of necessity, exercise their rights to expression or to equal protection under the law in ways that do not conform to the dominant group, but claims of "special rights" have been debunked.

All individuals can exercise their rights under international human rights law. The Universal Declaration of Human Rights (UDHR) specifies:

> Article 1. All human beings are born free and equal in dignity and rights. They are endowed with reason and conscience and should act towards one another in a spirit of brotherhood.
>
> Article 2. Everyone is entitled to all the rights and freedoms set forth in this Declaration, without distinction of any kind, such as race, colour, sex, language, religion, political or other opinion, national or social origin, property, birth or other status. Furthermore, no distinction shall be made on the basis of the political, jurisdictional or international status of the country or territory to which a person belongs, whether it be independent, trust, non-self-governing or under any other limitation of sovereignty.

Although less elegant and simple than "LGBTQI rights," we most often use "the human rights of LGBTQI persons/people" to underscore that we are speaking about universal rights common to all individuals.

It's extremely difficult to define the magnitude of the problem of LGBTQI discrimination, not least because it is extremely difficult to identify the number of queer people in the world. In addition to a paucity of data collection efforts, stigmatization hinders reporting. Estimates of the queer population hover at approximately 5 percent of the total population. But how queer people are perceived in a particular place may greatly affect how many publicly identify and how many are identified in public measurements like a census. In more accepting societies, estimates of queer people may be higher because more people feel safe to openly identify as queer. In societies where queer people are not as accepted, fewer people may openly identify as queer, but it does not mean that fewer people are queer. According to the Williams Institute, "an estimated 3.5% of adults in the United States identify as lesbian, gay, or bisexual and an estimated 0.3% of adults are transgender."[4] In a number of countries, documenting queer people in census and demographic data is becoming more common. For example, in India, the 2011 census counted almost

500,000 transgender people living in the country.[5] After Ireland became the first country in the world to vote (overwhelmingly) in a popular referendum to change the law to allow same-sex couples to marry, it saw a flurry of such marriages in the first few years before the number leveled out at around 3 percent of all marriages in the country.[6]

Violence and Disenfranchisement

Each year, thousands of individuals around the world are victims of violent attacks based on their sexual orientation or gender identity. In most countries—including those that have decriminalized homosexuality and gender-nonconformity— queer people, and especially queer people who are also part of other historically marginalized groups, are significantly more likely to experience violence, including murder.[7] The rise in murder rates of trans Americans (particularly trans women of color), the historically high rates of violent deaths of queer Brazilians, and the rising number of homophobic attacks in France are all indicative.[8] Trans people are often at heightened risk; the Trans Murder Monitoring Project documented the killings (often brutal) of 350 trans people around the world in the twelve months ending in October 2020.[9] In some countries, governments have taken the first step toward solving the problem by tracking these acts of violence and reporting on them. But in many places there are no reliable statistics, only frequent reports of individual incidents. And in some cases, law enforcement may be a part of the problem. Amnesty International reported data indicating discrimination against LGBTQI individuals in the United States, such as instances of "profiling . . . selective enforcement of laws, sexual, physical and verbal abuse, failure to respond or inadequate responses . . . to hate crimes and violence . . . inappropriate searches and mistreatment in detention and a lack of accountability for perpetrators."[10] It is likely this pattern of practice is present outside of the United States as well. It underscores the challenges with assembling reliable data: not only do many countries not document animus-based crimes against LGBTQI people, but in many places actors within law enforcement are part of the problem.

Centuries of social and economic marginalization also have had a compounding effect that leaves LGBTQI communities in the global North and South with diminished coping capacity in the face of cataclysmic events. The COVID-19 pandemic exposed the depth of this problem. Queer communities from Asia and Europe to Africa and the Americas suffered disproportionately from lack of healthcare access, job insecurity, domestic abuse, and disinformation attacks.[11] In 2020, a Georgian trans woman set herself on fire to protest the government lockdown policies that would ignore the economic realities of being queer; it made headlines, and her challenge resonated with many LGBTQI people around the world.[12]

Criminalization and Discrimination in Law

As of April 2021, some seventy countries still criminalize consensual sexual conduct between adults of the same sex, and eleven of these attach the death penalty to same-sex consensual sexual acts.[13] Additionally, many countries, including Egypt, Iraq, and Russia, use laws prohibiting certain forms of expression, prostitution, or public indecency and other related laws to de facto criminalize same-sex relations.[14] Others continue to curtail or deny certain legal rights for LGBTQI persons. Relatively few nations accord full civil rights protections and civil equality to LGBTQI persons (as of this writing, the United States has not yet enacted federal legislation that would do so). Where LGBTQI persons are not equal under law, legal barriers have a compounding effect. For example, discrimination in housing may also impact a person's access to employment or healthcare (and vice versa). Criminalization may impair access to justice for breach of contract or acts of violence.[15]

At the same time that these discriminatory laws are in conflict with universal human rights standards, they also result in substantial economic losses. The Williams Institute has found that each one-point increase in a country's rating on the Global Acceptance Index corresponds to an average GDP per capita that is $1,400 higher.[16] We have long known that protections for minority rights can be an indicator for the overall quality of rule of law in a country. However, discrimination itself has been shown to have specific negative economic impacts. In India, research has shown that workplace discrimination, health issues, and inadequate support for queer students in the education system stunt economic growth.[17]

Some leaders in countries that criminalize LGBTQI conduct or status say these laws are needed to protect against the "importing" of homosexuality, which they depict as foreign or Western. This is oddly ironic, because, in fact, it is the homophobia that was "imported": many laws criminalizing homosexuality are relics of colonialism or, more recently, directly inspired by US-based conservative groups (see Box 5.3).[18]

Box 5.3 The Colonial Legacy of Legalized Discrimination

Many of the existing laws banning homosexuality in African countries were introduced in the colonial period. The British, for example, left a trail of anti-sodomy laws in their wake.[19] Decolonization did not involve the retraction of laws imported and imposed by colonial powers. The only two surviving laws criminalizing homosexuality in the Russian neighborhood, in Uzbekistan and Turkmenistan, were introduced by the Russian colonial administration in the nineteenth century and updated in 1926 during the Soviet occupation.[20] The 2014 Ugandan Anti-Homosexuality Act presents an example of a new kind of legal import. It was written with the encouragement and assistance of conservative Christian activists from the United States.[21]

In addition to "bad old laws" on the books, a rash of bad new laws have been put in place recently. Broadly speaking, these laws curb freedom of expression or freedom of association and peaceful assembly. Some criminalize "gay propaganda" and make it illegal to talk about—and therefore to advocate for—greater acceptance of LGBTQI persons. Russia adopted such a law in early 2013 and has pressured other former Soviet countries to do the same.[22] Examples of similar legislative attacks aiming at restricting visibility of queer people include the wave of "LGBT-free zone" resolutions by Polish municipalities or the Hungarian ban on the retroactive change of legal gender.[23] Fundamentally, these laws limit the rights of all citizens in the countries where they are in place.

Religious teachings are often cited as formative influences on people's perspectives regarding LGBTQI rights and as guiding moral discussions on homosexuality and gender identity. In countries with an official or state religion, theistic interpretation is often used to justify discriminatory law and criminalization. For instance, the government of Brunei, which adopted Islamic law (sharia) in 2014, introduced in April 2019 a penal code making homosexual acts punishable by jail or death by stoning, and criminalizing "nonconforming gender expression."[24] A number of postcolonial leaders have argued that homosexuality is not only a question of religious belief but a question of rejecting a form of cultural neocolonialism as well. Some leaders—not only in Africa—have equated the rejection of LGBTQI rights with the rejection of Western imperialism, in some cases in tandem with affirming supposed religious teachings.[25]

Attacks on Civil Society

Where there has been progress advancing human rights, local civil society and independent journalism have been critical. Advocacy, service provision, and documentation are needed to effectively address violence, discrimination, and unjust laws. However, between 2014 and 2016 alone, more than sixty countries passed new laws restricting the activities of civil society organizations.[26] Organizations protecting queer people are often especially imperiled, and their members are more likely to have their fundamental freedoms violated.[27]

Journalists and civil society organizations document the nature and scope of violations of the human rights of LGBTQI persons (and others), creating a historical record. At the same time, it has become increasingly common for external actors seeking to influence politics in certain countries to use disinformation about queer people or legal protections for them in attempts to provoke popular backlash. For example, a wave of fake anti-LGBTQI news preceded the 2018 marriage equality vote in Taiwan.[28] Societies where institutions of journalism are weakened or suppressed are among those most affected by organized disinformation campaigns. In recent years, the Russian government has used disinformation to weaponize anti-queer sentiments in its attempt to retard closer relations between former Soviet republics—including Georgia, Moldova, and Ukraine—and the EU or other Western institutions.[29] Support for independent journalism is now an integral part of the toolbox for addressing LGBTQI discrimination, and for countering the disinformation and cynicism that seek to use the protection of human rights for queer people as a political provocation (see Box 5.4).

Box 5.4 Foreign-Fueled "Anti-Gender" Campaigns in Eastern Europe

Along with "LGBTQI," the word "gender" is an interchangeable trigger for anti-equality campaigns across Eastern Europe. Seeing queer and gender equality as foundational blocks for the larger "war on family" narrative, conservative groups lobby hard to exclude any mentions of the two words from any draft laws or official governing documents.[30] That way, they hope to arrest any public discourse regarding the topics and prevent civil rights groups from capitalizing on inclusive legislative language for further litigation.[31] In most countries of the region, these campaigns are financially and intellectually backed by conservative organizations from the United States and Russia.[32]

In sum, while it is often difficult to obtain reliable data on the scope of human rights violations experienced by LGBTQI people, we know that the problem remains widespread and global, even as it manifests itself in different ways in different places. Societal violence, stigma, and discriminatory laws reinforce each other in a toxic cocktail. And in countries that have seen democratic backsliding in the form of increasing restrictions on civil society and fundamental freedoms of expression and association, those problems have become ever more difficult to document and address.

Using Foreign Policy to Address the Problem: One Government's Approach to LGBTQI Rights

There are many ways to tell the story of the global LGBTQI human rights movement in foreign affairs, because there is not one story but many. Committed civil society activists were advocating domestically and internationally long before the topic received attention in foreign ministries and international organizations. This section recalls how one of the most influential actors in the world—the United States government—came to focus on the human rights of LGBTQI persons in foreign policy. The example is offered as a case study, not as a claim that the United States presents the first or best example of a country taking up the issue, even if it was surely a historically significant one.

Domestic Roots of Foreign Policy

The rise of LGBTQI rights in US foreign policy followed domestic developments. The modern US gay rights movement often traces its origins to the Stonewall riots in New York City in 1969, and gained tragic visibility through the AIDS crisis that began in the 1980s, which catalyzed LGBTQI community activism, particularly that of gay men.[33] The Human Rights Campaign (HRC)—the United States's first political action committee dedicated to queer rights—was founded in 1980, and activist groups like ACT UP, which emerged in protest of government inaction on HIV/AIDS, made headlines. As in many countries, activism and visibility led eventually to changes in law and, almost as predictably, to backlash.

The US Supreme Court ruled the criminalization of sodomy unconstitutional in *Lawrence v. Texas* in 2003.[34] The same year, marriage equality became law in Massachusetts.[35] Six months after that, political strategist Karl Rove engineered George W. Bush's reelection, in part by trying to stoke fears among conservatives in Florida and Ohio that marriage equality could become the law of the land.[36] When Barack Obama ran to succeed Bush in 2008, he promised, on the one hand, to end the policy that banned gay men and women from serving openly in the US military, a policy known as "Don't Ask Don't Tell," but he also reversed an earlier position he had expressed in support of marriage equality and averred that he believed marriage was between a man and a woman.[37] While the trajectory of progress was not linear, by the time Obama took office, the issue of the rights of LGBTQI persons had become part of mainstream domestic political discussions. By then, human rights organizations (including Human Rights Watch, Amnesty International, and Human Rights First) and LGBTQI organizations (including HRC and the International Gay and Lesbian Human Rights Commission, founded in 1990 and now renamed OutRight Action International) had formed a coalition called the Council for Global Equality that pressed the new administration to tackle the problem of discrimination and violence against LGBTQI persons internationally.

The Obama Administration and the Human Rights of LGBTQI Persons

As President Obama and the Democratic Party used an increasingly progressive approach to queer rights in domestic politics, the administration was cautious and purposeful in its foreign policy, carefully anchoring LGBTQI equality to international human rights law and to the bipartisan commitment to human rights leadership. While the Obama administration's elevation of the human rights of LGBTQI persons did not emerge from a vacuum with respect to foreign policy or domestic political developments, from a bureaucratic standpoint the administration's focus required innovations in the mechanics of foreign policy, including policy, facts, programming and grants, and diplomacy.

Policy

The most visible articulation of the Obama administration's policy was the speech delivered by Secretary of State Hillary Clinton in honor of Human Rights Day (December 10) on December 6, 2011, at the United Nations in Geneva.[38] Within days, it became Clinton's most-watched speech as secretary of state on the State Department website.[39] On the same day as Clinton's speech, the White House released a presidential memorandum that directed the US government to pursue several specific objectives—including decriminalization and improved responses to LGBTQI refugees and asylees—as part of the US commitment to the human rights of LGBTQI persons.[40] (Almost ten years later, President Biden would update the Obama memorandum and issue a similar directive in the opening weeks of his administration.)[41] The presidential memorandum and the speech by the secretary of state followed months of coordination by the State Department and the National Security Council at the White House. A year before her speech in Geneva, Secretary Clinton had sent a cable to all US ambassadors instructing them to treat the human rights of LGBTQI persons as they would the rights of individuals from other groups that had historically been targeted for human rights abuses (see Box 5.5).[42]

Box 5.5 Dan Baer

On one of my first trips as a deputy assistant secretary of state—before Secretary Clinton's cable instructing ambassadors and their teams to engage on the rights of LGBTQI persons—I visited a country in Eastern Europe where individuals who held public office had been credibly accused of a violent attack on a gay pride parade. When I asked the US ambassador if the matter had been raised with the host government, the ambassador replied with a (genuine) question: "Are we allowed to raise those issues?" This underscored to me the importance of communicating a clear policy to diplomats responsible for representing the US overseas.

Facts

The US State Department began publishing the Country Reports on Human Rights Practices, better known as the Human Rights Reports, in 1977.[43] Every year, the State Department releases documentation of known human rights abuses and developments in every other country around the world during the previous calendar year. Over decades, these reports, with their dry, technical prose, have become an important fact base not only for US policy but also for activists around the world whose claims and reporting are validated by the US government. Recognizing the importance of having a fact base to inform policy, the State Department created a new separate section in each country report examining the human rights record with respect to LGBTQI persons. The addition of this section meant that human rights and political officers at US embassies around the globe were now researching verified incidents and monitoring legal and other developments pertaining to the rights of LGBTQI persons. It also meant that policymakers in Washington had data to work with when developing public statements or diplomatic engagement plans.

Programming and Grants

By the time the US government elevated the human rights of queer people as a policy concern, both USAID and the State Department had millions of dollars of grant programs dedicated to supporting democracy and human rights around the world. Secretary Clinton announced in her Geneva speech a new effort to leverage US investment to attract funding from other donors in a Global Equality Fund that would support the human rights of LGBTQI people over the long term.[44] Grants programs included support for emergency evacuations, strategic litigation, legal assistance to help small NGOs accomplish onerous registration processes, advocacy campaigns, training for judges, and documentation efforts.

Diplomacy

New engagement by US diplomats was also needed. In the context of the bilateral relationships between the United States and other countries, this meant ramping up two forms of engagement. First, following Secretary Clinton's instructions, US ambassadors and their teams began to engage with host governments. Most often this was driven by a precipitating event—either a human rights concern, a legal development, or a public statement by an official.[45]

US embassies and consulates also significantly increased their contacts with relevant actors in the countries where they work. They began hosting International Day Against Homophobia and Transphobia (IDAHO-T, May 17) and pride events. Ambassadors marched in pride parades, wrote op-eds, and issued public statements advocating for the human rights of LGBTQI individuals. And US foreign assistance professionals and diplomats began investing time in meeting with civil society actors working on LGBTQI issues, getting to know them, and learning about the challenges they face. In some places, US embassies offered safe spaces for queer individuals and activists to come together to discuss common challenges and strategize solutions.

Additionally, the United States took an energetic leadership role in multilateral organizations. The United States supported South Africa's resolution at the UN Human Rights Council in 2011, which was the first UN resolution to recognize that universal human rights apply to LGBTQI persons.[46] The year before, the United States worked with other countries at the UN in New York to prevent removing reference to LGBTQI people from a resolution that condemned extrajudicial killings.[47] Additionally, the United States supported the naming of a special rapporteur in the Organization of American States (OAS) to monitor abuses and offer expert advice in the Western Hemisphere. Often the United States was not out in front; American diplomats worked with partners from other countries and in civil society, as well as with the leadership of the UN and other multilateral organizations, to advance change.

The coordination with international partners and the UN was an important part of the Obama administration's approach. It was an effective tactic for getting more governments to take the political step of affirming human rights protections for LGBTQI people while also helping ensure that addressing human rights abuses against queer people did not depend on any single government. This was important when Donald J. Trump replaced Obama as US president and the Trump administration aborted much of the work that was under way to support LGBTQI rights around the world. The Trump administration left the key position of assistant secretary of state for democracy, human rights, and labor vacant for over half of Trump's term, and it did not fill the position of special envoy for the human rights of LGBTI persons. Trump's first secretary of state, Rex Tillerson, did not overtly reverse Obama administration policies and (after pressure from Congress) raised the issue of violence against gay men in Chechnya with his Russian counterpart.[48] But under Tillerson's successor, US secretary of state Michael Pompeo, the State department removed the special envoy position from its website, directed embassies not to display pride flags (or other banners related to social justice), and championed a commission on human rights that was widely seen as an attempt to undermine commitments to the human rights of women and queer people.[49] Trump's ambassador to Berlin, Ric Grenell—arguably the highest-profile openly gay official in State Department history and the first openly gay ambassador to a G-7 country— nominally spearheaded an effort to maintain the Obama administration's policy to push for decriminalization of homosexuality around the world. However, Grenell's efforts lacked support from the administration and were criticized by activists as involving mainly "photo ops" for the notoriously brash diplomat (see Box 5.6).[50]

Box 5.6 Yogyakarta Principles

The active role that the United States played in multilateral forums in the 2010s was, at every step, encouraged and assisted by civil society. It also showed the value of civil-society-driven efforts, even when they are not immediately embraced by a majority of governments. In late 2006, a number of civil society actors and current or former UN special rapporteurs (UN-designated special representatives focused on topics like torture or freedom of expression) gathered in Yogyakarta, Indonesia, to articulate the human rights protections for LGBTQI persons under international law. The resulting Yogyakarta Principles, published in 2007 (and updated in 2017), defined how international human rights law should be applied to in relation to sexual orientation, gender identity, gender expression, and sex characteristics.[51] Even though the United States took a view that could be called disinterested in or even skeptical of the initial Yogyakarta effort (the United States was particularly unmoved by some of the language on economic, social, and cultural rights), the Yogyakarta principles informed much of the work that eventually went into the first successful UN resolutions on LGBTQI rights several years later.[52]

Change Is Possible: Examples of LGBTQI Rights Beyond the West

The story of the front-line struggle for LGBTQI rights is often told through the prism of Western historical background and experiences. This perspective tends to paint non-Western battles for queer equality in a narrative of linear progress and individualism. Yet the last decade provides case studies revealing a growing spectrum of successful battles for human rights equality that are not rooted in Western paradigms and do not follow popular Western strategies. The following three examples deepen understanding of how LGBTQI populations outside the West have succeeded in driving change.

Example A: Shifting Social Norms, Vietnam

Human rights protections for LGBTQI persons in South and East Asia remain limited. Same-sex relations are outlawed in many countries.[53] However, the issue's visibility has risen thanks to a number of factors, including the work of domestic and international NGOs and the visibility of queer people in global popular culture.

Popular opinion in Vietnam went through a rapid transformation in less than fifteen years. In 2001, more than 80 percent of Vietnamese citizens called homosexuality "never acceptable."[54] But in 2012, the Vietnamese queer community launched the country's first pride event, which was followed by a legislative pivot toward marriage equality. By 2016, 45 percent of the population backed marriage equality, with the state tolerating same-sex marriages without providing full legal recognition and protections.[55] Human rights equality for trans Vietnamese also expanded: a 2015 law allows individuals who have undergone reassignment surgery to register with a new gender.[56]

Many cite American diplomatic leadership as having helped solidify progress. Ted Osius, the US ambassador to Vietnam from 2014 to 2017, who is openly gay, publicly encouraged the country's move toward equality. Together with his husband, and as an openly gay, multiracial couple with children, they were part of the Vietnamese public debate about rights of LGBTQI persons, transcending a traditional diplomatic role to become ambassadors for the queer equality movement. Taking into account globally popular disinformation tactics labeling homosexuality "a Western invention," Ambassador Osius cautiously amplified messages and coordinated activities with local groups, supporting civil society "in doing what it is already doing."[57]

Example B: Challenging Failures in Rule of Law, Russia and Eastern Europe

Extreme dichotomies also characterize another global front line for LGBTQI equality, Russia and Eastern Europe. The 2017–2020 "gay pogroms" in the Russian region of Chechnya left dozens executed in extrajudicial killings or disappeared in secret government prisons, with hundreds subjected to brutal torture.[58] Anti-gay violence in Chechnya is not an isolated barbarity; it is a part of larger Kremlin-backed terror campaign against minorities and dissenting voices.[59] The Russian and Chechen governments abuse international anti-terrorism laws in the hunt for those fleeing pogroms.[60] In an example of diplomatic intervention, German chancellor Angela Merkel publicly addressed the issue at a live press conference with Russian president Vladimir Putin in Moscow in May 2017.[61] Hours later, activists on the ground in Chechnya confirmed that the anti-gay raids had been put on hold. But pogroms restarted in late 2018 (see Box 5.7).[62]

Box 5.7 Maksym Eristavi

In 2017–2019, I was part of global outreach bringing the stories of Chechen gay pogrom victims (predominantly Muslim minorities) to light, briefing a number of foreign governments and diplomats, including members of the US Congress. I faced a surprising knowledge gap among some key officials regarding the everyday life of queer communities outside North America and Europe. For example, some found it puzzling that LGBTQI victims from Muslim cultures would rather preserve relations with their homophobic families than sever ties to benefit individual freedom; to put it simply, it is harder for a queer Muslim person to leave an oppressive family behind than it is for LGBTQI people in the West. This knowledge gap results in misguided or sometimes damaging asylum and migration policies—most of those people fleeing the gay pogroms in Muslim-dominated southern Russia, Azerbaijan, and Tajikistan in 2017–2021 were denied asylum or visa requests by Western governments at least once.[63]

At the same time, since 2010 in Eastern Europe, there has been a historic shift toward greater human rights for queer persons, as countries have adopted norms that originated elsewhere in the international system, and as local civil society has adapted to the rapid, fundamental transformation of the global battle for LGBTQI equality.

Ukraine and its Kyiv Pride, the largest pride event in Eastern Europe, serve as both operational blueprint and illustration. Homophobia in Ukraine was predated by homophobic Soviet policies reinforced until 2014 by Russian geopolitical domination. The Maidan Revolution urged European Union integration, and with it came greater political will for progressive legislation. For example, Ukraine's only anti-discrimination law, which protects queer citizens from workplace discrimination, was passed to conform with a conditionality for greater integration with the EU.[64]

The Kyiv Pride civil rights march, which takes place in the Ukrainian capital, evolved from small gatherings in 2013–2015 marred by far-right violence. American and European diplomats facilitated negotiations between pride event organizers and the Ukrainian police, which had recently been reformed as a result of an international mandate. The first-ever violence-free Kyiv Pride was held in 2016 and spurred a number of regional pride marches.[65] The event became the largest in Eastern Europe as a result of the Ukrainian civil society decision to focus on the shared commitment to the rights of free speech and peaceful protest—values that Ukrainians prioritize after the bloodshed of the 2014 revolution. Pivoting away from an exclusive focus on "minority rights"—which would have obligated them to confront the extremely politicized LGBTQI discourse—helped political and public support for Kyiv Pride to skyrocket (see Box 5.8).

Box 5.8 International Pressure on Indigenous LGBTQI Rights Movements—Observations of Maksym Eristavi

---

During the 2018 Kyiv Pride, a sizable group of American conservative protesters tried to prevent me and other marchers from accessing the event's cordoned-off area. They revealed to me that they had traveled from Pittsburgh, Pennsylvania, to protect "traditional Ukrainians from Western homosexual conspiracy." The rising power of international homophobic groups and their export of disinformation places enormous pressure on indigenous human rights movements around the world.

Example C: Litigation, Belize

In 2016, the Supreme Court of Belize decriminalized homosexuality, citing a range of international and foreign jurisprudence, including cases from the United States Supreme Court and the European Court for Human Rights.[66] The case was launched by the United Belize Advocacy Movement (UNIBAM). The timing of the litigation wasn't accidental; the country's judiciary and government institutions had been signaling a growing acceptance of international human rights norms. And in 2014, citing the Universal Declaration of Human Rights, Kim Simplis Barrow, the

First Lady of Belize, made a public statement condemning anti-LGBTQI violence and supporting human rights protections for LGBTQI people.[67] Despite the victory for the local queer community, the court ruling also provoked accusations of "judicial imperialism."[68] The irony that Belize's sodomy law was imposed by British colonizers and then defeated with the assistance of British human rights and judicial activists didn't escape opponents. In another illustration of the growing power of trans-border anti-equality groups, UNIBAM and its allies faced pushback by local conservative and religious groups, reinforced by American religious groups. Specifically, they helped Belize's attorney general use international legal precedents, such as the dissenting opinion of Justice Antonin Scalia in *Lawrence v. Texas* in 2003, to defend the sodomy laws (see Box 5.9).[69]

Box 5.9　Third Gender in Asia

Dating back to the early modern period, Southeast Asia has fostered gender plurality in different dimensions.[70] Before colonialism in India, for example, hijras, a third gender group, were respected and considered to have spiritual assets in Hinduism.[71] India, Nepal, Bangladesh, and Pakistan all recognize more than two genders in the law.[72] Interestingly, Taiwan became the first Asian country to legalize marriage between same-sex couples in 2019.[73] Movements for gay rights and inclusive gender identities have not necessarily run parallel in Southeast Asia.

Lessons Learned and the Road Ahead

Robust international engagement around LGBTQI human rights has generated inspiring stories; it has also generated lessons for the road ahead.

- *Ground your inclusive foreign policy outreach firmly within indigenous civil society.* When it comes to diplomatic efforts to expand human rights equality for LGBTQI individuals, effective sustainable strategies can only thrive if primary ownership remains firmly with local civil society institutions. Being an outspoken ally and providing diplomatic leadership in responding to gross human rights violations remain key, but these are short-term remedies. And, if done ham-handedly, they can be counterproductive and upend the efforts of local advocacy groups. Civil society agents on the ground are essential in the long term. Regularly checking in with those local experts is critical to navigating political context and to calibrating foreign engagement for timeliness and precision.[74]

- *Study the shifting field of the global battles for LGBTQI and civil rights equality, which are going through rapid and fundamental transformations.* Encourage creative and inclusive messaging and monitor for new challenges facing front-line equality movements, such as organized disinformation, intentional abuse of identity politics by illiberal regimes, and the rise of trans-border anti-equality efforts.
- *Legislative activism is important, but implementation is even more so.* Even in countries where legal protections for queer communities were recently established, local governments often neglect implementation, and progress becomes a hostage to politicking or electioneering. Implementation mechanisms and deadlines must be embedded as conditionality, much like legislative agendas. And public local reporting on implementation, whether by journalists or human rights organizations, can help drive action.
- *Explore and experiment with unconventional diplomacy.* State policies are not enough to ensure that the pivot toward LGBTQI equality is sustained. Many transnational businesses are beginning to use "corporate diplomacy," whether by backing the UN LGBTI Standards of Conduct of Business, through the Partnership for Global LGBTI Equality at the 2019 World Economic Forum in Davos, or using emerging initiatives such as Open for Business, which utilizes corporate diplomacy to promote LGBTQI-inclusive business in challenging countries around the world.[75] The corporate sector is uniquely positioned to provide institutional leadership, and there is an opportunity to coordinate governmental and private sector efforts. US secretary of state Hillary Clinton successfully pioneered this type of convergence in 2009–2013 around issues such as women's empowerment.

Encouraging cultural evolution—particularly on an issue such as respect for the rights of LGBTQI people, which remains a taboo topic in many places—is particularly challenging. This is not an argument for cultural relativism; universal human rights must be universal. And activists do need support from the international community. But humility and sensitivity—in addition to courage and conviction—are critical if we want to successfully reinvent foreign policy to be truly inclusive.

How Work on LGBTQI Rights Contributes to an Effective Foreign Policy

The moral reason for governments to work on reinforcing the human rights of queer people—to uphold the equal dignity of all persons—is sufficient to warrant action, but it is not the only reason. A more inclusive foreign policy—inclusive in its scope (the issues that it addresses) and in its approach (the individuals and organizations with which it engages)—also pays dividends in other ways. Arguably the most successful and courageous assistance project of the George W. Bush administration's foreign policy was the President's Emergency Plan for AIDS Relief (PEPFAR), which has invested billions of dollars internationally in addressing the AIDS epidemic. The stigma and discrimination against LGBTQI populations in countries plagued by the AIDS epidemic have been a key hurdle in reaching affected individuals and developing maximally effective public health responses. The US government's support for anti-discrimination policies also contributed to making its public health assistance more likely to succeed. More broadly, the inclusion of LGBTQI human rights in US foreign policy has led to a more richly nuanced understanding of other societies by the US foreign policy bureaucracy. Crafting effective public diplomacy and foreign policy requires knowledge of other countries, and broadening the lens of understanding to include LGBTQI people, women, refugees, religious minorities, and so on makes foreign policy better informed and more likely to succeed.

Notes

1. Roosevelt 1949.
2. UN General Assembly 1948.
3. UN General Assembly 2018.
4. Gates 2011.
5. Census Organization of India 2011.
6. Power 2019.
7. McKay, Misra, and Lindquist 2017.
8. US Department of Justice 2017; De Oliveira 2017; SOS Homophobie 2019, 14. The term "trans" (also sometimes "transsexual," "transgender") refers to "someone who feels that they are not the same gender (i.e., sex) as the physical body they was born with, or who does not fit easily into being either a male or a female" (*Cambridge Dictionary*, s.v. "trans," https://diction ary.cambridge.org/us/dictionary/english/trans).
9. Transgender Europe 2019.
10. O'Flaherty and Fisher 2008, 209.
11. Thoreson 2020; LGBT Foundation 2020; Muhumuza 2020; Human Rights Campaign Foundation 2020; UNHCR 2020.
12. Sozashvili 2020.
13. This number varies due to Sri Lanka's law, which bans same-sex relations. This law is dormant, but Sri Lanka's constitutional laws cannot be removed, only reinterpreted.
14. Mendos 2019.
15. EU Agency for Fundamental Rights 2013.
16. Badgett et al. 2014, 45.
17. Badgett 2014.
18. Han and O'Mahoney 2014.
19. Human Rights Watch 2008.
20. Healey 2001.
21. Blake 2014.
22. Thoreson 2015.

23. Dan Baer, personal communication, April 2020.
24. Paris 2019; Human Rights Watch n.d.
25. Gera 2019; Kaoma 2009.
26. Brechenmacher 2017. Also see International Center for Not-for-Profit Law 2016.
27. United Nations 2017.
28. Steger 2018.
29. European External Action Service 2017.
30. Rowley 2019.
31. Ketelaars 2018.
32. Whyte 2018.
33. Morris 2009.
34. *Lawrence v. Texas*, 539 US 558 (2003).
35. *Goodridge vs. Massachusetts Department of Public Health*, 440 Mass. 309 (2003).
36. Kowal 2015.
37. Shanker and Healy 2007; Obama and McCain 2008.
38. Clinton 2011.
39. Clinton 2011.
40. Obama 2011.
41. Biden 2021.
42. Dan Baer, personal communication, April 2020.
43. US State Department 2017–2021.
44. Clinton 2011.
45. White House 2015.
46. UN General Assembly Human Rights Council 2011.
47. United Nations 2010; UN General Assembly 2016.
48. Lavers 2017.
49. Gauette and Hansler 2020; Hansler 2020.
50. Johnson 2020.
51. Transgender Europe n.d.
52. UNHCR n.d.
53. Mendos 2019.
54. Dalton and Ong 2001.
55. Carroll and Robotham 2016.
56. Human Rights Watch 2015.
57. Boudreau 2015.
58. Eristavi 2017.
59. Eristavi 2019; Baer 2017.
60. Eristavi 2018.
61. Putin and Merkel 2017.
62. Lytvynenko 2019; Roth 2019.
63. Gessen 2018; Eristavi 2019.
64. Wamberg Anderson 2015.
65. Williams and Zinets 2016.
66. *Oroaco v. Attorney General of Belize*, no. 668 (2016).
67. Belize Hub 2019.
68. Helfer 2002.
69. *Lawrence v. Texas*, 539 US 558 (2003).
70. Peletz 2006.
71. Harvard Divinity School 2018.
72. Ganguly 2018.

73. Feder 2019.

74. Thoreson 2015.

75. UN Human Rights Office n.d.; World Economic Forum 2019. The Open for Business website is https://open-for-business.org/.

Bibliography

Badgett, M. V. Lee. 2014. "The Economic Cost of Stigma and the Exclusion of LGBT People: A Case Study of India." World Bank. October. http://documents.worldbank.org/curated/en/527 261468035379692/pdf/940400WP0Box380usion0of0LGBT0People.pdf.

Badgett, M. V. Lee, Sheila Nezhad, Kees Waaldijk, and Yana van der Meulen Rodgers. 2014. "The Relationship Between LGBT Inclusion and Economic Development: An Analysis of Emerging Economies." Williams Institute. October. https://williamsinstitute.law.ucla.edu/wp-content/uploads/lgbt-inclusion-and-development-november-2014.pdf.

Baer, Daniel. 2017. "Anti-Gay Violence in Chechnya Exposes Putin's Weakness." *The Denver Post*, June 30.

Belize Hub. 2019. "First Lady of Belize Calls for End to Anti-Gay Violence." December 16. https://www.belizehub.com/first-lady-of-belize-calls-for-end-to-anti-gay-violence/.

Biden, Joseph R. 2021. "Memorandum on Advancing the Human Rights of Lesbian, Gay, Bisexual, Transgender, Queer, and Intersex Persons Around the World." February 4. https://www.whitehouse.gov/briefing-room/presidential-actions/2021/02/04/memorandum-advancing-the-human-rights-of-lesbian-gay-bisexual-transgender-queer-and-intersex-persons-around-the-world/.

Blake, Mariah. 2014. "Meet the American Pastor Behind Uganda's Anti-Gay Crackdown." *Mother Jones*, March 10. https://www.motherjones.com/politics/2014/03/scott-lively-anti-gay-law-uganda.

Boudreau, John. 2015. "Meet Vietnam's Gay Power Couple: U.S. Ambassador and His Husband." Bloomberg, August 2. https://www.bloomberg.com/news/articles/2015-08-02/meet-vietnams-gay-power-couple-u-s-ambassador-and-his-husband.

Brechenmacher, Saskia. 2017. "How State Restrictions Are Reshaping Civic Space Around the World." IPI Global Observatory. May 19. https://theglobalobservatory.org/2017/05/ethiopia-russia-egypt-civil-society/.

Carroll, Aengus, and George Robotham. 2016. "The Personal and the Political: Attitudes to LGBTI People Around the World." International Lesbian, Gay, Bisexual, Trans and Intersex Association. October. https://ilga.org/downloads/Ilga_Riwi_Attitudes_LGBTI_survey_Logo _personal_political.pdf.

Census Organization of India. 2011. "Transgender in India." Census 2011. http://www.census2 011.co.in/transgender.php.

Clinton, Hillary. 2011. "Remarks in Recognition of International Human Rights Day." Speech, Geneva, December 6. US Department of State: Diplomacy in Action. https://2009-2017.state. gov/secretary/20092013clinton/rm/2011/12/178368.htm.

Dalton, Russell J., and Nhu-Ngoc T. Ong. 2001. "The Vietnamese Public in Transition—The World Values Survey: Vietnam 2001." University of California, Irvine Center for the Study of Democracy. https://web.archive.org/web/20060901141246/http://www.democ.uci.edu/resour ces/virtuallibrary/vietnam/vietnam01.pdf.

De Oliveira, Feruchio. 2017. "Mortes Violentas de LGBT No Brasil Relatório 2017." Grupo Gay de Bahia. https://homofobiamata.files.wordpress.com/2017/12/relatorio-2081.pdf.

Eristavi, Maxim. 2019. "Time to Shame Putin Again." Atlantic Council. January 29. https://www. atlanticcouncil.org/blogs/ukrainealert/time-to-shame-putin-again.

Eristavi, Maxim. 2018. "Interpol Keeps Despots' Dissidents Close." Politico, December 13. https:// www.politico.eu/article/interpol-russian-abuse-keeps-despots-dissidents-close/.

Eristavi, Maxim. 2017. "This Is What We Know About the LGBT Executions in Russia's Chechnya." *Hromadske,* April 6. https://en.hromadske.ua/posts/lgbti-executions-in-russias-chechnya.

EU Agency for Fundamental Rights. 2013. "EU LGBT Survey: Results at a Glance." European Union Agency for Fundamental Rights. https://fra.europa.eu/sites/default/files/eu-lgbt-survey-results-at-a-glance_en.pdf.

European External Action Service. 2017. "Homophobic Hate Speech on Russian TV." EU vs. DISINFO. March 13. https://euvsdisinfo.eu/homophobic-hate-speech-on-russian-tv/.

Feder, J. Lester. 2019. "Struggle Among Progress as Countries Restrict L.G.B.T.Q. Rights." *New York Times,* June 23. https://www.nytimes.com/2019/06/23/world/global-lgbtq-rights.html.

Ganguly, Meenakshi. 2018. "South Asia's Third Gender Court Judgments Set Example: Netherlands Court Cites India, Nepal Cases." Human Rights Watch. June 6. https://www.hrw.org/news/2018/06/06/south-asias-third-gender-court-judgments-set-example#.

Gates, Gary J. 2011. "How Many People Are Lesbian, Gay, Bisexual, and Transgender?" Williams Institute. April. https://williamsinstitute.law.ucla.edu/wp-content/uploads/Gates-How-Many-People-LGBT-Apr-2011.pdf.

Gauette, Nicole, and Jennifer Hansler. 2020. "U.S. Embassy in Seoul Removes Black Lives Matter Banner and Pride Flag." CNN, June 15. https://www.cnn.com/2020/06/15/politics/us-embassy-seoul-blm-banner/index.html.

Gera, Vanessa. 2019. "Polish Leader Calls LGBT Rights an Imported Threat to Poland." Associated Press, April 25. https://www.usnews.com/news/world/articles/2019-04-25/polish-leader-lgbt-rights-an-import-that-threatens-nation.

Gessen, Masha. 2018. "Fleeting Anti-Gay Persecution in Chechnya, Three Young Women Are Now Stuck in Place." *The New Yorker,* October 1. https://www.newyorker.com/news/our-columnists/fleeing-anti-gay-persecution-in-chechnya-three-young-women-are-now-stuck-in-place.

Han, E. and J. O'Mahoney. 2014. "British Colonialism and the Criminalization of Homosexuality." *Cambridge Journal of International Affairs* 27, no. 2: 268–288.

Hansler, Jennifer. 2020. "Over 200 Human Rights Groups and Experts Denounce Pompeo's Unalienable Rights Commission Report." CNN, July 30. https://www.cnn.com/2020/07/30/politics/unalienable-rights-report-opposition-letter/index.html.

Harvard Divinity School. 2018. "Hinduism Case Study—Gender: The Third Gender and the Hijras." Harvard Divinity School Religious Literacy Project. https://rlp.hds.harvard.edu/files/hds-rlp/files/gender_hinduism.pdf.

Healey, Dan. 2001. *Homosexual Desire in Revolutionary Russia: The Regulation of Sexual and Gender Dissent.* Chicago: University of Chicago Press.

Helfer, Laurence L. 2002. "Overlegalizing Human Rights: International Relations Theory and the Commonwealth Caribbean Backlash Against Human Rights Regimes." *Columbia Law Review* 102: 1832–1911. https://scholarship.law.duke.edu/faculty_scholarship/2030/.

Herdt, Gilbert, ed. *Moral Panics, Sex Panics: Fear and Fight over Sexual Rights.* New York: NYU Press.

Human Rights Campaign Foundation. 2020. "The Lives and Livelihoods of Many in the LGBTQ Community Are at Risk Amidst COVID-19 Crisis." https://assets2.hrc.org/files/assets/resources/COVID19-IssueBrief-032020-FINAL.pdf?_ga=2.196211308.177186609.1589805247-397864020.1589805247.

Human Rights Watch. 2015. "Vietnam: Positive Step Toward Transgender Rights." November 30. https://www.hrw.org/news/2015/11/30/vietnam-positive-step-transgender-rights.

Human Rights Watch. 2008. "The Alien Legacy: The Origins of 'Sodomy' Laws in British Colonialism." December. https://www.hrw.org/sites/default/files/reports/lgbt1208_web.pdf.

Human Rights Watch. n.d. "Brunei." Human Rights Watch Country Profiles: Sexual Orientation and Gender Identity. Accessed September 20, 2020. https://www.hrw.org/video-photos/interactive/2020/06/22/human-rights-watch-country-profiles-sexual-orientation-and.

International Center for Not-for-Profit Law. 2016. "Survey of Trends Affecting Civic Space: 2015–16." https://www.icnl.org/resources/research/global-trends-ngo-law/survey-of-trends-affecting-civic-space-2015-16.

Johnson, Chris. 2020. "Ric Grenell Snaps at Reporter for Asking About Decriminalizing Homosexuality." *The Washington Blade*, September 4. https://www.washingtonblade.com/2020/09/04/ric-grenell-snaps-at-reporter-for-asking-about-decriminalizing-homosexuality/.

Kaoma, Kapya. 2009. "Globalizing the Culture Wars: U.S. Conservatives, African Churches, Homophobia." Political Research Associates. 2009. https://www.politicalresearch.org/2009/12/01/globalizing-culture-wars#The_African_Context.

Ketelaars, Elise. 2018. "When 'European Values' Do Not Count: Anti-Gender Ideology and the Failure to Comprehensively Address GBV in Ukraine." London School of Economics and Political Science. September 24. https://blogs.lse.ac.uk/gender/2018/09/26/when-european-values-do-not-count-anti-gender-ideology-and-the-failure-to-comprehensively-address-gbv-in-ukraine/.

Kowal, John F. 2015. "The Improbable Victory of Marriage Equality." Brennan Center for Justice. September 29. https://www.brennancenter.org/analysis/improbable-victory-marriage-equality.

Lavers, Michael. 2017. "Tillerson Raises Anti-Gay Chechnya Crackdown with Russian Counterpart." *The Washington Blade*, September 5. https://www.washingtonblade.com/2017/09/05/tillerson-raises-anti-gay-chechnya-crackdown-letter-russian-counterpart/.

LGBT Foundation. 2020. "Why LGBT People Are Disproportionately Impacted by Coronavirus." May 29. https://lgbt.foundation/coronavirus/impact.

Lytvynenko, Jane. 2019. "There Has Been a Resurgence of Detentions of LGBT People in Chechnya, According to Reports." BuzzFeed News, January 11. https://www.buzzfeednews.com/article/janelytvynenko/new-gay-crackdown-chechnya-activists-say.

McKay, Tasseli, Shilpi Misra, and Christine Lindquist. 2017. "Violence and LGBTQ+ Communities: What Do We Know, and What Do We Need to Know?" Research Triangle Institute International. March. https://www.rti.org/sites/default/files/rti_violence_and_lgbtq_communities.pdf.

Mendos, Lucas Ramón. 2019. "State-Sponsored Homophobia." International Lesbian, Gay, Bisexual, Trans and Intersex Association. March 2019. https://ilga.org/downloads/ILGA_State_Sponsored_Homophobia_2019.pdf.

Morris, Bonnie J. 2009. "History of Lesbian, Gay, Bisexual and Transgender Social Movements." American Psychological Association. https://www.apa.org/pi/lgbt/resources/history.

Muhumuza, Rodney. 2020. "LGBT Community Raided in Uganda over Social Distancing." ABC News, April 1. https://abcnews.go.com/International/wireStory/lgbt-community-raided-uganda-social-distancing-69915445.

O'Flaherty, Michael, and John Fisher. 2008. "Sexual Orientation, Gender Identity and International Human Rights Law: Contextualising the Yogyakarta Principles." *Human Rights Law Review* 8, no. 2: 207–248. https://globalfop.files.wordpress.com/2012/11/sexual-orientation-gender-identity-and-international-human-rights-law-contextualising-the-yogyakarta-principles.pdf.

Obama, Barack. 2011. "President Barack Obama to the Heads of Executive Departments and Agencies, December 6, 2011." Office of the Press Secretary, International Initiatives to Advance the Human Rights of Lesbian, Gay, Bisexual, and Transgender Persons. https://obamawhitehouse.archives.gov/the-press-office/2011/12/06/presidential-memorandum-international-initiatives-advance-human-rights-l.

Obama, Barack, and John McCain. 2008. "Saddleback Presidential Forum." Interview by Rick Warren in Lake Forest, CA, August 17. https://votesmart.org/public-statement/658545/full-transcript-saddleback-presidential-forum-sen-barack-obama-john-mccain-moderated-by-rick-warren/?search=saddleback#.XQJ6n29KjEZ.

Paris, Francesca. 2019. "Death by Stoning Among Punishments in New Brunei Anti-LGBT, Criminal Laws." National Public Radio, April 3. https://www.npr.org/2019/04/03/709359137/death-by-stoning-among-punishments-in-new-brunei-anti-lgbt-criminal-laws.

Peletz, Michael G. 2006. "Transgenderism and Gender Pluralism in Southeast Asia Since Early Modern Times." *Current Anthropology* 47 no. 2: 309–340. https://www.jstor.org/stable/pdf/10.1086/498947.pdf?refreqid=excelsior%3Aa6973b7d69f32228ddf4561129e61b98.

Power, Jack. 2019. "Number of Same Sex Marriages Dips After Post-Referendum Rush." *The Irish Times*, October 14. https://www.irishtimes.com/news/ireland/irish-news/number-of-same-sex-marriages-dips-after-post-referendum-rush-1.4050372.

Putin, Vladimir, and Angela Merkel. 2017. "Vladimir Putin and German Chancellor Angela Merkel Holding a Joint Press Conference." Press conference, May 2, 2017. https://www.yout ube.com/watch?v=HjSkzcZFZqw.

Rehman, Javaid, and Eleni Polymenopoulou. 2013. "Is Green a Part of the Rainbow? Sharia, Homosexuality and LGBT Rights in the Muslim World." *Fordham International Law Journal* 37 no. 1: art. 7. https://ir.lawnet.fordham.edu/cgi/viewcontent.cgi?article=2322&context=ilj.

Roosevelt, Eleanor. 1949. "Making Human Rights Come Alive." Speech, New York, March 30. Iowa State University Archives of Women's Political Communication. https://awpc.cattcenter. iastate.edu/2017/03/21/making-human-rights-come-alive-march-30-1949/.

Roth, Andrew. 2019. "Chechnya: Two Dead and Dozens Held in LGBT Purge, Say Activists." *The Guardian*, January 14. https://www.theguardian.com/world/2019/jan/14/chechnya-two-dead-and-dozens-held-in-lgbt-purge-reports.

Rowley, Thomas. 2019. "Ahead of Presidential Elections, 'Gender Ideology' Comes to Ukraine." OpenDemocracy. March 21. https://www.opendemocracy.net/en/odr/ahead-of-presidential-elections-gender-ideology-comes-to-ukraine/.

Shanker, Thom, and Patrick Healy. 2007. "A New Push to Roll Back 'Don't Ask, Don't Tell.'" *New York Times*, November 30. https://www.nytimes.com/2007/11/30/us/30military.html.

SOS Homophobie. 2019. *Rapport sur l'homophobie 2019.* https://www.sos-homophobie.org/sites/ default/files/rapport_homophobie_2019_interactif.pdf.

Sozashvili, Tamaz. 2020. "Transgender Woman Sets Herself on Fire in Tbilisi." OC Media, April 30. https://oc-media.org/transgender-woman-sets-herself-on-fire-in-tbilisi/.

Steger, Isabella. 2018. "How Taiwan Battled Fake Anti-LGBT News Before Its Vote on Same-Sex Marriage." *Quartz,* November 22. https://qz.com/1471411/chat-apps-like-line-spread-anti-lgbt-fake-news-before-taiwan-same-sex-marriage-vote/.

Thoreson, Ryan. 2020. "Covid-19 Backlash Targets LGBT People in South Korea." Human Rights Watch. September 17. https://www.hrw.org/news/2020/05/13/covid-19-backlash-targets-lgbt-people-south-korea.

Thoreson, Ryan. 2015. "From Child Protection to Children's Rights: Rethinking Homosexual Propaganda Bans in Human Rights Law." *Yale Law Journal* 124, no. 4. https://www.yalelawjour nal.org/comment/homosexual-propaganda-bans-in-human-rights-law.

Transgender Europe. 2019. "Trans Day of Remembrance (TDoR) Press Release 2019." Trans Murder Monitoring Project, press release. November 12. https://transrespect.org/en/tmm-update-trans-day-of-remembrance-2019/.

Transgender Europe. n.d. "The Yogyakarta Principles: How International Human Rights Protect LGBTI People." https://tgeu.org/yogyakarta-principles/.

UN General Assembly. 2018. "National Institutions for the Promotion and Protection of Human Rights, A/Res/72/181 (29 January 2018)." https://www.un.org/en/ga/search/view_doc. asp?symbol=A/RES/72/181.

UN General Assembly. 2016. "Extrajudicial, Summary and Arbitrary Executions, A/C.3/71/L.38, (31 October 2016)." https://undocs.org/A/C.3/71/L.38.

UN General Assembly. 1948. "Universal Declaration of Human Rights." 217 A (III). December 10. https://www.un.org/en/universal-declaration-human-rights/.

UN General Assembly Human Rights Council. 2011. "Resolution 17/19, Human Rights, Sexual Orientation and Gender Identity, A/HRC/RES/17/19 (14 July 2011)." http://arc-international. net/wp-content/uploads/2011/08/HRC-Res-17-191.pdf.

UN Human Rights Office. n.d. "Global Business Standards." UNFE. https://www.unfe.org/ standards/.

UNHCR. 2020. "COVID-19 and the Human Rights of LGBTI People." Office of the United Nations High Commissioner for Human Rights. April 17. https://www.ohchr.org/Documents/ Issues/LGBT/LGBTIpeople.pdf.

UNHCR. n.d. "United Nations Resolutions—Sexual Orientation and Gender Identity." Office of the United Nations High Commissioner for Human Rights. Accessed September 20, 2020. https://www.ohchr.org/EN/Issues/Discrimination/Pages/LGBTUNResolutions.aspx.

United Nations. 2017. "Action Needed to Stop Violations of LGBT People's Rights Worldwide, Expert Tells UN." UN News. October 27, 2017. https://news.un.org/en/story/2017/10/569492-action-needed-stop-violations-lgbt-peoples-rights-worldwide-expert-tells-un.

United Nations. 2010. "General Assembly Adopts 52 Resolutions, 6 Decisions Recommended by Third Committee on Broad Range of Human Rights, Social, Cultural Issues, GA/11041." Press release, December 21. https://www.un.org/press/en/2010/ga11041.doc.htm.

US Department of Justice. 2017. "Hate Crime Statistics (FBI)." https://ucr.fbi.gov/hate-crime/2017/topic-pages/victims.

US State Department. 2017–2021. "Country Reports on Human Rights Practices." https://www.state.gov/reports-bureau-of-democracy-human-rights-and-labor/country-reports-on-human-rights-practices/.

Wamberg Anderson, Johannes. 2015. "Ukraine Finally Passes Anti-Bias Law, a Prerequisite for Visa-Free Travel to EU." *Kyiv Post*, November 12. https://web.archive.org/web/20151112162819/http://www.kyivpost.com/content/kyiv-post-plus/ukrainian-finally-passes-anti-bias-law-a-prerequisite-for-visa-free-travel-to-eu-401906.html.

White House. 2015. "Fact Sheet: Promoting and Protecting the Human Rights of LGBT Persons: A United States Government Priority." White House Office of the Press Secretary. May 16. https://obamawhitehouse.archives.gov/the-press-office/2015/05/16/fact-sheet-promoting-and-protecting-human-rights-lgbt-persons-united-sta.

Whyte, Lara. 2018. "US and Russian Religious Right Unite Against 'Invasion of Radical Liberalism.'" OpenDemocracy. September 26. https://www.opendemocracy.net/en/5050/us-and-russian-religious-right-unite-against-radical-liberalism/.

Williams, Matthias, and Natalia Zinets. 2016. "Praise from West After Mostly Peaceful Kiev Pride March." Reuters, June 12. https://www.reuters.com/article/us-ukraine-pride-parade/praise-from-west-after-mostly-peaceful-kiev-pride-march-idUSKCN0YY0FD.

World Economic Forum. 2019. "Global Businesses Launch Partnership for Global LGBTI Equality." Press release. January 22. https://www.weforum.org/press/2019/01/global-businesses-launch-partnership-for-global-lgbti-equality/.

6

Advancing Disability-Inclusive Development

Janet E. Lord and Michael Ashley Stein

> Disability inclusion is an essential condition to upholding human rights, sustainable development, and peace and security. It is also central to the promise of the 2030 Agenda for Sustainable Development to leave no one behind. The commitment to realizing the rights of persons with disabilities is not only a matter of justice; it is an investment in a common future.
>
> —UN Secretary General, 2020

Introduction

At the dawn of the new millennium, persons with disabilities—a population of more than 1 billion worldwide—were unrecognized as stakeholders in development or humanitarian action.[1] To illustrate: the wildly successful Nobel Prize–winning campaign, the International Campaign to Ban Landmines, was heralded as a remarkable success and helped place the rights of landmine survivors on the international radar, yet there was little in the way of disability-inclusive laws and policies domestically within countries, or internationally in development assistance. Consequently, the adoption in 1997 of the Landmines Treaty resulted in a weakly worded provision that required states to facilitate the socioeconomic reintegration of landmine survivors into society.[2] This, in turn, led to an increase in funding of rehabilitation programs for landmine survivors, often by supplying prostheses to amputees and underwriting small-scale livelihood initiatives. These schemes were beneficial to landmine survivors, but in the broader context of international development and humanitarian assistance they had negligible impact. Specifically, funding to build schools, medical clinics, transport systems, and programs to feed people facing food insecurity and famine continued to be designed and implemented largely without taking into account the needs of beneficiaries with disabilities, whether physical, mental, or sensory.[3]

The adoption of the Convention on the Rights of Persons with Disabilities (CRPD) in 2006 brought about significant shifts in international policy on disability as well as domestic disability law, policy, and institutional change.[4] This was made possible by a drafting process initiated by Mexico, an unlikely champion of disability rights, and characterized by its participatory dynamic as well as the advocacy of persons with disabilities themselves from all corners of the globe. The promise of the convention—to ensure the fundamental human rights and freedoms of persons with disabilities—has manifested in greater disability awareness and prompted much-needed disability inclusion in development, diplomacy, and humanitarian action. Such inclusion of people with disabilities also applies in the Sustainable Development Goals (SDGs) metric "Leave no one behind."[5] Relatedly, in 2018, the United Nations released a flagship report outlining the future initiatives to achieve the SDGs "by, for, and with persons with disabilities."[6] Nevertheless, comprehensive and effective implementation of the CRPD's core principles is still very much a work in progress, and entire areas of programming remain neglected. The exclusion of persons with disabilities from development schemes is especially striking and detrimental given that 80 percent of disabled people live in the developing world.

This chapter provides the context for the global movement advancing disability inclusion in development and in humanitarian action, provides current examples of progress, and highlights some challenges and opportunities for advancement. First, we set out the conceptual framework for thinking about disability inclusion, pointing to the shift in perspective around disability brought about by the CRPD's adoption. Next, we trace the emergence of a new and distinct field of international development and humanitarian action, providing illustrations of disability inclusion. Finally, we turn to challenges that persist in bringing about the inclusion of persons with disabilities in development and humanitarian action, and note some avenues for improvement.

Conceptualizing Disability in Development and Humanitarian Action

Individuals with disabilities face isolation and exclusion in their communities and are routinely denied access to education, employment, health care services, and basic needs.[7] As a result, persons with disabilities have lower education and employment levels, have poorer health outcomes, are more likely to have incomes below established poverty thresholds, and are less likely to have savings and other assets than the wider population.[8] In all countries, disability prevalence rates are significantly higher among groups with lower economic status, underscoring the linkage between poverty and disability: one of every five of the world's poorest persons has a disability.[9]

Persons with disabilities, like other beneficiaries of development and humanitarian assistance programs, have a multitude of identity characteristics that produce different and intersectional barriers (see Box 6.1). A woman with a disability is more likely to be poor, and is at greater risk than her nondisabled peer of being a survivor of sexual violence. Her exposure to sexual violence makes her at high risk for HIV infection, and yet all too often she is left out of HIV programming.[10] This complexity and heterogeneity pose a significant challenge to development and humanitarian communities, who are, more than ever, cognizant of the need to ensure diversity, quality, and inclusion in order to do no harm and, further, to affirmatively ensure rights protection.

Box 6.1 Framing Disability

Persons with disabilities are individuals with long-term physical, mental, intellectual, or sensory impairments, which in interaction with various barriers may hinder their full and effective participation in society on an equal basis with others.

- Disability is an evolving concept.
- Disability is diverse, encompassing a wide range of impairments.
- Disability, like gender, is cross-cutting, with implications across law, policy, environmental, and social domains.

Traditional framing of disability as a medical problem needing a "fix" or "cure," or as a charity endeavor provoking paternalistic impulses, perpetuates stereotyping, undermines agency, and entrenches exclusion of persons with disabilities.[11] In particular, the "medical model" of disability pathologizes disability as a deficit that must be corrected as a prerequisite for full participation in society. In consequence, those who cannot be "cured" were and often are isolated and channeled into segregated settings, such as separate schools and residential institutions. This systemic exclusion makes persons with disabilities invisible and unheard, hence the refrain of the disability community globally: "Nothing About Us Without Us." Exclusion magnifies the very conditions that compromise stability and development in poor, fragile, and conflict-affected states. Consequently, the daily lives of persons with disabilities typically involve conditions of extreme poverty and social isolation.[12]

By contrast, a social model of disability frames disability-related disadvantage not as an inherent biological condition but rather as a condition arising from the interaction between individual impairment and the ways societies choose to construct physical, communicative, legal, and attitudinal barriers (see Box 6.1). Consider, for example, the impact on an individual who mobilizes with a wheelchair or has difficulty balancing when attempting to access a public venue that can only be entered via stairs. The social model identifies the sociocontextual understanding of disability and seeks to identify and dismantle gratuitous barriers for all persons with disabilities. Here, the emphasis is on questioning and amending the use of stairs rather than excluding persons with disabilities from social participation based on unnecessary criteria.

The emergence of disability rights standards set forth in the CRPD is contributing to a global shift away from the traditional conceptualization of disability as a narrow medical issue or charitable concern limited to beneficent ideas about rehabilitating disabled people or caring for wounded and disabled soldiers. Instead, the CRPD is precipitating the framing of disability in human rights law and policy changes that embrace the social model of disability.[13] In doing so, the CRPD is driving away from disability as an individual deficit and toward the identification and removal of hindrances that inhibit the full realization of personhood.

Movement Building: Globalizing Disability Rights

At the close of the twentieth century, an emerging global movement of persons with disabilities began to expose a major deficiency in the international human rights framework. Years of advocacy headed by civil society and NGOs, mostly in the West but expanding across the globe, preceded international policymaking.[14] No human rights treaty comprehensively focused on the specific barriers encountered by persons with disabilities, and the vast majority of governments around the world had little to no disability rights protection in law or policy.[15] Instead, references to disability were limited to the narrow confines of social protection.

A report issued in 2002 by the UN Office of the High Commissioner for Human Rights (OHCHR) demonstrated that the existing human rights system hardly ever addressed routine human rights violations to which people with disabilities were subjected.[16] While disability-based human rights were covered theoretically by human rights law and addressed in several disability-specific nonbinding international initiatives, in fact they did little to advance disability human rights.[17] This gap reinforced an advocacy gap whereby neither organizations of persons with disabilities (OPDs) nor mainstream human rights organizations (like Amnesty International and Human Rights Watch) engaged in rights work using existing human rights treaty frameworks for persons with disabilities. Mainstream human rights organizations possessed no disability expertise and focused their efforts on traditional civil and political rights issues, such as the rights of prisoners and the persecution of political dissidents. Concurrently, OPDs were typically narrowly focused, service-provision-oriented groups with limited law and policy advocacy experience and little to no engagement in the global human rights movement.

A successful initiative to develop a treaty on the human rights of persons with disabilities was launched by Mexico in 2001. Mexico prioritized disability issues as part of its national plan through an influential presidential candidate who made his way into President Fox's administration and also served on the Mexican delegation to the World Conference Against Racism in Durban, South Africa. The Mexican Durban delegation succeeded in having disability included in the platform of action adopted at the conference.[18] In the UN General Assembly session that followed, Mexico put forward a proposal that resulted in the adoption of a resolution calling for the establishment of an ad hoc committee mandated with elaborating "a comprehensive and integral international convention to promote and protect the rights and dignity of persons with disabilities, based on the holistic approach of the work done in the field of social development, human rights and non-discrimination."[19] While this effort came largely out of the blue, OPDs soon mobilized and, working closely with the Mexican government, pressured other UN member states to support the Mexican effort. Strikingly, it was Mexico that sought to engage the support of disability rights organizations for its treaty initiative.

Working closely with the Mexican delegation to the UN, disability rights advocates made the case for a thematically focused treaty on the rights of persons with disabilities that would foster law and policy change domestically and also bring about changes in the implementation of international development and humanitarian assistance programs.[20] OPDs noted, for example, that disability did not at all figure into the Millennium Development Goals, all of which were salient to disability.[21]

A concerted effort to support the participation of disabled activists from developing countries in the drafting of the CRPD also helped focus attention on efforts to ensure that the treaty text reflected the concerns of persons with disabilities from developing countries. A voluntary fund was established by the UN to facilitate participation in the New York treaty process by experts with disabilities from developing countries. Disabled Peoples International (DPI) and the Landmine Survivors Network (LSN) joined efforts to support diverse activists from developing countries in attending a three-day intensive advocacy workshop prior to the negotiations in 2003 in order to orient newcomers to the process.[22] A "rough guide" to the negotiations was developed for advocates, outlining tactics for effective advocacy. LSN also provided training supported by the Mexican delegation to the UN at their permanent mission for new government delegates attending drafting sessions, and shared detailed legal analysis of successive drafts of the treaty. LSN also drew on prior successes around environmental treaty processes and provided detailed day-by-day accounts of the negotiations, which made the process transparent and accessible.

A global caucus, the International Disability Caucus (IDC), which included DPI and LSN, among others, was formed and served as the focal point for a common lobbying position among disability organizations. While a common position was ostensibly forged around the shape of the text, the reality was far more complex and masked often significant disagreement regarding some of the more contentious treaty provisions. Disagreement surfaced around various provisions, including, for instance, the text on education and whether it should reflect only inclusive education or preserve choice for parents to place their children in separate schools. Significant disagreement also emerged around the protection of persons with psychosocial disabilities from forced medical intervention and involuntary institutionalization. The prevailing view within the IDC reflected the position of the World Network of Survivors and Users of Psychiatry that the treaty must prohibit all forms of forced treatment in all cases, whereas other advocates, including OPDs from Australia, cautioned against an approach that would prohibit involuntary treatment in all cases. OPDs from the global South, not present at the outset of the negotiations, were highly engaged in the second half of the process, and the resulting text, with its emphasis on issues such as inclusive development, poverty, and economic, social, and cultural rights, reflect their advocacy.

Negotiating sessions at the UN, regional meetings, and extensive networking harnessed, for the first time in the negotiation of a core UN human rights convention, technological advances by using email, Skype meet-up, and texting during the meeting itself. Side events sensitized governments to some of the issues disability rights advocates wanted reflected in the text. Alliances formed around particular provisions. The inclusion of a provision explicitly addressing women and girls with disabilities, for instance, reflected an effort by Korean disability advocates who worked closely with their government to see a specific article successfully included in the final text.[23]

Convention on the Rights of Persons with Disabilities

The adoption of the CRPD in 2006 proved to be the impetus for providing real and concrete guidance on the design of development and humanitarian interventions. Its principles of nondiscrimination, inclusion, participation, and accessibility, among others, offer a framework within which development and humanitarian work can be made more inclusive of persons with disabilities and responsive to their specific needs. Additionally, and critical to a holistic approach to inclusive development, the CRPD offers a guide for law reform efforts and institution-building processes that must adhere to human rights standards. To this end, development work that supports human rights and rule of law strengthening is supporting efforts to assist developing countries in the implementation of the CRPD. This is a long-term process, but such efforts have contributed to building understanding and agendas for reform based on the obligations set out in the CRPD.

One of the central requirements of the CRPD is to clarify and make applicable to persons with disabilities the existing human rights standards set out in earlier instruments of human rights law. This entails a generic standard—for instance, the right to equality and nondiscrimination, the prohibition against torture, the right to legal recognition before the law, or the right to education—to be squared with the specific barriers that persons with disabilities often experience in accessing those rights. In the context of development and humanitarian action in conflict situations, this necessitates attention to human rights principles as they impact persons with disabilities. Illustrative questions that arise include the following:

- How are nondiscrimination and equality to be achieved for a child refugee with a disability? Would, for example, a humanitarian organization in charge of distributing food in a refugee camp need to take specific measures to ensure that child refugees with disabilities have access to food?
- Does the prohibition against torture require any positive action on the part of prison authorities with respect to a prisoner with a disability? Would, for example, the failure to provide accessible toilet accommodations for a prisoner with a physical disability fall afoul of the prohibition against torture or other inhuman and degrading treatment or punishment?
- What does education law reform need to take into account to ensure the right to inclusive education for students with disabilities? Would provisions on reasonable accommodation and barrier removal need to be reflected in the legal framework on education?

Furthermore, Article 32 of the CRPD sets out obligations to ensure that international development programs—whatever the sector of development in question—are inclusive of persons with disabilities, both as beneficiaries of development and as participants in the processes of development.[24] Similarly, Article 11 of the CRPD requires positive measures of protection and safety for persons with disability who are affected by situations of risk, be it natural disaster, armed conflict, or other emergency.[25] This is further amplified by the language in the CRPD Preamble according to which "the observance of applicable human rights instruments are indispensable for the full protection of persons with disabilities, in particular during armed conflicts and foreign occupation."[26] Last, the Preamble to the CRPD, in paragraph (g), evokes disability inclusion as an essential strategy of sustainable development in pointing to the "mainstreaming disability issues as an integral part of relevant strategies of sustainable development."[27]

The implications of these provisions for international development, humanitarian action, and diplomacy are clear. They speak not only to the role of state actors in identifying and dismantling barriers to participation in development and engagement in humanitarian action and post-conflict reconstruction, but also to the important role of private actors, such as humanitarian actors or development agencies, in ensuring the CRPD's implementation. The impact of CRPD provisions requiring disability inclusion in development, diplomacy, and humanitarian action is demonstrable, as the rest of this chapter will illustrate. In sum, the tangible evidence of a shifting narrative around disability and the role of persons with disabilities in development can be seen in law, policy, and programming, although a long-term effort is required to bring about full implementation of a far-reaching and complex treaty.

Charting Progress in Making Development and Humanitarian Action Disability-Inclusive

The adoption of disability-inclusive strategies and plans by bilateral and multi-lateral development donors has been substantial since the adoption of the CRPD in 2006. It initiated, within the UN, an organization-wide interagency support group to consider the implications of the CRPD for the work of the UN system. UN agencies such as UNICEF, the United National Development Programme (UNDP), and the UN Population Fund all form part of an interagency working group designed to facilitate the application of CRPD principles to the work of the UN as a whole. These three agencies have adopted disability policies and are at various stages in the development of disability-inclusive programming. In 2016, for instance, UNDP commissioned the UNDP Independent Evaluation Office to undertake a global portfolio review of its programming to assess whether and how its programs around the world were inclusive of persons with disabilities.[28] A UN flagship report on disability and development was published in December 2018.[29] In 2019, a working group of the Inter-Agency Support Group steered the development of a United Nations Disability Inclusion Strategy.[30] Its aim is to provide the foundation for sustainable progress on disability inclusion throughout all work of the United Nations. Its adoption is tied to the role of the UN in achieving the 2030 Agenda for Sustainable Development and the Sustainable Development Goals.[31] The resulting United Nations Disability Inclusion Strategy provides policy direction and accountability measures in a strategy designed to ensure that the United Nations system is pursuing its work consistent with disability inclusion and guided by the principles of the CRPD.[32] It provides a foundation for sustainable and transformative change toward disability inclusion throughout all pillars of the UN's work. This includes removing barriers that inhibit the participation of persons with disabilities in the benefits of development; it also means developing policies and practices that will make the UN an inclusive place for persons with disabilities to work.

Also of note are efforts by development banks to ensure that their lending policies are aligned with disability-inclusive approaches. The most prominent example of a development bank embracing a disability inclusion mandate is the World Bank, a specialized UN agency (see Box 6.2). The adoption of the SDGs with a disability inclusion lens also pressed development donors to better account for persons with disabilities in their work.[33] Of special importance, SDG 4 ("Ensure inclusive and equitable quality education and promote lifelong learning opportunities") requires the design of education facilities responsive to the needs of students with disabilities; further, SDG 10 ("Reduce inequality within and among countries") requires the social, economic, and political inclusion of all, including persons with disabilities.[34]

Box 6.2 Disability Inclusion and the World Bank

- The World Bank committed to ensuring that all of its lending portfolio is disability-inclusive by 2025. This means that all World Bank funding will ensure that persons with disabilities are able to benefit from the development goals of a particular project and that barriers will be identified and removed or mitigated. The Bank employs a Global Disability Advisor who works across the Bank's portfolio to facilitate its move toward disability inclusion in its development work.[35]
- The World Bank adopted a Disability Inclusion and Accountability Framework in 2018 that aims to support the mainstreaming of disability in all World Bank activities.[36] It lays out a road map for the inclusion of disability in the Bank's policies, operations, and analytical work and details the building of internal capacity for supporting clients in implementing disability-inclusive development programs.
- A third major step toward disability inclusion is the adoption of a new World Bank Environmental and Social Framework (ESF).[37] It advances nondiscrimination for persons with disabilities in development operations supported through investment project financing. Environmental and Social Standard 1 (ESS1) emphasizes that prejudice and discrimination are risk factors that present risks for development projects.[38] This has clear implications for the identification of persons with disabilities. The ESF requires borrowers to identify the potentially differentiated risks and impacts of projects on persons with disabilities and to prevent and mitigate such risks. In sum, the ESF requires a disability-inclusive risk and impact analysis for identification projects by participating countries/counterparts and the application of principles of nondiscrimination, equal opportunity, and reasonable accommodation.

Bilateral agencies, including the United States Agency for International Development (USAID), the Australian Department of Foreign Affairs and Trade, and the United Kingdom's Department for International Development (DFID), have all made moves to enhance the inclusion of persons with disabilities as beneficiaries of development and humanitarian aid programs.[39] In 2017, DFID made disability a priority, adopting the slogan "Now Is the Time" and co-organizing its first Global Disability Summit.[40] It did so in partnership with the International Disability Alliance and the government of Kenya, and invited some 170 stakeholders (national governments, multilateral organizations, foundations, civil society organizations, businesses and research organizations, and academics), resulting in a series of commitments at the summit. Following the summit, DFID published its first-ever disability strategy, which runs for five years, until 2023. Among the four strategic pillars for action are economic empowerment to combat stigma and the promotion of economic and social participation and accessibility. The sector now boasts "disability inclusion" advisors and specialists. Increasingly, at the domestic level, "disability focal points" are situated in ministries, election commissions, and national human rights institutions, among others. Cross-ministerial bodies come together to advance coordination in the rollout of a national disability action plan or an inclusive education strategy.

Progress in socializing disability inclusion within development agencies is likewise reflected in the development of disability policies by international implementers of development and humanitarian assistance. Longtime organizations associated with the more traditional charity approach to disability—for instance, organizations narrowly focused on providing wheelchairs, attending to rehabilitation needs of amputees, or focusing on funding orphanages that care for disabled children—are reorienting their approach, in theory if not in practice. The French organization Handicap International, deeply associated with the provision of rehabilitation services in developing countries and not in building the local capacities of OPDs or empowering disability advocates, went so far as to change its name to Humanity and Inclusion in order to signal its shift to a more rights-based approach.[41] Similar moves are evident in human rights organizations that long have all but ignored the rights of persons with disabilities in their work. Human Rights Watch, for instance, developed a separate division focused on disability rights.[42]

Moreover, progress in ensuring that development and humanitarian action includes persons with disabilities is demonstrative and, to an extent, quantifiable. It is possible, for example, to count the number of organizations working in the development and humanitarian sectors that now have disability-inclusive policies or strategies, many of them linked specifically to the CRPD. Organizations of persons with disabilities are engaging in the design and implementation of development programs. Communities of practice bring together practitioners in the field, including groups linked to organizations and groups comprised of independent disability inclusion practitioners.

Disability Data and Identification

A major challenge in advancing implementation of disability rights is the absence of disability data in the vast majority of countries around the world.[43] Where a country has no data on how many individuals live with a disability or the prevalence of different types of disability, deciding how to allocate funding to meet the needs of persons with disabilities in education, workforce development, disaster assistance, election programming, or a myriad of other services is practically difficult. The absence of data also provides justification for those states inclined to continue neglecting the sector. Further, persons with disabilities are often denied their right to legal recognition in the context of applying for identity documents and other transactions such as opening bank accounts or voter registration. The absence of an official identity or the ability to prove who one is can reinforce already entrenched barriers to full participation in society, including access to basic public and private sector services. And it places persons with disabilities at risk during humanitarian crises, rendering them more vulnerable to human trafficking.[44]

Given the poor data on disability in many countries, it is not surprising that persons with disabilities are at high risk of not being served by education systems, health systems, and other important services.[45] This occurs very often, in part due to their invisibility in society. Research suggests that children with disabilities are less likely to be registered by their parents at birth and may remain isolated or hidden away due to the shame and stigma associated with disability. This complicates matters of notice and provision of aid to the individuals themselves, as well as to community schools. Procedures must be adopted to ensure that creation of a legal identity is part of an accessible and inclusive process, and that parents of children with disabilities are encouraged to register their children at birth and signal their presence in the community. Emerging evidence suggests the following barriers for persons with disabilities in the context of identification:

- Absence of legal frameworks that guarantee nondiscriminatory access to government services
- Procurement of poor quality and inaccessible technology, such as biometric systems that make capture challenging for atypical enrollees
- Lack of transport, including accessible transport, to enrollment centers
- Reliance on single-mode biometrics (e.g., fingerprints only) and lack of exception-handling protocols
- Enrollment processes that are cumbersome and hard to understand
- Burdensome fees associated with enrollment
- Physically inaccessible enrollment facilities
- Lack of procedures to accommodate persons with disabilities (e.g., seating for those who need to wait; trained personnel to provide orientation for blind persons or persons with low vision; lack of sign language interpreters)
- Lack of personnel trained to accommodate persons with disabilities in the enrollment process

Article 31 of the CRPD requires states to collect statistical and research data on disability and recognizes the need for disaggregation on disability and other factors such as sex, so that data may be used for monitoring purposes as required by domain-specific indicators of progress.[46] This obligation has helped to spur the development of methodologies designed to capture better disability data in national censuses and national surveys. Of special note is the work of the Washington Group on Disability Statistics, which has developed easy-to-deliver question sets in close collaboration with OPDs that are designed to facilitate cross-nationally comparable population-based measures of disability.[47]

This and other efforts are likely to help stimulate improved practices and help ameliorate widespread deficiencies in current data sets that have led to reporting of improbable variations in disability prevalence.[48]

The Turn to Inclusive Education

There are many reasons why gaps in educational attainment and learning persist for children with disabilities. Deciding what type of intervention to put into place and how resources should be allocated into educational development programs hinges on a better understanding of what types of programs can meaningfully reduce gaps. Absent data of this kind, the questions are unending:

- Should investments go into physical infrastructure improvements? For example, should priority be given to making toilets available, safe, and accessible for students with disabilities? Can children with disabilities get to school in the first place?
- Should the distance to schools be reduced, whether by building new and fully accessible schools in remote areas or by reducing transport barriers through accessible public transportation? And if so, will parents send their disabled children to school?
- Should families of children with disabilities be incentivized to enroll and keep their children in school through, for example, cash transfer programs, food vouchers, or scholarships? And in that event, will teachers be accommodating of students with disabilities?
- Should more funding go into teacher training? If so, should these funds be for specially trained teachers, or for empowering teachers already in the classroom setting? Should more teachers with disabilities be hired? If so, are they able to access higher education?
- Should more emphasis be placed on understanding and changing stereotypes about disability? How? Whose attitudes require change?
- Should interventions targeting students with disabilities be implemented in some instances, and if so, when and how?

Choosing between these and many other possible program approaches is challenging and will depend as well on the country context in question. The adoption of the CRPD and its commitment to inclusive education as a human right for persons with disabilities is working changes in law, policy, and practice within the framework of development cooperation, and even in the context of emergency education in humanitarian action. While small-scale pilot projects have been a long-standing but clearly limited approach to the inclusion of children with disabilities in mainstream schools, large-scale development programs are turning to strategies of inclusion.

The United States, although not a ratifying state party to the CRPD, nonetheless has forged ahead in some important respects to advance disability inclusion with an approach clearly tied to the CRPD. In 2017, USAID launched the first-ever large-scale assessment of higher education and its accessibility to persons with disabilities in Egypt under a mainstream contractual mechanism for the government of Egypt.[49] Interventions in the inclusive education sphere by USAID are the largest in its history, a marked departure from prior investments, and evident across a number of countries. USAID is likewise supporting added efforts to ensure disability inclusion in other aspects of education. In Côte d'Ivoire, for instance, a five-year project for access to justice included a budget for cross-cutting, integrative disability interventions, including the development of disability modules in judicial training.[50]

In another move to address disability inclusion in the context of education, the World Bank is supporting work to ensure that vocational education and training (VET) within its investment portfolio is advancing strategies of inclusion.[51] To that end, the Bank is undergoing assessments of the VET programs receiving support and providing country-specific assistance on how to ensure that VET is made accessible to persons with disabilities. The effort is, in effect, a move to retrofit the vocational education and training program design to ensure that it reaches persons with disabilities.

Disability-Inclusive Electoral Assistance

Development actors engaged in electoral assistance have conceptualized elections in terms of an electoral cycle.[52] Drawing from the social model of disability that understands disablement as barriers external to the individual with impairment (and not inherent deficit), the electoral cycle is used as a conceptual tool for thinking about design for disability inclusion in electoral programming.[53] Consider the following by way of illustration:

- The wheelchair user trying to find accessible transport to the polling center
- The blind voter wishing to cast her ballot independently
- The deaf voter who desires accessible information about the voting procedure
- The voter with an intellectual disability who hopes the ballot will be easy to understand

Each of the foregoing—and countless other examples one could identify—offers a shift in orientation away from an individualized deficit perspective (e.g., they are "confined" to a wheelchair, so they cannot travel to the polling center) and toward an orientation that asks what factors may inhibit full and complete participation in an electoral process and how supports can facilitate full participation in political and public life.

These factors—or better put, barriers—may exist in the physical environment (polling booths that are too narrow to fit a wheelchair, stairs that present obstacles for older voters), in the law (someone with a mental health issue can vote after they have received treatment, while someone with an intellectual disability is simply excluded from voting), in information or communication (inaccessible electoral information on a website, or lack of sign language interpreters at a polling center), and in the social environment (a disabled person is barred from choosing her own assistant in casting her ballot because she will be coerced into voting the way her assistant wishes her to vote, or an election official is rigid and unwilling to provide accommodations) (see Table 6.1).

Inclusion in Disaster Risk Reduction

The adoption of the CRPD helped highlight the lack of attention to the specific needs of persons with disabilities in humanitarian crises, such as natural disasters.[54] Several major natural disasters occurred during the drafting of the CRPD, including Hurricanes Rita and Katrina in 2005 and the 2004 Indian Ocean earthquake and tsunami. These events exposed the disproportionate impact of natural disasters on persons with disabilities and, in turn, resulted in the overwhelming support for a provision in the CRPD, ultimately Article 11, addressing disability inclusion in situations of risk. They also disclosed the risk to persons with disabilities and their households, especially in water-related disasters such as flooding. Specific risks can often include an absence of appropriate planning at the household level, including lack of flood-proofing; inaccessible warning systems; inability to evacuate; having to reside in inaccessible shelters and temporary housing with no accessible water, sanitation, and hygiene (WASH) facilities; and extra costs associated with reconstruction.[55]

Where the needs of persons with disabilities are not being included in community vulnerability assessments, community resilience-building activities, or capacity-building interventions, it can impact livelihoods, economic self-sufficiency, and a return to work, in many cases further reinforcing poverty. Disability-inclusive resilience planning and interventions, including financial assistance and social protection systems, can limit the negative effects of social, physical, housing, health, economic network, and resource disruptions. Including disability in disaster risk mitigation can address needs for accessibility at each stage of disaster recovery and rebuilding. The Inter-Agency Standing Committee, the UN mechanism responsible for coordinating humanitarian assistance across the UN system and with mainstream humanitarian actors, was recently constituted, along with the Guidelines on Inclusion of Persons with Disabilities in Humanitarian Action.[56] This effort, and other efforts such as the adoption of the World Charter on Disability Inclusion in Humanitarian Action, provide evidence of disability-inclusive agenda-setting by humanitarian actors.[57] For a further explanation of the rights of people

Table 6.1 Barriers to WASH for Persons with Disabilities

Persons with physical disabilities (mobility, dexterity, and physical strength)	• Uneven, unstable, narrow, or slippery surfaces • Traveling long distances • Reaching and operating controls; manipulating switches, parts, fasteners, and handles • Having difficulty squatting over pit latrines, balancing, and needing to sit • Holding, lifting, and carrying containers, hoses, and other equipment • Carrying heavy weights • Assistive aids or devices, such as wheelchairs and crutches, do not fit in water and sanitation facilities or have to be supported against dirty surfaces
Visual	• Having difficulty finding holes in pit latrines; danger of slipping with larger holes or damaged latrines • Assistive aids such as white canes do not fit in water and sanitation facilities or have to be supported against dirty surfaces • Having difficulty in accessing WASH information relayed through print media, text-only information on TV programs, or signing print-based documents and forms • Navigating new surroundings when all signage is in text • Entering, navigating, and using new physical spaces
Hearing	• Having difficulty in accessing information relayed through vocal media, such as radio programs, TV programs without captions, and community loudspeakers • Hearing sirens and other sounds (for example, in a flooding situation) • Facing barriers in communicating and interacting with relevant stakeholders, including in community meetings and consultations
Cognitive	• Having difficulty in communicating needs for water resources as well as personal hygiene needs • Needing information in visual formats • Needing incontinence aids, such as bedpans • Needing navigation and memory aids in finding, accessing, and using water resources • Relying on others to express their views and needs in community planning meetings and consultations
Psychosocial	• Experiencing social isolation and exclusion, which impedes receiving information on water resource management and participation in planning meetings and consultations • Having difficulty in communicating needs for water resources as well as personal hygiene needs • Needing navigation and memory aids in finding, accessing, and using water resources • Relying on others to express their views and needs in community planning meetings and consultations

Source: Adapted from World Bank 2017b, 8–9. License: CC BY 3.0 IGO.

with disabilities and the challenges they face in humanitarian crises and disaster recovery, see Chapter 13.

The Protection of Persons with Disabilities in Armed Conflict

The protection of persons with disabilities in armed conflict is now on the international agenda, and finds expression in Article 11 of the CRPD. The provision gives express recognition to the observance of international humanitarian law. Notably, the protection focus is a reminder of the historical record documenting the extermination of children and adults with disabilities in Nazi Germany, as well as the killing documented in the Armenian and Rwandan genocides.[58]

Recent attention by the UN Security Council highlights the particular toll that armed conflict has on children with disabilities. On June 20, 2019, the United Nations Security Council adopted Resolution 2475 to protect people with disabilities in armed conflict and ensure their equal access to humanitarian assistance.[59] Emerging evidence from recent conflicts additionally documents the impact of armed conflict on persons with disabilities. Research undertaken by Amnesty International, which adopted its first disability policy in 2019, highlights the egregious impact of armed conflict on persons with disabilities in Yemen.[60] Its report underscores the harsh impact of the conflict on children with disabilities in particular and calls on humanitarian actors to ensure that persons with disabilities are not left behind in aid efforts. Straightforward strategies are suggested, including directly seeking input from people with disabilities, providing more and better-suited assistive devices, and providing latrines in camps for internally displaced persons that meet their specific needs.[61] Research undertaken by Human Rights Watch exposes the toll that attacks by armed groups in the Central African Republic had on communities, including the finding that some ninety-six people with disabilities were abandoned or unable to escape when their homes came under attack; eleven were killed. In one case, the organization found seventeen people with disabilities left behind after fifteen hundred survivors fled the city of Bossemptélé.[62] A related issue is the need for disarmament, demobilization, and reintegration programs in post-conflict environments to account for the needs of disabled ex-combatants. Research demonstrates that the failure to do so in several countries (e.g., Sierra Leone, Mozambique, and Burundi) resulted in disaffected, disabled ex-soldiers resorting to violence in order to protest the lack of attention to their specific needs.[63]

Work undertaken by UNICEF demonstrates the toll of armed conflict on children with disabilities.[64] This includes compromised support systems as a result of violence, destruction of infrastructure, a loss or deterioration of essential services (medical, rehabilitation, access to food and water), and deepening poverty. According to available data, during armed conflict where there is a breakdown of social services and protection systems, children with disabilities are particularly at risk of violence.[65] Other studies show the unique risks that children with disabilities may face, including heightened protection challenges associated with the institutionalization of children with disabilities in some contexts and their vulnerability to sexual violence when supports break down.[66] Finally, emerging evidence is exposing heightened risk for persons with disabilities in clustered settlements, such as psychiatric hospitals, orphanages, social care homes, and other institutions, with documentation of the use of people with disabilities as human targets or shields by some combatants.[67]

Inclusive WASH

Specific obligations in the CRPD affirm the right of persons with disabilities to access water and sanitation facilities.[68] Far from a secondary concern, research shows clearly that poor WASH facilities pose serious barriers for persons with disabilities (see Table 6.1). They compromise access to schools and universities as well as other public services such as courts. Poorly constructed toilet facilities also pose major dangers for young children and persons with disabilities, as the grim reality of falling into and drowning in pit latrines illustrates. The health consequences of poor WASH can also be significantly aggravated for those persons with disabilities who are at high risk of experiencing urinary tract infections and related health risks.

Inclusive WASH also connects to the principles set forth in international disability law upholding principles of respect for inherent dignity and individual autonomy, nondiscrimination, full and effective participation, accessibility, and equality of opportunity, among others, for persons with disabilities (see Table 6.1).

Poor access can lead to serious and at times fatal secondary health conditions for persons with disabilities, such as dehydration, pressure sores, urinary tract infections, constipation, and other bowel and bladder health problems.[69] It is within this context that development agencies are beginning to turn their attention to the construction of accessible WASH facilities that are safe and well-constructed, provide separate spaces for girls and boys, and are physically accessible for persons with disabilities.[70]

Finally, persons with disabilities are not the only group that may experience functional difficulties that impede or restrict access to water resources across life domains.[71] Community members at large can benefit from barrier-free designed infrastructure and services. Accessible and universal design is good design, especially for older persons, pregnant women, children, women carrying children, and persons with temporary injuries. Good practice includes such features as railings for toilets, nonslip flooring, space for maneuvering wheelchairs or other assistive devices, and sink access.

Remaining Challenges

Challenges persist, not the least of which is the increasing sense that single-identity characteristics do not capture the reality of one's lived experience. The notion of intersectionality, first expressed in the context of gender and race by Kimberlé Crenshaw, has led to a growing recognition that all persons possess multiple identity statuses, each of which might be subject to its own or overlapping forms of discrimination, and that individuals do not neatly fit into discrete and mutually exclusive categories. Consider, for example, the real-life impact on a female refugee with a disability in a displacement camp who, because of her sex, is socially tasked with providing for her family and, due to her disability, may have difficulties carrying water allocations long distances. Within the disability field, recognizing the impact of intersectionality is a work in progress. The CRPD Committee's General Comment No. 6 expressly references multiple forms of discrimination created by intersecting attributes of identities and disability status.[72] Nevertheless, the Committee itself in a case involving a wrongly imprisoned Aboriginal person with a disability never once mentions that person's indigeneity.[73]

Notwithstanding the success of the CRPD in providing a much-needed platform from which to advocate for disability inclusion, the treaty envisages the kind of change that takes time to fully implement. The challenges posed to the international disability rights movement seeking to advance disability-inclusive development and humanitarian action are, in many respects, similar to those facing other civil society actors. Advancing law and policy is made difficult by the contraction of civil society space in countries across the world. The turn to restrictive NGO registration processes and limitations on freedom of speech by human rights defenders presents problems for all actors, and particularly for those already marginalized civil society actors who struggle for resources to build their networks and expand their influence.[74]

In other respects, the challenges posed to disability rights actors are different from those of other civil society networks. The heterogeneity of disability is a complicating factor for building a strong, cohesive, and unified voice for the movement as a whole. This, of course, was evidenced in the fractious and fragmented nature of the dynamic between various civil society organizations during the negotiations over the CRPD.[75] While the CPRD is characterized as a triumph of open and democratic treaty-making—and in many respects it was just that—relationships between participating disabled peoples organizations as well as other NGOs were anything but a model of congenial and collaborative consensus-building. Turf battles and ideological differences characterized a fair part of the process, and while they did not halt the adoption of the treaty, these dynamics suggest that challenges will persist in the implementation phase, creating lost opportunities for strong coalition-building in areas where it is sorely needed (e.g., inclusive education, building back better post-disaster, and domestic disability law reform).

In sum, the fractured nature of the global disability community persists. There is a lack of cohesion and structures for coordinated action among civil society organizations. This provides additional obstacles for advancing disability inclusion. At the same time, states obliged to implement their treaty obligations must engage as development donors and as recipients, in each case ensuring a process whereby development assistance is designed, implemented, and monitored with close attention to disability inclusion practices.

These real complexities lead to questions: How is it possible in a complex humanitarian setting, for example, to adequately account for the specific needs of refugees or displaced persons in all of their diversity?[76] Is this reducible to a checklist for field workers? What is the best approach to ensuring that protection risks are adequately addressed given the multitude of risk factors combined with the multiplicity of individual characteristics? On a national level, how can the issue of income inequality be addressed with particular awareness of the barriers that people with disabilities face in the workforce?[77] One approach has been to articulate guidelines to orient humanitarian field workers toward complexity in designing and implementing complex humanitarian assistance operations. An analysis of these guidelines reveals an earnest attempt to account for complexity and intersectionality, not only with regard to identity characteristics but also with regard to cross-cutting thematic issues.[78] What remains unclear is whether and how accounting for this complexity will be successfully operationalized with discernible impact on protecting at-risk populations who have unique needs and face multidimensional barriers.

Conclusion

The adoption of the CRPD and its nearly universal ratification is a major advance in setting a rights-based orientation for international and national development agendas. The imperative of ensuring that development and humanitarian action are designed and implemented inclusively is at last recognized as integral to success, and was demonstrably the consequence of the CRPD treaty process and its following practice. Further, the move away from declaring a vulnerable mass of "disadvantaged" or "marginalized" people as generalized targets of development has given way to an understanding that different groups, and indeed individuals, have different needs, and must therefore be included in the design and implementation of programs. The disability rights notion of directing attention to barriers that inhibit full participation and dismantling them, along with providing individualized supports, has implications for all marginalized groups. Specific attention must be directed to the needs of marginalized groups in order to facilitate their meaningful participation in the benefits of development.

Notes

1. WHO 2011.
2. United Nations 1997, art. 6(3)
3. Lord and Stein 2018.
4. UN General Assembly 2001b.
5. UN Committee for Development Policy 2018.
6. UN Department for Economic and Social Affairs 2019.
7. Lord 2002, 5.
8. Elwan 1999, 8. For more on disability and development generally, see Cobley 2018; Grech 2015.
9. UK Government 2006.
10. Stein, Lord, and McClain-Nhlapo 2013.
11. Lord and Stein 2008.
12. WHO 2011.
13. Stein and Stein 2014; Stein and Lord 2017.
14. Sabatello and Schulze 2013.
15. Stein 2007.
16. Quinn and Degener 2002.
17. Stein 2007, 76, 82.
18. United Nations 2001, ch. 1.
19. UN General Assembly 2001a.
20. Stein and Stein 2014.
21. United Nations 2011, ix. For a discussion of the MDGs and their implicit, but unstated, link to disability issues, see Lord and Guernsey 2005.
22. Among other assignments and activities during the ad hoc sessions, Michael Ashley Stein served as counsel to DPI, and Janet E. Lord represented LSN and, toward the end of the process, DPI.
23. CPRD, art. 6.
24. Lord and Stein 2018.
25. CRPD, art. 11.
26. CRPD, Preamble (o).
27. CRPD, Preamble (g).
28. See UNDP 2016.
29. United Nations 2018.
30. United Nations 2019.
31. United Nations 2015.
32. CRPD, art. 3.
33. United Nations 2015. The SDGs include seven targets that address persons with disabilities in specific terms with regard to education, accessible schools, employment, accessible public spaces and transport, empowerment and inclusion, and data disaggregation. Other targets refer to persons in vulnerable situations or are universal targets; these are therefore understood to include persons with disabilities. Finally, two other targets address discrimination, a major cause of inequality and unequal access to opportunities and services for persons with disabilities.
34. The International Disability Alliance and the International Disability and Development Consortium have published guides on the SDGs and disability. See especially IDA and IDDC n.d.
35. For the Bank's webpage detailing the work of the Bank in advancing disability inclusion, see https://www.worldbank.org/en/topic/disability.

36. McClain-Nhlapo et al. 2018.
37. World Bank 2017a.
38. World Bank 2017a, Environmental and Social Safeguard 1.
39. Australian Department of Foreign Affairs and Trade 2015.
40. For a summary overview, see Lord et al. 2010.
41. The website for Humanity and Inclusion's US office is https://www.hi-us.org/about.
42. The webpage for disability rights at Human Rights Watch is https://www.hrw.org/topic/disability-rights.
43. WHO 2011.
44. World Bank 2020; Lord 2018.
45. ICED 2019.
46. CRPD, art. 31.
47. Washington Group on Disability Statistics n.d. See generally Madans, Loeb, and Altman 2011.
48. Mont 2007.
49. USAID 2017.
50. Tetra Tech n.d.
51. See World Bank n.d.
52. ACE Electoral Knowledge Network n.d.
53. See Lord, Fiala, and Stein 2014.
54. Lord 2017; Lord 2014.
55. World Bank 2017b.
56. For the IASC Guidelines on Inclusion of Persons with Disabilities in Humanitarian Action, see http://www.internationaldisabilityalliance.org/art11/iasc.
57. Charter on Inclusion of Persons with Disabilities in Humanitarian Action, http://humanitariandisabilitycharter.org/.
58. Charter on Inclusion of Persons with Disabilities in Humanitarian Action, http://humanitariandisabilitycharter.org/.
59. UN Security Council Resolution 2475, "Protecting People with Disabilities in Armed Conflict and Ensuring Their Equal Access to Humanitarian Assistance," June 20, 2019.
60. Amnesty International 2019.
61. Amnesty International 2019.
62. Human Rights Watch 2017.
63. Lord and Stein 2015.
64. Thomas 2018.
65. Thomas 2018, 4.
66. European Coalition for Community Living 2010.
67. Devanda et al. 2017.
68. CRPD provisions of greatest relevance to the issue of WASH include the following: Article 28 (Adequate Standard of Living and Social Protection) requires states parties to ensure access to clean water services, as well as appropriate and affordable services. Article 19 (Living Independently and Being Included in the Community) addresses equity in needs-responsive community services and facilities. Article 9 (Accessibility) requires access to the physical environment and public spaces and services in rural and urban areas. In addition to these CRPD provisions, United Nations member states have affirmed the right of every individual to water and sanitation through a variety of other treaties, resolutions, and declarations.
69. World Bank 2017b, 4.
70. Researcher Hazel Jones has devoted much of her professional life to the issue of disability-inclusive WASH. For an overview of the field, see Jones and Wilbur 2014.
71. Singh et al. 2017.
72. CRPD 2018.

73. Harpur and Stein 2018.
74. See, e.g., Rutzen 2013.
75. Lord 2004.
76. See Reilly 2010.
77. For more information on this topic, see Mori, Reyes, and Yamagata 2014.
78. IASC 2011, 2012.

Bibliography

ACE Electoral Knowledge Network. n.d. "The Electoral Cycle." https://aceproject.org/electoral-advice/electoral-assistance/electoral-cycle.

Amnesty International. 2019. "Yemen: Excluded—Living with Disabilities in Yemen's Armed Conflict." MDE 31/1383/2019. December 3. https://www.amnesty.org/en/documents/MDE31/1383/2019/en/.

Australian Department of Foreign Affairs and Trade. 2015. "Development for All 2015–2020: Strategy for Strengthening Disability-Inclusive Development in Australia's Aid Program." http://dfat.gov.au/about-us/publications/pages/development-for-all-2015-2020.aspx.

Christensen, Darin, and Jeremy M. Weinstein. 2013. "Defunding Dissent: Restrictions on Aid to NGOs." *Journal of Democracy* 24: 77–91.

Cobley, D. 2018. *Disability and International Development.* London: Routledge.

CRPD. 2018. "General Comment No. 6, Article 5: Equality and Non-Discrimination." UN Committee on the Rights of Persons with Disabilities. CRPD/C/GC/6. April 26.

Devanda, Cristina, Shantha Rau Barriga, Gerard Quinn, and Janet E. Lord. 2017. "Protecting Civilians with Disabilities in Armed Conflicts." *NATO Review*, December 1. https://www.nato.int/docu/review/articles/2017/12/01/protecting-civilians-with-disabilities-in-conflicts/index.html.

Elwan, A. 1999. "Poverty and Disability: A Survey of Literature." World Bank Social Protection Discussion Paper 9932. https://documents1.worldbank.org/curated/en/488521468764667300/pdf/multi-page.pdf.

European Coalition for Community Living. 2010. "Wasted Time, Wasted Money, Wasted Lives . . . A Wasted Opportunity." http://www.community-living.info/documents/ECCL-StructuralFundsReport-final-WEB.pdf.

Grech, Shaun. 2015. *Disability and Poverty in the Global South: Renegotiating Development in Guatemala.* London: Palgrave Macmillan.

Harpur, Paul, and Michael Ashley Stein. 2018. "Children with Disabilities, Human Rights, and Sustainable Development." In *Children's Rights in International Sustainable Development Law*, edited by Claire Fenton-Glynn, 139–164. Cambridge: Cambridge University Press.

Human Rights Watch. 2017. "Central African Republic: People with Disabilities at High Risk." June 21. https://www.hrw.org/news/2017/06/21/central-african-republic-people-disabilities-high-risk#.

IASC. 2012. "Accountability to Affected Populations: Tools to Assist in Implementing the IASC AAP Commitments." July. Inter-Agency Standing Committee.

IASC. 2011. "Principles of Accountability to Affected Populations." Inter-Agency Standing Committee, Geneva.

ICED. 2019. "The Missing Billion: Access to Health Services for 1 Billion People with Disabilities." International Centre for Evidence in Disability. July. https://www.lshtm.ac.uk/research/centres/international-centre-evidence-disability/missing-billion.

IDA and IDDC. n.d. "The 2030 Agenda: The Inclusion of Persons with Disabilities Comprehensive Guide." IDA and IDDC, Geneva. http://www.internationaldisabilityalliance.org/sites/default/files/documents/2030_agenda_comprehensive_guide_for_persons_with_disabilities_comp.pdf.

Jones, Hazel, and Jane Wilbur. 2014. "Compendium of Accessible WASH Technologies." Water Aid. https://wedc-knowledge.lboro.ac.uk/resources/learning/EI_Compendium_of_accessibl e_WASH_Technologies.pdf.

Lord, Janet E. 2018. "Desk Review on Humanitarian Action Inclusive of Persons with Disabilities." Inter-Agency Standing Committee on Disability Inclusion in Humanitarian Action. March 1. https://interagencystandingcommittee.org/iasc-task-team-inclusion-persons-disabilities-humanitarian-action/documents/desk-review-humanitarian.

Lord, Janet E. 2017. "Desk Review on Humanitarian Action Inclusive of Persons with Disabilities." IASC Task Team on Inclusion of Persons with Disabilities in Humanitarian Action. December 15.

Lord, Janet E. 2014. "International Humanitarian Law and Disability: Paternalism, Protection or Rights?" In *Disability, Human Rights and the Limits of Humanitarianism*, edited by M. Gill and C. Schlund-Vials, 155–178. Burlington, VT: Ashgate.

Lord, Janet E. 2004. "Mirror, Mirror on the Wall: Voice Accountability and NGOs in Human Rights Standard Setting." *Seton Hall Journal of Diplomacy and International Relations* 5: 93–110.

Lord, Janet E. 2002. "A White Paper: Understanding the Role of an International Convention on the Human Rights of People with Disabilities." National Council of Disability, Washington, DC.

Lord, Janet E., Janos Fiala, and Michael Ashley Stein. 2014. "Facilitating an Equal Right to Vote for Persons with Disabilities." *Journal of Human Rights Practice* 6, no. 1: 115–139.

Lord, Janet E., and K. N. Guernsey. 2005. "Inclusive Development and the Comprehensive and Integral International Convention on the Protection and Promotion of the Rights and Dignity of Persons with Disabilities." Paper presented at the Fifth Session of the Ad Hoc Committee of the International Disability and Development Consortium, January. http://www.un.org/esa/socdev/enable/rights/ahc5docs/ahc5iddc.doc.

Lord, Janet E., Aleksandra Posarac, Marco Nicoli, Karen Peffley, Charlotte McClain-Nhlapo, and Mary Keogh. 2010. "Disability and International Cooperation and Development: A Review of Policies and Practices." World Bank Group, Washington, DC.

Lord, Janet E., and Michael Ashley Stein. 2018. "Commentary on Article 32." In *Commentary on the UN Convention on the Rights of Persons with Disabilities*, edited by Ilias Bantekas, Michael Ashley Stein, and D. Anastasiou. Oxford: Oxford University Press.

Lord, Janet E., and Michael Ashley Stein. 2015. "Peacebuilding and Reintegrating Ex-Combatants with Disabilities." *International* Journal of Human Rights 19, no. 3: 277–292.

Lord, Janet E., and Michael Ashley Stein. 2008. "The Domestic Incorporation of Human Rights Law and the United Nations Convention on the Rights of Persons with Disabilities." *University of Washington Law Review* 18: 449–479.

Madans, Jennifer H., Mitchell E. Loeb, and Barbara M. Altman. 2011. "Measuring Disability and Monitoring the UN Convention on the Rights of Persons with Disabilities: The Work of the Washington Group on Disability Statistics." *BMC Public Health* 11, suppl. 4: art. S4.

McClain-Nhlapo, C., L. Sivonen, D. Raja Samant, S. Palummo, and E. Acul. 2018. *Disability Inclusion and Accountability Framework*. Washington, DC: World Bank Group.

Mizunoya, S., and S. Mitra. 2013. "Is There a Disability Gap in Employment Rates in Developing Countries?" *World Development* 42: 28–43.

Mont, Dan. 2007. "Measuring Health and Disability." *Lancet* 369: 1658–1663.

Mori, Soya, Celia M. Reyes, and Tatsufumi Yamagata. 2014. *Poverty Reduction of the Disabled: Livelihood of Persons with Disabilities in the Philippines*. New York: Routledge.

Quinn, Gerard, and Theresia Degener. 2002. "The Moral Authority for Change: Human Rights Values and the Worldwide Process of Disability Reform." In *Human Rights and Disability: The Current Use and Future Potential of United Nations Human Rights Instruments in the Context of Disability*, 23–26. Geneva: United Nations.

Reilly, R. 2010. "Disabilities Among Refugees and Conflict-Affected Populations." *Forced Migration Review* 35: 8–10.

Rutzen, Douglas. 2015. "Authoritarianism Goes Global (II): Civil Society Under Assault." *Journal of Democracy* 26, no. 4: 28–39.

Sabatello, Maya, and Marianne Schulze. 2013. *Human Rights and Disability Advocacy*. Philadelphia: University of Pennsylvania Press.

Singh, R., H. Honda, B. Frost, and K. Urich. 2014. "Casting the Net Further: Disability-Inclusive WASH." World Vision International. http://www.wvi.org/clean-water-sanitation-and-hygi ene-wash/publication/disability-inclusive-wash-report.

Stein, Michael Ashley. 2007. "Disability Human Rights." *California Law Review* 95: 75–121.

Stein, Michael Ashley, and Janet E. Lord. 2017. "Charting the Development of Human Rights Law Through the CRPD." In *The United Nations Convention on the Rights of Persons with Disabilities: A Commentary*, edited by Valentina Della Fina, Rachele Cera, and Giuseppe Palmisano, 731–748.

Stein, Michael Ashley, Janet E. Lord, and Charlotte McClain-Nhlapo. 2013. "Education and HIV/ AIDS: Disability Rights and Inclusive Development." In *Millennium Development Goals and Human Rights: Past, Present and Future*, edited by M. Langford, A. Sumner, and A. E. Yamin, 274–294.

Stein, Michael Ashley, and Penelope J. S. Stein. 2014. "Disability, Development, and Human Rights: A Mandate and Framework for International Financial Institutions." University of California Davis Law Review 47: 1231–1278.

Tetra Tech. n.d. "Cote d'Ivoire Justice Sector Support Program." https://www.tetratech.com/en/ projects/justice-sector-support-program-c%C3%B4te-d%E2%80%99ivoire.

Thomas, Edward. 2018. "Children with Disabilities in Situations of Armed Conflict." UNICEF, New York. https://www.unicef.org/disabilities/files/Children_with_Disabilities_in_Situation s_of_Armed_Conflict-Discussion_Paper.pdf.

UK Government. 2006. *Disability Equality Scheme, 2006–2009*. London: DFID, Department for International Development.

UNDP. 2016. "Evaluation of Disability-Inclusive Development at UNDP." United Nations Development Programme. http://web.undp.org/evaluation/evaluations/thematic/disability. shtml.

UN Committee for Development Policy. 2018. "Leave No One Behind." https://sustainable development.un.org/content/documents/2754713_July_PM_2._Leaving_no_one_behind_ Summary_from_UN_Committee_for_Development_Policy.pdf.

UN Department of Economic and Social Affairs. 2019. "Disability and Development Report." https://social.un.org/publications/UN-Flagship-Report-Disability-Final.pdf.

UN General Assembly. 2001a. "Comprehensive and Integral International Convention to Promote and Protect the Rights and Dignity of Persons with Disabilities." Resolution 56/168.

UN General Assembly. 2001b. "Convention on the Rights of Persons with Disabilities." Resolution 61/106.

UN Secretary General. 2020. "Disability Inclusion in the United Nations System." Office of the Secretary General. https://www.un.org/sites/un2.un.org/files/un_disability_inclusion_strate gy_report_final.pdf.

United Nations. 2019. "United Nations Disability Inclusion Strategy." https://www.un.org/deve lopment/desa/disabilities/wp-content/uploads/sites/15/2019/06/un_disability_inclusion_st rategy_-_english.pdf.

United Nations. 2018. "UN Flagship Report on Disability and Development 2018—Realizing the SDGs by, for and with Persons with Disabilities." December. https://www.un.org/developm ent/desa/disabilities/publication-disability-sdgs.html.

United Nations. 2015. "Transforming Our World: The 2030 Agenda for Sustainable Development." A/RES/70/1.

United Nations. 2001. "Report of the World Conference Against Racism, Racial Discrimination, Xenophobia, and Related Intolerance," UN Doc A/CONF.189.12 (August 31–September 8).

United Nations. 1997. "Convention on the Prohibition of the Use, Stockpiling, Production and Transfer of Anti-Personnel Mines and on Their Destruction." September 18. https://www. refworld.org/docid/3ae6b3ad0.html.

USAID. 2017. "Needs Assessment of Persons with Disabilities in Egyptian Public Universities and Regional Technical Colleges (Final Report)." US Agency for International Development. https://pdf.usaid.gov/pdf_docs/PA00SVGS.pdf.

Washington Group on Disability Statistics. n.d. "Short Set of Disability Questions." http://www. washingtongroup-disability.com/washington-groupquestion-sets/short-set-of-disability-questions. Accessed March 23, 2017.

WHO. 2011. *World Report on Disability*. Geneva: World Health Organization and the World Bank.

World Bank. 2020. "Creating Disability-Inclusive ID Systems." World Bank Group, Washington, DC.

World Bank. 2017a. *Environmental and Social Framework: A Vision for Sustainable Development*. Washington, DC: World Bank.

World Bank. 2017b. "Including Persons with Disabilities in Water Sector Operations: A Guidance Note." https://openknowledge.worldbank.org/handle/10986/27542.

World Bank. n.d. "Systems Approach for Better Education Results (SABER)." http://saber.worldb ank.org/index.cfm?indx=8&pd=7&sub=0.

7

The Drive to Realize Indigenous Peoples' Rights

Valmaine Toki
With contributions from Lara Domínguez

> Fresh and creative approaches to mobilize the political will [are needed] to advance [the] agenda [of decolonization]. . . . We no longer have the luxury of indulging in rhetoric and rituals. . . . It is time for a new kind of fully inclusive dialogue about decolonization.
>
> —Ban-ki Moon, 2013[1]

Introduction

The struggle of Indigenous peoples for the recognition of their fundamental rights is ongoing and challenging.

Despite the strides made by the global Indigenous movement in the last fifty years, meaningful realization of their rights at the international and domestic levels remains elusive. The challenges are multifaceted. Indigenous peoples around the world continue to suffer marginalization, discrimination, poverty, and conflict. They are often disproportionately represented among those who are poor, disenfranchised, less educated, or in prison, or who suffer from poor health.[2] The consequences of this attainment gap are vividly illustrated by the plight of Indigenous peoples disproportionately impacted by the COVID-19 pandemic.[3] Making matters worse, some governments have used the cover of the pandemic to roll back hard-won environmental and social policies, eroding Indigenous land rights and fueling a rise in human rights abuses.[4]

Far from being exclusively a colonial phenomenon, dispossession of Indigenous territories has continued unabated in the postcolonial era. It stems from states' chronic failure to adequately recognize and protect Indigenous customary ownership rights. As competition for natural resources grows ever fiercer, Indigenous communities remain vulnerable to land grabs and violence perpetrated by government actors, corporations, and non-Indigenous settlers. Dispossession is undertaken for corporate profit and "development," and also, increasingly, for conservation. This is paradoxical in light of Indigenous peoples' unassailable track record as the world's best environmental custodians.[5] Whereas

Indigenous peoples are the least responsible for the drivers of environmental degradation, perversely, their livelihoods are the most vulnerable to its effects as well as to policies championed by the conservation establishment to counter climate change and biodiversity loss.[6] It is a stark example of how Indigenous worldviews and contributions are overlooked and made invisible by systems of knowledge creation and global governance that privilege Western scientific, legal, and political perspectives.

Despite the challenges, the dynamism of the global Indigenous movement cannot be overstated. It is evident in the robust rights framework that has been enshrined in the corpus of international law and in Indigenous peoples' direct participation in international lawmaking. The adoption of the United Nations Declaration on the Rights of Indigenous Peoples in 2007 represents a watershed not only for Indigenous peoples but also for the wider international community. It articulates defining standards that underpin the interpretation of binding international human rights treaties as applied to Indigenous peoples. Even though the Declaration is a nonbinding instrument (and one that certain states characterize as "aspirational"), the standards it articulates have had far-reaching effects. The impact of this milestone extends beyond the Indigenous rights regime. As scholar Sheryl Lightfoot has pointed out, the implementation of Indigenous rights as articulated in the Declaration requires a complete rethinking and reordering of sovereignty, territoriality, liberalism, and human rights.[7] In this sense, Indigenous peoples have accomplished more than perhaps any other rights-holder group at the international level. No small feat for a collective that is consistently among the most marginalized and vulnerable in the world.

In setting out the milestones achieved by the global Indigenous movement (as well as ongoing challenges), this chapter will first ask: who are Indigenous peoples? It will then provide an overview of the steps taken by Indigenous peoples to realize their fundamental rights at the international level, culminating in the adoption of the Declaration. With a focus on self-determination as a pivotal right, the second part will contextualize the Declaration. In pinpointing selective case studies, the chapter will examine the intersections between the fundamental rights enshrined in the Declaration, state obligations, and corporate responsibilities in extractive industries, as well as the implementation gap that persists. Finally, the chapter will discuss how the movement is progressing, emphasizing how the realization of Indigenous rights may hold the key to overcoming some of the world's most pressing global challenges, and review the UN's Special Committee on Decolonization as a vehicle through which Indigenous peoples can seek independence.[8]

Who Are Indigenous Peoples?

There are approximately 370 million Indigenous peoples belonging to five thousand groups, and they are located across every region.[9] They include the poorest of the poor and the most marginalized. With just 5 percent of the world's population, Indigenous peoples account for 15 percent of the world's extreme poor.[10]

Despite data collected on Indigenous peoples globally, the definition of "Indigenous" remains contentious (especially in Africa and Asia).[11] In the absence of a universally accepted definition of Indigenous peoples, varying definitions have emerged, although consensus exists around the factors that should be considered in determining whether a group is indigenous.[12] Jose R. Martínez Cobo, special rapporteur of the Sub-Commission on Prevention of Discrimination and Protection of Minorities, set out one of the most-cited definitions of the term "Indigenous" in his seminal "Study of the Problem of Discrimination Against Indigenous Populations" in 1981–1983. He provided the intellectual framework through which notions of indigeneity should be understood, centering on the rights of Indigenous peoples themselves to define what and who is "Indigenous." The working definition of "Indigenous communities, peoples and nations" provides:[13]

> Indigenous communities, peoples and nations are those which, having a historical continuity with pre-invasion and pre-colonial societies that developed on their territories, consider themselves distinct from other sectors of the societies now prevailing on those territories, or parts of them. They form at present non-dominant sectors of society and are determined to preserve, develop and transmit to future generations their ancestral territories, and their ethnic identity, as the basis of their continued existence as peoples, in accordance with their own cultural patterns, social institutions and legal system.
>
> This historical continuity may consist of the following factors:
>   a) Occupation of ancestral lands, or at least of part of them;
>   b) Common ancestry with the original occupants of these lands;
>   c) Culture in general, or in specific manifestations (such as religion, living under a tribal system, membership of an indigenous community, dress, means of livelihood, lifestyle, etc.);
>   d) Language (whether used as the only language, as mother-tongue, as the habitual means of communication at home or in the family, or as the main, preferred, habitual, general or normal language);
>   e) Residence on certain parts of the country, or in certain regions of the world;
>   f) Other relevant factors such as the identification of "waahi tapu" (sites of significance).

On an individual basis, an Indigenous person is one who belongs to an Indigenous community through self-identification as Indigenous (group consciousness) and is recognized and accepted by the community as one of its members (acceptance by the group). This preserves for Indigenous peoples the sovereign right and power to decide who belongs to them without external interference.

Historical Context

Indigenous peoples have relentlessly asserted their distinct sovereign autonomy, but have struggled to maintain it against the state. Indigenous peoples (particularly in settler colonial contexts) have entered into various treaties in a bid to preserve their sovereign rights as peoples. However, with a growing non-Indigenous settler population eager for lands and resources, states in various jurisdictions have proved less inclined to recognize and protect sovereign rights. Underlying this denial of Indigenous rights is the belief that Indigenous peoples belong to "subject races" rather than nations capable of self-government, able to represent their interests on equal footing with states as subjects, rather than objects, of international law.[14] Only in the 1980s did these attitudes begin to shift, paving the way for Indigenous peoples to participate in international lawmaking.

In seeking redress for breaches of their fundamental rights, Indigenous peoples have historically sought recourse beyond their domestic jurisdictions, particularly through the United Nations (and before that the League of Nations). In 1923, Cayuga chief Deskaheh, the representative of the Six Nations of the Iroquois (Native American Indian), traveled to the League of Nations in Geneva to seek redress for Canada's breaches of the Indian Act.[15] Similarly, Wiremu Ratana, from Aotearoa, New Zealand, traveled to the League of Nations seeking recourse for the state's breaches of the rights guaranteed to Māori under the Treaty of Waitangi.[16] Though both appeals were ultimately unsuccessful—a sign of the League of Nations' reluctance to challenge colonial paradigms that remained firmly entrenched after World War I—they show Indigenous peoples' willingness to resort to international fora when domestic advocacy has proved unavailing.

Following World War II, the international community treated Indigenous peoples much like any other ethnic minority group.[17] Their relative and historic disadvantage vis-à-vis non-Indigenous populations meant that Indigenous peoples were seen as needing to "catch up" and assimilate to achieve the same level of "development." Their concerns were to be addressed through the Universal Declaration of Human Rights, the International Covenant on Civil and Political Rights (ICCPR), and the Covenant on Economic, Social and Cultural Rights (CESCR) (together, "the Covenants").[18] These postwar instruments enact the universal human rights of individuals and frame minority group protection through the lens of nondiscrimination. With the exception of ICCPR Article 27 (which protects the right to culture of *an individual* belonging to a minority group), they do not contemplate special protections owed to vulnerable groups beyond the universal rights applicable to everyone.[19] Accordingly, this framework failed to address Indigenous peoples' most pressing concerns and, in particular, their need to preserve their cultures, territories, institutions, and ways of life following centuries of colonization, subjugation, dispossession, cultural erasure, and forced assimilation. It also reflects the lack of Indigenous participation in the lawmaking processes that engendered postwar human rights instruments.

The shortcomings of the postwar human rights regime were further compounded by Indigenous peoples' exclusion from the decolonization process that accelerated after World War II. For many years, states denied that Indigenous peoples were peoples within the meaning of the common Article 1 of the Covenants, which recognizes a people's right to self-determination (encompassing the right to freely determine their political status, including independence from the state). Consequently, many Indigenous peoples speak of an incomplete decolonization that has subjected them to the same ills of dispossession, assimilation, and marginalization that existed under colonialism.[20]

States' aversion to granting minorities and Indigenous peoples group-specific, collective rights after World War II is historically situated. The human rights regime that emerged under the Universal Declaration of Human Rights and the two Covenants is steeped in a postwar liberal tradition that believed that positioning human rights as universal did away with the need for group-specific rights and protections for vulnerable groups.[21]

This framing of minority rights represented a departure from established minority paradigms in the nineteenth century and the interwar period.[22] After World War I, a treaty system was established under the League of Nations whereby the rights of specific national minorities were protected through bilateral treaties between sovereign states. These treaties essentially recognized that national minorities had group-specific rights, not shared by the majority, that aimed to protect the group from disenfranchisement and unwanted assimilation. Because the Nazi regime had opportunistically seized on alleged breaches in the treaty rights of ethnic Germans in neighboring countries as a pretext for invasion, there was apprehension after the war that a regime based on group-specific rights could cause ethnic conflict.[23]

Another factor that deeply influenced the postwar minority rights regime is the ascendence of the United States, which skewed toward the adoption of an Anglo-American nondiscrimination model for minority rights. In the United States, laws and policies adopted to address the needs of disadvantaged minorities are centered on protection from discrimination and disenfranchisement by majority groups. Difference in treatment is permitted (via affirmative action policies) only until integration and equality vis-à-vis the majority are achieved.[24]

This integrationist approach to minority rights dovetails with the predominant view of "development" that emerged in the postcolonial era, which understood Indigenous cultures, institutions, and ways of life as essentially backward and needing to assimilate to dominant, industrialized societies to overcome poverty, marginalization and discrimination. Both miss the point. Where Blacks in the United States have been de jure and de facto segregated, Native Americans have been coercively integrated, their cultures, languages, and institutions actively erased.[25] It is not that Indigenous peoples "do not need protection against racism. But whereas racism against blacks comes from the denial by whites that blacks are full members of the community, racism against [Indigenous peoples] comes primarily from the denial by whites that [they] are distinct peoples with their own cultures and communities."[26] Indigenous peoples' insistence "that they are not minorities may in part reflect the complete inadequacy of the non-discrimination standard to their needs."[27]

The integrationist approach is even reflected in the first international treaty ratified to protect Indigenous peoples: ILO Convention No. 107, "concerning the protection and *integration* of indigenous and other tribal and semi tribal populations in independent countries," which was adopted in 1957. Dissatisfaction with the convention's assimilationist agenda led to the adoption of ILO Convention No. 169 in 1989. While it does not go as far as the Declaration, it made important strides on how the rights of Indigenous peoples are conceptualized in international law, recognizing Indigenous peoples as communities needing special protections vis-à-vis the majority.[28]

In sum, the postwar human rights regime failed to resonate with Indigenous peoples, their needs, and their worldviews. It did not encompass the collective and group-specific nature of Indigenous identities, claims, and values. This is perhaps best exemplified in the realm of culture and property. Introduced by colonizers, individualized property regimes in former colonies have driven conflict, inequality, and poverty and have accelerated the loss of Indigenous territories and cultures.[29] The idea that an individual could own property or lands is anathema to Indigenous worldviews. In Indigenous societies, lands are sacred and cannot be owned, at least not by individuals. Ownership, to the extent it exists, is collective: food, goods, and natural resources are shared among members of the group rather than accumulated and commodified for speculative return. Indigenous cultures and ways of life are thus enjoyed and exercised in community and inextricably linked to ancestral lands. In this context, the liberal conception of individual rights that runs through Western legal traditions can pose an impediment to (rather than a mechanism for) fulfilling Indigenous rights.

The Global Indigenous Movement and the Adoption of the Declaration

Resistance against acknowledging Indigenous peoples as peoples, imbued with group-specific rights to cultural identity, lands, non-assimilation, and self-determination, represented an important obstacle Indigenous peoples had to overcome as they sought to enact international standards capable of fulfilling their fundamental rights. The adoption of the Declaration therefore represents an enormous departure from dominant discourses around human rights, state sovereignty, and Westphalian politics. In this section, we will examine the global Indigenous movement's role in precipitating that change.

A series of events converged in the 1970s that sparked the global Indigenous movement. At that time, deep frustration and dissatisfaction with Indigenous peoples' relationships to their respective states bubbled over. It pushed Indigenous leaders from around the world to seek recourse at the international level for their communities' marginalization and for the repeated treaty breaches that had taken place since the mid-nineteenth century.[30] Through the erosion of treaty-based relationships, Indigenous peoples went from being recognized as nations to being seen as marginalized minority groups on the verge of extinction. This view of indigeneity was compounded by global governance systems focused on individual rights, nondiscrimination, and decolonization, all of which "problematically overlooked or even actively excluded Indigenous peoples."[31]

In this context, domestic activism by Indigenous peoples in several countries increasingly called for international recognition as peoples equal to all others, with the same human rights. To achieve this, Indigenous peoples understood they would have to secure collective rights to self-determination, ancestral lands, and a return to negotiated, nation-to-nation relationships with states.[32] Aided by improved travel and communication, domestic Indigenous movements began to link up transnationally, furnishing Indigenous activists with the opportunity to discuss common experiences of oppression and discrimination and begin strategizing on a global scale.[33]

The beginnings of the global Indigenous movement owe much to the American Indian Movement (AIM) in the United States. The standoff between AIM activists— who seized and occupied the town of Wounded Knee, South Dakota—and the federal government in 1973 represents a turning point.[34] In 1974, when negotiations with the federal government stalled, five thousand elders and traditional leaders representing ninety-eight Indigenous nations from nine countries came together at the Standing Rock Reservation in Lakota territory. There, they decided to take their treaty grievances to international fora and founded the International Indian Treaty Council (IITC), an organization of Indigenous peoples from North America, Central America, South America, the Caribbean, and the Pacific.[35]

Domestic activism in the United States coincided with events in Canada and the actions by First Nations to counter the government's 1969 white paper that, without consultation, proposed to revoke Indigenous constitutional recognition under a theory of equality and nondiscrimination.[36] In 1975, the first International Conference of Indigenous Peoples gathered in Canada. There, North American Indians, Saami from Scandinavia, Māori from New Zealand, and members from Aboriginal groups from Australia founded the World Council on Indigenous Peoples (WCIP).[37]

Shortly after being established, the WCIP and IITC obtained consultative status at the UN and, in 1977, over a hundred Indigenous delegates participated in the first NGO conference on discrimination in Geneva. During the conference, Indigenous participants drafted the Declaration of Principles for the Defence of the Indigenous Nations and Peoples of the Western Hemisphere, which defined the movement's founding principles and aims and shifted the conversation to focus on the right to self-determination, plural sovereignty arrangements, and collective rights (including to ancestral lands).[38] This position was reaffirmed at a follow-up NGO conference organized by the Sub-Committee on Racism and Racial Discrimination in Geneva in 1981, which drew 130 Indigenous representatives from North America, Central America, South America, Scandinavia, Australia, and New Zealand.[39]

These events coincided with the launch of a study on the problem of discrimination against Indigenous populations by the United Nations Sub-Commission on the Prevention of Discrimination and Protection of Minorities in 1972. The study report confirmed that the existing provisions in human rights instruments "are not wholly adequate for the recognition and protection of the specific rights of Indigenous populations."[40] It also recommended that the subcommission prepare a draft declaration on the rights of Indigenous peoples, triggering the creation of the UN Working Group on Indigenous Populations (WGIP), the first UN mechanism on Indigenous issues.[41]

WGIP held its first meeting in Geneva in 1982. It was the first time in the history of the UN that right-holders participated directly in the international standard-setting process. Participation by states, civil society organizations, and Indigenous peoples rose steadily over subsequent WGIP meetings. Growing Indigenous participation reflected WGIP's guiding principles, which departed from standard UN operating procedures. First, WGIP decided its meetings should be open to as many Indigenous organizations as possible, regardless of whether they had UN Economic and Social Council (ECOSOC) consultative status. Second, it established the UN Voluntary Fund for Indigenous Peoples in 1985 to cover the travel expenses of Indigenous participants so that they could attend UN meetings.[42] This helped ensure the direct participation of Indigenous peoples over time, and marks a significant shift from traditional international lawmaking, which is generally conducted by states.

Drafting of the Declaration started in 1985.[43] Elaboration began with the first meeting of the intersessional Working Group on the Draft Declaration on the Rights of Indigenous Peoples (WGDD) in 1995. Unlike the WGIP process, Indigenous representatives were observers rather than participants in the WGDD (which comprised state delegates and UN staff).[44] The road to the adoption of the final Declaration in 2007 was therefore fraught and drawn out.[45] By the second meeting of the WGDD in 1996, pressure to reopen the draft Declaration for review article by article led Indigenous representatives to insist they be able to participate directly in discussions to build consensus. The chair/rapporteur repeatedly ignored Indigenous delegates who attempted to speak during the meeting.

The Indigenous representatives then staged "a walkout in protest of the agenda and the lack of response to their collective proposals for change." As Haudenosaunee activist Kenneth Deer states, "We had some leverage in this because without Indigenous participation, the WGDD lacks credibility." The challenge, Deer says, "was how to get back in the room." The Indigenous delegates negotiated with states to establish an Indigenous cochair for the WGDD. Other process changes were made to increase Indigenous participation, meaning that consensus would have to be achieved between states and Indigenous peoples before votes could be called. As Deer describes, "This was a significant victory for Indigenous peoples, which those who entered the process after 1996 may not fully appreciate: if we have not been part of the consensus, we would not have the Declaration we have today."[46]

Although Indigenous representatives ultimately remained observers, they were allowed to make statements and participate. Some Indigenous representatives left in protest, but there was Indigenous Caucus consensus on the need to defend the content of the Declaration approved by the subcommission and fight against attempts to water it down. This negotiating position left little scope for change and led to an impasse that lasted from 1997 until 2004. During this time, no new articles were approved for adoption.[47]

In an effort to break the stalemate, in 2001 the Indigenous Caucus expressed that it would consider changes to the draft text adopted by the subcommission, provided the integrity of the text was retained. This led certain states to propose an amended draft Declaration in 2004 that substantially weakened a number of provisions. In response, six Indigenous delegates commenced a hunger strike to draw attention to continued attempts by some states to co-opt the process and dilute the fundamental protections approved by the subcommission. The situation was ultimately resolved by the Office of the UN High Commissioner for Human Rights, who promised Indigenous representatives that the Human Rights Council would not adopt a document that was not approved by consensus with them.[48]

By the following year, outstanding issues remained around self-determination, natural resources, lands, and collective rights. The chair therefore presented a compromise text that added protections around state sovereignty and territorial integrity. The chair's proposal was presented to the Human Rights Council in June 2006. The majority of states and Indigenous organizations voiced support for the compromise text, which was passed by the Human Rights Council on June 29, 2006, and forwarded to the General Assembly for adoption.[49]

Twenty-five years after negotiations under the WGIP first started, in September 2007, the General Assembly adopted the Declaration, with a majority of 143 states in favor. Eleven states abstained. Four states opposed adoption: Australia, Canada, the United States, and New Zealand (CANZUS). These states have since withdrawn their objections (which were largely premised on concerns around collective rights and self-determination). According to Sheryl Lightfoot, while states disrupted the emergence of the Indigenous rights movement in multiple ways, the final draft of the Declaration "live[s] up to the vast majority of its original intent, as articulated by the Indigenous rights movement in the 1970s."[50] It represents a major feat in international lawmaking.

The dramatic negotiations that led to the adoption of the Declaration reveal the high stakes involved and the Indigenous Caucus's negotiating prowess. Indigenous peoples insisted on remaining true to their identities and values, and their approach to UN advocacy reflects that. The Indigenous Caucus had a keen awareness of the pressure points at their disposal, a clear picture of what was ultimately beyond compromise, and deft negotiating skills in a hostile environment. Considering the odds—and the seemingly insurmountable structural changes required to effect Indigenous rights as articulated in the Declaration—it is remarkable that, by and large, recurrent controversies were resolved in favor of Indigenous peoples. The Indigenous Caucus's success is a product, at least in part, of the consensus-based approach to negotiation evident internally among members of the Indigenous Caucus, as well as with states. It is an important dynamic of Indigenous advocacy that originates in traditional consensus-based decision-making common to Indigenous communities globally.[51] The road to adoption shows the Indigenous Caucus's ability to remain steadfast on the fundamentals (i.e., direct participation, which is at the heart of self-determination) while at the same time displaying a willingness to work collaboratively with state representatives. Though these approaches to international lawmaking are painstaking and time-consuming, the Indigenous Caucus's success is a testament to the importance of fighting for a process capable of delivering the structural changes social movements seek to enact through their advocacy.

Contextualizing the Declaration: Case Studies

Perceived as a major triumph, the Declaration is the only international instrument that views Indigenous rights through an Indigenous lens.[52] For instance, Indigenous people no longer need to rely on ICCPR Article 27; rather, they can directly refer to the Declaration.[53]

The orthodox view is that the Declaration is not legally binding upon the states.[54] However, it provides a benchmark against which Indigenous peoples can measure state action, and a means of international appeal.[55] Portions may also represent binding international law. According to the former special rapporteur for Indigenous human rights, James Anaya:[56]

> Some aspects of the provisions of the Declaration can also be considered as a reflection of norms of customary international law. In any event, as a resolution adopted by the General Assembly with the approval of an overwhelming majority of Member States, the Declaration represents a commitment on the part of the United Nations and Member States to its provisions, within the framework of the obligations established by the United Nations Charter to promote and protect human rights on a non-discriminatory basis.[57]

The Declaration places Indigenous peoples within a human rights framework.[58] It contains more than twenty provisions affirming Indigenous peoples' right to participate, as a group, in decision-making. It emphasizes Indigenous peoples' right to participate as a core principle under international human rights law. The

Declaration affirms rights derived from human rights principles such as equality and self-determination, contextualizes those rights in light of their particular characteristics and circumstances, and promotes measures to remedy the rights' historical and systemic violation.[59]

The significance of the Declaration therefore lies in its effect as a minimum standard against which to assess state conduct. Breach of this standard provides Indigenous peoples a means of appeal in the international arena.[60] Thus the Declaration provides an additional international instrument for Indigenous peoples when their rights have been breached. It serves as an interpretative tool relied on by courts and human rights bodies to assess the scope of protections owed to Indigenous peoples under various human rights instruments. While the available remedy is uncertain, the Declaration nonetheless helps facilitate effective dialogue between governments and Indigenous peoples and provides leverage against states and others in the court of public opinion. The significance of public perception is evident in the CANZUS states' reversal toward support of the Declaration.[61]

Right of Self-Determination

The right to self-determination is one of the cardinal principles of international human rights law. Article 3 of the Declaration confirms that

> Indigenous peoples have the right to self-determination. By virtue of that right they freely determine their political status and freely pursue their economic, social and cultural development.

Article 3 is expressed in almost identical terms to the common Article 1 of the two Covenants, which provides:

> All peoples have the right of self-determination. By virtue of that right they freely determine their political status and freely pursue their economic, social and cultural development.

Yet the right of self-determination remains one of the most controversial articles of the Declaration. This controversy is, for the most part, based on a lack of understanding about the meaning and significance of the right to self-determination. Many states (particularly the CANZUS bloc) have resisted recognizing Indigenous peoples' right to self-determination on the false assumption that it entails a right to secede from the state. Rather, it confers a right to internal self-determination (i.e., a people's right to self-government without external interference) rather than external self-determination (which encompasses a people's right to form an independent state, free from alien domination).[62]

The UN Indigenous Rights Framework in the New Millennium

Prior to adoption of the Declaration, and as a result of continued advocacy by Indigenous peoples, the UN Permanent Forum on Indigenous Issues (UNPFII) was formed in 2000. The UNPFII provides expert advice to the Human Rights Council and UN agencies, raises awareness and promotes the integration of Indigenous issues within the UN system, prepares and disseminates information on Indigenous issues, and promotes respect for the Declaration. UNPFII's annual meeting provides an important platform where Indigenous peoples from all regions can voice their issues and concerns to states, UN agencies, NGOs, and other Indigenous peoples. This process is unique, as Indigenous peoples are "heard" and can contribute to a final report adopted by the Human Rights Council.

In 2001, the Commission on Human Rights established the UN Special Rapporteur on the Rights of Indigenous Peoples (SRRIP). The SRRIP promotes good practices, reports on the overall human rights situations of Indigenous peoples, addresses specific cases of alleged violations, and conducts thematic studies on promoting the rights of Indigenous peoples.

WGIP re-formed into the Expert Mechanism on the Rights of Indigenous Peoples (EMRIP) in 2007.[63] The continuation of the work undertaken by the WGIP through EMRIP reflects the importance of the forum for Indigenous peoples and the United Nations' recognition of the need to retain the platform. Collectively, the UNPFII, EMRIP, and SRRIP are the mechanisms within the UN system with an Indigenous mandate.

Indigenous Rights in Practice

Despite the formal recognition of Indigenous peoples' fundamental rights, breaches remain common. This implementation gap remains among the most intractable challenges facing the Indigenous rights movement today. The following brief examples highlight instances of noncompliance by states, corporate actors, and NGOs operating in diverse contexts and regions, and the strategies Indigenous communities have resorted to in asserting their rights.

Armed Resistance and Negotiated Autonomy: Bangladesh

Bangladesh's officially recognized Indigenous population, as of the 2011 census, totaled 1,586,141; however, according to Indigenous people in the country, the total is much higher, about 5 million.[64] The Chittagong Hill Tracts (CHT), in southeastern Bangladesh, is home to twelve Indigenous groups, collectively known as the Jumma people.[65] In Bangladesh, the government does not recognize Indigenous peoples as Indigenous; a 2011 constitutional amendment refers to Indigenous peoples as "tribes," "minor races," and "ethnic sects," recognizing cultural differences while ignoring the economic and political rights of Indigenous peoples, in particular vis-à-vis ancestral lands.[66]

Until the partition of British India in 1947, the Jummas' rights to land and autonomy were relatively well respected and their special status as a largely self-governing territory was recognized. Their situation began to decline as Pakistan took control of the CHT, and it rapidly deteriorated when their special status was revoked. Under Pakistani rule, Bengali settlers were permitted to move into the CHT.[67]

Following the civil war that resulted in the creation of Bangladesh, the Jumma hoped the change in government would pave the way for a return to self-government. However, the newly created government viewed the proposal as secessionist, launching raids into the CHT in 1972.[68] In response to a threat to settle Bengalis in the CHT, the Shanti Bahinis, an armed wing of the Jumma people's political party, Parbatya Chattagram Jana Samhati Samiti (PCJSS), initiated a low-intensity guerrilla war against the government. The reversion to an armed struggle occurred after its leaders failed to achieve autonomy through peaceful and constitutional means, including through participation in the national legislative bodies, delegations to the head of government, and peaceful strikes and demonstrations.[69] Sadly, it was followed by the "planned population transfer" of over half a million non-Indigenous Bengali plains settlers to CHT, the first in a long line of population transfers pursued by subsequent governments to forcibly assimilate the Jumma.[70]

The drivers of the conflict were the erosion of autonomy, denial of constitutional recognition, forced assimilation, and political, economic, and social marginalization. Serious human rights abuses against the Jumma—"including large scale massacres, arbitrary detention, torture, and extrajudicial executions" by Bangladeshi security forces and Bengali settlers—became frequent.[71] It "forced 70,000 Jummas, about 10 percent of the total Jumma population, to seek shelter in Tripura State of India in 1986, 1989 and 1993."[72]

Peace negotiations commenced in 1991, resulting in the 1997 Chittagong Hill Tracts Accord, signed by the government of Bangladesh and PCJSS.[73] The accord recognizes the CHT as a tribal inhabited region, acknowledges its traditional governance system and the role of its chiefs, and provides building blocks for regional autonomy. In 2013, amendments to the accord were approved by the Bangladesh cabinet to resolve long-standing land disputes. The accord, however, remained largely unimplemented, and the government has since supported programs that stand in opposition to the accord's aims and the Jumma's interests.[74] This has resulted in widespread human rights violations, violent conflict, and militarization.[75] On July 31, 2016, the cabinet approved the amendment of the CHT Land Disputes Resolution Commission Act, which empowers a commission to settle disputes, help to restore the rights of CHT Indigenous people to their lands, and address the roots of conflict between communities in the area.[76] The resulting Land Disputes Commission finally met in early 2018; however, the chair noted that approximately twenty-two thousand land-related complaints had been filed so far—with none resolved.[77]

As the model for an agreement that provides Indigenous autonomy, the 1997 Chittagong Hill Tracts Accord, including its implementation process, provides valuable lessons relating to the importance of community, Indigenous rights, and peacemaking. It illustrates the challenges of implementing a peace treaty, and how the failure to implement such a treaty can undermine progress. In terms of substance, the committee overseeing the implementation of the accord was not independent of the parties to the accord, and the absence of a third-party mediation clause has contributed to problems around implementation. This highlights the importance of robust legal instruments and transparent legal processes. In light of the stalemate and the fact that Indigenous peoples were very much the minority with weak electoral and economic power, activists sought recourse to international bodies such as the UNPFII and EMRIP. In the process, alliances with international and national civil society groups and Indigenous peoples were strengthened, underscoring the importance of collaboration and alliances when seeking, developing, and sustaining agreements.

Extractive Industries: The Porgera Mine in the Highlands of Papua New Guinea
Notwithstanding clear recognition of Indigenous peoples' right to ancestral lands, extractive activities on their territories often have negative, even catastrophic impacts on Indigenous peoples' economic, social, and cultural rights. A paradigmatic example is the recent surge of mining activities in Papua New Guinea (PNG).[78]

The Porgera mine in the Highlands of Papua New Guinea produces thousands of pounds of gold each year. The mine is owned and operated by Barrick, a Canadian corporation. Though it generates income and jobs for local Indigenous peoples, the mine has long been a source of controversy. The mine has been widely condemned for dumping over six million metric tons of liquid tailings into a nearby river.[79] Local Indigenous communities regard these destructive practices as a violation of their territorial, cultural, and self-governance rights.[80] This has created friction and grievances between Barrick and the Indigenous community. The tension is compounded by frequent allegations of rape, sexual assault, drownings, and shootings.[81] Protests by Indigenous communities indicate that human rights abuses continue.[82]

The Declaration affords Indigenous peoples rights to ancestral lands and natural resources and requires states and private actors to seek their free, prior, and informed consent before engaging in activities that will significantly impact their territories. However, Papua New Guinea, which was absent during the vote to adopt the Declaration, has weak rule of law and regulatory schemes, and weak governance and judicial systems. This provides fertile ground for transnational corporations to design grievance mechanisms that limit their legal liability and advance their reputation for protecting human rights without necessarily fulfilling their international obligations.[83] Regardless, this does not discharge corporations from minimizing adverse impacts, particularly environmental impacts, and from engaging meaningfully with Indigenous peoples to address concerns and violations.

A report on Barrick's grievance mechanism for sexual violence in Papua New Guinea authored by the Columbia and Harvard law schools' human rights clinics notes that

> rights holder engagement is consultation and requires early, proactive and comprehensive engagement with all stakeholders, particularly rights holders. Typical consultation models can maintain the unequal power relationship between rights holders and companies. The interests of rights holders are best served when they co-create a remedy mechanism with companies.[84]

This view is consistent with the spirit of the Declaration and can supplement its application. The most recent Barrick lease expired in April 2020, when Prime Minister James Marape refused to sign an extension.[85] Renegotiation provided an opportunity to ensure these rights were upheld. Initially, the PNG government sought to run the mine independently; however, economic and COVID-19-related health challenges hindered operations.[86] The loss of employment and revenue led the PNG government to negotiate a new lease arrangement with Barrick.[87]

Under the expired lease, Barrick held 95 percent ownership of the mining operation, and the PNG government and local landowners owned 5 percent.[88] Under the new agreement adopted in April 2021, ownership of the mine will transfer to a new joint venture that is 51 percent owned by the PNG government and 49 percent owned by Barrick.[89] The agreement also provides PNG stakeholders—the government and landowners—53 percent of the economic benefits from the mine.[90] Although this agreement appears to offer a sense of self-determination, the environmental concerns and the human rights abuses remain unresolved.[91] In addition, the landowners and those directly affected by the operation of the mine were not consulted, and details have not been released regarding how landowners will benefit economically.[92] This is unfortunate, and appears to be an opportunity lost, enabling economic gain over protection of the environment and human rights.

Infrastructure and Commercial Activities on Indigenous Territories: Chile

Traditional lands that are legally and/or ancestrally owned continue to be under serious threat from large extractive and infrastructure projects. In Chile, this is largely as a result of sector legislation (the 1981 Water Code) that has not been adapted to comply with ILO Convention 169.[93] As a result, third parties are able to establish rights over natural resources located on Indigenous territories.

This has resulted in various commercial activities on Mapuche ancestral lands, including logging, hydroelectric facilities, and salmon farming, with adverse impacts on their ways of life.[94] For example, the Ralco hydroelectric power plant is a large dam diverting water along the Bíobío River, which serves Mapuche communities.[95] Dam construction was undertaken without consulting with the Pehuenche (Mapuche) community, resulting in their displacement and the flooding of land, taking away their "resources and hunting grounds, and polluting the environment."[96]

Ultimately, it is up to the state to implement the Mapuche people's rights at the domestic level. A new constitution, which is being drafted, presents an opportunity for Indigenous recognition in Chile. Given the presence of strong corporate interests, Indigenous recognition will only succeed if a broad cross section of Chilean civil society comes together to back it.

Conservation, Litigation and Indigenous Rights: Africa

Indigenous peoples around the world are susceptible to dispossession not only in the name of development and corporate profit but also in the name of conservation. Premised on the mistaken belief that humans are at odds with the environment, an increasingly militarized approach to conservation, also known as fortress conservation, is disproportionately impacting Indigenous peoples because lands rich in biodiversity (which often overlap with Indigenous territories) are earmarked for "protection." Human habitation is prohibited, although tourism, safari hunting, and scientific research are permitted. As a result, many Indigenous communities are being evicted, even though they are among the most environmentally conscious communities in the world.

In Africa, conservation has become the number one threat to Indigenous territories.[97] The irreparable harms Indigenous communities suffer as a result of conservation-related displacements are vividly illustrated by the Batwa of the Democratic Republic of Congo (DRC) and the Ogiek and Endorois of Kenya.

The Ogiek and Endorois of Kenya

Litigation cannot undo the devastation to lives and communities after decades of forced separation from ancestral lands and ensuing landlessness. Nevertheless, seeking legal redress before supranational courts and human rights bodies is often the only avenue available to ensure the recognition of Indigenous peoples' land rights. Obtaining a favorable judgment is, however, only half the battle. As the Ogiek and Endorois cases show, after protracted legal campaigns, implementation often remains elusive.

The Endorois and Ogiek peoples are Indigenous communities evicted from their ancestral lands in the name of conservation. Both communities lodged cases before the African Commission on Human and Peoples' Rights (ACHPR). Following Kenya's failure to implement a favorable 2009 ruling ordering the Endorois to be restored to their ancestral lands, the ACHPR referred the Ogiek case to the African Court on Human and Peoples' Rights. In 2017, the African Court issued a landmark judgment vindicating the Ogiek's rights. To date, neither ruling has been fully implemented, and violations are ongoing.

The Endorois are a semi-nomadic Indigenous pastoralist community who have herded cattle and goats for many centuries in the Lake Bogoria area of Kenya's Rift Valley. Following independence, ownership of the land passed to the state, which held it in trust for the benefit of the community until 1973, when Kenya evicted the Endorois to create a game reserve. Their dispossession without consultation or compensation seriously interfered with their pastoralist livelihood and the exercise of their culture and religion. Following a series of failed attempts to have their customary rights recognized in domestic courts, the Endorois launched a case before the ACHPR.

In February 2010, the ACHPR rendered a decision recognizing Indigenous peoples' collective rights to their traditionally owned lands in Africa. It found that by restricting the Endorois' access to their ancestral lands, Kenya had violated several rights under the African Charter, including their right to development. It found Kenya had failed to obtain the Endorois' free, prior, and informed consent before creating the game reserve, and it established, for the first time, that governments must engage with Indigenous peoples in the development of policies that impact them.

The ACHPR recommended that the Kenyan government restore the Endorois to their lands and ensure their unrestricted access to Lake Bogoria and the surrounding area, pay compensation for the eviction, and pay royalties to the community from profits garnered from the reserve. Ten years later, Kenya has failed to comply with key recommendations of the decision, including restoring the Endorois to their ancestral lands and compensating the community for the losses suffered.

The Ogiek case appears to be following a similar pattern. The Ogiek are traditionally a forest-dwelling hunter-gatherer community that has lived in the Mau Forest of Kenya since time immemorial. They continue to depend on forest resources, though the community has become sedentarized following ongoing evictions since the colonial period. As a result, most of the community engages in agriculture and pastoralism, though they retain a strong cultural and spiritual connection to their ancestral lands and depend on forest resources (such as honey) to supplement their livelihoods.

Government policies of converting communal land to individual ownership led to much of the Ogiek's ancestral lands being sold off, jeopardizing their livelihood and their ability to live collectively on their lands. Resettlement schemes purportedly established for the Ogiek's benefit allocated large swaths of land to non-Ogiek, including political cronies. The government has also allowed substantial commercial and illegal logging to take place. These policies have spurred non-Indigenous settlers to illegally settle in the area.

In a bid to preserve the portions of the Mau Forest not degraded by settlement and resource exploitation, the Kenyan government implemented conservation measures that resulted in further evictions of Ogiek. These measures effectively labeled Ogiek as encroachers and banned them from the forest. These policies are misplaced for a number of reasons, among them that the environmental damage has been fueled by government policies, not the Ogiek.

In October 2009, the Ogiek successfully applied to the ACHPR for provisional measures barring Kenya from proceeding with the evictions. Citing the far-reaching implications of evictions for the Ogiek's survival, the commission eventually referred the case to the African Court, where it became the first Indigenous rights case the court has decided.

In a historic May 2017 judgment, the African Court recognized that the Ogiek have a right to use and occupy their ancestral lands. It held that, as Indigenous peoples, they have a critical role to play in safeguarding their local ecosystems and in conserving their ancestral lands. It concluded that the Ogiek could not be held responsible for the depletion of the Mau Forest, and it could not justify their evictions or the denial of their rights. The African Court reserved its ruling on reparations, but ordered Kenya to take measures to remedy the violations it found, including to the right to property, within six months of the judgment.

Since then, the Kenyan government has failed to implement the judgment, engaging in further evictions. The largest of these eviction campaigns took place between June and July 2020. More than a thousand Ogiek were illegally evicted from their homes, in the midst of the COVID-19 pandemic. Many have lost subsistence crops and livestock and have no way to feed themselves. Egregiously, these actions flout the judgment and actively prejudice its implementation.

These evictions, which the government disingenuously claimed had been carried out to implement the African Court judgment, fueled interethnic conflict between Ogiek and non-Ogiek settlers in the Mau Forest who fear its implementation will result in their removal. In a move that aimed to ease ethnic tensions, in September 2020 the government announced a land audit and titling scheme that would award five-acre plots of lands in eastern Mau to Ogiek and non-Ogiek alike. Problematically, the scheme disregards the African Court judgment (which recognizes that the underlying lands are ancestrally owned by the Ogiek) and the Ogiek's demand for collective land titles, which they see as the only way to preserve their culture. To put a stop to this, the Ogiek filed a case in local court arguing that the government's scheme failed to comply with the African Court judgment and their right to free, prior, and informed consent. In December 2020, the court issued a conservatory order directing the government to halt the land audit and titling scheme pending final adjudication of the case. While it offers a temporary respite, the conservatory order does not guarantee the ultimate outcome of the local court case nor that the government of Kenya will ultimately comply with the African Court judgment or its eventual reparations order.[98]

Both cases show that despite the progressive role international litigation plays in defining and expanding the scope of Indigenous peoples' rights, much work remains in the realm of implementation.

The Batwa of the Kahuzi-Biega Forest

The Batwa are the first inhabitants of the Congo Basin and one of the most marginalized communities in the Great Lakes region. Commonly referred to as "Pygmies," they are an Indigenous forest-dwelling community that has lived in symbiosis with the Kahuzi-Biega Forest in the South Kivu region of the DRC since time immemorial.[99] The Kahuzi-Biega Forest is also home to eastern lowland gorillas (a critically endangered species). In 1970, the government enacted a law creating a national park called the Parc National Kahuzi-Biega (PNKB). The creation of the PNKB (and its subsequent expansion in 1975) led to the forced eviction of three thousand to six thousand Batwa. It restricted their access to and use of their ancestral lands without consultation or compensation.

During these evictions, the Batwa were violently driven out without warning and forced to find shelter among non-Batwa communities that discriminated against them. No relocation arrangements were made to assist them, and they have lived in extreme poverty as squatters in various rural areas surrounding the PNKB ever since. Conversely, non-Batwa have been allowed to remain in the forest or have received compensation. Attempts to seek redress in domestic courts have been unavailing.

The consequences of the eviction have devastated the Batwa's traditional way of life. The forest from which they are now excluded provided them with security as well as food, medicine, and fuel. In addition, the Batwa's ancestral territory is seen as sacred, inextricably linked to the spiritual and cultural integrity of the community and its traditional way of life. As a result of the harsh living conditions they experience on the outskirts of the park, without access to basic infrastructure or public services, they suffer high rates of malnourishment, disease, and death. The human toll has been enormous: by the early 1980s, 50 percent of the Batwa expelled from their ancestral lands in the PNKB had perished.[100]

The situation has continued to deteriorate. The DRC has failed to protect Batwa ancestral lands from commercial poaching, illegal mining, and timber extraction, or to share the revenue from conservation and tourism activities on their land. Whereas the Batwa's traditional knowledge helped protect the forest, now some risk heavy fines, imprisonment, and even death by returning to collect herbs and wood and to hunt. Encounters with park guards have turned violent; the Batwa report being beaten, tortured, and arrested. Some have been shot dead; others have been harassed and intimidated for denouncing human rights abuses and standing up for their community's rights. The DRC has failed to hold park guards accountable even as several Batwa are in jail, accused of illegally accessing their lands.

The story of the Batwa of the Kahuzi-Biega forest is common across Africa and around the world. In the Congo Basin alone, victims of fortress conservation include the Batwa of Rwanda, Uganda, and two additional national parks in the DRC; the Babongo, Bakoya, Baka, Barimba, Bagama, Kouyi, and Akoa in Gabon; and the Baka of Cameroon and of the Republic of Congo.

These evictions and/or the ongoing human rights abuses are often carried out with the funding, support, and/or complicity of large Western conservation NGOs and donors. Although there has been a growing awareness within the conservation establishment of the problems attendant to fortress conservation, few of the standards, guidelines, and best practices have improved the situation on the ground.[101]

In 2003, the International Union for Conservation and Nature (IUCN) adopted the Durban Action Plan following Indigenous activism and lobbying. It is touted as effecting a paradigm shift in protected area management toward a rights-based approach to conservation.[102] Key goals include that: (1) all existing and future areas should be managed and established in full compliance with the rights of Indigenous peoples and local communities; (2) protected areas should have representatives chosen by Indigenous peoples and local communities proportionate to their rights and interests; (3) participatory mechanisms should be put in place for the restitution of Indigenous peoples' traditional lands in protected areas that were established without their free, prior, and informed consent by 2010; and (4) improved management should be undertaken that recognizes traditional governance structures.

Seventeen years later, none of these targets have been achieved in the PNKB. Several dialogues instituted with park authorities have broken down due to their repeated failure to deliver on promises. After years of protracted negotiations, many Batwa no longer believe dialogue offers any prospect of successfully resolving their situation. Reforms made to integrate Indigenous rights into protected area management have failed to materialize.[103]

Avenues for Future Advocacy

Decolonizing Conservation Policy

Fortress conservation is the latest in a long line of colonial interventions premised on separating Indigenous communities from their natural environments. Like prior colonial land policies, these conservation models are fundamentally flawed. Not only have they failed to adequately protect the environment, they have also devastated countless Indigenous and land-dependent communities, and they are facilitated by the non-recognition of customary title. Much of the degradation that has taken place in these pristine environments has resulted from non-Indigenous encroachment and exploitation of Indigenous lands. Although these dynamics date back to the colonial period, they have been carried forward by successor states.

Importantly, a growing body of evidence suggests that Indigenous and community ownership is more effective than state custodianship, conserving biodiversity at a fraction of the cost.[104] Examples of successful Indigenous and community-owned and conserved lands exist in Gambia, Tanzania, and Namibia, and across Latin America. NASA satellite images of recent forest fires in the Brazilian Amazon show that the only unburned areas are lands owned and controlled by Indigenous peoples. In Bolivia, Brazil, Colombia, and Guatemala, deforestation is two to three times lower in Indigenous and community-owned forest than on lands owned by states.[105] Accordingly, the struggle to secure Indigenous and local communities' land rights "will play a crucial role in global efforts to reduce greenhouse gas emissions and mitigate the global threat of climate change."[106] An approach to conservation centered on Indigenous peoples' right to self-determination will also avert the rights violations attendant to fortress conservation.

Recognition of Indigenous Rights Through Corporate Responsibility

Though the Declaration may not be incorporated into domestic legislation, states have a duty to protect the rights of Indigenous people against human rights violations and adverse corporate behavior. Further, private companies have a duty to act consistent with the Declaration and to respect the rights protected therein.[107] They must understand and be willing to comply with their obligations when corporate activities are undertaken on or near ancestral lands.

A state's failure to implement the rights contained in the Declaration through domestic legislation does not absolve companies of their responsibility to Indigenous peoples under the Declaration, which represents the minimum standard under existing human rights law. Corporations, like states, have an obligation to obtain Indigenous communities' free, prior, and informed consent when their property rights are at stake. A higher standard applies to Indigenous property rights because of the cultural significance of ancestral lands. Furthermore, Indigenous peoples' right to self-determination must be protected and upheld by corporations.

There are several reasons it behooves corporations to abide by these standards, including securing sustainable long-term profitability by avoiding conflict, improving corporate image, and bestowing social benefits.[108] Despite these important motivations, states and companies often fail to respect Indigenous peoples' rights. Companies blame governments for the failure to support Indigenous peoples and highlight the economic benefits of their projects, but economic benefit is often not a priority for Indigenous peoples, and many are skeptical they will derive any benefit (let alone one that could offset the detrimental impacts to their lands and ways of life).[109]

A new model is required, one that is centered on self-determination (and its derivative rights, including the right to free, prior, and informed consent). It must also apply the "protect, respect and remedy" framework articulated in the Guiding Principles on Business and Human Rights.[110]

UN Special Committee on Decolonization

To hasten the progress of decolonization, the UN General Assembly adopted the Declaration on the Granting of Independence to Colonial Countries and Peoples through Resolution 1514 (XV) on December 14, 1960. Article 1 recognizes that no peoples should be subjected to domination and exploitation. Article 2 states that all peoples have the right to self-determination, and by virtue of that right, they freely determine their political status and freely pursue their economic, social, and cultural development. This mirrors the language in Article 3 of the Declaration.

The UN Special Committee on Decolonization considers applications by Indigenous peoples to be instated or reinstated on the list of non-self-governing territories to which Resolution 1514 applies. Non-self-governing territories have a distinct legal personality from administering states, and they have a right to external self-determination under international law.[111] Consequently, the process afforded by the Special Committee on Decolonization provides an avenue for Indigenous peoples to renegotiate their relationships with states (particularly for colonized Indigenous peoples, such as in French Polynesia, Hawaii, and West Papua). Because Indigenous peoples lack standing to vote on UN resolutions, the process for reinscription is not immune from political and power dynamics within and between states. It, therefore, risks the same shortcomings that plague other UN procedures, to the detriment of Indigenous peoples. Although French Polynesia has recently been reinstated, Hawaii and West Papua have not.

Conclusions

Within the UN landscape, and despite the strides made through the advocacy of the global Indigenous movement, Indigenous peoples do not have the same standing as states. As a result, Indigenous peoples' rights are reliant on domestic legislation, an appeal to UN bodies, or litigation under various regional and international human rights instruments.

The adoption of the Declaration was a triumph, building on and manifesting the long-standing common body of principles that recognize Indigenous peoples' rights, providing a benchmark against which to measure state and corporate action at the international level. The Declaration articulates "a set of guidelines for state implementation of Indigenous rights, providing a framework for new Indigenous-state relationships, grounded in mutual respect."[112] It represents a global consensus among states, but also Indigenous peoples, who actively participated in the consensus-building process.[113] Under the auspices of the United Nations, this framework provides Indigenous peoples with a recourse of appeal in the international arena when states breach the standards articulated in the Declaration.

In reality, however, the struggle to fulfill Indigenous peoples' fundamental rights as articulated in the Declaration is onerous at best, and tragic at worst. When violations occur, as the case studies highlight, available remedies are uncertain, not least because enforcement of rights—even when successfully adjudicated through litigation—often remains elusive. Constitutional recognition of these fundamental rights would help provide clarity and certainty, but realization would still pose a challenge. In countries where rule of law and governance systems are weak, Indigenous rights are often violated. When Indigenous peoples seek redress, violence often ensues.

In response, Indigenous peoples as a collective have sought redress through the UN system by "naming and shaming." There are also formal processes, such as the Universal Periodic Review and other treaty review procedures, through which Indigenous peoples can bring their grievances. If there is a supranational judicial body able to hear claims brought by Indigenous peoples within their jurisdiction, this also provides an avenue for redress; but again, such redress is only as effective as the political will to comply with human rights obligations. In its absence, little will change.

Without constitutional recognition of the Declaration or other implementing legislation, it would be appropriate that dialogue between governments and Indigenous peoples take place when violations occur. The Declaration further provides Indigenous peoples with a standard to shame states in the court of public opinion. Given the implementation challenges, the international community (including states, donors, international financial institutions, and civil society) must leverage its considerable influence, pressing states and companies to comply with their international and domestic legal obligations vis-à-vis Indigenous peoples.

Reflections

This chapter discusses the movement to advance Indigenous rights. On a national level, the challenge has been constitutional or legislative recognition of these rights. To effect recognition requires political lobbying or protest movements, and even then, formal recognition may or may not be effective. On an international level, as they are not a "state" and therefore lack standing, Indigenous peoples are at the mercy of an array of political state agendas (which are often co-opted by corporate interests and the economic growth imperative).

Despite the challenges the global Indigenous movement has encountered along the way, Indigenous peoples have managed to participate directly in lawmaking and standard-setting at the international level. This represents a significant accomplishment in an international system premised on the primacy of states.

An Indigenous rights framework that falls short on implementation poses a legitimacy problem that is commonplace in the broader human rights system. It lays bare the cracks in the Westphalian system of international relations and the postwar human rights regime. In this context, despite the inherent and persistent challenges in making Indigenous rights effective, the Declaration is a harbinger of a new way of thinking about and engaging international politics. As Sheryl Lightfoot has underscored:

Like the Universal Declaration, the Indigenous rights declaration, if deployed in a consistent, widespread, and creative manner, could potentially represent the earliest stages of a new way of thinking and doing politics, a new way of being in the world, a new imagining of global politics beyond the constraints of the state system and hierarchical relations of domination and subordination.[114]

The shortcomings of a state-centered approach to international lawmaking are self-evident. Addressing complex global problems (including climate change) necessitates making space for rights-holders themselves to participate directly, forging strategic alliances across civil society in the face of opposition from states and powerful corporate actors. The global Indigenous movement has already shown its dynamism, commitment, and willingness to seek alliances in the struggle to make their rights effective. While offering new avenues for advocacy, the success of any strategic alliance will depend on the extent to which non-Indigenous allies are willing and able to support rather than co-opt, dilute, or stymie the movement. At a minimum, any joint advocacy must be premised on the principles of mutual respect and recognition of Indigenous peoples' fundamental rights, creating space for Indigenous worldviews and activism rather than stifling them.[115]

Notes

1. Ban 2013.
2. For instance, in New Zealand, Māori, the Indigenous peoples, comprise 15 percent of the population, yet 50 percent of prison populations identify as Māori; of women in prisons, 62 percent are Māori. Department of Corrections 2007, 6. See also Walters and Bradley 2019, 20–22. Similar data emerge from Australia, Canada and the United States of America. See, for example, Tyler 1999, 209, where he notes that the "very high rates of Aboriginal over-representation in the criminal justice systems of the white 'settler' societies are conventionally explained in terms of pervasive effects of cultural dispossession, and social and economic disadvantage and dislocation."
3. See, e.g., Curtice and Choo 2020, 1753; Al Saba 2020; Kristof 2020.
4. Forest Peoples Programme 2021.
5. Indeed, 80 percent of the world's remaining biodiversity is found in their territories even though they encompass only 22 percent of the world's land surface.
6. In particular, the creation of protected areas on indigenous territories displaces Indigenous peoples. Instead of rewarding them for successfully conserving their natural environments for generations, prevailing conservation strategies often fail to integrate Indigenous traditional knowledge or Indigenous rights to self-determination and ancestral territories, with devastating consequences for people and the environment. See generally Domínguez and Luoma 2020a.
7. Lightfoot 2018.
8. "Independence" applies when a colonized territory seeks independence from the colonizing state—e.g., French Polynesia. "Sovereignty" implies supreme authority within a territory. "Self-determination" is the process by which a country determines its own form of governing.
9. UNDESA 2009, 1.
10. UNSESA 2009, 1.
11. Some countries in Africa and Asia have maintained that the concept of Indigenous peoples applies only in the context of European settler colonialism. Under this view, Indigenous

communities invaded by their neighbors (i.e., subject to colonization from within) are not necessarily Indigenous. This understanding of indigeneity eschews the experience of conquest, oppression, marginalization, and forced assimilation that many Indigenous communities around the world have experienced, whether at the hands of European colonizers or other dominant groups. See Kingsbury 1998; African Group 2006; Sylvain 2017.
12. See, e.g., UN General Assembly 1998, para. 69; International Labour Organization Convention No. 169, art 1; ACHPR 2007, 30–31; ACHPR 2017, para 107; ACHPR 2010, 93.
13. Martínez Cobo 1981–1983.
14. As Will Kymlicka has explained, "Until recently, [Indigenous peoples] were seen as 'wards' or 'subject races,' lacking the political development to qualify as nations, incapable of self-government, and needing the paternalistic protection of their white 'superiors.' Traditional international law did not regard indigenous populations as subjects of international law, and treaties signed with them were not viewed as treaties according to international law, but unilateral acts pertaining to domestic law. These racist attitudes are slowly fading, but they have often been replaced, not with the recognition that Indigenous Peoples are distinct nations, but with the assumption that they are a disadvantaged 'racial minority' or 'ethnic group' for whom progress requires integration into mainstream society. While government policy toward Indians has run the gamut of genocide, expulsion, segregation, and assimilation, the one constant is that governments have never 'genuinely recognized Aboriginal peoples as distinct Peoples with cultures different from, but not inferior to, their own.'" Kymlicka 2013, 22. See also Barsh 1994. The title of Barsh's seminal article, "Indigenous Peoples in the 1990s: From Object to Subject of International Law?," borrows from a speech given by Mary Simon to the General Assembly on behalf of circumpolar peoples in 1992 where she noted: "We are no longer merely objects of international law; we are subjects of international law" (p. 66).
15. Anaya 2009, 4. A precursor to the United Nations, the League of Nations was established following World War I in 1920 to enable international cooperation; https://www.britannica.com/topic/League-of-Nations.
16. Anaya 2009, 16.
17. See Kingsbury 1998; African Group 2006; Sylvain 2017.
18. See generally Barsh 1994.
19. Although the UN Declaration on the Rights of Persons Belonging to National or Ethnic, Religious and Linguistic Minorities sets out special protections for individuals that belong to certain vulnerable minority groups on the basis of group membership, it was not enacted until 1992. And generally, minority rights, including under ICCPR Article 27, apply to individuals rather than the group.
20. Barsh 1994; Lightfoot 2018.
21. "Rather than protecting vulnerable groups directly, through special rights for the members of designated groups, cultural minorities would be protected indirectly, by guaranteeing basic civil and political rights to all individuals regardless of group membership. Basic human rights such as freedom of speech, association, and conscience, while attributed to individuals, are typically exercised in community with others, and so provide protection for group life. Where these individual rights are firmly protected, liberals assumed, no further rights needed to be attributed to members of specific ethnic or national minorities. . . . Guided by this philosophy, the United Nations deleted all references to the rights of ethnic and national minorities in its Universal Declaration of Human Rights." Kymlicka 2003, 2–3 (citations omitted).
22. See generally Kymlicka 2003, 49–58.
23. See generally Barsh 1994; Barsh 1989; Kugelmann 2007; Aukerman 2000.
24. As scholar Miriam Aukerman has explained: "In contrasting this 'equality in difference' approach to the Anglo-American non-discrimination model for minority rights, it is helpful to consider J. A. Laponce's distinction between 'minorities of force'—groups which desire

integration but are denied equality by the dominant society—and 'minorities of will'—groups which want to retain their distinctiveness and therefore seek treatment different from the dominant group. The distinction here is less about remedies than about goals. Both Central/ East European minorities and Indigenous Peoples choose to retain their unique societies, and argue for group-differentiated rights on that basis. In contrast, the predominant Anglo-American approach, which has largely shaped postwar international human rights law—envisions a limited, temporary role for differential treatment in pursuit of future equality and non-discrimination." Aukerman 2000, 1029.

25. "Where blacks have been forcibly *excluded* (segregated) from white society by law, Indians—aboriginal peoples with their own cultures, languages, religions and territories—have been forcibly *included* (integrated) into society by law. That is what is meant by coercive assimilation—the practice of compelling through submersion, an ethnic, cultural and linguistic minority to shed its uniqueness and identity and mingle with the rest of society." Kymlicka 2003, 60.

26. Kymlicka 2003, 60.

27. Aukerman 2000, 1030.

28. While it laid the groundwork for the Declaration, it has proven to be of limited utility given sparse ratification and the lack of effective implementation mechanisms. See generally Domínguez 2018.

29. See generally Kymlicka 2003, 43; Domínguez and Luoma 2020a, 3–4.

30. See generally Lightfoot 2018, 35–38; Minde 1996, 90–128.

31. Lightfoot 2018, 36.

32. Lightfoot 2018, 36.

33. By the 1960s, for example, Indigenous Peoples in North America had begun to establish networks with other Indigenous Peoples in Latin America and were increasingly aware of their plight. Lightfoot 2018, 36.

34. Lightfoot 2018, 37.

35. Founders included AIM members Russel Means (Lakota), Bill Means (Lakota), and Vernon and Clyde Bellecourt (Anishinaabe). Lightfoot 2018, 37.

36. Lightfoot 2018, 37, 67n6. The movement was led by George Manuel (Shuswap), Alex Denny (Mi'kmaw), Oren Lyons (Haudenosaunee Confederacy), Ted Moses and Harold Cardinal (Cree), Marie Smallface Marule (Blackfoot Confederacy), and Dan George (Salish).

37. Lightfoot 2018, 37.

38. Lightfoot 2018, 38–39, 41.

39. Lightfoot 2018, 41–42.

40. Martínez Cobo 1987.

41. Resolution 1982/34 of 7 May 1982.

42. Lightfoot 2018, 46; see also Barsh 1994.

43. While the principles it articulated were largely the same, the drafting style differed significantly, with the WCIP draft firmly rooted in the grassroots activism reflective of the organization's origins. Lightfoot 2018, 47–49.

44. Lightfoot 2018, 56.

45. Lightfoot 2018, 56–63.

46. Lightfoot 2018, 57.

47. Lightfoot 2018, 58–59.

48. Lightfoot 2018, 59–61.

49. Lightfoot 2018, 59–61.

50. Lightfoot 2018, 34.

51. See generally Lightfoot 2018, 78–89.

52. See Toki 2011, 29–43.

53. See, for example, UN Human Rights Committee 2000. The claim was that "the Government's actions violate the Maori's right to self-determination under article 1 of the Covenant, since this right is only effective when people have access to and control over their resources. They claim that the Treaty of Waitangi (Fisheries Claims) Settlement Act confiscates their fishing resources, denies them their right to freely determine their political status and interferes with their right to freely pursue their economic, social and cultural development."

54. Brownlie 2008, 4.

55. Toki 2011, 29–43.

56. UN Secretary General 2013, para. 64; Anaya 1991, 8.

57. UN Human Rights Committee 2008.

58. UN Human Rights Committee 2008.

59. UN Human Rights Committee 2008.

60. Toki 2011, 29–43.

61. Toki 2011, 29–43.

62. It is for this reason that the distinction between *people* and *peoples* is salient. For many years Indigenous peoples have fought to be recognized as peoples. While they have largely won this fight, Article 1(3) of ILO Convention 169 stipulates that use of the term "peoples" "shall not be construed as having any implications as regards the rights which may attach to the term under international law" (and is understood to be referring to the right to external self-determination). Similarly, Article 46 of the Declaration provides that none of its provisions will be interpreted as authorizing any action that would dismember "the territorial integrity or political unity of sovereign and independent States."

63. See IWGIA n.d.

64. Berger 2019.

65. Minority Rights Group 2018.

66. IWGIA n.d.

67. Minority Rights Group n.d.

68. Minority Rights Group n.d.

69. Roy 2012.

70. Minority Rights Group n.d.

71. Chakma 2004. See also Amnesty International 2000; Jamil and Panday 2008.

72. Chakma 2004.

73. Roy and M'Viboudoulou 2014.

74. Mikkelsen 2014, 323–326.

75. Roy and M'Viboudoulou 2014, para. 19. For more detailed information, see Roy 2000.

76. Minority Rights Group n.d.

77. Minority Rights Group n.d.

78. Columbia/Harvard 2015.

79. Porgera Gold Mine n.d.

80. Human Rights Watch 2010, 5.

81. Columbia/Harvard 2015; Radio New Zealand 2019.

82. Radio New Zealand 2019.

83. Columbia/Harvard 2015, 6.

84. Columbia/Harvard 2015, 4.

85. Barrick 2020.

86. Burton and Westbrook 2020.

87. Barrick 2021; Business Advantage PNG, 2021.

88. Jungk, Chichester, and Fletcher 2018, 19.

89. Barrick 2021.

90. Barrick 2021; Business Advantage PNG 2021.

91. Human Rights Watch 2020.
92. Columbia/Harvard 2015, 44.
93. Business and Human Rights Resource Centre 2013.
94. Mikkelsen 2014, 208.
95. Mikkelsen 2014, 208.
96. International Federation for Human Rights 2003.
97. Laltaika and Askew 2018.
98. See generally Minority Rights Group 2020.
99. "Pygmy" is a contested term, and some people consider it derogatory. Nevertheless, it is widely used in the DRC (in the phrase "peuples autochtones pygmées"), including by Indigenous peoples themselves.
100. See generally Barume 2000.
101. See generally Domínguez and Luoma 2020b.
102. See generally Tauli-Corpuz 2016, paras. 18, 39–50.
103. See also Tauli-Corpuz 2016.
104. See generally Domínguez and Luoma 2020a.
105. Blackman and Veit 2018; Rights and Resources 2016.
106. Rights and Resources 2018.
107. Columbia/Harvard 2015, 4.
108. O'Faircheallaigh and Ali 2008, 2.
109. Anaya 2011.
110. Columbia/Harvard 2015, 4.
111. General Assembly Resolution 1541 (which followed closely on Resolution 1514) contemplates three instances in which non-self-governing territories attain full self-government: "(a) Emergence as a sovereign independent State; (b) Free association with an independent State; or (c) Integration with an independent State." Each of these forms of decolonization is only effective if accomplished through "free consultation" with the non-self-governing territory.
112. Lightfoot 2018, 34 (emphasis omitted).
113. Lightfoot 2018, 35.
114. Lightfoot 2018, 34.
115. See generally Escárcega 2013.

Bibliography

ACHPR. 2017. *African Commission on Human and Peoples' Rights v. Republic of Kenya.* Application No. 006/2012. African Commission on Human and Peoples' Rights. https://www. escr-net.org/caselaw/2017/african-commission-human-and-peoples-rights-v-republic-kenya-acthpr-application-no.

ACHPR. 2010. "Report of the African Commission's Working Group on Indigenous Populations/ Communities, Research and Information Visit to Kenya." African Commission on Human and Peoples' Rights. https://www.iwgia.org/images/publications/0569_ACHPR_kenya_ENG.pdf.

ACHPR. 2007. "Advisory Opinion of the African Commission on Human and Peoples' Rights on the United Nations Declaration on the Rights of Indigenous Peoples." https://www.achpr.org/ public/Document/file/Any/un_advisory_opinion_idp_eng.pdf.

African Group. 2006. "Draft Aide Memoire: United Nations Declaration on the Rights of Indigenous People," New York. http://cendoc.docip.org/collect/cendocdo/index/assoc/ HASH0110/1b549795.dir/draft_africangroup.pdf.

Al Saba, Rasha. 2020. "Inequality and the Impact of COVID-19: How Discrimination Is Shaping the Experiences of Minorities and Indigenous Peoples During the Pandemic." Minority Rights Group International. September 10. https://minorityrights.org/publications/covid-briefing/.

Amnesty International. 2000. "Bangladesh: Human Rights in the Chittagong Hill Tracts." February 1. https://www.amnesty.org/en/documents/asa13/001/2000/en/.

Anaya, S. James. 2011. "Summary of Activities: Extractive Industries Operating Within or Near Indigenous Territories." Report to the Human Rights Council, A/HRC/18/35. https://www.ohchr.org/Documents/Issues/IPeoples/SR/A-HRC-18-35_en.pdf.

Anaya, S. James. 2009. *International Human Rights and Indigenous Peoples*. New York: Aspen.

Anaya, S. James. 1991. "Indigenous Rights Norms in Contemporary International Law." *Arizona Journal of International and Comparative Law* 8: 1–39.

Aukerman, Miriam J. 2000. "Definitions and Justifications: Minority and Indigenous Rights in a Central/East European Context." *Humarighquar Human Rights Quarterly* 22, no. 4: 1011–1050.

Ban Ki-moon. 2013. "Secretary-General's Remarks at the Opening of the 2013 Session of the Special Committee on Decolonization." February 21, https://www.un.org/sg/en/section/ban-ki-moon?page=836.

Barrick. 2021. "Porgera Mine Set to Restart as PNG and Barrick Niugini Limited Agree New Partnership." https://www.barrick.com/English/news/news-details/2021/Porgera-Mine-Set-to-Restart-as-PNG-and-Barrick-Niugini-Limited-Agree-New-Partnership/default.aspx.

Barrick. 2020. "Barrick Niugini Limited Challenges Non-Extension of Special Mining Lease." April. https://www.barrick.com/English/news/news-details/2020/barrick-niugini-limited-challenges-non-extension-of-special-mining-lease/default.aspx.

Barsh, Russel Lawrence. 1994. "Indigenous Peoples in the 1990s: From Object to Subject of International Law?" *Harvard Human Rights Journal* 7: 33–86.

Barsh, Russel Lawrence. 1989. "The United Nations and Protection of Minorities." *Nordic Journal of International Law* 582: 188–197.

Barume, Albert Kwokwo. 2000. *Heading Towards Extinction?: Indigenous Rights in Africa: The Case of the Twa of the Kahuzi-Biega National Park, Democratic Republic of Congo.* Copenhagen: IWGIA.

Berger, David Nathaniel. 2019. "Indigenous World 2019: Bangladesh." International Work Group for Indigenous Affairs. April 24, https://www.iwgia.org/en/bangladesh/3446-iw2019-bangladesh.html.

Blackman, Allen, and Peter Veit. 2018. "Titled Amazon Indigenous Communities Cut Forest Carbon Emissions." *Ecological Economics* 153: 56–67. https://doi.org/10.1016/j.ecolecon.2018.06.016.

Brownlie, Ian. 2008. *Principles of Public International Law*, 7th ed. Oxford: Oxford University Press.

Burton, Tom, and Melanie Westbrook. 2020. "Papua New Guinea to Take Control of Barrick Gold Mine." Reuters, April 24. https://www.reuters.com/article/us-papua-barrick-mining-idUSKCN2261TB.

Business Advantage PNG. 2021. "Barrick Gold and Papua New Guinea Government Strike New Deal over Porgera." April 12. https://www.businessadvantagepng.com/barrick-gold-and-papua-new-guinea-government-strike-new-deal-over-porgera/.

Business and Human Rights Resource Centre. 2013. "Agua Mineral Chusmiza Lawsuit (Re Chile)." April. https://www.business-humanrights.org/en/latest-news/agua-mineral-chusmiza-lawsuit-re-chile/.

Chakma, Leena. 2004. "Statement of Leena Chakma to the Commission on Human Rights, Sub-Commission on Promotion and Protection of Human Rights, Working Group on Minorities, 10th Session, 1–5 March 2004." https://www.ohchr.org/_layouts/15/WopiFrame.aspx?sourcedoc=/Documents/Issues/Minorities/WG/ASK(B)3a.doc&action=default&DefaultItemOpen=1.

Columbia/Harvard. 2015. "Righting Wrongs? Barrick Gold's Remedy Mechanism for Sexual Violence in Papua New Guinea: Key Concerns and Lessons Learned." Columbia Law School Human Rights Clinic and Harvard Law School International Human Rights Clinic. November. https://hrp.law.harvard.edu/wp-content/uploads/2015/11/FINALBARRICK.pdf.

Curtice, Kaitlin, and Esther Choo. 2020. "Indigenous Populations: Left Behind in the COVID-19 Response." *The Lancet* 395, no. 10239: 1753. https://doi.org/10.1016/S0140-6736(20)31242-3.

Department of Corrections. 2007. "Over-Representation of Māori in the Criminal Justice System: An Exploratory Report." Policy, Strategy, and Research Group, Department of Corrections, Government of New Zealand. September. https://www.corrections.govt.nz/__data/assets/pdf_file/0014/10715/Over-representation-of-Maori-in-the-criminal-justice-system.pdf.

Domínguez, Lara. 2018. "Litigating Indigenous Peoples' Rights in Africa: The Impact of Convention 169." *International Union Rights* 25, no. 4: 8–9.

Domínguez, Lara, and Colin Luoma. 2020a. "Decolonising Conservation Policy: How Colonial Land and Conservation Ideologies Persist and Perpetuate Indigenous Injustices at the Expense of the Environment." *Land* 9, no. 3: 1–22.

Domínguez, Lara, and Colin Luoma. 2020b. "Violent Conservation: WWF's Failure to Prevent, Respond to and Remedy Human Rights Abuses Committed on Its Watch." Minority Rights Group. December 17. https://minorityrights.org/publications/violent-conservation.

Escárcega, Sylvia. 2013. "The Global Indigenous Movement and Paradigm Wars: International Activism, Network Building, and Transformative Politics." In *Insurgent Encounters: Transnational Activism, Ethnography, and the Political*, edited by Jeffrey S. Juris and Alex Khasnabish, 129–150. Durham, NC: Duke University Press.

Forest Peoples Programme. 2021. "Rolling Back Social and Environmental Safeguards in the Time of COVID-19: The Dangers for Indigenous Peoples and for Tropical Forests." February 18. 2021. https://www.forestpeoples.org/en/rolling-back-safeguards/global.

Human Rights Watch. 2020. "World Report 2021: Rights Trends in Papua New Guinea." December 17. https://www.hrw.org/world-report/2021/country-chapters/papua-new-guinea.

Human Rights Watch. 2010. "Gold's Costly Dividend: Human Rights Impacts of Papua New Guinea's Porgera Mine." https://www.hrw.org/report/2011/02/01/golds-costly-dividend/human-rights-impacts-papua-new-guineas-porgera-gold-mine.

International Federation for Human Rights. 2003. "The Mapuche People: Between Oblivion and Exclusion." August. https://www.refworld.org/pdfid/46f146420.pdf.

IWGIA. n.d. "Bangladesh." International Work Group for Indigenous Affairs. Accessed May 16, 2021. https://www.iwgia.org/en/bangladesh.html.

Jamil, Ishtiaq, and Pranab Panday. 2008. "The Elusive Peace Accord in the Chittagong Hill Tracts of Bangladesh and the Plight of the Indigenous People." *Commonwealth and Comparative Politics* 46: 464–489. doi:10.1080/14662040802461141.

Jungk, Margaret, Ouida Chichester, and Chris Fletcher. 2018. "In Search of Justice: Pathways to Remedy at the Porgera Gold Mine." BSR, San Francisco. https://www.bsr.org/reports/BSR_In_Search_of_Justice_Porgera_Gold_Mine.pdf.

Kingsbury, Benedict. 1998. "'Indigenous Peoples' in International Law: A Constructivist Approach to the Asian Controversy." *American Journal of International Law* 92, no. 3: 414–457.

Kristof, Nicholas. 2020. "The Top U.S. Coronavirus Hot Spots Are All Indian Lands." *The New York Times*, May 30. https://www.nytimes.com/2020/05/30/opinion/sunday/coronavirus-native-americans.html.

Kugelmann, Dieter. 2007. "The Protection of Minorities and Indigenous Peoples: Respecting Cultural Diversity." *Max Planck Yearbook of United Nations Law* 11: 233–263.

Kymlicka, Will. 2013. *Multicultural Citizenship: A Liberal Theory of Minority Rights*. Oxford: Clarendon Press.

Laltaika, E. I., and K. Askew. 2018. "Modes of Dispossession of Indigenous Lands and Territories in Africa." UN Expert Group Meeting on Sustainable Development in Territories of Indigenous Peoples, New York.

Lightfoot, Sheryl R. 2018. *Global Indigenous Politics: A Subtle Revolution*. New York: Routledge.

Martínez Cobo, José. 1987. "Study of the Problem of Discrimination Against Indigenous Populations, Volume V: Conclusions, Proposals and Recommendations." E/CN.4/Sub.2/1986/7/Add.4. United Nations. https://digitallibrary.un.org/record/133666?ln=en.

Martínez Cobo, José. 1981–1983. "Study of the Problem of Discrimination Against Indigenous Populations." Final report submitted by the Special Rapporteur. Introduction, July 30, 1981 (E/CN.4/Sub.2/47610); August 10, 1982 (1982E/CN.4/Sub.2/1982/2), August 5, 1983 (1983E/CN.4/Sub.2/1983/21). United Nations. https://www.un.org/development/desa/indigenous peoples/publications/martinez-cobo-study.html.

Mikkelsen, Caecille, ed. 2014. *Indigenous World.* Copenhagen: IWGIA.

Minde, Henry. 1996. "The Making of an International Movement of Indigenous Peoples." In *Minorities and Their Right of Political Participation,* edited by Frank Horn, 90–128. Rovaniemi, Finland: Northern Institute for Environmental and Minority Law.

Minority Rights Group. 2020. "Update: One Step Forward for the Ogiek as Kenyan Court Issues Conservatory Orders, Stopping Government's Titling Process in Eastern Mau." December 18. https://minorityrights.org/2020/12/18/ogiek-update/.

Minority Rights Group. 2018. "World Directory of Minorities and Indigenous Peoples— Bangladesh: Adivasis." July. https://www.refworld.org/docid/49749d5841.html.

Minority Rights Group. n.d. "Adivasis." https://minorityrights.org/minorities/adivasis/.

O'Faircheallaigh, Ciaran, and Saleem H. Ali, eds. 2008. *Earth Matters: Indigenous Peoples, the Extractive Industries and Corporate Social Responsibility.* London: Routledge, 2008.

Porgera Gold Mine. n.d. "Riverine Tailings and Waste Rock Management." http://q4live.s22.clie ntfiles.s3-website-us-east-1.amazonaws.com/788666289/files/porgera/Porgera-Riverine-Taili ngs-and-Waste-Rock-Management.pdf.

Radio New Zealand. 2019. "Pressure at PNG's Porgera Mine to Act on Human Rights Redress." February 6. https://www.rnz.co.nz/international/pacific-news/381841/pressure-at-png-s-porgera-mine-to-act-on-human-rights-redress.

Rights and Resources. 2018. "A Global Baseline of Carbon Storage in Collective Lands." September. https://rightsandresources.org/wp-content/uploads/2018/09/A-Global-Baseline_RRI_Sept-2018.pdf.

Rights and Resources. 2016. "The Facts Are In: Community Governance Supports Forest Livelihoods and Sustainability." IFPRI and Rights and Resources Factsheet. January. https://rig htsandresources.org/wp-content/uploads/Factsheet-Community-Governance.pdf.

Roy, Raja Devasish. 2012. "Promoting Partnerships in Implementing Intra-State Autonomy Agreements—Lessons from the Chittagong Hill Tracts, Bangladesh." Office of the United Nations High Commissioner for Human Rights. July. https://www.ohchr.org/Documents/Iss ues/IPeoples/Seminars/Treaties/DevasishRoy.pdf.

Roy, Raja Devasish, and Simon William M'Viboudoulou. 2014. "Study on Best Practices and Examples in Respect of Resolving Land Disputes and Land Claims, Including Consideration of the National Commission on Indigenous Peoples (Philippines) and the Chittagong Hill Tracts Land Dispute Resolution Commission (Bangladesh) and the Working Group on Indigenous Populations/Communities of the African Commission on Human and Peoples' Rights." E/C 19/2014/4. UN Permanent Forum on Indigenous Issues. https://digitallibrary.un.org/record/767536?ln=en.

Roy, Rajkumari Chandra. 2000. "Land Rights of the Indigenous Peoples of the Chittagong Hill Tracts, Bangladesh." IWGIA Document No. 99. https://www.iwgia.org/images/publications//0128_Chittagong_hill_tracts.pdf.

Sylvain, Renee. 2017. "Indigenous Peoples in Africa." *Oxford Research Encyclopedia of African History.* Online. Oxford: Oxford University Press.

Tauli-Corpuz, Victoria. 2016. "Report of the Special Rapporteur of the Human Rights Council on the Rights of Indigenous Peoples." Doc. A/71/229. United Nations. July 29.

Toki, Valmaine. 2011. "Indigenous Rights, Hollow Rights?" *Waikato Law Review* 19, no. 2: 29–43.

Tyler, William. 1999. "Aboriginal Criminology and the Postmodern Condition: From Anomie to Anomaly." *Australian and New Zealand Journal of Criminology* 32, no. 2: 209–221. https://doi.org/10.1177/000486589903200209.

UN General Assembly. 1998. "Standard-Setting Activities: Evolution of Standards Concerning the Rights of Indigenous People." E/CN.4/Sub.2/AC.4/1996/2. Report of the Working Group on Indigenous Populations, United Nations.

UN Human Rights Committee. 2008. "Promotion and Protection of All Human Rights, Civil, Political, Economic, Social and Cultural Rights, Including the Right to Development: Report of the Special Rapporteur on the Situation of Human Rights and Fundamental Freedoms of Indigenous People, S. James Anaya." A/HRC/9/9. August 11. https://undocs.org/A/HRC/9/9.

UN Human Rights Committee. 2000. *Apirana Mahuika v. New Zealand.* CCPR/C/70/D/547/1993. October 13. http://www.worldcourts.com/hrc/eng/decisions/1995.10.13_Mahuika_v_New_Zealand.htm.

UN Secretary General. 2013. "Report of the Special Rapporteur on the Rights of Indigenous Peoples." A/68/317. August 14. https://undocs.org/A/68/317.

UNDESA. 2009. "State of the World's Indigenous Peoples." United Nations, New York.

Walters, Reece, and Trevor Bradley. 2019. *Introduction to Criminological Thought.* Auckland: Edify.

8

Fostering Inclusion for Ethnic, Religious, and Linguistic Minority Communities

Joshua Castellino

They cannot make history who forget history.

—Dr. B. R. Ambedkar[1]

Introduction

Notions of identity influence human history around the globe. They are reified regularly through nationalist narratives that seek to emphasize specific imagined histories of "nations."[2] In general, individuals cooperate to face threats and challenges, overcoming the "natural" Hobbesian competition for scarce resources. The arrival of rival groups in the same space can enhance intra-group cohesion and cooperation, but it can also sow rivalries with the "Other." As human migration, forced and voluntary, brings diverse communities into greater contact, identity politics is playing a significant role in regional, national, and international societies.[3] As societies face challenges that push against the limits of current governance capacities (such as addressing climate change when political leaders are deeply indebted to and buttressed by industries that pollute), it becomes hard to resist the temptation of falling back onto "us versus them" narratives in order to seize and consolidate political power. This is even easier when mechanization has replaced jobs, leaving significant parts of the population disenfranchised, frustrated, and looking for someone to blame for their plight.

History shows that societies and policymakers are often fully aware of the role of identity politics, and of the possibility of catastrophes that have befallen numerically inferior and nondominant groups in societies around the world.[4] The threats to these individuals and communities usually arise from their differing ethnic (racial), religious, or linguistic cleavages, which often cause tensions in societies and contribute to deep roots of conflict.[5] The manner in which national histories are constructed—emphasizing victor's justice while airbrushing all but powerful or "significant" men out of the narrative—gives the impression that subaltern communities, women, minorities, and others, contributed nothing to the building of the modern state, merely basking in its magnanimous and paternalistic protection.

This chapter seeks to emphasize why the inclusion of minorities is the only pragmatic way to guarantee peacebuilding and development, and suggests that a strong focus ought to lie in reimagining the historical narrative of each state. Many of the perspectives presented here are drawn from the work of Minority Rights Group International (MRG), a fifty-year-old nongovernmental organization that operates globally. The chapter draws on scenarios in postcolonial states where the formulations of "national identities" have often acted against inclusivity, but equally through the lens of growing xenophobia in "liberal" democracies. It concludes by reiterating the urgent need for inclusion, highlighting its benefits from a moral and pragmatic perspective. The chapter is divided into four sections. The first identifies the parameters of the "definition" of minorities. It includes two explanatory boxes addressing why the term "ethnic" is preferred in international law to the term "racial," which is more commonly used in North America. A second box casts further light on contested components of the widely accepted definition. The second section enunciates the rich legacy of minority rights in international legal history, with additional text boxes that frame this evolution: the quest to prevent genocide, and the attempt to direct society away from "the strongest wins" principles through a concerted effort to enshrine equality as a cornerstone principle in law. The third section paints the evolution of contemporary forms of exclusion to the impact of colonization, which first treated people beyond Europe as "objects" and not "subjects," but then also had a salutary effect on how new states (imagined communities) emerged. The concept of "nationhood" as a form of governance derived from more homogeneous European states was perched atop multilingual, multireligious, and multiethnic communities, disenfranchising many. A separate box explains how the etymology of exclusion not only impacts former colonial states but is particularly rife in developed former colonizing powers too. The final section examines why a rewiring of the future is possible only through a reconciliation with the past. It emphasizes that without such a reckoning, the supremacist, masculine notions of identity that currently dominate nationalist narratives will flourish to the detriment of peace and security, incorrectly painting over significant parts of the body politic and sowing the discontent and division that characterize the modern state.

Minorities Defined

Close to two-sevenths of the world's population could be considered minorities. That number, close to two billion people, may seem high, but it needs to be put into a context where two of the world's largest "minorities"—the Dalits and Muslims in India alone—account for over 200 million people each. (The numbers come from the 2011 census and are therefore dated.)[6] To add further context, those two

groups are not the only minorities in India. In the modern world, second-genera-
tion migrant populations that have acquired the citizenship of the state they are in
would also fit within the definition, with a significant number among populations
in Europe. Further, in many countries, a growing share of people belong to more
than one ethnic, religious or linguistic community. See Box 8.1.

Box 8.1 Why "Ethnic" and Not "Racial"

It is common in many parts of the world to use the term "race" in seeking to
differentiate between ethnic groups.[7] This reflects a phenomenon of discrimination against individuals for their perceived membership in a particular
group, defined by a different skin color. One of the earliest references to the
word "race" in published English likely occurred around 1508, but this became amplified through colonial activities and greater interactions between
peoples of different origins and cultures.[8] The history of the term "race" has
encompassed ideas based on the superiority of a dominant category of people,
who sought to structure their domination over others whom they placed in a
hierarchically lower position. Spanish colonization of the Americas brought
this concept into wider public awareness in the famous Valladolid Controversy,
discussing the treatment of "natives" encountered by the Europeans in their
quest to colonize the Americas.[9] The existence of different "races" among the
human population gained further traction through treatises such as *The Races
of Men: A Philosophical Enquiry into the Influence of Race over the Destinies of
Nations* (1862), where Knox confidently declared that "race in human affairs
is everything, is simply a fact, the most remarkable, the most comprehensive,
which philosophy has even announced."[10] Darwin's *The Descent of Man* in 1871
treats the question of race in some detail, but his position is far more nuanced
than often credited. Darwin states:

> Man has been studied more carefully than any other organic being, and yet
> there is the greater possible diversity among capable judges whether he should
> be classed as a single species of a race. . . . The naturalist will end by uniting all
> the forms which graduate into each other as a single species: for he will say to
> himself that he has no right to give names for objects which he cannot define.[11]

Darwin's work spawned others, such as his relative Francis Galton, to write
about the science of "improving stock . . . to give the more suitable races or strains
of blood a better chance of prevailing over the less suitable." In fact, Galton went
significantly further, suggesting that race ought to be a permanent subject of
consideration since "the very foundation and outcome of the human mind is dependent on race."[12] Galton played a major role in the development of eugenics,
a key point of reference during the atrocities of World War II, despite critiques

of its existence in works such as *Man's Most Dangerous Myth* (1942), where Montagu stated emphatically: "The idea of 'race' represents one of the greatest errors, if not the greatest error, of our time, and the most tragic."[13]

The lessons of the Holocaust have meant that the word "race" has become taboo in a number of countries. For instance, Sweden abolished use of the word from its legal lexicon in 2011 on account of the country's fraught history, specifically its widespread adoption of eugenic thinking during the decades before and after the war, when 63,000 people, mostly women, were sterilized in pursuit of racial purity. There was even a race biology institute established in 1922 at the prestigious Uppsala University; at the time, it represented the general consensus.[14]

The proposal to use "ethnic group" instead of "race" was put forward by Huxley and Haddon in 1935, on the grounds that the adjective "ethnic" more clearly indicated a course of social (rather than biological) differences.[15] Keane's authoritative explanation summarizes the best reason for seeking not to use the term "race" other than in a description of "racial discrimination," which is a factor that continues to impact populations irrespective of the philosophical nonexistence of "race" as a divisor among human populations. Warning about a straight replacement of "race" with "ethnicity," Keane asks:

> Do race and ethnicity represent very different concepts? A possible difference between them is that race has been developed as an exclusive criterion built on arbitrary classifications of populations, with the intention of drawing hierarchical rankings of these groupings. Ethnicity, by contrast, could be said to be based on shared culture and heritage, and should be considered an inclusive term through which groups identify themselves, and are identified by others. The suggestion to substitute ethnicity for race could . . . be an erroneous one, due to the particular semantic position occupied by ethnicity. It should be noted, however, that ethnicity is as indeterminate as race. Neither concept has any basis in biology, for there are no biological differences between ethnic groups or racial groups that have been found to be constant.[16]

Who Are the World's Minorities?

The definition of who fits within the legal concept of "minority" is an emotive one since it includes both small groups far from sites of power and larger groups whose claim to sovereignty (and therefore separate statehood) has been denied. The components in the definition proposed by Italian jurist Francesco Capotorti in 1977 (discussed later) are problematic, mainly since the definition seeks to capture in text a term that is necessarily rooted in context. Thus, two groups that may have the same characteristics and live across the border from each other, such as Kosovars, may be perceived as a minority in one state (Serbia) and as the dominant majority in another (Albania). In this example, the Kosovar claim to separate statehood (self-determination) as the independent state of Kosovo itself is contested in the global community.

The challenge lies in finding a set of words in a definition that will reflect as accurately the situation of hunter-gatherer communities that have been subsumed by the establishment of a modern state around them, of which they are nominally a part, as they would a group that may constitute as much as 70 percent of the state, as with the Shia in Bahrain, who remain in a subjugated, nondominant position.

The fundamental elements of the definition could be broken down to, first, protected characteristics that create group cohesion and a shared identity against the backdrop of the dominant group(s) in the state; second, their distance from sites of power, as a consequence of which they face structural discrimination that impinges their equal enjoyment of rights; and, third, a clearly articulated position that advocates for the maintenance of their distinct identity while seeking equal protection of the law and the guarantee of human rights. This approach includes Indigenous peoples, though many would accurately consider them as sui generis entities since they existed as nations since time immemorial and prior to the arrival of the communities that may dominate in their lands. (See Chapter 7 for a discussion focused on the movement for Indigenous peoples' rights.) It may include other groups far from sites of power, such as those without nationality, be they stateless peoples, asylum-seekers, refugees, migrants, immigrants, or emigrants. "Minority rights" defined narrowly to cover "ethnic, linguistic and religious" minorities could offer some protection to these categories in and of themselves as minimal standards where their rights are being denied on the basis of these protected characteristics; however, since they share characteristics with the dominant majority, it may be difficult to consider them as "minorities" per se, except when the category is justifiably broadened to include sexual minorities. Those facing intersectional discrimination, where women, LGBTQI, and others come from a minority community, fall squarely within the more restricted definition of a minority. In a strict legal sense other existing legal regimes may apply to some of the groups listed previously.

Despite these questions of definition, in the world of practice it is clear that the term "minorities" subsumes groups far from sites of power who are being deprived and denied access to rights. MRG, for example, makes no distinction between "minorities," "Indigenous peoples," "tribal peoples," and "forest peoples," or even "the stateless," "migrants," and "refugees," many of whom come from minority backgrounds. This differs sharply from intergovernmental bodies, including the United Nations, which distinguishes between these groups. MRG also increasingly places work on intersectional discrimination at the forefront of its approach, both as a countermeasure to tackling discrimination and problematic attitudes *within* minority communities and to address unmet needs of individuals from such groups who may be beyond the reach of human rights law.[17] See Figure 8.1 and Figure 8.2.

Levels of Religious Diversity

Countries are shaded according to level of religious diversity

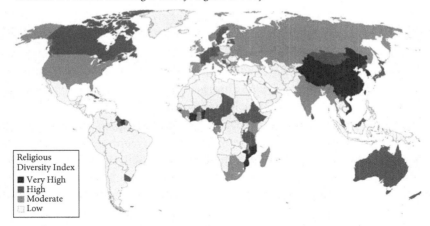

Religious Diversity Index
- ■ Very High
- ■ High
- ■ Moderate
- □ Low

Based on Religious Diversity Index scores. For more information about how the index is calculated, see the Methodology. Data are for 2010.
"Global Religious Diversity," April 2014
PEW RESEARCH CENTER

Figure 8.1 Levels of Religious Diversity

Credit line: Levels of Religious Diversity in "Global Religious Diversity." Pew Research Center, Washington, D.C. (2014) https://www.pewforum.org/2014/04/04/global-religious-diversity/.

Cultural Diversity Around the World

The countries with the most and least cultural diversity

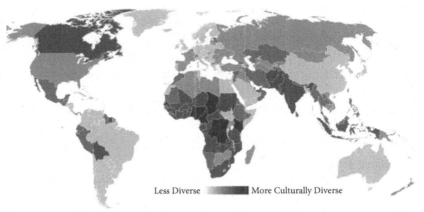

Less Diverse ▬▬▬ More Culturally Diverse

Based on Table A1 in "Economic Effects of Domestic and Neighboring Countries' Cultural Diversity" by Erkan Goren. Center for Translational Studies, University of Bremen Working Paper No. 16/2013
PEW RESEARCH CENTER

Figure 8.2 Cultural Diversity Around the World

Credit line: Cultural Diversity Around the World in "The most (and least) culturally diverse countries in the world." Pew Research Center, Washington, D.C. (2013) https://www.pewresearch.org/fact-tank/2013/07/18/the-most-and-least-culturally-diverse-countries-in-the-world/.

The Evolving Legal Context for Minorities

The catastrophes that dominate historical lexicons give us terms such as "genocide," "crimes against humanity," "ethnocide," and "ethnic cleansing."[18] International legal regimes have evolved seeking to eradicate these phenomena, with international law playing a role as the "gentle civilizer of nations."[19] Despite the development of these norms, the mass killings of minorities have continued: in Rwanda, Srebrenica, Darfur, and Iraq most recently. This has spawned significant legal activity to determine accountability for such genocide, war crimes, crimes against humanity, and aggression. The institutional effort to ensure against impunity for such crimes has led to establishment of the International Criminal Court; however, its acceptance as a tool in the fight for accountability has been hindered by its political nature and questions regarding who is bound by its jurisdiction, when an investigation is launched, who is indicted, and who is actually brought before the court. And yet, definitions of these atrocities still vary depending on context. (See Box 8.2.)

Box 8.2 The Vexed Question: When Mass Killing or Gross Human Rights Violations Are "Genocide" in Law

The term "genocide" conjures up powerful historical images and is billed as "the crime of crimes."[20] Persistent debate remains about its meaning, its treatment in law, whether there are specific thresholds that have to be crossed for a determination of genocide, and the relationship between genocide and equally egregious or marginally less egregious atrocities perpetrated.

According to the Oxford Dictionaries, genocide is "the deliberate killing of a large group of people, especially those of a particular nation or ethnic group." Coined by a Polish lawyer, Raphael Lemkin, the term has a precise definition in law, reflected in article 2 of the Genocide Convention, which states:

In the present Convention, genocide means any of the following acts committed with intent to destroy, in whole or in part, a national, ethnical, racial or religious group, as such:
(a) Killing members of the group;
(b) Causing serious bodily or mental harm to members of the group;
(c) Deliberately inflicting on the group conditions of life calculated to bring about its physical destruction in whole or in part;
(d) Imposing measures intended to prevent births within the group;
(e) Forcibly transferring children of the group to another group.[21]

The definition focuses on the intent of the persons perpetrating the mass violence. The critical difference between a mass killing and a "genocide" hinges on whether the perpetrators were seeking to "wipe out" or "exterminate" a particular category of individuals.[22] There has also been considerable discussion about whether the categorization of persons as a recognizable group is necessary for the definition to apply.

In light of this high threshold, international law has codified other crimes that could be considered equally egregious, including "crimes against humanity," "war crimes," "ethnic cleansing," and even the crime of "aggression," which often provides the backdrop for other gross violations of human rights.[23] These concepts are enshrined in the Rome Statute of the International Criminal Court, with that body given jurisdiction for action when these crimes have been proven.[24]

The term "cultural genocide" has been determined not to fall within the legal scope of the definition of genocide.[25] Nonetheless, when used, the term references when a group is actively stripped of its culture, or where conditions are imposed to ensure that the culture of a group fails. Advocates argue that the outcome is the same: the destruction in whole or part of a particular group.[26] That said, though such actions may be deliberate, without a concerted policy of mass killings that can be evidenced, they fall short of genocide as agreed in the 1948 Convention.

Application of the term "genocide" is often vigorously debated. During the Rwandan genocide in 1994, for example, officials in many governments resisted use of the term to describe the rampant killing under way, because of the investigation and punishment that might be required if a "genocide" was declared.[27]

The effort to unravel structural discrimination has not warranted as much attention in international law. As a consequence, it has been less successful in helping create egalitarian legal, educational, and policymaking systems that eliminate the deep-seated sense of "Otherness" that permeates the human psyche, though domestic courts and activists have continued to push for such outcomes with relative success.[28] Despite the growth of modern human rights, born of the attempt to erect a more just society in the aftermath of World War II, the mission to foster full and meaningful inclusion for ethnic, linguistic, and religious communities has been relatively unsuccessful at the international level, when compared to the domestic legal systems of states.[29] While legal systems now ostensibly recognize equality in law (de jure equality), inequality in fact (de facto inequality) continues to be the norm, particularly hurting individuals from communities that are ethnically, linguistically, and religiously different from the majority population of the state. The burden is even greater on women from these communities who face multiple forms of discrimination, the continued gender bias in legal systems and societal norms compounding their disadvantage.[30] The justice and political sectors the world over are synonymous with this problem: they tend to be dominated by males from the majority community and, perhaps as an indirect consequence, the women's "equality" agenda, while recognized, is not at the forefront of societal change.

Law has sought to evolve "minority rights" standards, tracing back to the treatment of dhimmi communities in the Ottoman era from the eighth century onward, through bilateral agreements such as the Promise of St. Louis of France to the Maronites in the thirteenth century, and in more contemporary international society through the growth of international human rights law.[31] Yet the emphasis has largely been on the legal protection of civil and political (rather than economic, social, and cultural) rights of minorities.[32] Such efforts have also spawned discussions about who ought to be considered a "minority" and what the limits of the contours should be.[33] The universally known, though flawed, working definition is that by Italian jurist Francesco Capotorti, who in 1977 determined a minority to be

> a group, numerically inferior to the rest of the population of the state, in a non-dominant position, whose members being nationals of the state possess ethnic, religious and linguistic characteristics that differ from the rest of the population, and who show if only implicitly, a sense of solidarity directed towards preserving their identity.[34]

The definition has been the source of much writing.[35] It does effectively "divide" marginalized and vulnerable groups: distinguishing those who are nationals from those who are not, ignoring the claims of migrants and refugees; distinguishing those of a "different" community from others who are equally disenfranchised as a consequence of being far from sites of power, such as the poor or the "working classes"; and justifying the creation of a sui generis category for "Indigenous peoples."[36] Without engaging the merits of the definitional debate, it is important to highlight that the justification for thinking of minorities as ethnically, linguistically, or religiously distinct is actually a throwback to when the discourse first evolved in Europe, where these bases of identity made specific communities more visibly distinct and vulnerable to unique existential threats. See Box 8.3.

Box 8.3 The Development of the Equality Agenda in Law and Policy

While it could be argued that the very concept of law is linked intrinsically to that of "justice," the historical development of law is skewed toward guaranteeing "order" rather than "justice." The earliest laws in the Western world were developed by landowners, and their subject matter was the protection of their land from other claimants through the creation of rules that would ostensibly govern society and create stability and order. While the Magna Carta and other celebrated but less well-known instruments such as the Code of Hammurabi magnify the link between law and justice, the more mundane task of drafting, implementing, and upholding law was still largely dominated by questions concerning order rather than justice.[37]

This changed in the postwar world with the idea of centralizing the concept of human rights as a bulwark against mass atrocities. The Universal Declaration of Human Rights (1948) not only made a positive statement about the need to protect the inherent dignity and rights of every individual but also called upon states to adopt legislative, administrative, and judicial measures to make this a reality.[38] The growth of core instruments of international human rights law has sought to build on that foundation, and this has found significant traction within the domestic laws of nearly every state on the planet.

Today the concept of equality is a fundamental general principle of law, and nondiscrimination is considered to be a norm of jus cogens—that is, globally recognizable law that is binding upon states irrespective of its specific codification in law.[39] Despite the exalted treatment of the issue in legal systems, significant problems remain in realizing the equality agenda, including (1) determining who should be able to shelter under its protection (questions concerning gender, LGBTQI communities, refugees, undocumented migrants, and stateless populations); (2) how groups far from power can access to legal mechanisms that tend to be elitist; (3) the extent to which the legal profession itself largely reflects dominant groups and therefore lacks the empathy and the ability to dispense the equality agenda; (4) the extent to which unconscious bias runs unchecked and unacknowledged through governance systems, creating practical hurdles to the realization of equality in society; (5) the extent to which specific communities dominate the social policy and, as a consequence, are unable to make policies that effectively combat inequality; and (6) the renewed political mobilization by segments of dominant groups in societies to push back against evolving norms of equality that challenge their hegemony.

An Etymology and Evolution of Exclusion

In the annals of international law, only territory that was unoccupied, *terra nullius*, could be open for acquisition.[40] This natural extension of the regime of private property law did not prevent colonial expansion into territories where local communities lived. By declaring the populations that inhabited them as less than human based on notions of racial superiority, colonial powers justified expansion on the grounds of a "civilizing" or "Christianizing" mission accompanied by a quest for "commercial expansion."[41] These "three Cs," postulated by powerful mercantile European states, envisioned and placed Europe in the middle of the global map, with the rest of the world on its periphery, awaiting incorporation onto the European stage, but with lesser roles.[42]

While notions of "Otherhood" did not come to American, African, Asian, and Pacific lands with Europeans, Europeans' arrival brought the concept into sharper focus as groups responded to the strangers who arrived seeking territorial domination. Differentiations based on identity kindled wars and conflicts all around the world, just as they did in Europe. The case of the first arrival of White settlers (called Parekha in Māori) in New Zealand is instructive. Having established British sovereignty over Australia, against firmly established principles in international law that prohibited the colonization of inhabited territory, the British sought to do the same in New Zealand. However, when confronted by the relatively better organized Māori tribes (in comparison to Australian Aboriginals, whose societal structures were more diffuse), the British resorted to signing the famous Treaty of Waitangi of 1840.[43] The subterfuge of the treaty obligations varies wildly between the English and Māori versions of the treaty, and effectively resulted in the Crown extending a legal right to Māori lands. While the Māori welcomed the settlers as friends, the Parekha in fact annexed New Zealand. History shows us that the guns, germs, and steel that came with the settlers resulted in the decimation of the Māori population through war and disease.[44]

Colonization is relevant to this discussion in two ways. First, it brings with it an assumption that the sovereign state was the ideal model for reorganizing societies everywhere in the world—with fixed boundaries, defined populations, a formal government, and the ability to trade with other, similar entities.[45] The idea, derived from the annals of European Enlightenment history, traces back to 1648 and the signing of the Peace of Westphalia, which brought the Thirty Years' War to an end.[46] Second, decolonization, which presented the opportunity to reimagine nearly 80 percent of the world's sovereign states, usually placed in power members of a dominant ethnic, religious, or linguistic group, with the hope that egalitarian principles brought in through colonial law and stated in the de jure equality of all "citizens" would yield inclusive societies where development and opportunity would be determined by more than an accident of birth.[47] Of course, the edifice of colonial law was not without its own prejudices: most notably, Victorian values criminalized homosexuality, contributed to the establishment of corporal punishment and the death penalty, and even led to the criminalization of certain tribes. By and large, however, the aspirations concerning the rule of law and order proved attractive to emerging independent countries; however, these countries also inherited entrenched legal structures and institutions that would prove difficult to unwind, and many of which persist today.

The divide-and-rule policies of the colonial leaders (which were designed to maintain power in unfamiliar theaters) coupled with precolonial historical animosities, convenient interpretations of difference based on sacred and cultural readings of history, and factors such as loyalty or animosity toward new rulers to generate newer roots for ancient differences.[48] As a result, at the time of transition to independence, groups that were ethnically, religiously, or linguistically "different" from the new governments were perceived to be threats and felt threatened by postcolonial structures.[49]

The trappings of modern statehood provide incumbent governments with exclusive powers that include a monopoly on the use of force (in countries other than the United States, where guns are legal) and an unfettered ability to put in place administrative, legislative, and judicial structures that are often used to ensure hegemonies for the majorities at the cost of subjugation of the minorities.[50] Whether through direct bias born out of a perceived threat to the state or an unconscious bias built on ancient intragroup cohesions against the "Other," minorities and Indigenous peoples became the marginalized and disenfranchised populations in most newly independent states.[51] The lack of coherence in the colonial boundary-drawing process also meant that communities were cut across and often left on different sides of the boundaries of the new postcolonial states.[52] Their own intragroup relations often featured greater cohesion with kin in a neighboring state than with their new fellow "citizens" from other groups.[53] In Africa, for example, artificial borders in South Africa and Sudan, among other countries, have profound consequences for stability, as there is significant strife among identity groups.[54] It is thus unsurprising that a significant proportion of the conflicts in the second half of the twentieth century were based around identity and contestations for power and territory.[55]

Europe in particular, and the Western Hemisphere in general, reaped significant financial reward from colonization.[56] Yet as former colonial countries transitioned to independence without any payment of reparations, development gaps grew internationally, leading to growing inequality between the so-called global North and global South.[57] Additionally, the failure to structure postcolonial states as egalitarian entities resulted in wealth being amassed by a few members of majority communities.[58]

One means of survival for those further from power was (and is) to seek livelihoods in countries that were former colonial powers.[59] The result is the birth of significant diversity in the United Kingdom, France, Belgium, the Netherlands, Portugal, and Spain, reflective of the communities they impacted in previous centuries.[60] The phenomenon is also apparent in former Dominion states of the United Kingdom: Canada, Australia, New Zealand, and South Africa, all of which attracted immigrants from predominantly English-speaking Commonwealth states.

Meanwhile, the United States, billed as "the land of opportunity" from the time of its independence from the United Kingdom, also was a beacon for people around the world willing to move and start afresh. This non-European migration echoed previous European migration to the so-called New World, which included Latin American states. The result is a sudden and startling diversity within these states. Migrants are often given equal rights in law but discriminated against in practice. They face continued discrimination from host populations who feel overrun, and they are expected to conform and accept the intrinsically "European" values of the adopted states. Education, mainly through the narration of history and the trappings of the insignia of the state, reifies the image of these states as essentially part of the "European" world. See Box 8.4.

Box 8.4 Treatment of Minorities in Developed Countries

It has often been assumed that strong democracies adhering to the rule of law and fundamental human rights protections do not discriminate against citizens based on identity. The basis for this belief rests in exhortations and statements within laws, upheld by institutions. However, history shows us that the negation of overt bias does not yield equality if institutions do not follow suit at all levels, and if existing unconscious biases are not addressed.

Women, minorities, and Indigenous peoples (and in particular Indigenous women and minority women) continue to face inordinate obstacles to inclusion. De jure statements of equality in developed countries are well rehearsed, and sporadic bouts of policymaking seek to address this issue. Yet the vast majority of nations still have discriminatory laws.[61] The lessons gleaned from an increased focus on gender in the last two decades show that while equality can gain traction in achieving societal change, it is not a continued arc of success and inevitably faces backlash by those who feel threatened by its trajectory.

The issue came to a head recently in the United Kingdom with its long history of immigration from former colonies.[62] Anti-racism protests sprang up in 2020, alongside those in the United States and elsewhere following the death of George Floyd at the hands of US police.[63] The official historical narrative in the United Kingdom often suggested that the generations of people from the British Commonwealth came to rebuild the country and were worthy of respect. This narrative was used to trumpet greater engagement with such communities (labeled "Black and Minority Ethnic," or BAME) in combating street violence underpinned by racism.[64] However, the study of history as a subject in the United Kingdom did not include the serious violations of land and property perpetrated by the imperial state against these communities' lands of origin. Instead, British history is narrated as an uncontested arc of progress that eventually yielded a fair multicultural society with an existing "diversity dividend."[65]

This multicultural society is under serious threat in the face of hostile governmental policies perpetrated by all political parties in power, in a bid to gain the popular vote. The vast majority of the population was never taught British "overseas" history and, as a consequence, failed to realize its devastating effect on communities abroad while wealth accumulated at home. Further, documents have come to light in the Windrush Files, documents that point to a continually racist governmental stance in the context of migration, making past policies and current discourse around immigration and xenophobia unsurprising.[66]

In the period immediately following colonial withdrawal from African and Asian states, the movement of people into former colonial states was largely tolerated as important to the rebuilding of these societies after the war.[67] While they gained employment in low-skilled jobs, wealth became concentrated in fewer hands within the dominant communities, leaving immigrants in a subjugated position. At the dawn of the twenty-first century, the growth in automation significantly slowed down job creation for the low-skilled, generating employment scarcities that have affected the entirety of society. Climate change and the realization that unlimited growth is unsustainable highlight the need for significant changes in lifestyles and priorities.[68] Rather than address these challenges through policy, those with wealth have generated crises based on the "Other," dismissing climate science as alarmist, and seeking to break down egalitarian models of society carefully constructed since the eighteenth century.[69]

Outside the Western Hemisphere, in the world's largest economies, including China, Russia, Brazil, and India, the sense of urgency and crisis around identity is accentuated.[70] This is accompanied by the arrival of new opportunities for wealth accumulation as the global economy relies on these countries' robust population and ability to produce and supply goods at lower cost. That said, the wealth being accumulated is once again following existing ethnosocial and religious fault lines, reinforcing identity and leaving communities behind; greater national wealth is occurring alongside growing inequalities. For example, in India, the top 1 percent of households control 25 percent of the wealth and the bottom 40 percent control just over 3 percent of the wealth nationally. Similarly, Hindu high castes control most wealth relative to other socioreligious groups.[71] At the same time, politics is dominated by those who can scare large swaths of populations over engineered threats to jobs and "culture" posed by the "Other," thereby consolidating political power, even as leaders downplay the scientifically proven, collective existential threat posed by climate change.

Rewriting the Past to Rewire the Future

If identity differences continue to heavily influence who runs governments and who occupies legislative bodies, there are likely to be greater threats to the inclusion of minorities within societies. Thus, the ascension to power by groups that overtly adhere to a specific identity differentiator will likely divide a polity, especially if the concerned state is multicultural. For instance, when French-speaking Cameroonians achieve the mandate to govern by highlighting their linguistic rights, it has an automatic dampening effect on the country's English-speaking population, who become the hated "Other." Similarly, if Shia Iraqis assert a right to govern based on their presence as a majority and their past oppression at the hands of Saddam Hussein's Sunni government, it creates additional tensions among the significant Sunni and Kurdish populations, never mind the smaller Christian communities that have always formed part of ancient Mesopotamia and modern Iraq. The rise of Hindu nationalism in multicultural, multireligious, and multilingual India poses an immediate threat, since it generates division rather than uniting populations that have largely been thrown together at the whim of colonial powers. The assertion of sharia law and a stronger Islamic identity in Nigeria has a similar effect on the Christian and animist populations, who are dominant in the south of the country.

These divisions negatively impact the development prospects of these economies, creating uncertainties and social tensions that are disincentives to investment.[72] They also rupture the fledgling social fabric of composite national identities by "Othering" particular groups. When coupled with existing structural discrimination, this can impede certain communities' access to basic services and the factors of production, leading to further exclusion and contributing to social tension that can lead to conflict. Outside factors such as climate change further exacerbate these effects.[73]

International human rights law has been attempting to chip away at structural discrimination incrementally, as the international community is mindful of the threat it poses. For example, the articulation of the "leave no one behind" principle is firmly enmeshed in the Sustainable Development Goals as a cross-cutting theme; implementing such a principle and monitoring progress toward implementing it are likely to be key to whether the Sustainable Development Goals are achieved by 2030. Additionally, one goal (Goal 10) specifically addresses inequalities.

Consequences of Exclusion

There are many consequences to leaving groups behind. First, there is a security imperative that suggests that grinding poverty, perceptions of injustice, and the marginalization and exclusion of particular identity groups contribute to the politics of desperation that has become the scourge of societies around the world.[74] The use of absolute force against those who aid, abet, and resort to terrorism has been of limited utility, as subsequent attacks highlight. While it may be possible to safeguard key assets through an increasingly militarized presence, this sows fear among those not involved in terrorism, who are often innocent bystanders, and breeds resentment and grievance.[75] The tools of this policy, which usually include extensive use of surveillance and racial profiling, increase stigmatization of particular communities and create new sources of injustice that refuel the exclusion and marginalization that help drive radicalization. Worse, it has created deeply divided polities, as visible in the United States, the United Kingdom, France, Germany, Italy, Spain, Hungary, and Poland, where divisiveness has been used to benefit extreme political views across the spectrum.

Measures to include *all* the populations of the state are much more likely to dissipate differences and enhance harmony than measures designed to stigmatize, especially where blame is difficult to pinpoint and apportion, and where the identification of specific "culprits" risks fomenting hate and a sense of anger and injustice.[76] Addressing poverty and ethnoreligious marginalization is far more likely to harness forces that can control extremism. Growing exclusion, alienation, and stigmatization are the greatest allies of conflict.[77] This applies directly to places like Iraq, Syria, and Afghanistan, but also to others such as India, Pakistan, Sri Lanka, Russia, Saudi Arabia, and Jordan, where identity politics and politics of privilege fuel a sense of exclusion for communities far from power.[78]

Second, contemporary crises are exacerbating and reinforcing inequities and polarization. Climate change—whether manifest in increased drought, greater climate uncertainty, or greater propensity to flooding—is a reality in many parts of the world, and has already fueled conflict as communities scramble to access dwindling resources.[79] Minority Rights Group's 2019 *Key Trends Report* shows the palpable failures that minorities and Indigenous peoples around the world are facing as communities on the front lines of climate change. The same has proven true during the COVID-19 pandemic; disadvantage and discrimination have placed indigenous communities at greater risk and left them facing disproportionate harm.[80] Similarly, the failure to generate employment commensurate with population growth and the automation-driven loss of jobs also threaten peace and stability. What is needed is a change in economic thinking and a reskilling to embrace artificial intelligence and automation.[81] At the same time, it is important to note that the wage gap between White and minority workers persists even within "low-skill" jobs in the United States and elsewhere.[82] Furthermore, OECD research found that obstacles including education levels, racism, and discrimination in hiring, as well as negative stereotypes of ethnic minorities, among other factors, explain why "young people from ethnic minorities tend to have poorer employment outcomes than young people from non-minority backgrounds."[83] Thus, minority workers face obstacles in securing employment in their youth, and continue to face inequalities after being hired, even in "low-skill" jobs.

In this context, the groups being left behind are unlikely to be able to contribute solutions. European men dominate lists of the most accomplished people of the last century; this is not due to their innate superiority over European women and the rest of the world. Rather, as in the case of European women, it is because others have been denied equal access. Greater participation by women has seen them entering lists of high achievers. But this is not true yet for minorities, and it is even less true for Indigenous peoples. Denying equal education to a child from a minority community undermines our ability to harness that child's human potential for society. It is the equivalent of deciding to pick a national soccer team only from among those who go to church on Sunday, and then being upset when they fail to compete effectively against others. Identity, or rather the accident of birth, still plays the greatest role of all in determining the future achievements of a child. There has not yet been a concerted effort to generate and design systems that generate equality of opportunity beyond the accident of birth.

This is not to dismiss significant efforts to overcome inequality and marginalization. Affirmative action measures in all areas of public life are attempts to level the scales.[84] These measures, whether the addition of extra points to give minorities access to university education in the United States, the creation of reserved seats for members of excluded minorities in India, or the creation of bespoke "minority nationality"–oriented opportunities in China, seek to promote excluded "Others"— women, Indigenous peoples, minorities—and to generate change by providing voice closer to sites of power.[85] When carefully designed and effectively monitored and strengthened, these measures can yield strong results: accruing benefits to individuals and their immediate communities, and changing majoritarian perspectives on minority populations.[86] Poor design of such measures proves counterproductive, leading to ineffectiveness, ratcheting up talk of "unfair privileges," and sowing discord. Thus, there are allegations that affirmative measures benefit a "creamy layer" (privileged people within specific communities) rather than creating a more level playing field for all.[87] Regardless, while they increase inclusion of voices from excluded communities, affirmative measures have not resulted in systemic structural change at the scale needed. Similarly, approaches seeking greater political participation by way of autonomous arrangements for territorially concentrated minorities, or personal autonomy laws where minorities are scattered, have also yielded limited results.

Moving Toward Inclusion

To generate a system-wide trigger for inclusion, something more is necessary, something that speaks as much to the majority population as it benefits excluded minorities. Since nearly 80 percent of countries in the world are newly independent and emerged from colonization, and since a significant proportion of the remaining 20 percent were involved in colonization, rethinking and rewriting history from a wider perspective is a better way to harness inclusion.

Feminist critiques of history make the compelling point that the historical narrative privileges certain types of activities while largely ignoring others, notably the role played by women in the growth and development of societies.[88] Others have argued that history only narrates the story from the perspective of the "winners," often ignoring the "losers" or glossing over details and substituting perspective for fact.[89] In most countries, national histories are constructed as an unbroken and relatively smooth series of events in which the forces of "good" overcome forces of "evil." This lazy, politically motivated narrative may have been justifiable to mobilize the population to support the state or kingdom.[90] But when placed into a multicultural environment where the "enemy" lives within, it nurtures the roots of conflict.

Besides the question of morality, the narratives are flawed, since they are often told from a deeply ethnicized perspective, treating loss of life on the "other side" as justified, and relying on ancient interpretations of just-war theory that crystallized during the Crusades.[91] See Box 8.5.

Box 8.5 Biased Narratives: The Example of Myanmar

In Myanmar, a largely Buddhist country with minority Muslim and Christian populations, the current threat to Rohingyas, an ethnically distinct Muslim population in the region, is fueled by a narrative that sees them labeled "foreign" because of the religion they profess.[92] This has led to calls to "maintain the state's purity" as a Buddhist homeland, portraying Islam as foreign to the region, having come in through "invaders." While there has always been identity-based tension around religion in the country and in the region (because of the mixture of religions, homeland claims, and ethnic and linguistic groups), it has taken the hue of a moral panic in recent decades as the new independent and democratic state emerged from military rule.

The ascendance to power of Aung San Suu-Ki, who benefited from global solidarity over her previously disallowed claim to govern, was seen as the best guarantee of human rights for all. Yet the reverse has taken place. Populations long silenced in a brutal dictatorship but fed a biased history of the Rohingya now see their independence as extending to "taking back" their state. It has resulted in greater incitement to violence against the Rohingya and their expulsion through brutal ethnic cleansing from many of the lands they inhabited. The irony lies in labeling the Rohingya "foreign" based on their religion: history books and popular narratives of the "Burmese" state fail to highlight that while Islam did come from the west and could therefore be deemed "foreign," Buddhism also came from the west, only slightly nearer, and would be equally "foreign." Further, state boundaries were demarcated by the British, who drew lines on maps for administrative reasons, making questions of "foreign" and "Indigenous" meaningless.

Conclusion

In postcolonial states, recent histories are dominated by people from majoritarian communities. While this is inevitable—they had a near-monopoly on access to education and literacy—the politicized narration has fostered bigotry and xenophobia, proving counterproductive to long-term societal cohesion. Such histories also undermine stability and constrain development. In former colonial states, the failure to scrutinize past events with equanimity and circumspection has led to a triumphalist interpretation of issues such as war, conquest, and exploitation. In addition to benefiting primarily the elite by allowing them to accumulate wealth through theft, it has led to a sense of entitlement to unfettered growth despite planetary and human constraints. It is not surprising that those from "outside," who are often portrayed as ill-deserving "scroungers" seeking a redistribution of wealth, face collective angst.[93] The impression is of people seeking to "steal" hard-won rewards unjustifiably, not—as is most often the case—seeking a subsistence-level return that may have accrued to them had resources not been taken in the first place.

Engagement in collective history-writing may seem counterintuitive at this time of heightened hysteria in the public square. But if led by enlightened historians, it may emphasize the importance of listening. This involves listening to critiques— some justified, others politically motivated, including many flawed narratives based on a deeply held sense of injustice rather than fact. If engaged within national communities with equal access to the public discussion, this listening may place society in a more reflective, rather than reactionary, mode. If narrated well, the histories will show the ebbs and flows of force, persuasion, treachery, and valor, and how they accumulate on every side of every event. This may finally lead to the realization that a time of peace—where swords could be beaten into plowshares—was the overarching driver of the decision to wield swords in the first place.[94] Such an exercise, if done well, could recast perpetrators and victims in a nuanced manner, rather than perpetuating a simplistic good-versus-evil narrative that reiterates ancient division and allows generational reliving of enmities based on flawed and politically skewed narration of "fact."

Fake news was not invented in this century. It is part of our official history books, and its retelling with every generation excludes many—women, minorities, and Indigenous peoples among them. It fuels ancient conflict by contributing new strands to it, and it actively undermines peaceful and inclusive development.

Notes

1. Dr. B. R. Ambedkar was an Indian scholar, jurist, economist, politician, and social reformer who is regarded as the father of the Indian constitution.
2. See, for example, Ndlovu-Gatsheni and Mhlanga 2013.
3. For an emerging research agenda on the subject, see Todd 2018.
4. See Kumar et al. 2018; Kinloch and Mohan 2005. Also see Anderson 2006.
5. See Cordell and Wolff 2009; Bozeman 2015. The term "ethnic" is used in this context to include "racial," as explained in Box 8.1.
6. Census India 2011.
7. One of the earliest expositions of this can be traced to a column raised by Pharaoh Sesotris III (1887–1849 BCE) above the second cataract of the Nile. See Comas 1958.
8. See the discussion of William Dunbar's poem "The Dance of the Seven Deadly Sins" in Keane 2007, 72.
9. See Keane 2007, 75–85.

10. Knox 1862, i.
11. Darwin 1981, 226–227.
12. Galton 1883, 217.
13. Montagu 1942, 1. On Galton, see Buchanan et al. 2000, 29.
14. For more, see Hartley 2015.
15. Huxley and Haddon 1935, xi–xii (cited in Keane 2007, 105).
16. Keane 2007, 105.
17. Information on minorities in their specific national contexts can be found in the World Directory of Minorities, available at the Minority Rights Group International webpage.
18. UN General Assembly 1948; Robertson 2006; Clavery 2008; Mann 2005. For more on the legal nuance between "genocide" and other mass killings that are claimed as genocide, see Box 8.2.
19. Koskenniemi 2004.
20. For a brief and accessible explanation of the issue, see Schabas 2008. For a seminal work on this issue, see Schabas 2009.
21. UN General Assembly 1948. On Lemkin, see Irvin-Erickson 2016.
22. See Schabas 2009, 12, 241–306.
23. Statute of the International Criminal Court (1994), art. 7, art. 8, art. 8 bis. While "ethnic cleansing" is not recognized as a specific crime in international law, the United Nations has used the term regularly in describing particular situations, commencing with the crisis in Yugoslavia. For a more comprehensive explanation, see https://www.un.org/en/genocidepre vention/ethnic-cleansing.shtml.
24. For the Rome Statute, see https://www.icc-cpi.int/NR/rdonlyres/ADD16852-AEE9-4757-ABE7-9CDC7CF02886/283503/RomeStatutEngl.pdf.
25. Schabas 2005.
26. See Kingston 2015.
27. Jehl 1994.
28. Sustainable Development Solutions Network 2013.
29. For an assessment of the extent to which legal standards exist and are accessible to minorities and Indigenous peoples in three areas of the world, see Castellino and Dominguez-Redondo 2006; Castellino and Keane 2009; Castellino and Cavanaugh 2013.
30. See Crenshaw 1991.
31. See Castellino 2010; Hashemi 2006; Hukuku 2016. General background information on St. Louis can be found on the *Encyclopaedia Britannica* website at: https://www.britannica.com/biography/Louis-IX. For more on other historical treaties protecting minorities, see Thornberry 1992, chapter 1.
32. See Thio 2005.
33. Valentine 2004.
34. Capotorti 1977: Also see Martínez Cobo 1987.
35. See Pentassugglia 2002.
36. Kingsbury 2001, 189.
37. See generally Ishay 2008.
38. For an authoritative commentary on the Universal Declaration, including the working documents and discussions that framed it, see Schabas 2013.
39. Hossain 2005.
40. Castellino 2008, 503.
41. For an indicative tone of this "discussion," see Carey 1876.
42. Said 1991.
43. New Zealand History n.d.
44. See Diamond 2017.

45. See Montevideo Convention on the Rights and Duties of States, December 26, 1933, 49 Stat. 3097 T.S.881.
46. See Crawford 2006.
47. Mylonas 2012.
48. See, e.g., Wesseling 2015; Keita 2002.
49. See, e.g., Jackson 1989. For many states the threat posed by minorities lies in the possibility of secession. For more, see Pavkovic and Radan 2001.
50. See Miller 2003.
51. See, e.g., Ganguly 2017. For a review of general issues concerning minorities, see Minority Rights Group 2018.
52. See especially Keese 2015.
53. See Kemp, Popovski, and Thakur 2011.
54. Deng 1997.
55. See Gurr 1993. Also see Minority Rights Group n.d. b.
56. See Drayton 2005.
57. See Hickel 2018.
58. For an illustration of this phenomena in sub-Saharan Africa, see Austin 2010.
59. See Bosma, Lucassen, and Osstindie 2012.
60. For data that looks at long-term migration in Europe, see Van Mol and de Valk 2015.
61. World Bank 2020.
62. Olusoga 2019.
63. BBC 2020.
64. Belchem 2014.
65. Kirk, Stein, and Fischer 2018.
66. See Kirby and Ross 2019.
67. See Lairson and Skidmore 2017.
68. See Sachs 2015.
69. Glaser 2017.
70. For a contemporary comparison between the two largest states in the world, China and India, and how the rise of majorities could compromise the existence of each state, see Castellino 2020.
71. Tagade, Naik, and Thorat 2018.
72. See Gwatipedza and Janus 2019.
73. Klein 2016.
74. See Schwartz, Dunkel, and Waterman.
75. See, e.g., Zhao 2013.
76. This was the subject of the classic text entitled *Nation Building* (Deutsch and Folz 1963).
77. Otsby 2007.
78. See Franzen 2011; Castellino and Keane 2012; Aldoughli 2018; Rostami-Povey 2012; Castellino 2020b; Durrani 2008; Stokke 1998; Semenenko 2013; Rich and MacQueen 2017; Bani Salameh and El-Edwan 2016. For an intriguing analysis of the gaps that are emerging in this discussion in many societies, see Richter, Antonakis, and Harders 2018.
79. Rockstrom, Klum, and Miller 2015. For a specific impact on minorities, see Minority Rights Group 2019.
80. Minority Rights Group, 2021.
81. See Ernst, Merola, and Samaan 2018.
82. See, for example, Acs and Loprest 2009; Nopo 2012; Gerard et al. 2018.
83. Froy and Pyne 2011.
84. See, e.g., Spann 2000.
85. See Ricks 2004; Deshpande 2013; Ding, Myers, and Price 2017.

86. See, e.g., Fredman 2017, 124. Also see Castellino 2004.
87. See, e.g., Economist 2019.
88. See Morgan 2006.
89. Mazower 2012.
90. See, e.g., Elshtain 2005.
91. These ideas are discussed in Fotion 2007.
92. For more on the Rohingya community and the existential crisis faced, see Abdul Bari 2018. Also see Minority Rights Group n.d. a.
93. For an insight into how financial outflows among the super-rich have contributed to development financing gaps, see Bullough 2018.
94. An echo from the compelling text written in the 1960s by a scholar who was arguing for the natural tendency of societies toward peace. See Claude 1965.

Bibliography

Abdul Bari, Muhammad. 2018. *The Rohingya Crisis: A People Facing Extinction*. UK: Kube Publishing.

Acs, Gregory, and Pamela Loprest. 2009. "Job Differences by Race and Ethnicity in the Low-Skill Job Market." The Urban Institute. Brief no. 4. February. https://www.urban.org/sites/default/files/publication/30146/411841-Job-Differences-by-Race-and-Ethnicity-in-the-Low-Skill-Job-Market.PDF.

Aldoughli, Rahaf. 2018. "The Symbolic Construction of National Identity and Belonging in Syrian Nationalist Songs (from 1970–2007)." *Contemporary Levant* 4, no. 2: 141–154. https://doi.org/10.1080/20581831.2018.1554233.

Anderson, Benedict. 2006. *Imagined Communities: Reflections on the Origin and Spread of Nationalism*. Revised ed. London: Verso.

Austin, Gareth. 2010. "African Economic Development and Colonial Legacies' Dossier—Africa: 50 Years of Independence—Review; Major Development Policy Trends." *International Development Policy* 1: 11–32. https://journals.openedition.org/poldev/78.

Bani Salameh, Mohammed Torki, and Khalid Issa El-Edwan. 2016. "The Identity Crisis in Jordan: Historical Pathways and Contemporary Debates." *Journal of Nationalism and Ethnicity* 44, no. 6: 985–1002.

BBC. 2020. "George Floyd Death: Thousands Turn out for UK Anti-Racism Protests." BBC News, June 7. https://www.bbc.com/news/uk-52949014.

Belchem, John. 2014. *Before the Windrush: Race Relations in Twentieth-Century Liverpool*. Liverpool: Liverpool University Press.

Bosma, Ulbe, Jan Lucassen, and Gert Osstindie, eds. 2012. *Postcolonial Migrants and Identity Politics: Europe, Russia, Japan and the United States in Comparison*. New York: Berghahn Books.

Bozeman, Adda Bruemmer. 2015. *Conflict in Africa: Concepts and Realities*. Princeton, NJ: Princeton University Press.

Buchanan, Allen, Dan W. Brock, Norman Daniels, and Daniel Wikler. 2000. *From Chance to Choice: Genetics and Justice*. Cambridge: Cambridge University Press, 2000.

Bullough, Oliver. 2018. *Moneyland: The Inside Story of the Crooks and Kleptocrats Who Rule the World*. New York: Profile Books.

Capotorti, Francesco. 1977. "Study on the Rights of Persons Belonging to Ethnic, Religious and Linguistic Minorities." United Nations. E/CN.4/Sub.2/384/Rev.1.

Carey, H. C. *Commerce, Christianity, Civilization Versus British Free Trade: Letters in Response to the London Times*. Philadelphia: Collins, 1876.

Castellino, Joshua. 2020a. "The Rise of Majorities and Emerging Existential Threats to China and India." *Chinese Journal of Comparative Law* 8, no. 3: 538–557.

Castellino, Joshua. 2020b. "The Threat to the Unity and Integrity of India." Lecture, Cornell India Law Center, March 19. https://indialawcenter.lawschool.cornell.edu/2020/03/19/the-thr

eat-to-the-unity-and-territorial-integrity-of-india-the-dangers-and-implications-of-unravell
ing-the-constitutional-minority-rights-package/.

Castellino, Joshua. 2010. "The Protection of Minorities and Indigenous Peoples in International Law: A Comparative Temporal Analysis." *International Journal on Minority and Group Rights* 17, no. 3: 393–422.

Castellino, Joshua. 2008. "Territorial Integrity and the Right to Self-Determination: An Examination of the Conceptual Tools." *Brooklyn Journal of International Law* 33, no. 2: 503–568.

Castellino, Joshua. 2004. "Affirmative Action for the Protection of Linguistic Rights: An Analysis of International Human Rights Legal Standards in the Context of the Irish Language." *Dublin University Law Journal* 25: 1–43.

Castellino, Joshua, and Kathleen Cavanaugh. 2013. *Minority Rights in the Middle East: A Comparative Legal Analysis.* Oxford: Oxford University Press.

Castellino, Joshua, and Elvira Dominguez-Redondo. 2006. *Minority Rights in Asia: A Comparative Legal Analysis.* Oxford: Oxford University Press.

Castellino, Joshua, and David Keane. 2012. "Transcending Sectarianism Through Minority Rights in Iraq." *International Journal of Contemporary Iraqi Studies* 5, no. 3: 387–407.

Castellino, Joshua, and David Keane. 2009. *Minority Rights in the Pacific: A Comparative Legal Analysis.* Oxford: Oxford University Press.

Census India. 2011. "Population Enumeration Data (Final Population)." Office of the Registrar General & Census Commissioner, India. http://censusindia.gov.in/2011census/population_enumeration.html.

Claude, Inis. 1965. *Swords into Ploughshares.* London: Hodder & Stoughton 1965.

Clavery, Bartolome. 2008. *Genocide or Ethnocide 1933–2007: How to Make, Unmake and Remake Law with Words.* Milan: Giuffre.

Cohen, Julie, and Betsy West, producers. 2018. *RBG.* Los Angeles, CA: Magnolia Home Entertainment, 2018. Film.

Comas, J. 1958. *Racial Myths.* Paris: UNESCO.

Cordell, Karl, and Stefan Wolff. 2009. *Ethnic Conflict: Causes, Consequences, Responses.* Cambridge: Polity Press.

Crawford, James. 2006. *The Creation of States in International Law.* 2nd ed. Oxford: Oxford University Press.

Crenshaw, Kimberlé. 1991. "Mapping the Margins: Intersectionality, Identity Politics, and Violence Against Women of Color." *Stanford Law Review* 43, no. 6 (1991): 1241–1299.

Darwin, Charles. 1981. *The Descent of Man and Selection in Relation to Sec.* Princeton, NJ: Princeton University Press.

Deng, Francis M. 1997. "Ethnicity: An African Predicament." Brookings Institution. June 1. https://www.brookings.edu/articles/ethnicity-an-african-predicament/.

Deshpande, Ashwini. 2013. *Affirmative Action in India.* Oxford Short Introductions. New Delhi: Oxford University Press.

Deutsch, Karl, and William Folz. 1963. *Nation Building.* New York: Atherton Press.

Diamond, Jared M. 2017. *Guns, Germs, and Steel: The Fates of Human Societies.* New York: W. W. Norton.

Ding, Sai, Samuel L. Myers Jr., and Gregory N. Price. 2017. "Does Affirmative Action in Chinese College Admissions Lead to a Mismatch? Educational Quality and the Relative Returns to a Baccalaureate Degree for Minorities in China." *International Journal of Anthropology and Ethnology* 1, no. 3. https://ijae.springeropen.com/articles/10.1186/s41257-017-0006-7.

Drayton, Richard. 2005. "The Wealth of the West Was Built on Africa's Exploitation." *The Guardian.* August 20. https://www.theguardian.com/politics/2005/aug/20/past.hearafrica05.

Durrani, Naureen. 2008. "Schooling the 'Other': The Representation of Gender and National Identity in Pakistani Curriculum Texts." *Compare: A Journal of Comparative and International Education* 38, no. 5: 595–610. https://doi.org/10.1080/03057920802351374.

Economist. 2019. "Quotas for All: Almost All Indians Will Soon Qualify for Affirmative Action in India." *The Economist,* January 12. https://www.economist.com/asia/2019/01/12/almost-all-indians-will-soon-qualify-for-affirmative-action-in-india.

Elshtain, Jean Bethke. 2005. "The Just War Tradition and Natural Law." *Fordham International Law Journal* 28, no. 3: 742–755.

Ernst, Ekkehard, Rossana Merola, and Daniel Samaan. 2018. "The Economics of Artificial Intelligence: Implications for the Future of Work." ILO Future of Work Series. ILO, Geneva. https://www.ilo.org/wcmsp5/groups/public/---dgreports/---cabinet/documents/publication/wcms_647306.pdf.

Foblets, Marie-Claire, Michele Graziadei, and Alison Dundes Renteln. 2017. *Personal Autonomy in Plural Societies: A Principle and Its Paradoxes.* London: Routledge.

Fotion, Nicholas. 2011. *War and Ethics: A New Just War Theory.* London: Bloomsbury.

Franzen, Johan. 2011. "The Problem of Iraqi Nationalism." *National Identities* 13, no. 3: 217–234. https://doi.org/10.1080/14608944.2011.591371.

Fredman, Sandra. 2017. "Reimagining Power Relations: Hierarchies of Disadvantage and Affirmative Action." *Acta Juridica* 17, no. 1: 124–145.

Froy, F., and L. Pyne. 2011. "Ensuring Labour Market Success for Ethnic Minority and Immigrant Youth." OECD Local Economic and Employment Development Working Papers, 2011/09. http://dx.doi.org/10.1787/5kg8g2l0547b-en.

Galton, Francis. 1883. *Inquiries into Human Faculty and Its Development.* London: Macmillan.

Gerard, François, Lorenzo Lagos, Edson Severnini, and David Card. 2018. "Assortative Matching or Exclusionary Hiring? The Impact of Firm Policies on Racial Wage Differences in Brazil." National Bureau of Economic Research. October 22. https://doi.org/10.3386/w25176.

Ganguly, Meenakshi. 2017. "Engaging in Whataboutery Rather than Protecting Rights." *Brown Journal of World Affairs* 24, no. 1: 39–52.

Glaser, Eliane. 2017. *Anti-Politics: On the Demonization of Ideology, Authority and the State.* London: Repeater Books.

Gurr, Ted. 1993. *Minorities at Risk: A Global View of Ethnopolitical Conflicts.* Washington, DC: United States Institute of Peace.

Gwatipedza, Johnson, and Thorsten Janus. 2019. "Public Investment Under Autocracy and Social Unrest." *Economics and Politics* 3, no. 1: 112–135. https://doi.org/10.1111/ecpo.12123.

Hartley, Emma. 2015. "Revival of a Swedish Taboo." Politico, September 30. https://www.politico.eu/article/revival-of-a-swedish-taboo/.

Hashemi, Kamran. 2006. "The Right of Minorities to Identity and the Challenge of Non-discrimination: A Study on the Effects of Traditional Muslims' Dhimmah on Current State Practices." *International Journal on Minority and Group Rights* 13, no. 1: 1–26.

Hickel, Jason. 2018. *The Divide: Global Inequality from Conquest to Free Markets.* London: W. W. Norton.

Hossain, Kamrul. 2005. "The Concept of Jus Cogens and the Obligation Under the UN Charter." *Santa Clara Journal of International Law* 3, no. 1: art. 3. https://digitalcommons.law.scu.edu/cgi/viewcontent.cgi?article=1011&context=scujil.

Hukuku, Kamu. 2016. "Ottoman Human Rights Practice: A Model of Legal Pluralism." *Yildirim Beyazit Hukuk Dergisi* 2: 201–222.

Huxley, Julian, and A. C. Haddon. 1935. *We Europeans: A Survey of Racial Problems.* London: Jonathan Cape.

Irvin-Erickson, Douglas. 2016. *Raphael Lemkin and the Concept of Genocide.* Philadelphia: University of Pennsylvania Press.

Ishay, Micheline. 2008. *The History of Human Rights: From Ancient Times to the Globalization Era.* Los Angeles: University of California Press.

Jackson, Pamela Irving. 1989. *Minority Group Threat, Crime and Policing: Social Context and Social Control.* Westport, CT: Praeger.

Jehl, Douglas. 1994. "Officials Told to Avoid Calling Rwanda Killings 'Genocide.'" *New York Times*, June 10. https://www.nytimes.com/1994/06/10/world/officials-told-to-avoid-calling-rwanda-killings-genocide.html.

Keane, David. 2007. *Caste Based Discrimination in International Human Rights Law.* New York: Ashgate.

Keese, Alexander. 2015. *Ethnicity and the Colonial State: Finding and Representing Identifications in a Coastal West African and Global Perspective (1850–1960)*. Leiden: Brill.

Keita, Maghan, ed. 2002. *Conceptualizing/Re-conceptualizing Africa: The Construction of African Historical Identity*. Leiden: Brill.

Kemp, Walter, Alexander Popovski, and Romesh Thakur, eds. 2011. *Blood and Borders: The Responsibility to Protect and the Problem of the Kin State*. Tokyo: UNUP.

Kingsbury, Benedict. 2001. "Reconciling Five Competing Conceptual Structures of Indigenous Peoples' Claims in International and Comparative Law." *New York University Journal of International Law and Politics* 34, no. 1: 189–250.

Kingston, Lindsey. 2015. "The Destruction of Identity: Cultural Genocide and Indigenous Peoples." *Journal of Human Rights* 14, no. 1: 63–83.

Kinloch, Graham C, and Raj P. Mohan, eds. 2005. *Genocide: Approaches, Case Studies and Responses*. New York: Algora.

Kirby, Tom, and James Ross, dir. 2019. *The Unwanted: The Secret Windrush Files*. London: Uplands Television Limited.

Kirk, Tom, Danielle Stein, and Annette Fischer. 2018. "The Relationship Between Ethnic Diversity and Development: A Diversity Dividend?" Konung International. June 21. https://assets.publishing.service.gov.uk/media/5b507c88e5274a73380f7b3e/The_Relationship_between_Ethnic_Diversity___Development-__A_Diversity_Dividend_Kirk__Stein___Fisher_21.6.18.pdf.

Klein, Naomi. 2016. "Let Them Drown: The Violence of Othering in a Warming World." Edward W. Said London Lecture, May 4. https://vimeo.com/166018049.

Knox, Robert. 1862. *The Races of Men: A Philosophical Enquiry into the Influence of Race over the Destinies of Nations*. London: H. Renshaw.

Koskenniemi, Martti. 2004. *The Gentle Civilizer of Nations: The Rise and Fall of International Law 1870–1960*. Cambridge: Cambridge University Press.

Kumar, Ashok, Adam Elliot-Cooper, Shruti Iyer, and Dalia Gebrial. 2018. "An Introduction to the Special Issue on Identity Politics." *Historical Materialism* 26, no. 2: 3–20. https://doi.org/10.1163/1569206X-00001776.

Lairson, Thomas D., and David Skidmore. 2017. *International Political Economy: The Struggle for Power and Wealth in a Globalizing World*. New York: Routledge.

Mann, Michael. 2005. *The Dark Side of Democracy: Explaining Ethnic Cleansing*. Cambridge: Cambridge University Press.

Martínez Cobo, José. 1987. "Study on the Problem of Discrimination Against Indigenous Populations, Volume V: Conclusions, Proposals and Recommendation." United Nations. E/CN.4/Sub.2/1986/Add.4. https://undocs.org/en/E/CN.4/Sub.2/1986/7/Add.4.

Mazower, Mark. 2012. *Governing the World: The History of an Idea*. London: Allen Lane.

Miller, Russell A. 2003. "Self-Determination in International Law and the Demise of Democracy." *Columbia Journal of Transnational Law* 41, no. 3: 601–648.

Minority Rights Group. 2021. Minority and Indigenous Trends 2021: Lessons of the COVID-19 Pandemic. https://minorityrights.org/trends2021/.

Minority Rights Group. 2019. *Key Trends Report 2019: Focus on Climate*. London: Minority Rights Group.

Minority Rights Group. 2018. *Minority and Indigenous Trends 2018*. London: Minority Rights. https://minorityrights.org/trends2018/.

Minority Rights Group. n.d. a. "Muslims and Rohingya." https://minorityrights.org/minorities/muslims-and-rohingya/.

Minority Rights Group. n.d. b. "Peoples Under Threat." Minority Rights Group. https://peoplesunderthreat.org/.

Montagu, Ashley. 1942. Man's *Most Dangerous Myth: The Fallacy of Race*. New York: Columbia University Press.

Morgan, Sue. 2006. *The Feminist History Reader*. London: Routledge.

Mylonas, Harris. 2012. *The Politics of Nation-Building: Making Co-Nationals, Refugees and Minorities*. Cambridge: Cambridge University Press.

Ndlovu-Gatsheni, Sabelo J., and Brilliant Mhlanga. 2013. *Bondage of Identity Politics in Postcolonial Africa: The Northern Problem and Ethno-Future.* Oxford: African Books Collective.

New Zealand History. n.d. "Treaty of Waitangi Signed." Government of New Zealand. Accessed September 29, 2020. https://nzhistory.govt.nz/the-treaty-of-waitangi-is-signed.

Nopo, Hugo. 2012. *New Century, Old Disparities: Gender and Ethnic Earnings Gaps in Latin America and the Caribbean.* Kyiv: World Bank Publications.

Olusoga, David. 2019. "Windrush: Archived Documents Show the Long Betrayal." Observer Special Report. *The Guardian*, June 16. https://www.theguardian.com/uk-news/2019/jun/16/windrush-scandal-the-long-betrayal-archived-documents-david-olusoga.

Otsby, Gudrun. 2007. "Horizontal Inequalities, Political Environment, and Civil Conflict: Evidence from 55 Developing Countries, 1986–2003." World Bank Policy Research Working Paper No. 4193. April 1. https://ssrn.com/abstract=979665.

Pavkovic, Aleksandar, and Peter Radan, eds. 2001. *The Ashgate Research Companion to Secession.* Surrey: Ashgate.

Pentassugglia, Gaetano. 2002. *Minorities in International Law: An Introductory Study.* Strasbourg: Council of Europe.

Reid, Carolina. 2009. "Addressing the Challenges of Unemployment in Low-Income Communities." Federal Reserve Bank of San Francisco. https://www.frbsf.org/community-development/files/Reid_Carolina_CI_Spring_2009.pdf.

Rich, Ben, and Ben MacQueen. 2017. "The Saudi State as an Identity Racketeer." *Middle East Critique* 26, no. 2: 105–121.

Richter, Carola, Anna Antonakis, and Clija Harders, eds. 2018. *Digital Media and the Politics of Transformation in the Arab World and Asia.* Wiesbaden: Springer VS. https://link.springer.com/book/10.1007/978-3-658-20700-7#toc.

Ricks, Irelene. 2004. "The 50th Anniversary of *Brown v. Board of Education*: Continued Impacts on Minority Life Science Education." *Cell Biology Education* 3, no. 3: 146–149. doi: 10.1187/cbe.04-05-0044.

Robertson, Geoffrey. 2006. *Crimes Against Humanity: The Struggle for Global Justice.* London: Penguin.

Rockstrom, Johan, Matthias Klum, and Peter Miller. 2015. *Big World Small Planet.* New Haven: Yale University Press.

Rostami-Povey, Elaheh. 2012. "Afghan Women's Resistance and Struggle: Gender, Agency and Identity." In *Women and Fluid Identities*, edited by H. Afshar 146–165. London: Palgrave Macmillan.

Sachs, Jeffrey D. 2015. *The Age of Sustainable Development.* New York: Columbia University Press.

Said, Edward. 1991. *Orientalism: Western Conceptions of the Orient.* London: Penguin Books.

Schabas, William A. 2013. *The Universal Declaration of Human Rights.* Cambridge: Cambridge University Press.

Schabas, William A. 2009. *Genocide in International Law: The Crime of Crimes.* Cambridge: Cambridge University Press.

Schabas, William A. 2008. "Convention for the Prevention and Punishment of the Crime of Genocide." United Nations Audiovisual Library of International Law. http://legal.un.org/avl/pdf/ha/cppcg/cppcg_e.pdf.

Schabas, William. 2005. "Cultural Genocide and the Protection of the Right to Existence of Aboriginal and Indigenous Groups." In *International Law and Indigenous Peoples*, edited by Joshua Castellino and Niamh Walsh, 117–132. Leiden: Martinus Nijhoff.

Schwartz, Seth J., Curtis S. Dunkel, and Alan S. Waterman. 2009. "Terrorism: An Identity Theory Perspective." *Studies in Conflict and Terrorism* 32, no. 6: 537–559. doi: 10.1080/10576100902888453.

Semenenko, Irina. 2013. "The Quest for Identity: Russian Public Opinion on Europe and the European Union and the National Identity Agenda." *Perspectives on European Politics and Society* 14, no. 1: 102–122.

Spann, Girardeau A. 2000. *The Law of Affirmative Action: Twenty-Five Years of Supreme Court Decision on Race and Remedies.* New York: New York University Press.

Stokke, Kristian. 1998. "Sinhalese and Tamil Nationalism as Post-Colonial Projects from 'Above', 1948–1983." *Political Geography* 17, no. 1:83–113.

Sustainable Development Solutions Network. 2013. "Achieving Gender Equality, Social Inclusion and Human Rights for All: Challenges and Priorities for the Sustainable Development Agenda." Sustainable Development Solutions Network, New York. September. http://unsdsn.org/wp-content/uploads/2014/02/TG3-Final-Report.pdf.

Tagade, Nitin, Ajaya Kumar Naik, and Sukhadeo Thorat. 2018. "Wealth Ownership and Inequality in India: A Socio-Religious Analysis." *Journal of Social Inclusion Studies* 4, no. 2: 1–18. doi: 10.1177/2394481118808107.

Thio, Li-Ann. 2005. *Managing Babel: The International Legal Protection of Minorities in the Twentieth Century.* Leiden: Martinus Nijhoff/Brill.

Thornberry, Patrick. 1992. *International Law and the Rights of Minorities.* Oxford: Clarendon Press.

Todd, Jennifer. 2018. "The Politics of Identity Change and Conflict: An Agenda for Research." *Politics* 38, no. 1: 84–93. *https://doi.org/10.1177/0263395717715857.*

UN General Assembly. 1948. "Convention on the Prevention and Punishment of the Crime of Genocide." Adopted December 9. https://treaties.un.org/doc/publication/unts/volume%2078/volume-78-i-1021-english.pdf.

Valentine, J. R. 2004. "Toward a Definition of National Minority." *Denver Journal of International Law and Policy* 32, no. 3: 445–474.

Van Mol, Christof, and Helga de Valk. 2015. "Migrants and Immigrants in Europe: A Historical and Demographic Perspective." In *Integration Processes and Policies in Europe*, edited by Blanca Garcés-Mascareñas and Rinus Penninx, 31–55. IMISCOE Research Series. Cham: Springer. https://link.springer.com/chapter/10.1007/978-3-319-21674-4_3.

Wesseling, H. L. 2015. *The European Colonial Empires 1815–1919.* London: Routledge.

World Bank. 2020. "Women, Business, and the Law." Global Indicators Group, World Bank, Washington, DC. https://wbl.worldbank.org/.

Zhao, Suisheng. 2013. "Foreign Policy Implications of Chinese Nationalism Revisited: The Strident Turn." *Journal of Contemporary China* 22, no. 82: 535–553. https://doi.org/10.1080/10670564.2013.766379.

SECTION III

PREVENTING AND RESOLVING CONFLICT INCLUSIVELY

Tactics and Approaches

The evidence is clear: when ending wars or breaking cycles of conflict, the engagement of diverse stakeholders can determine whether there is continuing bloodshed or a solid foundation for rebuilding societies. Peace negotiations are more likely to succeed when diverse players are engaged. Accords are more likely to stick when the population as a whole is invested in peace. Societies are more likely to successfully reunite when reconciliation and reconstruction efforts strive to meet the varied needs of all citizens.

But success requires intentionality. In a world where peace talks often prize secrecy and exclusion, strategies and tactics need to shift to leverage the benefits of inclusion. When conflict resolution has often simply meant a division of spoils among combatants, a focus on inclusion and equity necessitates changes in approach. This section focuses on key components of efforts to address fragility and conflict, discussing why attention to diversity and inclusion are fundamental in each specific stage of conflict resolution and peacebuilding processes, and provides examples of strategies that successfully leverage diversity to promote long-term stability (and some that fail). The chapters are rich with examples, including from Brazil, Democratic Republic of Congo, Jordan, and Vanuatu.

Featuring collaboration among leading practitioners and scholars, the chapters examine moments when an inclusive approach is particularly critical to consolidating stability and building peace. Katia Papagianni and Sarah Federman discuss how to advance inclusion in peace negotiations, using recent efforts in Yemen, Syria, Libya, and Nigeria to draw lessons for the future. Colette Rausch and Zuhra Halimova carry forward the discussion in analyzing the import of inclusiveness when implementing peace accords, particularly reflecting on examples from Nepal and Tajikistan. Hugo Van der Merwe and Nomathamsanqa Masiko look at where there has (and has not) been progress creating transitional justice processes that address the priorities and concerns of varied stakeholders in post-conflict societies; their analysis is combined with reflections from Eduardo González regarding the Peruvian experience. Meaghan Shoemaker and Michelle Barsa consider strategies for transforming the security sector—how to bring diverse voices into forces, and how to ensure that security services protect and defend the rights of all members of society during and after conflict. Leading expert practitioners Kate Sutton, Pip Henty, and Charlie Damon, reflect on inclusion in providing humanitarian assistance, especially for older people and women. Finally, Tatiana Moura, Elis Borde, Henny Slegh, and Gary Barker consider how to address societal violence inside and outside of conflict, reflecting particularly on how norms of masculinity drive violence.

Each of the chapters discusses how a critical juncture can create or break faith in the effort to transition toward stability and prosperity, offering or extinguishing citizens' hope for a better future. What becomes clear is that the trajectory toward equity and inclusion is either reinforced or undermined at various stages in the process. For example, an inclusive peace negotiation is important because it is likely to result in an agreement that is more durable, but it is insufficient to guarantee an equitable and inclusive post-conflict society unless it is followed by focus to implement that accord inclusively.

9

Enabling Inclusive Peace Mediation and Negotiation

Structures and Tactics

Katia Papagianni and Sarah Federman

> The outcomes, at least in terms of specific policies, are uncertain. But this messy process is unavoidable and healthy in new and established democracies.
>
> —Leigh Payne, University of Oxford

Introduction

On October 31, 2000, the UN Security Council adopted Resolution 1325, applying a gender lens to analyses of armed conflicts and peacebuilding processes. Other related resolutions have further codified commitments to broader engagement of civil society.[1] Over twenty years, these resolutions have lent support to initiatives seeking to engage community-level actors in conflict analysis and resolution. Yet genuine representation and participation by a wide range of stakeholders in formal, national-level processes remain limited, albeit crucial for lasting peace.

This chapter first advocates for inclusion of these groups for their intrinsic and strategic value. The authors then examine specific inclusive peacebuilding efforts in Yemen, Syria, Libya, and Nigeria to demonstrate approaches and challenges faced by those leading these efforts over the past two decades. It concludes by advocating for increased inclusion of civil society representatives at all levels of peace processes and post-conflict governance, even when such inclusion does not produce the immediate strategic outcomes outlined by elites.

Why Inclusion

The post–Cold War period at the close of the twentieth century brought with it a series of successful negotiated agreements ending devastating conflicts in different parts of the world. The West emerged with a belief that negotiations among leaders were a pathway to peace. But the limitations of elite-generated accords are increasingly apparent: agreements have collapsed and negotiations have stagnated around the world. In response to the limitations of these top-level negotiations, those interested in peacebuilding turned toward local communities as sites of intervention for long-term peace.[2]

There are myriad reasons for including women and other civil society representatives in peace processes. First, military actors alone can rarely create lasting peace; those seeking to end the fighting must focus on strategies to disrupt immediate violence and destruction. Moreover, multiple and often fragmented communities, not militaries, will have to live with and uphold the peace accord. Additionally, the complexities of conflict resolution are growing, with consequences for negotiation processes. As Whitfield writes, "The dramatic combination of external and internal fragmentation in contemporary conflicts erodes the possibility of reaching agreement with political and military elites alone."[3] Further, though agreements can outline terms, they cannot heal the divisions between groups. Inclusive processes can help.

The benefits of inclusive mechanisms in the peace processes of the 1990s and early 2000s are well documented and indisputable. From Guatemala to Liberia, women and other civil society representatives made their marks on the conflict resolution process. They opened channels of communication among conflicting parties, shaped the negotiation agenda, managed the contributions of civil society to the official negotiations, facilitated meetings between conflict parties, and drafted provisions in peace agreements.[4]

In 2018, Krause, Krause, and Bränfors published their analysis of the effect of women signatories on peace agreements. Their examination of eighty-two peace agreements in forty-two conflicts between 1989 and 2011 revealed a statistically significant correlation between women delegates (with signing power) and durable peace. Their study also found that agreements made with the involvement of women signatories contained more provisions aimed at political reform and a higher rate of implementation of these provisions.[5] Overall, women's security directly correlates to stability and security.[6]

Inclusion should not be judged exclusively for its strategic value. To evaluate the contribution of women and civil society organizations (CSOs) based only on their instrumental value positions these actors as tools of war, rather than as intrinsically valuable members of society.[7] When high-level processes position members of civil society as victims or simply "sources of hope," it diminishes and marginalizes them.[8] The inclusion of women and civil society organizations at all levels of the peacemaking processes should occur because these groups are affected by violence, not simply because they can help resolve it.

Making a solely strategic argument for inclusion carries another risk: if community participants are perceived by elites as spoilers or disruptive, they risk exclusion when they express a desire for alternative futures. A liberal democratic approach promotes stakeholder inclusion as a human right. The following discusses where greater participation in peacebuilding processes can and does occur.

Track I and Track II Inclusive Peace Processes

Peace processes are increasingly multilevel, multitrack, and multiparty.[9] This means that processes often have an official track along with discreet, informal tracks run by nongovernmental actors or by subnational dialogues. They may serve in an advisory capacity or focus on particular aspects of the dispute. In some contemporary peace processes, the official negotiation track is dormant, ceremonial, or simply unproductive. Other tracks, therefore, emerge to bring together various configurations of conflicting parties at various levels of seniority and in various geographical regions. These tracks are often quietly endorsed by those managing the formal tables, even as they work toward incremental progress. When official processes stall or are dormant, separate tracks may bring together a variety of nongovernmental actors to discuss long-term options for constitutional design, transitional governance, and/or justice. These dialogues may not directly contribute to immediate conflict resolution, but they boost efforts to build a healthier political system. This multitrack, multistage environment creates numerous potential entry points for women's groups and other civil society organizations. Since 2000, inclusion attempts have targeted formal negotiations (Track I) and peacebuilding efforts usually driven by influential nongovernment actors (Track II).

Track I: Formal Negotiations

We will start with a short review of inclusive Track I negotiations, which usually involve senior officials convening armed actors to secure ceasefires, create power-sharing agreements, or craft constitutions. Participation in Track I can include helping set the agenda, adding substantive clauses to a draft agreement, helping implement the agreement, and moving the process toward closure.[10]

Inclusion can support successful Track I negotiations: nongovernmental actors can set in motion official negotiations and can foster the continuation of these negotiations through backchannel talks and discreet passing of messages among conflict parties when negotiations falter.[11] Civil society actors are not always satisfied with these roles. Some advocate to participate more directly by strategically seeking entry points using assets they have, such as the trust of one or more of the armed conflict actors; technical skills; wide social networks valued by the conflict parties and intermediaries; and/or legitimacy earned through their work, role, or stature in the country.[12]

Direct representation of civil society in Track I processes occurred, for example, in Northern Ireland and Yemen; some civil society representatives achieved observer status during official negotiations in Liberia, meaning they could attend but not vote on outcomes; and civil society members participated via consultative forums in Guatemala.[13] In the past few years, we have also seen a few high-profile efforts by those intervening in conflicts to formalize the role of women and civil society in official negotiation processes.[14] The women's and civil society advisory committees established by the previous UN envoy to Syria, Staffan de Mistura, and more recently of the current UN envoy to Yemen, Martin Griffiths, point to a recent trend.[15] In sum, Track I participation ranges from consultations with the public and civil society organizations on issues discussed at the negotiation table to direct participation in national dialogues and official consultative forums.[16] Through this work, various civil society groups try to support and influence official negotiations directly. Yet the reality is that despite their key contributions and their status as key stakeholders, civil society actors often remain excluded from these formal negotiations, especially in their early stages.

Relatedly, while we see an increase in supplementary participation, women rarely are included as mediators or negotiating parties. Between 1992 and 2018, women accounted for 3 percent of mediators, 4 percent of signatories, and 13 percent of negotiators.[17] As of 2020, UN Women and the UN Department of Political and Peacebuilding Affairs (DPPA) report that resistance to the inclusion of women at these levels remains high. Increasing these numbers will help but not guarantee the influence of women in these processes. Women need to have presence, power, and legitimacy in these meetings.[18] This requires the parties involved in armed conflict to cede some power and control.

Even when women-directed organizations are invited to offer input at certain junctures in Track I negotiations, they rarely control the timing of that invitation or how their contributions are handled. Irregular engagement controlled by others makes it difficult to stay abreast of the shifting situation. Participants are thrown off balance by their treatment as outsiders and by constantly needing to play catch-up. This controlled participation reduces their ability to influence the outcomes of Track I discussions. Furthermore, expecting these actors to play substantive roles on short notice and in an ad hoc manner is unrealistic and contributes to the perception that they are unable to understand political complexities. This impedes their becoming or being seen as experts. According to feminist scholar Cynthia Enloe, if they are listened to at all, women will be heard "only later—that is after the crisis has passed, after the crucial decisions have been made, when it no longer matters; after the new constitution is written."[19]

The costs of this exclusion in Track I discussions remains high. The majority of peace agreements do not explicitly address gender equality or the rights of women. For example, in 2018, out of fifty-two agreements addressing a range of issues, only four contained gender-related provisions.[20] The participation of women in these agreements, however, does not necessarily correlate to gender-related considerations.[21] The UN and other intervening parties often insert these provisions.

Track II: Consultations with Civil Society Actors

To date, Track II discussions serve as the most active site of inclusion. According to the Georgetown Institute for Women, Peace and Security, Track II diplomatic processes include dialogues and consultative processes involving nonpolitical stakeholders who wish to end violent conflict.[22] In these sometimes parallel or intersecting practices we see greater engagement with women and civil society. Between 1989 and 2017, roughly 60 percent of peace processes included informal Track II processes occurring at the same time as Track I negotiations. Of these, 71 percent engaged women's groups.[23] The number would be higher if civil society groups are included. At times, women and civil society groups were called upon to support ceasefires so that humanitarian efforts could move in, or so that Track I negotiations could occur.

When Track II processes occur in parallel to the official negotiations, they can open and maintain lines of communication among conflicting parties to encourage them to enter a negotiation and to help them identify solutions once negotiations have commenced. During preparatory talks, conflicting parties are made aware of various substantive issues that are negotiated in eventual formal talks. Parties in conflict may, for example, hold preliminary talks on modalities of ceasefires, on the timing of elections, on political participation in the post-agreement transition, and on strengthening judicial institutions. Such discussions offer civil society organizations opportunities to influence the conflicting parties' understanding of issues civil society cares about, and to suggest ways to address them.[24] This is crucial, as it prepares the ground for negotiations and helps make negotiations productive. Because Track I negotiations succeed only if communities abide by the results, Track II processes can help prepare societies for the longer-term work of peacebuilding.

Unfortunately, though the power of women's groups is often used to create the contexts for peace, that rarely translates to a voice in or influence over Track 1 efforts. A broad study conducted by Dayal and Christien confirmed that women's inclusion in Track II efforts was often used to "legitimate formal peace processes."[25] Women were asked to create the peaceful context for elites to succeed at their negotiations, but they were kept out of formal peace processes, which marginalized their framing of the conflict and their view of appropriate responses.

Inclusive Peacebuilding: Examples

Having made the argument for inclusion in Track I and Track II processes, a few brief examples reveal the complexities. No single approach or model works for every conflict, and case studies remain an important complement to broader surveys.[26] Instructive are the Yemeni National Dialogue Conference (NDC) of 2013; the Civil Society Support Room established by the UN special envoy for Syria in 2016; and the National Conference process launched by the UN special envoy for Libya, Ghassan Salame, in 2018–2019.

The United Nations played a role in each of these processes, which all encouraged participation by a wider range of stakeholders. While some readers may be tempted to label these efforts as failures, particularly given the inability to create lasting peace, we offer a different lens for evaluation. The challenges highlight broken places in the social system or larger geopolitical environment; at times, the challenges result from top-down directives rather than the failure of inclusion as an approach to peace. Local inclusion efforts may fail to bring peace on a national level because the government is not in control or is caught in a proxy war between global powers. The failure of inclusive efforts to bring about peace can help bring into sharper focus structural issues within the United Nations itself. The veto power of each of the permanent members of the UN Security Council often paralyzes intervention, limiting the UN's ability to support inclusion efforts.[27] In sum, removing the inclusion efforts because they fail to bring peace is akin to removing the warning lights in your car rather than exploring the source of the problem. Engaging women and civil society in the long term will help them, and us, to better understand and respond to the complex conflict dynamics both at home and geopolitically. The challenges of Yemen's National Dialogue highlights some of these multilevel challenges.

Yemen (2012–2013): National Dialogue Enlarges Official Processes

The November 2011 Yemen Implementation Mechanism was an important peacemaking achievement in a very difficult context. Earlier in 2011, Yemenis poured into the streets in massive demonstrations, demanding political rights and freedoms. In May 2011, fifty-two protesters were killed by snipers. Later in the same month, dozens more were killed in clashes between the supporters of President Ali Abdullah Saleh and tribal groups. In September, following a government crackdown on protests, another fifty people were killed. President Saleh signed what became known as the Yemen Implementation Mechanism, which transferred power to his vice president. This agreement implemented a transitional process, which sought to accommodate the interests of the country's major political actors and bring Yemen back from the brink of civil war. To achieve this, the Implementation Mechanism put in place a short-term, power-sharing government consisting of the country's traditional political elites but excluding some key actors.[28] The agreement excluded, for example, the Houthis (an armed Islamic political movement), who had fought six wars during the decade of the 2000s against the government in Sanaa and had not recently participated in the central government. The agreement also excluded the Southern Movement as well as youth, women, and other representatives of civil society who had participated actively in the 2011 street demonstrations.[29] The Southern Movement served as an umbrella of diverse interests in the south of the country, some demanding independence. Excluding these key actors threatened the success of the provisional government.

Understanding the importance of greater inclusion, those leading this transitional government organized a national dialogue to address the main issues facing the country and to agree on the principles for a new constitution.[30] The UN played a crucial role in supporting this national dialogue, which would include civil society, including women and youth leaders who had played leading roles during the 2011 street demonstrations. By explicitly including these actors in the dialogue's mandate in addition to the Houthis and the Southern Movement, the transitional government secured broad participation in the process, which eventually commenced in 2013. This explicit provision for inclusion facilitated the dialogue process.

Yemeni civil society actors, however, had mixed feelings about participating. The Implementation Mechanism offered an imperfect agreement that elevated old elites in the transitional government and made almost no references to human rights issues. At the same time, it offered the possibility of more inclusive politics through the national dialogue. Civil society remained divided over whether to work with the transitional government toward a more democratic future or whether to push for change outside the official process. Their decision was made more difficult by the fact that the Implementation Mechanism only vaguely stated that the members of the Gulf Cooperation Council, UN Security Council (UNSC), and EU would support implementation of the mechanism. In 2012, UNSC Resolution 2051 only requested the secretary-general to continue his role, including through his special advisor, and to continue engaging in Yemen through a small team of experts to support the transition and the national dialogue.[31]

Between 2011 and 2014, civil society organizations, including women's groups and human rights activists, remained divided concerning the dialogue. Would participation lead to greater voice in the long term or simply legitimize the new power-sharing agreement of the elites? To work toward the former, they advocated for greater representation in the national dialogue, argued over the method of selecting representatives, and requested clarity over whether or not they were guaranteed participation in *all* working groups and executive bodies of the National Dialogue Conference.[32]

Planners agreed to structure the national dialogue using a 50-30-20 formula: 50 percent of its participants had to be originally from the southern part of the country, even if currently living in the north; 30 percent had to be women; and 20 percent had to be younger than forty.[33] The formula applied to the composition of the NDC as a whole and to every one of its organs and working groups, including the executive bodies, and the deadlock-breaking mechanism. As a result, every constituencies represented in the NDC had to ensure that their representatives were 50 percent southerners, 30 percent women, and 20 percent below forty years old.[34] By the time the NDC was launched in March 2013, and throughout its duration, the formula was a widely understood norm among the Yemeni elite; no one challenged its implementation. This structured form of inclusion was in itself an impressive achievement. In addition, 120 out of the 565 participants of the NDC were independents, unaffiliated with any of the political parties or armed factions. These seats were divided equally among the constituencies of youth, women, and civil society. Some representatives of these constituencies argued that they should have been granted a greater share of the seats, as the country's transitional government was dominated by old elites and given that the reform-minded spirit of the 2011 revolution. Additionally, some argued that these constituencies should have been able to select their representatives in a more direct manner, and that the chosen representatives were handpicked by the traditional political parties. Conversely, the traditional political parties resisted the concept of "independent" representatives, arguing that the 120 seats should have been divided among the parties. Regardless, thanks to the provisions in the Implementation Mechanism, the rights of women, youth, and civil society to participate in the NDC was not questioned.

Many independents opted to participate in the national dialogue and had a significant impact on the hundreds of recommendations produced, including important, groundbreaking provisions on human rights, including women's rights. Throughout the ten-month NDC, they participated in each of the nine working groups and reached out to their constituencies outside the NDC to consult and inform. Thousands of events took place all over the country in an effort to reach out to the wider population, consult, receive contributions, and inform NDC discussions. The independents' sustained participation in the NDC proved substantively invaluable to the final document. The recommendations produced by the NDC placed a strong emphasis on human rights, accountability, social justice and equality before the law.[35] That said, some independents boycotted the NDC and continued their work outside the official political process, arguing that it was dominated by the country's traditional powerholders and offered no hope of genuine change.

The NDC completed work on January 21, 2014, after ten months of deliberations. It produced agreements on the federal nature of the Yemeni state, on power-sharing, and on the structure of the constitution-making process. Unfortunately, a year later, on January 22, 2015, following the takeover of the country's capital by Houthi militia in September 2014, the country's president, Abd Rabbuh Mansur Hadi, resigned after receiving the resignation of Prime Minister Khaled Bahah and his government. On March 25, 2015, Saudi Arabia launched air strikes in Yemen in support of President Hadi and against the Houthis.

More than six years later, the conflict continues, and Yemen's political and military landscape remains extremely fragmented. Talks since 2015 have only involved two armed actors, marginalizing women and civil society. Saudi Arabia proposed a ceasefire in early 2021 that was quickly rejected by the Houthi.[36] There are calls to involve women and civil society in any future talks, given their contributions to the NDC and their successes brokering local truces, opening roads, and freeing prisoners throughout the crisis.[37] But the path to a durable inclusive peace remains long and fraught.

With the exception of radical Islamic groups, the 2011 Implementation Mechanism and the national dialogue successfully kept many of the country's military and political actors engaged in the political process until the middle of 2014. In the challenging context of Yemeni politics and regional competition, this was a significant achievement.[38] Unfortunately, Yemeni political leaders did not ultimately use the transitional period and the national dialogue to genuinely negotiate the key challenges facing the country. The Yemeni National Dialogue Conference had seemingly clear goals: to discuss the structure of the constitution-making process, define the key principles to be included in the new constitution, and address questions of Saada (a predominantly Houthi region) and of the southern part of the country.[39] However, these were extremely contentious issues that had not been discussed adequately by the political and military leaders before the launch of the NDC. The political groundwork had therefore not been laid. National dialogues require commitment by the country's leadership to conduct inclusive negotiations, to resolve disputes, and to broker compromises. This commitment did not exist in Yemen.

Nonetheless, the NDC was a genuine effort to include women, youth, and civil society in a challenging political process. It was also a groundbreaking effort in a country that had not practiced inclusive politics before. It remains to be seen whether the outcomes of the national dialogue will inform future negotiations in Yemen and the new constitution. The NDC itself was, nonetheless, an unprecedented moment of free political expression, inclusive of multiple points of view. Importantly, it prevented the country's descent into war for more than two years: a noteworthy achievement in an extremely difficult situation.

Syria (2016–2020): The Civil Society Support Room

As the Arab Spring continued to unfold across the Middle East, Syrians similarly found themselves on the path to a civil war. Protestors demanded the removal of Syrian president Bashar al-Assad, and the government responded with violent suppression, including the use of chemical weapons. In March 2011, a civil war erupted among several factions. Over time, Russia, the United States, and Turkey began supporting various groups, and the civil war became a proxy struggle between powerful foreign nations. In the early stages of the Syrian conflict, the United Nations and the Arab League co-led peacemaking efforts through appointed special envoys, starting with the former UN secretary general Kofi Annan (February to August 2012), followed by Algerian diplomat Lakhdar Brahimi (August 2012 to May 2014). They were followed by Italian-Swedish diplomat Staffan de Mistura (July 2014) and then Norwegian diplomat Geir Pedersen (November 2018; as of 2021, Pedersen remains the UN special envoy for Syria). During these mediation attempts, the conflict raged on, killing hundreds of thousands of people and displacing millions.

Initially, UN special envoys Kofi Annan and Lakhdar Brahimi worked almost exclusively with the parties to the armed conflict and with the regional powers, placing little emphasis on civil society's involvement. They framed the conflict as an international one, believing its resolution required focusing on regional and international supporters of the conflict parties. Based on this logic, in June 2012, Annan convened the Action Group for Syria in Geneva, which consisted of China, France, Russia, the United States, the United Kingdom, Turkey, and the European Union, as well as a few Arab League member states. In what became known as Geneva I, negotiation efforts explicitly emphasized that peace required regional and international actors. The Geneva Communiqué also called for a ceasefire and outlined a transitional plan that was never implemented.

When Brahimi brought the parties together for the first time for the Geneva II meeting in early 2014, the talks broke down within a few days.[40] In advance of the Geneva II meetings, fifty Syrian women launched the Syrian Women's Initiative for Peace and Democracy (SWIPD) to influence the Geneva talks and protect women's rights. But when Geneva II launched ten days later, Brahimi was unwilling to consider any form of civil society presence in the talks.[41]

The next UN special envoy, Staffan de Mistura, recognized the importance of regional and international governments as well as civil society; he established the Women's Advisory Board (WAB) and the Civil Society Support Room (CSSR). The CSSR provides a physical space in the UN's compound in Geneva managed by Swisspeace, a practice-oriented peace research institute, and the Norwegian Centre for Conflict Resolution (NOREF). Here Syrian civil society could meet, advise the special envoy's team and the various UN agencies, engage with the Women's Advisory Board, and receive technical assistance as needed.[42] The aspiration was to influence the political process through interactions with the Office of the Special Envoy (OSE) and with the parties when Geneva talks took place.

To participate in the Civil Society Support Room, the participants had to be active members of civil society organizations or civilian initiatives and possess relevant technical expertise. Participation was based on a rotational system, with some civil society actors invited to several rounds to enable continuity of discussions and others rotated in to allow for greater inclusivity. There was an effort to ensure geographic and demographic representation among the participants. By December 2017, more than three hundred people had traveled to Geneva to attend CSSR rounds during intra-Syrian talks. In summer 2017, the CSSR began to hold regional meetings in Beirut, Gaziantep, and Amman in an effort to maintain engagement with civil society actors in between official rounds in Geneva.[43]

The main dilemma facing Syrian civil society actors resembled that of Yemeni civil society back in 2012–2013: whom to include and the extent of their influence. The first challenge facing the CSSR was the selection of its participants. For the CSSR to genuinely represent a wide variety of Syrian views and inform peace efforts accordingly, its participants had to come from diverse backgrounds. However, there is a natural bias toward actors that are "easily identifiable because they are well established, institutionalized, and accustomed to dealing with their international counterparts."[44] This has increased skepticism about the usefulness of the mechanism in transmitting local developments and opinions to the peace process. The CSSR lacks any Kurdish affiliation, for example, and CSOs working in opposition-held areas outnumber those coming from government-held areas.[45]

The second challenge was ensuring meaningful engagement. As much as the CSSR had the potential to be useful, the mere presence of civil society actors in the room proved insufficient.[46] The OSE found it difficult to engage with the participants in the CSSR while also maintaining the confidentiality of the official talks.[47] A group of Syrian human rights organizations, for example, published a statement in late 2017 arguing that the UN special envoy did not report fully in his briefings to the UN Security Council on the results of the CSSR consultations in Geneva, and that the CSSR participants were not adequately consulted ahead of time regarding the agenda for the meetings.[48] When the Syrian peace process stalled, civil society actors questioned the purpose of their participation in the CSSR; their networks back home also began to doubt whether participation had become merely symbolic. CSSR participants had to choose between prioritizing urgent humanitarian and civilian protection work on the ground and participating from the sidelines of a stalled process delivering few tangible benefits to civilians in Syria; at best, they hoped to make a long-term contribution to the resolution of the conflict.[49] Some groups pressured CSSR participants to take a particular stance; for example, "a strong movement in Gaziantep was initiated against the presence of civil society in the talks, claiming that . . . civil society should defend the opposition delegation and adopt the 'revolution narrative.' "[50]

It remains to be seen how the CSSR and the WAB will contribute to genuine participation in the peace process when and if meaningful negotiations eventually occur. However, in an extremely challenging conflict, the CSSR provided one mechanism through which civil society could engage in the conversation and develop valuable networks and skills.[51] (Note that a similar mechanism was created in Yemen in mid-2018, the Yemeni Women's Technical Advisory Group).[52] The contribution of these mechanisms demonstrates the value of inclusive approaches, even though the conflict rages on.

Today, new technologies facilitate broader participation; for example, "The Syrian Women Advisory Board and the Technical Advisory Group for Yemen have been able to meet more regularly through online platforms and have engaged with the offices of the respective UN Special Envoys as well as with the main protagonists in the conflict."[53] Those advocating for inclusion do well to make use of these tools for engagement.

Libya (2018–2020): Unfinished Inclusive Peacemaking

We now turn to Libya. Since the fall of Muammar Gaddafi's regime, the security situation in Libya has deteriorated, resulting in major clashes and loss of civilian lives. UN envoys' attempts to establish a transitional governance process culminated in the signed Libyan Political Agreement (LPA) in 2015, but the accord was never implemented. In late 2018 and early 2019, under the leadership of Acting Special Representative of the Secretary-General for Libya Stephanie Williams, the UN-backed Government of National Accord, led by Prime Minister Fayez al-Serraj, and the rival administration in the east, supported by General Khalifa Haftar, agreed to hold elections and end the country's eight-year transition; attendees at a meeting in Palermo, Italy, noted that "no space was made for Libyan women to contribute their input, perspectives, and stories to decision-making."[54]

In a hopeful sign, the October 2020 signing of a ceasefire opened the door to negotiations under the auspices of the UN Special Mission in Libya (UNSMIL). Since the signing of the ceasefire, the Libyan Political Dialogue Forum (LPDF) has created a road map for advancing a comprehensive peace.[55] The LPDF brings together "75 participants[,] Libyan women and men representing the full social and political spectrum of the Libyan society"; it includes elected representatives of the warring factions who were signatories to the LPA as well as representatives of diverse political and geographic interests, youth, women, ethnic groups, and tribes.[56] The LPDF met several times, virtually and in person, successfully advancing progress toward a unified Libyan government, selecting an interim prime minister and Presidency Council in February 2021, and has begun planning for December 2021 elections.[57] In 2020, a series of broadly participatory digital dialogues augmented outreach as well, particularly engaging youth.[58] UN special envoy Ján Kubiš met and pledged to work "very closely" with women, youth, and civil society activists to prepare for elections and beyond.[59]

In March 2021, the interim government under the leadership of prime minister Abdelhamid Dbeibah was sworn in. The government backed away from an initial pledge that 30 percent of ministerial posts would go to women, and five women were among thirty-one appointees, including Libya's first female foreign and justice ministers.[60] While there is hope for the future of Libya, there is still substantial instability.

The seeds for a more participatory, transparent peacebuilding process were planted years before the convening of the LPDF. In September 2017, the UN Special Representative of the Secretary General (SRSG), Ghassan Salamé, issued the UN Plan of Action of Libya, which proposed negotiations among the main parties to amend the LPA; a Libya-wide inclusive dialogue process, called the National Conference, offering ordinary Libyans the opportunity to discuss their visions for the future of the country; amending and adopting a national constitution; and holding presidential and parliamentary elections.[61] The meetings among the main parties, which took place in Italy and Abu Dhabi, did not include women or civil society. However, through the National Conference, civil society, women, and young people would be able to express their opinions.

In April 2018, the Centre for Humanitarian Dialogue (HD Centre)—a private diplomacy organization based in Switzerland—launched local consultations across Libya, as the first phase of the National Conference process. The SRSG and major Libyan stakeholders collaborated closely with the HD Centre to ensure that the dialogues engaged ordinary Libyans and segments of society previously excluded from the elite political dialogues. In total, seventy-seven consultations were held over fourteen weeks in forty-three locations in Libya and with diaspora groups abroad (in Tunis, Cairo, Istanbul, and London). In some cases, multiple meetings occurred in the same city in order to include a variety of groups excluded from the political process. To encourage women's free participation, nine events were open only to women. In total, 25 percent of the participants were women. Some consultations also targeted youth groups. The stalled political transition and elite unwillingness to change the status quo created an opportunity for these smaller consultations and the larger National Conference to give Libyans a voice and to participate in the political process. These consultations produced a National Charter to be considered in the larger national conference.[62]

Participants in the National Conference, to be held April 14–16, 2019, in Libya, would decide whether to endorse the National Charter produced through the consultative process. The conference participants would also adopt a road map to conclude the transitional period, which included elections. The National Conference participants could also offer recommendations on how to deal with the draft constitution produced by the Constitutional Drafting Assembly.[63]

In his briefing to the Security Council in January 2019, UN special envoy Salamé acknowledged the risks of the peace process. He stated, "There will be those who seek to undermine the National Conference and its outcomes; particularly individuals hoping to delay elections so they may remain in their seats. Without the concerted support of the international community, spoilers will sabotage the political advancement and undo any progress made."[64] In April 2019, a few days before the National Conference was to convene, fighting escalated as the Libyan National Army, led by General Haftar, attacked Tripoli. As a result, the National Conference did not take place. Fast- forward, and we can see how greater transparency and a broader, more participatory consultative effort have potentially, created a foundation for peace.

Middle Belt of Nigeria (2013–2017): Parallel Processes

When Track I deliberations remain closed to civil society participation, Track II and other multitrack processes offer a pathway for engagement and community building. When these dialogues work in parallel with official negotiations, participants amplify their influence. The following example of an inclusive local process in Nigeria demonstrates how these dialogues can unfold.

From 2013 to 2017, the HD Centre facilitated intercommunal dialogues in the Middle Belt of Nigeria, starting with eight communities in the city of Jos, the capital of Plateau State; in southern Kaduna, among twenty-nine communities; and in Southern Plateau state, with fifty-six communities. These dialogues focused on preventing violence around local elections and between farmer and herder communities. The dialogues resulted in jointly drafted agreements endorsed by the communities. The agreements called upon federal, state and local governments and local leaders, including religious and business leaders, to contribute to implementation.

Representatives of all communities were invited, and extensive preparatory discussions took place with the leaders of the communities and various groups, including women's groups. In Jos, the model of the dialogue emerged after lengthy engagement with eight communities in the city. Each community was represented by seven delegates, one for each social group: traditional leaders, religious leaders, herders, farmers, women, youth, and persons of standing within the community. The dialogue also included an official from the state government and one from the local government. The agenda covered a number of issues, including religious intolerance, discriminatory governance, displacement of people, compensation for lives and property lost in the violence, and resource clashes between herders and farmers, among others.[65]

The effort to ensure women's participation started in the preparatory process. In preparation for the Jos dialogue, women's groups met regularly to discuss marketplace networks, education, or religious affairs, and were consulted on the format of women's participation in the dialogue and on the content of the dialogue. They agreed that local women would be involved in the talks with the leaders from the various communities, but would also hold separate talks involving only women from all of the communities. To identify the women and groups that would be interested in the two approaches—participation in the main process but also in a separate, women-only track—the facilitators gathered the various local groups for preparatory talks. The goals were to create the agenda for discussions and to form a steering committee that would organize meetings throughout the process and maintain contact with participants and constituencies.[66]

Two parallel processes took place over a period of several months, resulting in two declarations under which communities agreed to work together to prevent future violence. The agreements recognized the need to take action locally to address the damage the conflict had inflicted on their societies, and to do things differently in the future. They agreed not to wait for the government to take action to reduce violence, but to take responsibility for doing so. They established implementation mechanisms, sometimes in the form of local NGOs carrying out early warning work, in which women were active participants. The declaration produced by the women's dialogue focused more explicitly on the gendered aspects of local history and the conflict, including sexual violence. Additionally, the women agreed to continue working more closely to encourage trust-building among themselves and across their communities, and to remain active in conflict prevention efforts.[67]

The processes in southern Kaduna and southern Plateau did not include separate tracks for women but ensured more expansive participation of women and youth in the wider community dialogue. Agreements related to the rebuilding of churches and mosques; the establishment of tension management mechanisms that included positions for women; the setting up of a group of female peace monitors; and provisions on women's access to credit and skills training.

Sustaining the gains achieved and the networks created during the dialogues remains a challenge. One approach has been to officially include women in monitoring the agreements and all aspects of the implementation process. Their participation was supported by the research finding that "civil society monitors may offer local knowledge, access to communities, as well as a capacity and expertise in monitoring. Civil society may also contribute to the legitimacy of monitoring and verification because of the credibility they have stemming from their status as non-partisan or bipartisan."[68]

These local dialogues demonstrate the crucial importance of including women from the very beginning: in designing the dialogue, participating in the dialogue, drafting the agreement, and implementing the agreement. When this happens, women influence the process consistently and reflect their concerns in the content of the agenda and any resulting agreements. Rather than trying to interject community participation at certain key points, a local, intercommunal focus was the point of departure. External factors were less able to disrupt these community-grounded events. As facilitator, the HD Centre focused on interests of local actors and explained to them the benefits of an inclusive approach. This inclusive orientation from the beginning helped the group continue work regardless of the external factors that derailed some other attempts. These examples help make visible some of the local challenges and possibilities for inclusion. Working toward more inclusive processes, however, also requires understanding the larger geopolitical context.

Geopolitical Fragmentation and Inclusive Peace Processes

In the past decade, those supporting peacebuilding efforts have worked in an increasingly constrained political space. Diffused authority internationally and rising geopolitical rivalry have led to paralysis within the UN Security Council around major conflicts, including those in Syria, Yemen, and Libya. It has also impeded response to mass violence. Disagreements also persist between regional and international powers on the management and ultimate goal of peace processes. Specifically, the disagreement focuses on (1) the ingredients to be included in a final agreement, (2) the relevance of universal values and principles in peacemaking strategies, (3) the choice of mediator, and (4) the definition of the conflict parties that can legitimately participate in a peace process.

The division within the international community is reflected in a normative polarization between those supporting democracy and human rights as prerequisites for sustainable peace and alternative models that emphasize stability and a strong state as requirements for peace and security. In civil wars, for example, "the goal of stabilization has displaced the quest for democratization."[69] When conflict endures, the stability promised by authoritarian approaches can appeal to local populations as well as to elites who can retain power. The absence of political (and even local) will to invest in long-term interventions supporting a form of liberal or positive peace that includes rights results in less ambitious and far-reaching agreements.

Many recent peace agreements, for example, have weak implementation provisions and do not focus on democratic institutions and human rights protections. Peacemaking is moving away from comprehensive agreements, which used to provide for an ambitious transformative political agenda as well as a strong third-party role in their implementation.[70] Contemporary peace processes produce narrower deals that are often accompanied by international missions with a "light footprint." Agreements are often subnational, addressing only a few of the issues linked to the conflict; many include only some of the conflict parties, hoping to incorporate the rest gradually; they focus on ceasefires; they may usher in transitional political processes meant to decide the important social and political issues facing the country; often they lack serious implementation provisions. In sum, many of these peace processes are far less ambitious in scope.

Great-power rivalries have also led to an increasing number of mediation actors and a fragmentation of conflict parties. In contemporary peace processes, for example, the lead mediation actor may be the United Nations, a regional institution, a government or a group of governments, a private actor or NGO, or a combination of these. Furthermore, as a process evolves, the relationship among the various actors as well as the role of the mediating parties can change as the negotiations evolve. As a result, the strategies women's groups and civil society use to influence peace processes need to be flexible and constantly adapted.

To manage the challenges of fragmentation and great-power competition, peacemakers increasingly promote a multitrack approach at national and/or subnational levels as well as in parallel among different sets of actors. A multitrack strategy helps official negotiation processes develop stronger links with dialogues among unofficial representatives of conflict parties and of civil society actors.[71]

Challenges for Community Stakeholders

Geopolitical realities create and compound operational dilemmas for civil society and women's groups eager to contribute to peace processes. When official negotiation tracks are dormant, ceremonial, or simply unproductive for many years, possibilities for inclusion remain unclear. What would people be included in? What results would engagement yield? Advocates of inclusive approaches ask: How much should be invested in stalled formal negotiations given that they can last for many years and produce agreements lacking transformational ambitions? Might energy be better invested in focusing on other tracks, such as local dialogues and building civil society coalitions that may produce concrete results in the medium term? Given the reality of limited resources for most of these actors, these are important questions.

Furthermore, futile participation in formal processes has long-term consequences. As Hellmüller and Zahar write, civil society's "continuous inclusion into a stalled process risks sending a wrong impression of progress and legitimacy and may mask fundamental challenges instead of addressing them."[72] Elites sometimes retain power and preserve structural inequalities while telling participants they have voice. Eventually, participants see whether their participation leads to any shifts. Participating in ongoing consultation without tangible results, they may respond with anger or despair. Burdened with the struggles of daily life in war zones, people may be less willing to engage in future forums and reflect that prior ones yielded unsatisfying or no outcomes.

The need for productive engagement in both the short term and the long term urges us to engage with an additional dilemma; how can women's groups and civil society identify productive entry points? Multiple alternatives of varying effectiveness exist and may change as the process progresses. Some of the actors leading mediation efforts may not have the capacity or political will to consider the recommendations and advice of civil society. To be heard, civil society actors may need to target their message and methodology to different actors and be willing to adjust their strategies along the way. For example, the openings for discussing human rights issues with a UN mediation team may be different from those available for discussion with a team from the Gulf Cooperation Council, an East African Community team, or an NGO team. These varied communication efforts certainly improve links between political and military leaders, on one hand, and civil society, women, and human rights activists, on the other. Achieving this requires enormous time and energy, not just from mediators but also from war-weary communities.

To these challenges add the constant challenge of selecting participants and legitimizing participation. Questions around criteria leading to the selection of participants, the credentials of participants, and the extent to which they actually represent a constituency remain sensitive and unresolved. Simply having civil society members seated at a table does not guarantee their voices will be heard. In these forums, there are privileged ways of speaking and conceptualizing problems/solutions. When forums value only comments that align with conceptions espoused by elites, participants can remain pawns in a structure.[73] When their personal lives and responses have weight, a shift has occurred. Until then, marginalization persists, even if representatives are seated at the table. Working with and through allies can be a valuable pathway to deeper inclusion. In certain contexts, elite members will be the most effective advocates for women and civil society. These relationships need to be cultivated. In sum, civil society and women sometimes must decide whether to invest time and resources advocating for their engagement in Track I negotiation processes that may lead to modest peace agreements, or to invest in Track II efforts where they face less resistance. Cultivating relationships that cross tracks remains key to their long-term influence.

Conclusion

In the two decades since the passage of Resolution 1325 and related resolutions, many UN special envoys have advocated for more inclusive peace processes. UN involvement has also contributed to the addition of gender provisions in a number of agreements.[74] The inclusion attempts in Yemen, Syria, Libya, and Nigeria provided examples of how these efforts can unfold and the kinds of challenges they face. Their inability to bring an end to violence may reflect national and geopolitical fractures more than the failure of inclusion as a vital component of peacebuilding. The veto power of the permanent five members of the UN Security Council limits liberal democratic nations from more fully supporting these efforts. Proxy wars between world powers often fuel these conflicts, leaving those on the ground with less control over the futures of their countries. Women and civil society groups can grow weary of participation in initiatives that lead nowhere and do little to lessen the struggles of daily life. Given the complexities of violent conflicts, outsiders eager to help may be better advised to support local initiatives rather than launching their own well-intentioned interventions.

In many ways, the image of a small room of stakeholders agreeing to terms is now an antiquated one. This structure is less feasible in an increasingly globalized, post–Cold War context. Today's interventions need to adapt to the fragmentation of groups and interests, with outside interveners supporting civil-society-initiated efforts. Unfortunately, the contribution civil society actors are able to make depends upon the political openings and space available and made available through advocacy, and the political will of the armed conflict parties to include them.

Those most affected by violence have the right to a seat at any table discussing their future. Framing such participants as "useful" or "good" creates the opportunity to exclude them when someone questions their utility or reframes them as spoilers. We cannot always anticipate the role these groups will play; not all women have feminist agendas, and not every civil society group will advocate for the greater good. They are political stakeholders nonetheless. Furthermore, the role of these groups is not static.

Despite the challenges, civil society actors and women's groups should seek participation in the top-level negotiations (Track I), even if progress is limited. While such engagement entails opportunity costs, this long-term strategy can help women's issues to be properly considered in agreements. While advocating for this inclusion, strong allies must promote their causes at the negotiation table. The cultivation of allies will always remain key to success.

While the national-level negotiation remains a crucial component of a long-term strategy, engagement in other dialogue platforms (Track II) can deliver valuable results. Linking formal negotiating tables with parallel dialogue tracks and inclusive forms of peacemaking remains critical. Serious questions remain as to whether the various tracks reinforce or detract from each other, and whether they create too great a coordination burden. The advantage of the multitrack approach, however, is that it gives flexibility to the main table to explore issues the official parties may be reluctant to include definitively in the formal agenda. It also allows the main table to engage excluded groups and bring them closer to the talks, including armed groups, civil society organizations, and other relevant social groups. Finally, multitrack processes allow the main table to maintain confidentiality on some issues while adopting a transparent approach on others. Multitrack processes lack the ambition of unified processes and comprehensive solutions, but they retain flexibility and the ability to separate tracks. To be powerful players, civil society organizations must continue diversifying their strategies and identifying where they can make tangible contributions. While the national-level negotiation remains a crucial component of a long-term strategy, engagement in other dialogue platforms can deliver valuable results.

Notes

1. See UN Resolutions 1261, 1265, 1296, 1314.
2. Cobb, Federman, and Castel 2019.
3. Whitfield 2019, 6.
4. Institute for Inclusive Security 2009, 2013; O'Reilly, Ó Súilleabháin, and Paffenholz 2015.
5. Krause, Krause, and Bränfors 2018.
6. Hudson et al. 2008–2009.
7. Enloe 2013.
8. See Enloe 2013.
9. Harlander et al. 2019.
10. Paffenholz et al. 2016.
11. O'Reilly, Ó Súilleabháin, and Paffenholz 2015.
12. Paffenholz, Kew, and Wanis-St. John 2006.
13. Council on Foreign Relations 2020; Jalal 2019; Joshi, Quinn, and Regan 2015; Krznaric 1999.
14. Paffenholz 2014; Institute for Inclusive Security 2013; Bell and Forster 2019.
15. Hellmüller and Zahar 2019.
16. Paffenholz 2014.
17. UN Women and CFR 2019.
18. Paffenholz et al. 2016.
19. Enloe 2013, 6.
20. Hudson et al. 2008–2009.
21. There has been conflicting data on whether women's participation leads to greater gender provisions. One study analyzing ninety-eight peace agreements across fifty-five countries between 2000 and 2016 found that agreements are likely to include gender provisions when they result from processes that enabled women's participation. These agreements

highlighted issues that would otherwise have been left out, such as the protection of displaced persons, sexual violence, and social justice. But Bell (2015) and Anderson (2016) found that presence of gender provisions in settlements correlates with heavy international involvement, rather than advocacy by women' groups. Dayal and Christien (2020) conclude from their research that gender provisions do not correlate with women's engagement.

22. Dayal and Christien 2019.
23. Dayal and Christien 2020.
24. Papagianni 2017; Verweijen 2019; Cuhadar 2019.
25. Dayal and Christien 2020.
26. Ragin and Becker 1992.
27. Trahan 2020.
28. United Nations Peacemaker 2011.
29. International Crisis Group 2011.
30. International Crisis Group 2012.
31. Security Council Resolution 2051, June 12, 2012, article 16.
32. For a breakdown of the division of seats among the participating constituencies in the National Dialogue, see Secretariat of the Yemeni National Dialogue Conference 2014, 6.
33. Technical Committee 2012, 15–17.
34. Secretariat of the Yemeni National Dialogue Conference 2014, 17.
35. Secretariat of the Yemeni National Dialogue Conference 2013–2014.
36. Middle East Eye 2021.
37. Crisis Group 2021.
38. Day 2014.
39. Office of the President of Yemen 2012, articles 3.2.a and 3.2.b.
40. Hellmüller and Zahar 2019.
41. Alzoubi 2017, 1–2.
42. Swisspeace n.d.
43. Hellmüller and Zahar 2018, 5.
44. Hellmüller and Zaher 2019.
45. Alzoubi 2017, 2, 4.
46. Hellmüller and Zahar 2018, 4.
47. Hellmüller and Zahar 2018, 4.
48. Al-Kawakbi Center for Transitional Justice and Human Rights et al. 2017.
49. Hellmüller and Zahar 2018, 3–4.
50. Alzoubi 2017, 4.
51. Turkmani and Theros 2019.
52. Whitfield 2019, 6.
53. UN Women et al. 2020.
54. Bel and Warren 2018.
55. UNSMIL 2020.
56. UNSMIL n.d.; Williams and Feltman 2021.
57. UNSMIL n.d.
58. Williams and Feltman 2021.
59. UNSMIL 2021.
60. TRT World 2021.
61. Miller 2018.
62. ReliefWeb 2018.
63. United Nations 2019b.
64. United Nations 2019a.

65. Centre for Humanitarian Dialogue 2020.

66. Centre for Humanitarian Dialogue n.d.

67. Centre for Humanitarian Dialogue n.d.

68. Ross 2017, 4.

69. Howard and Stark 2017–2018.

70. For similar conclusions, see Buchhold et al. 2018, 6.

71. Buchhold et al. 2018, 6.

72. Hellmüuller and Zahar 2019, 87.

73. Cobb 2013.

74. See Anderson 2016. See also Bell 2015.

Bibliography

Al-Kawakbi Center for Transitional Justice and Human Rights et al. 2017. "Statement by Syrian Human Rights Organizations on the Invitation to the Civil Society Support Room in Geneva." December 5. https://syriaaccountability.org/updates/2017/12/05/statement-by-syrian-human-rights-organizations-on-the-invitation-to-the-civil-society-support-room-in-geneva/.

Alzoubi, Zedoun. 2017. "Syrian Civil Society During the Peace Talks in Geneva: Role and Challenges." *New England Journal of Public Policy* 29, no. 1: 1–4. https://scholarworks.umb.edu/nejpp/vol29/iss1/11/.

Anderson, Miriam. 2016. *Windows of Opportunity: How Women Seize Peace Negotiations for Political Change*. New York: Oxford University Press.

Arendt, Hannah. 1998. *The Human Condition*. Chicago: University of Chicago Press.

Bel, Amber, and Michael James Warren. 2018. "Libya Talks Embody Missing Participation of Women in Peace Processes." IPI Global Observatory. December 5. https://reliefweb.int/report/libya/libya-talks-embody-missing-participation-women-peace-processes.

Bell, Christine. 2015. "Text and Context: Evaluating Peace Agreements for Their 'Gender Perspective.'" UN Women Political Settlements Research Programme, New York. https://www.unwomen.org/en/digital-library/publications/2017/8/evaluating-peace-agreements-for-their-gender-perspective.

Bell, Christine, and Robert Forster. 2019. "Women and the Renegotiation of Transitional Governance Arrangements." PA-X Report, Spotlight Series. Edinburgh Global Justice Academy, University of Edinburgh. https://www.politicalsettlements.org/wp-content/uploads/2019/08/PA-X-Spotlight-Interim-Power-Sharing-Digital.pdf.

Buchhold, Christina, Jonathan Harlander, Sabrina Quamber, and Oyvind Ege. 2018. "The End of the Big Peace? Opportunities for Mediation." Oslo Forum Meeting Report, Centre for Humanitarian Dialogue. https://www.africaportal.org/publications/oslo-forum-2018-end-big-peace-opportunities-mediation/.

Burton, John. 1997. "Needs Theory." In *Violence Explained: The Sources of Conflict, Violence, and Crime and Their Prevention*, 32–40. New York: Manchester University Press.

Centre for Humanitarian Dialogue. n.d. "Including Women in Peace Processes at Local Levels: Reflections from HD's Experiences." Internal document, in author's files.

Cobb, Sara. 2013. *Speaking of Violence: The Politics and Poetics of Narrative Dynamics in Conflict Resolution*. New York: Oxford University Press.

Cobb, Sara, Sarah Federman, and Alison Castel. 2019. *Introduction to Conflict Resolution: Discourses and Dynamics*. Milton Keynes: Rowman & Littlefield International.

Council on Foreign Relations. 2020. "The Northern Ireland Peace Agreement." March 5. cfr.org/backgrounder/northern-ireland-peace-process.

Crisis Group. 2021. "The Case for More Inclusive—and More Effective—Peacemaking in Yemen." March 18. https://www.crisisgroup.org/middle-east-north-africa/gulf-and-arabian-peninsula/yemen/221-case-more-inclusive-and-more-effective-peacemaking-yemen.

Çuhader, Esra. 2019. Inclusion and the Kurdish 'Resolution Process in Turkey In *Inclusion in Peace Processes*, edited by Andy Carl, 80–83. London: Accord. https://www.c-r.org/accord/inclusion-peace-processes.

Day, Stephen W. 2014. "The 'Non-Conclusion' of Yemen's National Dialogue." *Foreign Policy*, January 27. https://foreignpolicy.com/2014/01/27/the-non-conclusion-of-yemens-national-dialogue/.

Dayal, Anjali, and Agathe Christien. 2020. "Women's Participation in Informal Peace Processes." *Global Governance: A Review of Multilateralism and International Organizations* 26, no. 1: 69–98.

Dayal, Anjali, and Agathe Christien. 2019. "Tracking Women's Participation in Informal Peace Processes." Georgetown Institute for Women, Peace and Security. https://giwps.georgetown.edu/resource/tracking-womens-participation-in-informal-peace-processes/.

Enloe, Cynthia. 2013. *Seriously! Investigating Crashes and Crises as if Women Mattered.* Berkeley: University of California Press.

Harlander, Jonathan, Sabrina Quamber, Chizitera Njoku, Eve Cheri Krassner, and Spencer McMurray. 2019. "Rebooting Mediation: Connecting Tracks, Processes and People." Oslo Forum Meeting Report, Centre for Humanitarian Dialogue. https://www.africaportal.org/publications/oslo-forum-2019-rebooting-mediation-connecting-tracks-processes-and-people/.

Hellmüller, Sara, and Marie-Joelle Zahar. 2019. "UN-Led Mediation in Syria and Civil Society: Inclusion in a Multi-Layered Conflict." In *Inclusion in Peace Processes*, edited by Andy Carl, 84–87. London: Accord. https://rc-services-assets.s3.eu-west-1.amazonaws.com/s3fs-public/Navigating_inclusion_in_peace_processes_Accord_Issue_28.pdf.

Hellmüller, Sara, and Marie-Joelle Zahar. 2018. "Against the Odds: Civil Society in the Intra-Syrian Talks." International Peace Institute. March. https://www.ipinst.org/2018/03/against-the-odds-civil-society-intra-syrian-talks.

Howard, Lise Morje, and Alexandra Stark. 2017–2018. "How Civil Wars End: The International System, Norms and the Role of External Actors." *International Security* 42, no. 3: 127–171. https://www.researchgate.net/publication/322781299_How_Civil_Wars_End_The_International_System_Norms_and_the_Role_of_External_Actors.

Hudson, Valerie M., Mary Caprioli, Bonnie Ballif-Spanvill, Rose McDermott, and Chad F. Emmett. 2008–2009. "The Heart of the Matter: The Security of Women and the Security of States." *International Security* 33, no. 3: 7–45. https://www.belfercenter.org/publication/heart-matter-security-women-and-security-states.

Institute for Inclusive Security. 2013. "Nine Models for Inclusion of Civil Society in Peace Processes." July. https://www.inclusivesecurity.org/wp-content/uploads/2013/11/9-Models-for-Inclusive-Peace-Processes-w-footers.pdf.

Institute for Inclusive Security. 2009. "Bringing Women into Peace Negotiations." Strategies for Policymakers, no. 2. https://www.inclusivesecurity.org/publication/strategies-for-policymakers-bringing-women-into-peace-negotiations/.

International Crisis Group. 2012. "Yemen: Enduring Conflicts, Threatened Transition." Middle East Report no. 125. July 3. https://www.crisisgroup.org/middle-east-north-africa/gulf-and-arabian-peninsula/yemen/yemen-enduring-conflicts-threatened-transition.

International Crisis Group. 2011. "Breaking Point? Yemen's Southern Question." Middle East Report no. 114. October 20. https://www.crisisgroup.org/middle-east-north-africa/gulf-and-arabian-peninsula/yemen/breaking-point-yemen-s-southern-question.

Jabri, Vivienne. 1996. *Discourses on Violence: Conflict Analysis Reconsidered.* Manchester: Manchester University Press.

Jalal, Ibrahim. 2019. "Yemen's Peace Process: The Hodeida Agreement That Never Was?" Middle East Institute. September 16. https://www.mei.edu/publications/yemens-peace-process-hodeida-agreement-never-was.

Joshi, Madhav, Jason Michael Quinn, and Patrick M. Regan. 2015. "Annualized Implementation Data on Comprehensive Intrastate Peace Accords, 1989–2012." *Journal of Peace Research* 52: 551–562. https://peaceaccords.nd.edu/accord/accra-peace-agreement.

Krause, J., W. Krause, and P. Bränfors. 2018. "Women's Participation in Peace Negotiations and the Durability of Peace." *International Interactions* 44, no. 6: 985–1016. https://pure.uva.nl/ws/files/26826416/Krause.pdf.

Krznaric, Roman. 1999. "Civil and Uncivil Actors in the Guatemalan Peace Process." *Bulletin of Latin American Research* 18, no. 1: 1–16 . https://doi.org/10.1016/S0261-3050(98)00001-1

Kurtzleben, Danielle. 2020. "What the 'Wall of Moms' Protests Say About Motherhood, Race in America." NPR. July 28. https://www.npr.org/2020/07/28/896174019/what-the-wall-of-moms-protests-say-about-motherhood-race-in-america.

Middle East Eye. 2021. "Yemen War: Saudi Arabia Proposes Peace Initiative but Houthis Say Little New in It." March 22. https://www.middleeasteye.net/news/yemen-saudi-arabia-offers-houthi-rebels-ceasefire-end-fighting.

Miller, Elissa. 2018. "One Year Later the UN Action Plan for Libya Is Dead." Atlantic Council. September 17. https://www.atlanticcouncil.org/blogs/menasource/one-year-later-the-un-action-plan-for-libya-is-dead/.

Office of the President of Yemen. 2012. "Presidential Decree No 30 (2012) on the Technical Committee for the National Dialogue Conference." In author's files.

O'Reilly, Marie, Andrea Ó Súilleabháin, and Thania Paffenholz. 2015. "Reimagining Peacemaking: Women's Roles in Peace Processes." International Peace Institute. June. https://www.ipinst.org/wp-content/uploads/2015/06/IPI-E-pub-Reimagining-Peacemaking.pdf.

Paffenholz, Thania. 2014. "Broadening Participation in Peace Processes: Dilemmas and Options for Mediators." Mediation Practice Series, no. 4. Centre for Humanitarian Dialogue. June. https://www.inclusivepeace.org/wp-content/uploads/2021/05/paper-broadening-participation-peace-processes-en.pdf.

Paffenholz, Thania, Daren Kew, and Anthony Wanis-St. John. 2006. "Civil Society and Peace Negotiations: Why, Whether and How They Could Be Involved." Background paper, Oslo Forum. Centre for Humanitarian Dialogue. https://gsdrc.org/document-library/civil-society-and-peace-negotiations-why-whether-and-how-they-could-be-involved/#:~:text=Participation%20of%20civil%20society%20gives,sustainability%20of%20the%20peace%20agreement.&text=It%20is%20necessary%20to%20analyse,solution%20to%20fit%20the%20process.

Paffenholz, Thania, Nick Ross, Steven Dixon, Anna-Lena Schluchter, and Jacqui True. 2016. "Making Women Count—Not Just Counting Women: Assessing Women's Inclusion and Influence on Peace Negotiations." Inclusive Peace and Transition Initiative, Graduate Institute of International and Development Studies, Geneva, and UN Women. April. https://www.unwomen.org/en/digital-library/publications/2017/5/making-women-count-not-just-counting-women.

Papagianni, Katia. 2017. "Human Rights Issues and Dilemmas in Contemporary Peace Mediation." In *Human Rights and Conflict Resolution: Bridging the Theoretical and Practical Divide*, edited by Claudia Fuentes Julia and Paula Drumond, 61–77. London: Routledge. https://www.academia.edu/36583206/Human_Rights_and_Conflict_Resolution_Bridging_the_Theoretical_and_Practical_Divide.

Power, Samantha. 2019. *The Education of an Idealist: A Memoir*. New York: HarperCollins.

Ragin, Charles C., and Howard S. Becker. 1992. *What Is a Case? Exploring the Foundations of Social Inquiry*. Cambridge: Cambridge University Press.

ReliefWeb. 2018. "The Libyan National Conference Process—Final Report, November 2018 [EN/AR]—Libya." https://reliefweb.int/report/libya/libyan-national-conference-process-final-report-november-2018-enar.

Ross, Nicholas. 2017. "Civil Society's Role in Monitoring and Verifying Peace Agreements: Seven Lessons from International Experience." Graduate Institute Geneva. https://repository.graduateinstitute.ch/record/295150.

Rustad, Siri Aas, Gudrun Østby, and Ragnhild Nordås. 2016. "Artisanal Mining, Conflict, and Sexual Violence in Eastern DRC." *The Extractive Industries and Society* 3, no. 2: 475–484. https://www.prio.org/Publications/Publication/?x=9133.

Secretariat of the Yemeni National Dialogue Conference. 2014. "A Year in Dialogue." February. In author's files.

Secretariat of the Yemeni National Dialogue Conference. 2013–2014. "Final Communiqué of the National Dialogue Conference, Sanaa 2013–14." http://www.pdf-yemen.com/PDF/Democra tic/NDC%20English2.pdf.

Swisspeace. n.d. "Civil Society Support Room." https://www.swisspeace.ch/projects/mandate/ civil-society-support-room.

Technical Committee. 2012. "Report of the Technical Committee to Prepare for the Comprehensive National Dialogue Conference." December 12. In author's files.

Trahan, Jennifer. 2020. *Existing Legal Limits to Security Council Veto Power in the Face of Atrocity Crimes.* Cambridge: Cambridge University Press.

TRT World. 2021. "Libya's New Interim Government Sworn In." March 16. https://www.trtworld. com/africa/libya-s-new-interim-government-sworn-in-45035.

True, J., and Y. Riveros-Morales. 2019. "Towards Inclusive Peace: Analysing Gender-Sensitive Peace Agreements 2000–2016." *International Political Science Review* 40, no. 1: 23–40. https:// doi.org/10.1177/0192512118808608.

Turkmani, Rim, and Marika Theros. 2019. "A Process in Its Own Right: The Syrian Civil Society Support Room." Conflict Research Programme, London School of Economics and Political Science. http://eprints.lse.ac.uk/101034.

UN Security Council. 2019. "Report of the Secretary-General on Women Peace and Security." S/ 2019/800. https://www.securitycouncilreport.org/atf/cf/%7B65BFCF9B-6D27-4E9C-8CD3- CF6E4FF96FF9%7D/s_2019_800.pdf.

UN Women. 2012. "Women's Participation in Peace Negotiations: Connections Between Presence and Influence." https://reliefweb.int/sites/reliefweb.int/files/resources/03AWomenP eaceNeg.pdf.

UN Women and CFR. 2019. "Women's Participation in Peace Processes." UN Women and Council on Foreign Relations. https://www.cfr.org/womens-participation-in-peace-processes/.

UN Women and UN DPPA. 2020. "COVID-19 and Conflict: Advancing Women's Meaningful Participation in Ceasefires and Peace Processes." Policy Brief No. 19. UN Women and UN Department of Political and Peacebuilding Affairs. https://peacemaker.un.org/sites/peacema ker.un.org/files/Policy%20Brief%20No19_COVID-19%20and%20Conflict_August2020.pdf.

United Nations. 2019a. "Remarks of SRSG Ghassan Salamé to the United Nations Security Council on the Situation in Libya." January 18. https://unsmil.unmissions.org/remarks-srsg- ghassan-salam%C3%A9-united-nations-security-council-situation-libya-0.

United Nations. 2019b. "Remarks of SRSG Ghassan Salamé to the United Nations Security Council on the Situation in Libya." March 20. https://dppa.un.org/en/remarks-of-srsg-ghas san-salame-to-united-nations-security-council-situation-libya-20-march-2019.

United Nations Peacemaker. 2011. "Agreement on the Implementation Mechanism on the Transition Process in Yemen in Accordance with the Initiative of the Gulf Cooperation Council (GCC)." May 12. http://peacemaker.un.org/yemen-transition-mechanism2011.

UNSMIL. 2021. "Transcript of the Opening Remarks of the Special Envoy for Libya, Jan Kubis in the Virtual Meeting of LPDF—Verbatim." March 27. https://unsmil.unmissions.org/transcr ipt-opening-remarks-special-envoy-libya-jan-kubis-virtual-meeting-lpdf-verbatim.

UNSMIL. 2020. "For the Preparatory Phase of a Comprehensive Solution." Libya Political Dialogue Forum. https://unsmil.unmissions.org/sites/default/files/lpdf_-_roadmap_final_en g_0.pdf.

UNSMIL. n.d. "Libyan Political Dialogue Forum." https://unsmil.unmissions.org/libyan-politi cal-dialogue-forum.

UN Women, UN Department of Political and Peacebuilding Affairs. 2020. COVID-19 and con- flict: Advancing women's meaningful participation in ceasefires and peace processes. https:// www.unwomen.org/en/digital-library/publications/2020/08/policy-brief-covid-19-and- conflict.

Verweijen, Judith. 2019. "Inclusion and Fragmentation: Mai-Mai proliferation in the Democratic Republic of Congo." In *Inclusion in Peace Processes,* edited by Andy Carl. London: Accord, 74– 78. https://www.c-r.org/accord/inclusion-peace-processes.

Whitfield, Teresa. 2019. "Mediating in a Complex World." Oslo Forum Background Paper. https://www.hdcentre.org/publications/mediating-in-a-complex-world/.

Williams, Stephanie Turco, and Jeffrey Feltman. 2021. "Can a Political Breakthrough Mend a Broken Libya?" Brookings Institution. February 17. https://www.brookings.edu/blog/order-from-chaos/2021/02/17/can-a-political-breakthrough-mend-a-broken-libya/.

10

Implementing Peace Accords

Colette Rausch and Zuhra Halimova

It was good that the peace was declared, but it would have been better if words had been translated into action.

—Anoja Guruma[1]

Introduction

In terms of sheer numbers, this is a golden age for peace agreements. "Some 50 percent of civil wars have terminated in peace agreements since 1990, more than in the previous two centuries combined, when only one in five resulted in negotiated settlement. Numerically, these settlements amount to over three hundred peace agreements in some forty jurisdictions."[2] While the objectives and goals vary, the accords are generally designed to halt violence and steer countries toward peace. Frequently, however, they fail to achieve those goals, especially following civil wars, which account for the vast majority of today's armed conflicts. One study of peace agreements from 1989 to 2004 found a failure rate of approximately "45 percent within five years."[3] Many agreements, without failing outright, lead to a "no war, no peace" limbo often more devastating than the conflicts they were supposed to end. "By a huge magnitude," notes one study of negotiated settlements, "more people died after the peace accords in Angola and Rwanda than during the civil wars that preceded them."[4] Why is the record for implementation of peace accords not better?

This chapter argues that one of the chief explanations lies in the neglect of inclusivity during agreement implementation. Although the management of the negotiation phase and the wording of the peace accord provisions are crucial to the prospects for enduring peace, the signing of a peace deal does not signal the end of conflict in the minds of the people who have experienced it. Nor do even the most artfully constructed terms of an agreement suffice to resolve the underlying problems that drove the conflict. Changing the minds of citizens and addressing deep-rooted conflict drivers can only be accomplished by including citizens and marginalized groups in the process of implementation. The international community tends to emphasize the negotiation phase, but, as Thania Paffenholz of the

Graduate Institute Geneva has shown, "many processes fail or substantial gains of inclusive negotiations get lost during implementation."[5] Although inclusion during peace negotiations is important, observes Paffenholz, "implementation is key but often neglected."[6]

This chapter starts by outlining what "inclusivity" means in the context of implementation, then explains why inclusivity matters to the success of the implementation process. Subsequently, the text presents an overview of the challenges faced during implementation and explores why inclusivity is often elusive. The chapter concludes by highlighting strategies and tools for enhancing inclusivity.

What Does "Inclusivity" Mean?

In the context of peace accord implementation, "inclusivity" means at a minimum that a wide range of groups from within the conflict-affected society are involved in translating the terms of an agreement into practice. Instead of participation in that process being restricted to the government and its political and military opponents in the recent conflict, inclusive implementation features active roles for many other stakeholders who stand to benefit from and can contribute to sustainable peace. These may include not only the direct parties to the peace accord but also the general public, including segments likely to have been marginalized in the past, such as women, youth, and minorities—including ethnic and racial minorities, religious groups, and the LGBTQI community—as well as the many and varied components of civil society, including nongovernmental organizations, religious groups, media, labor organizations, and business groups. In practical terms, the participation of the public and previously marginalized groups could take many forms, such as public education through workshops and media campaigns, discussions through dialogues, and surveys and consultations that allow the public to air concerns but also funnel those concerns back to decision-makers.

A truly inclusive process, however, should also offer roles for actors who have *not* been traditionally marginalized but who are marginalized now because of a change in regime or other recent shifts in the political, economic, and social landscape. These previously powerful players may include former government officials, members of recently disbanded or purged security forces, and demobilized rebel fighters who foresee little prospect of reintegration into society. Such actors have the potential to act as spoilers, determined to torpedo any hopes of successful implementation through politically destabilizing activities, the use of violence, or more passive forms of resistance such as creating delays in reform initiatives. Some of these groups will resist overtures to become part of the implementation process, and some will see the peace accord as fundamentally antithetical to their interests. In short, some spoilers will prove intractable. But others may be persuaded to work with, rather than against, the process as long as they do not fear that participation threatens them in some significant way.

A mapping of the entire country will help identify traditionally marginalized groups and the newly marginalized potential spoilers. It can also help deepen understanding of the diverse roles of stakeholders that can run counter to stereotypes, such as female combatants. These may differ at the national and local levels, so the mapping should focus not only on capitals but also regional and local centers of power, both rural and urban.

Inclusivity means not only broader participation but also greater impact in terms of being listened to, shaping the peacebuilding agenda, enacting change, and becoming part of society's decision-making processes. If implementation is to lay the foundations for an enduring peace, then the society needs not merely to disarm fighters and enact new policies but to undergo a transformation from a society engaged in violent conflict to one that uses nonviolent tools such as dialogue, mediation, negotiation, and problem-solving to nurture peace. Providing the space and opportunity for groups to work together on reforms can help build social cohesion, which can help transform divisions that may lead to conflict. It can also help seed the ground for reconciliation, which can strengthen social cohesion.

Why Inclusivity in Implementation Matters

How these stakeholders participate will depend on context, but it is crucial that inclusion is a feature of all elements of an implementation process. If sustainable peace is the ultimate goal of a peace accord, then it is imperative to acknowledge that the signing of the accord is not by itself going to accomplish that goal. In fact, if lasting peace is to have the best chance for success, the signing of the peace accord, while important, needs to be seen as part of a broader process. That process must include both a carefully conceived and inclusive negotiation process and an equally well-formulated and inclusive post-accord implementation phase. Ideally, inclusivity will begin at the negotiating table and continue far beyond not only the signing ceremony but also elections and other milestones on the path to societal and political reconciliation. Even if inclusivity was not adequately addressed during the negotiation stage, it is imperative that it begin at the outset of the implementation phase.

Inclusivity, it should be admitted, can be unpalatable for many involved in implementation. Inclusivity means bringing in spoilers. It means bringing in people from groups that have long been marginalized in society, and groups that, until their recent removal from power, were responsible for that marginalization. But if a society resilient to violence is the ultimate goal of a peace agreement, then its implementation must at least aim toward inclusion. The more inclusive that implementation is, the more enduring the peace is likely to be. Further, given the role that factors such as discrimination and marginalization often play in stoking violent conflict, it is all the more important to ensure that implementation strategies and processes include rights-based approaches, such as promoting participation and representation, as well as rule of law and accountability.

Inclusivity Can Help Keep Implementation on Track

One reason why inclusivity is so important is that implementation of a peace accord is far from straightforward. The accord may specify the kinds of activities that will be part of the implementation process, but usually the details of those activities are left to be defined during the process itself. This task typically precipitates disagreements that can endanger the entire peace process. An inclusive implementation process, however, increases the number of actors who are in a position to resolve such disagreements, especially actors who have a firsthand understanding of the problem.

Take the case of women's groups in the Liberian peace process, described in Chapter 3. Liberian women were successful in terms of participating—formally as observers, informally through consultations with the parties—in the peace talks and influencing the agreement, although their impact waned during implementation "despite women's groups being directly represented in the transitional government and various implementation commissions."[7]

Strong public buy-in, supportive regional and international actors, strong women's groups, preexisting personal networks, and regional women's networks all contributed to women's influence on the talks. That said, the ad hoc and unstructured nature of women's transfer and communication strategies meant that the impetus for change was not sustained throughout the implementation process. Limited decision-making power, lack of funding, and heterogeneity among the groups also constrained women's continued influence.[8]

Despite this waning influence, women proved invaluable in keeping the disarmament, demobilization, and reintegration (DDR) process on track. The DDR process had not met its goals and was suspended prematurely. After riots over conditions had erupted in the camps, injuring male and female combatants, women's groups in Liberia stepped in to help. Prior to the DDR suspensions, they had already identified the DDR weaknesses, so they were well prepared to help get the DDR process back on track. The DDR process was relaunched with the assistance of the women's groups, including addressing the needs of the female combatants.[9] (For a discussion of inclusion in the security sector, see Chapter 11.)

The monitoring and verification of DDR and of progress toward other goals laid out in a peace accord typically require the participation of independent organizations and institutions. So, too, does the task of addressing past human rights abuses through transitional justice (TJ) mechanisms such as war crimes tribunals, traumahealing programs, and reparations (see Chapter 12). These mechanisms seek "to accomplish such goals as establishing the truth of what happened, acknowledging the suffering of victims, holding perpetrators accountable, compensating for wrongs, preventing future abuses, and promoting social healing."[10]

In addition, institutional reforms may be mandated by a peace accord and therefore will be part of the implementation phase. These often include police and military reforms and can be linked in practice to DDR and TJ efforts. Power-sharing agreements affecting the structure of government can also be part of an accord, and thus part of the implementation process (see Chapter 16). They can be a powerful tool for addressing inadequate representation in government institutions.

Addressing past human rights abuses and creating bodies to address past exclusion can—if they involve the groups who have suffered from abuse and marginalization—help recognize and tackle grievances and injustices that have helped to perpetuate the conflict and that could reignite violence.

Inclusivity in Implementation Can Compensate for a Lack of Inclusivity During Negotiations

A large and growing body of research suggests that diversity and inclusion in peace processes implementation can help consolidate peace. For instance, the results of the analysis of eighty-three peace agreements mentioned at the outset of this chapter "show that if civil society is included in a peace agreement the risk of peace breaking down between the signatories is reduced by 64 per cent. This finding suggests an important role for civil society in peace processes: we may expect that if actors from civil society are allowed a place at the negotiation table, or are stipulated to play a role in the implementation of an agreement, the post-agreement peace among the signatories stands a better chance of lasting."[11] Another study found that "in the short term, peace processes that included women as witnesses, signatories, mediators, and/or negotiators demonstrated a 20 percent increase in the probability of a peace agreement lasting at least two years. This percentage continues to increase over time, with a 35 percent increase in the probability of a peace agreement lasting fifteen years."[12] Another study showed "a robust correlation between peace agreements signed by female delegates and durable peace" and found that "agreements signed by women show a significantly higher number of peace agreement provisions aimed at political reform, and higher implementation rates for provisions."[13] (For a discussion of inclusion in peace negotiations, see Chapter 9.)

Even if negotiations have not been inclusive, it is not too late to turn to inclusivity to bolster the chances of a comprehensive peace. In Nepal, despite the fact that the peace process that led to the signing of the accord in 2006 was not considered inclusive in practice, it was the post-accord constitutional drafting process that became the primary flashpoint test for whether the peace accord would hold, and an opportunity for inclusion to be realized in order to head off a potential reignition of war. In fact, the constitutional drafting process lasted until 2015, when a new inclusive constitution was signed.[14] The years-long period of negotiation over the new constitution was in essence a negotiation of a new social contract among a multitude of political, economic, and social divisions and interests. It included periods of unrest that led to political violence and instability. Yet it continued as a form of trying to resolve issues left unresolved in the peace process, the primary one being inclusion, which focused on envisioning what an inclusive Nepal society would look like.

Groups that had been historically excluded from full participation in society—for instance, by being denied access to high-level positions in the police force, or by being assigned a lowly position in the caste system—engaged in activism to have their voices heard. Eventually, some members of the politically powerful in-group reached out and began to work with members of the out-groups to negotiate a constitution.

The peace accord itself did not, nor could it realistically be expected to, resolve the grievances and divisions that helped fuel the civil war. Further, as one Northern Ireland political leader who had been involved in that country's peace process said during a visit in 2007 to help advise a group of Nepalese civil society, political, and security representatives on building peace, the Nepal peace agreement was on paper inclusive and covered international norms, yet it was done so quickly that the long road of peace had not yet begun. He was essentially saying that the implementation phase was where the peace agreement would rise or fall.

What Challenges Confront Efforts to Promote Inclusivity in the Implementation Process?

Some of the same challenges face all types of implementation processes, not just inclusive ones. For instance, peace accords are usually multidimensional, and, by extension, implementation processes are typically complex, involving multiple actors, institutions, and issues. Colombia's 2016 peace agreement ran to more than three hundred pages and included such varied components such as introducing comprehensive rural reform; encouraging political participation; stipulating a ceasefire, cessation of hostilities, and laying down of arms; tackling illicit drugs; creating a comprehensive system for truth, justice, reparations, and nonrepetition of human rights abuses; and establishing an implementation and monitoring commission.[15] Yet despite the comprehensive nature of the accord and strides made toward inclusion, as of the end of 2020, implementation of the accord continues to be challenging.[16] Thousands of militants have resumed fighting, hundreds of community leaders and activists have been killed, and hundreds of thousands have been newly displaced amid continued fighting. Complexity—which is increased by efforts to be more inclusive because they bring additional actors and issues into the process—can make it much harder to orchestrate the different elements of implementation.

Another formidable challenge encountered in many different types of implementation processes is ambiguity. Perhaps in part because many agreements cover so much ground, they are often worded in an ambiguous fashion that can greatly complicate the task of implementation. The ambiguity may be deliberate; where the parties are not able to agree on an issue, they may "paper over their disagreement by using ambiguous languages" so that the stalemate will not derail the negotiations, and in hopes that the unresolved issue can be dealt with at some future point.[17] In the Good Friday Agreement, for instance, constructive ambiguity played a role both

in negotiating the peace agreement and in implementing it. While constructive ambiguity "aided the political progress" in Northern Ireland, it was "unhelpful to the
improvement of inter-communal relations."[18] But when it comes to implementing
a provision that is vaguely defined, the potential for disagreement and discord to
reignite is considerable.

The international community may be able to offer both advice and resources to
help tackle complexity and ambiguity, but as every post-conflict society has discov-
ered, the international community—in the shape of international NGOs, intergovernmental organizations, neighboring countries, donors, and sometimes global or
regional powers—also presents its own set of challenges. Fully coordinating their
efforts can be difficult if not impossible, resulting in duplication of effort, con-
fusion, and competing efforts that retard rather than advance the peace process.
Moreover, the differing agendas of international actors may not align with the goals
of the peace accord or with the interests of national and local actors. For example, in
Nepal, the push for inclusion of marginalized groups in the 2006 peace agreement
was driven largely by international actors supporting the peace process together
with those historically marginalized groups and aligned political parties. Other political parties and Nepal's army, however, saw the move for inclusion as a threat to
their interests.

Some challenges, however, while not perhaps unique to inclusive processes, are
common to them. This is in part because they are related to the need to change the
perspectives and attitudes of a large and diverse array of groups, if not of society as
a whole, and in part because inclusion presents a threat to the status quo and entrenched power structures.

The Need for Longevity

Achieving the kind of societal and conflict transformation set as a goal in some
accords can take a generation or more, but even implementing the technical
provisions of a complex peace accord can take many years. For example, the Tajik
Peace Accord signed in 1997, designed to end a five-year-old civil war, contained
twenty-one provisions, ranging from those concerning the executive branch and
the constitution to those addressing DDR and prisoner release. After ten years,
Tajikistan had reportedly implemented 76 percent of the accord's provisions—although some observers were uncertain if those gains could be solidified.[19]

Too Fast a Pace

A fast pace of implementation may, in fact, not be advantageous, because there is
a limit to the amount of change that societies can absorb at any one time. Many
reforms, especially in the security sector, cannot be successfully implemented until

some level of trust and capacity has been built up. Willingness and readiness to listen to the "Other" also need to be established before bringing together groups that have a history of mutual isolation and hostility.

Including a group in an implementation process where there is a history of intergroup conflict demands careful consideration and should not be put to one side or hastily addressed in an attempt to keep the process moving swiftly. Nepal learned this lesson when its quickly signed peace agreement headed into the implementation phase and Nepal realized it could not gloss over the fact that it had societal divisions that ran along ethnic, caste, and regional divides. A more inclusive constitutional drafting and adoption process had to be devised, which pushed back the timetable for finalizing and promulgating a new constitution by five years—but those five years were a wise long-term investment toward securing a constitution that reflected Nepal's diversity.

Lack of Trust

Lack of trust in the aftermath of conflict also tends to extend to the government and its ability or even its readiness to implement the terms of the accord it has just signed. Lack of trust tends to be acute in societies where some groups have been historically marginalized or subject to structural impediments to full participation in government. For instance, Guatemala's 1996 peace accords included provisions designed to counter the long-standing marginalization of the Indigenous population, but implementation has been slow and piecemeal, and concern persists about the lack of accountability for disappearances and human rights violations during the conflict.

Many citizens need to see some form of "peace dividend"—some improvement, often economic, in their quality of life—in order to believe that the peace agreement is desirable and workable.[20] "Quick wins," such as the reopening of businesses or the reappearance of police on the streets, are important to rebuilding public confidence in the government, but they must be accompanied by a long-term process of developing the institutions mandated by the accord and building human capacity to implement accord provisions and reforms. The parties to the agreement share this desire to see some kind of peace dividend. The dividend might be political or economic, for example, but it must be perceived as valuable by the parties (not least their rank-and-file supporters) if they are to retain confidence in the agreement they signed and support its implementation.

Lack of Engagement

The combination of a dearth of institutional and human capacity, insufficient financial capacity to support implementation, and threadbare political will to find resources for institutions and personnel are formidable challenges to implementation, taxing the commitment of the government and the patience of the public. Without a broad engagement and outreach effort together with effective communication, a good expectations-management strategy, and a transparent implementation plan, those working to implement the peace accord will face public frustration and lack of trust in the process.

Engagement can take many forms, such as providing civil society organizations across the political and social spectrum with roles in elections and governance, in institutions, and in reform efforts. In Nicaragua, the role of civil society organizations expanded during implementation of the 1990 peace agreement between the Sandinistas and the new anti-Sandinista liberal government that had defeated the Sandinistas in elections. Eventually, however, starting in 1997, the government, feeling threatened by the influence of civil society organizations and particularly those perceived as "leftist," pursued restrictions on the activities of civil society organizations, such as instituting audits and trying, unsuccessfully, to limit foreign funding to organizations.[21] In El Salvador and Guatemala, inclusive voices did have an influence on the wording of peace agreements, but civil society was never able to secure a foothold in implementation efforts, in part because civil society actors were not always well organized, and in part because national leaders made little effort to engage civil society. As a consequence, public disillusionment set in.

Translating inclusive provisions into practice is evidently challenging. Governments and elites may agree during negotiations to inclusive measures, but during implementation old habits resurface and previous patterns of exclusionary rule reassert themselves.

Spoilers

In the absence of trust, the danger posed by "spoilers"—groups and individuals who try to block or sabotage implementation of an agreement to advance their own goals and interests—is exacerbated. Some are political factions who reject the peace agreement on ideological grounds; some are criminal gangs who fear the agreement will curtail their activities; some are armed splinter groups who believe their former comrades have "sold out" by signing an accord; and some are members of those groups who previously held power but have now seen their political, social, or economic status significantly diminished and regard the implementation process as a process of entrenching their exclusion from government and ostracization from society. As Stephen John Steadman noted in his influential 1997 article on spoilers, "By signing a peace agreement, leaders put themselves at risk from adversaries who may take advantage of a settlement, from disgruntled followers who see peace as a betrayal of key values, and from excluded parties who seek either to alter the process or to destroy it. By implementing a peace agreement, peacemakers are vulnerable to attack from those who oppose their efforts."[22]

Spoilers will use whatever means they have at their disposal to frustrate implementation and drive a wedge between groups who have supported the agreement, while undermining public confidence in the practicability and even the desirability of its implementation. They may even resort to violence. In Libya after the fall of the Gaddafi regime and in Iraq after the ouster of Saddam Hussein's regime, those who had for years filled the ranks of the civil service and the security forces suddenly found themselves purged, unemployed, and legally prohibited from working for the state.[23] Their resentment and anger not only alienated them from the post-conflict peace process but also drove many of them into the ranks of the Sunni insurgency that fought to overthrow the US-supported Shiite government.

Lack of Local Input

One way to bolster public confidence and persuade skeptical citizens that they are about to experience real and positive change in their lives is to create or demonstrate synergy between the national-level accord and local-level peacemaking and peacebuilding endeavors. In Nepal, accomplishing this was complicated by the fact that the country historically had a highly centralized government and that the 2006 peace agreement did not explicitly mandate local-level peacebuilding initiatives. To establish local-level dialogues (such as those between civil society and the police that addressed justice and security issues) required those working within the system to get permission to engage locally while international human rights organizations applied pressure from outside.[24]

Multiple Social and Other Divisions

The sheer number and scale of divisions within society can make inclusivity hard to achieve. Take the example of Nepal. Inclusion in the implementation phase of Nepal's peace process had to be widely defined because the civil war in Nepal was fueled by long-standing factors such as marginalization and was conducted in a brutal fashion that created deep divisions between Maoist rebels, government forces, and the civilians who suffered at the hands of both sides. Plus, the country suffered from regional divisions (Kathmandu-centered groups could not adequately represent rural areas, and the populations of the hill areas and the plains had differing views and identities), as well as having numerous ethnic, caste, gender, and religious fault lines. There were also sharp ideological divisions between different political parties and movements, between human rights activists and security forces, and so forth. With so many competing but also often overlapping identities, all of which could shift within the dynamic post-conflict context, Nepalis had to accept that their peace process would be a messy, drawn-out business requiring compromise and perseverance.

Conflict Parties Dictate Who Has a Role in Implementation

Why inclusivity is not more prized is in part attributable to a lack of know-how and capacity about how to promote inclusivity, but it also has much to do with the attitudes of the most powerful actors within conflict-affected societies. According to Paffenholz, "conflict parties tend to initiate inclusion largely in order to strengthen their legitimacy, and the legitimacy of the process" in the eyes of the general population and the states and societies involved in the conflict.[25] The parties invite the participation of actors such as national political and business elites, hard-liners, and the military, as well as international and regional powers. An "exception to this general rule is women's organizations, which are rarely included in order to increase legitimacy—and when they are, it is often due only to significant outside pressure and lobbying efforts by civil society groups, women's NGOs and international organizations."[26]

The Illusion of Inclusion and Elite Resistance to Real Participation

Even when women and other marginalized groups are involved in a peace process, their participation by itself does not mean that broader views and interests will be reflected in the peace process. The design of a peace process can profoundly enable or constrain the ability of included actors to exercise influence. Often elites continue to dominate outcomes despite the presence of less powerful groups at the table. In the 2001 Somali peace process, for example, "women were allocated a quota in all six 'reconciliation' committees, but any decision by the committees required the authorisation of a leadership committee of male clan elders, effectively muting women's influence."[27]

Furthermore, the presence of women in peace negotiations is no guarantee that gender equality or women's rights issues will be placed on the peace agenda. In the El Salvador peace process, "although approximately 30 percent of the Farabundo Marti National Liberation (FMLN) negotiators were women, gender equality was not included in the peace agreements."[28] Moreover, "the El Salvador peace agreements included discriminatory provisions in the accords, such as barring women to varying degrees from reconstruction programmes, with far-reaching consequences for adolescent girls, women and their dependents."[29]

In Guatemala's peace process, which culminated in a 1996 agreement, a wide range of interest groups were consulted during negotiations through a civil society assembly. For example, women were members of the negotiation teams, larger groups of women were consulted through the assembly, and women's specific needs were directly acknowledged—yet women's interests did not continue to be respected during implementation.

The Guatemalan peace agreement included eleven accords on the issues of addressing human rights violations, the resettlement of groups displaced by the conflict, the rights of Indigenous peoples, socioeconomic issues, land rights, civilian power, the role of the armed forces in post-conflict Guatemala, constitutional reforms, and the integration of the Guatemalan National Revolutionary Unity (URNG) into civilian life. Each of the thematic accords included language on women's rights and gender equality as they related to participation in all sectors of society, ending all forms of discrimination against women, and recognizing the vulnerability of Indigenous women.[30]

The inclusive negotiation process was not replicated during the implementation phase. "Elite resistance coupled with lack of public buy-in prevented the implementation of the peace accord."[31] The legacies of the failure to consolidate the peace are clear from the levels of inequality, violence, femicide, corruption, and illegal criminal organization activity that persist in Guatemala.[32]

There are many examples of how, during the implementation phase, established power structures and powerful elites can push back against moves in the direction of inclusiveness. The "inclusive constitution-making process in Fiji from 2006 to 2013 produced a widely accepted constitution. However, the military government rejected the constitution altogether and stopped the process."[33] During implementation, forward-looking plans for reform and wider participation confront such harsh realities as corrupt elites, self-serving politicians, donors with waning enthusiasm for pushing for inclusion, and militaries and militias nervous about being held accountable for past human rights abuses.

Members of groups who have been traditionally privileged economically and politically can resist inclusion that they perceive will challenge or be a threat to their status or economic security. This resistance can be compounded where a lack of trust exists and those in elite positions trust neither the implementation process nor those who are part of the implementation process, such as opposition leaders or groups. There is also the possibility of backlash during the implementation phase following the signing of an inclusive peace agreement. For example, six to nine years after the 2006 Nepal peace agreement, donors were confronted with pressure from Nepal's government to not fund activities and groups that promoted inclusion.[34]

Resistance to Inclusion from Civil Society

Civil society groups, too, can be an obstacle. For instance, even though "the National Assembly in Guatemala has been a highly representative body, one of the most influential civil society organizations, the landowners' association, was excluded. Together with the political establishment the landowners were able to lobby against the implementation of the peace agreement."[35] Civil society can help bring greater public representation into peacebuilding, but it speaks with diverse voices and comes in many different organizational forms. Civil society groups may pursue not only divergent but also conflicting approaches to implementation, and may compete for the same funds from donors. Furthermore, groups have varying degrees of autonomy from the state, so their participation may not in fact inject a strictly nongovernmental perspective into the process—or the state may restrict the role they can play. In Nicaragua in the late 1990s, for instance, President Arnoldo Alemán tried to introduce legislation to prevent NGOs from receiving foreign funding.[36]

Neural Resistance to Inclusion

Another reason for the elusiveness of inclusivity may be rooted not in a society's power structure but in the wiring of the human brain. According to Maddalena Marini, "social beliefs reflect associations that are strongly ingrained in our brains, and changing them will likely entail the reconfiguration of their underlying biological processes."[37] Neuroscience is currently illuminating the processes underlying "us-versus-them" attitudes that fuel a great deal of conflict. "Fear and hatred towards out-groups that are deemed different (ethnically, ideologically, religiously, etc.) and the urgency to barricade oneself from 'outsiders' or 'intruders' is largely based on fear and ancestral predispositions, which regard belonging to a tribe, a group, as pivotal to survival."[38] In other words, inclusivity is elusive because our brains are wired to exclude groups that are different from us. Whichever group is most powerful in society and can dictate who participates in a peace process will therefore exclude groups it sees as different from itself, unless those groups are also powerful and cannot be ignored, such as the other side in the conflict. However, there are ways that peace processes, through inclusivity, can help build constructive intergroup relations. The research around intergroup dynamics and contact theory—the theory that conflict between groups and prejudice can be reduced if members of the groups interact with each other under appropriate conditions—shows that by creating opportunities and processes that enable positive interactions between members of groups in conflict, intergroup relations and empathy can improve while intergroup anxiety and stress can decrease.[39]

What Strategies and Tools Can be Used to Enhance Inclusivity in Implementation?

Given the challenges of implementing peace accords and enhancing inclusivity, policymakers and peacebuilding practitioners can find it helpful to plan ahead of the implementation phase, anticipating what provisions are likely to be included in the final agreement, what priorities will dominate the peacebuilding agenda, and how best to sequence and coordinate their activities. Each transition, of course, is different, and each demands context-specific knowledge. But there are a number of strategies and tools that have been used in a variety of transitions around the world and that have helped to make the implementation of peace accords more inclusive.

Each of the following merits consideration and, if deemed to be relevant, could be adapted to the specific transition context.

Ensure Inclusivity Is Part of Formal Implementation Structures and Government and Institutional Reform Efforts

Post-accord institutions could include monitoring, oversight, peace support, and ombudsperson offices. The peace accord itself may provide for the establishment of mechanisms or institutions to support peace accord implementation. The 2015 South Sudan peace agreement, for instance, called for the creation of the Joint Monitoring and Evaluation Commission; transitional commissions, including a peace commission; and a public grievances chamber.[40] The 1999 Lomé Peace Agreement between the government of Sierra Leone and the Revolutionary United Front called for the reestablishment of the Commission for the Consolidation of Peace that had originally been part of the failed 1996 Abidjan Peace Accord.[41] Alternatively, the government itself may initiate such structures, as the Kenyan government did in 2008 when it created by statute the National Commission on Integration and Cohesion following the outbreak of violence in the aftermath of elections.[42]

The mere existence of such mechanisms, however, does not guarantee that they will promote inclusivity. To do that, the membership of a mechanism must be sufficiently varied so as to reflect its inclusive goals, and the members themselves must be committed to translating the ideal of inclusivity into practice.[43]

Post-agreement benchmarking systems can be created to track "whether the various aspects of gender equality, inclusion, and other provisions are progressing or implemented."[44] One such mechanism is the Peace Accords Matrix, which is the largest existing collection of implementation data on intrastate peace agreements.[45] It provides the opportunity to track implementation of, for example, the Colombian accord. Such mechanisms can reveal when implementation is slipping off track, thereby encouraging course corrections to be made.

Donors can directly tie their funds to the implementation of specific provisions that enable inclusion. Donors can also craft their assistance in a way that ensures inclusivity is part of implementation-support programs, including offering technical assistance to implementation mechanisms that can provide monitoring, evaluation, oversight, and peace support. Two examples of such assistance are the Third-Party Monitoring Team in the Philippines and the Kroc Institute's Barometer Initiative in Colombia.[46] Both of these initiatives help support peace agreement implementation by enabling watchdog organizations and the media to call attention to a lack or slow pace of progress. Even the parties to the agreement may be grateful for independent assessments of the extent and nature of implementation.

Additionally, reform efforts undertaken by the government can be instituted with inclusion as a priority, thereby laying a foundation for inclusive governance and citizen participation. When inclusion is accepted as a fundamental building block of peace and a requisite for making societies more cohesive and more resilient to conflict triggers, then its prioritization in reforms becomes apparent. There are ample opportunities to do this across reform efforts, from constitution-making to security sector reform, elections, budgeting, finance, and administration. In Nepal, for example, the United States Institute of Peace (USIP) focused on supporting programs that shared comparative lessons learned for constitutional drafting processes as well as transitional justice. USIP was careful to take an inclusive approach in its education programs, including traditionally marginalized groups as well as former combatants, security forces, and members of all political parties. Some donors focused exclusively on certain marginalized groups, which sparked a backlash by other marginalized groups as well as by members of the political elite, who felt that those donors were creating more divisions.

When political actors, whether from marginalized communities or traditional elite communities, play politics by stoking the fears of their own narrow constituencies rather than working together to create reforms for the country as whole, a peace accord can be undermined. This occurred in Nepal seven years after the peace accord was signed, where the multiyear constitutional reform process sparked a "violent escalation of minority grievances in 2015, thereby transforming the country's new constitution from the 'end of the peace process' into a 'catalyst' for violence."[47] "As observers of Nepal's reform process have argued: without legitimate politics in the institutional reform process, any institutional design that is an outcome of such reform can generate the risk of new violence."[48]

Establish Community-Level Monitoring Mechanisms

One way of combating a loss of confidence, both among the public and the parties to the agreement, is to develop monitoring mechanisms to track the progress of implementation and to ensure that milestones are reached. For instance, in 2003 in Mindanao in the Philippines, civil society organizations created a grassroots-based system known as the Batay Ceasefire. The system involves community volunteers monitoring the ceasefire between the government and the Moro Islamist Liberation Front, reporting violations, and generally working to improve the security of local residents.[49] Another example, inspired by the Philippines experience, is in Myanmar, where civilian ceasefire monitoring projects were implemented in two states in support of the peace process.[50]

Unfortunately, creating and maintaining such mechanisms is often a multifaceted challenge, with issues of logistics, costs, political obstruction, and credibility all threatening progress from the very start of implementation. A related challenge is establishing effective conflict resolution mechanisms to address issues that will naturally arise in implementation. Such mechanisms might include bodies to provide mediation, dialogue, and negotiation when problems arise, but setting these bodies up and giving them the credibility, the trained staff, and the financial and material support they need can be extremely difficult in poor and deeply divided societies.

At a minimum in such conditions, where mechanisms writ large are not immediately possible, one could work at the community level, on a small scale, with locally trusted and perceived neutral actors who could be equipped with the skills to facilitate dialogues. This could also include providing education on impediments to peacebuilding such as trauma, or on the neurobiological dynamics around group conflict and violence. When travel or other deeper engagement is not possible from a resource perspective, something as basic as putting written educational material on a thumb or shared drive and getting it to local actors or setting up a WhatsApp or call can be better than nothing. Simply being a support source for brainstorming or mentoring for those working on the ground can be helpful.

For example, in Nepal, in the days after the king relinquished political power on the heels of the People's Revolution in spring 2006, USIP representatives met with civil society leaders and human rights activists who had led the protests against the king, as well as with Nepali police. The civil society and human rights actors were keen to discover what other countries had done in similar transitions, looking for lessons that could guide the Nepal experience. For their part, the Nepali police were concerned about security during transitions and sought examples of how other countries had coped. So, USIP assembled material on constitution-making, transitional justice, combating serious crimes in post-conflict societies, and law reform and put them on CDs to share. In Libya in the aftermath of its revolution, a different approach was used in training local facilitators to conduct dialogues between communities to help resolve conflicts before they spiraled into violence. Additionally, a shared Dropbox folder was created to provide curated resources such as publications and handbooks on a variety of topics including transitional justice, rule of law, constitution-building, and combating serious crimes. USIP also held workshops to educate government officials and civil society actors about the threats that serious crimes posed to the transition and about the importance of inclusive dialogues among community members to help address potential spoilers. These trainings were wide-ranging; for instance, trauma was discussed to explain how it can impede successful dialogues.

Understand What Came Before

A number of agreements are often made along the winding path to a formal peace agreement. These may include agreements related to the cessation of hostilities, ceasefires, the conduct of the parties to the agreement, and humanitarian access to conflict zones. The agreements may be concluded at different levels, including the local level, and cover different regions and groups.[51]

Understanding these agreements and how they were negotiated and implemented can be instructive in the implementation phase of the final peace accord, highlighting conflict dynamics, inclusivity gaps, the progress already made in terms of conflict resolution, and the distance still to travel to reconciliation. One study indicated that while 80 percent of ceasefire agreements are broken, they can nonetheless be important stepping-stones toward peace: "What we found was that the best predictor that any one ceasefire agreement will be successful—and by successful I mean: not followed by renewed conflict or violence— . . . is how many failed peace agreements came before."[52] In other words, the larger the number of ceasefires that are arranged, even if they do not endure, the greater the likelihood that a ceasefire will eventually lead to sustainable peace.

Explore How to Expand the Participation of Civil Society

Civil society can play a number of roles in support of peace accord implementation: from advocacy and watchdog roles to involvement in local peace committees and dialogue processes. In some cases, civil society can achieve more in terms of reconciliation by itself than it can by working alongside government and political actors. In Nepal, for instance, local-level mechanisms, such as local peace committees patterned on those used in post-apartheid South Africa, had limited impact because they were controlled by political parties and elites.[53] USIP's Justice and Security Dialogue program experienced greater success because it supported its very diverse participants to shape agendas and activities.[54]

More work needs to be done to determine how to expand participation to include citizens, especially at the local level and beyond the capital region. A variety of low-tech methods such as holding town hall meetings, convening focus groups, and conducting inexpensive surveys via mobile phones can allow many more citizens to engage in the many moving parts of implementation.[55]

Plan Ahead

Although it is often difficult to predict if and when a peace accord will be signed, what form it may take, and when and how the implementation phase will begin, those who will manage or monitor that phase should plan ahead as much as possible, using a variety of scenarios so as to anticipate an array of directions that the peace process might take. Ideally, this planning will be led by those already in the country (e.g., not only national governments and local NGOs, but also international bodies with field offices or other representatives in the country), who will then be better prepared to engage with international donors and others that will provide transition support during the implementation phase should a peace agreement be signed.

In Nepal, months before the 2006 peace accord was signed, and in Libya, in the midst of the 2011 civil war just before Gaddafi was killed, individuals and groups from civil society sought to become informed and ready to engage in the impending transition. They gathered case studies and material on other post-conflict transitions, sought guidance from people experienced with transitions, and began to have conversations on topics ranging from transitional justice to constitution-making. A more structured form of pre-transition planning took place in Colombia (as it emerged from its long-running conflict) and Venezuela (when it was mired in turmoil), where in-country expert groups were formed and developed working relationships with advisors from around the world who had experience with transitions. Together, they shared knowledge and conducted research to help them anticipate problems and possible solutions during the forthcoming transitional period.[56]

In both the pre-negotiation and formal negotiation phases of the process that led to the 2005 peace agreement between the government of Indonesia and the Free Aceh Movement, considerable attention was devoted to thinking through the design, composition, and responsibilities of implementation mechanisms. This included, for example, discussions during the first round of talks on the funding of monitoring missions and other forms of support to sustain a peace agreement.[57]

Sustain Dialogue to Keep Implementation on Track

A successful peace process depends in part on civil society leaders being able to work with the parties to the agreement to help resolve the problems that inevitably arise during the lengthy implementation phase. To this end, a post-conflict process needs to include the creation of "formal or informal platforms for ongoing dialogue between actors that go beyond the end of official negotiations" and narrow the gap between postwar power elites and local constituencies.[58] Creating and maintaining a space for continued dialogue among political and social stakeholders on crucial issues can help a society not only navigate short-term crises during implementation but also achieve the long-term transformation essential to sustainable peace.

"Sustained dialogue" is a well-tested approach to conflict resolution that focuses on transforming conflicted relationships into more constructive ones through changing perceptions, attitudes, and relationships so that the parties themselves overcome their internal divisions and become capable of constructively dealing with the economic, social, and political issues in the conflict.[59] This is the approach modeled by the Inter-Tajik Dialogue (ITD), which began in 1993 and involved a core of ten to fourteen influential citizens of Tajikistan divided among the different political factions. The ITD paved the way for negotiations to end the country's civil war. The official UN-mediated negotiations included three ITD members as delegates. A peace agreement was concluded and signed in 1997, ushering in a transitional period for establishing a process of national reconciliation. Four ITD members became members of the Commission on National Reconciliation, which was entrusted with overseeing the implementation of the peace accords. Others became active members of civil society organizations, such as the Public Committee for Promoting Democratic Processes, which sought to foster dialogue in public forums and economic development benefiting all communities.[60]

Provide Civil Society with Resources and Training

Implementation of peace accords "is a costly endeavor and often exceeds the capacities of domestic players in post-conflict societies. Through financial aid and technical support, international donors and NGOs can contribute to the implementation of peaceful transition in post-war political arenas."[61] In practice, however, such support falls short of what is required. As the 2002 UN report *Women, Peace and Security* report points out, women involved in informal peacebuilding processes have identified lack of access to sources of funding as a major constraint for local and national donors. Thus, many women are largely dependent on international NGOs and international governmental and intergovernmental institutions, yet the procedures for obtaining such funding are complicated and protracted. There are also conflicting priorities between donors and local groups. Women cite leadership training and skills training programs, in such areas as peace education, trauma healing, and counseling, as essential for carrying out their peace work.[62] Like women, other traditionally marginalized groups need to be empowered through funding and training to develop the capacity to help implement peace accords. Structural barriers, such as obstructive gatekeepers and the lack of financial support required to travel or participate in implementation processes, must be removed so that trained women can actually use their skills.

Following the signing of the 2003 peace agreement in Liberia, civil society organizations were active in seeking out training and capacity-building opportunities on a number of fronts, including rule-of-law reform, transitional justice, and gender violence. In 2003–2004, at the request of Liberian officials and human rights defenders, USIP traveled to Liberia to share comparative experiences on post-conflict law reform. Simultaneously, on their own initiative, a coalition of Liberian women was able to push through stronger laws against rape, thanks not least to their ability to organize and garner national and international support.

In Burundi in 2015, when a political crisis threatened to open up wounds from the civil war that had ended with a 2000 peace accord, the United Nations stepped in and provided support for over five hundred women community leaders to help reduce tensions through local dialogues between communities and the security forces.[63] This example underscores the need to be ready to conduct or support conflict prevention and mediation efforts long after the signing of a peace accord.

Conclusion

As discussed in this chapter, peace agreement implementation is a complex endeavor that involves working to prevent a resurgence of violence by addressing conflict drivers and strengthening the social fabric of a society torn apart by war. Success in such an endeavor requires a multidimensional approach.

Moving forward, efforts should be made to ensure that the process of implementing an accord is closely linked with the processes of negotiating and drafting that accord. Achieving this goal will require those individuals and organizations who lead and support negotiation and implementation to see themselves as part of a continuous process and a single team. Too often, negotiations and implementation are consigned to separate "silos," with different actors confined to those silos and separate resources assigned to them. Individuals and organizations need to stop regarding themselves as either negotiators or implementers and start seeing themselves as both—as players on a team that is involved in a continuous, organic process of conflict resolution, undertaking multiple activities simultaneously.

That team, it should be admitted, is likely to be large and varied. It will include the negotiators and drafters: the parties themselves, as well as third parties such as ambassadors from countries trusted by the parties, and high-level officials from organizations such as the United Nations. Also on the team will be those who provide support to the negotiators and use their good offices to lend credibility to the process, whether representatives of think tanks and universities, or experts from regional or international organizations, such as the European Union and the United Nations. UN participation is likely to feature personnel from the UN Department of Political and Peacebuilding Affairs, which is mandated to provide, among other things, assistance on mediation, preventive diplomacy, and peacemaking activities such as peace negotiations. Nongovernmental organizations and other civil society entities and individuals also have a part to play, such as civil society representatives having a seat at the negotiation table, providing support to dialogues that feed information into peace processes, helping to shape public advocacy for an inclusive peace process, and supporting local peacebuilding efforts. Citizens, communities, and civil society should be integrated into all aspects of the peace process, and not as an afterthought or a check-the-box exercise.

The work of those who have helped craft a peace agreement must link up with the work of those who seek to implement that agreement. The latter include the institutions within the country that are charged with implementing the peace agreement and civil society organizations that will be involved in activities in support of implementation, such as holding parties accountable for implementing the term of the peace accord, monitoring government reform efforts, and providing early warning of renewed potential for violence. Citizen participation should reflect societal diversity and include, for instance, members of women's groups, former combatants, business leaders, and members of historically marginalized groups. Also playing important roles will be local, national, and international NGOs, as well as international organizations such as the UN Department of Peacekeeping Operations, the UN Development Programme, the UN High Commissioner for Human Rights, and regional organizations such as the African Union, the Organization of American States, and the Organization for Security and Co-operation in Europe. Researchers from academia and think tanks can also contribute expertise, monitor progress, and otherwise support the work of the team members.

Achieving cooperation among these diverse actors will not be easy, of course, and a mechanism to enable coordination of activities and sharing of information will have to be customized to suit the specific context. But if the process of implementing a peace accord is to be inclusive, then the team involved in guiding and supporting that process must also adopt an inclusive approach to their own work.

Notes

1. Rausch 2015.
2. Bell 2006, 373.
3. Westendorf 2015, 7.
4. Downes 2004.
5. Paffenholz 2015, 3.
6. Paffenholz 2015, 2.
7. Zanker 2018.
8. See Zanker 2018.
9. See Geneva Center for the Democratic Control of Armed Forces 2011.
10. Rausch 2017.
11. Nilsson 2014.
12. Stone 2015, 34.
13. Krause, Krause, and Bränfors 2018.
14. See Phuyal 2015.
15. Oficina del Alto Comisionado para la Paz 2016.
16. Casey 2019.
17. Snodderly 2018.
18. Mitchell 2009, 321.
19. Kroc Institute for International Peace Studies n.d. a. Today, some critics contend that the agreement, previously hailed as a triumph, has seen democratic backsliding and has lost its positive trajectory. See Torfeh 2016. Whatever the merits of the assessments of Tajikistan's progress, the larger point is that one should always be wary of rushing to premature judgments as to the success of an implementation process.
20. See, for example, UNDP 2011.
21. See Borchgrevink 2006.
22. Stedman 1997, 5.
23. See, for example, Hosenball 2016.
24. Quinney 2011.
25. Paffenholz 2016, 2.
26. Paffenholz 2016, 2.
27. Paffenholz 2015, 3.
28. United Nations 2002, 64.

29. United Nations 2002, 64.
30. See Chang et al. 2015.
31. See Zachariassen 2017.
32. Reilly 2009.
33. See Paffenholz et al. 2015, 3.
34. See Ghale 2019.
35. Paffenholz 2015, 4.
36. See Borchgrevink 2006. See also Nilsson 2018.
37. Marini, Banaji, and Pascual-Leone 2018.
38. Al-Rodhan 2016.
39. Levy, Dovidio, and Saguy 2021.
40. Intergovernmental Authority on Development 2015, 17.
41. The text of the Lomé agreement is available at https://peacemaker.un.org/sierraleone-lome-agreement99.
42. National Cohesion and Integration Commission Kenya n.d.
43. Verjee 2020.
44. UN Women 2018, 8.
45. Kroc Institute for International Peace Studies n.d. b.
46. See Centre for Humanitarian Dialogue n.d.; Kroc Institute for International Peace Studies n.d. c.
47. Strasheim 2017, 15.
48. Strasheim 2017, 16.
49. For details, see Ross 2017.
50. For details, see Bächtold 2016.
51. Chounet-Cambas 2016.
52. Snyder 2016.
53. Giessmann 2016, 32–33.
54. Quinney 2011.
55. See, for example, Dubow 2017.
56. Institute for Integrated Transitions n.d.
57. See Herrberg 2008.
58. Schernbeck and Vimalarajah 2017, 4.
59. "This approach Sustained Dialogue has its roots in a high level, U.S.–Soviet, now U.S.–Russia, dialogue, known as the Dartmouth Conference, which first met at Dartmouth College in 1960 and held its 137th session in October 2015. Its focus on transformation of relationships enables Sustained Dialogue to be effective in addressing a very wide range of conflicts, from a civil war in Tajikistan, to tensions between Israeli Arabs and Jews, to ethnic and racial tensions on 60 college campuses around the world and to intracommunity and intra-institutional conflicts." Stewart and Shamsi 2015, 158. See also Vorhees 2002.
60. Slim and Saunders 2015, 47.
61. Schernbeck and Vimalarajah 2017, 8.
62. UN Women 2002, 68.
63. See UN Women 2016.

Bibliography

Al-Rodhan, Nayef. 2016. "Us Versus Them: How Neurophilosophy Explains Our Divided Politics." World Economic Forum. October 3. http://www.weforum.org/agenda/2016/10/us-versus-them-how-neurophilosophy-explains-populism-racism-and-extremism.

Bächtold, Stefan. 2016. "Final Evaluation Report: Civilian Ceasefire Monitoring Project." Swisspeace. January. https://www.nonviolentpeaceforce.org/images/publications/16.01.15._External_Evaluation_Report_NP__Shalom_1.pdf.

Bell, Christine. 2006. "Peace Agreements: Their Nature and Legal Status." *American Journal of International Law* 100, no. 2: 373–412. http://www.jstor.org/stable/3651152.

Borchgrevink, Axel. 2006. "A Study of Civil Society in Nicaragua: A Report Commissioned by NORAD." Norwegian Institute of International Affairs, no. 699. https://www.files.ethz.ch/isn/27865/699.pdf.

Casey, Nicholas. 2019. "Colombia's Peace Deal Promised a New Era: So Why Are These Rebels Rearming?" *New York Times*, May 17. https://www.nytimes.com/2019/05/17/world/americas/colombia-farc-peace-deal.html.

Centre for Humanitarian Dialogue. n.d. "The Third Party Monitoring Team (TPMT) and Its Terms of Reference." https://www.hdcentre.org/the-third-party-monitoring-team-tpmt-and-its-terms-of-reference-philippines/.

Chang, Patty, Mayesha Alam, Roslyn Warren, Rukmani Bhatia, and Rebecca Turkington. 2015. "Women Leading Peace: A Close Examination of Women's Political Participation in Peace Processes in Northern Ireland, Guatemala, Kenya and the Philippines." Georgetown Institute for Women, Peace and Security. https://giwps.georgetown.edu/wp-content/uploads/2017/08/Women-Leading-Peace.pdf.

Chounet-Cambas, Luc. 2016. "Ceasefires." GSDRC. June. https://gsdrc.org/professional-dev/ceasefires/.

Downes, Alexander B. 2004. "The Problem with Negotiated Settlements to Ethnic Civil Wars." *Security Studies* 13, no. 4: 230–279.

Dubow, Talitha. 2017. "Civic Engagement: How Can Digital Technologies Underpin Citizen-Powered Democracy?" Corsham Institute. https://www.rand.org/content/dam/rand/pubs/conf_proceedings/CF300/CF373/RAND_CF373.pdf.

Geneva Center for the Democratic Control of Armed Forces. 2009. "Gender-Sensitive Disarmament, Demobilization and Reintegration: Examples from the Ground." Training Resources on Defense Reform and Gender Series, Liberia. https://issat.dcaf.ch/esl/download/4956/43716/Examples%20from%20the%20ground.pdf

Ghale, Shradha. 2019. "Backlash Against Inclusion." Conciliation Resources, March. http://www.c-r.org/accord/nepal/backlash-against-inclusion.

Giessmann, Hans J. 2016. "Embedded Peace Infrastructures for Peace: Approaches and Lessons Learned." Berghof Foundation and UNDP. https://www.undp.org/content/undp/en/home/library/democratic-governance/conflict-prevention/infrastructures-for-peace--approaches-and-lessons-learned.html.

Herrberg, Antje. 2008. "Aceh-Indonesia: The Brussels Backstage of the Aceh Peace Process." Conciliation Resources, September. https://www.c-r.org/accord/aceh-indonesia/brussels-backstage-aceh-peace-process.

Hosenball, Mark. 2016. "Inquiry Finds UK, U.S. Failed to Curb Destabilizing Purge of Iraqi Ba'athists." Reuters, July 7. https://www.reuters.com/article/us-britain-iraq-inquiry-purge-idUSKCN0ZN2I5.

Institute for Integrated Transitions. n.d. "Transition Assistance Practice Group." https://www.ifit-transitions.org/issue-areas/transition-assistance/transition-assistance-practice-group.

Intergovernmental Authority on Development. 2015. "Agreement on the Resolution of the Conflict in South Sudan." https://peacemaker.un.org/sites/peacemaker.un.org/files/Agreement%20on%20the%20Resolution%20of%20the%20Conflict%20in%20the%20Republic%20of%20South%20Sudan.pdf.

Krause, Jana, Werner Krause, and Piia Bränfors. 2018. "Women's Participation in Peace Negotiations and the Durability of Peace." *International Interactions* 44, no. 6: 985–1016. https://doi.org/10.1080/03050629.2018.1492386.

Kroc Institute for International Peace Studies. n.d. a. "General Agreement on the Establishment of Peace and National Accord in Tajikistan." Peace Accords Matrix. https://peaceaccords.nd.edu/accord/general-agreement-on-the-establishment-of-peace-and-national-accord-in-tajikistan.

Kroc Institute for International Peace Studies. n.d. b. "About." Peace Accords Matrix. https://peaceaccords.nd.edu/about.

Kroc Institute for International Peace Studies. n.d. c. "Colombia Barometer Initiative." Peace Accords Matrix. https://kroc.nd.edu/research/peace-processes-accords/pam-colombia/.

Levy, Aharon, John F. Dovidio, and Tamar Saguy. 2021. "Reducing Intergroup Conflict and Promoting Commonality and Cooperation." May 15. *NeuroPeace* 2: 5–28. Mary Hoch Center for Reconciliation, George Mason University. https://www.neuropeace.org/volumes.

Marini, Maddalena, Mahzarin R. Banaji, and Alvaro Pascual-Leone. 2018. "Studying Implicit Social Cognition with Noninvasive Brain Stimulation." *Trends in Cognitive Sciences* 22, no. 11: 1050–1066.

Mitchell, David. 2009. "Cooking the Fudge: Constructive Ambiguity and the Implementation of the Northern Ireland Agreement, 1998–2007." *Irish Political Studies* 24, no. 3: 321–336. doi: 10.1080/07907180903075751.

National Cohesion and Integration Commission Kenya. n.d. "NCIC at a Glance." http://www.cohesion.or.ke/index.php/about-us/ncic-at-a-glance.

Nilsson, Desirée. 2014. "Civil Society in Peace Accords and the Durability of Peace." Conciliation Resources. April, p. 30. https://rc-services-assets.s3.eu-west-1.amazonaws.com/s3fs-public/Accord25_CivilSocietyInPeaceAccords.pdf.

Nilsson, Manuela. 2018. "Civil Society Actors in Peace Negotiations in Central America." *Journal of Civil Society* 14, no. 2.

Oficina del Alto Comisionado para la Paz. 2016. "Final Agreement to End the Armed Conflict and Build a Stable and Lasting Peace." http://especiales.presidencia.gov.co/Documents/20170620-dejacion-armas/acuerdos/acuerdo-final-ingles.pdf.

Paffenholz, Thania. 2016. "Inclusion and Legitimacy in Contemporary Peace and Transition Processes: Results from the Broadening Participation Project (2011–2015)." Working Paper, Institute for Human Security, March. https://sites.tufts.edu/ihs/files/2016/03/Thania-Paffenholz-article-carnegie.pdf.

Paffenholz, Thania. 2015a. "Can Inclusive Peace Processes Work? New Evidence from a Multi-Year Research Project." Policy Brief, Graduate Institute Geneva. https://www.inclusivepeace.org/wp-content/uploads/2021/03/briefing-note-can-inclusive-processes-work-en.pdf.

Paffenholz, Thania. 2015b. "Beyond the Normative: Can Women's Inclusion Really Make for Better Peace Processes?" Policy Brief, Graduate Institute Geneva. https://www.peacewomen.org/sites/default/files/Graduate%20Insitute%20of%20Geneva-%20Beyond%20the%20Normative.pdf.

Paffenholz, Thania, et al. 2015. "Expert Views on Findings from the 'Broadening Participation' and 'Civil Society and Peacebuilding' Projects." Graduate Institute Geneva, Policy Brief. https://cmi.fi/wp-content/uploads/2016/04/Gender_policy_brief_FINAL.pdf.

Phuyal, Hari. 2015. "Nepal's New Constitution: 65 Years in the Making." *The Diplomat*, September 18. https://thediplomat.com/2015/09/nepals-new-constitution-65-years-in-the-making/.

Quinney, Nigel. 2011. "Justice and Security Dialogue in Nepal." Building Peace no. 1. United States Institute of Peace, Washington, DC. https://www.usip.org/publications/2011/06/justice-and-security-dialogue-nepal.

Rausch, Colette. 2017. "Reconciliation and Transitional Justice in Nepal: A Slow Path." Peace Brief. United States Institute of Peace, Washington, DC. August 2, https://www.usip.org/publications/2017/08/reconciliation-and-transitional-justice-nepal-slow-path.

Rausch, Colette. 2015. *Speaking Their Peace: Personal Stories from the Frontlines of War and Peace.* Berkeley, CA: Roaring Forties Press.

Reilly, C. A. 2009. "Introduction: Easier Signed than Done." In *Peace-Building and Development in Guatemala and Northern Ireland*, 1–8. New York: Palgrave Macmillan. https://doi.org/10.1057/9780230617889_1.

Ross, Nick. 2017. "Civil Society's Role in Monitoring and Verifying Peace Agreements: Seven Lessons from International Experiences." Inclusive Peace and Transition Initiative, Graduate Institute Geneva. January. https://www.inclusivepeace.org/wp-content/uploads/2021/03/report-civil-society-monitoring-en.pdf.

Schernbeck, Nico, and Luxshi Vimalarajah. 2017. "Paving the Way for the Effective and Inclusive Implementation of Peace Accords: A Strategic Framework." Berghof Foundation, Berlin. https://berghof-foundation.org/library/paving-the-way-for-the-effective-and-inclusive-imp lementation-of-peace-accords.

Slim, Randa M., and Harold H. Saunders. 2015. "The Inter-Tajik Dialogue: From Civil War Towards Civil Society." *Conciliation Resource*, July 24 http://www.c-r.org/accord-article/inter-tajik-dialogue-civil-war-towards-civil-society.

Snodderly, Dan. 2018. *Peace Terms: Glossary of Terms for Conflict Management and Peacebuilding*, 2nd ed. Washington, DC: United States Institute of Peace Press.

Snyder, Stephen. 2016. "Why Broken Ceasefires Are Actually Good for Peace." Public Radio International, October 20. https://www.pri.org/stories/2016-10-20/why-broken-ceasefi res-are-not-all-bad.

Stedman, Stephen John. 1997. "Spoiler Problems in Peace Processes." *International Security* 22, no. 2: 5–53. https://www.jstor.org/stable/2539366?seq=1.

Stewart, Philip D., and Nissa Shamsi. 2015. "Transformative Experience, Conflict Resolution and Sustained Dialogue." *International Journal of Conflict Engagement and Resolution* 3, no. 2: 158–179.

Stone, Laurel. 2015. "Quantitative Analysis of Women's Participation in Peace Processes." Annex II in Marie O'Reilly, Andrea Ó Súilleabháin, and Thania Paffenholz, *Reimagining Peacemaking: Women's Roles in Peace Processes*. New York: International Peace Institute. https://www.ipinst.org/wp-content/uploads/2015/06/IPI-E-pub-Reimagining-Peacemaking.pdf.

Strasheim, Julia. 2017. "The Politics of Institutional Reform and Post-Conflict Violence in Nepal." GIGA Working Papers no. 296. German Institute of Global and Area Studies, Hamburg. https://www.econstor.eu/bitstream/10419/149880/1/877337144.pdf.

Torfeh, Massoumeh. 2016. "Tajikistan: The Success Story That Failed." *Al Jazeera*, December 10. https://www.aljazeera.com/opinions/2016/12/10/tajikistan-the-success-story-that-failed.

UN Women. 2018. "Women's Meaningful Participation in Negotiating Peace and the Implementation of Peace Agreements: Report of the Expert Group Meeting." May. http://www. unwomen.org/en/digital-library/publications/2018/10/egm-report-womens-meaningful-participation-in-negotiating-peace.

UN Women. 2016. "Women Mediators Promote Peace in Burundi." January. https://www.unwo men.org/en/news/stories/2016/1/women-mediators-promote-peace-in-burundi.

UNDP. 2011. "Peace Dividends: Consolidating Peace in Northern Kenya Through Peace Dividend Projects." *Amani Papers* 2, no. 5. https://nscpeace.go.ke/resources/item/5-amani-papers-peace-dividends.

United Nations. 2002. *Women, Peace and Security*. New York: United Nations Publications. http://www.un.org/ruleoflaw/files/womenpeaceandsecurity.pdf.

Verjee, Aly. 2020. "After the Agreement: Why Oversight of Peace Deals Implementation Mechanisms Succeeds or Fails." Peaceworks. United States Institute of Peace, Washington, DC. https://www.usip.org/publications/2020/09/after-agreement-why-oversight-peace-deals-succeeds-or-fails.

Vorhees, James. 2002. *Dialogue Sustained: The Multilevel Peace Process and the Dartmouth Conference*. Washington, DC: USIP Press.

Westendorf, Jasmine-Kim. 2015. *Why Peace Processes Fail: Negotiating Insecurity After Civil War*. Boulder, CO: Lynne Rienner. https://www.rienner.com/uploads/55bfbb90085b6.pdf.

Zachariassen, Anne. 2017. "Women in Peace and Transition Processes: Guatemala (1994–1999)." Case Study, Inclusive Peace and Transition Initiative. Graduate Institute Geneva. May. https://www.inclusivepeace.org/sites/default/files/IPTI-Case-Study-Women-Guatemala-1994-1999.pdf.

Zanker, Franzisca. 2018. "Women in Peace and Transition Processes: Liberia (2003–2011)." Case Study, Inclusive Peace and Transition Initiative. Graduate Institute Geneva, April. https://www.inclusivepeace.org/wp-content/uploads/2021/05/case-study-women-libe ria-2003-2011-en.pdf.

11

Creating Representative and Responsive Security Sector Forces

Meaghan Shoemaker and Michelle Barsa

In the face of complex new security threats associated with pandemics, climate change, artificial intelligence, and cyber, we need to employ all resources available. Increasingly, we're understanding that meaningful inclusion is a national and international security imperative.
— Jacqueline O'Neill, Ambassador for Women,
Peace and Security, Canada

Introduction

At the height of the war in Afghanistan, the United States prohibited soldiers from growing beards because of their incompatibility with gas masks. Those opting to maintain beards for cultural and religious reasons were meant to choose: their beliefs or their service. Consider Harjit Sajjan, who changed this calculus through his service with the Canadian Armed Forces prior to his election as Canada's first Sikh minister of defense. While advising a US general in Afghanistan in 2011, he designed a patented gas mask that could be worn with a beard, which enabled him to keep his beard while serving his country. In 2017, the US Army changed its policy to enable soldiers to wear turbans, beards, and hijabs, noting "successful examples of soldiers currently serving with these accommodations."[1] While only scratching the surface of conversations on diversity in security and defense, this example illustrates how the conformity that defines identity within security forces can inadvertently exclude those with a desire to serve their country. Such barriers to inclusion both infringe upon the rights of individuals to serve and impair the efficacy of security forces. In some cases, security institutions have demonstrated an understanding of how inclusion and diversity are vital to operations. The North Atlantic Treaty Organization (NATO), for example, has adapted to gender mainstreaming and understands the operational-effectiveness imperative that a gender-conscious organization can support.[2] However, as

a multilateral organization, NATO is ultimately defined by the states that constitute its membership. Due to the historical reliance on tradition and masculinities,
many security forces are inhibited when it comes to innovation, creativity, and
learning with regard to diversity and inclusion, by vesting control in authorities
often dominated by one group in society.

This chapter examines the case for diversity in the composition of security sector
forces and institutions. The chapter begins with an overview of how diversity is
framed in the security sector and why it is important, with a foundation in both
normative and operational effectiveness arguments. The chapter then provides two
deeper dives into the application and relevance of diversity and inclusion to security
sector reform (SSR), disarmament, demobilization, and reintegration (DDR), and
community security. Within community security, we consider rule-of-law promotion, community resilience, and conflict prevention. The chapter also summarizes
resistances and challenges observed in academia and in practice with regard to diversity and inclusion within the security sector.

What Is "Diversity and Inclusion" in the Security Sector?

Diversity and inclusion can be examined in several ways within the security
sector. The most common inference is sex-based diversity—particularly focused
on increasing the recruitment and retention of cis-gendered women in security
forces. Even here, nation-states continue to fall short; in 2019, NATO reported
that women constitute an average of 10.9 percent of their member state militaries.[3]
The reality is, however, that this conversation is not just about women. To be effective in responding to the unique security needs of the diverse groups that constitute communities, security forces must go beyond the integration of women to
include broader intersections of identities and lived experiences. The phrase "diversity and inclusion" here refers to the representation and participation of those
of various races, ethnicities, sexes, genders, religions, physical abilities, and sexual
orientations in the composition of the forces themselves, the security sector writ
large, and the planning of security-related processes. While literature that spans beyond the scope of sex-based diversity is growing, as reflected in what follows, the
majority of resources available consider diversity in terms of women's representation or participation.

Why It Is Important: A Rights-Based Argument

A myriad of international and national legal instruments protect the rights of all
individuals, irrespective of identity, to serve in security forces. A rights-based approach from both service provider and end-user perspectives enables greater

clarity as to the case for inclusion. Still, the case for increased representation of women in security institutions, in particular, often falls to the rationale that diversity and inclusion will increase the effectiveness of security operations. This is not without criticism: some scholars suggest these arguments instrumentalize women in the name of security, while some recommend a broadened understanding of efficacy that leverages less essentializing examples of diverse groups.[4] Understanding that different rationales are salient with varying audiences, the argument holds that, when actors are integrated meaningfully into security sector institutions and organizations, and barriers to participation are reduced, individuals are able to be their full and authentic selves. The Inter-Parliamentary Union, an international organization of parliaments, describes inclusion as foundational to democratic practice, concluding that gender equality in "modern democratic societies, is nothing less than a new social contract in which men and women work in equality and complementarity, enriching each other mutually from their differences . . . what is basically at stake is democracy itself."[5]

This sentiment is echoed in the resolutions of a range of multilateral organizations. When it comes to the more specific post-conflict SSR and DDR processes, there are several international mandates requiring inclusion and diversity. These include United Nations Security Council Resolution 1325 and related resolutions on women, peace, and security, and the first UN Security Council resolution on SSR, Resolution 2151 (2014).[6] Resolution 2151 stresses the need for "gender sensitive security sector reform [as] key to developing security sector institutions that are non-discriminatory, representative of the population and capable of effectively responding to the specific security needs of diverse groups."[7] These international resolutions, and others, reflect the international community's consensus around global norms recognizing the importance of women's integration and participation in peace and security processes.

In addition to calling for gendered peace processes, DDR, and SSR, there has been a shift in international policy and guidance in regard to the focus of SSR and DDR processes. The European Union recently adjusted its approach to SSR initiatives by elevating attention to human rights and expanding missions' focus on SSR, capacity-building, and security force improvement.[8] In 2014, the African Union released its Policy Framework on Security Sector Reform, in which it committed to the integration of women and gender equality in SSR, including women-specific activities, gender awareness, and gender-responsive programming, and to supporting transformative change for gender equality within the security sector.[9] Beyond gender, the African Union policy stresses the importance of context-specific solutions for change and development, as well as the importance of cognizance when working with the diversity of nations and populations in SSR and DDR processes.[10] For both, the increased focus on strengthening security forces and institutions requires greater attention to gender and diversity within the institutions themselves.

Why It Is Important: An Operational Effectiveness Argument

Reinforcing rights-based arguments, the inclusivity of security forces is argued to directly impact the ability of those forces to achieve their mission objectives—commonly referred to as "operational effectiveness" among security actors.[11] Peacekeeping research suggests, for example, that the level of diversity in a mission's military forces has direct bearing on the protection of civilians and reduces the number of civilian casualties.[12] Diversity implies a larger pool of skills and experiences from which to draw—consider this in relation to culture and language and the ways it may facilitate connections with and understanding of the target population. Diversity also implies a collection of various individual profiles, each of which is better positioned to conduct outreach to the groups with whom they share identity factors—consider women military officers in Afghanistan conducting outreach to Afghan women, who were otherwise off-limits to male military officers. Diversity can be pivotal in the aftermath of war, particularly in restoring the rule of law and preventing a reemergence or remanifestation of wartime violence. Inclusion, particularly of nontraditional security actors, in defining new security paradigms expands the range of options available and builds local ownership. While operational effectiveness can be deconstructed vis-à-vis a range of security operations (e.g., intel preparation, search and seizure, civil-military relations), this chapter spotlights the ways in which diversity and inclusion enhance SSR and DDR outcomes, and correlate to rule of law, violence prevention, and efforts to counter violent extremism (CVE).[13] See Figure 11.1 and Box 11.1.

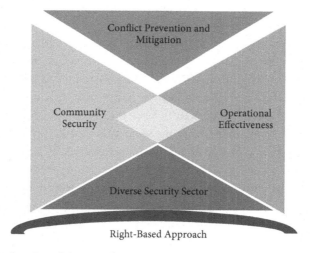

Figure 11.1 Rights-Based Approach
Credit line: Meaghan Shoemaker and Michelle Barsa.

Box 11.1 Inclusive Analysis in Action

During NATO's Kosovo Force (KFOR) mission, inclusive analysis of the battlespace supported the design of more effective operations. In this example, Major Elisabeth Schleicher and Major Andrew Young identified the north of Kosovo as an area where ethnic tensions were rising and resulting in violence. Reviewing the environment through multiple lenses, and through the vantage points of different stakeholders, they realized:

> The frustrations of the Kosovo Serbians boiled into civil unrest and led to them setting up roadblocks. The roadblocks decreased freedom of movement, which was a part of the KFOR mandate. . . . It was identified that it was mostly unemployed men who worked with the roadblocks. They were paid to guard them and thus were motivated to keep them in place. It was also identified that the roadblocks interrupted the supply of food and supplies to the communities. This impacted women and children more than the men since some of the men had begun to establish new resupply routes.[14]

As a result of identifying these gendered ethnic dynamics, responses in Kosovo were tailored and contextualized to local circumstances. The stakeholders suggest that casualties were minimized and the relationship between KFOR and the Kosovo Serbian communities was improved. This case provides a strong example of the ways in which the diversity of individuals and local populations must be taken into account in the planning and execution of operations.

SSR and DDR

Ending armed conflict requires the challenge of defining new norms that will quell current violence and sustainably prevent the reemergence of violence at local and national levels, as well as in both public and private spaces. SSR and DDR approaches rooted in diversity and inclusion acknowledge that individuals experience security and insecurity differently. Encouraging gendered and diverse approaches to the provision of security enables responsive and sustainable stabilization and post-conflict reconstruction.[15]

The security sector, which focuses in part on conflict prevention and mitigation, will typically carry the mandate for the execution of SSR and DDR processes. The internal diversity of security sector institutions, in turn, influences SSR and DDR, and vice versa. In some cases, SSR efforts have supported institutions to become more diverse and representative.[16] In other cases, organizational diversity has been used to shape SSR and DDR efforts that enable equity and inclusion within post-conflict societies. As a result, there is a case to be made that diversity and inclusion can be both an end and a means to support responsive SSR and DDR. Ultimately, SSR and DDR in the aftermath of war can only be as successful as the broader post-conflict reconstruction framework, which itself relies on inclusion and citizen engagement for its success (see Chapter 10).[17]

With this in mind, the role of diverse security forces in SSR and DDR processes must be probed further. The increased emphasis on human security in UN and EU policies, as referenced earlier, has resulted in new types of missions that do not fall within the purview of traditional warfighting. These missions often require substantial civil-military relationships as well as bilateral coordination across national militaries. Diversifying military contributions to peacekeeping operations supports local ownership, improves the effective delivery of justice and security services, and strengthens inclusion, oversight, and accountability.[18] This accountability manifests in a tangible way, as diversity in operations may support lower incidences of sexual misconduct and enhance the reputation of peacekeeping forces by improving trust.[19] While the assumption is often prevalent that diversity in security forces exclusively refers to women's integration—and therefore the impact of women on operational effectiveness—this is not the argument the authors necessarily intend to make. Recall that diversity in security forces is framed to include broader intersections of identities and lived experiences: representation and participation of various races, ethnicities, sexes, genders, religions, physical abilities, and sexual orientations in the composition of the forces themselves and in the planning of security-related processes. In some instances, this may require diversity in security forces to access particular populations, but it also requires all security forces to approach operations with a diverse and inclusive lens—an analytical frame that security actors must build the skill of applying in order to provide responsive support for diverse populations.

Security Sector Reform

SSR is multidimensional and complex. Levels of external assistance may extend from "the professionalization of military and police services, to the democratic transformation of security governance and the reform of oversight institutions."[20] As the approach to SSR has arguably remained unchanged since the 1990s and been executed with varying degrees of success, scholars and practitioners have criticized the normative state-centric approach and characterized SSR as the "ineffective and inefficient provision of security and, increasingly, justice, in part because the providers may themselves be a source of insecurity; and the inadequacy of accountability and oversight in the security sector."[21] Where the state has been a source of insecurity and injustice, local communities often turn to alternative authority structures for protection, further entrenching customary practice over statutory compliance.[22] Moving beyond the state-centric approach necessarily requires increased diversity in the types of institutions playing integral roles—particularly expanding to include civil society organizations, traditional leaders, and traditional justice mechanisms. This is in contrast to SSR processes led exclusively by the state that tend to have limitations reaching local populations—who Rosenbaum and Lurigio posit are the "user level of conflict-affected societies."[23] Inclusion can also enable bridging of informal and formal justice mechanisms in a way that meaningfully expands access to justice across population segments.[24] This is reinforced by Resolution 2151, which encourages states to consult local populations, particularly those most affected by conflict, to inform development of an inclusive national vision for security sector reform.[25]

SSR processes typically require reconstitution, in part or in full, of security forces. That process calls for an intentional rethinking of the profiles of individuals in those forces and the extent to which their makeup reflects the constituencies they serve. For the security sector to be representative and responsive to a broader population in local contexts, recognizing patterns of marginalization in society is critical; it makes it possible to ensure that those patterns are not replicated within the forces themselves.[26] In Burundi and South Africa, women in security forces, despite some being survivors of sexual violence by colleagues, felt they had a role in continuing to serve in order to protect local populations from their male colleagues. Wilén quotes a South Afircan female soldier, "If the woman [soldier] is there, this violence [against other women] will perhaps diminish, this violence which is committed by the military."[27] Some suggest that the inclusion of women within security forces may decrease the "demand" for sexual exploitation and abuse.[28] Others note the potential influence of a critical mass of women in security forces to improve sexual violence reporting.[29] Accordingly, inclusion may be a technique for enhanced protection of populations vulnerable to sexual exploitation and abuse.[30] It is important to recognize, however, that these pro-diversity arguments can place a double burden on groups that comprise a minority of the forces in question. The expectations may be larger than the capability, given the small numbers. This emphasizes the need to manage expectations while prioritizing recruitment and retention of diverse individuals.

Disarmament, Demobilization, and Reintegration

A DDR process is typically used to support former fighters from insurgent or violent extremist groups to hand over weapons, leave formal or informal armed groups, and reintegrate back into civilian communities. These are crucial steps for securing a sustainable cessation of hostilities and preventing a return to armed conflict. DDR has traditionally overemphasized the role of the armed fighter, typically male, to the exclusion of those who provided support roles within the group, often women. The narrow focus on male combatants overlooks women as perpetrators and agents of violence, while simultaneously compartmentalizing them as victims of violence.[31] Resolution 1325 calls for the "different needs of female and male ex-combatants . . . and the needs of their dependents" to be considered in planning. However, most DDR processes remain underresourced and either intentionally or inadvertently blind to the needs of diverse population sets. DDR processes require a greater understanding of the unique experiences and traumas exacerbated by gender, particular types of violence, and norms of expected behavior.[32] Women aligned with insurgent groups are in many cases prohibited from bearing arms. Yet many DDR processes continue to require weapons handover as a means of entry. In Sierra Leone and East Timor, this restriction essentially barred women combatants from accessing the benefits of the DDR process.[33] Negotiations over DDR and planning for DDR processes are a key entry point for discussion of how to build diversity and inclusion into the design and implementation processes for DDR. The more inclusive the negotiation process is, the more likely it will be that the outcome reflects the needs of a diverse cross section of affected populations.

But the role of diverse security forces and their operational effectiveness is not just with regard to post-conflict reconstruction; it also applies to the demobilization of violent extremists, whether they be domestic or foreign fighters. Efforts to stem or transform violent extremism approaches must be gender- and identity-sensitive, and prioritize the meaningful inclusion of key stakeholders in their development and implementation. Without diversity—both among engaged civil society actors and among those in the security sector—these initiatives are likely to overlook many of the factors that have driven individuals toward violent extremism, and will likely compromise the relevance and efficacy of attendant CVE policies. Importantly, when diverse groups are a core component of the development and implementation of CVE-related decision-making, this can have the added effect of elevating women and minority groups to be seen as equal partners in decision-making related to peace and security. This equal partnership can foster a sense of trust with military and security organizations, without which, evidence has found, conditions conducive to violent extremism may be perpetuated.[34]

Community Security: Rule of Law, Community Resilience, and Conflict Prevention

Rule of Law

The optimal way to contend with security threats is through productive and collaborative relationships between security forces, particularly police and peacekeeping forces, and the communities they are tasked to serve. For the rule of law to prevail, citizens must report crimes, incidences of rule-breaking, and warning signs of future criminality. Citizens will typically do so when (1) they are informed of the laws and rules, and of how to report breaches; (2) they do not fear retribution or abuse by law enforcement; and (3) they have some faith that the response will be effective. All aspects imply a needed degree of trust and communication between communities and security forces. Communities that do not trust authorities, do not feel represented within governmental bodies, or are disproportionately targeted by law enforcement or government bodies, are unlikely to cooperate with them. Strengthening networks across groups requires intentional forums for intergroup interaction and dialogue that are oriented toward trust-building. Security forces that are representative of the communities with which they engage have a higher likelihood of building stronger trust. Anecdotal evidence from Minneapolis, Minnesota, for example, suggests that residents of Somali origin expressed distrust of law enforcement, citing a lack of diversity of race, religion, and ethnicity within law enforcement. This tension decreased to some extent when the city and the US Transportation Security Administration hired Somali American individuals for policing and airport security roles.[35]

Restoring the rule of law is a prerequisite for rebuilding states in the aftermath of war.[36] Take, for example, the post-conflict environment in Liberia following the civil war. It was defined by limited social trust and low legitimacy of state institutions—a context in which dependence on formal state institutions alone for SSR or transitional justice would have had limited or, more critically, negative implications.[37] Yet, ownership of the institutional reforms was vested in a state committee composed of the warring parties, who proved to have little interest in implementation. Louise Andersen points out that a "lack of political will" is a primary indicator of mis-assigned ownership—where the citizens who maintained peace during war were shut out and ownership of the reconstruction process was left to those armed actors who had destroyed the very nation they were tasked to rebuild.[38] In 2016, after a decade of reform, Liberians continued to perceive state security and justice institutions as "ill-equipped, inaccessible, and ineffective."[39] Attempting to rectify this, the Liberian National Police set up Confidence Patrols—teams of ten to fifteen officers who travel to towns and villages throughout rural Liberia to raise awareness, demonstrate police capacity, and sensitize citizens to increased police presence in and around their communities. Blair and colleagues found that the program "increased knowledge of the police and Liberian law, reduced the incidence of some crimes, increased reporting of crimes to the police and courts, and enhanced security of property rights"—all positive contributors to the rule of law.[40] While the program did not serve to build citizen trust in the police, researchers speculated that it did shift social norms around the appropriateness of engaging with the police and courts. In short, inclusion of local communities and diversification of those we understand to be security stakeholders can be transformative.

Community Resilience

Community resilience—understood as the ability of a community to resist or recover quickly from natural or human-made stressors and shocks when they occur—is typically fortified by strengthening vertical and horizontal social integration across diverse stakeholders to improve trust and confidence.[41] More generally, it is accomplished by promoting adaptive social capabilities proven to reduce violence—such as information and communication infrastructure and/or systems facilitating nonviolent conflict resolution. According to resilience scholars, to build collective resilience, "communities must reduce risk and resource inequities, engage local people in mitigation, create organizational linkages, boost and protect social supports, and plan for not having a plan, which requires flexibility, decision-making skills, and trusted sources of information that function in the face of unknowns."[42] Multisectoral committees inclusive of community representatives, security forces, and local government collectively and collaboratively enable the diversity of skills and adaptability required to support risk reduction and improve trust with populations—ultimately increasing community resilience. While information-sharing is a central pillar of community resilience and crisis management, it is effective only if the networks for dissemination of information function and people trust the information received. Neuroscientific research confirms that people are more likely to trust information delivered by an individual from a similar identity group.[43] Again, this reinforces that a diverse force may enable key resiliency factors.

Conflict Prevention and Mitigation

Violence, or the threat of violence, can destroy the social fabric of communities, again harming trust across and within groups. In the absence of trust, groups and subgroups tend to take on an inward-focused, insular posture, which reduces the propensity to serve and protect others outside of their bonded group.[44] Authors argue that there is little coincidence that "countries whose security forces are more gender balanced and ethnically representative are some of the most peaceful in their region. And this pattern is global—from Sweden to Nicaragua to Botswana."[45] Just as diversity of security sector actors can increase social trust, it may also support conflict prevention through increased early warning capabilities. A diversity of views and inputs can identify locally relevant metrics to track changes that may indicate the imminent onset of violence or conflict. For example, women in Kosovo were the first to flag that men were amassing weapons and training for battle, long before the violence erupted.[46] Inclusion of local populations and diverse groups in designing conflict prevention and mitigation approaches is a direct countermand to the normative patterns that typically contribute to the onset of war—social exclusion, systemic discrimination, and security force abuse, among others.[47] Local understandings and social assessments of marginalization are a critical first step in fostering more inclusive practices—the markers of which should serve as indicators for conflict and potential for lasting peace processes.

Challenges and Barriers That Present Opportunities

Despite the rationales just given for including diverse perspectives in peacekeeping, SSR, and DDR, there remain limitations and resistance.

Sexism, Homophobia, and Transphobia

Gender and sexuality should be understood as constitutive categories that cannot be disentangled from each other. Normative gender ideals shape our perceptions of sexuality, particularly heterosexuality, in a way that affects the identity not only of individuals but also of institutions. Armed forces and military institutions have traditionally reflected hypermasculine gender norms that are intimately connected to, and co-constructed with, heteronormative ideals.[48]

Historically, the soldier has served as the "quintessential figure of masculinity." It was in the military that boys, according to the popular saying found in many languages, were made into men. Here, masculinity was (and is) actively and consciously constructed and consolidated, oftentimes in relation and in contrast to notions of femininity, as well as, in late modern history, homosexuality.[49]

Exclusion of and blatant discrimination against LGBTQI service members is intimately linked to these gendered institutional identities. These normative social beliefs have been codified in law and/or regulation by a number of states, including the United States, where in 2017 the repeal of discriminatory regulation was later threatened by a presidential ban on transgender service members.[50] In the same way that women may be penalized for not adhering to particular performances of masculinity (for example, "not being manly enough"), so too can men be punished for demonstrating traditionally feminine characteristics and/or not aligning with hypermasculine expression.

Assumptions About Unit Cohesion

A common counterdiversity argument from military institutions is that diversity—particularly that of gender and sexual orientation—will negatively impact "unit cohesion," or the bonding of soldiers in a way that sustains their will and commitment to each other, the unit, and mission accomplishment. Studies have found within the armed forces, for example, "ingrained views according to which the presence of homosexuals in the armed forces compromises cohesion and leads to unit conflict and division."[51] While unit cohesion is essential for the safety and efficacy of military units, assumptions about how diversity interferes with cohesion may be highly flawed. The Hague Centre for Strategic Studies finds instead that "morale is higher when people feel recognized and respected at work. Cohesion is improved when colleagues can communicate openly. Trust is enhanced when there is no suspicion that colleagues have something to hide."[52] This implies that cohesion does not necessarily rest on identity-based conformity but, instead, relies on communication skill sets and the ability to construct social capital.

Imposition of Western Values

A tension often perceived in SSR and DDR interventions involves presumptions around local and global values in regard to gender equality. There is often reluctance from international actors to advocate for gender equality in SSR in places where gender discrimination and patriarchal values define local norms.[53] These concerns are warranted: critical development and international relations scholars highlight the often colonial, racial, and gendered practices that interventions—particularly Western interventions—can impose on countries in the global South.[54] In Afghanistan, for example, failure to meaningfully consult diverse groups of local actors meant that intervening nations designed interventions based on their assumptions of the local context. These assumptions often proved false and resulted in at best limited impact and at worst heightened tensions and conflict.[55] To respond to these challenges, context sensitivity is key.[56] There can be no one-size-fits-all approach to inclusion and diversity in SSR and DDR; what works in some ethnocultural contexts will likely not work in others for a multitude of reasons, including but not limited to economic divergences, security considerations, heterogeneity of views, and social norms.

Homogeneity in Troop-Contributing Countries

The increased emphasis on diversity is challenged by accusations of hypocrisy when donor nations fail to deploy diverse peacekeeping forces, either intentionally or unintentionally. Countries calling for increased participation of diverse groups, often women, in security forces continue to fail at assembling their own diverse units for deployment. Ultimately, "if the premise of [military] intervention is to have competing ethnicities cooperate, then the intervening countries and their forces need to practice what they preach and model that to the people on the ground."[57] A number of troop-contributing nations cite differences in Western and non-Western contexts, claiming that local norms prohibit them from deploying women to serve in peacekeeping operations abroad. Anecdotal evidence suggests, however, that the peacekeeping deployments are seen as highly lucrative opportunities and men are reluctant to relinquish spots to women for this reason.[58]

Education and Training: Availability and Quality

Well-informed, culturally specific, research-based education and training for military and security personnel are essential both to create inclusive security forces and to support SSR and DDR practices that attend equally to all segments of the population. The role of professional military education may be an opportunity to keep pace with and improve the socialization of new policies advancing equity; however, there are challenges with regard to the quality of training and education and the importance placed on diversity as a core competency in promotions. Often, security force training for human security and diversity focuses on sexual exploitation and abuse—on the messaging that "rape is wrong." Although such training is relevant and critical, participants in the Congolese army, for example, found it personally insulting and ineffective in strengthening relevant skill sets.[59] This approach, all too common, focuses on deficits (what not to do) instead of assets (what to do). Despite challenges, there are demonstrated best practices and clear opportunities for fostering diversity and inclusion among security forces in developing and post-conflict contexts—and these should be the focus of education and training. The risks of poor training and education on this issue are high: condescending training, or training that is not articulated in a way that speaks to the audience, may result in disengagement from the conversation altogether.

Policy Change Outpacing Normative Change

Security institutions have experienced increasing pressure to demonstrate compliance with and champion international calls for diversity in security forces. In some cases, there has been a rush to change policies and laws to reflect these international calls, but implementation lags behind as the slow process of changing institutional and social norms begins. In Serbia, for example, there are concerns that the nation is adopting laws and strategies faster than it can change practice.[60] Nina Wilén found in her research in South Africa and Burundi that three norms directly influenced post-conflict military reform: (1) resistance to women in the army, (2) women as primary caregivers, and (3) men's perceived superiority over women.[61] Policy change that ignores existing social norms will not typically yield concrete effect. Inclusive processes, through which buy-in is garnered and participatory consultation processes are utilized to define these proposed changes, increase the likelihood that individuals and institutions will comply.[62]

The Way Forward: Policy Implications and Research

There remain opportunities for academic and practitioner contributions to the study of diversity and inclusion in security forces, SSR, and DDR. With a surge of attention and research on women's experiences since the 1980s within critical feminist approaches to international relations, political economy, and development studies, expansion of studies across all lines of diversity and their intersections would be welcome. Diversification of authorship is also essential as research on and by LGBTQI, visible minorities, and Indigenous peoples remains limited or marginalized in discussions of human security and development studies.

Beyond Gender

It is widely acknowledged that SSR and DDR planning and operations need to be gendered because the security sector and development fields require a diversifying of security forces in order to be responsive in local contexts.[63] However, the words "gender" and "women" are often used interchangeably.[64] Within the current gender-focused debate, this conflation of gender and women stifles attention to masculinities, which are often strongly correlated to drivers of violence. Consider, for example, the role of military masculinities in sexual misconduct and harassment in military forces, where an organization steeped in tradition and an "old-boys' club" mentality has perpetuated sexual violence and misconduct.[65] There is also an opportunity here to consider the role of masculinities, positive leadership, and male allyship in addressing diversity and inclusion in military forces. But there is a need to push the discussion of "gender analysis and women's inclusion" to be more inclusive of diversity broadly understood: the intersection of identities and lived experiences, which includes gender, and how they improve our interactions and work within the security field.

Beyond Active Duty

With an increased call for diversity of lived experiences and identities within security forces, one must also consider proactively the transition of these individuals to civilian life. Research from Canada and the United States, for example, has brought to light the assumption of homogeneity in understandings of who security actors are, and the programs, services, and policies available to them.[66] Understanding how discrimination and biases reify themselves beyond employment in the security and defense sector during program delivery for veterans is an emerging body of research that requires immediate focus. Understanding that, with demands for increased representation and participation of diverse groups, transition plans must reflect differences in experiences.

Beyond Numbers

Historically, metrics of diversity have been quantitative, with the institutional default being to report on the numbers of individuals recruited, promoted, and/or consulted within each identity group. Quotas for increasing representation of certain groups in security forces have also been a default for many states and multilateral organizations. However, quotas rarely work in isolation, and instead must be bolstered by enabling measures and programs that support increased recruitment, promotion, and retention through systemic and institutional change.[67] Select security institutions have begun to move beyond numbers to evaluate institutional policies, doctrine, systems, and cultural norms.[68] Researchers Sabrina Karim and

Kyle Beardsley, for example, have pushed beyond the numbers on women's participation in peacekeeping operations to ask how the culture of UN peacekeeping needs to change if gender equality in peace operations is to become an attainable goal.[69] More research is needed to compile a meaningful body of metrics to evaluate not just the numbers but the extent of the enabling environment.

Conclusion

This chapter identified how diverse and inclusive perspectives within security institutions can provide adaptable and responsive post-conflict support. The diversity of security forces results in improved and inclusive SSR and DDR responses, while narrow conceptions of "gender" within these dialogues limits understanding of local populations and their distinct needs. Critically, diversity and inclusion of security sector stakeholders, which includes local populations, can also help mitigate the effects of conflict. Future research and initiatives should emphasize the importance of rigorous data collection and analysis, both qualitative and quantitative, as well as inclusive conversations of ways to integrate intersecting identities. Local populations benefit from diverse security actors, and diversity in security forces enables meaningful and lasting change.

Notes

1. Department of Defense 2017.
2. Hardt and von Hlatky 2020.
3. NATO 2019.
4. Jennings 2012.
5. IPU 1997.
6. United Nations 2014b.
7. United Nations 2014b.
8. Dursun-Ozkanca and Vandemoortele 2012.
9. African Union 2014.
10. African Union 2014.
11. Egnell 2016.
12. Bove and Ruggeri 2016.
13. US Joint Staff 2009; Jennings 2012, 20; Barsa 2013.
14. NCGM 2015, 16.
15. Bastick 2008.
16. Bastick and Valasek 2009.
17. Ebo 2006.
18. Hendricks 2012.
19. Bridges and Horsfall 2009.
20. Schroeder and Chappuis 2014, 152.
21. Detzner 2017, 119, citing Nicole Ball. See, for example, Sedra 2010; Baker 2010.
22. Lawrence 2012.

23. Baker and Scheye 2007. Rosenbaum and Lurigio 1994.
24. Burian 2018.
25. United Nations 2014a.
26. Wilén 2019, 7.
27. Wilén 2019, 7.
28. Crawford and Macdonald 2013, 86–87.
29. Karim and Beardsley 2017.
30. UNDP 2016.
31. Hauge 2019.
32. Gutiérrez Sanín and Carranza Franco 2017.
33. Rehn and Sirleaf 2002.
34. Giscard d'Estaing 2017.
35. In-person interview between Michelle Barsa and a representative of the US Department of Homeland Security Office of Civil Rights and Civil Liberties, 2017.
36. Blair, Karim, and Morse 2016.
37. Andersen 2006.
38. Andersen 2006.
39. Blair, Karim, and Morse 2016.
40. Blair, Karim, and Morse 2016, 12.
41. Norris et al. 2008.
42. Norris et al. 2008, 130.
43. See, for example, Williams 2001; Tanghe, Wisse, and Ven Der Flier 2010; Tanis and Postmes 2005.
44. Siegler 2014.
45. Burian 2018.
46. Hill 2003, 18.
47. O'Reilly 2016, 119.
48. Sundevall and Persson 2016.
49. Sundevall and Persson 2016.
50. In January 2021, US president Joe Biden signed an executive order repealing the transgender ban instituted by US president Donald Trump in July 2017.
51. Rokvić and Stanarević 2016.
52. Polchar, Sweijis, Marten, and Galdiga 2014, 11.
53. Gordon, Welch, and Roos 2015; Ansorg and Gordon 2019.
54. For example, in South Sudan, tensions exist between calls and interventions for diversity and gender equality in SSR and DDR processes, which often uphold the current power dynamic and further marginalize the groups most affected by post-conflict environments. See Gordon, Welch, and Roos 2019, 2. See also Kunz 2014; Teissen 2014.
55. Barley 2008.
56. Mobekk 2010.
57. Leuprecht 2009, 573.
58. Conclusions draw from in-person interviews conducted by Michelle Barsa with senior Southeast Asia police officers in 2015.
59. Baaz and Stern 2017.
60. Rokvic and Stanarevic 2016.
61. Wilén 2019.
62. Andersen 2006.
63. Baaz and Utas 2012, 5.
64. Carver 1996, 5.
65. Taber 2018; Lee 2016.

66. See, for example, Shoemaker and von Hlatky 2020; Eichler and Smith-Evans 2018; Perkins et al. 2020.
67. UN Women 2018, 33.
68. Okros 2009.
69. Karim and Beardsley 2017.

Bibliography

African Union. 2014. "Policy Framework on Security Sector Reform." https://www.peaceau.org/uploads/au-policy-framework-on-security-sector-reform-ae-ssr.pdf.

Andersen, Louise. 2006. "Post-Conflict Security Sector Reform and the Challenge of Ownership in the Case of Liberia." Danish Institute for International Affairs. www.jstor.org/stable/resrep13223.

Ansorg, Nadine, and Eleanor Gordon. 2019. "Co-operation, Contestation and Complexity in Post-Conflict Security Sector Reform." *Journal of Intervention and Statebuilding* 13, no. 1: 2–24. https://doi.org/10.1080/17502977.2018.1516392.

Baker, Bruce. 2010. "The Future Is Non-State." In *The Future of Security Reform*, edited by Mark Sedra, 208–228. Waterloo: CIGI.

Baker, Bruce, and Eric Scheye. 2007. "Multi-Layered Justice and Security Delivery in Post-Conflict and Fragile States." *Conflict, Security and Development* 7, no. 4: 503–528. doi: 10.1080/14678800701692944.

Barley, Duncan. 2008. "Rebuilding Afghanistan's Security Forces: Security Sector Reform in Contested State-Building." *RUSI* 153, no. 3: 52–57. doi: 10.1080/03071840802249596.

Barsa, Michelle. 2013. "Challenges to Securing Afghan Women's Gains in a Post-2014 Environment." Prepared Testimony for the House Armed Services Committee. HASC No. 113–67: Hearing Before the Subcommittee on Oversight and Investigations, 113th Congress, 1st Session, October 29.

Barsa, Michelle, Olivia Holt-Ivry, and Allison Muehlenbeck. 2017. "Inclusive Ceasefires: Women, Gender and a Sustainable End to Violence." Inclusive Security, Washington, DC. https://www.inclusivesecurity.org/wp-content/uploads/2016/03/Inclusive-Ceasefires-ISA-paper-Final-3.10.2016.pdf.

Bastick, Megan. 2008. "Integrating Gender in Post-Conflict Security Sector Reform." DCAF, Geneva.

Bastick, Megan, and Kristin Valasek. 2009. "Gender and Security Sector Reform Training Resource Package." DCAF, Geneva. https://www.dcaf.ch/gender-and-security-sector-reform-training-resource-package.

Bastick, Megan, and Tobie Whitman. 2013. "A Women's Guide to Security Sector Reform." Institute for Inclusive Security and DCAF, Washington, DC. https://www.inclusivesecurity.org/publication/a-womens-guide-to-security-sector-reform/.

Blair, Robert, Sabrina Karim, and Benjamin Morse. 2016. "Building Trust in a Reformed Security Sector: A Field Experiment in Liberia." Policy Brief. International Growth Center, London. August.

Bloom, Mia. 2011. *Bombshell: Women and Terrorism*. Philadelphia: University of Pennsylvania Press.

Bove, Vincenzo, and Andrea Ruggeri. 2016. "Kinds of Blue: Diversity in UN Peacekeeping Missions and Civilian Protection." *British Journal of Political Science* 46 no. 3: 681–700. doi:10.1017/S0007123415000034.

Bridges, Donna, and Debbie Horsfall. 2009. "Increasing Operational Effectiveness in UN Peacekeeping: Toward a Gender-Balanced Force." *Armed Forces and Society* 36, no. 1: 120–130.

Burian, Alexander. 2018. "Security Sector Reform and Conflict Prevention." World Bank blog, April 25. https://blogs.worldbank.org/dev4peace/security-sector-reform-and-conflict-prevention.

Carver, Terrell. 1996. *Gender Is Not a Synonym for Women*. Boulder, CO: Lynne Rienner.

Community Policing Consortium. 1994. "Understanding Community Policing: A Framework for Action." US Department of Justice, Office of the Justice Programs, Bureau of Justice Assistance, Washington, DC.

Crawford, Kerry, and Julia Macdonald. 2013. "Establishing a Marketplace of Women in Peacekeeping: An Analysis of Gender Mainstreaming and Its Viability in United Nations Peacekeeping Operations." *ASPJ Africa and Francophonie*, first quarter, 80–96.

Department of Defense. 2017. "Policy for Brigade-Level Approval of Certain Requests for Religious Accommodation." Army Directive 2017-03, Secretary of the Army, Washington, DC. http://s3.amazonaws.com/becketpdf/Army-Directive-2017-03-Policy-for-Brigade-Level-Approval-of-Certain-Requests-for-Religious-Accommodation.pdf.

Detzner, Sarah. 2017. "Modern Post-Conflict Security Sector Reform in Africa: Patterns of Success and Failure." *African Security Review* 26, no. 2: 116–142. https://doi.org/10.1080/10246029.2017.1302706.

Dursun-Ozkanca, Oya, and Antoine Vandemoortele. 2012. "The European Union and Security Sector Reform: current practices and challenges of implementation." *European Security* 21, no. 2: 139–160. doi: 10.1080/09662839.2012.665881.

Ebo, Adedeji. 2006. "The Challenges and Lessons of Security Sector Reform in Post-Conflict Sierra Leone." *Conflict, Security, and Development* 6, no. 4: 481–501. doi: 10.1080/14678800601066447.

Egnell, Robert. 2016. "Gender Perspectives and Military Effectiveness: Implementing UNSCR 1325 and the National Action Plan on Women, Peace, and Security," *PRISM* 6, no. 1: 73–89. https://genderandsecurity.org/projects-resources/research/gender-perspectives-and-military-effectiveness-implementing-unscr-1325.

Eichler, Maya, and Kimberley Smith-Evans. 2018. "Gender in Veteran Reintegration and Transition: A Scoping Review." *Journal of Military, Veteran, and Family Health* 4, no. 1: 5–19. doi: 10.3138/jmvfh.2017-0004.

Eriksson Baaz, Maria, and Maria Stern. 2017. "Being Reformed: Subjectification and Security Sector Reform in the Congolese Armed Forces." *Journal of Intervention and Statebuilding* 11, no. 2: 207–224. https://doi.org/10.1080/17502977.2017.1337338.

Eriksson Baaz, Maria, and Mats Utas, eds. 2012. *Beyond "Gender and Stir": Reflections on Gender and SSR in the Aftermath of African Conflicts*. Uppsala: Nordic Africa Institute. https://uu.diva-portal.org/smash/get/diva2:850978/FULLTEXT02.pdf.

Giscard d'Estaing, Sophie. 2017. "Engaging Women in Countering Violent Extremism: Avoiding Instrumentalisation and Furthering Agency." *Gender and Development* 25, no. 1: 103–118. doi: 10.1080/13552074.2017.1279823.

Global Center on Cooperative Security and the Institute for Inclusive Security. 2015. "Strengthening Rule of Law Responses to Counter Violent Extremism: What Role for Civil Society in South Asia?" Global Center on Cooperative Security Policy Brief.

Gordon, Eleanor, Anthony Cleland Welch, and Emmicki Roos. 2015. "Security Sector Reform and the Paradoxical Tension Between Local Ownership and Gender Equality." *International Journal of Security and Development* 4, no. 1: 1–23. https://doi.org/10.5334/sta.gj.

Gutiérrez Sanín, Francisco, and Francy Carranza Franco. 2017. "Organizing Women for Combat: The Experience of the FARC in the Colombian War." *Journal of Agrarian Change* 17, no. 4: 770–778. https://doi.org/10.1111/joac.12238.

Hardt, Heidi, and Stéfanie von Hlatky. 2020. "NATO's About-Face: Adaptation to Gender Mainstreaming in an Alliance Setting." *Journal of Global Security Studies* 5, no. 1: 136–159. https://doi.org/10.1093/jogss/ogz048.

Hauge, Wench Iren. 2019. "Gender Dimensions of DDR—Beyond Victimization and Dehumanization: Tracking the Thematic." *International Feminist Journal of Politics* 2, no. 22: 206–226. doi: 10.1080/14616742.2019.1673669.

Hendricks, Cheryl. 2012. "Research on Gender and SSR in Africa." In *Beyond "Gender and Stir": Reflections on Gender and SSR in the Aftermath of African Conflicts*, 11–17. edited by Maria Eriksson Baaz and Mats Utas. Uppsala: Nordic Africa Institute.

Hill, Felicity. 2003. *Women's Contribution to Conflict Prevention, Early Warning and Disarmament.* United Nations Institute for Disarmament Research. http://www.peacewomen.org/assets/file/Resources/UN/unifem_womencontributrconprevewdisarm_2003.pdf.

Hudson, Valerie. 2012. *Sex and World Peace.* New York: Columbia University Press.

IPU. 1997. "Towards Partnership Between Men and Women in Politics: Concluding Statement by the President of the Inter-Parliamentary Union at the Specialized Inter-Parliamentary Conference Held in New Delhi." February 18. http://archive.ipu.org/splz-e/Ndelhi97.htm.

Jennings, Kathleen M. 2012. "Women's Participation in UN Peace Operations: Agents of Change or Stranded Symbols?" In *Beyond "Gender and Stir": Reflections on Gender and SSR in the Aftermath of African Conflicts*, edited by Maria Eriksson Baaz and Mats Utas, 18–30. Uppsala: Nordic Africa Institute.

Karim, Sabrina, and Kyle Beardsley. 2017. *Equal Opportunity Peacekeeping: Women, Peace, and Security in Post-Conflict States.* New York: Oxford University Press.

Kunz, Rahel. 2014. "Gender and Security Sector Reform: Gendering Differently?" *International Peacekeeping* 21, no. 5: 604–622.

Lawrence, Michael. 2012. "Towards a Non-State Security Sector Reform Strategy." CIGI SSR Issue Paper. https://www.cigionline.org/sites/default/files/ssr_no_8_0.pdf.

Lee, Peter. 2016. "This Man's Military: Masculine Culture's Role in Sexual Violence." Drew Paper no. 26. Air University, Montgomery, AL.

Leuprecht, Christian. 2009. "Diversity as Strategy: Democracy's Ultimate Litmus Test." *Commonwealth and Comparative Politics* 47, no. 4: 559–579. https://doi.org/10.1080/14662040903388383.

Mobekk, Eirin. 2010. "Gender, Women and Security Sector Reform." *International Peacekeeping* 17, no. 2: 278–291. http://dx.doi.org/10.1080/13533311003625142.

NATO. 2019. "Summary of Annual National Reports—2017." IMS Office of the Gender Advisor. Brussels.

NCGM. 2015. "Whose Security? Practical Examples of Gender Perspectives in Military Operations." Swedish Armed Forces.

Norris, Fran, et al. 2008. "Community Resilience as a Metaphor, Theory, Set of Capabilities and Strategy for Disaster Readiness." *American Journal of Community Psychology* 41: 127–150. doi: 10.1007/s10464-007-9156-6.

Okros, Alan. 2009. "Rethinking Diversity and Security." *Commonwealth and Comparative Politics* 47, no. 4: 346–373.

O'Reilly, Marie. 2016. "Inclusive Security and Peaceful Societies: Exploring the Evidence." *PRISM* 6, no. 1: 21–33. https://www.inclusivesecurity.org/publication/inclusive-security-and-peaceful-societies-exploring-the-evidence/.

OSCE. 2014. *Preventing Terrorism and Countering Extremism and Radicalization That Lead to Terrorism: A Community Policing Approach.* Vienna: OSCE.

Perkins, Daniel, et al. 2020. "Veterans' Use of Programs and Services as They Transition to Civilian Life: Baseline Assessment for the Veteran Metrics Initiative." *Journal of Social Service Research* 46, no. 2: 241–255. https://doi.org/10.1080/01488376.2018.1546259.

Polchar, Joshua, Tim Sweijs, Philipp Marten, and Jan Galdiga. 2014. "LGBT Military Personnel: A Strategic Vision for Inclusion." The Hague Centre for Strategic Studies. https://hcss.nl/wp-content/uploads/2014/06/HCSS_LGBT_webversie.pdf.

Rehn, Elisabeth, and Ellen Johnson Sirleaf. 2002. "Women, War and Peace: The Independent Expert's Assessment on the Impact of Armed Conflict on Women and Women's Role in Peace-Building." United Nations Development Fund for Women, New York. https://www.unwomen.org/en/digital-library/publications/2002/1/women-war-peace-the-independent-experts-assessment-on-the-impact-of-armed-conflict-on-women-and-women-s-role-in-peace-building-progress-of-the-world-s-women-2002-vol-1#view.

Rokvic, Vanja, and Svetlana Stanarevic. 2016. "Toward Gender and LGBT Equality in the Serbian Armed Forces." *Women's Studies International Forum* 55: 26–34. https://doi.org/10.1016/j.wsif.2016.02.003.

Rosenbaum, Dennis P., ed. 1994. *The Challenge of Community Policing.* Thousand Oaks, CA: Sage, 1994.

Rosenbaum, Dennis P., and Arthur J. Lurigio. 1994. "An Inside Look at Community Policing Reform: Definitions, Organizational Changes, and Evaluation Findings." *Crime and Delinquency* 40, no. 3: 299–314. https://heinonline.org/HOL/LandingPage?handle=hein.journals/cadq40&div=21&id=&page=.

Schroeder, Ursula C., and Fairlie Chappuis. 2014. "New Perspectives on Security Sector Reform: The Role of Local Agency and Domestic Politics." *International Peacekeeping* 21, no. 2: 133–148. https://doi.org/10.1080/13533312.2014.910401.

Sedra, Mark. 2010. *The Future of Security Reform.* Waterloo: CIGI. https://www.cigionline.org/sites/default/files/the_future_of_security_sector_reform.pdf.

Shoemaker, Meaghan, and Stefanie von Hlatky. 2020. "Unblurring the Lines of Responsibility: The Puzzle of Veteran Service Provision and Its Gendered Implications." *Journal of Veterans Studies* 6, no. 2: 88–100. http://doi.org/10.21061/jvs.v6i2.181.

Siegler, Veronique. 2014. "Measuring Social Capital in the UK." Office of National Statistics, London. https://www.researchgate.net/publication/281293496_Measuring_Social_Capital_in_the_UK_July_2014_Office_for_National_Statistics.

Sundevall, Fia, and Almsa Persson. 2016. "LGBT in the Military: Policy Development in Sweden 1944–2014." *Sexuality Research and Social Policy* 13: 119–129. https://www.ncbi.nlm.nih.gov/pmc/articles/PMC4841839/.

Taber, Nancy. 2018. "After Deschamps: Men, Masculinities, and the Canadian Armed Forces." *Journal of Military, Veteran, and Family Health* 4, no. 1: 100–107. doi: 10.3138/jmvfh.2017-0005.

Tanghe, Jacqueline, Barbara Wisse, and Henk Ven Der Flier. 2010. "The Role of Group Member Affect in the Relationship Between Trust and Cooperation." *British Journal of Management* 21, no. 2: 359–374. https://doi.org/10.1111/j.1467-8551.2009.00643.x.

Tanis, Martin, and Tom Postmes. 2005. "A Social Identity Approach to Trust: Interpersonal Perception, Group Membership, and Trusting Behavior." *European Journal of Social Psychology* 35, no. 3: 413–424. doi: 10.1002/ejsp.256.

Teissen, Rebecca. 2014. "Gender Equality and the Two CIDAs: Successes and Setbacks, 1976–2013." In *Rethinking Canadian Aid*, edited by Stephen Brown, Molly den Heyer, and David Black, 195–209. Ottawa: University of Ottawa Press.

UN Women. 2018. "Women's Meaningful Participation in Negotiating Peace and the Implementation of Peace Agreements: Report of the Expert Group Meeting." UN Women, New York. https://iknowpolitics.org/sites/default/files/egm-womens-meaningful-participation-in-negotiating-peace-en_0.pdf.

UNDP. 2016. "Preventing Violent Extremism Through Inclusive Development and the Promotion of Tolerance and Respect for Diversity." United Nations Development Programme, New York. https://www.undp.org/content/undp/en/home/librarypage/democratic-governance/conflict-prevention/discussion-paper---preventing-violent-extremism-through-inclusiv.html.

United Nations. 2014a. "Unanimously Adopting Resolution 2151 (2014), Security Council Underscores Need for National Ownership of Security-Sector Reform." SC/11369. https://www.un.org/press/en/2014/sc11369.doc.htm.

United Nations. 2014b. "Resolution 2151." Adopted by the Security Council on April 28, 2014. https://www.securitycouncilreport.org/atf/cf/%7B65BFCF9B-6D27-4E9C-8CD3-CF6E4FF96FF9%7D/s_res_2151.pdf.

US Joint Staff. 2009. "Joint Intelligence Preparation of the Operational Environment." Joint Publication 2-01.3. https://www.bits.de/NRANEU/others/jp-doctrine/jp2_01_3%2809%29.pdf

Wilén, Nina. 2019. "Achieving a Gendered Transformation of the Post-Conflict Military Through Security Sector Reform: Unpacking the Private-Public Dynamics." *International Feminist Journal of Politics* 22, no. 1: 86–105. doi: 10.1080/14616742.2018.1559749.

Williams, Michele. 2001. "In Whom We Trust: Group Membership as an Affective Context for Trust Development." *Academy of Management Review* 26, no. 3: 377–339.

12

Addressing Legacies of Abuse Through Transitional Justice Mechanisms

Hugo van der Merwe and Nomathamsanqa Masiko-Mpaka
With contributions from Eduardo González

True peace must be anchored in justice and an unwavering commitment to universal rights for all humans, regardless of ethnicity, religion, gender, national origin or any other identity attribute.

—Desmond Tutu[1]

Introduction

Today, confronting legacies of mass abuses is generally accepted to be a component of efforts to build peaceful and democratic societies. These transitional justice (TJ) processes have increasingly sought ways to address the needs of victims and marginalized communities. The last thirty years have seen rapid growth in new strategies to make these processes more responsive to the diverse segments of society affected by conflict, and to look more seriously at how they can be empowered in more sustainable ways. While there is a danger that victim's experiences can be co-opted simply as symbols of reconciliation or martyrdom in national debates and rituals, these marginalized voices have become increasingly assertive regarding their needs, priorities, and perspectives in transitional justice debates. In response, transitional justice policy processes and the implementation of these mechanisms have become more responsive, both in the diversity of stakeholders they include and in the way they understand their goals. Political transitions provide an opportunity to shift the trajectory of political participation and set new precedents for diversity and inclusion. Drawing on lessons from other countries and international norms, policy innovators have created exciting opportunities for giving voice to marginalized communities. Donor inputs and international collaborations have been key to shaping these innovations.

The Emergence of TJ as a More Inclusive Response to Past Abuses

Transitional justice is defined by the United Nations as

> the full range of processes and mechanisms associated with a society's attempts to come to terms with a legacy of large-scale past abuses, in order to ensure accountability, serve justice and achieve reconciliation.[2]

Historically, most conflicts simply ended with the pursuit of victor's justice (and victor's truth), and/or some form of amnesty and amnesia in cases where parties had reached a bilateral negotiated settlement. Over the last thirty years, campaigns for human rights, as well as demands for truth and more creative ways to come to terms with the past, have led to transitional justice and reconciliation processes that confront the past in more even-handed and inclusive ways. Since the mid-1970s, over thirty-five truth commissions have been established across the globe, and even more countries instituted processes of trials and amnesties.[3] Over the last three decades, transitional justice has "moved from the margins to the mainstream of global politics."[4] Since its normalization as an essential component of any peacebuilding process, it is now almost inconceivable for peace agreements not to provide some provisions for addressing truth, accountability, or justice needs. Increasingly, these processes have sought to engage with issues of inclusion and diversity.

In the context of conflicts that divided society along ethnic, racial, religious, or ideological lines, the conventional starting point for inclusion was to ensure that transitional justice processes addressed the concerns and were representative of all sides of the conflict. However, it became quickly apparent that only having political leaders of the main contending factions at the table still led to the marginalization of a myriad of other voices and experiences. Whom to include and how to include them has been a central point of contention in transitional justice processes across the globe.

At the center of the growth of transitional justice has been the explicit goal of inclusion of victims of human rights abuses as a key constituency that should benefit from, be consulted in, and participate in TJ processes. Yet, explicit claims of the victim-centeredness of these processes have been criticized as often just amounting to empty rituals rather than substantive commitments.[5] Victim-centeredness has not necessarily translated into an acknowledgment of the diversity of victim voices and the right of these constituencies to participate in all aspects of transitional justice. Over the past three decades, there has been a significant normative shift in support for inclusivity and diversity in transitional justice processes. Through public declarations and within policy statements at least, there is now near universal support for the principles of inclusion and diversity. Translating this into practice has, however, proven a lot more challenging.

The norm of victim-centeredness has become a key principle driving contemporary conceptions of transitional justice in policy and academic arenas. This norm affirms the vital significance of addressing victims' rights, including them in consultation regarding transitional justice policy, and ensuring that interventions are effective in addressing their needs. These rights of victims have been incorporated into the policy commitments of various regional and global bodies (e.g., the United Nations, African Union, and European Union) and have been increasingly formalized through international law precedents (e.g., through decisions of the Inter-American Court of Human Rights and the African Commission for Human and People's Rights) and through new institutions of international justice, such as the International Criminal Court.[6]

Victims of human rights abuses in settings of war and mass atrocity involve a broad range of different people, targeted or made vulnerable for different reasons, experiencing different forms of violations, and presenting different needs in relation to accessing redress and rebuilding their lives. In recognizing the full diversity of victims' experiences and needs, the importance of recognizing these as key constituencies who need to be consulted and understood becomes clear. Taking victims seriously, therefore, translates into taking the diversity of victimized groups seriously, rather than treating them as a uniform mass.

A second critical normative shift in the transitional justice field has been the recognition of the need for consultation and participation. Recognizing that transitional justice processes will not succeed without effective input and participation by those directly affected by conflict, policy frameworks and mainstream practice have increasingly acknowledged the centrality of inclusion in all aspects of the process. The African Union Transitional Justice Policy goes as far as to include it in its definition of transitional justice:

> Transitional justice refers to the various (formal and traditional or non-formal) policy measures and institutional mechanisms that societies, through an inclusive consultative process, adopt in order to overcome past violations, divisions and inequalities and to create conditions for both security and democratic and socioeconomic transformation.[7]

This principle of inclusion goes beyond just including direct victims to also include all those affected by the conflict and who are expected to benefit from transitional justice processes. It thus speaks potentially to the perspectives of those who are vulnerable to future violence and whose exclusion creates conditions for future conflict, opening the door for processes that go beyond just narrowly targeted consultations with select beneficiary groups. The African Union's definition also offers an expanded set of goals for transitional justice—namely, to "overcome past violations, divisions and inequalities and to create conditions for both security and democratic and socio-economic transformation." This highlights the preventive function of transitional justice, an approach that makes inclusion even more relevant as societies seek to uncover and address the various causes of past conflicts.

However, transitional justice praxis is often fraught with empty rituals rather than substantive commitment to these principles.[8] While those involved in high-level political negotiations over transitional justice processes cannot ignore these obligations, they have not always translated them into effective processes of consultation and participation. Many transitional justice processes are still heavily criticized for their failure to recognize the diversity of experiences and their failure to include key sectors in policy development and implementation. The inclusion of marginalized groups is often merely an afterthought rather than treated as a central element of the policy development and transitional justice implementation process.

Simon Robins, for instance, argues that transitional justice mechanisms are driven by the needs of the state and not by the needs of victims. This is evidenced by a bias toward state-centric legalistic solutions that prioritize prosecutions of perpetrators rather than addressing the needs victims often prioritize, such as reparations. Policy-makers rarely assess victim needs, and while many processes claim to be victim-centered, victims are not given the opportunity to engage on their own terms. As a result, victims have little agency; instead, they merely participate as instruments of those mechanisms.[9]

Alongside these official transitional justice mechanisms, which resist victim inclusion or struggle to give it meaning, victims, affected groups, and civil society organizations have also established their own processes to document their experiences, promote dialogue, and redress past abuses. Such innovations have had mixed results but have demonstrated the possibility of putting marginalized groups at the center of these solutions. Though they do not have the authority inherent in formal state or international mechanisms, such processes have given greater voice and agency to those excluded from conventional policy spaces.

Dimensions of Inclusion

The term "inclusivity" lacks conceptual clarity in the transitional justice field.[10] Inclusivity means different things to different stakeholders, and as a result, even if inclusivity is accepted in principle as a necessary element of transitional justice, its implementation proves contentious. Inclusion can be broadly understood as the process of including individuals who might otherwise be excluded or marginalized (such as women, youth, people with disabilities, and members of minority groups) from decision-making processes.

The meaning of inclusion in transitional justice can be broadly framed in relation to key aspects of the process: (1) the nature and scope of human rights violations addressed by transitional justice processes; (2) consultation and participation in policy development; (3) representation in transitional justice mechanisms; and (4) participation in transitional justice implementation and monitoring. The question of inclusion thus goes beyond setting up processes of participation in predetermined and prescribed frameworks where transitional justice simply gets synchronized to particular unique needs. Inclusion can present challenges to existing power dynamics that may require a reconceptualization of key assumptions of pillars of transitional justice.

There are some forms of transitional justice that have proven quite malleable and innovative in how they respond to issues of diversity and inclusion, while others such as courts, which are subject to stricter conventions, have been much slower to adapt.

Redefining the Scope of Human Rights Violations Addressed by Transitional Justice Processes

The scope of human rights violations addressed by transitional justice processes continues to expand. While initially there was a focus on physical violence (killings; torture; cruel, inhumane, and degrading treatment; enforced disappearances), more recently there has been growing acknowledgment of other human rights violations, such as psychological trauma; economic, social, and cultural rights abuses; sexual and gender-based violence; sexual torture; and structural and systemic violence. This expansion has sometimes been driven by groups seeking to shape transitional justice as an avenue for addressing their concerns. Feminists have, for example, entered the transitional justice arena with an overt intention of shifting its parameters to speak to broader injustices than those conventionally contained in the transitional justice mandate. This expanded agenda also raises more fundamental questions about what we mean by transitional justice. Explicitly recognizing sexual and gender-based violence or violence targeting LGBTQI individuals and communities as included in transitional justice mandates required rethinking the meaning of political transitions, the term "reconciliation," and the methodologies of pursuing these outcomes.[11]

Early truth commissions and war crimes trials adopted "gender-neutral" conceptions of human rights violations. Years of awareness-raising and lobbying resulted in the recognition of sexual violence as a strategy in war and rape as a tool of genocide, which shifted how these mechanisms define the range of violations they address and the tools required for engaging victim populations.[12]

Youth have mobilized to incorporate into transitional justice mandates a focus on the political and economic exclusion carried out by repressive and authoritarian regimes. Rather than just focusing on physical abuses, transitional justice mechanisms in Sierra Leone, Kenya, and Tunisia broadened their scope to expose the corrupt practices of economic elites that excluded the bulk of their populations from access to economic and political opportunities.

So far, the Colombian transitional justice process has explicitly included in its mandate a focus on violations of the rights of LGBTQI individuals.[13] These more radical shifts in agendas (LGBTQI in Colombia and economic crimes in Tunisia) have, however, often subsequently been reversed when more conservative forces reassert themselves in subsequent years. See Box 12.1.

Box 12.1 The Peruvian Experience
By Eduardo González

Peru's Truth and Reconciliation Commission (2001–2003) was the linchpin of that country's transitional justice processes. The TRC provided the central arena to examine the abuses committed between 1980 and 2000, during the confrontation between the state and Marxist-Leninist armed groups. The commission's report is the platform upon which reparations, criminal justice, and memorialization policies and projects continue to be developed.

The TRC emerged in the heat of mass mobilizations that led to the resignation and flight of authoritarian leader Alberto Fujimori. Civil society organizations advocated for a quick, generic presidential decree to establish the commission during the democratic springtime, rather than risking a protracted and unpredictable legislative negotiation. This choice had consequences for the commission's mandate.[14] It enumerated human rights abuses in a mostly generic manner, and called for specific attention only to abuses suffered by Indigenous communities. That said, the generic nature of the decree left members of the commission ample room for interpretation.

Truth commissions have evolved toward highly detailed legal mandates negotiated in the legislative branch, so Peru's approach seems confounding. However, it can be argued that in an environment marked by mass mobilization and led by sophisticated human rights advocates, the trade-off worked: a generic mandate did not prevent expansive interpretations of the mandate while taking full advantage of the quick pace of the transition.

There was one notable omission in the decree, though: a glaring silence on rape and sexual violence, which was not formally included in the list of abuses being investigated. Women's groups actively engaged the commission to ensure that interpretation of the mandate would encompass all forms of sexual violence. Their advocacy included publishing opinion pieces in the press and online, bringing attention to rape cases, and offering the TRC technical assistance to secure the inclusion of a gender perspective. As a result, the commission established a Gender Unit, organized public hearings focused on women's experiences, and included chapters on sexual violence and the experiences of women in the commission's final report.[15] This was quite an achievement considering that only two of twelve commissioners were women, and the TRC was only active for twenty-three months.

The internally displaced were also successful in securing attention to their situation, in spite of the absence of the crime of forced displacement from the formal enumeration of crimes in the mandate. Also, the civil society organizations of several regions pushed to ensure that the commission would be decentralized, creating offices in a number of provinces to conduct region-specific research, hold local public hearings, and contribute to sections of the final report.[16]

Paradoxically, the explicit inclusion of an Indigenous perspective in the legal mandate did not result in extensive attention to Indigenous peoples, probably because of the nature of Indigenous politics in Peru, which is strongly marked in the Andes by the campesino class identity, rather than by cultural identity. While the final report included a chapter on anti-Indigenous racism and documented massive instances of racist violence, the greatest focus of the chapter was on the experience of Amazonian—not Andean—communities, where Indigenous identity is represented by strong organizations.

Inclusion of LGBTQI communities' perspectives was more rudimentary. In the early 2000s, the LGBTQI movement was small, had little visibility, and was mostly represented by one pioneering organization led by gay men. The acronym "LGBTQI" was not in use and sexual dissidences were publicly absent, with the exception of sparsely attended pride parades. It was, in fact, a chance encounter of activists with gay and ally TRC staff during a pride event that resulted in the only effort to reflect an LGBTQI perspective and document LGBTQI experiences during the armed conflict.

A small group of gay activists used pride events to memorialize the massacre of eight trans women in 1989, committed by a Marxist-Leninist group to "punish common criminals" who had a "negative influence on youth." TRC staff participating in the pride parade encouraged the activists to present the cases to the TRC only a few weeks before release of the final report.[17] TRC allies, in turn, mobilized within the commission to corroborate the allegations using existing testimony and contemporary press reports. This resulted in the inclusion of a brief passage about "acts of terror against sexual minorities."[18] In the years following issuance of the final report, LGBTQI researchers and organizations scoured it for clues regarding additional homophobic crimes, identifying and publicizing several more committed by armed actors in Peru's conflict.[19] Post-commission work resulted in memorialization of hate crimes and a National Day of Struggle Against Hate Crimes as well as numerous related performing arts and documentary film projects.[20]

The Peruvian experience, particularly for LGBTQI communities, failed to achieve effective inclusion; it was particularly rudimentary compared to a successive truth commission in Brazil (2012–2014), which included a full chapter on the persecution of LGBTQI communities, also going beyond the explicit legal mandate of the commission, which was silent on hate crimes. More recently, the truth commission of Colombia (2017–2021) had the gender perspective and violence against LGBTQI persons explicitly included in its legal mandate, and it conducted extensive research and outreach on the experiences of LGBTQI communities during that country's armed conflict. However, the Peruvian case does show that civil society can use advocacy and expertise to shape the way truth commissions interpret their mandates and design key processes, overcoming the weaknesses of legal mandates.

From Policy to Implementation: Inclusive Participation Throughout TJ Processes

Inclusion involves an ongoing struggle to ensure that the needs and voices of less powerful actors are involved in key decisions and processes. It should not be limited to one part of the TJ process; it needs to be an integral aspect of the entire process, from the development of TJ policy to its implementation and monitoring. Sustained engagement is critical to ensure that commitments are fulfilled and followed up beyond the life of short-term mechanisms.

State-driven transitional justice mechanisms are often developed through peace negotiations or within formal frameworks of parliamentary processes. Traditionally, these were exclusive forums driven by polarized political agendas; as a result, public debate and consultation with targeted sectors and marginalized groups were not key elements of the design process. Where civil society has mobilized around transitional justice agendas, these policy spaces have been contested, and they have opened up to new voices such as women, youth, and organizations representing victims. Where international donors have supported transition processes, they have also funded national consultation processes where a range of constituencies have been brought into these debates and a much greater diversity of voices are consequently heard in the policy development process.

In contexts of ongoing political tension and with little history of broad democratic participation, such broad consultations may be quite limited. In some countries, consultations amount to little more than a national survey of opinions that makes little effort to document the needs of particularly marginalized sectors of society. In others (e.g., Burundi), those being consulted are just given a menu of options to choose from. Where women and youth have been more actively engaged in policy design, transitional justice policies and mechanisms have been more effectively tailored to engage with their priorities.[21]

Formal transitional justice mechanisms have also shifted from being mainly state-led mechanisms to including a more diverse range of nonstate or semi-state processes, many of which draw on representation from different societal sectors and often explicitly include gender quotas. Nonlegal mechanisms have been particularly innovative in pursuing inclusivity (rather than just technical expertise and reputation) as a means for ensuring legitimacy, reach, and therefore an ability to deliver on their goals.

The need for gender balance in the composition of truth commissions (TCs) has become commonly recognized. While earlier commissions had very few women (e.g., South Africa in 1995 with only seven women out of seventeen commissioners, Peru in 2001 with only two out of twelve, and Morocco in 2014 with one out of seventeen), more recent commissions such as Kenya in 2009 had 50 percent women commissioners. Additionally, the Gambian commission established in 2018 had five women among its eleven commissioners. This increased representation is significant for a number of reasons:

> Gender equality should also be a criterion for selecting commissioners. Although equal representation of men and women as commissioners will not guarantee a gender-sensitive approach, it does demonstrate the importance of recognizing different understandings of reality and the differential impacts of human rights violations on different types of people. The appointment of women as commissioners also facilitates the investigation of cases of sexual violence, where victims are mostly women. The selection of staff, interviewers, and researchers responsible for the TC's daily work should also follow this gender balance requirement—to send a positive message to the TCs.[22]

Many transitional justice processes also now recognize the need for continued consultations with communities affected by conflict. Maintaining a relationship with particular sectors and collaborating with civil society organizations with particular expertise in these areas has occurred in some countries.[23] Such "outreach" or "popularization" processes are, however, often just one-way channels for communication and have been criticized by the communities they are intended to serve for not providing avenues for effective engagement and accountability. This has led to a critique of many transitional justice mechanisms as being responsive to national and international political elites rather than to local communities most directly affected by conflict.

In some cases, this has led to the establishment of nonstate transitional justice processes that have much greater scope to place victims, women, youth, and other marginalized sectors at the center of the process. Civil society has sometimes taken the lead in collecting victims' stories, holding public hearings, facilitating art projects and exhibitions, developing documentaries, facilitating dialogues, and promoting a range of other interventions that are not dependent on the state's convening authority. These processes sometimes offer a dramatic shift in not only including marginalized voices but also putting them at the center of convening forums and shaping new narratives.[24]

Many state-led transitional justice processes are designed as short-term interventions that present findings and recommendations to guide future state action. While they often succeed admirably in achieving their goals, it is still up to the state to ultimately implement these recommendations and facilitate a longer-term process of justice, transformation, and reconciliation. This has been the aspect of transitional justice that has been the most severely criticized as states have consistently failed to fulfill this promise. This can undo much of the goodwill and trust initially built by transitional justice mechanisms. After the truth commission's robust engagement with victims in South Africa, the government's subsequent marginalization of their role in developing and implementing reparations and prosecutions led to protests and court challenges.

Civil society has increasingly lobbied for more responsive transitional justice processes and has monitored and engaged these mechanisms to ensure that they deliver on their mandates and that the state follows through on recommendations that arise from these mechanisms. Any commitment to addressing the needs of women, youth, or other marginalized groups means little in the absence of continued monitoring and pressure to deliver. Such engagement requires significant resources and investment in collaboration and networks, which are difficult to maintain indefinitely. Funders often treat transitional justice as a short-term process and see the closure of a truth commission or the end of a big trial as the end of the story, instead of as the foundation on which effective justice for marginalized groups can be pursued.

The laudatory findings of the Sierra Leone truth commission for reparations for people with war-related disabilities, as well as the recommendations for reparations and accountability for victims of sexual and gender-based violence by the Kenya truth commission, have seen little in the form of delivery by the state. Efforts to seek redress by these affected communities and sectors continue for years, if not decades, beyond the conclusion of these mechanisms.[25]

Similarly, after an extensive consultation process with victims during the Sierra Leone Truth and Reconciliation Commission (SLTRC), the commission developed recommendations that were viewed as responsive and appropriate to the range of perspectives collected. However, ten years later, victims were not much closer to receiving redress. A 2014 report by the country's Amputee and War-Wounded Association called on the government and international community to ensure that the recommendations of the SLTRC from 2004 are respected and are implemented. People who sustain severe injuries during a conflict have long-term health, rehabilitative, and social care needs that must be prioritized in a sustainable way. The fact that victims' rights have not been respected will have ramifications. It has also caused mistrust toward the government and international community about getting involved in peace and justice processes.[26]

The Benefits of Inclusion

There are a few state-specific studies that provide empirical evidence of benefits for victims as well as for the legitimacy and reach of transitional justice processes. However, concerns have been raised by studies that show the dark side of short-sighted participatory processes that expose vulnerable groups to retraumatization or raise unrealistic expectations. That said, a number of benefits have been identified in favor of more inclusive and diverse transitional justice processes.

First, there is significant knowledge gained by inclusion in such processes. Knowledge of the dynamics of conflict in a particular context is enriched by diverse voices, for there is a greater understanding of the causes of conflict, the conditions that produced a conducive environment for the conflict or repression to emerge, and the nature and extent of the human rights abuses committed. This knowledge is enriched by diverse voices, because conflict or repression impacts individuals in society differently depending on their identity.[27] For example, women, LGBTQI individuals, youth, and other marginalized groups all have different experiences of conflict. Therefore, any attempt to address the wrongs of the past needs to begin by understanding the varied lived experiences of a diverse group of people to enable a more complete and nuanced picture of the conflict or authoritarian period and ensuing human rights violations.

Second, transitional justice gains legitimacy from inclusion. Transitional justice is often regarded as a Western concept (or even a Western imposition), birthed in Europe and parachuted into developing countries to resolve their conflicts and authoritarian legacies.[28] It stands accused of being a concept that is deeply embedded in Western liberal ideals, and often not in line with contextual realities of the global South. Transitional justice (as it is conventionally framed in Western legalistic conceptions) is accused of being technocratic, elitist, and alien to the societies and communities it is supposed to benefit. Where transitional justice has failed to address inclusion and build local ownership, this challenge to its legitimacy is impossible to refute. Those activists who have sought to indigenize transitional justice have developed processes that are more attuned to local needs and realities. This can only be done through inclusive design and implementation efforts. Therefore, bringing transitional justice to "the people" and "the people" to transitional justice is important in ensuring that the process is deemed legitimate, is locally owned, and reflects the ideals of all in society, including victim groups and other marginalized groups. The conditions that necessitated the establishment of transitional justice processes—injustice, inequality, exclusion, dehumanization—need to be overcome, not reproduced. All too often, exclusionary politics are replicated in transitional justice mechanisms as certain sections of society are completely left out of meaningful spaces of participation and control. Inasmuch as transitional justice seeks to prevent future conflict by addressing its root causes, inclusion and legitimacy are interdependent and necessary conditions.

Third and most significantly, more inclusive transitional justice processes hold a greater prospect of preventing the recurrence of conflict through addressing its causes. Transitional justice processes are conventionally backward-looking processes focusing on the overt abuses committed during a conflict. When they are opened up to include the voices of sectors of society that are vulnerable, they are also placed under pressure to address the sources of this vulnerability. Gender, youth, and LGBTQI advocates have pushed these processes to address the underlying power inequalities and social norms that would simply reproduce conditions of vulnerability, inequality, and violence if left unattended.

Who Is Included in Transitional Justice?

The scope of the diversity and extent of inclusivity addressed by transitional justice is constantly expanding. The United Nations Approach to Transitional Justice (2010), the European Union's Policy Framework on Support to Transitional Justice (2015), and the recently adopted African Union Transitional Justice Policy (2019) all emphasize inclusion as a key principle and focus on particular dimensions of diversity, including but not limited to women, youth, and members of other historically marginalized groups.[29]

These policies provide strong affirmations of the centrality of inclusion of certain voices in transitional justice processes. The United Nations document focuses particularly on the inclusion of women and children:

> National consultations are a critical element of the human rights-based approach to transitional justice, founded on the principle that successful transitional justice programmes necessitate meaningful public participation, including the different voices of men and women.[30]
> The United Nations should facilitate the process of national consultations by organizing forums for discussions, providing legal and technical advice, promoting the participation of traditionally excluded groups, such as victims, minorities, women, and children, supporting capacity building, and mobilizing financial and material resources.[31]
> Encouraging women and children to actively participate in the peace process, by sharing their gender-specific experiences of the conflict, and their priorities for achieving sustainable peace and accountability through appropriate transitional justice mechanisms.[32]

The European Union's policy on transitional justice spells this commitment to inclusion out more clearly and concretely, recognizing children particularly as key stakeholders with a right to be included:

> A victim-centered approach requires the early involvement and active participation of victims and affected communities, including diverse ethnic, racial, religious and other groups or minorities.[33]
> Transitional justice can only reach its goals if the process of its design and implementation is nationally and locally-owned and inclusive....[34]
> Therefore, the participation of civil society, victims, persons belonging to minority groups, women and youth in such processes plays an important role.[35]

Children are thus important stakeholders in transitional justice processes; they hold a unique view of what happened, and are a crucial constituent for building a more peaceful future. Not to involve children in these processes would fail to comply with the UN Convention on the Rights of the Child that guarantees the right of children to life, survival and development, as well as the right to express their views freely in all matters affecting them.[36]

The African Union takes this commitment to diversity and inclusion a few steps further. It explicitly focuses on youth and people with disabilities as key constituencies that need to be included. It also highlights within its nine foundational principles "inclusiveness, equity and non-discrimination" and "due regard to the gender and generational dimensions of violations and transitional processes."[37] The policy also has a whole section on "cross-cutting issues," which includes subsections on women and girls; children and youth; persons with disabilities; internally displaced persons, refugees, and stateless persons; and older persons.[38]

Another whole section of the policy is dedicated to "diversity management" that "addresses the group dimension of conflicts and violations where violence was organized and perpetrated on the bases of race, ethnicity, colour, sex, language, religion, political or any other opinion, national and social origin, fortune, birth or other status."[39]

Women and Transitional Justice

Feminist scholars and practitioners have highlighted the critical yet often neglected gendered impact of conflict and the importance of interventions that speak to this reality in its aftermath. Sirkku Hellsten argues that in light of the fact that women are disproportionately and uniquely affected by conflict and have a unique experience even in the period of transition, gender analyses need to be given prominence in transitional justice processes.[40]

A key problem for transitional justice is the way that it has been narrowly conceptualized as addressing specific political conflicts, blinding it to various underlying and ongoing "nonpolitical" divisions and forms of violence, such as gender-based violence. Violence against women is thus often ignored by mechanisms that focus on politically motivated abuses. Excluding such cases as "ordinary" or "apolitical" crimes ignores the fact that gender-based violence is embedded in a sociopolitical system of gender inequality.

While there has been increased recognition of sexual violence as a weapon of political conflict, policymakers have been more reluctant to deal with the deeply embedded gender roles and inequalities that create vulnerabilities that are simply exacerbated during conflict. Violence against women cannot be framed outside the context of gender inequality. It is no wonder violence against women does not end with the signing of peace agreements and transitions to democracy, but can be understood as taking place along a continuum (before, during, and after armed conflict).[41] A case in point is South Sudan. While a revitalized peace deal was signed in September 2018, sexual violence perpetrated against women continues to be on the rise and remains endemic. Structural challenges that limit women's access to opportunities and resources are coupled with unequal gender dynamics to create an environment conducive to women's insecurity in places such as refugee camps and camps for internally displaced persons in South Sudan. Similarly, in countries as diverse as Guatemala, Liberia, and South Africa, levels of violence against women are similar and at times higher than those experienced during periods of conflict.[42]

Transitional justice processes have historically failed to address the multifaceted issue of gender justice, particularly where women's voices have been absent in policy development or the implementation of these processes. The South African Truth and Reconciliation Commission's failure to engage in a gender analysis of the abuses it documented, to provide appropriate avenues for women to engage with the commission, or to make significant recommendations for how entrenched gender-based violence can be prevented was strongly critiqued, and provided the basis for future commissions to improve their strategies. Subsequently, the SLTRC attempted to highlight the gendered experiences and impact of conflict by paying special attention to sexual violence perpetrated against women.[43] However, the impact of the Special Court of Sierra Leone is yet to be realized, and its gender-responsive and gender-sensitive recommendations are yet to be implemented. There were few prosecutions, and there were contentious issues relating to command responsibility and the post-conflict rate of gender-based violence in the country.[44] The commission is generally perceived to have failed to address gender justice in the country.

Similarly, the Tunisian Truth and Dignity Commission (TDC) demonstrated the political will and innovation to go beyond women's experiences of sexual violence during the various authoritarian regimes in the country, and to also examine violations of socioeconomic and cultural rights. A Women's Committee was established by the TDC as a way of showing commitment to women's full and meaningful participation in the transitional justice process. This led to the presence of women in the TDC, and consequently opened points of access through which women in civil society and women victims of human rights violation could participate.[45] However, critiques of the Women's Committee contend that the committee used its powers to shine a light on certain types of harms and certain types of victims—generally along partisan lines—thereby creating victim hierarchies. This has caused divisions in Tunisian society since the revolution began in 2011. "The Tunisian case study shows that reliance on technical innovations within traditional transitional justice mechanisms does not necessarily guarantee the pursuance of transformative justice outcomes which cross political divides."[46]

LGBTQI and Transitional Justice

While gender justice and the need to address sexual and gender-based violence are increasingly recognized as key aspects of justice in the transitional justice field, those categories have seldom been viewed as inclusive of repression of and violence against sexual and gender minorities. In addition, "there is a tendency in the transitional justice field to equate gender with women, thereby 'exclusive gender': gender about women, for women, and primarily by women." If transitional justice is to be more inclusive in its response to past abuses, then it is critical that everyone's gendered experiences and gendered harms are appreciated and addressed—men, women, boys, girls, and gender-nonconforming persons.

While there is a normative shift in support for gender sensitivity in transitional justice processes, global policy frameworks are slow to recognize LGBTQI individuals and communities as a group disproportionately or uniquely affected by conflict. There have, however, been significant developments, especially within Latin American transitional justice processes, that have included in the mandates of such processes cases of violence against gender and sexual minorities as human rights violations.[47] The Brazil Truth Commission (2012–2014) held a public hearing on dictatorship and homosexuality in recognition of the repression suffered by sexual and gender minorities.

The transitional justice process in Colombia created new precedents for addressing LGBTQI populations. The 2011 Victim's and Land Restitution Law made special provision for needs relating to sexual orientation and gender identity. The National Centre for Historical Memory established by this law also conducted extensive research on the repression of LGBTQI populations, which resulted in a book published in 2015.[48] These developments came as a result of decades of documentation and mobilization by local LGBTQI activists, and their direct involvement in the Colombian peace negotiations.[49]

Youth and Transitional Justice

While young people are key stakeholders in transitional justice processes and have much to contribute and gain, they also are often given little space to engage in such processes, or are completely marginalized.[50] There has been an increase in rhetoric about the need for youth inclusion, but this has seldom translated into serious efforts at inclusion through participation or a focus on youth experiences of conflict. While children have become a serious focus for transitional justice processes, these engagements have treated them as victims or passive recipients of attention, rather than actively seeking their input or mobilizing them as a sector expected to shape and implement policy.

Given the direct role of youth in driving or supporting political change and their direct participation in violent conflict as combatants, this is a serious oversight. Many political conflicts have at their roots a society's inability to address problems that disproportionately affect youth— unemployment, poverty, inequality, and public exclusion from political power. The role of youth, and particularly students, in driving political campaigns relating to democracy, anti-corruption, and social justice have flourished in the last ten years. The role of youth in using new technology in these settings has also shown their ability to drive new forms of mobilization and protest. This rise in influence is yet to be fully comprehended by transitional justice mechanisms, which have been slow in adopting technological innovations or viewing youth as a critical constituency or partner in driving reform. Transitional justice processes have used conventional forms of public outreach and media engagement that have not effectively tapped into social media for collecting information or publicizing stories of abuse. While youth and social media may serve as key drivers of social protest, they remain marginal actors in the social change strategies promoted by many transitional justice mechanisms.

There are. however, some innovative examples of transitional justice processes that have sought to engage youth as key players who bring unique perspectives and needs. Virginie Ladisch recounts two promising examples:

> Sierra Leone blazed the trail with its explicit focus on children and youth in the truth commission process, and with the "Accountability Now" clubs set up by the Special Court for Sierra Leone to involve youth in educating their peers and communities about human rights. More recently, in Canada, the Truth and Reconciliation Commission (TRC) did not initially have an explicit focus on youth. However, at the first national event, the commissioners were impressed by the participation of a group of youth and their testimonies reflecting the severity and magnitude of the intergenerational impact of the residential schools. In response, the TRC created "Education Day," to be included at each of the remaining national events. Several hundred students attended each of the Education Days to witness cultural ceremonies, listen to survivors' testimonies, and view an exhibit about the history and impact of the Indian Residential Schools (IRS). This initiative was complemented by a teaching unit about the IRS. In this way, the TRC in Canada listened to young voices, recognized a gap in its process, and added a new and unique element to its truth-seeking efforts.[51]

Conclusion

Transitional justice has emerged as a field that built its credibility largely on its claims of inclusion and of being victim-centered. While such claims were often more rhetoric than reality, many groups who have traditionally been marginalized in peacebuilding processes have used transitional justice as a lens and a set of mechanisms through which to claim a voice and claim their rights. As transitional justice has become part of the mainstream and its principles are captured in international and regional conventions and norms, it has also been pushed to address a broadened scope of exclusions. In taking the needs of victimized groups more seriously, transitional justice policy-makers and practitioners have had to recognize the diverse experiences of violence, the diverse forms of vulnerability, and the diverse demands for truth, justice, and reparative interventions from a range of communities and social sectors. The fight for recognition for and by women, youth, and LGBTQI people illustrates the possibilities but also the challenges of using this avenue for social change.

Recommendations: Thoughts on Advancing Inclusion Through Transitional Justice

Transitional justice is a contested terrain that provides some tools in the struggle for diversity and inclusion. It is, however, a terrain that requires active engagement and mobilization to ensure progress for any context. The following are suggestions that are critical for advancing this agenda:

1. Inclusion is an ongoing battle that requires sustained efforts. Early victories during consultation processes (when things are in transition) are often reversed when the state reverts to business as usual. Therefore, state commitments should be monitored and the state should be held accountable for the implementation of inclusive policies and initiatives.
2. To address diversity in transitional justice contexts, the boundaries and definition of "transition" and "justice" need to be challenged to promote transformative change that addresses broader social injustices embedded in cultural norms that perpetuate exclusion. These cultural norms are evident in the racialized, patriarchal, and gerontocratic nature of most societies (including transitional justice processes themselves).
3. Addressing diversity and inclusion of marginalized groups requires the empowerment of these groups. Sustained inclusion requires support for local capacity to organize and mobilize.
4. Efforts should be made in transitional justice processes to continue to expand the range of abuses addressed and to maintain the involvement of different marginalized groups. There is scope to highlight, for example, violations of economic, social, and cultural rights.
5. Intersectional approaches should be undertaken when considering the different identities of marginalized groups to allow for greater inclusion in transitional justice processes. Critical engagements with sex, gender, and sexual identity, together with race, ethnicity, religion, class, and other sources of marginalization, serve as tools to ensure inclusivity in transitional justice processes

6. Victims can be portrayed as helpless and voiceless—particularly women, LGBTQI communities, and people with disabilities. This often leads to these groups becoming invisible during transitional justice processes. By challenging this image of the helpless victim and allowing marginalized groups to participate in all transitional justice processes, there can be more room for inclusion and diversity.

7. Diversity and inclusion efforts need to be responsive to what the concepts of "diversity" and "inclusion" mean and look like in local context. International approaches and norms can undermine local experiences and capacities if they impose simple templates regarding whom to include or what inclusion looks like.

8. Where official state-led transitional justice initiatives exclude some who have been affected by conflict and violence, alternative nonstate transitional justice approaches can still play a key role in providing acknowledgment and facilitating reconciliation and justice.

9. International transitional justice policy frameworks provide a strong basis for arguing for a broadened and deepened approach to diversity and inclusion, but they still provide many loopholes for leaving out certain groups. Further advocacy is needed to ensure more explicit international acknowledgment of the experiences and rights of various excluded groups.

10. Gender justice in the transitional justice field has advanced significantly through critical evaluation of various mechanisms over the last twenty years. New benchmarks have been set as the field advances. This same critical analysis should become standard practice in advancing other rights of marginalized groups such as youth and LGBTQI communities.

Notes

1. Tutu 2010.
2. United Nations 2004.
3. Hayner 2017; Olsen, Payne, and Reiter 2010.
4. Dancy, Kim and Wiebelhaus-Brahm 2010.
5. Taylor 2014.
6. United Nations 2010; UN Human Rights Council 2011; African Union 2019, 4; European Union 2015; Pena 2010.
7. African Union 2019, 4. Emphasis added.
8. Taylor 2014.
9. Robins 2017.
10. Jamar 2018.
11. Mbwana 2019.
12. Russell-Brown 2003.
13. Bueno-Hansen 2018. The Victims' and Land Restitution Law mandated the Unit for the Service to and Reparation of Victims to offer attention, assistance, and holistic reparations to victims of internal armed conflict, including a differential approach that recognizes sexual orientation and gender identity.

14. Presidencia de la República (Peru) 2001.
15. Comision de la Verdad y Reconciliación (Peru) 2003, sección cuarta, capítulo 1.5, "La violencia sexual contra la mujer"; segunda parte, capítulo 2.1, "Violencia y desigualdad de género."
16. Comision de la Verdad y Reconciliación (Peru) 2003, primera parte, sección tercera, "Los escenarios de la violencia."
17. Movimiento Homosexual de Lima 2003.
18. Comision de la Verdad y Reconciliación (Peru) 2003, primera parte, sección segunda, capítulo 1.4.3, "Actos de terror contra minorías sexuales."
19. Montalvo 2017.
20. Infante 2013; Vidarte 2017; Goicochea 2018.
21. Gyimah 2009.
22. World Bank 2006.
23. Meintjes 2009.
24. See, for example, a range of civil society initiatives covered in Brankovic and van der Merwe 2018.
25. Ndonga 2018.
26. Conteh and Berghs 2014.
27. Murphy 2018.
28. Nagy 2008.
29. United Nations 2010; European Union 2015; African Union 2019.
30. United Nations 2010, 9.
31. United Nations 2010, 9.
32. United Nations 2010, 11.
33. European Union 2015, section IV, para. 7.
34. European Union 2015, section IV, para. 1.
35. European Union 2015, summary.
36. European Union 2015, section IV, para. 8.
37. African Union 2019, 6, 7.
38. African Union 2019, 21–24.
39. African Union 2019, 15.
40. Hellsten 2012.
41. Sigsworth and Valji 2012; Scanlon and Muddell 2009.
42. Sigsworth and Valji 2012.
43. Teale 2009.
44. The Special Court indicted and prosecuted individuals who held the greatest responsibility in terms of command structure during the civil war. One of the greatest critiques of the court is its failure to indict foot soldiers who were notorious for committing heinous human rights violations during the conflict.
45. Warren et al. 2017.
46. Ketelaars 2018.
47. Bueno-Hansen 2018.
48. Bueno-Hansen 2018, citing "Aniquilar la Diferencia: Lesbianas, Gays, Bisexuales y Transgeneristas en el Marco del Conflicto armado Colombiano."
49. Subsequently, though, a national referendum in 2016 that rejected the peace plan also threatened the gains made for LGBTQ + rights. Shaw 2017.
50. Ladisch 2018.
51. Ladisch 2018.

Bibliography

African Union. 2019. "Transitional Justice Policy." https://au.int/en/documents/20190425/trans itional-justice-policy.

Brankovic, Jasmina, and Hugo van der Merwe, eds. 2018. *Advocating Transitional Justice in Africa: The Role of Civil Society*. Cham: Springer.

Bueno-Hansen, Pascha. 2018. "The Emerging LGBT+ Rights Challenge to Transitional Justice in Latin America." *International Journal of Transitional Justice* 12, no. 1: 126–145. https://doi.org/ 10.1093/ijtj/ijx031.

Centro Nacional de Memoria Histórica. 2015. *Aniquilar la Diferencia. Lesbianas, gays, bisexuales y transgeneristas en el marco del conflicto armado colombiano*. Bogotá: CNMH, UARIV, USAID, and OIM. http://www.centrodememoriahistorica.gov.co/descargas/informes2015/ aniquilar-la-diferencia/aniquilar-la-diferencia.pdf.

Comision de la Verdad y Reconciliación (Peru). 2003. "Informe Final." August 28. https://www. cverdad.org.pe/ifinal/.

Conteh, Edward, and Maria Berghs. 2014. "'Mi at Don Poil': A Report on Reparations in Sierra Leone for Amputee and War-Wounded People." Sierra Leone Amputee and War-Wounded Association. https://disability-studies.leeds.ac.uk/wp-content/uploads/sites/40/library/ AWWA%20Report%20on%20Reparations.pdf.

Dancy, Geoff, Hunjoon Kim, and Eric Wiebelhaus-Brahm. "The Turn to Truth: Trends in Truth Commission Experimentation." *Journal of Human Rights* 9, no. 1 (2010): 45–64. doi: 10.1080/ 14754830903530326. https://www.semanticscholar.org/paper/The-Turn-to-Truth%3A-Tre nds-in-Truth-Commission-Dancy-Kim/9851d368e49c7634ad5327572116b00c65879dfb.

European Union. 2015. "The EU's Policy Framework on Support to Transitional Justice." http:// eeas.europa.eu/archives/docs/top_stories/pdf/the_eus_policy_framework_on_support_to_t ransitional_justice.pdf.

Goicochea, Juan Carlos. 2018. *El Pecado Social*. Documentary. Trailer available on YouTube: https://www.youtube.com/watch?v=INM5OSqqTX8.

Gyimah, A. 2009. "Gender and Transitional Justice in West Africa: The Cases of Ghana and Sierra Leone." Research Report No. 4. African Leadership Centre. https://www.africanleadershipcen tre.org/attachments/article/43/ALC%20Report%20No.%204%20Gyimah.pdf.

Hayner, Priscilla. 2017. "Truth Commission." https://www.britannica.com/topic/truth-com mission.

Hellsten, Sirkku K. 2012. "Transitional Justice and Aid." Working Paper No. 2012/06. World Institute for Development Economics Research. United Nations University. https://www. wider.unu.edu/sites/default/files/wp2012-006.pdf.

Infante, Gio. 2013. "Las otras memorias." Lamula. https://gioinfante.lamula.pe/2013/08/28/las- otras-memorias/gioinfante/.

Jamar, Astrid. 2018. "Victims' Inclusion and Transitional Justice: Attending to the Exclusivity of Inclusion Politics." PA-X Report, Transitional Justice Series. Political Settlements Research Programme, University of Edinburgh. http://www.politicalsettlements.org/wp-content/uplo ads/2018/12/2018_Jamar_Victims-Report.pdf.

Ketelaars, E. 2018. "Gendering Tunisia's Transition: Transformative Gender Justice Outcomes in Times of Transitional Justice Turmoil?." *International Journal of Transitional Justice* 12, no. 3: 406–426. https://academic.oup.com/ijtj/article-abstract/12/3/407/5146418?redirectedF rom=fulltext.

Ladisch, Virginie. 2018. "A Catalyst for Change: Engaging Youth in Transitional Justice." ICTJ Briefing. International Center for Transitional Justice. https://www.ictj.org/sites/default/files/ ICTJ-Briefing-Youth-TJ-2018.pdf.

Mbwana, Thokozani. 2019. "Transitional Justice and the Inclusion of LGBTQIA+ Rights." Policy Brief. Centre for the Study of Violence, Johannesburg. https://media.africaportal.org/docume nts/Transitional_Justice_and_Inclusion_of_LGBTQIAL_Rights_Policy_Brief_2020.pdf.

Meintjes, Sheila. 2009. "'Gendered Truth'? Legacies of the South African Truth and Reconciliation Commission: Views from the Field." *African Journal on Conflict Resolution* 9, no. 2: 101–112. https://journals.co.za/doi/10.10520/EJC16350.

Montalvo Cifuentes, José Julio. 2017. "Crimenes de odio durante el conflicto armado interno en el Perú (1980–2000)." *Memorias* 1: 57–67 Lugar de la Memoria, Perú. https://www.scribd.com/document/434321010/Crimenes-de-odio-durante-el-CAI-pdf.

Montalvo Cifuentes, José Julio. 2003. "Crímenes de homofobia en el contexto de la violencia política." August 6. https://www.scribd.com/document/159713611/Crimenes-por-homofo bia-Peru-Montalvo-et-al.

Murphy, Colleen. 2018. "The Ethics of Diversity in Transitional Justice." *The Georgetown Journal of Law and Public Policy* 16: 821–836. https://www.law.georgetown.edu/public-policy-journal/wp-content/uploads/sites/23/2018/11/16-S-Ethics-Diversity-Transitional-Justice.pdf.

Nagy, Rosemary. 2008. "Transitional Justice as Global Project: Critical Reflections." *Third World Quarterly* 29, no. 2: 275–289. https://tjcentre.uwo.ca/documents/Nagy%203rd%20Wo rld%20Quarterly%202008.pdf.

Ndonga, Agatha. 2018. "Kenya: Still Grappling with a Stalled Transitional Justice Mandate." International Center for Transitional Justice. https://www.ictj.org/news/kenya-still-grappling-stalled-transitional-justice-mandate.

Olsen, Tricia D., Leigh A. Payne, and Andrew G. Reiter. 2010. "Transitional Justice in Balance." United States Institute of Peace. https://www.usip.org/events/transitional-justice-balance.

Pena, Mariana. 2010. "Victim Participation at the International Criminal Court: Achievements Made and Challenges Lying Ahead." *ILSA Journal of International and Comparative Law* 16, no. 2: art. 8. https://nsuworks.nova.edu/ilsajournal/vol16/iss2/8.

Presidencia de la República (Peru). 2001. "Decreto Supremo 065-2001-PCM: Crean Comisión de la Verdad." June 2. https://reparations.qub.ac.uk/assets/uploads/2001-Peru-DS-N-065-2001-PCM.pdf.

Robins, Simon. 2017. "Failing Victims? The Limits of Transitional Justice in Addressing the Needs of Victims of Violations." *Human Rights and International Legal Discourse* 11, no. 1: 41–58. https://eprints.whiterose.ac.uk/122438/1/Robins_Failing_victims_The_limits_of_transitio nal_justice.pdf.

Russell-Brown, Sherrie L. 2003. "Rape as an Act of Genocide." *Berkeley Journal of International Law* 21: 350–374. https://genderandsecurity.org/sites/default/files/Russell-Brown_-_Rape_as _an_Act_of_Genocide.pdf.

Scanlon, H., and K. Muddell. 2009. "Gender and Transitional Justice in Africa: Progress and Prospects." *African Journal on Conflict Resolution* 9, no. 2: 9–28.

Shaw, Ari. 2017. "Why Colombia's Peace Process Could Mean Trouble for LGBT Rights." World Politics Review. July 21. https://www.worldpoliticsreview.com/articles/22765/why-colombia-s-peace-process-could-mean-trouble-for-lgbt-rights.

Sigsworth, R., and N. Valji. 2012. "Continuities of Violence Against Women and the Limitations of Transitional Justice: The Case of South Africa." In *Gender in Transitional Justice*, edited by S. Buckley-Zistel and R. Stanley, 115–135. Governance and Limited Statehood Series. London: Palgrave Macmillan. https://link.springer.com/chapter/10.1057/9780230348615_5.

Taylor, David. 2014. "Victim Participation in Transitional Justice Mechanisms: Real Power or Empty Ritual?" Impunity Watch. https://www.impunitywatch.org/post/victim-participation-in-transitional-justice-mechanisms-real-power-or-empty-ritual.

Teale, L. 2009. "Addressing Gender-Based Violence in the Sierra Leone Conflict: Notes from the Field." *African Journal on Conflict Resolution* 9, no. 2: 69–90. https://www.ajol.info/index.php/ajcr/article/view/52173.

Tutu, Desmond. 2010. "Divesting from Injustice." HuffPost, June 13. https://www.huffpost.com/entry/divesting-from-injustice_b_534994.

UN Human Rights Council. 2011. "The EU's Policy Framework on Support to Transitional Justice." http://eeas.europa.eu/archives/docs/top_stories/pdf/the_eus_policy_framework_ on_support_to_transitional_justice.pdf.

United Nations. 2010. "Guidance Note of the Secretary-General: United Nations Approach to Transitional Justice." https://www.un.org/ruleoflaw/files/TJ_Guidance_Note_March_2010FI NAL.pdf.

United Nations. 2004. "The Rule of Law and Transitional Justice in Conflict and Post-Conflict Societies." Report of the Secretary-General. https://digitallibrary.un.org/record/527647?ln=en.

Vidarte, Giuliana. 2017. "La noche de las gardenias. Prácticas de arte y archive sobre crímenes de odio en la Amazonía peruana." Micromuseo. https://www.micromuseo.org.pe/rutas/noche-gardenias/sinopsis.html.

Warren, R., A. Applebaum, B. Mawby, H. Fuhrman, R. Turkington, and M. Alam. 2017. "Inclusive Justice: How Women Shape Transitional Justice in Tunisia and Colombia." Georgetown Institute for Women, Peace and Security, Washington, DC. https://giwps.georgetown.edu/resource/inclusive-justice/.

World Bank. 2006. "Gender, Justice, and Truth Commissions." http://siteresources.worldbank.org/INTLAWJUSTINST/Resources/GJTClayoutrevised.pdf.

13

Providing Humanitarian Assistance That Reaches All

Kate Sutton, Pip Henty, and Charlie Damon

> Too often it is the most vulnerable people and the people most in need who fall through the cracks.
>
> —Elhadj As Sy, former IFRC secretary general[1]

Introduction

Globally documented evidence highlights the fact that disasters and conflict impact people differently.[2] Due to preexisting inequalities, women, children, people with disabilities, the elderly, sexual and gender minorities, and other marginalized groups experience differing impacts.[3] For example, people with disabilities are four times more likely to die when a disaster strikes.[4] And in some crisis settings, over 70 percent of women have been documented to experience gender-based violence.[5]

Since the onset of the COVID-19 pandemic, these inequalities have intensified. For example, measures aimed at reducing the spread of infection have had disproportionate impacts on women. They have increased the incidence and severity of gender-based violence (GBV) due to economic strains, restrictions of movement, emotional burden, and changed household and social roles. This is further exacerbated by women's reduced access to support and ability to seek safety. In the Pacific, for example, where women already experience high rates of violence, rapid gender analysis found that COVID-19 isolation and quarantine increased the risk of GBV.[6]

The preexisting inequalities and differentiated impacts of disasters and conflicts are not always identified or addressed in humanitarian response strategies. This can inhibit certain groups from accessing assistance, arguably undermining the humanitarian principle of impartiality, which clearly states that humanitarian aid must be provided on the basis of need, without discrimination (see Box 13.1). It also results in poorly targeted and inappropriate assistance. Examples include the provision of food rations that cannot be cooked by women because no one has asked what cooking facilities are familiar and available; the provision of information that cannot be read by different language groups in the population; or the establishment of evacuation centers that cannot be accessed by people with disabilities.

Box 13.1 An Overview: Humanitarian Response

Humanitarian action aims to "save lives, alleviate suffering and maintain human dignity during and after man-made crises and disasters caused by natural hazards, as well as to prevent and strengthen preparedness for when such situations occur."[7] Inclusive humanitarian action "refers to actions taken to ensure the right to information, protection, and assistance for all persons affected by crisis, irrespective of age, sexual and gender identity, disability status, nationality, or ethnic, religious, or social origin or identity."[8]

Within the humanitarian sector there has been an increasing focus on prioritizing inclusion, as articulated in the World Humanitarian Summit. The concept of "leave no one behind" is a central theme to the 2030 Agenda. As a key document that guides the sector, it lays out a transformative agenda:

> To end poverty and hunger everywhere; to combat inequalities within and among countries; to build peaceful, just and inclusive societies; to protect human rights and promote gender equality and the empowerment of women and girls; and to ensure the lasting protection of the planet and its natural resources.[9]

Inclusion must be considered in all stages of a humanitarian action, including disaster risk reduction and preparedness work, response, and recovery. There are specific entry points for greater inclusion throughout the program cycle, including at program design; during identification of relevant populations; as part of monitoring the impact of programs; throughout implementation and targeting of programs; and as part of the final program evaluation. Two important concepts should underpin the program to support inclusion: (1) accountability to affected populations (AAP), which means taking account of, and being held accountable by, different stakeholders, primarily those who are affected by crises and disasters; and (2) protection, which encompasses all activities aimed at ensuring full respect for the rights of the individual in accordance with the letter and the spirit of the relevant bodies of law (i.e., international human rights law, international humanitarian law, international refugee law).[10]

This chapter will unpack how different groups of people experience humanitarian action and the barriers that exist to their participation and ability to benefit from action. It will further explore what efforts humanitarian actors have taken to improve inclusion of all groups and examine why these efforts have not always been successful. It will conclude by proposing the way forward to ensure that future action is more effective.

Who Is Excluded?

In its World Disasters Report for 2018, the International Federation of the Red Cross (IFRC) identified five categories of people that are overlooked in humanitarian action.[11] These include the one billion people who don't have basic identity documents that may be required to receive assistance, and the 68 million older people with mobility constraints who are unable to access assistance in environmentally vulnerable and politically fragile countries.[12] The categories articulated by IFRC are useful for understanding who is excluded and why. They include people who are out of sight, left out of the loop, out of reach, out of money, or out of scope.[13] In this chapter, we focus on the first two categories.

The first category relates to those that are "out of sight"—that is, people we fail to see. This group includes people who may not be visible for practical reasons, such as older people or people with disabilities who are confined to their homes or have mobility issues. For example, according to a 2015 study, 75 percent of disabled people affected by a humanitarian crisis feel they do not have adequate access to essentials such as water and shelter.[14] Research highlights that activities targeting older people were included in less than 1 percent of projects submitted to the UN Consolidated Appeals Process.[15] This category also includes people who are not seen because they choose to remain out of sight to protect themselves. People may be undocumented with the government and so not included on assistance lists. They may be from a minority group that fears being targeted and therefore wants to remain anonymous. For example, during Cyclone Pam in Vanuatu, sexual and gender minority groups intentionally remained out of sight to avoid being targets of violence and discrimination (see Box 13.2).[16]

Box 13.2 Sexual and Gender Minorities: Case Study, Cyclone Pam

Sexual and gender minorities are one of the most vulnerable populations, and this vulnerability is often compounded during a crisis. Gender minorities face stigma, violence, exploitation, and exclusion from community resources and relief assistance. This risk becomes especially heightened in displacement contexts.

Tropical Cyclone Pam hit Vanuatu in March 2015, impacting all six provinces and displacing many communities. During the response phase, sexual and gender minorities reported harassment and exclusion at distribution sites—including from humanitarian staff—and violence when using communal bathroom facilities. Informal networks that normally supported sexual and gender minorities were disrupted and unable to help reach and engage with their stakeholders. No humanitarian organization specifically targeted support to sexual and gender minorities, and many people chose not to identify themselves publicly. Below are some of the quotes from people who identify with a sexual and gender minority group that were captured in research:

"Discrimination through actions, attitudes and disrespect."

"I am scared because they say many bad things about me and this brings shame to me."

  "They did not want us to join in the workshop because I was gay, even though it was an NGO-run workshop."[17]

The second category identified by IFRC includes people who are "left out of the loop"—those who are present and visible in the response but unintentionally excluded by humanitarian actors from specific activities (see Box 13.3).[18] This group may overlap with those who are "out of sight," but their exclusion is the result of generic programming approaches that do not consider people's different capacities and needs. Communications may not be inclusive of different languages, abilities, or levels of literacy, and thereby fail to reach key groups of people. Assistance may be generic and fail to meet specific needs, such as extra nutrition for pregnant and lactating mothers, medication for people with disabilities, or continence supplies for older people. Similarly, provisions may not be offered in ways that adapt to different skills and abilities of different beneficiaries. Rations may be unwieldy for women or older people to receive and transport safely and easily; supplies that need to be prepared, such as rice or beans, may not be suitable for individuals (such as unaccompanied children) or families who do not have access to appropriate cooking facilities or skills.

Box 13.3 Disaster, Conflict, or Complex Emergency

The specific vulnerabilities and capacities of different individuals and groups will be greatly impacted by the context, and importantly whether humanitarian assistance is required in the context of a disaster, conflict, or complex emergency. Although there may be similar inclusion challenges, there are also significant differences.

The Sendai Framework defines a disaster as a serious disruption of the functioning of a community or a society due to hazardous events interacting with existing vulnerabilities and capacities that lead to human, material, economic, and environmental losses and impacts.[19] Disasters include contexts where a natural hazard has occurred, such as a cyclone, flooding, or tsunami. People's existing vulnerabilities may be impacted by their inability to access services or networks that are disrupted as a result of the disaster.

In a conflict or complex emergency setting there is total or considerable breakdown of authority resulting from internal or external conflict that may be exacerbated by natural hazard events—for example, conflict in a drought-affected context. The vulnerabilities associated with a disaster exist, but in addition, there may be conflict dynamics that impact groups differently. Particular race, gender, or ethnic groups may be discriminated against or become targets of violence. Furthermore, conflict settings result in the long-term breakdown of essential services such as health and education that will impact different groups. In the countries surrounding Syria, humanitarian agencies are working to enroll 1.35 million children (five to seventeen years of age) in formal education who would otherwise have no access to basic education.[20]

The humanitarian sector has also progressed in its understanding of diversity and inclusion by adopting intersectional approaches.[21] These approaches recognize that individuals have multiple identities that will interact to either promote or hinder inclusion in humanitarian action, as well as to either potentially exacerbate vulnerabilities or protect from harm. An individual's gender, age, ability, and sexual identity, for example, will interact to create different capacities or vulnerabilities (see Box 13.4). A rapid gender analysis in the Mekong subregion (Cambodia, Lao PDR, Myanmar, Thailand, and Vietnam) in the context of COVID-19, conducted by UNICEF, UN Women, and CARE in September 2020, found that those particularly at risk of GBV were sexual and gender minorities, women with disabilities, and migrant women.[22] The Women's Refugee Commission has undertaken a lot of work to understand how gender and ability intersect to make women with disabilities far more vulnerable to sexual and gender-based violence. Between 2009 and 2011, the commission reported, 49 percent of Bhutanese adult rape survivors in Nepali refugee camps were persons with mental and/or physical impairments.[23] At the United Nations, the High Commissioner for Refugees has taken an intersectional approach to inclusion by adopting an age, gender, and diversity policy that guides staff to meaningfully include in operational humanitarian programs all persons of concern with these intersecting identities.[24] As a concrete example, UNHCR develops child-friendly information materials and consultation exercises for boys and girls of different ages.

Box 13.4 The Gendered Nature of Vulnerability

Women and girls are disproportionately vulnerable to gender-based violence during humanitarian crises, and this violence has long-term negative impacts on individuals', families', and communities' health, poverty, and socioeconomic outcomes. The UN secretary general's report on conflict-related sexual violence noted that sexual violence was evident across a number of settings in 2017, including the Democratic Republic of Congo, Central African Republic, South Sudan, Myanmar, Yemen, and besieged areas of the Syrian Arab Republic. The majority of those impacted were economically marginalized women and girls lacking institutional protection. Many were targeted on the basis of their perceived ethnic, religious, or political affiliation.[25] Displacement also increases

the risk of early and forced marriage for refugee girls, especially in the Middle
East, and particularly for Syrians.[26]

At the same time, the unique capacities or contributions different groups can
bring to disaster preparedness, response, and recovery may also be overlooked (see
Box 13.5). A recent analysis undertaken by the Humanitarian Policy Group in partnership with Age International and HelpAge International finds that formal traditional humanitarian response operations have not considered either the specific
needs or capacities of older people, resulting in negative coping mechanisms and
less effective response.[27]

**Box 13.5 The Role of Older People in Drought Preparedness and
Response in East Africa**

Drought impacted the East African region for consecutive years and resulted in
food insecurity and humanitarian need for about fifteen million people across
Ethiopia, Uganda, Kenya, and Somalia in 2017. Older people in the community
had a critical role in preparation and response to drought. Their knowledge and
wisdom were critical to educate and advise younger generations on traditional
coping mechanisms such as wild foods to use when crops fail. Older people also
played a role as community leaders, conveners, mediators, and decision-makers.
However, this role shifted in the context of drought, both positively and negatively. Typically, community disputes related to resource allocation and livelihood issues increased during scarcity, and the elders played an increasing role
in conflict mediation. At the same time, as the climate became increasingly unpredictable, traditional knowledge of past patterns was sometimes considered
less relevant, and the burden of providing food and support to older people
increased. Humanitarian actors need to better understand the changing roles
and specific gaps as relevant to older people and adopt practices that promote the
inclusion of older people in all stages of humanitarian action.[28]

What Are the Barriers?

There are many barriers to the inclusion of different groups in a response setting. Practical barriers to inclusion may include location, accessibility, and timing
(length of meeting, time of day) of humanitarian activities. This may exclude
women in particular, who have other domestic, income-generation, and protection
considerations to factor into their daily schedules.[29] Physical and communication
barriers may affect many different groups. For people with disabilities, physical
barriers include steps or physically difficult terrain, while communication barriers

include information and resources not being available in accessible formats such as Braille, sign language, or simple language.[30]

There are also larger societal and attitudinal barriers that affect the inclusion and voice of women, children, people with disabilities, and sexual and gender minorities. People with disabilities face stigma and discrimination in their communities, and are frequently denied basic rights such as food, education, employment, and access to health services.[31] This stigma leads to them being "hidden" at home, being hard to find during post-disaster rapid assessments, lacking active voice or participation in discussions regarding their own needs, and being confronted by negative assumptions regarding their capabilities. Sexual and gender minorities often experience harassment, discrimination, exclusion, and violence in everyday life. This gets worse in times of crisis.[32] For women, there are social norms that limit women's attendance and participation in relief activities due to male-dominated decision-making structures. This is particularly evident in countries where the patriarchal system impedes women from aspiring to higher positions because both men and women believe consciously or subconsciously that women are not able to perform outside of the traditional gender role assigned to them. The result can be an approach to humanitarian aid that is shaped by patriarchal norms.[33] The impact may be, for example, that funding allocations and policy commitments to issues such as gender equality, protection, and women's empowerment are lacking. Between 2011 and 2014, the Financial Tracking System of the UN's Office for the Coordination of Humanitarian Affairs showed that less than 2 percent of all humanitarian programs had an explicit focus on gender equality, women, and girls.[34]

Another barrier is the traditional "international" approach to humanitarian action. Local organizations have local knowledge and a contextual understanding that could highlight and help address barriers to women, children, people with disabilities, and sexual and gender minorities.[35] However, local organizations, which are closest to the front line and often have a better understanding of the needs and priorities of the most affected populations, have limited access to direct funds, have little influence in decision-making, and often aren't included in coordination mechanisms (see Box 13.6).[36] They also face barriers to accessing direct funding. In total, 99.6 percent of humanitarian funding goes directly to international agencies, while 0.4 percent goes directly to local and national agencies.[37]

Box 13.6 Women's Leadership in COVID-19

Women and women's rights organizations have been underrepresented in national COVID-19 responses. Women's leadership and participation in decision-making spaces—where policies and strategies are determined—is critical for ensuring responses consider different needs based on gender.[38] Recent research conducted by the Humanitarian Advisory Group and UN Women found that there was limited evidence women were able to have a leadership role, contribute to, or influence national approaches to COVID-19 response.[39] For example, only 35 percent of women's rights organization representatives participated in national interagency task forces. This limited access resulted in "a lack of programming and support to address the gendered impacts of the pandemic and the needs of diverse women."[40] In contrast, at the community level women have sometimes led in the COVID-19 response. Research in the Pacific highlights the strong role women's rights organizations played in community engagement and messaging, emphasizing the critical role women play in the health sector.[41]

It is often too late to address barriers to inclusion in the midst of a response. The critical stage to identify marginalized groups and address barriers is during disaster risk reduction (DRR) and preparedness stages; it is during these stages that systematic efforts are made to analyze and reduce exposure and lessen vulnerability (see Box 13.7).[42] For all involved, it may involve specific preparations to be safe in the event of an emergency. The success of these processes was evidenced in the 2011 Great East Japan Earthquake and tsunami, when groups of residents with psychosocial disabilities were evacuated in a timely manner due to their involvement in planning processes and community training in preparation for emergencies.[43]

Box 13.7 Gender-Responsive Disaster Risk Reduction Study, Cyclone Pam, Vanuatu

From 2013 to 2015, CARE's DRR and preparedness work in Vanuatu aimed to increase the resilience of at-risk communities and schools to the impact of natural disasters, including an explicit aim of building women's leadership in disaster preparedness and response. This was done by setting up and training Community Disaster and Climate Change Committees (CDCCCs) and supporting them over time with planning, capacity-building, and coordination assistance. CDCCCs had gender-balanced membership and were training on gender and protection. Men and women in the CDCCCs were trained to understand early warning information, prepare communities, conduct rapid assessments, and undertake emergency simulations. The study conducted after Cyclone Pam struck Vanuatu in 2015 found that the approach had increased the representation of women in community leadership roles, including in some cases as chairs of the CDCCCs. Additionally, the training helped increase respect for women's leadership in disasters. It found that voices of women were heard more loudly, women's membership and leadership in CDCCCs were greater and more respected, and the greater involvement of women in disaster leadership contributed to more inclusive preparedness and response.

The study also found that after the cyclone, communities where CARE had worked could provide evidence of specific actions taken to seek out and support women, children, and people with a disability in preparing, responding to, and recovering from the cyclone. For example, in evacuation centers in Aniwa, women and girls were escorted by trusted community members to access washing and toilet facilities to ensure that they were safe. In contrast, in communities where this approach was not used, women were less likely to speak up in the community meetings and were not able to participate in community decision-making. Finally, it found that through the DRR program, disaster management evolved from a family responsibility to a community obligation, and people with disabilities, the elderly, and children were also seen to be community responsibilities.[44]

What Has the Humanitarian Sector Done to Ensure More Inclusive Humanitarian Action?

The international development sector has increasingly tried to document and understand different experiences across affected populations in order to better address needs. Following large-scale disasters such as the 2004 Indian Ocean tsunami, and in the context of long-running conflicts such as those in the Middle East, scholars and practitioners observed and analyzed the impact of these disasters on different groups.[45] Research explores issues such as differences in mortality or morbidity, including which groups of people are most affected by gender-based violence or psychosocial impacts in the event of a crisis or disaster. Research also tries to understand different groups' abilities to access assistance; the appropriateness of assistance provided to specific groups; and the voice or representation of marginalized groups, such as religious minorities, in disaster response.[46] As a result, the sector is building up a more complete picture of who is excluded and why. This shared understanding provides an important platform for developing comprehensive and sector-wide responses to support inclusion.

As awareness and research have increased, so too have sector guidance and approaches to promote inclusive humanitarian action. Some actors and donors have adopted and promoted a twin-track approach to inclusion, addressing needs of a specific group in two ways (see Box 13.8). First, targeted programming is being used to reach specific groups or individuals with a specific set of needs; for example, the International Committee of the Red Cross (ICRC) often establishes centers to support the physical rehabilitation of people who were injured—often by landmines—and have permanent physical disabilities. One of the largest centers was opened in Myitkyina, northern Myanmar, in 2016. Second, inclusion-related considerations have been mainstreamed into general humanitarian programming—for example, by providing information about a humanitarian program in different mediums to ensure that visually or hearing-impaired people receive the same information as others in the community. The twin-track approach has been adopted particularly to support disability inclusion in humanitarian action.

Box 13.8 Disability Inclusion in Humanitarian Response: Twin Track Approach

---

Disasters disproportionately impact people with disabilities. Not only can humanitarian disasters, and specifically natural disasters, cause disabilities, they can also "exacerbate pre-existing conditions through the loss of equipment or medication."[47] Often, people with disabilities are unable to access information, utilize traditional evacuation routes, or find appropriate care and support in the aftermath of a crisis.[48] For example, deaf people and people with hearing loss will not have access to information transmitted through sirens, televisions without closed captioning, radios, phone messages, and oral communication of emergency plans.[49] Donors and organizations have worked to promote inclusion, and the Australian government in particular has made disability inclusion a thematic priority for humanitarian action.[50]

The twin track approach to disability inclusion in Australian humanitarian response programs includes:

1. Disability-specific initiatives that target people with disabilities to provide the support required to ensure full participation in all aspects of programming. This might include providing direct support to disabled persons' organizations, funding provision of support devices such as wheelchairs or hearing aids, and ensuring that rehabilitation services are available.
2. Disability mainstreaming focused on ensuring that people with disabilities participate in, and are reached by, all humanitarian action. This might include identifying and addressing barriers to education for children with disabilities and adapting humanitarian services to make them accessible (for example, ramps and handrails for toilets).[51]

Targeted programs during all phases of program development and implementation ensure that the sector is engaging with and better understanding the needs of specific groups. For example, the establishment of child-friendly and women-friendly spaces has been increasingly adopted and become standard practice in response operations.[52] These are normally physical spaces within a response context that provide a range of activities that may be tailored to the needs of the group, but which also provide groups an opportunity to safely engage with the humanitarian community and raise concerns or issues. A number of women's organizations have developed sophisticated models to deliver these programs, and they have been found to be particularly effective in conflict contexts, where the value of a safe space that also provides psychosocial support cannot be overestimated. An example of this type of program is the UN Women safe spaces provided in the refugee camps responding to the Syria crisis (see Box 13.9).[53]

Box 13.9 Women-Safe Spaces in Refugee Camps in Jordan

UN Women operates Oasis centers within the Za'atari and Azrak camps in Jordan for highly vulnerable refugee women. The Oasis centers provide training, income-generating opportunities, childcare support, and linkages to other programs and psychosocial support initiatives, reaching 16,000 people per year.[54] In some cases, women are supported to access paid positions within the camp—for instance, within the World Food Program's Healthy Kitchens program.[55] The Oasis centers have had a positive impact on those who access them—among program participants, there has been a 20 percent reduction in domestic violence, and 91 percent of participants report an increase in household and community decision-making power as a result of the cash-for-work programs.[56]

A number of organizations have inclusion as an intrinsic programming approach. CARE has taken an explicit approach to gender inclusion that includes ensuring long-term gender-responsive programs (such as its DRR program in Vanuatu), preparing "Gender in Brief" documents before a disaster that give an overview of the gender context, and conducting a rapid gender analysis immediately post-disaster. The rapid gender analysis provides essential information about gender roles and responsibilities, capacities, and vulnerabilities.[57] It increasingly also includes other protection considerations such as looking at issues affecting people with disabilities or those affecting sexual and gender minorities (where data is safely able to be collected). The analysis is based on primary data (collected by local relief staff) and secondary data and is therefore contextualized both to the country and to specific disaster impacts. The analysis results in sector-specific program recommendations to address issues being faced by different groups; these recommendations are communicated to humanitarian actors, usually through sector working groups or through the cluster system (the formal sector coordination groups in disaster response).

There has also been a lot of momentum in the sector to strengthen protection and accountability to affected populations (AAP). This is considered critical to mainstreaming in all humanitarian action, and to promoting and supporting the inclusion of potentially vulnerable groups. "Protection" refers to "all activities aimed at obtaining full respect for the rights of the individual in accordance with the letter and the spirit of the relevant bodies of law (i.e. international human rights law (IHRL), international humanitarian law, international refugee law (IRL))."[58]

The concept of protection recognizes that all people are entitled to safe access to humanitarian programs, including preparedness, response, and recovery. It has promoted inclusion by identifying the needs of particular groups and providing concrete tools to ensure their needs are met.

AAP promotes active engagement with affected communities in humanitarian response and provides a framework for gathering input into design processes, supporting feedback on existing programs and approaches, and encouraging engagement in monitoring and evaluation processes. If done well, AAP can provide an avenue for different voices to effectively influence disaster planning, response, and recovery processes. The ICRC explicitly links accountability to affected populations and inclusion, recognizing that "not making the effort to understand people's specific needs, taking into account factors such as gender, age or disability, could end up excluding people who need our help."[59]

Finally, the sector has invested heavily in the creation and dissemination of standards and guidance. The Sphere Handbook, which is used extensively across the sector and translated into more than thirty different languages, provides protection principles that guide the approach to humanitarian action.[60] One of the principles, "Ensure people's access to impartial assistance, according to need and without discrimination," specifically aims to ensure inclusive humanitarian action and provides a number of guidance notes to assist in operationalizing the principle. Guidance notes cover the importance of identifying and addressing barriers for any groups or individuals to assistance, and promoting outreach to "hidden" at-risk groups such as persons with disabilities.[61] The Inter-Agency Standing Committee has also invested in standards as they relate to prevention of sexual and gender-based violence, child protection, and protection of older people and people with disabilities.[62] These guidance documents are typically hundreds of pages long, extremely detailed, and translated into a number of languages. Though there is some evidence that the guidance documents and standards are used, there are very few evaluations analyzing the appropriateness, relevance, and effectiveness of these tools.

Where To from Here?

Despite all of these efforts, humanitarian action continues to struggle to effectively and consistently include marginalized groups. In recent responses, such as the Sulawesi earthquake response (2018), famine response in Yemen (2017), and response to ongoing conflict in Myanmar, agencies have highlighted significant gaps and problems in services and support for specific groups, such as lack of spaces for women, gender-insensitive feedback mechanisms, and lack of consideration of the needs of people with disabilities and older persons.[63] It is important for the sector to ask why this continues to happen and what can be done to address it. It is clear that resources in the sector are finite and that there may always remain a gap in terms of how many people can be reached; however, are we using the resources we have as effectively as possible, and do investments reach those that are most in need?

The authors of this paper suggest three areas that could support more inclusive responses moving forward. The first area relates to an increased focus on DRR and preparedness: increased investment and support to marginalized groups to participate in analysis and planning for crises and disasters. The second area relates to a shift of focus: away from creation of lengthy and expensive tools (standards and guidance) specific to inclusion of particular groups and toward more context-specific mentoring and support that focuses on understanding and applying intersectional approaches. The third area relates to looking internally: taking stock of how inclusive the sector is and how that may (or may not) impact its ability to deliver inclusive humanitarian action.

When diverse groups are included in DRR planning and preparedness processes, they are more likely to be included and involved in disaster response and recovery.[64] If effectively engaged, marginalized groups can make valuable contributions to risk reduction efforts. For example, in the Philippines, the Dumaguete Effata Association of the Deaf has been working with the local government to develop early-warning systems that are not dependent on sirens or spoken materials.[65] In addition, by mapping and understanding the capacities of different groups of people, relief providers are in a better position to understand how these groups may contribute to response and recovery efforts.

Recent research suggests that the proliferation of tools and associated training is overwhelming the sector and not leading to concrete changes in programming.[66] This is especially true in the context of increasingly localized humanitarian responses, where national and local actors are responsible for decision-making and leadership. National and local actors often perceive international standards and training events to be constructed at global levels and to lack relevance to their contexts. Such events are also frequently not available in the format or language that is accessible to the organizations and staff that are on the front lines of response. Furthermore, the proliferation of standards tends to result in more and more guidance targeting the inclusion of specific groups of people. The sector could reconsider the emphasis placed on the development and dissemination of tools and training resources for inclusion of specific groups, and instead consider a shift to focus more on mentoring and on-the-job support for understanding and applying intersectional approaches. This shift may build on the learning and frameworks developed, but be driven by and more tailored to context. Potential areas for support are outlined in the Inclusion Charter that was created to support the UN Secretary General's Agenda for Humanity; it provides five steps to impartial humanitarian response for the most vulnerable, encouraging humanitarian actors to commit to the charter and take action in relation to participation, data, funding, capacity, and coordination.[67] A shift in approach also needs to be informed by more reviews and evaluations that specifically ask questions such as: "How relevant and appropriate are the various standards and guidance tools that relate to inclusion of different groups?" "Do these approaches deliver value for money?" "What alternative approaches could better support inclusive humanitarian action?"

Finally, there is evidence that the sector may need to look internally to bring about lasting change in the way the field programs humanitarian aid. The Humanitarian Advisory Group recently suggested that the sector is unlikely to achieve inclusive humanitarian action until leadership teams within the sector better reflect the populations it intends to serve.[68] Of over 1,400 staff in the sector surveyed in the research, only 38 percent felt that their leadership teams were diverse, and only 42 percent perceived their leadership teams to be inclusive. The research suggests that this impacts the quality of programming. In particular, the research suggests that where teams are more diverse and inclusive, they are six times more likely to be perceived to listen to and act on the views of communities.[69] The sector needs to be more intentional about creating diverse and inclusive leadership teams in order to improve the way programs understand and appropriately respond to the needs and capacities of diverse groups in humanitarian response.[70]

Conclusion

The humanitarian sector has a strong understanding of the ways in which different groups of people are impacted by crises and disasters. For the most part, humanitarian actors agree that all phases of humanitarian action should be inclusive—actively seeking and responding to the perspectives and contributions of different groups of people in affected communities. This is important to upholding the humanitarian principle of impartiality, but also because the evidence is growing that it results in better humanitarian outcomes.

This increased understanding and commitment have translated into a great deal of work on tools, guidance, and different approaches to inclusion that are still being tested. There is positive evidence of programs that adopt a twin-track approach to inclusion for groups, such as people with disabilities, and innovative programs or cross-sector initiatives to promote improved communication with communities. There is also growing evidence of the applicability and utility of intersectional approaches to considering and implementing inclusion in humanitarian action. However, it is incredibly challenging to ensure that inclusion is consistently considered and that best practices are universally applied.

This chapter recognizes the inclusion challenge and proposes three key ways to better approach inclusion in humanitarian action. The first relates to increased investment and focus on inclusion in disaster risk reduction and preparedness processes. Humanitarian agencies and donors need to review resource allocation, and there is an important role for the research and academic community to provide a strong evidence base regarding the return on investment from preparedness. Essentially, as a sector, we need to be able to draw clearer linkages between investment and impact, asking ourselves, "What was better and/or avoided as a result of this investment?"

The second approach relates to a shift of focus from developing tools and standards for specific groups to providing mentoring and on-the-job support to field-based staff on intersectional approaches. The value of a focus on intersectionality—the multiple identities of people and the implications for people's ability to be seen and assisted—has been demonstrated in other sectors, especially health, but has yet to be fully understood and applied in the humanitarian sector. The proliferation of tools and standards that often cannot be used or understood by national actors needs to be slowed. Researchers and academics have an important role to play in providing an evidence base regarding which tools and approaches really work in supporting inclusion.

Finally, the sector needs to improve the diversity and inclusiveness of humanitarian sector leadership teams, so that they better reflect and are more capable of meeting the needs of diverse affected populations. Policymakers and senior decision-makers need to create a leadership culture that promotes inclusion and diversity. Academics and researchers can support the sector by providing an evidence base for leadership practices. Sector professionals need to be able to ask, "What impact do diverse and inclusive leadership teams have on the inclusiveness and quality of our humanitarian response operations?"

Notes

1. IFRC 2018a, foreword.
2. IFRC 2018b.
3. United Nations 2019.
4. OHCHR 2015.
5. ActionAid 2016.
6. See CARE 2020a, 2020b.
7. Good Humanitarian Donorship 2018.
8. Searle 2016.
9. United Nations 2015a.
10. IASC 1999.
11. IFRC 2018b.
12. Desai, Diofasi, and Lu 2018; IFRC 2018b.
13. IFRC 2018b.
14. Handicap International 2015.
15. Delgado, Skinner, and Calvi 2013.
16. Humanitarian Advisory Group 2018.
17. Humanitarian Advisory Group 2018.
18. IFRC 2018b.
19. UNISDR 2015.
20. UNHCR 2019.
21. Crenshaw 2017.
22. UNICEF 2020; CARE 2020a, 2020b.

23. Women's Refugee Commission 2013.
24. UNHCR 2018.
25. UN Security Council 2018.
26. Karasapan and Shah 2019; Mourtada, Schlecht, and DeJong 2017.
27. Barbelet, Samuels, and Plank 2018.
28. Barbelet, Samuels, and Plank 2018.
29. CARE 2015.
30. CARE 2015; DFAT 2018.
31. Twigg and Lowell 2018.
32. Humanitarian Advisory Group 2018.
33. Hashem 2019.
34. ActionAid 2016.
35. ActionAid 2016.
36. Grand Challenges Canada 2019.
37. ALNAP 2018.
38. United Nations 2020; CARE 2020b.
39. Humanitarian Advisory Group 2021.
40. Humanitarian Advisory Group 2021, 22.
41. Australian Red Cross 2020.
42. Twigg and Lowell 2018.
43. United Nations 2015.
44. CARE 2017a.
45. Human Rights Center 2005; United Nations 2019; Barbelet, Samuels, and Plank 2018.
46. Bell, Jackson, and Bakrania 2019.
47. Twigg and Lowell 2018, 3.
48. Twigg and Lowell 2018.
49. Guernsey and Scherrer 2017, 20.
50. DFAT 2016.
51. DFAT 2018.
52. IASC 2011.
53. DFAT 2019.
54. UN Women, 2018.
55. DFAT 2019.
56. UNICEF 2020.
57. CARE 2017b, CARE n.d.
58. IASC 2016.
59. ICRC 2018, 2.
60. Sphere 2018.
61. Sphere 2018.
62. IASC 2011, 2014, 2016, 2017
63. Catholic Relief Services 2018; DFAT 2018.
64. United Nations 2015b.
65. IFRC 2018b.
66. Australian Red Cross 2017.
67. Inclusion Charter 2016.
68. Humanitarian Advisory Group 2019.
69. Humanitarian Advisory Group 2019.
70. Humanitarian Advisory Group 2019.

Bibliography

ActionAid. 2016. "On the Frontline: Catalysing Women's Leadership in Humanitarian Action." https://actionaid.org.au/wp-content/uploads/2018/08/On-the-Frontline-Catalysing-Womens-Leadership-in-Humanitarian-Action.pdf.

ALNAP. 2018. "State of the Humanitarian System." https://sohs.alnap.org/help-library/the-state-of-the-humanitarian-system-2018-full-report.

Australian Red Cross. 2020. "Local Response in a Global Pandemic: Case Study of the Red Cross Response to Tropical Cyclone Harold During COVID-19 in Vanuatu and Fiji." https://www.redcross.org.au/getmedia/7c374bd0-90c8-423d-a0e4-8c0a26ea4bc5/ARC-TC-Harold-Full-report-Final-Electronic-041120.pdf.

Australian Red Cross. 2015. "Disability Inclusion and Disaster Management." https://www.redcross.org.au/getmedia/1283d6b8-c755-4455-82b5-a81afd8a29ee/Disability-Inclusion-Report-LR.pdf.aspx.

Australian Red Cross. 2017. "Going Local: Achieving a More Appropriate and Fit-for-Purpose Humanitarian Ecosystem in the Pacific." https://www.redcross.org.au/getmedia/fa37f8eb-51e7-4ecd-ba2f-d1587574d6d5/ARC-Localisation-report-Electronic-301017.pdf.aspx.

Barbelet, Véronique, Fiona Samuels, and Georgia Plank. 2018. "The Role and Vulnerabilities of Older People in Drought in East Africa." ODI. https://odi.org/en/publications/the-role-and-vulnerabilities-of-older-people-in-drought-in-east-africa-progress-challenges-and-opportunities-for-a-more-inclusive-humanitarian-response/.

Bell, Joe, Paul Jackson, and Shiv Bakrania. 2019. "Security and Justice Evidence Mapping Update." GSDRC. July. https://gsdrc.org/publications/security-and-justice-evidence-mapping-update/.

CARE. 2020a. "CARE Rapid Gender Analysis COVID-19 Pacific Region." March 26. Version 1. https://www.care.org.au/wp-content/uploads/2020/03/Pacific-RGA-FINAL-APPROVED-26March2020.pdf.

CARE. 2020b. "Where Are the Women? The Conspicuous Absence of Women in COVID-19 Response Teams and Plans, and Why We Need Them." https://www.care-international.org/files/files/CARE_COVID-19-womens-leadership-report_June-2020.pdf.

CARE. 2017a. "Does Gender Responsive Disaster Risk Reduction Make a Difference When a Category 5 Cyclone Strikes?" https://reliefweb.int/sites/reliefweb.int/files/resources/Vanuatu-DRR-Impact-Study-Summary_12-Oct-2016-3.pdf.

CARE. 2015. "CARE Australia Disability Framework." https://www.care.org.au/wp-content/uploads/2015/10/CARE-Australia-Disability-Framework-Revised-FINAL-PDF.pdf.

CARE. 2017b. "Gender in Brief." http://gender.careinternationalwikis.org/_media/gie_guidance_note_gender_in_brief.pdf.

CARE. n.d. "Rapid Gender Analysis." Retrieved from https://insights.careinternational.org.uk/in-practice/rapid-gender-analysis.

Catholic Relief Services. 2018. "Gender Protection Analysis in the CRS Central Sulawesi Response." https://www.crs.org/sites/default/files/tools-research/crs_sulawesi_gender_and_protection_analysis_indonesia_december_2018.pdf.

Crenshaw, Kimberlé. 2017. On Intersectionality: Essential Writings. New York: The New Press.

Delgado, Andrea, Marcus Skinner, and Piero Calvi. 2013. "Disasters and Diversity: A Study of Humanitarian Financing for Older People and Children Under Five." ALNAP. April. https://www.alnap.org/help-library/disasters-and-diversity-a-study-of-humanitarian-financing-for-older-people-and-children.

Desai, Vyjayanti T., Anna Diofasi, and Jing Lu. 2018. "The Global Identification Challenge: Who Are the 1 Billion People Without Proof of Identity?" Voices (World Bank blog). April 25. https://blogs.worldbank.org/voices/global-identification-challenge-who-are-1-billion-people-without-proof-identity.

DFAT. 2019. "Independent Evaluation of the Syria Crisis Humanitarian and Resilience Package." Department of Foreign Affairs and Trade, Australian Government. https://www.dfat.gov.au/sites/default/files/syria-crisis-humanitarian-resilience-package-evaluation-report.pdf.

DFAT. 2018. "Development for All: Evaluation of Progress Made in Strengthening Disability Inclusion in Australian Aid." Department of Foreign Affairs and Trade, Australian Government. https://www.dfat.gov.au/development/performance-assessment/aid-evaluat ion/strategic-evaluations/development-for-all-evaluation.

DFAT. 2016. "Humanitarian Strategy." Department of Foreign Affairs and Trade, Australian Government. https://www.dfat.gov.au/sites/default/files/dfat-humanitarian-strategy.pdf.

Good Humanitarian Donorship. 2018. "24 Principles and Good Practice of Humanitarian Donorship." https://www.ghdinitiative.org/ghd/gns/principles-good-practice-of-ghd/princip les-good-practice-ghd.html.

Global Protection Cluster. n.d. "Tools and Guidance." http://www.globalprotectioncluster.org/ tools-and-guidance/.

Grand Challenges Canada. 2019. "Analysis of Barriers Affecting Innovations in Humanitarian Contexts." https://humanitariangrandchallenge.org/wp-content/uploads/2019/05/BarrierAn alysis_Final_EN.pdf.

Guernsey, Katherine, and Valérie Scherrer. 2017. "Disability Inclusion in Disaster Risk Management: Promising Practices and Opportunities for Enhanced Engagement." Global Facility for Disaster Reduction and Recovery, Washington, DC. https://www.gfdrr.org/sites/ default/files/GFDRR%20Disability%20inclusion%20in%20DRM%20Report_F.PDF.

Handicap International. 2015. "Disability in Humanitarian Contexts: Views from Affected People and Field Organisations." July. https://d3n8a8pro7vhmx.cloudfront.net/handicapinternatio nal/pages/1500/attachments/original/1449158243/Disability_in_humanitarian_context_ 2015_Study_Advocacy.pdf?1449158243.

Hashem, A. 2019. "Impact of Patriarchy on Humanitarian Assistance in Yemen." Al-Madaniya. https://almadaniyamag.com/2019/02/19/impact-of-patriarchy-on-humanitarian-assistance-in-yemen/.

Human Rights Center. 2005. "After the Tsunami: Human Rights of Vulnerable Populations." Human Rights Center at the University of California, Berkeley, School of Law. https://huma nrights.berkeley.edu/publications/after-tsunami-human-rights-vulnerable-populations.

Humanitarian Advisory Group. 2021. "Tracking the Progress and Impact of Women's Leadership in COVID-19 Responses in the Philippines." https://humanitarianadvisorygroup.org/wp-cont ent/uploads/2021/03/HAG-UNWomen-Baseline_Final_05032021.pdf.

Humanitarian Advisory Group. 2019. "Data on Diversity." https://humanitarianadvisorygroup. org/insight/data-on-diversity-humanitarian-leadership-under-the-spotlight/.

Humanitarian Advisory Group. 2018. "Taking Sexual and Gender Minorities out of the Too-Hard Basket." https://humanitarianadvisorygroup.org/insight/taking-sexual-and-gender-min orities-out-of-the-too-hard-basket/.

IASC. 2017. "Gender Handbook for Humanitarian Action." Inter-Agency Standing Committee, Save the Children. https://reliefweb.int/report/world/iasc-gender-handbook-humanitarian-action-2017-enar.

IASC. 2016. "Policy on Protection in Humanitarian Action." Inter-Agency Standing Committee, Save the Children. https://interagencystandingcommittee.org/iasc-protection-priority-glo bal-protection-cluster/iasc-policy-protection-humanitarian-action-2016.

IASC. 2014. "Inter Agency Guidelines for Case Management and Child Protection." Inter-Agency Standing Committee, Save the Children. https://resourcecentre.savethechildren.net/library/ inter-agency-guidelines-case-management-and-child-protection.

IASC. 2011. "Guidelines for Child Friendly Spaces." Inter-Agency Standing Committee, Save the Children. https://resourcecentre.savethechildren.net/library/iasc-guidelines-child-friendly-spaces.

IASC. 1999. "Guiding Principles on Internal Displacement." Inter-Agency Standing Committee. https://interagencystandingcommittee.org/focal-points/documents-public/guiding-princip les-internal-displacement-1999.

ICRC. 2018. "Accountability to Affected People: Institutional Framework." International Committee of the Red Cross. https://www.alnap.org/help-library/accountability-to-affected-people-institutional-framework.

IFRC. 2018a. "World Disasters Report." https://media.ifrc.org/ifrc/wp-content/uploads/2018/10/B-WDR-2018-EN-LR.pdf.

IFRC. 2018b. "Leaving No One Behind." International Federation of the Red Cross. https://relief web.int/report/world/2018-world-disasters-report-leaving-no-one-behind.

Inclusion Charter. 2016. http://www.inclusioncharter.org.

Karasapan, Omer, and Sajjad Shah. 2019. "Forced Displacement and Child Marriage: A Growing Challenge in MENA." Brookings Institution. June 19. https://www.brookings.edu/blog/fut ure-development/2019/06/19/forced-displacement-and-child-marriage-a-growing-challe nge-in-mena.

Mourtada, R., J. Schlecht, and J. DeJong. 2017. "A Qualitative Study Exploring Child Marriage Practices Among Syrian Conflict-Affected Populations in Lebanon." *Conflict and Health* 11, supp. 1: art. 27. https://doi.org/10.1186/s13031-017-0131-z.

OHCHR. 2015. "Report on the Rights of Persons with Disabilities Under Article 11 of the CRPD Relating to Situations of Risk and Humanitarian Emergencies." UN Office of the High Commissioner for Human Rights. November 30. https://www.ohchr.org/EN/Issues/Disabil ity/Pages/Article11.aspx.

Searle, Louise. 2016. "Inclusive Humanitarian Action: A Study Into Humanitarian Partnership Agreement (HPA) in Practice in the Nepal Earthquake Response." Humanitarian Advisory Group. https://reliefweb.int/sites/reliefweb.int/files/resources/Nepal%20Inclusion%20Study_May%202016_email%20%282%29.pdf.

Sphere. 2018. *The Sphere Handbook*. Geneva: Sphere.

Twigg, John, and Emma Lowell. 2018. "Disability Inclusion and Disaster Risk Reduction." ODI. https://www.odi.org/sites/odi.org.uk/files/resource-documents/12324.pdf.

UN Security Council. 2018. "Report of the Secretary-General on Conflict-Related Sexual Violence." S/2018/250. https://undocs.org/en/S/2018/250.

UNHCR. 2019. "Regional Refugee and Resilience Plan (3RP)." United Nations High Commissioner for Refugees. http://www.3rpsyriacrisis.org/wp-content/uploads/2020/03/3RP_brochure_150dpi.pdf.

UNHCR. 2018. "UNHCR Policy on Age, Gender and Diversity." United Nations High Commissioner for Refugees. https://www.unhcr.org/protection/women/5aa13c0c7/policy-age-gender-diversity-accountability-2018.html.

UNICEF. 2020. "Rapid Gender Analysis during COVID-19 Pandemic: Mekong Sub-Regional Report." UNICEF, UN Women, and CARE. https://www.unicef.org/eap/media/6871/file/Rapid%20Gender%20Analysis%20during%20COVID-19%20Pandemic.pdf.

UNISDR. 2015. "Sendai Framework for Disaster Risk Reduction." United Nations Office for Disaster Risk Reduction. https://www.undrr.org/publication/sendai-framework-disaster-risk-reduction-2015-2030.

United Nations. 2015a. "2030 Agenda for Sustainable Development." https://www.un.org/ga/sea rch/view_doc.asp?symbol=A/RES/70/1&Lang=E.

United Nations. 2020. "Policy Brief: The Impact of COVID-19 on Women." https://reliefweb.int/sites/reliefweb.int/files/resources/policy-brief-the-impact-of-covid-19-on-women-en.pdf.

United Nations. 2019. "Humanitarian Assistance in Emergencies: Mainstreaming Gender and Protection." United Nations Mozambique and Protection Cluster Mozambique. https://www.globalprotectioncluster.org/_assets/files/field_protection_clusters/Mozambique/files/protect ion-mainstreaming_pocket-guide-gender-and-protection-brochure.en.

United Nations. 2015b. "UN World Conference on Disaster Risk Reduction." https://www.un.org/sustainabledevelopment/un-world-conference-on-disaster-risk-reduction/.

UN Women. 2018. Empowerment Through Employment for Syrian Refugee Women in Jordan. https://arabstates.unwomen.org/en/news/stories/2018/8/feature-empowerment-through-employment-for-syrian-refugee-women-in-jordan.

Women's Refugee Commission. 2013. "Gender-Based Violence Among Displaced Women and Girls with Disabilities: Findings from Field Visits 2011–2012." https://www.womensrefuge ecommission.org/research-resources/gender-based-violence-among-displaced-women-and-girls-with-disabilities-findings-from-field-visits-2011-2012/.

14

Understanding Linkages

Conflict, Societal Violence, and Masculinities in and Outside of Wars

Tatiana Moura, Elis Borde, Henny Slegh, and Gary Barker

What if war is just a male version of dressing up, a game devised to avoid profound spiritual questions?

—Louise Gluck

Introduction

This chapter makes a case for applying a masculinities lens to understand multiple forms of violence in conflict and non-conflict settings. It discusses how violence is tied to inequalities, marginalization, patriarchal and other power structures, masculinities, and young men's identities. It further examines how those dynamics shape the differential impact of conflict on females versus males and individuals of other gender identities. Further, it brings an intersectional understanding of how race, social class, and gender, in particular, masculinities interact in conflict and high-violence settings.

The chapter concludes with reflections on the implications for programs and policies focusing on urban violence prevention (including prevention of sexual and gender-based violence [SGBV], harassment, and sexual exploitation) as well as post-conflict recovery. As we have worked extensively in reducing and understanding urban violence in favelas in Brazil and in understanding and responding to SGBV in eastern Democratic Republic of Congo, we bring in research and case studies from those settings.

Masculinities, Patriarchy, Armed Conflict, and Public Violence

Conflict, war, and violence have historically been tied to masculinities. Men, often younger men from lower-income and historically marginalized groups, are predominantly those either socialized, voluntarily conscripted, or recruited, sometimes in brutal ways, into the roles of soldier and combatant. Similar trends hold for other forms of armed violence, particularly urban-based gang-related violence, where low-income men from groups that have been historically discriminated against also predominate. Masculinist posturing and use of power are often also tied to how male political leaders, military leaders, and leaders of armed groups, including gangs, project their identities, wield power over others, and treat women and other non-male gender identities, both through policies and in their individual behavior.

Conflict and armed violence also affect masculinities. Men's lives, their identities, and their livelihoods—and clearly also those of women, girls, boys, and others—are disrupted in gendered ways by conflict and armed violence. Specifically, for some men participation in armed violence is a way to achieve status, income, and sexual partnership. In post-conflict settings, some men face trauma, loss of livelihood, loss of status, or imprisonment. In sum, some men achieve a sense of socially recognized manhood in wars, conflict, or armed violence, and other men have their sense of gendered identity, or manhood, affected by the results of war, conflict, and armed violence.

The most obvious indicator of how conflict, war, and armed violence affect men is mortality. Globally, men are more than 80 percent of victims of homicide and direct war-related deaths. This does not imply that women and girls suffer less from conflict. Indeed, there is a vast literature and attention from key civil society groups on the impact of conflict, war, and urban violence on women, including experiences of sexual and gender-based violence, lost livelihoods, and marginalization in peace processes. In calling attention to men and masculinities, the chapter seeks to evidence how conflict affects masculinities and how masculinities affect conflict, and to present a relational perspective that acknowledges how masculinities—in terms of identities, power, and individual and collective actions by men—affect women and girls, as well as individuals of other gender identities.

A growing body of academic literature discusses how masculinities and patriarchy shape militaries and gendered patterns of political support for war, as well men's use of and victimization by rape and sexual violence in war.[1] There is also important research on how masculinities are part of other forms of violence, including gang-related violence.[2] This chapter explores two specific settings—eastern Democratic Republic of Congo and urban Brazil—to understand how patriarchal power, race-based and class-based inequalities, men's gendered identities, and men's sense of thwarted adult manhood influence conflict and violence, individuals, and communities. The authors bring an intersectional approach to understand how men's armed violence and especially gun-related violence is often part of a deliberate reinforcement of power structures among groups of men, and of the power of some men over women. While the historical and contextual origins of and effects of conflict and violence are distinct geographically, power between specific groups, some men's power over other men, and men's gendered reactions to trauma and displacement—along with the reactions from the state, the UN, and other bodies—shape post-conflict realities. In sum, the cases demonstrate what it means to apply an intersectional masculinities lens to conflict and post-conflict settings.

We deliberately include and apply this lens to one setting recognized as post-conflict (DRC) and one setting not generally thought of as a conflict or post-conflict setting (urban Brazil). These examples are included because the distinction between war and peace, or between wartime violence and other forms of public violence, is increasingly being questioned.[3] Further, global data affirm that other forms of armed and societal violence, and more specifically urban violence, contribute to far more deaths than wartime violence, and in some countries affect more people. Globally, there were an estimated 409,000 homicide deaths in 2018, over 84 percent of whom were males, surpassing the 105,000 killed in armed conflicts in the same year.[4]

Over 30 percent of all homicides are in the Americas—a region that accounts for only 13 percent of the world's population.[5] Indeed, Latin America, while not currently the region with the largest number of armed conflicts in the world, has and continues to have the highest per-capita homicide rates in the world.[6] This strongly relates to persistent and deep inequalities in the region. Inequality is the most well-established environmental determinant of levels of violence, tied to processes of social marginalization and exclusion that shape the patterns of violent death.[7] Brazil officially registered 63,895 homicides in 2017, the world's highest absolute number of homicides, which corresponds to a homicide rate of 30.5 deaths per 100,000 people.[8] For comparison, India, which has five times the population of Brazil, had 42,678 homicides in 2016.[9] "Armed conflict" in Brazil can be considered an example of what have been termed "newest wars," undeclared and chronic wars or chronically high lethal violence in "times (and settings) of formal peace."[10] Several Central American countries, such as Honduras and El Salvador, also constitute tragic examples, with homicide rates of 41.7 and 62.1 deaths per 100,000, respectively, in 2017.[11] Venezuela also had a high homicide rate, with 56.8 deaths per 100,000 in 2017.[12] Such situations resemble wars in that violence and the fear of violence deeply shape the daily lives of the millions who live there.[13]

The mainstream debate on public security and urban violence in Latin America and elsewhere generally focuses on drug-related violence, kidnappings, and violence between rival gangs. Considerable research has explored risk factors such as alcohol consumption, access to and availability of guns, population density, poverty, unemployment, lack of governance, and weakness of the state.[14] Yet these analyses often fail to fully explain the complex, tragic persistence of violence in urban settings. They also often overlook the drivers of the inequitable gendered distribution of violent deaths, which are intimately linked to and neatly reflect gendered, societal hierarchies and power relations, disproportionately affecting young, nonwhite, and poor men in deeply polarized, unequal, and segregated cities. A recent Brazilian Public Safety Yearbook, for example, indicates that homicide victims in Brazil are mostly Black (75.4 percent), between eighteen and twenty-nine years old (68.2 percent), and only completed primary school (81.5 percent).[15] Similar trends have been observed in other countries of the Americas.[16]

This Latin American violence does not present a classic conflict; there is no one identifiable, organized group declaring war against another organized group. But it is a complex interaction of historical social exclusion, expectations that men will be providers and breadwinners, and salient norms about manhood. It would not be an exaggeration to say that the persistently high homicide rates among young, low-income men represent a form of war against them, waged by an interplay of historical social injustices.

Men are overrepresented among deaths directly related to conflict and in homicides, and specific groups of disempowered young men even more so. Men are also overrepresented as perpetrators of most forms of lethal and physical violence (homicide, suicide, assault, intimate partner violence, conflict-related sexual violence, and nearly every other form of lethal and nonlethal physical violence). This is not to say that violence is essentially masculine or associated with being biologically male, but rather that it reflects complex processes involving gender norms and identities, power structures, and marginalization. In this regard, we argue on the basis of our case in Brazil that (gun) violence is part of a deliberate reinforcement of power structures between groups of men with more power against less powerful men.[17] Furthermore, women and girls are affected in gendered ways by all these forms of violence, for example: they suffer from men's perpetration of violence against them, as well as from the economic and other forms of hardship that result from men's victimization and death.

The analysis of the involvement of men and women in conflict, war, violence, and peacebuilding has long been characterized by simplistic universalizing and stereotyping, focusing on the most visible practices and actors. Women have predominantly been associated with peace and informal peacebuilding, while men have been associated with violence and formal, state-involved peacemaking. While these patterns do exist, analyses have frequently focused on these traditional gender roles, undervaluing women (and nonprivileged men) and their experiences, and failing to critically discuss the weight of historical gender constructions in the (re)production of cultures and contexts of violence. Some international-relations feminists have argued that we must not essentialize being male and social constructions of masculinities as inherently violent, though men are historically overrepresented as casualties and combatants in war.[18] Similarly, it is important to acknowledge that the type of violence (domestic, armed, economic, etc.) and the local context matter.[19] Some researchers also have said that application of a masculinities lens should focus on patriarchal systems and the power dynamics that have historically placed power in the hands of some men over other men and women.[20]

So what, then, is meant by a masculinities lens applied to violence and conflict? First, we affirm that while the socioeconomic and racial dimensions of urban violence have received attention, gender (and within that masculinities) has not garnered significant attention.[21] "Gender-neutral" concepts of urban violence continue to prevail. As a result, with some notable exceptions, gender relations, gender power dimensions, and gender norms and identities have rarely or only superficially been considered in urban violence scholarship.[22] Other gender analyses of conflict, urban violence, and war simply disaggregate data on mortality or participation in armed groups by sex and call it a gender analysis.

Our analysis is informed by diverse theorists—from Raewyn Connell's work on hegemonic and subaltern masculinities to Judith Butler's work on gender as performative (and masculinities as performed and judged by other men) to the vast array of work by Michael Flood and others on men's use of violence in the context of partnered relationships and the complex interplay of individual, childhood, and societal conditions driving violence.[23] We see masculinities as (1) power structures, (2) relational in that they are constructed in relation to women, (3) contextual, (4) performed, and (5) varying over the life cycle. Five common, internationally salient dynamics affect the likelihood that men participate in or are victims of violence:

1. *The need to maintain socially recognized manhood status.* Often at the core of masculine gendering and the use of violence is the demand that male-identifying persons achieve and continually reassert their manhood.
2. *Constant policing of masculine performance.* The concept of "being a man" is held in place through continual policing of men's and boys' performance. For many, context-specific violence relates to being judged by other men.
3. *Pressure to hide emotions.* Around the world, men are encouraged to refrain from showing emotional vulnerability and to evidence a limited range of emotions. Aggressivity and violence are acceptable, while vulnerability, cooperation, and nonviolence are judged to be nonmasculine.
4. *Gender-segregated spaces and cultures.* Gender norms produce many harmful and unnecessary divisions and fractures within societies. Social spaces (and even "microcultures") associated with men often become places where violence is rehearsed and reinforced. These include armies, male-specific social groups, certain sports, and armed groups such as gangs.
5. *Reinforcement of patriarchal power.* Violence is ultimately about reinforcing power structures that advantage men over women and that favor particular men over other men.[24]

Rather than demonstrating any "natural" inclination toward violence, research affirms that violence is encouraged and reinforced as part of gender-specific socialization processes that boost violent masculinities and hypermasculine norms.[25] In this regard, masculinities—which can be defined as norms, social expectations, and power dynamics—often contribute to violence.[26] (See Chapter 19 for a discussion of norms.) With this overview of how we define masculinities and the relationship between violence and masculinities, we explore the case studies.

The Case of Rio de Janeiro: A War Against Poor Black Young Men?

Low-income urban areas in Brazil provide a useful case study for understanding how poverty, urban insecurity, and masculinities interact. Brazil continues to have the largest absolute number of homicides per year in the world. Over forty years of large-scale killing means that there are now over 4 million more women than men in the country. And though overall homicide rates have fallen in Brazil, they have not come down for Black men, and an alarming proportion of all violent deaths were committed by security forces—a phenomenon that has been growing since 2016, according to the latest Brazilian Public Safety Yearbook. In 2018, police killed 1,444 people in the state of Rio de Janeiro alone.[27]

Many of the young men who are murdered—or who murder—in Brazil are connected to drug trafficking gangs. Most killings take place in urban areas, where the drug trade emerged as a response to unemployment, where there is limited state presence, and where there is easy access to firearms.[28]

A recent study by Promundo on linkages between masculinities, public violence, and violence at home—the International Men and Gender Equality Survey Urban Violence (IMAGES-UV) study, conducted in Rio de Janeiro between 2013 and 2016—found that homicide and other forms of violence persist at high levels in favelas and other low-income settings in Rio de Janeiro, and that this violence over-whelmingly affects low-income young Black men. The study included interviews with respondents in the city from the "south," where homicide rates are lower, and from the "north," where homicide rates are higher. Results found that men's exposure to urban violence before age eighteen was strongly linked to their later use of violence—including gender-based violence—as adults. Of the men interviewed, 82.8 percent had experienced or witnessed at least two of the following before age eighteen: aggravated assault, violent treatment by the police, battering, exchange of gunfire, house or workplace hit by bullets, death threats, or being shot by a firearm. At the same time, nearly 95 percent of men surveyed viewed gun ownership and use favorably, although a relatively small proportion of individuals reported that they owned or had ever used firearms. Over 70 percent of all female respondents also reported supporting gun ownership and use.

One of the key findings of IMAGES-UV connected exposure to urban violence and childhood experiences of domestic violence to the use of violence in adulthood.[29] In this regard, the IMAGES-UV results illustrate the implications of "newest wars" in cities of the global South and the pervasive connections between gendered socialization and violence, pointing at the severe implications of what the authors understand as "militarized" childhoods, shaped by daily exposure to guns and weaponry.[30] Guns and crossfire among drug factions and the police have long been common, both when communities are controlled by drug traffickers and there are intermittent police raids, and when militias or (military) police assumes militarized control, the latter for example, in the context of the creation of the Unidade de Polícia Pacificadora program (UPP), which employs units that use heavy "war" machinery including helicopters and *caveirão* tanks, as well as armored urban combat vehicles with skull-and-crossbones images painted on them. Boys and girls are exposed to power hierarchies and confrontational approaches to security and governance, largely carried out by men who embody power over other men and women. Power may shift between police, drug lords, militias, and paramilitary groups, but it overwhelmingly lies with those who have used and are willing to use weapons; this reinforces hypermasculine identities around "being tough" and sometimes even encourages boys to play with guns from an early age.[31] Though many young men socialized in such settings do not become perpetrators of violence, the relationships between weapons and masculinities are increasingly recognized. A recent study from the United States, for example, showed how the symbolic value of a gun is intimately tied to hegemonic masculinity and validated by narratives of self-reliance, security, protection, and defense.[32]

In Brazil, among low-income young men who perceive themselves to be powerless, guns and participation in armed groups increase the likelihood of gang participation, especially when combined with other vulnerabilities and inequalities such as lack of employment, lack of other sources of identity, and limited ties to social institutions.[33] Gang participation (in which guns are wielded for power and controlled by those who hold more power in a given gang) is also related to competition for reputation—recognition, honor, and prestige among potential female partners—among young men who have few things that make them feel socially recognized, and by adult men facing social marginalization and exclusion.[34] In this regard, men's armed-group-related violence and gun-related violence deliberately reinforce power structures; even guns themselves are distributed and controlled within gangs based on a hierarchy of power and rank.[35]

The vast majority of victims of homicide in Brazil are low-income urban-based men of African descent, victims of legacies of social inequality. The vast majority of perpetrators are also men, sometimes from rival drug gangs, and often from police and armed vigilante or militia groups. In this way, power by the state and nonstate actors interacts with young men's desire to achieve socially recognized manhood. Some young men turn to armed violence to achieve this manhood, and their actions are often brutally repressed by state-sanctioned homicide carried out by other men.

The Case of Eastern DRC: A War of Emasculated Men Against Women?

Since 1993, eastern Democratic Republic of Congo has been the site of a series of conflicts that have involved standing militaries from multiple countries, proxy armed groups for those countries, and ethnic-based combatant groups, with considerable fluidity between and among the groups. This series of conflicts, along with chronic poverty and inequality in the region, has given rise to armed groups that still operate in the Kivu regions and have participated in large-scale human rights violations, including high rates of sexual and gender-based violence by combatants against noncombatant women, girls, men, and boys.[36] The number of active armed forces in eastern DRC was estimated in 2012 at about two dozen, most of which have committed serious human rights abuses.[37] Over four-fifths (81 percent) of the incidents of human rights abuse involving armed groups occurred in South Kivu.[38]

In such a context, women and girls are exposed to many risks, including various forms of gender-based violence. Sexual violence has largely and consistently been used as a weapon of war in DRC. It also emerges from historical and contextual norms and practices related to sexuality, and to women's and girls' limited power relative to men and boys. Successive violent crises have resulted in millions of women, men, girls, and boys being subjected to human rights abuses and widespread conflict-related and post-conflict-related SGBV.

Worldwide, studies and media coverage have reported the prevalence of those gross human rights abuses of women and girls, with men mainly portrayed as brute and monstrous rapists and women as victims. Maria Eriksson Baaz was among the first researchers exploring the motivations of Congolese soldiers and examined how conflict, suffering, and disempowerment of men can fuel emasculation, leading to new, specific forms of sexualized violence.[39] Rather than the simplistic portrayals of Congolese men (and Congolese male combatants, whether in the military or other armed groups) as inherently violent or prone to rape, they describe how men's use of rape is shaped by childhood experiences, power dynamics within armed groups, race and ethnic-based tensions, gender norms, and widespread impunity for rape and other rights violations.

A growing body of research from the DRC looks at how masculinities and men's realities feed into conflict and are shaped by it. Several studies have examined the impact of the conflict on gender relations, encompassing the disempowerment or emasculation many men perceive in the face of lost livelihoods, and loss of status born of displacement and victimization by armed conflict.[40] Lwambo's study in 2011 was one of the earliest to look at how men's sense of identity is severely impacted by the conflict, with consequences for men themselves, their partners, and their families.[41]

Promundo and partners also studied how trauma and displacement in eastern DRC influence men's use of violence against female partners. In a household survey in 2014, approximately 70 percent of men and 80 percent of women reported at least one conflict-related traumatic event, including loss of property, displacement, loss of a family member or child, personal injury, or the experience of sexual violence.[42] Nearly two-thirds of men and women who experienced the conflict reported negative psychological consequences. In general, men tended to cope with extreme stress and trauma by seeking to reduce feelings of vulnerability, including through alcohol and substance abuse. Women more frequently sought help or turned to religion. The study also found high rates of male support for various forms of violence. Sixty-two percent of women and 48 percent of men said that a man has a right to sex even if a woman refuses. Seventy-eight percent of women agreed that they have to tolerate violence to keep the family together, and 48 percent of women agreed that women sometimes deserve to be beaten.

The research also found that sexual violence and other forms of violence by men in eastern DRC can be seen partly as expressions of failed masculinity in a failing state. When, because of war and poverty, men are unable to fulfill the culturally defined male roles as protectors and providers for their families, self-perceptions of failure and loss of power and control lead many to alcohol abuse and violence against women. For some, this sense of lost masculinity, together with a sense of hopelessness and early exposure to violence, provides a motive to join armed groups. Constructions of masculinity based on rigid and traditional notions of power, control, and honor also contribute to the perception that fighting and violence are the only ways to resolve interpersonal and intercommunal conflicts.

The analysis also found complex ways that sexual violence affects women and is used to shame men. Clearly, rape and sexual violence mostly affect women as victims, with serious and long-lasting physical, psychological, and social consequences. Rape of a woman as daughter, mother, and wife has huge consequences for the family, due to stigma, health issues, and traditional perceptions of gender relations. Yet sexual violence against women also affects men, both directly and indirectly, and that explains why the rape of women is potently used as a strategy of war to humiliate and emasculate men. For example, men forced to rape relatives, neighbours or even strangers, as well as men forced to watch the rape of relatives suffer from extreme guilt and shame, as illustrated in the experience of a man in Luvungi, DRC:

> I saw how my daughter was raped: I wished they had killed me. What kind of man am I not able to protect my family? I am not able to revenge those men, I have not the courage and physical strength anymore. My life is destroyed; I lost my sexual life and I have no will to live anymore.

Men's guilt and shame are strongly associated with social stigma rooted in perceptions of masculinity, particularly the notion that men are supposed to be able to protect female relatives. Men explain how they lose courage and pride after being forced to watch armed men rape a woman or girl; it makes them feel "less of a man," unable to live up to the gendered ideal of men as protectors. As one man stated:

> The wife is the heart of the family, those men that penetrated her, destroyed the family and they took my heart away.

In addition, local social norms in the DRC frequently hold that a man is supposed to reject his wife after she is raped (affirmed by 46 percent of men), and if he does not reject her, he may face sanctions or reproach from his extended family. Women who are raped are stigmatized, and men too are stigmatized by association with "damaged" women. Even though most men participating in the qualitative research admit that a woman should not be blamed for being raped, some men see no alternative to rejecting her in an attempt to save social position and not be associated with the shame of sexual violence.

The accounts of husbands whose wives were raped reveal high levels of traumatic stress. Men and women describe how most men react with intense anger and violence upon hearing that their wives were raped.[43] Some men disclosed feelings of depression, staying in bed all day, headaches, no appetite, and suicidal thoughts. The male perpetrators (mostly combatants) who carry out the rapes know the impact of these social norms. Thus, the conflict-related sexual violence against women that has defined eastern DRC is partly also against men; armed groups rape women in part to emasculate men.

Women and girls do face the most substantial lifelong physical, psychological, social, and economic consequences of sexual violence. Women speak of the effects of being abandoned, stigmatized, and expelled from homes by male partners after being raped by combatants before, during, and after conflict. Some women who survive rape by combatants tell of male partners using violence against them, in effect revictimizing them, because their husbands blame them for not stopping the rape and because of men's own trauma. Women are keenly aware of their husbands' limited coping skills and of the cycles of alcohol abuse and men's self-harm that often accompanied violence against their wives. Any masculinities lens must encompass an understanding of how men's perceptions and actions directly impact women and girls, and vice versa. Additionally, though not addressed here, is the issue of children born out of rape, who are often also socially excluded, are living with the mother (with or without a male partner), and often face higher rates of trauma and poverty than other households. With limited access to health care or psychosocial support, women and girls in DRC often cope with physical and psychological injuries in isolation. In the absence of a system for protection and care, they are extremely vulnerable to reabuse and retraumatization.[44]

Discussion

Masculinities and the Effects of Conflict

The two case examples demonstrate how masculinities, power, patriarchy, and poverty feed violence; how violence in public settings affects violence in homes; and how violence must be seen as gendered.[45] There is increasing recognition that a gendered perspective is necessary to understand wars and to build effective peacebuilding responses. This applies equally to violent urban conflict, which has taken on dimensions that fundamentally challenge the traditional divide between war and peace, as violent urban conflict "occurs before, during, after and even in the absence of war," and sometimes can be considered an undeclared, chronic war in "times of formal peace."[46] As Giles and Hyndman argue, the blended category "womenandchildren"—to use Cynthia Enloe's apt expression—is no longer spatially separate from the waging of war.[47] In other words, "everyone is at the battlefront," whether directly or indirectly."[48]

How Emasculation Leads to Repeating Cycles of Violence

The International Men and Gender Equality Survey (IMAGES) in Brazil and in the DRC reveals links between traumatic and disempowering experiences of men and the reproduction of violence in other settings. Studies show that men who feel humiliated and abused by armed groups tend to be more prone to violence themselves.[49] Paradoxically, men in conflict settings generally do not perceive themselves as perpetrators; rather, men perceive themselves as the aggrieved ones, as the ones who have been wronged. They sometimes justify their violence by victim-blaming and by distancing themselves from the victims' suffering, a psychological defense mechanism of externalization—also framed as "othering."[50]

The case studies show that men tend to cope with humiliation and disrespect using violence. Young men in socially excluded settings often try to reclaim power by using violence against someone they see as more vulnerable or weaker, in order to come to terms with their feelings of powerlessness. A group of Congolese women participating in the qualitative research identified three types of men: (1) "men as lions," who are very violent and aggressive at home; (2) "men as volcanoes," who are very silent but who can suddenly explode; and (3) "men as lakes," who are very calm and quiet. (The last group is very rare.) The lion men impose their superiority and power, driven by the need to be privileged and respected and the head of the family. The volcano men use violence when they are out of control due to trauma, substance abuse, and unbearable frustration; they can use extreme forms of violence against their wives, but also against themselves or others. Lake men remain calm and stand beside their wives and family, using mutual support to sustain them. "Lake men" provide the evidence that men are not born violent; rather, an extreme violent, unjust, and unequal environment creates the conditions under which men are more likely to behave violently.

These examples are important in calling attention to the diversity of men's experiences of and responses to violence. It's clear that men's use of violence, their responses to it, and their actions and participation in conflict settings vary. Male violence is neither natural nor universal. Though this chapter has focused on masculinities and men's lived experiences, it is important to emphasize that this does not imply that women's experiences of violence and of conflict are less tragic, complex, or egregious.

Implications for Programs and Policy

What implications emerge from applying this lens of power, patriarchy, and masculinities to conflict- and violence-affected areas? While the settings are quite varied, several conclusions and recommendations emerge.

Understand Salient Power Structures and Masculine Norms in Context

Given the strong associations among masculinities, power, patriarchy, and violence, research in conflict and high-violence settings should analyze how social norms, power structures, patriarchy, and childhood socialization shape violence in any given setting. Use the evidence gathered to directly challenge masculine norms in violence prevention programming, using approaches that deliberately seek to change social norms related to gender.

Focus on and Identify Resistance to Patriarchal Violence

Studies and programming should focus on examining men's resistance to violence and resilience within contexts of violence. Though feminist literature increasingly focuses on men's multiple experiences and expressions of gender, there remains a tendency to emphasize men's involvement in violence rather than to understand their noninvolvement (that is, how men resist or cope with dominant versions of masculinities).[51] Risk and vulnerability, rather than resilience, are often the starting point for research on violence (among men). It is crucial to understand how to negotiate models of masculinity away from violence and how to produce alternative models of masculinity that resist violence and promote equality. Theoretical discussions of masculinities have shifted from a more singular "male sex role" view to a conceptualization of "multiple masculinities."[52] The emphasis on changing identity expressions sheds light on alternatives to dominant/hegemonic forms of masculinities and draws attention to nonviolent pathways. Understanding what leads men to prioritize pathways to nonviolent and peaceful versions of manhood is essential to reducing violence in the public and private sphere.

Help Men (and Women) Find Alternative Identities Not Associated with Violence

Numerous qualitative studies affirm the importance of employment that provides visible identity as a provider for young men in settings where combatant or delinquent versions of manhood hold strong power.[53] Other aspects that have been shown to promote nonviolent male life trajectories are fatherhood; active caregiving for biological and nonbiological children; and additional constructive engagements, such as membership in social groups that have the potential to widen life perspectives and eventually engender nonviolent, caring versions of manhood. Involved fatherhood and fatherhood training in settings of high violence provide some men with tremendous coping skills, connection, and resilience through their care of children; others can be encouraged to find these benefits through structured fatherhood training groups that include couples communication, a trauma-response component, and nonviolent child-rearing training.[54]

Provide Alternative, Meaningful Pathways to Support Peaceful, Gender-Equitable Life Choices

Limited research has explored abandonment of gangs, drug trafficking, or criminal activity; post-conflict transformation and masculinities following war; transitions following incarceration; and programs and public policies designed to end men's use of intimate partner violence and other types of violence.[55] Resilience frameworks can also be found in the humanitarian and disaster response literature, and to a lesser extent in urban contexts.[56]

Understand the Masculine Dimensions of Trauma

Men and women in settings of high violence typically experience and witness multiple forms of violence, loss, and displacement. Given salient patterns of socialization in many parts of the world promulgating the idea that men should not seek help or show vulnerability, men typically cope poorly after traumatic violence. It is exactly in the intimacy of partner relations where experiences of lost manhood emerge as an unbearable shame and humiliation, and may turn into extreme forms of violence. However, not all economically stressed men use violence; many employ nonviolent coping strategies to deal with loss and trauma. These strategies may include communicating with their partners and others about the problems, and taking up a more caring and protective role at home. On the negative side, the strategies may involve isolation, silence, shutting down, or substance abuse. An acknowledgment of men's suffering in dealing with grief, loss, and feelings of emasculation is a way to dismantle an artificial distance between "them" and "us." Dealing with anger, humiliation, and hurt in nonviolent ways is learned through interactions in early childhood, lifetime experiences, role models, and positive responses. In DRC, Promundo and the Institut Supérieur du Lac created a community-based psychosocial support methodology to address the psychosocial needs of men by using a therapeutic group design to reduce effects of trauma and foster positive and nonviolent gender-transformative coping strategies to deal with distress. The model relies in part on the deliberate engagement of men in conflict-affected communities who showed positive coping and generally did not use physical violence against their wives. These "men of good standing" participated in group therapy sessions along with men who had used violence against their wives (often who also had experienced sexual violence in the conflict) as a way to build on the positive coping skills of some men. The impact evaluation three years after implementation showed that intimate partner violence had stopped in thirty out of forty families, and positive involvement of men in the household had increased, including in the care of children. Relapses in men's behaviors to using psychological and economic violence in ten families were related to alcohol abuse by men and severe mental health issues; no physical violence against women was reported.[57]

Consider How Masculine Norms Are Reinforced and Taught to Children in Conflict and High-Violence Settings

In Brazil and DRC, youth were engaged as agents of change through Youth Living Peace, a gender-transformative intervention program designed to help adolescent boys and girls heal from violence while providing school-based training for violence prevention. The program's overall goal was to enable adolescent girls and boys to experience greater gender equality and increased freedom from violence through individual and community change, as well as through supportive school environments.

Men's violence is produced—not innate—and nonviolent, pro-social masculinities exist alongside violent versions of manhood in any setting, including in conflict settings. While we must work at all levels to end conflict and violence, efforts to achieve peace work better when we see men and masculinities in their complexity rather than reducing men, or women, to stereotypical roles and norms. Understanding masculinities is never, on its own, the way to end conflict, and it should be done together with understanding women's lived realities. By understanding patriarchy and masculinities together with the array of other drivers of conflict and violence, and the experiences of women and girls, solutions are likely to be more effective and more enduring.

Notes

1. Cockburn 2004; Higate 2003.
2. Baird 2018.
3. Cockburn 2004.
4. Hideg and del Frate 2021.

5. Hideg and del Frate.
6. UNODC 2019.
7. Wilkinson 2004.
8. UNODC 2019.
9. UNODC 2019.
10. Moura 2007; Moura, Garraio, and Roque 2012.
11. UNODC 2019.
12. UNODC 2019.
13. Penglas 2014.
14. Muggah 2012; Briceño-León, Villaveces, and Concha-Eastman 2008.
15. Cerqueira et al. 2017.
16. Hideg and del Frate 2021.
17. Barker 2016.
18. Detraz 2012.
19. Moser 2001; Moura, Garraio, and Roque 2012.
20. Barker 2016.
21. Sampson and Wilson 1995; Bennett and Fraser 2015.
22. See Pearce 2006; Wilding 2011, 2014; Peake and Rieker; Kern and Mullings 2013; Baird 2012.
23. Connell 2016; Butler 1988. Flood 2011.
24. Heilman and Barker 2018.
25. Barker 2016.
26. Lindsay and Miescher 2003, 4.
27. Cerqueira et al. 2017.
28. Cerqueira et al. 2017.
29. Taylor et al. 2016.
30. Taylor et al. 2016; Borde, Page, and Moura 2020.
31. Barker et al. 2012.
32. Gahman 2015.
33. Barker et al. 2010.
34. Barker 2005.
35. Barker 2016.
36. Kelly et al. 2012; Brown 2012; Elbert et al. 2013.
37. Stearns, Verweijen, and Baaz 2013.
38. Taback, Painter, and King 2008.
39. Baaz and Stern 2013.
40. Lwambo 2011; Baaz and Stern 2010.
41. Lwambo 2011.
42. Slegh, Barker, and Levtov 2014.
43. Slegh, Barker, and Levtov 2014.
44. Slegh 2011; Liebling and Slegh 2011.
45. It is important to note that SGBV is not just a feature of the conflict in DRC. Indeed, rape has a particular role, as Giles and Hyndman (2004) emphasize referencing landmark indictments issued by the International Crimes Tribunal for Yugoslavia in 1996 for the arrest of eight men charged with sexual assault for the purpose of torture and enslavement. For the first time in history, rape was prosecuted as a weapon of war and a "crime against humanity," and the "ample evidence that men used rape to terrorize, humiliate, and 'contaminate' the women of opposing ethnic groups in Bosnia-Hercegovina led to these indictments" (Giles and Hyndman 2004, 310). Further reference is made to the fact that some men were raped in an effort to emasculate their identities. But the gendered aspects of violent conflict go beyond rape. Research has, for example, emphasized gender-specific effects of displacement and loss of livelihoods, and the links between gender, coping, and violence use.

46. Giles and Hyndman 2004; Moura 2007; Moura, Garraio, and Roque 2012.
47. Giles and Hyndman 2004; Enloe 1993, 165–166.
48. Giles and Hyndman 2004, 4.
49. Baaz and Stern 2013.
50. Staub 2006.
51. Barker 2005; Moura, Garraio, and Roque 2012.
52. Connell 2005.
53. Barker 2005.
54. Marsiglio and Pleck 2005.
55. Baird 2012; Campbell and Hansen 2012; Moura, Garraio, and Roque 2012; Theidon 2009; Visher and Travis 2003.
56. Almedom and Tumwine 2008; Christensen 2008.
57. Tankink and Slegh 2017.

Bibliography

Almedom, Astier M. 2008. "Resilience to Disasters: A Paradigm Shift from Vulnerability to Strength." *African Health Sciences* 8, no. 1: S1–S4.

Alsaba, Khuloud, and Anuj Kapilashrami. 2016. "Understanding Women's Experience of Violence and the Political Economy of Gender in Conflict: The Case of Syria." *Reproductive Health Matters* 24, no. 47: 5–17.

Anderlini, Sanam Naraghi. 2007. *Women Building Peace: What They Do, Why It Matters.* Boulder, CO: Lynne Rienner.

Baaz, Maria Eriksson, and Maria Stern. 2013. "Sexual Violence as a Weapon of War?" In *Perceptions, Prescriptions, Problems in the Congo and Beyond.* London: Zed Books.

Baaz, Maria Eriksson, and Maria Stern. 2010. "Understanding and Addressing Conflict-Related Sexual Violence: Lessons Learned from the Democratic Republic of Congo." Nordiska Afrikainstitutet, Uppsala. https://www.files.ethz.ch/isn/116630/2010_3.pdf.

Baird, Adam. 2018. "Becoming the 'Baddest': Masculine Trajectories of Gang Violence in Medellín." *Journal of Latin American Studies* 50, no. 1: 183–210. https://doi.org/10.1017/S0022216X17000761.

Baird, Adam. 2012. "The Violent Gang and the Construction of Masculinity Amongst Socially Excluded Young Men." *Safer Communities* 11, no. 4: 179–190. https://doi.org/10.1108/17578041211271445.

Barker, Gary. 2016. "Male Violence or Patriarchal Violence? Global Trends in Men and Violence." *Sexualidad, Salud y Sociedad* 22, no. 14: 316–330. https://doi.org/10.1590/1984-6487.sess.2016.22.14.a.

Barker, Gary. 2005. *Dying to Be Men: Youth, Masculinity and Social Exclusion.* London: Routledge.

Barker, Gary, et al. 2012. "Boys and Education in the Global South: Emerging Vulnerabilities and New Opportunities for Promoting Changes in Gender Norms." *Boyhood Studies* 6, no. 2: 137–150.

Barker, Gary, et al. 2010. "What Men Have to Do with It: Public Policies to Promote Gender Equality." International Center for Research on Women and Instituto Promundo, Washington, DC. https://promundoglobal.org/resources/what-men-have-to-do-with-it-public-policies-to-promote-gender-equality/

Bennett, Mark, and Daniel Fraser. 2015. "Urban Violence Among African American Males: Integrating Family, Neighborhood, and Peer Perspectives." *Journal of Sociology and Social Welfare* 27, no. 3: 93–117.

Borde, Elis, Victoria Page, and Tatiana Moura. 2020. "Masculinities and Nonviolence in Contexts of Chronic Urban Violence." *International Development Planning Review* 42, no. 1: 73–91.

Briceño-León, Roberto, Andrés Villaveces, and Alberto Concha-Eastman. 2008. "Understanding the Uneven Distribution of the Incidence of Homicide in Latin America." *International Journal of Epidemiology* 37, no. 4: 751–757. https://doi.org/10.1093/ije/dyn153.

Brown, Carly. 2012. "Rape as a Weapon of War in the Democratic Republic of the Congo." *Torture: Quarterly Journal on Rehabilitation of Torture Victims and Prevention of Torture* 22, no. 1: 24–37.

Butler, Judith. 1988. "Performative Acts and Gender Constitution: An Essay in Phenomenology and Feminist Theory." *Theatre Journal* 40, no. 4: 519–531. https://doi.org/10.2307/3207893.

Campbell, Howard, and Tobin Hansen. 2012. "Getting out of the Game: Desistance from Drug Trafficking." *International Journal of Drug Policy* 23, no. 6: 481–487. https://doi.org/10.1016/j.drugpo.2012.04.002.

Cerqueira, Daniel, et al. 2019. "Atlas da Violência 2019." IPEA e FBSP, Rio de Janeiro. http://www.ipea.gov.br/portal/images/stories/PDFs/relatorio_institucional/190605_atlas_da_violencia_2019.pdf.

Cerqueira, Daniel, et al. 2017. "Atlas da Violência 2017." IPEA e FBSP, Rio de Janeiro. http://www.ipea.gov.br/portal/index.php?option=com_content&view=article&id=30253.

Christensen, Lene. 2008. "From Trauma to Resilience." *African Health Sciences* 8, no. 1: 39–40.

Cockburn, Cynthia. 2004. "The Continuum of Violence: A Gender Perspective on War and Peace." In *Sites of Violence: Gender and Conflict Zones*, edited by Wenona Giles and Jennifer Hyndman, 24–44. Berkeley: University of California Press.

Cockburn, Cynthia. 2001. "The Gendered Dynamics of Armed Conflict and Political Violence." In *Gender, Armed Conflict and Political Violence; Victims, Perpetrators or Actors?*, edited by Caroline O. N. Moser and Fiona C. Clark, 13–29. London: Zed Books.

Connell, Raewyn. 2016. "Masculinities in Global Perspective: Hegemony, Contestation, and Changing Structures of Power." *Theory and Society* 45, no. 4: 303–318. https://doi.org/10.1007/s11186-016-9275-x.

Connell, Robert. 2005. *Masculinities*. Cambridge: Polity Press.

Connell, Robert, and James W. Messerschmidt. 2005. "Hegemonic Masculinity: Rethinking the Concept." *Gender and Society* 19, no. 6: 829–859. https://doi.org/10.1177/0891243205278639.

Detraz, Nicole. 2012. *International Security and Gender*. Cambridge: Polity Press.

Enloe, Cynthia. 2007. *Globalization and Militarization: Feminists Make the Link*. London: Rowman and Littlefield.

Elbert, Thomas, et al. 2013. "Sexual and Gender-Based Violence in the Kivu Provinces of the Democratic Republic of Congo: Insights from Former Combatants." World Bank, Washington, DC. https://openknowledge.worldbank.org/handle/10986/17852.

Enloe, Cynthia. 1993. *The Morning After: Sexual Politics at the End of the Cold War*. Berkeley: University of California Press.

Flood, Michael. 2011. "Involving Men in Efforts to End Violence against Women." *Men and Masculinities* 14, no. 3: 358–377.

Gahman, Levi. 2015. "Gun Rites: Hegemonic Masculinity and Neoliberal Ideology in Rural Kansas." *Gender, Place and Culture* 22, no. 9: 1203–1219.

Giles, Wenona, and Jennifer Hyndman. 2004. *Sites of Violence: Gender and Conflict Zones*. Berkeley: University of California Press.

Heilman, Brian, and Gary Barker. 2018. "Making the Connections: Masculine Norms and Violence." Promundo-US and Oak Foundation, Washington, DC. https://promundoglobal.org/resources/masculine-norms-violence-making-connections/

Hideg, Gergely, and Anna Alvazzi del Frate. 2019. "Darkening Horizons Global Violent Death Scenarios." Briefing Paper, Graduate Institute Geneva. https://repository.graduateinstitute.ch/record/297260.

Higate, Paul. 2003. *Military Masculinities: Identity and the State*. London: Praeger.

Kelly, Jocelyn, J. Kabanga, W. Cragin, L. Alcayna-Stevens, S. Haider, and M. Vanrooyen. 2012. "'If Your Husband Doesn't Humiliate You, Other People Won't': Gendered Attitudes Towards Sexual Violence in Eastern Democratic Republic of Congo." *Global Public Health* 7, no. 3: 285–298.

Kern, Leslie, and Beverley Mullings. 2013. "Urban Neoliberalism, Urban Insecurity and Urban Violence: Exploring the Gender Dimensions." In *Rethinking Feminist Interventions into the Urban*, edited by Linda Peake and Martina Rieker, 23–40. https://doi.org/10.4324/9780203568439.

Kivel, Paul. 2010. *Men's Work: How to Stop the Violence That Tears Our Lives Apart.* New York: Simon and Schuster.

Liebling, Hellen, and Henny Slegh. 2011 "'I Became a Woman with a Bad Reputation in My Society': Gendered Responses to Women and Girls Bearing a Child from Rape in Eastern Congo." *African Journal of Traumatic Stress* 2, no. 2: 60–68.

Lindsay, Lisa, and Stephen Miescher. 2003. *Men and Masculinities in Modern Africa.* Portsmouth: Heinemann.

Lwambo, Desiree. 2011. "'Before the War, I Was a Man': Men and Masculinities in Eastern DR Congo." HEAL Africa, Goma.

Marsiglio, William, and Joseph H. Pleck. 2005. "Fatherhood and Masculinities." In *The Handbook of Studies on Men and Masculinities,* edited by Michael S. Kimmel, Jeff Hearn, and Robert W. Connell, 249–269. Thousand Oaks, CA: Sage.

Moser, Caroline. 2001. "The Gendered Continuum of Violence and Conflict: An Operational Framework." In *Gender, Armed Conflict and Political Violence; Victims, Perpetrators or Actors?,* edited by Caroline O. N. Moser and Fiona C. Clark, 30–52. London: Zed Books.

Moura, Tatiana. 2007. *Rostos Invisíveis da Violência Armada. Um Estudo de Caso Sobre o Rio de Janeiro.* Rio de Janeiro: 7Letras.

Moura, Tatiana, Júlia Garraio, and Sílvia Roque. 2012. "Sexual Violence in Armed Conflicts." *Revista Crítica de Ciências Sociais* 96, no. 205: 1989–2009.

Muggah, Robert. 2012. "Researching the Urban Dilemma: Urbanization, Poverty and Violence." IDRC/CRDI. https://idl-bnc-idrc.dspacedirect.org/handle/10625/53538.

Notar, Susan. 2006. "Peacekeepers as Perpetrators: Sexual Exploitation and Abuse of Women and Children in the Democratic Republic of the Congo." *Journal of Gender, Social Policy, and the Law* 14, no. 2: art. 5.

Peake, Linda, and Martina Rieker. 2013. *Rethinking Feminist Interventions into the Urban.* London: Routledge.

Pearce, Jenny. 2006. "Bringing Violence 'Back Home': Gender Socialisation and the Transmission of Violence Through Time and Space." *Global Civil Society* 7: 42–61.

Penglase, R. Ben. 2014. *Living with Insecurity in a Brazilian Favela: Urban Violence and Daily Life.* New Brunswick, NJ: Rutgers University Press, 2014. http://www.jstor.org/stable/j.ctt9qh1fx.

Sampson, Robert, and William Julius Wilson. 1995. "Toward a Theory of Race, Crime and Urban Inequality." In *Crime and Inequality,* edited by John Hagan and Ruth Peterson, 37–54. Stanford, CA: Stanford University Press.

Slegh, Henny. 2011. "Listening to Women in the Congo: Hearing Being Human." In *Roads and Boundaries: Travel in Search of Reconnection,* edited by M. Tankink and M. Vysma. Diemen: AMB. https://www.amb-press.nl/roadsandboundaries.

Slegh, Henny, Gary Barker, and Ruti Levtov. 2014. "Gender Relations, Sexual and Gender-Based Violence and the Effects of Conflict on Women and Men in North Kivu, Eastern Democratic Republic of the Congo: Results from the International Men and Gender Equality Survey (IMAGES)." Promundo-US and Sonke Gender Justice, Washington, DC, and Cape Town. https://promundoglobal.org/resources/gender-relations-sexual-violence-and-the-effects-of-conflict-on-women-and-men-in-north-kivu-eastern-drc-preliminary-results-images/

Stearns, Jason, Judith Verweijen, and Maria Eriksson Baaz. 2013. "The National Army and Armed Groups in the Eastern Congo Untangling the Gordian Knot of Insecurity." The Rift Valley Institute, UK. https://riftvalley.net/publication/national-army-and-armed-groups-eastern-congo.

Staub, Ervin. 2006. "Reconciliation After Genocide, Mass Killing, or Intractable Conflict: Understanding the Roots of Violence, Psychological Recovery, and Steps Toward a General Theory." *Political Psychology* 27, no. 6: 867–894. https://doi.org/https://doi.org/10.1111/j.1467-9221.2006.00541.x.

Taback, Nathan, Robin Painter, and Ben King. 2008. "Sexual Violence in the Democratic Republic of the Congo." *JAMA: Journal of the American Medical Association* 300, no. 6: 653–654.

Tankink, Marian, and Henny Slegh. 2017. "Living Peace in Democratic Republic of the Congo: An Impact Evaluation of an Intervention with Male Partners of Women Survivors of Conflict-Related Rape and Intimate Partner Violence." Promundo–US, Washington, DC. https://promundoglobal.org/resources/living-peace-democratic-republic-congo-impact-evaluation-intervention-male-partners-women-survivors-conflict-related-rape-intimate-partner-violence/

Taylor, Alice, Tatiana Moura, Jeferson de Lara Scabio, Elis Borde, João Afonso, and Gary Barker. 2016. "'This Isn't the Life for You': Masculinities and Nonviolence in Rio de Janeiro, Brazil. Results from the International Men and Gender Equality Survey (IMAGES) with a Focus on Urban Violence." Promundo, Washington, DC, and Rio de Janeiro. https://promundoglobal. org/resources/isnt-life-masculinities-nonviolence-rio-de-janeiro-brazil/

Theidon, Kimberly. 2009. "Reconstructing Masculinities: The Disarmament, Demobilization, and Reintegration of Former Combatants in Colombia." *Human Rights Quarterly* 31, no. 1: 1–34. https://doi.org/10.1353/hrq.0.0053.

True, Jacqui. 2012. *The Political Economy of Violence Against Women.* New York: Oxford University Press.

UNODC. 2019. "Global Study on Homicide 2019." United Nations Office on Drugs and Crime, Vienna. https://www.unodc.org/unodc/en/data-and-analysis/global-study-on-homicide.html.

UNODC. 2018. "Global Study on Homicide 2018. Gender-Related Killing of Women and Girls." United Nations Office on Drugs and Crime, Vienna. https://www.unodc.org/documents/data-and-analysis/GSH2018/GSH18_Gender-related_killing_of_women_and_girls.pdf.

Visher, Christy, and Jeremy Travis. 2003. "Transitions from Prison to Community: Understanding Individual Pathways." *Annual Review of Sociology* 29: 89–113. https://doi.org/10.1146/annurev.soc.29.010202.095931.

Wilding, Polly. 2014. "Gendered Meanings and Everyday Experiences of Violence in Urban Brazil." *Gender, Place and Culture* 21, no. 2: 228–243. https://doi.org/10.1080/0966369X.2013.769430.

Wilding, Polly. 2011. "'New Violence': Silencing Women's Experiences in the Favelas of Brazil." *Journal of Latin American Studies* 42, no. 4: 719–747. https://doi.org/10.1017/S0022216X10001343.

Wilkinson, Richard. 2004. "Why Is Violence More Common Where Inequality Is Greater?" *Annals of the New York Academy of Sciences* 1036, no. 1: 1–12. https://doi.org/10.1196/annals.1330.001.

SECTION IV

INCLUSIVE GLOBAL DEVELOPMENT
Strategies for Progress

Extreme poverty will only be eliminated with a concerted effort to foster development inclusively. Otherwise, substantial pockets of extreme poverty and under-development will persist, even if national measures of overall well-being improve. That pattern is evident today. Many countries are getting wealthier and developing at a macro level, but inequalities are growing and large segments of society are being left behind. Often it is members of marginalized or vulnerable communities who are not keeping pace.

The failure to ensure universal progress fundamentally signals that societies around the world aren't successfully delivering for all their residents. As explored in Chapter 1, the costs of inequity, marginalization, and exclusion are vast; they create vulnerabilities and represent missed opportunities to boost prosperity and stability around the world.

Proactive, explicit efforts are needed to ensure that cultural, social, political, and economic well-being improves across all subcommunities and segments of societies. Barriers to equity and inclusion must be removed. Further, a willingness to focus on closing gaps in the status of different subpopulations is required. Global development practice must transform to truly leverage and deliver for all segments of society.

This section focuses on specific interventions that are needed to ensure that investments and activities benefit everyone within societies and communities. Each of the chapters speaks to an essential development domain, explaining why a greater focus on diversity, equity, and inclusion is needed. Further, the chapters consider how to realize that emphasis through changes in orientation and practice. Given the growing overlap among fragile, conflict-affected, and less-developed countries, several authors focus on post-conflict environments to discuss how to advance inclusion and leverage diversity for both stability and development.

Maitreyi Bordia Das and Sabina Anne Espinoza open the section discussing the need for economic and social development efforts to focus on inclusive development as a means to maximize returns on investment; they delve into strategies for better ensuring that interventions reach a wider range of communities. The second chapter in the section, by Atifete Jahjaga, Madison Schramm, and Teuta Avdimetaj, looks at promoting inclusion in structures of government and through governance; they focus particularly, though not exclusively, on efforts to foster women's inclusion around the world, exploring Kosovo and Sierra Leone in greater depth to bring forward many of the real-world challenges involved in fostering inclusive governance. Lisa Hilbink and Claudia Escobar Mejía then carry forward the discussion by examining inclusion in the justice sector; they look at why and how a focus on equity and inclusion can and must be advanced to create an equitable society, drawing on the scholarly literature as well as Escobar's experience as a judge in Guatemala. Shaazka Beyerle and Sayed Ikram Afzali then consider how to leverage and elevate the work of local civil society organizations, both in pushing for progress and in delivering programs that advance equity and inclusion; a focus on anti-corruption work in Afghanistan grounds the discussion. Complementing those analyses is an exploration of societal norms and narrators by Ann Towns, Wazhma Frogh, and Amelia Cotton Corl, who discuss how efforts to leverage diversity and advance equity and inclusion necessitate navigating and transforming attitudes within societies; revealing of the challenges is their exploration of the struggle Afghan women face in advancing their status.

Taken together, the chapters in Section IV focus on providing a broad road map for advancing equity and inclusion as part of development interventions, especially as part of post-conflict peacebuilding. They make a compelling case for weaving a focus on diversity and inclusion as a priority across sectors, and offer important strategic insights for more effectively advancing well-being globally.

15

Socioeconomic Inclusion in International Development

Maitreyi Bordia Das and Sabina Anne Espinoza

We will not march back to what was, but move to what shall be.

—Amanda Gorman[1]

Introduction

The commitment to "leave no one behind" is at the core of the global 2030 Agenda for Sustainable Development, adopted by all United Nations member states in 2015.[2] The focus on those who have not benefited equally from progress is motivated by the observation that in every country of the world, there are certain groups who face barriers to social inclusion, to fully participating in society. They are excluded from access to markets, to services, and to political and social spaces in their communities and countries. The global COVID-19 pandemic made existing socioeconomic cleavages more visible than ever. Those already in precarious jobs were at highest risk of being laid off. The poorest children were least likely to be able to access online learning while schools were closed. Children with disabilities were often unable to access support services administered through the school system. Women and children suffered increased domestic violence. Certain ethnic groups—often minority groups that already faced stigmatization before the pandemic—were scapegoated for the disease in many countries. And these are only some examples.

There are many kinds of exclusion in various domains. Exclusion is perpetuated through formal and informal mechanisms, from laws stipulating the inferior status of certain groups to discriminatory and stigmatizing norms, practices, and social mores. Social exclusion occurs when individuals and groups are left behind based on their identity. Identities most commonly resulting in exclusion encompass gender, disability status, sexual orientation and gender identity (SOGI), caste, ethnicity, or religion, but also migrant or citizenship status, location, socioeconomic status, and others. The overlay of identities multiplies exclusion.[3]

Social inclusion matters because exclusion is unjust, has devastating impacts on individuals' lives, and denies people their dignity. But today there is also a greater awareness than ever that social exclusion carries significant economic and social costs, and that inclusion matters for poverty reduction and sustainable development. The costs of exclusion accrue through different channels and over different time spans. They range from lost wages for individuals to forgone gross domestic product (GDP) and human capital accumulation for entire societies.[4] This chapter defines social inclusion and explains why it matters from a development perspective. It draws out the costs of social exclusion for individuals and for society at large and presents data on the exclusion of groups in different regions of the world. It then discusses how change toward inclusion comes about, and who the key actors are in the quest for social inclusion. Presenting a range of examples from development interventions, the chapter provides concrete pointers on how inclusion can be propelled through policies and programs. The chapter draws on examples from the *Inclusion Matters* and *Inclusion Matters in Africa* reports.[5]

What Do We Mean by Social Inclusion in Development?

Although "inclusion" and "inclusive" are now widely used in international development discourse, these terms mean many things to many people. At times, they are used almost interchangeably with any positive development outcome.[6] We define social inclusion based on the World Bank report on social inclusion, *Inclusion Matters*, as "the process of improving the ability, opportunity, and dignity of people, disadvantaged on the basis of their identity, to take part in society."[7]

Inclusion Matters postulates that individuals and groups are included in (or excluded from) three interrelated domains: markets, services, and spaces. *Markets* encompass land, housing, labor, and credit markets. *Services* encompass education, health, transport, water, social protection, electricity, information, communication, and technology, among others. And *spaces* include not just physical space but also space in a broader sense: social, political, and cultural spaces may solidify exclusion or foster inclusion.[8] Social inclusion thus goes beyond poverty reduction. The discourse on poverty has largely centered on outcomes—from traditional measures of poverty focused on measuring consumption or income to multidimensional poverty measures that include, among others, indicators on education, health, and living standards to assess poverty.[9]

A social inclusion lens emphasizes the importance of understanding the processes that drive certain outcomes. It also emphasizes the importance of *ability*, *opportunity*, and *dignity* for individuals and groups to take part in society. Excluded groups and individuals routinely confront stigma, discrimination, and treatment that undermine their sense of worth. Lack of dignity can affect the extent to which they benefit from services, engage in markets, or make their voices heard in the social and political space of their communities and countries.[10] Social inclusion thus

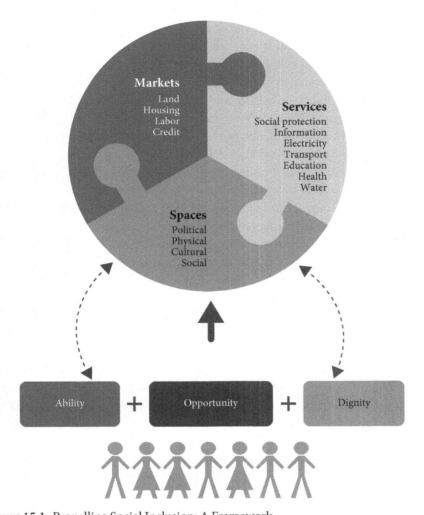

Figure 15.1 Propelling Social Inclusion: A Framework

departs from a traditional poverty focus in that it focuses on the processes that underlie adverse outcomes for certain groups. See Figure 15.1.

Why Inclusion Matters for Development

The idea that inequalities between different social groups not only are unfair but can be detrimental to economic growth is not new to the economic and development literature.[11] Stiglitz has argued that in countries like the United States, the United Kingdom, and Italy, overall economic growth would have been six to nine percentage points higher in the last two decades if income inequality had not grown.[12] Studies on *inequality of opportunity* (i.e., inequalities driven by differences at birth, such as gender, ethnicity, or parental background) have also shown a negative relationship between inequality and growth.[13]

There is also increasing evidence that specific social groups fare worse across a range of development indicators and have been less likely to benefit from growth the world over. To name some examples: The *World Development Report 2012: Gender Equality and Development* made the economic (and moral) case for greater gender equality.[14] Observing that women in many countries were more likely to die, less likely to be enrolled in primary or secondary school, more likely than men to work in the informal sector, and less likely to have a say over decisions and control over resources, the report argued that focused policies for women were needed to ensure that economic progress would also translate into greater gender equality. In Europe, data demonstrate that people of Roma ethnic minority origin are overrepresented among the poor and have lower access to services and limited economic opportunities.[15] In Latin America, those of African descent are revealed to have fewer years of education, to be more likely to become victims of crime and violence, to be underrepresented in decision-making positions, and to have fewer chances of social mobility.[16] (See Figure 15.2.)

Exclusion has multiple costs for society, in both the short and long terms, and at individual, household, community, and societal levels. Measuring the costs of social exclusion is complex, as many different groups may be affected by exclusion. And exclusion impacts virtually every area of socioeconomic life, so costs can accrue in myriad ways. In the development literature, costs of exclusion are perhaps most commonly calculated at the individual level. One way to quantify individual-level costs of exclusion is in terms of lower earnings and employment outcomes. Using that measure, those of African descent, for instance, have nearly twice the

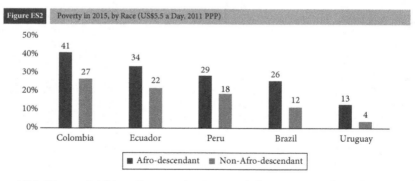

Figure 15.2 Those of African Descent Are More Likely to Be Poor than Those Not of African Descent Across Different Latin American Countries (Poverty Rates in 2015, by Race [US $5.50 a day, 2011 PPP])

Credit line: Freire, German; Diaz-Bonilla, Carolina; Schwartz Orellana, Steven; Soler Lopez, Jorge; Carbonari, Flavia. 2018. *Afro-descendants in Latin America: Toward a Framework of Inclusion*. World Bank, Washington, DC. © World Bank. https://openknowledge.worldbank.org/handle/10986/30201 License: CC BY 3.0 IGO unemployment rate of those not of African descent in many Latin American countries, at around 13 percent compared to 6 percent.[17]

Such outcomes, in turn, may be driven by lower human capital endowments (in particular lower health, education, and skills) which may be caused by prior disadvantage in accessing health and education services, but also by discrimination in the hiring process or in the workplace.[18] Roma children, for instance, are much more likely to be born into a family at the bottom of the income distribution. Across Central and Eastern Europe, between 55 and 70 percent of Roma children (ages three to six) do not attend preschool, half as many as their non-Roma neighbors. Moreover, many Roma children are at risk of malnutrition and, in growing up in severely impoverished families, often have limited exposure to cognitive stimulation at home.[19] These early childhood gaps then lead to unequal access to quality primary education. A majority of Roma children drop out between ages twelve (in Bulgaria) and fifteen (in the Czech Republic and Hungary). Only 11 to 31 percent of young Roma reach upper secondary education. (See Figure 15.3 and Figure 15.4.)

In addition to lower levels of education, Roma also face discrimination when looking for jobs: according to the Regional Roma Survey (RRS), between 27 and 62 percent of Roma report having experienced discrimination while searching for jobs.[20] All this results in significantly lower employment and earnings outcomes for Roma compared to non-Roma. For instance, irregular work is two to six times more common for Roma than their non-Roma neighbors, and while Roma have similar labor participation rates as non-Roma, Roma are half as likely to be employed. In the Czech Republic, for example, Roma workers earn only a third of their non-Roma neighbors' wages.[21]

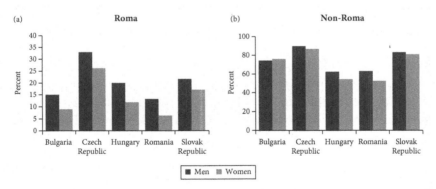

Figure 15.3 Roma Versus Non-Roma Upper Secondary School Completion Rates for Men and Women (Ages 25–64)

Note: "Secondary school completion" is defined as having completed either a vocational/technical or a general secondary school program, or a higher level of education. Sample restricted to individuals ages 25–64.

Credit line: Gatti, Roberta; Karacsony, Sandor; Anan, Kosuke; Ferre, Celine; de Paz Nieves, Carmen. 2016. *Being Fair, Faring Better: Promoting Equality of Opportunity for Marginalized Roma*. Directions in Development- Human Development. Washington, DC: World Bank. © World Bank. https://openknowledge. worldbank.org/handle/10986/23679 License: CC BY 3.0 IGO.

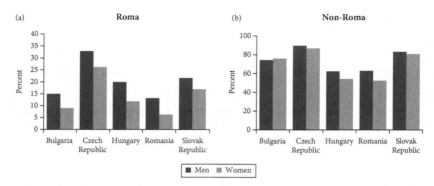

Figure 15.4 Roma Men and Women Are Less Likely to Complete Upper Secondary School than Non-Roma

Note: "Secondary school completion" is defined as having completed either a vocational/technical or a general secondary school program, or a higher level of education. Sample restricted to individuals ages 25–64.

Credit line: Gatti, Roberta; Karacsony, Sandor; Anan, Kosuke; Ferre, Celine; de Paz Nieves, Carmen. 2016. *Being Fair, Faring Better: Promoting Equality of Opportunity for Marginalized Roma*. Directions in Development- Human Development. Washington, DC: World Bank. © World Bank. https://openknowledge. worldbank.org/handle/10986/23679 License: CC BY 3.0 IGO.

Discrimination is not only costly in preventing individuals from accessing health services, education, and opportunities in the labor market. It can also have severe physical and mental health costs for individuals and households, and ultimately, large costs at the national level—both for treatment and in terms of lost productivity.[22] And when individuals are unable to receive health services, either because they are denied access as a result of discrimination or because they feel they are not treated with respect by service providers, it can result in high costs of emergency treatment rather than more efficient preventive and in-time care. (See Box 15.1.) A study conducted in the European Union, for instance, calculated the cost of exclusion of migrants lacking legal status from various preventive healthcare services.[23] It found that it would be significantly less expensive for governments to provide all pregnant, irregular migrant women access to prenatal care rather than only treating the resulting low-birth-weight children. It is estimated that savings would be between 48 percent (or €56 per woman) in Germany and 60 percent (or €177 per woman) in Sweden.[24]

Box 15.1 The Importance of Dignity in Development: It Matters How Services Are Supplied

---

The effective delivery of services to excluded groups often hinges upon the respectful treatment by, and cultural competency of, service providers.[25] Where stereotypes against certain groups are widely held by society, service providers are often no exception, and their attitudes can affect how they treat their clients.

This, in turn, can cause members of excluded groups to opt out of services—for example, discouraging them from seeking health care or pursuing education. The COVID-19 pandemic provided a stark example of how stigmatization, both actual and anticipated, can act as a barrier to accessing health care—people avoiding testing for the virus because of fear of being discriminated against, patients and their families feeling judged by others, those diagnosed with COVID-19 being ostracized within their communities.[26] But attitudes and behaviors can be changed, as shown by examples from health care and social work, and increasingly from education and other sectors.

In the context of the COVID-19 pandemic, interventions to counter social stigma were focused on education and communication. The World Health Organization stressed the importance of focusing on factual information, educating people about the disease, and avoiding associations of the disease with countries or specific ethnicities.[27]

Evaluations of cultural competence training, although only starting to emerge, show that such training can improve the attitudes of health care providers and increase patient satisfaction.[28] Evidence from Romania suggests that Roma cultural "mediators" have had a positive impact on a number of issues by improving communication and mutual understanding between service providers and Roma. They have successfully helped to decrease school dropout and nonenrollment rates, reduced absenteeism among students, reduced segregation in the classroom, and improved the educational attainment and academic performance of Roma students. Mediators have also helped improve teachers' attitudes toward the Roma.[29] From Serbia, there is evidence that Roma health mediators achieved better immunization, facilitated the provision of personal documents and health cards, and improved access to reproductive health services for Roma women and other vulnerable groups, including the elderly and persons with disabilities.[30]

Language is another key cultural attribute affecting the effectiveness of development policy and interventions. Those who speak minority languages often lag behind in schooling, jobs, and other endowments, and evidence suggests that teaching children in their mother tongue improves educational outcomes and can also improve the support of parents for education.[31]

Social exclusion also has significant costs for society and the economy. In the economic and development literature, such costs are most commonly calculated in terms of forgone GDP and human capital. When excluded groups are prevented from achieving their potential, or when perceived exclusion leads them to opt out of education and the labor market, it translates into lower human capital achievements, lost productivity for employers, and lost GDP. For example, the cost of exclusion of LGBTQI people in the United States alone has been estimated to be around $64 billion per year.[32] The current gender gap in the labor force has been calculated to cost countries around 35 percent of GDP.[33] For Africa, Wodon and de la Brière estimate that the region lost $2.5 trillion in human capital due to gender inequality and 11.4 percent of total wealth in 2014.[34] Exclusion also means that societies fail to benefit from diversity: companies in the top quartile for gender, racial, and ethnic diversity have been found to be 15 to 35 percent more likely to have financial returns above their industry medians.[35] And, importantly, the beneficial effect of inclusion is not only due to the addition of workers to the labor force; diversity in itself may increase productivity.[36] In the United States, it has been estimated that reduced discrimination against women and Blacks and the resulting more optimized allocation of talent in the labor market drove a quarter of the productivity increase between 1960 and 2010.[37]

Moving Toward Social Inclusion

Social exclusion is about power relations, and societies across the world have complex ways of upholding the social structures that relegate some groups to subordinate status. Exclusion is sustained through structures and systems, but also through covert processes. Structures and systems include, among others, families, communities, legal and political systems, labor, land markets, and knowledge systems. Exclusionary processes can encompass discriminatory or stigmatizing attitudes, beliefs, perceptions, and practices.[38] Inclusion often progresses when excluded groups can assert their voice and agency through social and political participation: whether and to what extent they are able to do so depends, in part, on the implicit and explicit political choices of those in power. It is also influenced by the momentum of nonstate social movements and changing norms and attitudes in broader society at any given time. (See Chapter 14 and Chapter 19.)

Attitudes, perceptions, and social practices matter for inclusion because they affect the actions and behaviors of dominant and subordinate groups. They affect whether service providers and state institutions treat all equally. They also affect whether or not excluded groups take up opportunities, such as for education or employment, or whether or not they choose to engage in the political processes of their community or country. When perceptions of unequal treatment accumulate, this can lead to social tensions and conflict. At the same time, such perceptions may also lead to the political organization of excluded groups and pave the way for movement toward social inclusion.[39]

The state plays a central role in facilitating change toward social inclusion. It can create the enabling environment that allows citizens to challenge the status quo and to move toward better outcomes for all. It can design explicit legislation, policies, and programs to foster social inclusion. The state can facilitate voice and accountability for all within the selection of government and policy processes, such as by ensuring that all citizens are able to participate in selecting their government, and by ensuring a political environment that fosters freedom of expression, freedom of association, and free media.[40] Finally, the state has a preeminent role in the enforcement and implementation of an inclusive legal and policy framework.[41]

The impact of state-led actions, however, also depends on other actors and their stakes in making the change successful, such as social movements, civil society organizations, and business leaders, which can all be powerful propellers for new political agendas and push for change toward inclusion. The media can be used as a tool for spreading misinformation about excluded groups, but it can also play an important role in fostering awareness for inclusion.[42]

What Works for Inclusion?

Examples of Inclusive Projects and Policies

This section highlights some examples of how national legislation and policies, as well as development programs and projects, can advance social inclusion. The section draws primarily from the experience of sub-Saharan Africa.[43]

Social inclusion interventions are as diverse as the multifarious types of exclusion that they can address. Furthermore, their implementation is often a complex long-term agenda, necessitating political choices and alliances. Nevertheless, examples abound where policies or programs have made a positive difference for inclusion.

Legislation

Laws can be discriminatory and institutionalize exclusion, but they are also one of the most important instruments for social change. At the apex of legal systems, constitutions can be instruments to signal and trigger change toward inclusion. In South Africa, for instance, the constitution prohibits discrimination on the basis of race, gender, sex, color, sexual orientation, or disability, among others. Mozambique and the Seychelles recently decriminalized same-sex relations (2015 and 2016, respectively), and same-sex relations are not criminalized in a number of other African countries.[44] The Botswana Supreme Court ruled in 2017 that the constitution requires the government to legally recognize transgender people's gender self-identification, and Namibia's courts interpreted their 1963 law on registrations of births, marriages, and deaths as allowing official recognition of gender change. Other laws ban all or some forms of anti-LGBTQI discrimination. (Countries that ban some forms include Angola, Botswana, Cabo Verde, Mauritius, Mozambique, and the Seychelles; South Africa bans all forms.)[45] (See Chapter 5 for a discussion of the movement for LGBTQI rights.)

Many African countries have also seen extensive legal reforms promoting gender equality, from reforms that allow women to register businesses, open bank accounts, sign contracts, get jobs, and choose where to live to laws addressing workplace sexual harassment and domestic violence.[46] Hallward-Driemeier and Gajigo have argued that changes in Ethiopia's family law that gave women increased control over property and removed restrictions in pursuing employment led to significant improvements in women's employment: the legal reforms led to a 15 to 24 percent increase in the proportion of women working in occupations that require non-home-based employment, in occupations with more educated workers, and in paid and full-time jobs.[47]

Affirmative Action or Quotas

Affirmative action or quotas can be controversial but are still considered among the more effective policy mechanisms to address entrenched group-based disparities.[48] South Africa has been much cited for its affirmative action policies, including notably the 1998 Employment Equity Act and the Broad-Based Black Economic Empowerment (B-BBEE) legislation of 2007. There is evidence to suggest that affirmative action has had positive effects on wages and led to growing returns to education for Black South African men.[49] The Ugandan constitution has established quotas for women, youth, persons with disabilities, and other groups in parliament and local government.[50] Affirmative action has also been used in other regions to promote the inclusion of excluded groups. In Romania, for instance, evidence suggests that affirmative action has contributed to expanding the pool of Roma intellectuals and professionals. This, in turn, has been argued not only to benefit the individuals who received affirmative action but also to create role models and make a positive difference in Roma communities.[51]

Targeting Excluded Groups Within Broader Programs

Targeting particular groups within universal access programs such as health or education programs is another way to foster inclusion. Health programs in several countries focus on particular identity groups, such as children, adolescents, the elderly, or pregnant women. Accessibility will have different components for different excluded groups: It may mean that school buildings are adapted to the physical needs of learners, or that children from remote minority groups can go to school at a convenient geographic location or access adequate mobile learning. It may also involve the adaptation of learning materials to the needs of children with different abilities or from different linguistic groups. It may entail providing safe spaces for students who belong to sexual or gender minorities, or adapting school curricula to ensure that ethnic or sexual and gender minorities see themselves positively and made visible.[52] Both Uganda, through the 2006 Persons with Disabilities Act, and Ghana, through its Inclusive Education Policy since 2013, committed to disability-inclusive education and are requiring educational institutions to eliminate barriers to accessibility and prohibit discrimination.[53]

Another way of addressing particular excluded groups within service delivery is to involve them in the monitoring and evaluation mechanisms. Innovative means of community-based monitoring can enhance downward accountability of providers and maintain a system of checks and balances. Traditionally excluded groups can be involved in the surveillance of health facilities to monitor their opening and closing hours, as well as the availability of health personnel, amenities, and infrastructure. Simultaneously, incentives may be given to service providers to reach and stay in remote areas.[54]

Land Reform

Providing land titles or de facto recognition of land use patterns of historically excluded groups can be effective in increasing their inclusion and enhancing their dignity.[55] In particular, Indigenous groups and women still face significant barriers to owning land in many countries. Establishing ownership rights for these groups can be a powerful means to increase access to labor markets and contribute to economic empowerment. One example is Rwanda's nationwide land tenure regularization program from 2010. The legislative reforms that were implemented eliminated bias against land ownership by women, put in place a single statutory system of land tenure to end parallel customary and formal tenure systems, and introduced a low-cost registration process. The reform achieved the registration of 10.7 million parcels out of an estimated 11.5 million parcels of land in Rwanda overall, in under three years. The reforms also had a positive impact on attitudes around women's land rights, with the perceived land ownership rights of women increasing from 33 percent to between 67 and 94 percent, depending on the program area.[56]

Social Safety Nets

Social safety nets encompass a wide range of cash or in-kind transfers, social pensions, public works, and school feeding programs targeted to poor and vulnerable households. Social safety nets have a historical track record of shielding households from the negative effects of shocks and, more recently, of building household and community assets. Social safety net programs that go beyond addressing income poverty to target the specific needs of excluded groups, including behavioral constraints to accessing social services, have been successful in different regions of the world. Sistema Chile Solidario has been described as one of the first comprehensive programs to move from a traditional social assistance paradigm of providing services and goods to the poor toward an approach that seeks to personalize interventions and to equip individuals and families with the skills that they need to actually benefit from existing services. To this end, Chile Solidario established a service to help families navigate the social protection system, establish relationships of trust, and develop greater self-confidence and self-efficacy. Red Unidos, implemented in Colombia, has taken a similar approach, supporting individuals and families in accessing existing programs.[57] In Africa, there is evidence that social safety nets can promote social inclusion by increasing the sense of self-confidence and the dignity of recipients, in addition to addressing income poverty and strengthening human capital.[58] In Ghana, for instance, safety net programs contributed to reducing stigma among persons with disabilities; in Lesotho and Zimbabwe, they allowed children to go to school well dressed. There is evidence that safety net programs can raise the social status of the poorest by allowing them to meet social obligations and engage in relations of reciprocity, such as contributing to group savings or attending weddings.[59]

Fostering Stakeholder Alliances for Inclusion

Making a change toward social inclusion is often about addressing power relations at various levels, from the local to the national. The global HIV response provides a powerful example of how voice influences decisions and how political alliances of different actors can be powerful catalysts of change for inclusion. Under the slogan "Nothing for us without us," AIDS activists globally influenced budget allocations, research priorities, drug approval procedures, drug availability, and service delivery models.[60]

Another example revealing the importance of coalition-building and of fostering normative change across society involves efforts to abolish female genital cutting (FGC). Burkina Faso saw the most striking drop in FGC between 2000 and 2010. First efforts to end FGC go back to Catholic missionaries who during colonization tried—unsuccessfully—to put an end to the practice by threatening to excommunicate those who practiced it. But from the late 1970s onward, partnerships began to form between civil society, government, the judiciary, and communities. FGC began to be widely denounced by a range of actors, along with widespread national awareness and information campaigns. In 1997, FGC was criminalized in Burkina Faso, and implementation of the law has since been accompanied by stronger enforcement as well as normative change—including, for instance, sending patrols into communities to raise awareness of harmful consequences and of the criminalization of the practice.

Groups' Advocacy, and Programs That Enable and Empower

In Uganda, an Empowerment and Livelihood for Adolescents program implemented by Building Resources Across Communities combined training for small-scale enterprises with education for health and to reduce risky behaviors. An impact evaluation found that the program had positive outcomes for the adolescent girls: it increased girls' income-generating activities by 32 percent, primarily through increased self-employment.[61] Self-reported condom use by those who were sexually active increased by 50 percent, fertility rates dropped by 26 percent, and there was a 76 percent reduction in adolescent girls reporting having had sex against their will during the past year.[62] Experts believe that the program was particularly effective because it simultaneously addressed multiple constraints for young women.

Empowerment programs that combine multifaceted assistance have also proven useful for survivors of physical and sexual violence. While economic empowerment for survivors is often key to reducing their economic dependence on the perpetrator, experience from the World Bank's engagement around gender-based violence shows that collaboration between law enforcement, legal aid services, health care organizations, public health programs, educational institutions, and agencies devoted to social services and economic development are most successful.

Technology and Social Inclusion

Empirical evidence on the economic and social impacts of mobile saving accounts is only beginning to emerge. However, there are indications that M-PESA, a money transfer system operated by Kenya's largest cellular phone provider, has had positive effects for the poorest, and for women in particular.[63] Bastian and colleagues find that the promotion and registration of a mobile savings account among women micro entrepreneurs in Tanzania led women to save substantially more and that additional business training bolstered this effect.[64] It has been argued that providing women access to individual (private) accounts can increase control over financial resources, especially when they have limited decision-making authority in the household. Allocating money to a savings account makes the money less fungible and may help women feel less obligated to share the money with others.[65]

Conclusion: The Road Ahead

This chapter, having made the case for a focus on inclusion in development interventions, emphasized that there is no one-size-fits-all inclusion intervention. Social exclusion is as complex a phenomenon as the societies in which it plays out. In turn, solutions for greater inclusion need to be designed to consciously tackle the power relations and social dynamics that underlie the exclusion of any given group, in any given context. Political choices and alliances at the local and national levels are key to facilitate the right environment and policies for inclusion. A multitude of nonstate actors can act as catalysts for inclusion by putting inclusion concerns on the political agenda, by fostering normative change within society, and by informing and monitoring government actions. This said, a multitude of development interventions can foster inclusion. Their common starting point is that they ask, first and foremost, who is (likely to be) left out, how they are left out, and why they are not benefitting on par with other groups in society. *What* policies do is as important as *how* they do it. The best opportunities can come to naught unless they are cognizant of the cultural and social preferences of their clients and are implemented with sensitivity, enhancing the dignity of those for whom they are designed.

The chapter presented evidence from a range of development projects and policies that have been tried or that have shown promising results for inclusion. Change toward inclusion is a long-term agenda. It requires an array of actors to work together. Exclusionary processes, practices, and outcomes will rarely be undone within a few years of the implementation of inclusive policy. And change toward inclusion is not always linear: previously dominant groups may resist and even fight back against the inclusion of others. Policies may have unintended effects, both positive or negative. Inclusion is also aspirational by nature: As societies evolve, new forms of exclusion and new opportunities for inclusion appear on the horizon, and new groups may be recognized to be excluded. In the quest for developing increasingly effective interventions for social inclusion, data will be an important part of the puzzle. For too many excluded groups, disaggregated data are still limited. One example is that of data on disability in Africa: emerging data in some African countries has highlighted poorer outcomes for persons with disabilities in employment and education.[66] Many countries in the region, however, still lack reliable quantitative data on different types of disability and their impact on different dimensions of individual welfare and development outcomes.[67]

Given the diversity of excluded groups around the world and the breadth of arenas from which they can be excluded, the best way to develop interventions for inclusion is to start by asking the right questions. A clear identification of the problem that needs to be solved and the questions to be answered is the foundation for good design of social inclusion interventions.[68] And in doing so, those people who are to be reached by interventions must be brought into the process of problem diagnosis, policy design, and implementation.[69]

The World Bank Social Inclusion Assessment Tool provides four key overarching questions to guide analysis:

1. *Who is excluded?* Identifying who is excluded is a first step toward assessment. Exclusion, though often seen and treated as synonymous with poverty, is often about more than poverty, and at times it is not about poverty at all. Minority Roma men and women in many parts of Europe may be discriminated against and excluded from economic and political spaces regardless of their wealth status. Whether poor or not, transgender individuals may face restricted access to public spaces. When identities overlap, they can create cumulative disadvantage. For example, an Indigenous woman with a disability who is living in a remote area may be more likely to face disadvantages than an Indigenous woman without a disability who is living in an urban area.

2. *How are they excluded?* Social inclusion analysis aims to understand how certain groups may be left out of growth and prosperity, and through which processes. It looks at institutional, historical, legal, or other circumstances that affect excluded groups in various domains, to understand the processes that solidify exclusion (e.g., discrimination, stigma, stereotyping, lack of role models, etc.). Oftentimes, it makes sense to ask whether norms and practices impede access and participation for some groups.

3. *Why are they likely to be excluded?* Why people are excluded can be the most difficult question to ask and answer. Roots of exclusion are often historical and political. One can ask: How do underlying power relations affect who is included and who is left out? For example, do some land ownership patterns affect who gets access to services? It is also important to explore institutional or organizational underpinnings. Do informal norms or institutions exclude

some groups from decision-making? Are some groups invisible? Other questions can relate to the history of the area or earlier projects and programs, and may tell us how groups can be left out.

4. *What can be done toward greater social inclusion?* The analysis should identify the wrong to be addressed or the right to be deepened; whom the intervention seeks to include; and who is at risk of being left out. After determining why those groups or areas are at risk of being left out, channels can be selected through which inclusion can take place, consideration can be given to what could be done differently, and innovations can be adopted.

But eventually, even the best analysis of data and design of legislation or projects are only the starting point. Any intervention for inclusion then requires political commitment and concerted effort, often from multiple social actors, for implementation. Social inclusion must be a conscious choice for societies and governments. As this chapter has laid out, there are many different policies and interventions that can successfully promote more inclusive societies, from creating the enabling legislative and institutional environment to fostering individual and collective mindsets and behaviors for inclusion. But governments need to commit to financing such programs, and there needs to be sufficient political and social momentum to implement and transform. In the wake of the COVID-19 pandemic, the odds may be better than ever before. Last but not least, there needs to be recognition that as societies evolve, new challenges and new opportunities for inclusion will continually arise. Social inclusion is always aspirational in nature—yet much can and has been done to foster it today, to honor the pledge to leave nobody behind.

Notes

1. Gorman 2021.
2. UN General Assembly 2015.
3. World Bank 2013.
4. Das and Espinoza 2020.
5. World Bank 2013; Das and Espinoza 2020.
6. Das 2016.
7. World Bank 2013.
8. World Bank 2013.
9. For an excellent overview of poverty measurement, see Alkire and Santos 2013; Alkire et al. 2015.
10. World Bank 2013.
11. Rodrik 1999; Berg and Ostry 2011; IMF 2017.
12. Stiglitz 2016.
13. For example, Ferreira et al. 2014; Marrero and Rodríguez 2013; Atinc et al. 2005.
14. World Bank 2012.
15. Ringold, Orenstein, and Wilkens 2004; Gatti et al. 2016; Robayo-Abril and Milan 2019.
16. Freire et al. 2018.

17. Also see, for instance, Lamichhane and Sawada 2013 and Male and Wodon 2017 on people with disabilities. On people with HIV, see Sprague, Simon, and Sprague 2011. On racial minorities in the United States, see Turner 2013. On gender, see World Bank 2012; Wodon et al. 2017; Wodon and de la Brière 2018; Buehren et al. 2019. On youth employment in Africa, see World Bank 2014. On Roma, see Gatti et al. 2016; Robayo-Abril and Milan 2019.
18. Buckup 2009; Lamichhane and Sawada 2013; Morgon Banks and Polack 2015.
19. Gatti et al. 2016, 3.
20. Gatti et al. 2016, 4.
21. Gatti et al. 2016, 97ff.
22. Lereya et al. 2015; Chisholm et al. 2016.
23. Calculations were made for Germany, Greece, and Sweden.
24. FRA 2015.
25. World Bank 2013.
26. Sotgiu and Dobler 2020.
27. WHO 2020.
28. Betancourt and Green 2010, 583.
29. Gatti et al. 2016.
30. Das et al. 2017.
31. Das and Espinoza 2019.
32. Burns 2012.
33. The finding applies for countries ranking in the bottom half of gender inequality. Ostry et al. 2018.
34. Wodon and de la Brière 2018; Das and Espinoza 2020.
35. Hunt, Layton, and Prince 2015; Hunt et al. 2018.
36. Ostry et al. 2018.
37. Hsieh et al. 2013; Cavalcanti and Tavares 2015.
38. World Bank 2013; Das and Espinoza 2020.
39. World Bank 2013; Das and Espinoza 2020.
40. "Voice and accountability" is one dimension of governance reported on by the World Bank Worldwide Governance Indicators, which report on six broad dimensions of governance for over 200 countries and territories. See https://info.worldbank.org/governance/wgi/ and https://info.worldbank.org/governance/wgi/pdf/va.pdf.
41. World Bank 2013.
42. World Bank 2013.
43. Drawing on evidence from Das and Espinoza 2019.
44. Benin, Burkina Faso, the Central African Republic, the Democratic Republic of Congo, the Republic of Congo, Côte d'Ivoire, Djibouti, Equatorial Guinea, Gabon, Guinea-Bissau, Lesotho, Madagascar, Mali, Niger, São Tomé and Príncipe, the Seychelles, and South Africa do not criminalize same-sex relations.
45. Das and Espinoza 2020.
46. Over the past decade, Africa has implemented most reforms promoting gender equality of any region world-wide. See World Bank 2019.
47. Hallward-Driemeier and Gajigo 2013.
48. Langer, Stewart, and Schroyens 2016.
49. Burger and Jafta 2010.
50. Muriaas and Wang 2012.
51. Gatti et al. 2016.
52. World Bank 2019.
53. Das and Espinoza 2019.
54. Das et al. 2017.

55. World Bank 2013.
56. Ali, Deininger, and Goldstein 2011; Ali et al. 2015.
57. Camacho et al. 2014.
58. Camacho et al. 2014.
59. Beegle, Coudouel, and Monsalve 2018; Pavanello et al. 2016.
60. De Cock et al. 2011.
61. The evaluation used a randomized control trial and tracked 4,888 girls over two years. Bandiera et al. 2013.
62. Bandiera et al. 2013.
63. Van Hove and Dubus 2019, 568; Suri and Jack 2016.
64. Bastian et al. 2018.
65. Buvinic and O'Donnell 2016; Hoff and Stiglitz 2016.
66. E.g., Mitra 2018, drawing on data from the Living Standards Measurement Survey (LSMS), which looks at employment and educational outcomes for persons with disability in Ethiopia, Malawi, Tanzania, and Uganda.
67. Das and Espinoza 2019.
68. Das et al. 2017.
69. World Bank 2012, 23.

Bibliography

Ali, D. A., K. Deininger, and M. Goldstein. 2011. "Environmental and Gender Impacts of Land Tenure Regularization in Africa: Pilot Evidence from Rwanda." Africa Region Gender Practice Policy Brief 2. https://openknowledge.worldbank.org/handle/10986/25527.

Ali, D. A., K. W. Deininger, M. P. Goldstein, and E. LaFerrara. 2015. "Empowering Women Through Land Tenure Regularization: Evidence from the Impact Evaluation of the National Program in Rwanda." Development Research Group Case Study. World Bank, Washington, DC. https://documents1.worldbank.org/curated/en/241921467986301910/pdf/97833-BRI-PUBLIC-Box391490B-ADD-SERIES-TITLE-See-73154.pdf.

Alkire, S., J. E. Foster, S. Seth, M. E. Santos, J. M. Roche, and P. Ballon. 2015. *Multidimensional Poverty Measurement and Analysis*. Oxford: Oxford University Press.

Alkire, S., and M. E. Santos. 2013. "A Multidimensional Approach: Poverty Measurement and Beyond." *Social Indicators Research* 112, no. 2: 239–257. https://doi.org/10.1007/s11205-013-0257-3.

Atinc, T. M., A. Banerjee, F. H. G. Ferreira, P. Lanjouw, M. Menendez, B. Ozler, G. Prennushi, V. Rao, J. Robinson, M. Walton, and M. Woolcock. 2005. *World Development Report 2006: Equity and Development*. Washington, DC: World Bank Group. https://documents.worldbank.org/en/publication/documents-reports/documentdetail/435331468127174418/world-development-report-2006-equity-and-development.

Bandiera, O., N. Buehren, R. Burgess, M. Goldstein, S. Gulesci, I. Rasul, and M. Sulaiman. 2020. "Women's Empowerment in Action: Evidence from a Randomized Control Trial in Africa." *American Economic Journal: Applied Economics* 12, no. 1: 210–259.

Bandiera, O., N. Buehren, R. Burgess, M. Goldstein, S. Gulesci, I. Rasul, and M. Sulaiman. 2013. "Empowering Adolescent Girls: Evidence from a Randomized Control Trial in Uganda." EnGender Impact: The World Bank's Gender Impact Evaluation Database. World Bank, Washington, DC. https://openknowledge.worldbank.org/handle/10986/25529.

Bastian, G., I. Bianchi, M. Goldstein, and J. Montalvao. 2018. "Short-Term Impacts of Improved Access to Mobile Savings, with and Without Business Training: Experimental Evidence from Tanzania." CGD Working Paper 478. Center for Global Development, Washington, DC. https://www.cgdev.org/publication/short-term-impacts-improved-access-mobile-savings-business-training.

Beegle, K., A. Coudouel, and E. Monsalve, eds. 2018. *Realizing the Full Potential of Social Safety Nets in Africa*. Washington, DC: World Bank and Agence Française de Développement. https:// openknowledge.worldbank.org/handle/10986/29789.

Berg, A. G., and J. D. Ostry. 2011. "Inequality and Unsustainable Growth: Two Sides of the Same Coin?" IMF Staff Discussion Note 11/08. International Monetary Fund, Washington, DC. https://www.imf.org/external/pubs/ft/sdn/2011/sdn1108.pdf.

Betancourt, J. R., and A. R. Green. 2010. "Commentary: Linking Cultural Competence Training to Improved Health Outcomes: Perspectives from the Field." *Academic Medicine* 85 no. 4: 583–585.

Buckup, S. 2009. "The Price of Exclusion: The Economic Consequences of Excluding People with Disabilities from the World of Work." Employment Working Paper No. 43. International Labour Organization, Geneva. http://ilo.org/skills/pubs/WCMS_146260/lang--en/index.htm.

Burger, R., and R. Jafta. 2010. "Affirmative Action in South Africa: An Empirical Assessment of the Impact on Labour Market Outcomes." CRISE Working Paper No. 76. Centre for Research on Inequality, Human Security and Ethnicity, Oxford. https://assets.publishing.service.gov.uk/ media/57a08b2ced915d622c000b5d/workingpaper76.pdf.

Burns, C. 2012. "The Costly Business of Discrimination: The Economic Costs of Discrimination and the Financial Benefits of Gay and Transgender Equality in the Workplace." Center for American Progress, Washington, DC. https://www.americanprogress.org/issues/lgbtq-rights/ reports/2012/03/22/11234/the-costly-business-of-discrimination/.

Buvinic, M., and M. O'Donnell. 2016. "Revisiting What Works: Women, Economic Empowerment and Smart Design." Washington, DC: Center for Global Development. https://www.cgdev.org/ publication/revisiting-what-works-women-economic-empowerment-and-smart-design.

Camacho, A., W. Cunningham, J. Rigolini, and V. Silva. 2014. "Addressing Access and Behavioral Constraints Through Social Intermediation Services: A Review of Chile Solidario and Red Unidos." Policy Research Working Paper no. WPS 7136. World Bank Group, Washington, DC. https://openknowledge.worldbank.org/handle/10986/20695.

Cavalcanti, T. V., and J. Tavares. 2015. "The Output Cost of Gender Discrimination: A Model-Based Macroeconomic Estimate." *Economic Journal* 126, no. 590: 109–134.

Chisholm, D., K. Sweeney, P. Sheehan, B. Rasmussen, F. Smit, P. Cuijpers, and S. Saxena. 2016. "Scaling Up Treatment of Depression and Anxiety: A Global Return on Investment Analysis." *Lancet Psychiatry* 3, no. 5 (2016): 415–424.

Das, M. B. 2016. "Social Inclusion in Macro-Level Diagnostics: Reflecting on the World Bank Group's Early Systematic Country Diagnostics." Policy Research Working Paper 7713. World Bank, Washington, DC. https://openknowledge.worldbank.org/handle/10986/24630.

Das, M. B., and S. A. Espinoza. 2020. *Inclusion Matters in Africa*. Washington, DC: World Bank. https://openknowledge.worldbank.org/bitstream/handle/10986/32528/IM-Africa.pdf.

Das, M. B., T. G. Evans, T. Palu, and D. Wilson. 2017. "Social Inclusion: What Does It Mean for Health Policy and Practice?" Health, Nutrition and Population Discussion Paper. World Bank, Washington DC. https://openknowledge.worldbank.org/bitstream/handle/10986/28941/121 584-WP-SocialInclusionHealth-PUBLIC.pdf?sequence=1&isAllowed=y.

De Cock, Kevin M., Harold W. Jaffe, and James W. Curran. 2011. "Reflections on 30 Years of AIDS." *Emerging Infectious Diseases* 17, no. 6 (June): 1044–1048. doi: 10.3201/eid1706.100184.

Ferreira, F. H. G., C. Lakner, M. A. Lugo, and B. Özler. 2014. "Inequality of Opportunity and Economic Growth: A Cross-Country Analysis." Policy Research Working Paper 6915. World Bank, Washington, DC. https://openknowledge.worldbank.org/handle/10986/18764.

Filmer, D., et al. 2014. *Youth Employment in Sub-Saharan Africa*. Washington, DC: World Bank. https://openknowledge.worldbank.org/handle/10986/16608.

FRA. 2015. "Cost of Exclusion from Healthcare: The Case of Migrants in an Irregular Situation." European Union Agency for Fundamental Rights, Vienna. https://fra.europa.eu/en/publicat ion/2015/cost-exclusion-healthcare-case-migrants-irregular-situation.

Freire, G., C. Diaz-Bonilla, O. Schwartz, L. Soler, and F. Carbonari. 2018. "Afro-Descendants in Latin America: Toward a Framework of Inclusion." World Bank, Washington, DC. https:// openknowledge.worldbank.org/handle/10986/30201.

Gatti, R. V., S. I. Karacsony, A. Kosuke, C. Ferre, and C. De Paz Nieves. 2016. "Being Fair, Faring Better: Promoting Equality of Opportunity for Marginalized Roma." World Bank, Washington, DC. https://openknowledge.worldbank.org/handle/10986/23679.

Gorman, A. 2021. *Hill We Climb and Other Poems.* New York: Penguin.

Hallward-Driemeier, M., and O. Gajigo. 2013. "Strengthening Economic Rights and Women's Occupational Choice: The Impact of Reforming Ethiopia's Family Law." Policy Research Working Paper no. 6695. World Bank, Washington, DC. https://openknowledge.worldbank.org/handle/10986/16919.

Hoff, K., and J. E. Stiglitz. 2016. "Striving for Balance in Economics: Towards a Theory of the Social Determination of Behavior." *Journal of Economic Behavior and Organization* 126: 25–57.

Hsieh, C.-T., E. Hurst, C. I. Jones, and P. J. Klenow. 2013. "The Allocation of Talent and U.S. Economic Growth." NBER Working Paper 18693. National Bureau of Economic Research, Cambridge, MA. https://www.nber.org/papers/w18693.

Hunt, V., D. Layton, and S. Prince. 2015. "Diversity Matters." McKinsey & Company, New York. https://www.mckinsey.com/insights/organization/~/media/2497d4ae4b534ee89d929cc6e3aea485.ashx.

Hunt, V., S. Prince, S. Dixon-Fyle, and L. Yee. 2018. "Delivering Through Diversity." McKinsey & Company, New York. https://www.mckinsey.com/~/media/mckinsey/business%20functions/organization/our%20insights/delivering%20through%20diversity/delivering-through-diversity_full-report.ashx.

IMF. 2017. "Fiscal Monitor: Tackling Inequality." October. International Monetary Fund, Washington, DC. https://www.imf.org/en/Publications/FM/Issues/2017/10/05/fiscal-monitor-october-2017.

Lamichhane, K., and Y. Sawada. 2013. "Disability and Returns to Education in a Developing Country." *Economics of Education Review* 37: 85–94.

Langer, A., F. Stewart, and M. Schroyens. 2016. "Horizontal Inequalities and Affirmative Action: An Analysis of Attitudes Towards Redistribution Across Groups in Africa." WIDER Working Paper Series 119. World Institute for Development Economic Research. https://www.wider.unu.edu/publication/horizontal-inequalities-and-affirmative-action.

Lereya, S. T., W. E. Copeland, E. J. Costello, and D. Wolke. 2015. "Adult Mental Health Consequences of Peer Bullying and Maltreatment in Childhood: Two Cohorts in Two Countries." *Lancet Psychiatry* 2, no. 6: 524–531.

Male, C., and Q. Wodon. 2017. "The Price of Exclusion: Disability and Education." Global Partnership for Education and the World Bank. December. https://www.edu-links.org/sites/default/files/media/file/Disability_gaps_in_educational_attainment_and_literacy.pdf.

Marrero, G. A., and J. G. Rodríguez. 2013. "Inequality of Opportunity and Growth." *Journal of Development Economics* 104: 107–122.

Mitra, S. 2018. "Measurement, Data and Country Context." In *Disability, Health and Human Development.* Palgrave Studies in Disability and International Development. New York: Palgrave Pivot.

Morgon Banks, L., and S. Polack. 2015. "The Economic Costs of Exclusion and Gains of Inclusion of People with Disabilities: Evidence from Low and Middle Income Countries." International Centre for Evidence in Disability and London School of Hygiene and Tropical Medicine. https://www.cbm.org/fileadmin/user_upload/Publications/Costs-of-Exclusion-and-Gains-of-Inclusion-Report.pdf.

Muriaas, R. L., and V. Wang. 2012. "Executive Dominance and the Politics of Quota Representation in Uganda." *Journal of Modern African Studies* 50 no. 2: 309–338.

Ostry, J., J. Alvarez, R. A. Espinoza, and C. Papageorgiou. 2018. "Economic Gains from Gender Inclusion: New Mechanisms, New Evidence." IMF Staff Discussion Note 18/06. International Monetary Fund, Washington, DC. https://www.imf.org/en/Publications/Staff-Discussion-Notes/Issues/2018/10/09/Economic-Gains-From-Gender-Inclusion-New-Mechanisms-New-Evidence-45543.

Pavanello, S., et al. 2016. "Effects of Cash Transfers on Community Interactions: Emerging Evidence." *Journal of Development Studies* 52, no. 8: 1147–1161.

Ringold, D., M. A. Orenstein, and E. Wilkens. 2004. "Roma in an Expanding Europe: Breaking the Poverty Cycle." World Bank, Washington, DC. https://openknowledge.worldbank.org/handle/10986/14869.

Robayo-Abril, M., and N. Milan. 2019. "Breaking the Cycle of Roma Exclusion in the Western Balkans." World Bank, Washington, DC. https://openknowledge.worldbank.org/handle/10986/31393.

Rodrik, D. 1999. "Where Did All the Growth Go? External Shocks, Social Conflict, and Growth Collapses." *Journal of Economic Growth* 4, no. 4: 385–412.

Sotgiu, G., and C. C. Dobler. 2020. "Social Stigma in the Time of Coronavirus Disease 2019." *European Respiratory Journal* 56: 2002461. https://doi.org/10.1183/13993003.02461-2020.

Sprague, L., S. Simon, and C. Sprague. 2011. "Employment Discrimination and HIV Stigma: Survey Results from Civil Society Organisations and People Living with HIV in Africa." *African Journal of AIDS Research* 1, no. 3: 311–324.

Stiglitz, J. 2016. "Inequality and Economic Growth." *The Political Quarterly* 86, no. 1: 134–155.

Suri, T., and W. Jack. 2016. "The Long-Run Poverty and Gender Impacts of Mobile Money." *Science* 354, no. 6317: 1288–1292. https://www.science.org/doi/10.1126/science.aah5309.

Turner, M. A. 2013. "Housing Discrimination Against Racial and Ethnic Minorities 2012: Executive Summary." US Department of Housing and Urban Development, Washington, DC. https://www.huduser.gov/portal/Publications/pdf/HUD-514_HDS2012_execsumm.pdf.

UN General Assembly. 2015. "Transforming Our World: The 2030 Agenda for Sustainable Development." Resolution 70/1. https://sustainabledevelopment.un.org/content/documents/21252030%20Agenda%20for%20Sustainable%20Development%20web.pdf.

Van Hove, L., and A. Dubus. 2019. "M-PESA and Financial Inclusion in Kenya: Of Paying Comes Saving?" *Sustainability* 11, no. 3: 568. https://doi.org/10.3390/su11030568.

Wodon, Q., et al. 2017. "Economic Impacts of Child Marriage: Global Synthesis Report." World Bank and International Center for Research on Women, Washington, DC. https://www.icrw.org/wp-content/uploads/2017/06/EICM-Global-Conference-Edition-June-27-FINAL.pdf.

Wodon, Q., and B. de la Brière. 2018. "Unrealized Potential: The High Cost of Gender Inequality in Earnings." Cost of Gender Inequality Notes Series. World Bank, Washington, DC. https://openknowledge.worldbank.org/handle/10986/29865.

World Bank. 2019. "Women, Business and the Law 2019: A Decade of Reform." World Bank, Washington, DC. https://openknowledge.worldbank.org/handle/10986/31327.

World Bank. 2013. *Inclusion Matters: The Foundation for Shared Prosperity*. Washington, DC: World Bank. https://openknowledge.worldbank.org/handle/10986/16195.

World Bank. 2012. *World Development Report 2012: Gender Equality and Development*. Washington, DC: World Bank. https://openknowledge.worldbank.org/handle/10986/4391.

WHO. 2020. "Social Stigma Associated with COVID-19." World Health Organization, UNICEF, and International Federation of the Red Cross and Red Crescent Societies. https://www.who.int/docs/default-source/coronaviruse/covid19-stigma-guide.pdf.

16

Democracy and Diversity in
Post-Conflict States

Atifete Jahjaga, Madison Schramm, and Teuta Avdimetaj

To make peace long-lasting and strengthen democracy, diversity and inclusion must be central to peacebuilding efforts following war. Lingering
divisions and disunity among the people must be addressed by tackling
grievances without prejudice to background—while building institutions
that offer citizens an equal chance to raise their voice and take action."
—Atifete Jahjaga, former president of Kosovo

Introduction

States emerging from intrastate conflict face particularly acute challenges
cultivating liberal, inclusive democracies.[1] While scholars have long identified the
challenge social cleavages pose to democracy following war, diversity and inclusion
are often relegated to a secondary priority.[2]

In this chapter, we investigate the specific contours of democratic institutions and
interventions that facilitate diversity in post-conflict states. We focus on ethnicity
and gender, reviewing some of the existing literature and bringing in the insights of
leaders in Kosovo and Sierra Leone.[3] Both of these countries have experienced recent war and grappled with the development of democratic institutions.[4]

Diversity and Inclusion in Governance

Countries (re)establishing systems of governance following conflict undergo multiple transformations at the same time. Many post-conflict countries experience an
overhaul of their social, economic, and political structures. In these efforts, diversity and inclusion are instrumental in determining the quality of democratic governance and the responsiveness to its citizens. This period of transition provides an
opportunity to include those traditionally left behind, such as women and ethnic

minorities, enabling them to influence the changes in their circumstances through decision-making processes.[5]

Post-conflict countries also face challenges in maintaining stability and effectively providing public goods and services due to demolished governing structures.[6] Leveraging a diversity of perspectives through inclusion offers a chance to better navigate these complexities and recognize that identities (salient before and after the conflict) will always be revisited, influenced, and renegotiated.[7]

Instrumentally, diversity and inclusion are important to obtaining positive outcomes.[8] However, diversity in national office has intrinsic value, and it is imperative we commit to the development of inclusive structures.[9] There is no silver bullet, and the schema for democratization will need to vary in accordance with states' existing institutions, social and economic cleavages, histories of conflict, and the timing of policy interventions. However, *building* inclusive and diverse societies should be a normative orientation, a good in and of itself, and a virtue that we should embrace.

Diversity and Inclusion in Democracy Building: The Range of Issues

States engaging in peacebuilding and democratization—overlapping processes addressing postwar stability, reconstruction, and the transition to a democracy— must consider a variety of complex challenges regarding diversity.[10] The war-to-democracy transition, encompassing the transitions from violent conflict to peace and from authoritarian rule to democracy, creates a number of dilemmas relating to the inclusion and representation of various societal groups (e.g., warring parties, democratic political parties, civil society); the relationships and connections between elite and mass politics; local versus international ownership of democratization and peacebuilding processes; and the short-term versus long-term effects of democratization on peacebuilding processes and vice versa.[11]

Inclusion in Post-Conflict Transitions

In post-conflict transitions, who is included in the negotiations, and what interests are addressed in formal agreements?[12] During conflict, the unequal situation of women and other marginalized groups makes them more vulnerable to human rights abuses such as sexual violence during conflict, as witnessed across case studies, including Liberia's civil war (1989–2003) and the civil war in Sri Lanka (1983–2009).[13] Yet while women and minority groups endure particular challenges in war, their distinct needs often become secondary concerns in the transition process.[14] However, as evidence from peace processes in Northern Ireland (1996–1998) and in the Philippines (2001–2014) shows, women's inclusion in peace negotiations makes peace agreements more comprehensive and more likely to last.[15] (For an in-depth discussion on inclusion in negotiations, see Chapter 9.) Transition governments, civil society leaders, and national and international non-governmental organizations need to work together to ensure diversity in Track I and II negotiations.[16]

Transitional Justice Mechanisms

Are there transitional justice mechanisms in place to address conflict-related human rights abuses? Women are rarely consulted in processes to establish transitional justice mechanisms with the purpose of tackling impunity or facilitating truth-telling and reconciliation.[17] Since the experience of women in conflict can differ based on their roles within the conflict, it is imperative to include their diverse views in efforts to address past grievances and achieve transformative social change. (See Chapter 12.)

Building Inclusive and Representative Structures

In the process of democratization, how can states build inclusive and representative electoral and state structures that cultivate legitimacy? Once peace negotiations are finished, establishing systems open to participation, both numerically and substantively, is integral to generating long-term stability.[18] The design of electoral systems often depends on the basis and intensity of social cleavages, as well as the nature of the dispute that initially gave way to conflict.[19] For instance, in many electoral transitions with a legacy of social divides, proportional representation (PR) systems have facilitated the inclusion of diverse groups in parliament and helped build consensus in South Africa (1994), Mozambique (1994), Indonesia (1999), Kosovo (2001), and Timor-Leste (2001).[20]

Access to Social Services and Welfare

Post-conflict states have to navigate the development of inclusive and accessible infrastructure including schooling, healthcare, food subsidies, and local security services.[21] Questions that need to be asked include who has access to social services and welfare, and whose needs these systems are built to address. A number of studies note that post-conflict reconstruction/reform in service provision often lacks gender sensitivity, making it harder to analyze the impacts of particular policies on women. For instance, research on health system reforms post-conflict has been marred by a lack of understanding of the differential health issues facing men and women.[22]

These questions are critical for developing stability in post-conflict states. The exclusion or subjugation of ethnic minorities can increase the likelihood of civil war.[23] Having more women in national office reduces the likelihood of renewed conflict, and a recent study of more than fifty conflict-affected states found that when women were absent in the legislature, states face an increased risk of conflict recurrence.[24] Furthermore, countries that elect more women have better child health outcomes and may be more likely to invest in social welfare programs. Researchers have also pointed to the positive economic impact of including voices from diverse ethnic groups in the policy process.[25] For instance, Chattopadhyay and Duflo found that the election of women to one-third of village council head positions in India through mandated representation significantly affected the provision of public goods.[26] Women elected to these positions invest more in public goods that are more closely related to women's concerns, such as drinking water to improve child health, and that potentially free up time and opportunities to facilitate women's greater involvement in income-generating activities.[27]

While all of these considerations are essential, it is impossible to address the breadth and depth of the myriad issues surrounding diversity, peacebuilding, and democratization within a single chapter. For this reason, we direct our focus to the structures that facilitate the numerical or descriptive inclusion of women and ethnic minorities in post-conflict democracies.

Identity and Inclusion in Elected National Governments

Within the context of this discussion, we use Dahl's definition of democracy as a regime that has relatively high degrees of contestation and participation.[28] There is tremendous variation between democracies in terms of their constitutional and electoral systems and their legal frameworks. Democracies can be characterized according to the distribution and structure of executive authority (e.g., presidential, parliamentary, and mixed or semi-presidential systems), the number of houses or legislative bodies (unicameral or bicameral), or the state's electoral system (often roughly categorized into majoritarian and proportional representation systems; in majoritarian or winner-take-all systems, positions are allocated by the majority of the electorate, whereas in PR systems, seats are allocated to leaders according to the portion of the electorate that casts votes in their favor).[29]

We focus primarily on the numerical or descriptive inclusion of ethnic minorities and women in post-conflict democracies.[30] Ethnicity is used in a variety of ways: it can refer to an affiliation or identification with particular mores, culture, or religion, and it is occasionally deployed as synonymous with race. Ethnicity operates as a social fact, significantly informing how individuals think of themselves and others.[31] However, it would be a mistake to think of ethnicity as immutable—individuals have a variety of identities that can be role- or context-specific.[32] Civil wars are often framed along the lines of identity, and cleavages do present unique challenges; treating identities as hardened facts can contribute to the reification of certain narratives, which can hamstring progress.[33] Furthermore, when we discuss ethnicity, we are often talking about a combination of facets, including ethnolinguistic and religious identity. These traits can have differential effects on the prospects for inclusion and democracy.[34] As of 2018, 11 percent of countries still have formal restrictions (by constitution or statute) on the eligibility of national candidates based on their ethnicity, race, religion, or language.[35] Appreciating ethnicity as complex and multifaceted is key to creating truly inclusive democracies. (See Figure 16.1.)

Transitions to democracy alone do not tend to increase women's political inclusion in the national legislature, as democracies can all too easily fail to integrate the voices of historically marginalized populations into the deliberative processes.[36] By their very nature, democracies can slow the passage of sweeping reforms, including those regarding women's inclusion. However, conflict itself provides unique opportunities for women to come into political office. During conflict, women frequently take on roles traditionally reserved for men, such as participation in militant networks or paid work outside the home.[37] However, the extent to which women are able to maintain these political and social gains in the post-conflict period varies substantially between cases. For example, women took on prominent political and military positions during the conflict in

Figure 16.1 Countries That Restrict Candidates for National Office by Race, Religion, and/or Ethnicity in 2018 (in red)

Credit line: Data Source: *Varieties of Democracy Dataset.*

Coppedge, Michael, John Gerring, Carl Henrik Knutsen, Staffan I. Lindberg, Jan Teorell, Vlad Ciobanu, and Lisa Gastaldi. "V-Dem Country Coding Units V9." *Varieties of Democracy*. 2019.

El Salvador but were largely sidelined from these positions in the post-conflict state.[38] (See Figure 16.2.)

Although leadership positions are often taken on out of necessity during conflict, they can empower women to renegotiate gender norms and to make greater demands during the transition process. Intrastate conflicts in particular are more likely to require substantial institutional reform and rebuilding, opening up opportunities for women to advance their political inclusion in national political office.[39] The intensity and durability of these political and institutional shifts, however, vary within and between countries and regions, depending on variables including the pre-conflict social and political arrangements, the length and intensity of the conflict, and the nature and content of the peace agreement. Societal perceptions of women as "natural" peacemakers may incline voters to be more supportive of women candidates for president in the aftermath of conflict. While these gendered stereotypes are not always borne out, they mean that women may have some advantage when running for high-profile positions in post-conflict states.[40] Additionally, the election of women heads of government may not translate to broader political representation; while women became heads of government following the brutal Liberian civil war (Ellen Johnson Sirleaf), the fall of the Marcos regime in the Philippines (Corazon Aquino), and the transition from military dictatorship in Burma (Aung San Suu Kyi), for example, women's representation in these countries' parliaments stalled.[41]

0.003 ▭▬▬▬▬ 0.613

Figure 16.2 Percent of Women in the Lower/Single House as of February 2019

Credit line: Data Source: *International Parliamentary Union.*

Inter-Parliamentary Union. "Sierra Leone Parliament." Accessed February 19, 2019. http://archive.ipu.org/parline-e/reports/2281.htm.

State Structure: Constitutional and Electoral Systems

The design of power-sharing systems has important implications for peace and stability. Hartzell and Hoddie found that the more specific the rules of power-sharing among former adversaries, the more likely it is for peace to last.[42] Specifically, in cases of bargained resolution of civil wars, they argue that power-sharing is not a dichotomous variable that is either present or absent; rather, it encompasses political, military, territorial, and economic components.[43] As the drivers of civil war vary, the design of power-sharing institutions to address concerns must encompass different dimensions.[44] When conflict parties feel that no other stakeholder group can dominate any of the domains, they are more likely to feel safe and remain committed to keeping the peace.[45] We explore several types of these structures in what follows.

Two organizational structures are often the focus of research regarding ethnic inclusion: federalism and consociationalism.[46] (See Table 16.1.) Within these subcategories there is tremendous variation, and many states have aspects of both federalism and consociationalism.[47] However, both of these systems present challenges for long-term cooperation and inclusion. Within federal systems, there are few incentives for cooperation along identity lines, as power is distributed to substate entities. Within both systems existing cleavages may become reified.[48] For instance, Lebanon's consociational model is often lauded as a model of a plural and stable democracy in the Middle East due to its guarantees of power-sharing and political representation. However, such cases of highly institutionalized consociational arrangements can lead to sectarianism, institutional instability, clientelism, and state frailty.[49] In line with Horowitz's argument that consociationalism can lead to reification of ethnic divisions, consociationalism in Lebanon is considered to have created divisive effects through the politicization of ethnicity and an inability to ward off communal conflicts.[50] Calfat argues that in Lebanon's consociationalism, electoral stimuli calcify voters' identification and politicians' affiliation on a sectarian basis, producing electoral results along denominational lines while disregarding ideological changes or migratory movements and reifying communal bonds.[51]

Table 16.1 Constitutional Systems

Federal systems	Substate territories/groups have some independent executive power from the central government. Examples include Brazil, United States, and Australia.
Consociational systems	Power-sharing among groups and often characterized by proportional representation systems and minority veto.* Examples include Belgium, Switzerland, South Africa

* Wolff 2011.

Post-conflict states' electoral systems have significant implications for inclusion. Although the relative benefits of majoritarian and proportional representation systems across democracies writ large is outside the scope of this chapter, PR systems provide natural benefits for inclusion in divided post-conflict societies.[52] In PR systems, seats are distributed by the percentage of votes candidates receive. These can be contrasted with majoritarian or winner-take-all systems. As Cammett and Malesky have argued, countries with closed-list PR systems have superior governance outcomes and tend to experience more enduring peace and stability.[53]

We attempt to disaggregate ethnic and gender diversity in post-conflict states, but of course these considerations must be made in tandem and affect each other in important ways. For example, Bird found that while women and ethnic minorities benefit from PR systems, the benefits to minority ethnic groups are contingent on the presence of ethnic parties.[54] Hughes found that minority women are more likely to benefit when gender quotas are adopted in tandem with minority quotas.[55]

Proportional representation systems have been correlated with women's representation in legislative bodies.[56] Undemocratic or unconstitutional breaks in the national legislature more generally have also been shown to have a positive effect on bringing women to office.[57] Like proportional representation systems, these legislative breaks result in turnover and thus more opportunities for women to come to office. Alternatively, states with higher incumbency rates elect fewer women to the national legislature.[58]

Different constitutional systems do benefit or impede ethnic minorities' and women's candidacies in meaningful ways.[59] As Liphardt has argued, "Wherever significant differences appear, the parliamentary-PR systems almost invariably post the best records, particularly with respect to representation, protection of minority interests, voter participation, and control of unemployment."[60]

Mandated Protections: Ethnic and Gender Quotas

Another mechanism for increasing diversity in post-conflict states is quotas. In post-conflict countries, inclusive initiatives such as quotas can increase the likelihood of democratic survival.[61] Ethnic quotas can be organized to establish special electoral districts, to reserve seats for ethnic parties, or to create multiethnic parties.[62] Both gender and ethnic quotas can be found in autocratic and democratic states. However, not all ethnic or gender quotas are equally effective.

Gender quotas have been adopted by 127 states, more than half of which have experienced conflict since the end of the Cold War.[63] However, the particular type of gender quota and the associated enforcement mechanism(s) matter.[64] Some quotas are legally mandated by the constitution and/or electoral laws and can include reserved seats for women; others are voluntarily adopted by political parties. Requirements regarding the inclusion of women can be implemented as early as the candidate stage, and/or coincide with the nomination of candidates for the ballot.

Some laws have severe penalties for noncompliance, whereas others have few to no sanctions.[65] These, of course, intersect with ethnic quotas in a variety of ways.

While most countries that have succeeded in electing a national legislature that is more than 30 percent women have some type of quota system, quotas are not a panacea. For example, although women's representation in France has been steadily increasing over the past twenty years, it wasn't until President Emmanuel Macron gave winning seats to women that women reached more than 30 percent of the national legislature.[66] Even Rwanda, long held up as a positive example for having achieved gender parity in the national legislature after the genocide, is ultimately not a democracy, limiting the ability of women to govern effectively. And governments have gone to great lengths to evade and subvert the effectiveness of quota provisions.[67] Furthermore, researchers have warned against conflating gains in numerical representation with gains in women's interests, while others have noted how gender quotas can entrench patronage politics and inadvertently create backlash against women.[68] Overall, the evidence on quotas seems to be positive.[69] Though they are sometimes depicted as quick anti-meritocratic fixes, they can play an important role in changing social norms. Researchers examining India, for example, found that quotas (here called "reservations") for different castes improved social and legal norms of interaction.[70] Similarly, gender quotas accelerate the rise of women to leadership positions and offer long-term gains.[71] For example, Campbell and Wolbrecht found that greater visibility of women politicians increased the likelihood that adolescent girls indicated an intention to be politically active.[72]

While we have emphasized various structural interventions to increase ethnic and gender diversity in post-conflict states, it is worth reemphasizing the importance of embracing inclusion as a normative orientation. Unfortunately, today we are witnessing a backlash against diversity and inclusion, even in consolidated democracies. While structural interventions are important, enduring inclusive governance depends on broad social and attitudinal acceptance of inclusion as an ethical priority.

Evidence from Kosovo and Sierra Leone

Case Study: Kosovo

> Legislation is the key to ensuring inclusiveness. We made sure that inclusiveness was reflected in our Constitution—the very foundation of our state.
> —President Atifete Jahjaga[73]

Kosovo is a multiparty, parliamentary republic built upon power-sharing principles, where the government exercises executive power, the assembly exercises legislative power, the president represents the unity of the people, and the judiciary is independent. Its system of proportional representation implies that a single party is not likely to have a parliamentary majority, and the government of Kosovo is required to have a composition that includes minority parties.[74] By constitution, Kosovo is "a multi-ethnic society consisting of Albanian and other communities governed democratically with full respect for the rule of law through its legislative, executive and judicial institutions."[75] Although the majority of the population consists of Albanians, it is estimated that ethnic minorities make up around 13 percent of the population.[76] (See Box 16.1.)

Box 16.1 President Jahjaga

"Some of the key challenges in post-conflict Kosovo were related to the unique makeup of our society. Kosovo is home to around two million people with diverse backgrounds, including ethnicity, gender and age. And while this diversity is a blessing, it also means that each group needs a customized approach to ensure that they are fully included in society, which is not easy for a post-conflict country."

Conflict transforms countries in numerous and meaningful ways, but the process of change—particularly toward democracy—is often context-specific. There are significant differences between places where democracy takes hold with pre-existing systems of governance and those that lack any form of institutional governance structure. Building democracy and inclusive institutions in post-conflict settings can be especially challenging.

A customized approach that ensures inclusion is often anchored in legislation that does not discriminate based on gender, ethnicity, or other background. As Kosovo built its democratic institutions from scratch, an inclusive legislative framework was a key starting point, though gaps between laws and their implementation persist. Throughout this process, the role of the international community has been critical. In the immediate post-conflict setting in Kosovo, the international community had executive powers, which extended until the end of supervised independence in 2012, with continuous influence in Kosovo's institutional structures and performance.[77] Yet, as multiple international missions conflated peacebuilding with state-building, there was a struggle as to how to accommodate and transform ethnic cleavages while resolving claims for statehood.[78] Though Kosovo and Serbia have yet to normalize relations, achieving European Union integration may push the countries toward an eventual peace deal.

With the ultimate goal of achieving Euro-Atlantic integration, Kosovo has been undertaking reforms to make sure that its laws across sectors—including equal representation—are in full compliance with EU *acquis* and NATO standards. It is within this framework that Kosovo's legislation is being advanced.

The constitution of Kosovo guarantees political representation for nonmajority community representatives. Out of 120 seats in the Assembly, twenty are reserved for nonmajority ethnic groups, allocated based on the relative size of their populations—Serb representatives are guaranteed ten seats, four for Romani, Ashkali, and Egyptians jointly, three for Bosniaks, two for Turks, and one for a Gorani representative.[79] Importantly, any amendment of the Constitution requires a double two-thirds majority, of both the Assembly and the deputies holding seats guaranteed for communities.[80] This provision ensures that minorities are part of decision-making processes, though by various accounts it has also been considered a barrier in fulfilling the state-building process for Kosovo. For instance, the transformation of the Kosovo Security Force (KSF) into an army, required for completing the country's security sector infrastructure, was blocked for a period of time due to the Serb minority veto. Thus, due to the lack of double majority that is necessary for making changes to the constitution, the parliament opted instead to amend existing laws that extend KSF's mission and start the slow and lengthy process of transformation.[81] The creation of Kosovo's army is an additional step in consolidating Kosovo's statehood, which the Serbian members of parliament in Kosovo—largely backed by Belgrade—oppose as a way of contesting the country's territorial integrity.[82]

Despite challenges, the consociational model in the case of Kosovo has managed to achieve common interethnic governance and proportional representation of all communities, as evidenced by the participation of all minorities in each government since Kosovo declared independence in 2008.[83] (See Box 16.2.)

Box 16.2 President Jahjaga

"We created a legal framework that guaranteed seats for minorities in Kosovo's assembly to ensure fair representation. And to ensure that they can raise their voices on matters that pertain to their communities specifically, and also issues that pertain to all of us. I firmly believe that this is what helped us address many serious issues immediately after the end of the war in our country."

Further, "in the democracy we built within our country, everyone has a say. Everyone can influence policy through their vote, through petition, through conversations with policymakers. Challenges to inclusive decision-making and policymaking were gradually addressed with the input of our citizens. We learned from them what could be done to bring the necessary change. For example, women's organizations and activists for gender equality raised their voices and worked constantly for a legal framework that supports gender equality."

Since 2000, Kosovo has adopted gender quotas to ensure that women hold at least 30 percent of the seats in the Assembly of Kosovo. (See Box 16.3.) Although in most instances the technical requirements of Kosovo's electoral quota have been followed, the spirit of the law often is not— women are often less cultivated as candidates or leaders compared to their male counterparts.[84] There are even cases when male candidates refer to the quota to argue that there is no need for parties to support women during the campaign process, since their seats are already guaranteed.[85]

Box 16.3 President Jahjaga

"We established gender quotas to address the underrepresentation of women in Kosovo's assembly, and at the central and local level of government. This was not an easy process, as it implied a social change that is slow to take place, even in countries that are far more developed than we are."

The National Democratic Institute (NDI) in Kosovo argues in a report that the gender quota has helped increase women's representation in parliament and in decision-making positions in Kosovo.[86] In each successive election, more women are getting into parliament based on the number of preferential votes personally received, rather than through apportionment to fulfill quota numbers.[87] In the 2014 parliamentary elections, 20 percent of the top five or ten most-voted candidates on most parties' lists were women, despite the fact that they were competing against high-profile male candidates.[88] In the parliamentary elections of 2017, women won 38 out of 120 seats in the Assembly; 17 of them won seats due to the quota, while 21 won their seats on their own merit, even though male candidates outnumbered women candidates threefold.[89] In October 2019 elections, only 13 out of 39 women elected deputies got their seat based on the quota.[90] In the most recent parliamentary elections, in February 2021, women won a new record number of seats—43 out of 120 seats, exceeding the 30 percent quota. Notably, 35 out of these 43 women candidates did not need the quota to secure a seat in the parliament.[91] As the trends in these successive elections show, women in Kosovo are increasingly being voted for by the public and even constitute the top-voted candidates across the major political parties, rendering quotas less necessary over time.

At the central level of governance, women hold a record number of senior positions in Kosovo's new government; five of the fifteen ministries are led by women. For the first time, there are two women deputy prime ministers, one of whom comes from the Bosniak community, which did not hold a similar position until now. It is a significant increase from previous governments, which had only three women ministers out of sixteen ministries in total. The numerical representation of women in the government is hailed as a positive development, but advocates for inclusion caution that these appointments should be coupled with a mindset among men and women representatives to be sensitive to gender issues, "installing equality between women and men as a criterion, anytime they make a decision or manage [Kosovo's] financial resources."[92]

In another historic milestone, in April 2021, Kosovo elected its second female head of state—Vjosa Osmani, who was also the most-voted candidate when she ran in the recent parliamentary elections.[93] Thus, within a decade, Kosovo is one of the few countries in the world to have elected not only one but two women to the highest office. In her previous role, Osmani was the first woman head of Assembly in Kosovo. Numerical representation is currently lacking at the local level of governance, however; none of the thirty-eight municipalities in Kosovo is led by a woman. Thus, it is difficult to determine whether progress can be sustained if political parties continue not to fully abide by the Law on Gender Equality, which requires a minimum representation of 50 percent for each gender in governing and decision-making bodies at both central and local levels of governance.[94]

In addition to internally led development efforts, reforms required as part of Kosovo's EU integration process hold the potential for continued progress, and having minority and gender quotas is a reassuring means for ensuring greater representation. Overall, the system of laws is critical for enabling inclusion, but these laws were crafted for the specifics of Kosovo's context and must be implemented at the central and local levels. To push for implementation, political will is necessary. And as the conflict recedes into the past, realization of these reforms is increasingly important for achieving inclusiveness and for making peace more durable. As President Jahjaga argues, "Women and minorities are an integral part of society and their participation and representation is not only a determining factor in the transformative process from conflict to peace, but also pivotal in any efforts to strengthen democracy and make peace enduring."[95]

Case Study: Sierra Leone

> When you are rebuilding following a failure of governance, it's political marginalization, it's economic collapse: it's completely different . . . you can't just use the same analysis.
>
> —Minister Zainab Hawa Bangura[96]

Sierra Leone is a presidential representative republic where the president exercises executive power as the head of state and head of government, the parliament exercises legislative power, and the judiciary is independent.[97] In the context of Sierra Leone, Minister Bangura explains, one of the main challenges has been to merge post-conflict reconstruction efforts with the peace accord that is being implemented.

Sierra Leone is quite diverse in terms of ethnicity. Among sixteen ethnic groups, each with their own language and customs, Temme and Mende are the most influential and collectively make up 63.8 percent of the population.[98] The third-largest group is the Limba, with 8.4 percent, while the four smallest ethnic groups are Vai, Krim, Yalunka, and Krio, which collectively constitute 2.3 percent of the population.[99]

While ethnic identity is not considered to have been a key contributing factor in the eruption of the civil war in Sierra Leone, ethnic groups sought to obtain political representation within the national government through the democratization process.[100]

To spur economic development and achieve better governance, key political reforms undertaken in Sierra Leone included the restoration of the multiparty system and the reconstitution of local government or "decentralization" after more than thirty years.[101] The international donor community has been instrumental in supporting decentralization efforts in Sierra Leone through the devolution of key political, fiscal, and administrative functions from the central government to local councils.[102] This has led to political power-sharing beyond Freetown and better provision of services at the subnational level, though resources available to the local councils remain limited and may make them susceptible to central influence in the long run. (See Box 16.4.)

Box 16.4 Minister Bangura

"I think the shift postwar has been a big challenge from a diversity perspective, because the focus is on fixing the effects and the consequences of the war, the damage that's been done, rather than saying, what really caused the war? That's where inclusion and participation, diversity, become important. They come in when you are addressing root causes: what caused the war?"

Furthermore, "in countries coming out of conflict, often as a result of political marginalization or bad governance, one of the best ways to give people a voice and influence is to introduce multi-party democracy." One of the challenges about democracy is that "people just think democracy entails elections." But where a country has been marred by political marginalization and economic marginalization, to have a sustainable democracy in which everybody has a voice "you really have to build institutions, independent and effective institutions that represent, [and] you have to embark on [reforming] the security sector."

In many ethnically diverse post-conflict settings, policies such as decentralization are used to help reduce conflict risk, promote community cohesion and reconciliation, and/or enhance the legitimacy of the state.[103] But decentralization can also become a source of contention if principles of equity and distributive fairness aren't used to drive resource allocation among local and central actors.[104] (See Box 16.5.)

Box 16.5 Minister Bangura

"We need to look to proper devolution. Because if the marginalization has to do with ethnicity or religion . . . clusters of ethnic groups are basically in certain areas. The best way you can have them involved is a decentralized system of government in which they can deal with . . . needs of the local community when they have representatives.

"However, we can have decentralization in theory, but we cannot have decentralization in practice in the case of Sierra Leone. . . . Even though they have the councils, they don't have money, they don't have power, so it's a lot of challenges rebuilding the states that reflects, and to make sure it's inclusive and diversified."

Post-conflict efforts in building inclusive democracy in Sierra Leone have diminished due to the lack of local capacity, lack of information-sharing about decision-making processes, and imported policies that are not customized to the local context.

The process of building inclusive institutions, including the pace of interventions, has a critical impact on the future of diversity and inclusion. Including women, minority ethnic groups, and diverse voices in the transition and the constitution-building process will have implications for the future of inclusion. However, these choices will inevitably be constrained by the capacity of existing institutions, security, and path dependence. The multiple actors involved in post-conflict reconstruction condition this. This can further marginalize the voices of women and minorities, since women may lack the knowledge and capacities to be part of these platforms. (See Box 16.6.)

Box 16.6 Minister Bangura

"Most of these [post-conflict reconstruction] processes lack inclusion, lack participation, because they are controlled and directed by foreign partners. . . . There are too many players, the international NGOs, the national NGOs, the multilateral and the bilateral partners. So you have a whole lot of players, international players as well as national players. Many processes are going on at the same time."

Even though there is a lingering gap between the drafting of policies and their implementation, legislation that promotes inclusiveness can often be viewed as a prerequisite to increasing diversity in governance. In the case of Sierra Leone, a major obstacle to inclusive policies, particularly in relation to gender equality, remains the unfavorable legal framework. The OECD Development Centre's Social Institutions and Gender Index (SIGI), which measures discrimination against women in social institutions, ranks Sierra Leone as high in terms of gender-based discrimination in laws and institutions.[105] (See Box 16.7.)

Box 16.7 Minister Bangura

"Legislation is extremely important because it has to mainstream and institutionalize inclusion." She sees an important opening for such legislation in the immediate post-conflict setting, which leaves countries needing international help or recognition. As foreign countries offer their support for post-conflict reconstruction, they also have more leverage to push for legislation that advances inclusion.

It is important to work with "people who have been protected or who the law intends to protect, to strengthen them to take advantage of the law." At the same time, if rights and protections are not codified in law, the political class may always become stronger and may reverse or impede progress.

Civil society and women's organizations are quite active in promoting inclusiveness in Sierra Leone. The Women's Movement for Peace played a crucial role in 1995, creating the conditions for the end of military rule and the elections of 1996, which paved the way for the peace process in Sierra Leone.[106] However, women were marginalized in the peace agreement as well as in the newly elected government.[107] (See Box 16.8.)

Box 16.8 Minister Bangura

"Women led in all the discussions, we participated, we took part, we did everything in the security sector, informing the DDR in the peace processes and everything. But once the state started rebuilding itself, little by little, women were left behind."

In the current parliament of Sierra Leone, out of 146 elected members, only 18, or 12.6 percent, are women, a figure that is regarded as resulting from the failure to legislate women's inclusion in politics through tools such as gender quotas.[108] Women are also underrepresented in the government; only five of twenty-seven ministries are led by women.

Members of the parliament of Sierra Leone recently adopted a resolution calling on government and parliamentarians to address issues highlighted by UN Security Council Resolutions 1325 and 1820 on women, peace, and security.[109] These include the recognition of the systematic abuse of women and girls during the conflict and women's exclusion from peace processes important for post-conflict recovery and reconciliation in Sierra Leone.[110]

The passing of this resolution is felt to pave the way for additional legal reforms in support of gender equality, including "amendments to a section of the 1991 Constitution, which currently allows for discrimination against women in certain instances, bringing to the Table of the House, an Affirmative Action Bill, and fast-tracking the adoption of amendments to the Child Rights Act of 2007."[111] This resolution was put forward by the Female Parliamentary Caucus, which has also been pushing for adoption of the Gender Equality Bill and institutionalizing the 30 percent quota to increase the number of women in government.[112]

Minister Bangura sees quotas as essential, but she cautions that "they must be implemented with very clear guidelines; or with a lot of consultation and engagement. It should be done in a very transparent and participatory manner."[113] Drawing from the experience in Sierra Leone, her concern is that often male leaders get to handpick women to fill the quotas, and they do so by choosing unqualified women.

In the context of Sierra Leone, there is a general sense that progress has been made in terms of expanding opportunities for women and girls to promote gender equality and empowerment of women, but challenges persist.[114] There is a need to complete the legal infrastructure in a way that is nondiscriminatory and reflects the country's diversity. At the same time, the impact of those laws will depend on national will and the capacity to implement legal mandates. In addition to legislation, policies such as decentralization, which will ensure the participation of minority groups in political processes, depend on whether resources have been equally allocated to the decentralized units. Only by fully including women and minority groups within society and tapping the country's diversity will it be possible to address the root causes of the conflict and not merely deal with its repercussions.

Findings and Conclusion

This chapter explores the various contours of democratic institutions that promote and enable diversity and inclusion in post-conflict states, focusing on the numerical or descriptive inclusion of women and ethnic minorities. It argues that diversity and inclusion in governance present an intrinsic value that should be pursued in and of itself. Following are some of the key findings/observations:

- *Expanding equal rights and opportunities is fundamental to peacebuilding and democratization.* The transitions to peace and democracy entail complex challenges regarding diversity and inclusion, along a range of issues. It's important to consider the inclusiveness of processes to negotiate peace, address past grievances, and build representative electoral systems. (See Chapters 9, 10, and 12.) These considerations are instrumental in cultivating legitimate post-conflict governance structures that support durable peace, sustainable development, and citizens' social well-being, regardless of their background.

- *Post-conflict settings provide an opening for diversity and inclusion by challenging preexisting norms.* Notwithstanding enormous devastation, the post-conflict period offers a unique opening to challenge preexisting norms and for traditionally marginalized groups to expand their roles as substantial institutional reforms take place.

- *Non-discriminatory legislation is foundational for diversity and inclusion, though implementation often hinges upon political will and the resources available.* Legislation that is free from discrimination is key in facilitating diversity and inclusion in post-conflict states. As the case of Sierra Leone illustrates, discriminatory laws prevent inclusive policymaking, but a broader space for women and minorities to advocate for parity may open up new pathways in this regard. However, even when laws are enacted, their implementation will also depend on the state's capacity and political will to implement these laws. This is also evident in the case of Kosovo, which shows that having advanced laws is not enough if there is no political will to make them a reality.

- *Electoral systems in post-conflict countries have significant implications for inclusion.* The relative benefits of majoritarian and proportional representation systems vary across democracies, though PR systems are particularly conducive to inclusion in post-conflict societies, especially in terms of representation, protection of minority interests, and voter participation.

- *Mandated protections such as ethnic and gender quotas are useful tools in facilitating diversity and inclusion.* The effectiveness of mandated protections often depends on the way in which countries institute and enforce them. Although some view mandated protections as quick and anti-meritocratic measures, such criticism is offset by the largely positive impact of ethnic and gender quotas in increasing diversity, shifting social norms, accelerating the ascension of women to leadership positions, and securing long-term gains.

- *Structural interventions and numerical representation are necessary but not sufficient to advance equity and inclusion.* To advance diversity, leaders must explicitly commit to the values of diversity and inclusion and work with national and subnational power brokers, such as local and provincial officials, the press, and civil society, to establish inclusive government structures. This is required in tandem with building capacity for historically marginalized groups, security sector reforms, and anti-corruption efforts. Perhaps most important is to design these interventions for local contexts. The best designs to promote diversity and inclusion, particularly regarding women and minority ethnic groups, will depend on a variety of complex considerations and needs. Further, they are integrated with approaches that engage with local communities to articulate the issues that matter to them and consider power asymmetries and cleavages along multiple lines.

- *While building liberal, stable democracies is a desirable goal, the means and methods should not minimize diversity and inclusion for short-term gains.* Liberal theory highlights fair processes as a prerequisite for just societies. An ethical question must also pervade institutional development: that of means and consequences. As Minister Bangura argued, "I do not have a good example of any country in which it has worked. Because the principles are not being followed, the results that people are looking for are short-term, and the international community does not invest in the long-term democratic development. It's expensive, and it's time-consuming for them; they just give power to the government and then they disappear. So, I don't have a country that I could tell you what we're talking about, the right thing, has been done."[115] We should be wary of utilitarian arguments that are contingent on demonstrable short-term outcomes. Building a liberal democracy will not be seamless.

- *Policy-makers need to consider a host of factors when developing inclusive infrastructure in a new democracy.* These factors include the degree to which ethnicity is politicized, the intensity of conflict as well as the number of groups and the demographic and geographic distribution of those groups within a given country. In particular, when striving for women's inclusion, the effects of wartime sexual violence, the status of women's education, sociohistorical norms regarding women, and how gender intersects with ethnic identity all must be considered.

- *There is a lack of research in documenting women's and other marginalized groups' experiences and their contributions to peacebuilding and democratization.* In recent decades, there have been increasing efforts to record the experience of women and other marginalized groups, particularly in conflict and post-conflict settings. There is greater interest in examining the impact of war on women and marginalized groups, the role of women and minorities in mobilizing for peace, and women's and minorities' contributions to strengthening democracies. However, in many cases, there continues to be a dearth of data that would enable a consistent cross-country analysis of diversity and inclusion as measured through key indicators. Further research in this regard is needed to advance our thinking on the myriad of ways in which women and marginalized groups are affected by these transitional processes, on their agency, and on their contributions to the development of policy—with the purpose of extracting important insights on best practices.

Notes

1. Especially as the arrangements supported by international actors to end the conflict may be incongruous with democracy promotion. See Aitken 2007; Jung 2012; Simonsen 2005.
2. See Dahl 2006; Diamond 1988.
3. The Kosovo War (1998–1999) was sparked when the former Yugoslav president Slobodan Milosevic unleashed an ethnic cleansing campaign targeting the majority Albanian population

in Kosovo. The war ended with NATO's intervention and a political agreement that required an immediate end to violence and a rapid withdrawal of the Serbian military, police, and paramilitary forces as prescribed by UN Security Council Resolution 1244. The war resulted in the death of over thirteen thousand civilians, the displacement of around a million people, an estimated twenty thousand women and men raped (where rape was used as a tool of war), and over sixteen hundred people still missing. After the war ended, UNSC Resolution 1244 established the United Nations Interim Administration Mission in Kosovo (UNMIK) to oversee the civilian administration of the territory, offer provisional mechanisms of self-government, and help determine Kosovo's political status. Kosovo declared its independence in 2008, and the role of the international community has been crucial throughout the state-building process.

The Sierra Leone Civil War (1991–2002) began when the Revolutionary United Front (RUF) under Foday Sankoh, with the support of Liberian rebel leader Charles Taylor and his National Patriotic Front of Liberia (NFPL), sought to overthrow the government of Sierra Leonean president Joseph Momah. The war resulted in seventy thousand casualties and 2.6 million displaced people. Child abductions and rape were also widespread. The war erupted due to "a repressive predatory state, dependence on mineral rents, the impact of structural adjustment, a large excluded youth population, the availability of small arms after the end of the Cold War, and interference from regional neighbors." Kaldor and Vincent 2006, 4.

The war ended in 2002, following British military intervention to support the Sierra Leone government and the UN peacekeeping mission on the ground (UNAMSIL), which repelled the RUF advance.

4. Although there are numerous aspects of inclusion and identity, we focus on structural interventions to promote diversity in national office.

5. O'Driscoll 2018. Zuckerman and Greenberg (2004) argue for a more inclusive and normative/rights-based approach in post-conflict reconstruction, including the right to participate meaningfully in policymaking and resource allocation; the right to benefit equally from public and private resources and services; and the right to build a gender-equitable society for lasting peace and prosperity.

6. Cliffe and Manning 2006.

7. Simonsen 2005.

8. Krause, Krause, and Bränfors 2018.

9. See, for example, Swiss, Fallon, and Burgos 2012; Best, Shair-Rosenfield, and Wood 2019; Bashevkin 2014.

10. See Barnett 2007, 35; Graham, Miller, and Strøm 2017.

11. Jarstad and Sisk 2008.

12. See, for example, Vandeginste and Sriram 2011, 489; Chinkin and Charlesworth 2006.

13. Swiss 1998.

14. See, for example, Denov and Gervais 2007.

15. Georgetown Institute for Women, Peace, and Security 2017.

16. See, for example, Eisenstadt, LeVan, and Maboudi 2015; Gibson 2006.

17. Georgetown Institute for Women, Peace, and Security 2016.

18. See, for example, Cammett and Malesky 2012; Simonsen 2004.

19. Reilly and Reynolds 2000.

20. Reilly n.d.

21. See Creighton, Post, and Park 2016; Tenret 2016; Mickelson et al. 2001 .

22. Percival et al. 2014.

23. See, for example, Cederman, Hug, and Krebs 2010.

24. Demeritt and Nichols 2014, 362.

25. Birnir and Waguespack 2011.

26. Chattopadhyay and Duflo 2004.
27. Chattopadhyay and Duflo 2004.
28. Dahl 1971, 1–3. Many quantitative attempts to operationalize democracy emphasize institutional or procedural qualities (e.g., Cheibub et al. 2010; Boix et al. 2013; and Coppedge et al. 2019). Although these data sets have attempted to standardize a threshold of democracy through aggregate indicators, significant questions regarding the conceptualization of "democracy" as an objective, measurable construct persist. The minimalist criteria for democracy includes direct elections for the legislature, political rights, and civil liberties.
29. Fish and Kroenig 2009.
30. Substantive inclusion must be considered along with numerical representation.
31. Anderson 2006.
32. Wendt 1992.
33. See Mamdani 2009.
34. Gerring, Hoffman, and Zarecki 2018.
35. Coppedge et al. 2019.
36. Matland and Montgomery 2003; Deveaux 2016.
37. See Turshen, Meintjes, and Pillay 2001; Bop 2001. For example, during the Troubles, Republican women in Northern Ireland created networks to organize around feminist issues while imprisoned together. This facilitated the creation of the Women's Department in Sein Fein.
38. Kaufman and Williams 2010.
39. Hughes 2009.
40. Schramm and Stark 2019.
41. Inter-Parliamentary Union. n.d. b.
42. Hartzell and Hoddie 2003.
43. Hartzell and Hoddie 2003.
44. Hartzell and Hoddie 2003.
45. Hartzell and Hoddie 2003.
46. See Horowitz 2014; Agarin 2019.
47. Fish and Kroenig 2009.
48. See Lijphart 1977; Ciepley 2013; Howard 2012; Simonsen 2005; and Graham, Miller, and Strøm 2017.
49. Calfat 2018.
50. Calfat 2018.
51. Calfat 2018.
52. See also Kittilson and Schwindt-Bayer 2010.
53. Cammett and Malesky 2012; Htun 2004.
54. Bird 2014 .
55. Hughes 2011. See also Murray 2016; Folke, Freidenvall, and Rickne 2015.
56. Hughes 2007.
57. Hughes 2007, 26. However, the effects are not linear. The frequency and duration of the interruptions will have differential effects on women's inclusion.
58. Heath, Schwindt-Bayer, and Taylor-Robinson 2005.
59. See Lijphart 1991.
60. Lijphart 1991, 81.
61. Graham, Miller, and Strøm 2017.
62. Anderson and Choudhry 2019.
63. See Dittrich Hallberg 2012; International IDEA 2019.
64. Rosen 2017.
65. International IDEA 2018; Krook 2006.

66. Kelly 2017.
67. On Brazil's "ghost candidates," see Douglas and Preissler Iglesias 2018.
68. Goetz 1998; Franceschet, Krook, and Piscopo 2012; Berry, Bouka, and Kamuru 2020; Clayton, Josefsson, and Wang 2014; Lake and Berry 2020.
69. Tripp and Kang 2008.
70. Chauchard 2014.
71. O'Brien and Rickne 2016.
72. Campbell and Wolbrecht 2006.
73. Jahjaga 2019. Interviewed August 16, 2019. Atifete Jahjaga served as the fourth president of the Republic of Kosovo from 2011 to 2016. She was also the first woman president of Kosovo, the first nonpartisan candidate, and the youngest woman head of state to be elected to lead a country at that time. Previously, she served as deputy director of the Kosovo police, holding the rank of general lieutenant colonel, the most senior among women officers in south-eastern Europe. In 2018, she established the Jahjaga Foundation, an initiative that focuses on achieving positive social change in Kosovo by empowering women and youth.
74. Assembly of the Republic of Kosovo 2008, Article 96.
75. Assembly of the Republic of Kosovo 2008, Article 3.
76. European Center for Minority Issues in Kosovo n.d. a.
77. Relevant international presence in Kosovo has included UNMIK (United Nations Interim Administration Mission), which from 1999 to 2008 had executive powers; the International Civilian Office (ICO) from 2008 to 2013, overseeing Kosovo's independence; and the European Union Rule of Law Mission (EULEX), which has operated in Kosovo since 2008 with the mission to strengthen rule of law.
78. Oxford Research Group 2019.
79. Assembly of the Republic of Kosovo 2008, Article 96.
80. European Center for Minority Issues in Kosovo n.d. a.
81. Selimi 2019; Balkan Insight 2018.
82. Selimi 2019; Balkan Insight 2018.
83. Semini 2019; Balkan Insight 2018.
84. National Democratic Institute 2015, 5.
85. National Democratic Institute 2015, 5.
86. National Democratic Institute 2015, 7.
87. National Democratic Institute 2015, 7.
88. National Democratic Institute 2015, 7.
89. Halili 2019.
90. Central Election Commission 2019.
91. Central Election Commission 2021.
92. Sopi 2020.
93. On Osmani, see https://president-ksgov.net/en/.
94. Assembly of the Republic of Kosovo 2015.
95. Jahjaga 2019. Interviewed August 16, 2019.
96. Bangura 2019. Interviewed remotely August 15, 2019. Zainab Hawa Bangura is an advo-cate for conflict resolution and reconciliation who served as Special Representative of the Secretary-General on Sexual Violence in Conflict from 2012 to 2017. She was Minister of Health and Sanitation (2010–2012) and Minister of Foreign Affairs and International Cooperation (2007–2010) for the Government of Sierra Leone. Bangura also served as Executive Director of the National Accountability Groups as well as Coordinator and Co-founder of the Campaign for Good Governance. Currently, she is the Director-General of the United Nations Office at Nairobi (UNON).
97. Parliament of Sierra Leone 1991.

98. Statistics Sierra Leone 2015, 9.
99. Statistics Sierra Leone 2015, 9.
100. Assadi 2013, 10.
101. Assadi 2013, 10.
102. Srivastava and Larizza 2011, 141.
103. Wall 2016, 899.
104. Schou and Huag 2005.
105. OECD 2019.
106. Kaldor and Vincent 2020.
107. Kaldor and Vincent 2020.
108. Inter-Parliamentary Union n.d. Quotas already in place include those that guarantee seats for paramount chiefs in the national parliament and those that mandate geographical or population quotas. See Dahlerup 2010.
109. UNDP 2019.
110. Peacewomen n.d.
111. Peacewomen n.d.
112. Bangura 2019. Interviewed remotely August 15, 2019.
113. Bangura 2019. Interviewed remotely August 15, 2019.
114. UNFPA Sierra Leone 2020.
115. Bangura 2019. Interviewed remotely August 15, 2019

Bibliography

Agarin, Timofey. 2019. "The Limits of Inclusion: Representation of Minority and Non-Dominant Communities in Consociational and Liberal Democracies." *International Political Science Review* 41, no. 1: 15–29. https://doi.org/10.1177/0192512119881801.

Aitken, Rob. 2007. "Cementing Divisions? An Assessment of the Impact of International Interventions and Peace-Building Policies on Ethnic Identities and Divisions." *Policy Studies* 28, no. 3: 247–267. doi: 10.1080/01442870701437568.

Anderson, Benedict. 2006. *Imagined Communities: Reflections on the Origin and Spread of Nationalism.* London: Verso.

Anderson, George, and Sujit Choudhry. 2019. "Territory and Power in Constitutional Transitions." doi: 10.31752/idea.2019.1.

Assadi, Nina. 2013. "Natural Resources and Prolonged Conflict: The Case of Sierra Leone." *Cornell International Affairs Review* 7, no. 1: 10.

Assembly of the Republic of Kosovo. 2015. "Official Gazette—Law on Gender Equality." https://gzk.rks-gov.net/ActDocumentDetail.aspx?ActID=10923.

Assembly of the Republic of Kosovo. 2008. "The Constitution of the Republic of Kosovo." https://gzk.rks-gov.net/ActDetail.aspx?ActID=3702.

Balkan Insight. 2018. "Kosovo Votes to Turn Security Force into Army." https://balkaninsight.com/2018/12/14/kosovo-votes-ksf-transformation-into-army-12-14-2018/.

Bangura, Jariatu S. 2018. "Women Push for Enactment of Gender Equality Bill & 30% Quota." *Sierra Leone Concord Times,* May 4. http://slconcordtimes.com/women-push-for-enactment-of-gender-equality-bill-30-quota/.

Bangura, Zainab Hawa. Remote interview by authors. August 15, 2019.

Barnett, Michael. 2007. "Peacebuilding: What Is in a Name." *Global Governance* 13, no. 1: 35.

Bashevkin, Sylvia. 2014. "Numerical and Policy Representation on the International Stage: Women Foreign Policy Leaders in Western Industrialised Systems." *International Political Science Review* 35, no. 4: 409–429. doi: 10.1177/0192512113516029.

Berry, Marie E., Yolande Bouka, and Marilyn Muthoni Kamuru. 2020. "Implementing Inclusion: Gender Quotas, Inequality, and Backlash in Kenya." *Politics and Gender*, online, March 5. https://doi.org/10.1017/S1743923X19000886.

Best, Rebecca H., Sarah Shair-Rosenfield, and Reed M. Wood. 2019. "Legislative Gender Diversity and the Resolution of Civil Conflict." *Political Research Quarterly* 72, no. 1: 215–228.

Bird, Karen. 2014. "Ethnic Quotas and Ethnic Representation Worldwide." *International Political Science Review* 35, no. 1: 12–26.

Birnir, Jóhanna Kristín, and David M. Waguespack. 2011. "Ethnic Inclusion and Economic Growth." *Party Politics* 17, no. 2: 243–260. doi: 10.1177/1354068810391149.

Boix, Carles, Michael Miller, and Sebastian Rosato. 2013. "A Complete Data Set of Political Regimes, 1800–2007." *Comparative Political Studies* 46, no. 12: 1523–1524.

Bop, Codou. 2001. "Women in Conflicts, Their Gains and Their Losses." In *The Aftermath: Women in Post-Conflict Transformation*, edited by Sheila Meintjes, Anu Pillay, and Meredith Turshen, 19–34. London: Zed Books.

Calfat, Natalia Nahas. 2018. "The Frailties of Lebanese Democracy: Outcomes and Limits of the Confessional Framework." *Contexto Internacional* 40, no. 2: 269–293. doi: 10.1590/s0102-8529.2018400200002.

Cammett, Melani, and Edmund Malesky. 2012. "Power Sharing in Postconflict Societies: Implications for Peace and Governance." *Journal of Conflict Resolution* 56, no. 6: 982–1016. doi: 10.1177/0022002711421593.

Campbell, David E., and Christina Wolbrecht. 2006. "See Jane Run: Women Politicians as Role Models for Adolescents." *The Journal of Politics* 68, no. 2: 233–247.

Cederman, Lars-Erik, Simon Hug, and Lutz F. Krebs. 2010. "Democratization and Civil War: Empirical Evidence." *Journal of Peace Research* 47, no. 4: 377–394.

Central Election Commission. 2021. "Elections for Assembly of Kosovo 2021." https://rezultatet2021.org/.

Central Election Commission. 2019. "Results of Snap Elections for the Parliament of the Republic of Kosovo 2019." http://www.kqz-ks.org/an/zgjedhjet-e-pergjithshme/zgjedhjet-per-kuvend-te-kosoves-2019/.

Chattopadhyay, Raghabendra, and Esther Duflo. 2004. "Women as Policy Makers: Evidence from a Randomized Policy Experiment in India." *Econometrica* 72, no. 5: 1409–1443.

Chauchard, Simon. 2014. "Can Descriptive Representation Change Beliefs About a Stigmatized Group? Evidence from Rural India." *American Political Science Review* 108, no. 2: 403–422.

Cheibub, José Antonio, Jennifer Gandhi, and James Raymond Vreeland. 2010. "Democracy and Dictatorship Revisited." *Public Choice* 143: 67–101. https://doi.org/10.1007/s11127-009-9491-2.

Chinkin, Christine, and Hilary Charlesworth. 2006. "Building Women into Peace: The International Legal Framework." *Third World Quarterly* 27, no. 5: 937–995.

Ciepley, David. 2013. "Dispersed Constituency Democracy: Deterritorializing Representation to Reduce Ethnic Conflict." *Politics and Society* 41, no. 1: 135–162.

Clayton, Amanda, Cecilia Josefsson, and Vibeke Wang. 2014. "Present Without Presence? Gender, Quotas and Debate Recognition in the Ugandan Parliament." *Representation* 50, no. 3: 379–392.

Cliffe, Sarah, and Nick Manning. 2006. "Building Institutions After Conflict: The International Peace Academy's State Building Project." World Bank. http://siteresources.worldbank.org/INTLICUS/Resources/388758-1094226297907/Building_instiutions_after_conflict.pdf.

Coppedge, Michael, John Gerring, Carl Henrik Knutsen, Staffan I. Lindberg, Jan Teorell, Vlad Ciobanu, and Lisa Gastaldi. 2019. "V-Dem Country Coding Units V9." Varieties of Democracy. https://www.v-dem.net/media/filer_public/3a/b4/3ab4f110-25c3-40b7-88c8-c600a21d91ae/v-dem_country_coding_units_v9.pdf.

Creighton, Matthew J., David Post, and Hyunjoon Park. 2016. "Ethnic Inequality in Mexican Education." *Social Forces* 94, no. 3: 1187–1220.

Dahl, Robert A. 1971. *Polyarchy*. New Haven: Yale University Press.

Dahl, Robert A. 2006. *A Preface to Democratic Theory*. Expanded ed. Chicago: University of Chicago Press.

Dahlerup, Drude. 2010. "Introducing Gender Quotas in Sierra Leone: How to Make Electoral Gender Quotas Work." Campaign for Good Governance in Sierra Leone. https://www.stats

vet.su.se/polopoly_fs/1.232192.1428917626!/menu/standard/file/gender_quotas_in_Sierra_
Lenone_Dahlerup_1_Febr_10.pdf.

Demeritt, Jacqueline H. R., and Angela D. Nichols. 2014. "Female Participation and Civil War
Relapse." *Civil Wars* 16, no. 3: 346–368. https://www.tandfonline.com/doi/abs/10.1080/13698
249.2014.966427.

Denov, Myriam, and Christine Gervais. 2007. "Negotiating (In) Security: Agency, Resistance, and
Resourcefulness Among Girls Formerly Associated with Sierra Leone's Revolutionary United
Front." *Signs: Journal of Women in Culture and Society* 32, no. 4: 885–910.

Deveaux, Monique. 2016. "Effective Deliberative Inclusion of Women in Contexts of Traditional
Political Authority." *Democratic Theory* 3, no. 2: 2–25.

Diamond, Larry. 1988. *Class, Ethnicity, and Democracy in Nigeria: The Failure of the First Republic.*
Syracuse, NY: Syracuse University Press.

Dittrich Hallberg, Johan. 2012. "PRIO Conflict Site 1989–2008: A Geo-Referenced Dataset on
Armed Conflict." *Conflict Management and Peace Science* 29, no. 2: 219–232. doi: 10.1177/
0738894211433168.

Douglas, Bruce, and Simone Preissler Iglesias. 2018. "Ghost Candidates Plague Brazil's Push for
Women in Politics." Bloomberg, July 10. https://www.bloomberg.com/news/articles/2018-07-
10/phantom-candidates-plague-brazil-s-push-for-women-in-politics.

Eisenstadt, Todd A., A. Carl LeVan, and Tofigh Maboudi. 2015. "When Talk Trumps Text: The
Democratizing Effects of Deliberation During Constitution-Making, 1974–2011." *American
Political Science Review* 109, no. 3: 592–612.

European Center for Minority Issues in Kosovo. n.d. a. "Communities in Kosovo." http://www.
ecmikosovo.org/en/Community-Profiles.

European Center for Minority Issues Kosovo. n.d. b. "Kosovo's Legal Framework." http://www.
ecmikosovo.org/en/Kosovo's-Legal-Framework.

Fish, M. Steven, and Matthew Kroenig. 2009. *The Handbook of National Legislatures: A Global
Survey.* Cambridge: Cambridge University Press.

Folke, Olle, Lenita Freidenvall, and Johanna Rickne. 2015. "Gender Quotas and Ethnic Minority
Representation: Swedish Evidence from a Longitudinal Mixed Methods Study." *Politics and
Gender* 11, no. 2: 345–381.

Franceschet, Susan, Mona Lena Krook, and Jennifer M. Piscopo. 2012. "Conceptualizing
the Impact of Gender Quotas." In *The Impact of Gender Quotas*, 3–26. New York: Oxford
University Press.

Georgetown Institute for Women, Peace, and Security. 2017. "Women from Civil Society Leading
Peace." https://giwps.georgetown.edu/wp-content/uploads/2018/03/WomenLeadingPe
ace.pdf.

Georgetown Institute for Women, Peace, and Security. 2016. "Women and Transitional Justice."
https://giwps.georgetown.edu/wp-content/uploads/2017/08/Occasional-Paper-Series-Vol
ume-II-Women-and-Transitional-Justice-July-2016.pdf.

Gerring, John, Michael Hoffman, and Dominic Zarecki. 2018. "The Diverse Effects of Diversity
on Democracy." *British Journal of Political Science* 48, no. 4: 283–314.

Gibson, James L. 2006. "The Contributions of Truth to Reconciliation: Lessons from South
Africa." *Journal of Conflict Resolution* 50, no. 3: 409–432.

Graham, Benjamin A. T., Michael K. Miller, and Kaare W. Strøm. 2017. "Safeguarding
Democracy: Powersharing and Democratic Survival." *American Political Science Review* 111,
no. 4: 686–704. doi: 10.1017/s0003055417000326.

Halili, Dafina. 2019. "Gender Inequality Is Still Pervasive in Decision-Making and Politics."
Kosovo 2.0. February 8. https://kosovotwopointzero.com/en/gender-inequality-is-still-pervas
ive-in-decision-making-and-politics/.

Hartzell, Caroline, and Mathew Hoddie. 2003. "Institutionalizing Peace: Power Sharing and Post–
Civil War Conflict Management." *American Journal of Political Science* 47, no. 2: 318–332.

Heath, Roseanna Michelle, Leslie A. Schwindt-Bayer, and Michelle M. Taylor-Robinson. 2005.
"Women on the Sidelines: Women's Representation on Committees in Latin American
Legislatures." *American Journal of Political Science* 49, no. 2: 420–436.

Horowitz, Donald L. 2014. "Ethnic Power Sharing: Three Big Problems." *Journal of Democracy* 25, no. 2: 5–20. https://www.journalofdemocracy.org/articles/ethnic-power-sharing-three-big-problems/.

Howard, Lise Morjé. 2012. "The Ethnocracy Trap." *Journal of Democracy* 23, no. 4: 155–169.

Htun, Mala. 2004. "Is Gender Like Ethnicity? The Political Representation of Identity Groups." *Perspectives on Politics* 2, no. 3: 439–458.

Hughes, Melanie M. 2011. "Intersectionality, Quotas, and Minority Women's Political Representation Worldwide." *American Political Science Review* 105, no. 3: 604–620.

Hughes, Melanie M. 2009. "Armed Conflict, International Linkages, and Women's Parliamentary Representation in Developing Nations." *Social Problems* 56, no. 1: 174–204.

Hughes, Melanie M. 2007. "Windows of Political Opportunity: Institutional Instability and Gender Inequality in the World's National Legislatures." *International Journal of Sociology* 37, no. 4: 26–51.

International IDEA. 2019. "Gender Quotas Database." www.idea.int/data-tools/data/gender-quotas/country-overview.

International IDEA. 2018. "Gender Quotas." www.idea.int/data-tools/data/gender-quotas/quotas.

Inter-Parliamentary Union. n.d.a. "Sierra Leone Parliament." Accessed February 19, 2019. http://archive.ipu.org/parline-e/reports/2281.htm.

Inter-Parliamentary Union. n.d.b. "Women In Parliaments: World Classification." Accessed February 2, 2020. http://archive.ipu.org/wmn-e/classif.htm.

Jahjaga, Atifete. Interview August 16, 2019.

Jarstad, Anna K., and Timothy D Sisk, eds. 2008. *From War to Democracy: Dilemmas of Peacebuilding.* Cambridge: Cambridge University Press.

Jung, Jai Kwan. 2012. "Power-Sharing and Democracy Promotion in Post-Civil War Peace-Building." *Democratization* 19, no. 3: 486–506.

Kaldor, Mary, and James Vincent. 2020. "Evaluation of UNDP Assistance in Conflict-Affected Countries: Case Study Sierra Leone." United Nations Development Programme. http://web.undp.org/evaluation/documents/thematic/conflict/SierraLeone.pdf.

Kaufman, Joyce P., and Kristen P. Williams. 2010. *Women and War: Gender Identity and Activism in Times of Conflict.* Sterling, VA: Kumarian Press.

Kelly, Jemima. 2017. "France Elects Record Number of Women to Parliament." Reuters, June 18. https://www.reuters.com/article/us-france-election-women/france-elects-record-number-of-women-to-parliament-idUSKBN19911E.

Kittilson, Miki Caul, and Leslie Schwindt-Bayer. 2010. "Engaging Citizens: The Role of Power-Sharing Institutions." *The Journal of Politics* 72, no. 4: 990–1002.

Krause, Jana, Werner Krause, and Piia Bränfors. 2018. "Women's Participation in Peace Negotiations and the Durability of Peace." *International Interactions* 44, no. 6: 985–1016. doi: 10.1080/03050629.2018.1492386.

Krook, Mona Lena. 2006. "Gender Quotas, Norms, and Politics." *Politics and Gender* 2, no. 1: 110–118.

Lake, Milli, and Marie E. Berry. 2020. "When Quotas Come Up Short." *Boston Review*, September 14. bostonreview.net/global-justice-gender-sexuality/marie-e-berry-milli-lake-when-quotas-come-short.

Lijphart, Arend. 1991. "Constitutional Choices for New Democracies." *Journal of Democracy* 2, no. 1: 72–84. https://muse.jhu.edu/article/225619/pdf?casa_token=mBNRwPWrLx0AAAAA:y7m93cB9cHL0K1LzK7zaKAIQimoEeqeJMtyMvKj6GVmdFVnLk85_mcbai1EV0seHZtKJWjqWNQ.

Lijphart, Arend. 1977. *Democracy in Plural Societies: A Comparative Exploration.* New Haven: Yale University Press.

Mamdani, Mahmood. 2009. *Saviors and Survivors: Darfur, Politics, and the War on Terror.* New York: Doubleday.

Matland, Richard E., and Kathleen A. Montgomery. 2003. *Women's Access to Political Power in Post-Communist Europe.* Oxford: Oxford University Press.

Meintjes, Sheila, Anu Pillay, and Meredeth Turshen, eds. 2001. *The Aftermath: Women in Post-Conflict Transformation*. New York: Zed Books.

Mickelson, Roslyn Arlin, Mokubung Nkomo, and Stephen Samuel Smith. 2001. "Education, Ethnicity, Gender, and Social Transformation in Israel and South Africa." *Comparative Education Review* 45, no. 1: 1–35. doi: 10.1086/447643.

Murray, Rainbow. 2016. "The Political Representation of Ethnic Minority Women in France." *Parliamentary Affairs* 69, no. 3: 586–602.

National Democratic Institute. 2015. "Kosovo: Overcoming Barriers to Women's Political Participation." https://www.ndi.org/Kosovo_gender_report.

O'Brien, Diana Z., and Johanna Rickne. 2016. "Gender Quotas and Women's Political Leadership." *American Political Science Review* 110, no. 1 (2016): 112–126.

O'Driscoll, Dylan. 2018. "Good Practice in Post-Conflict Reconstruction." Knowledge, Evidence and Learning for Development (K4D). UK Department for International Development. https://assets.publishing.service.gov.uk/media/5c6bdb23ed915d4a343cb9dd/494_Good_P ractice_in_Post-Conflict_Reconstruction.pdf.

OECD. 2019. "Social Institutions and Gender Index (SIGI)." https://www.genderindex.org/rank ing/?region=&order=field_sigi_cat19_value.

Oxford Research Group. 2019. "Intervention and Statebuilding in Kosovo: An Interview with Gëzim Visoka." April 30. https://www.oxfordresearchgroup.org.uk/blog/an-interview-with-gezim-visoka.

Parliament of Sierra Leone. "Constitution of Sierra Leone." 1991. http://parliament.gov.sl/dnn5/AboutUs/ConstitutionofSierraLeone.aspx.

Peacewomen. n.d. "National Action Plan: Sierra Leone." Women's International League for Peace and Freedom. https://www.peacewomen.org/nap-sierraleone.

Percival, Valerie, Esther Richards, Tammy MacLean, and Sally Theobald. 2014. "Health Systems and Gender in Post-Conflict Contexts: Building Back Better?" *Conflict and Health* 8, no. 1: 1–14. doi: 10.1186/1752-1505-8-19. https://conflictandhealth.biomedcentral.com/articles/10.1186/1752-1505-8-19.

Reilly, Ben. n.d. "Electoral Assistance and Post-Conflict Peacebuilding—What Lessons Have Been Learned?" Australian National University. http://aceproject.org/ero-en/topics/elections-security/Reilly-2505.pdf.

Reilly, Ben, and Andrew Reynolds. 2000. "Electoral Systems and Conflict in Divided Societies." In *International Conflict Resolution After the Cold War*, edited by Paul C. Stern and Daniel Druckman, 420–482. Washington, DC: National Academy Press.

Rosen, Jennifer. 2017. "Gender Quotas for Women in National Politics: A Comparative Analysis Across Development Thresholds." *Social Science Research* 66: 82–101.

Schou, A., and M. Huag. 2005. "Decentralisation in Conflict and Post-Conflict Situations." GSDRC. https://gsdrc.org/document-library/decentralisation-in-conflict-and-post-conflict-situations/.

Schramm, Madison, and Alexandra Stark. 2019. "Peacemakers or Iron Ladies? Women and International Conflict." *Security Studies* 29, no. 3: 515–548.

Selimi, Behar. 2019. "Minority Veto Rights in Kosovo's Democracy." *The Age of Human Rights Journal* 12: 148–157. doi: 10.17561/tahrj.n12.8.

Simonsen, Sven Gunnar. 2005. "Addressing Ethnic Divisions in Post-Conflict Institution-Building: Lessons from Recent Cases." *Security Dialogue* 36, no. 3: 297–318.

Simonsen, Sven Gunnar. 2004. "Ethnicising Afghanistan? Inclusion and Exclusion in Post-Bonn Institution Building." *Third World Quarterly* 25, no. 4: 707–729. doi: 10.1080/01436590410001678942.

Sopi, Arta. 2020. "Record Number of Women in Government 'Inspirational.'" Prishtina Insight. https://prishtinainsight.com/record-number-of-women-in-government-inspirational/.

Srivastava, Vivek, and Marco Larizza. 2011. "Decentralization in Postconflict Sierra Leone: The Genie Is Out of the Bottle." In *Yes Africa Can: Stories from a Dynamic Continent*, edited by Punam Chuhan-Pole and Manka Angwafo, 141–154. Washington, DC: World Bank. http://documents.worldbank.org/curated/en/304221468001788072/930107812_201408252042023/additional/634310PUB0Yes0061512B09780821387450.pdf.

Statistics Sierra Leone. 2015. "Sierra Leone Population and Housing Census: National Analytic Report." https://www.statistics.sl/images/StatisticsSL/Documents/Census/2015/2015_census_national_analytical_report.pdf.

Swiss, Liam, Kathleen M. Fallon, and Giovani Burgos. 2012. "Does Critical Mass Matter? Women's Political Representation and Child Health in Developing Countries." *Social Forces* 91, no. 2: 531–558. doi: 10.1093/sf/sos169.

Swiss, Shana. 1998. "Violence Against Women During the Liberian Civil Conflict." *JAMA* 279, no. 8: 625–629. doi: 10.1001/jama.279.8.625.

Tenret, Elise. 2016. "Exclusive Universities: Use and Misuse of Affirmative Action in Sudanese Higher Education." *Comparative Education Review* 60, no. 2: 375–402.

Tripp, Aili Mari, and Alice Kang. 2008. "The Global Impact of Quotas: On the Fast Track to Increased Female Legislative Representation." *Comparative Political Studies* 41, no. 3: 338–361.

UNDP. 2019. "UNDP'S Work with Parliaments Contributes to Sierra Leone Adoption of Resolution on Women, Peace and Security." United Nations Development Programme. https://www.sl.undp.org/content/sierraleone/en/home/presscenter/articles/undp_s-work-with-parliaments-contributes-to-sierra-leone-adoptio.html.

UNFPA Sierra Leone. 2020. "Gender Equality." https://sierraleone.unfpa.org/en/node/6135.

Vandeginste, Stef, and Chandra Lekha Sriram. 2011. "Power Sharing and Transitional Justice: A Clash of Paradigms." *Global Governance* 17: 489–505. https://www.jstor.org/stable/23104288.

Wall, Gareth J. 2016. "Decentralisation as a Post-Conflict State-Building Strategy in Northern Ireland, Sri Lanka, Sierra Leone and Rwanda." *Third World Thematics: A TWQ Journal* 1, no. 6: 898–920. doi: 10.1080/23802014.2016.1369859.

Wendt, Alexander. 1992. "Anarchy Is What States Make of It: The Social Construction of Power Politics." *International Organization* 46, no. 2: 391–425.

Wolff, Stefan. 2011. "Post-Conflict State Building: The Debate on Institutional Choice." *Third World Quarterly* 32, no. 10: 1777–1802.

Zuckerman, Elaine, and Marcia Greenberg. 2004. "The Gender Dimensions of Post-Conflict Reconstruction: An Analytical Framework for Policymakers." *Gender and Development* 12, no. 3 (2004): 70–82.

17

Closing Gaps in Access to Justice and Rights

Lisa Hilbink and Claudia Escobar Mejía

> Peace cannot exist without justice, justice cannot exist without fairness, fairness cannot exist without development, development cannot exist without democracy, democracy cannot exist without respect for the identity and worth of cultures and peoples.
>
> —Rigoberta Menchu[1]

Introduction

Access to justice is integral to the rule of law, human rights protection, and human development.[2] It refers to the ability of any person to call on justice institutions to aid in the peaceful and effective resolution of individual or collective conflicts, and to receive adequate counsel and due process when accused of legal violations. It also encompasses the ability of individuals and communities to turn to the justice system to claim legal rights—to bodily integrity, to land and water, to nondiscrimination and political participation, to education and healthcare, and beyond. It is thus both a fundamental right in and of itself and crucial to the protection of all other rights.[3] (See Box 17.1.)

Box 17.1 Access to Justice in Human Rights Conventions

The principle of access to justice and legal remedy is clearly established in:

- *The Universal Declaration of Human Rights.* Article 8 states: "Everyone has the right to an effective remedy by the competent national tribunals for acts violating the fundamental rights granted him by the constitution or by law."
- *The International Covenant on Civil and Political Rights.* Article 2, section 3a and 3b, requires states to "ensure that any person whose rights or freedoms as herein recognized are violated shall have an effective remedy, notwithstanding that the violation has been committed by persons acting in an

official capacity" and "that any person claiming such a remedy shall have his right thereto determined by competent judicial, administrative or legislative authorities . . . and to develop the possibilities of judicial remedy."

Both documents also enshrine equal protection of the law (Article 7, UDHR; Article 26, ICCPR).

- The following regional rights charters:
  - European Convention on Human Rights, Article 13
  - Charter of Fundamental Rights of the European Union, Article 47
  - American Convention on Human Rights, Article 8, paragraph 1
  - African Charter on Human and Peoples' Rights, Article 7

Yet, as of 2019, an estimated 5.1 billion people around the world are unable to resolve their conflicts and claim rights through any justice system.[4] Living or working without formal legal status or protection, unaware of their rights and options for engaging the legal system, alienated from or intimidated by law and justice institutions, and/or unable to overcome physical, linguistic, or financial barriers, enormous swaths of the global population cannot or do not claim rights or seek legal redress when faced with harms and abuses perpetrated by private or public actors.[5] Moreover, if and when they do manage to make legal claims, members of marginalized groups are often met with unresponsiveness, and sometimes hostility, from the administration of justice.[6] Rather than assert their legal agency, then, many people either resign themselves to living with injustice or may be compelled to take matters into their own hands and seek private revenge.[7]

To be sure, high levels of impunity fuel violence in many places, and unresolved conflicts and grievances have negative repercussions for the economic, social, and political well-being of individuals and communities. Human rights and justice monitoring organizations have repeatedly underscored the ways that the lack of an effective legal response to past and present violence feeds its recurrence at both the macro and micro levels.[8] The 2019 Task Force on Justice notes that those with unresolved justice problems "lose an average of one month's wages" and often suffer damage to their physical and mental health. Such issues cost OECD countries between 0.5 percent and 3 percent of their annual GDP, and more than 2 percent of GDP in low-income countries.[9] Politically, a justice gap may render people susceptible to appeals by populist authoritarians, who capitalize on their disaffection with government institutions to rise to power, and then leverage it further to weaken institutional checks in their path.[10]

Most of those facing limited access to justice today are poor people and/or members of vulnerable groups such as women, children, older people, Indigenous populations, ethnic and religious minorities, people with disabilities, those who belong to the LGBTQI community, and migrants and refugees.[11] People with low or unstable incomes, who often have limited formal education, inadequate housing, and/or poor physical and mental health, face multiple, overlapping barriers to justice. Women often face discriminatory laws and practices, as well as insufficient legal and social services to respond to intimate partner violence and other forms of sexual assault and harassment. Children, a shocking 50 percent of whom are victims of violence globally, are also "highly vulnerable to exploitation, abuse, and neglect," and require specialized justice services absent in many parts of the world.[12] Racial and ethnic minorities, disabled people, and LGBTQI people encounter discrimination and disproportionately suffer violence in both private and public spaces.[13] Indigenous people often find that justice system operators are unfamiliar with their cultural and moral values, and dismissive of their claims.[14] And migrants and refugees, dependent on courts for voicing rights claims, are extremely susceptible to abuse in a world of ascendant ethnonationalism.[15]

With these grave consequences and severe disparities in mind, we argue that closing gaps in access to justice and rights requires a three-pronged approach, grounded squarely in diversity and inclusion. The technical and elite-focused reforms that have characterized rule-of-law building programs in past decades have proven inadequate in advancing equal access to justice around the world. A new approach is needed, one that puts diversity and inclusion at the center of the endeavor, aiming not just at the incorporation of more people but in the transformation of systems.

First, at the formal institutional level, staffing, training, and incentive structures must promote cultural competency, including an understanding of systemic inequities affecting diverse and marginalized members of the community. Special attention should be given to the recruitment and appointment of more diverse personnel, such that a fuller variety of social views and experiences are represented in the justice system.

Second, mechanisms of legal empowerment (through direct or technologically facilitated outreach) must be created or enhanced to enable all persons to identify and claim rights, to secure remedies when rights are violated, and "to make effective and proactive use of law and legal processes when and as desired in the pursuit of all legitimate life objectives."[16] As a preliminary step, programs to universalize legal registration and identity are crucial.

Third, given the limitations of a narrowly legal conception of and approach to justice, alternative, non-formal, and integrated service sites for obtaining remedies and redress should be introduced, such that previously excluded and marginalized people can access justice as they understand it, and not simply legal services. To boost the legitimacy and effectiveness of these alternative fora, targeted communities should be encouraged to participate in their design and operation.

In this chapter, we discuss each of these three prongs in turn, first explaining the logic behind the recommendation and then offering examples from various countries around the world. Interspersed throughout the chapter are text boxes that provide first-person reflections by coauthor Claudia Escobar, a former magistrate of the Court of Appeals of Guatemala. All of the examples we offer are illustrative, and, in many cases their scalability and transferability remain to be determined.[17] In any case, the specific forms any access-to-justice initiatives should take will vary depending on the context.[18] The goal of this chapter, then, is not to provide a template for practitioners, but rather to suggest how reframing access to justice around diversity and inclusion will help advance the "people-centered approach to justice" that is now advocated as part of the international sustainable development agenda.[19]

The Importance of Staffing, Training, and Incentivizing Diversity and Inclusion

The conventional approach to justice sector reform—or what Stephen Golub has called the "rule of law orthodoxy"—tends "to define the legal system's problems and cures narrowly, in terms of courts, prosecutors, contracts, law reform, and other institutions and processes in which lawyers play central roles."[20] While a diversity- and inclusion-anchored approach necessarily moves the focus away from legal elites, it nonetheless begins with formal institutional rules and practices, and includes the objectives of the traditional approach: judicial independence, impartiality, and integrity. However, the pursuit of these objectives should not mean insulating the judiciary or failing to attend to its composition and how it is perceived and experienced by the public.

Choices About Appointments and Staffing Matter

To serve the rule of law, courts must function independently from the control of powerful actors, such that they are able to adjudicate cases *nic spe nic metu*—without the fear of punishment or the hope of reward—and to offer impartial and fair treatment to the parties in cases before them, regardless of who they are. Most obviously, judges cannot be handpicked by any sitting government, nor subject to threats, bribery, or other forms of unilateral influence by public or private interests.[21] The Bangalore Principles of Judicial Conduct, adopted by the Judicial Group on Strengthening Judicial Integrity, acknowledge that "judicial independence is a prerequisite to the rule of law and a fundamental guarantee of a fair trial. A judge shall therefore uphold and exemplify judicial independence in both its individual and institutional aspects." As they further emphasize, the application of this principle requires that a judge "not only *be* free from inappropriate connections" and influences "but must also *appear to a reasonable observer to be* free therefrom."[22] In this vein, and with regard to the appointment of judges, the Inter-American Court of Human Rights has stressed that "the State has the duty to guarantee an appearance of independence of the magistracy that inspires legitimacy and sufficient confidence not only to the justiciable but to the citizens in a democratic society."[23] (See Box 17.2.)

Box 17.2 Judge Claudia Escobar on Corruption and Financial Barriers to Justice in Guatemala

---

Corruption in Guatemala's judicial system is prevalent, but it disproportionately affects people with fewer resources. Cases range from petty corruption to grand corruption. Individuals with more resources are better able to navigate the justice system and get the outcome they want. Some people are charged unlawful "fees" in the justice system. In criminal cases, the bribes can be as much as several thousand dollars per case. Generally speaking, those who are able to pay will not face penalties, and those who cannot pay will be convicted. Complainants who cannot pay or do not want to pay bribes cannot pursue their case. Clearly this presents a financial barrier to justice. Furthermore, corruption is prevalent in the selection process for magistrates. Judges with relationships to the politicians are elevated to magistrate on the court of appeals or the Supreme Court— representing an egregious violation of the independence of the judiciary. This situation has been denounced by many human rights defenders and acknowledged by the UN rapporteur on judicial independence, but corrupt politicians use all their power to prevent the reform of the judicial system.

A perspective anchored in diversity and inclusion shares the goals of a fair administration of justice and the appearance thereof. However, to achieve these goals, the justice system must not be so "far removed" from the various kinds of people that it serves that judges (and other justice system personnel) might be suspected, correctly or incorrectly, of approaching cases with a built-in bias.[24] As Argentine legal scholar Roberto Gargarella has argued, the traditional understanding of impartiality that has motivated institutional design of the judiciary in liberal republics since the late eighteenth century required that judges be socially distanced from the persons whose cases they might adjudicate, and especially distanced from ordinary people, who were often deemed to have "irrational" demands and expectations. The way in which this distance was achieved was not only via the institutional insulation of the judiciary from popular influence but also, argues Gargarella, via judicial selection rules that ensured that judicial posts were occupied by people socially separate from the common people (and from their supposed irrational tendencies). In historical practice, this meant that judicial posts were reserved for wealthy, White, elite-educated men.[25] Today, an absence of social pluralism continues to characterize the judiciary in many countries.[26] It has become increasingly clear that this lack of social diversity in the judicial system is problematic. Rather than securing impartiality, a socially homogeneous justice system permits the (inescapable and often unconscious) partiality of one social sector to go unchallenged. And rather than neutrality, it projects to the public an image of potential bias, implicit or explicit.

To begin, a justice system lacking in social diversity excludes the possibility that a wide range of experiences and points of view are applied in the administration of justice. Without this range, it is less likely that the courts will be sensitive and receptive to the perspectives, needs, and concerns of different citizens.[27] This does not mean, for example, that only women (or members of other historically disfavored social groups) can understand or represent the perspectives of women (or of these other groups).[28] Nor, to continue with the example of gender, does it mean that female judges decide in a manner distinct from their male counterparts (that they speak, in Carol Gilligan's famous phrase, "in a different voice").[29] There is no solid empirical evidence to support such claims, at least not as a general matter.[30] But there *is* evidence, for example from the United States, that the presence of one (or more) women on a collegial court influences decisions on sex discrimination and harassment, and that the inclusion of one African American judge on a judicial panel affects decisions in voting rights and affirmative action cases—that is, that a more diverse group reasons and decides differently than a homogeneous one ("panel effects").[31] In addition, the incorporation of more women in the justice system as a whole influences the way in which all of its members frame and discuss gender issues.[32] A first argument for greater diversity in the judicial system, then, is that it broadens the perspectives and "check[s] the partiality" of those from the historically dominant community, adding more voices to deliberations within and across courts and cases, thereby improving the quality of justice.[33] (See Box 17.3.)

Box 17.3 Judge Claudia Escobar's Reflections on the Role of Women in Anti-Corruption Efforts in Guatemala

While I do not believe that women are inherently less corruptible than men, as outsiders to the established networks of power in Guatemala, a number of women judges and prosecutors have taken the lead in fighting against corruption and impunity. In 2010, Claudia Paz y Paz, the first woman to be elected as attorney general, investigated serious crimes committed by the army during the civil war and presented the case against former president General Efraín Ríos-Montt for the 1982–1983 genocide of the Maya-Ixil people. Paz y Paz was succeeded by another woman, Thelma Aldana, who led the fight against corruption and sent the sitting president (at the time) and his cabinet to jail. Meanwhile, in the judiciary, a group of women judges, myself included, have defended the independence of the judiciary from political interference. In 2009, we created an organization called the Judiciary Institute (Instituto de la Judicatura) that promotes transparency and efficiency in the judicial system. As a magistrate in the court of appeals, I denounced the head of Congress for influence-peddling and bribery.[34] He was found guilty and sentenced to fourteen years in prison by another woman judge.

A second and related matter is the importance of diversity to public perceptions of justice institutions. If citizens of diverse origins and backgrounds see few justice system operators who share their demographic profile (in terms of gender, class, race, ethnicity, sexual orientation, disability, etc.), they may suspect, correctly or not, that those in charge of the administration of justice don't know, don't understand, or don't consider their perspectives when interpreting and applying the law.[35] A perception that their views are not taken seriously enough can lead to low reporting rates, as has been documented in cases of violence against women and children.[36] More generally, if the judiciary projects an image of unequal composition, this could easily be interpreted by the citizenry as institutionalized inequality, putting at risk the trust and support of the public necessary to an effective judiciary.[37] As judge Brenda Hale contends, "The public should be able to feel that the courts are their courts; that their cases are being decided and the law is being made by people like them, and not by some alien beings from another planet."[38] A few recent studies in the United States lend empirical support to the idea that increased diversity in courts and other deliberative bodies boosts their perceived legitimacy and that of their decisions.[39]

What, then, are some mechanisms that might contribute to a more diverse and inclusive formal justice system? First, diversity targets can be established at the stage in which vacancies are announced, signaling that diversification is an institutional priority. One example comes from Jordan, where, beginning in 2005, the Ministry of Justice set a minimum quota of 15 percent for the admission of women aspirants to the judicial studies institute.[40] Such targets can help in advancing beyond piecemeal and token recruitment of personnel from underrepresented groups, promoting "cluster" hires, which are thought to be more sustainable.[41] Second, women and members of other underrepresented groups can be proactively recruited, helping to address the problem that such candidates, although they are well qualified, oftentimes think they don't have a chance of being selected and thus don't apply for higher positions.[42] Traditional candidates tend to have networks that offer them informal access to the workings of the system and to information regarding how to best present themselves. In addition, in many countries, there is a system (informal, of course) of the "tap on the shoulder" of a prospective candidate, which functions within established social networks. In order to even the playing field, then, what has been proposed, for example in Great Britain, is using that system to "tap on the shoulder" of underrepresented candidates. The idea is to reorient the established practice of "identify[ing], counsel[ing], encourage[ing], and persuad[ing]" highly qualified individuals so that it benefits new types of candidates.[43] What must be avoided, in any case, are methods of informal and secret recruitment among those who are already members of the metaphorical club.[44] In this vein, a 2018 International Development Law Organization report on women and justice underscores the importance of building and supporting women's law networks, allowing younger women, among other things, "to meet mentors, to access promotional and scholarship opportunities, and . . . to collectively push for reform of discriminatory laws."[45] This same logic could apply to racial, ethnic, and sexual minorities, or to those with disabilities.

These sorts of initiatives do not imply abandoning the concept of merit in judicial selection. For permanent posts, in particular, it is extremely important to name people who are highly qualified. But two points deserve emphasis. First, literature on women candidates for government office suggests that, even when by objective standards they are equally or more qualified than their male counterparts, women "may be required to demonstrate more competence and experience before being perceived as qualified enough."[46] Second, there is not a neutral way of defining merit; its definition and interpretation will always involve value and status hierarchies.[47] The criteria will always be based on the skills and qualities of the group of potential candidates, as well as on the particular activities and experiences that such candidates can demonstrate in a curriculum vitae.[48] And those who lead the selection tend to define criteria on the basis of qualities and experiences that are familiar to them and similar to their own.[49] This tendency is amplified in spaces where the selectors have a lot of discretion. Thus, in order to counteract self-replication and promote diversification in the judiciary, merit criteria need to be rethought in accordance with the experiences, skills, and characteristics that diverse candidates might have. Furthermore, there must be a transparent selection process, in which the criteria and rules are clearly and publicly articulated in advance, and selectors are trained on how to recognize implicit bias.[50] (See Box 17.4.)

Box 17.4 Judge Claudia Escobar on Anti-Corruption and the Intersection with Domestic Violence

During my experience in family court, I saw how the burden of corruption affected people who filed cases against their abuser. Corrupt employees in the court who hear evidence for cases would often illegally bribe complainants (usually women). They were also unwelcoming for victims of abuse who had to recall traumatic events to state their cases. Women with fewer resources often came without lawyers and without knowledge of how the court system works. In cases of domestic violence, I made some changes to the system in my court that helped speed up proceedings and granted protection immediately, so that women and children were protected by the law when they needed it. For other family issues, I implemented alternative resolution mechanisms as well.

Of course, the construction of a more descriptively representative justice system, staffed by people who look more like the general population, does not necessarily ensure that those people will be more in touch with and sensitive to the needs and perspectives of those they serve, or solve the problem of perception for any given office, where fully diverse staffing may be impossible to realize in practice. In addition to diversifying the ranks of different institutions in the justice system, then, closing gaps in access to justice and rights must involve equipping all justice system operators, through training and professional development, with knowledge of the social reality of those who come before the courts and the skills necessary to engage effectively with them.[51]

Using Training, Exposure, and Performance Reporting to Increase Understanding

There are different mechanisms for achieving this. One is legal aid clinics that bring aspiring lawyers and judges into direct contact with members of communities to which they might not belong. This experience can help to render legal professionals more familiar with and more sensitive to the needs and perspectives from below, as well as to give them the opportunity to develop "soft" skills, which are so important to the perception of fair treatment.[52] Another mechanism, introduced by the Canadian Judicial Council as part of judicial training in that country, is a "social context awareness program" that includes sessions on poverty, literacy, Aboriginal issues, disability, and domestic violence, among others. The goal is to ensure that judges are "aware of diverse social views and invited to be receptive to arguments from different sections of the society," with the hope that, thus, judges "may be trusted to reach a decision acceptable to the community, or, at least, to express reasons with appropriate sensitivity."[53] Some analysts caution, however, that there are often serious limits to what such programs can achieve, particularly if they are not designed with care.[54] As Daniel Brinks notes regarding access to justice initiatives for Indigenous peoples in Latin America, "Efforts to train judges to be more sensitive to cultural issues have largely failed." He attributes this to the fact that "justice systems more often than not incorporate the pathologies of their surrounding political and social systems, and it is difficult if not impossible to turn those who are second-class citizens outside the justice system, into first-class citizens inside."[55]

Moreover, training will not make a difference if the incentive structure of the institution does not reward justice system operators who show a commitment to and excel in the provision of more sensitive and inclusive justice. One possible way to move in this direction is via judicial evaluation mechanisms that invite public participation—not necessarily in the review of individual judges, but rather in global evaluations of institutional performance on specific criteria.[56] As Rottman and Tyler argue, judicial performance "might be rated highly by legal professionals but at the same time be poorly rated by the public." In particular, the public puts more emphasis than do legal professionals on procedural justice, especially on the quality of treatment (if judges listen attentively to all parties, if they treat all parties with dignity and respect, and if they are in touch with the community). Thus, judicial performance evaluation programs that encompass public input can and should include mechanisms for evaluating how judges treat the people who come before them.[57] This would permit the establishment of improvement goals in line with public expectations, and might create a dialogue between the judiciary and those it is meant to serve.

Inclusion of Diverse Populations via Legal Empowerment

Reforms that focus on legal professionals and formal justice system institutions might be called the supply side of access to justice.[58] But any approach fostering diversity and inclusion must move beyond this and prioritize legal empowerment, such that the vast sectors of people today unable to access justice develop the capability "to experience and assert the full range of their legal endowment in their everyday lives."[59] This requires viewing citizens not as "victims requiring a technical service" but rather as (potential) legal agents who can and should be empowered "to understand and use the law themselves."[60]

Empowerment means giving people "opportunities that [they] can use to make effective choices and take action."[61] An empowered actor "is able to envisage and purposely choose options" within a given opportunity structure.[62] Legal empowerment is thus defined as "a process of systemic change through which the poor and excluded become able to use the law, the legal system, and legal services to protect and advance their rights and interests as citizens and economic actors."[63] It involves training people to be able to identify (1) legal rights, (2) legal problems, (3) how to claim legal rights, and (4) how to enforce rights.[64] The objective can be summarized in the concept of "legal competence," understood in the following terms:

> The competent subject will be aware of the relation between the realization of [their] interests and the machinery of law making and administration. [They] will know how to use this machinery and when to use it. Moreover, [they] will see assertion of [their] interests through legal channels as desirable and appropriate. The legally competent person has a sense of [themselves] as a possessor of rights and [they] see the legal system as a resource for validation of those rights. [They] know when and how to seek validation.[65]

Public policies to advance access to justice must thus include programs of "[citizen] education in routes of access to the administration of justice . . . making it possible for those who have experienced violations and ask for the restoration of their rights to know where to turn and how to go about activating the judicial apparatus."[66] For example, to increase access to justice, Ushindi, a program in eastern Democratic Republic of Congo, provides medical, psychosocial, economic, and legal assistance to victims of sexual and gender-based violence; legal clinics were placed at hospitals and provided services to over sixteen thousand survivors, exceeding project goals.[67]

Before elaborating on programs for legal empowerment, it is important to emphasize the foundational importance of legal registration to closing gaps in access to justice. Indeed, giving people legal identity might be considered a first and necessary step to their legal empowerment. It is indispensable to the ability to "vote, claim entitlements, inherit property, and access financial services" (e.g., open bank accounts and take out loans), sometimes even to finding formal employment, and it allows people to be "taken into account when policymakers use national and subnational statistics to inform the design and implementation of government projects and programs."[68] According to the Task Force on Justice, in 2019 over one billion people worldwide lack legal identity.[69] This exclusion disproportionately affects girls and women, and it is an important source of discrimination against disfavored ethnic and religious minorities.[70] In some countries, there is a gender gap in birth registration, and in many more, women are less likely than men to possess legal identification. This makes laws against child marriage, for example, more difficult to enforce, and means "women cannot take advantage of economic opportunities and exercise their rights as citizens."[71] A crucial access to justice policy tool is thus "to make birth registration free, simple and available at the local level" and "to reach out to those who have previously been left out of the system, including the estimated 750 million children still under the age of 16 whose births have not been recorded."[72]

Successful programs include one conducted through mobile courts in Côte d'Ivoire, which benefited some 900,000 persons in the wake of the 2007 peace agreement, and a UNICEF program in Bangladesh that "combined birth registration with primary health and education services," equipping "health workers and teachers . . . [to] register children who came in for immunizations or primary school enrollment" and thereby increasing the percentage of legally registered children under the age of five from less than 10 percent in 2006 to 53.6 percent in 2009.[73] Government cash grant programs for the poor have been shown to incentivize registration of all births in these populations, closing the gender gap.[74] And while there has been some enthusiasm for new technologies such as biometrics for creating more integrated, universal, and secure national databases of citizen identification, rights defenders have recently raised challenges to digital identification systems, such as the National Integrated Identification Management System in Kenya, because of insufficient data protection and because of the risks of "exclusion by design" of vulnerable groups (in Kenya, of Nubians and other Muslims).[75] As one set of critics puts it, "Tech-utopian schemes don't make systemic bias disappear. They make it worse."[76] This is because "to obtain a digital ID, you need proof of your identity, something people who face discrimination often lack;" and "under the proposed scheme, the consequences of not having an ID will be even greater," as "nearly all public services—enrolling in school, accessing health care, registering for an electricity connection—would be contingent on possessing a digital ID."[77]

This is not to say that technology has no role to play in legal empowerment and access to justice. "There is vast potential in technology-based approaches to legal services, such as smart forms, mobile banking applications to pay fines, electronic case filing, and mobile alert systems that litigants in rural areas could use to confirm hearing dates prior to travel to courts in distant cities."[78] Each of these makes it less costly, in both time and resources, for citizens to engage the justice system. In Uzbekistan, UNDP, USAID, and the Supreme Court of the Republic of Uzbekistan implemented a national electronic case management system for the civil courts, known as E-SUD National E-justice System. E-SUD has two main components: a web portal giving public access to any court connected through the system, and the electronic case management system, which provides an internal virtual station for the courts. This tool has been useful for citizens and legal representatives, who can now file and get information about civil cases online. It also helps judges and clerks in the preparation of judicial documents, since it provides an enormous database of materials. By 2018, all civil courts of Uzbekistan had implemented the E-SUD system, cutting the average number of visits to civil courts from six to seven times per case to just two to three times per case, and thereby reducing the trial expenses of the parties. In addition, the E-SUD system has proved to be very useful in family cases to secure alimony for women and children with minimal difficulty.[79] (See Box 17.5.)

Box 17.5 Judge Claudia Escobar on Lack of Physical Accessibility for People with Disabilities

---

People with disabilities are often barred from accessing justice due to physical barriers. In Guatemala, court buildings are not designed for easy access. My office in the court system was on the third floor, and there was no elevator for people who could not access that floor by using the stairs. Restrooms were also not accessible to the public. As a result, I seldom witnessed a person with physical disabilities in the courtroom. These physical barriers are not just a problem in Guatemala; other countries in Latin America also have the same barriers. Technology is key to bridging this gap: it can make the justice system more accessible not only to people with disabilities who cannot come to the courtroom but also to people who live in remote locations or who face communication barriers. As technology becomes more widely used in the justice system, some of the impediments to justice for vulnerable populations may be mitigated.

Technology can also facilitate outreach to communities to provide otherwise excluded or marginalized people with "access know-how." In Sierra Leone, for example, BBC Media Action worked with local partners from 2014 to 2016 to broadcast a radio drama and discussion program, *Leh Wi Know* (Let us know), to provide women in target regions with information on human rights and gender violence.[80] Episodes were created by local journalists and delivered in local languages, which, facilitated by mobile technology, "reached 15% of adults (40% of whom were women)."[81] This is just one of many projects being carried out in developed and developing countries alike, aimed at building people's rights consciousness and their understanding of when, where, and how to seek legal remedies and solutions and/or to navigate judicial processes. Some examples include the Welfare Rights Advisers in the United Kingdom, Housing Court Navigators in New York City, and the Women's Justice Initiative in Guatemala. Some of these are administered by justice institutions, while others are led by NGOs. In many places, they involve the training of and subsequent outreach by community paralegals. A notable example is the Popular Legal Promoters program in Brazil.[82] Since 1990, civil society organizations have been training local female leaders on gender issues, legal instruments, and justice system institutions, based on the understanding that "the experience and knowledge of local female leaders can be strengthened with knowledge about the law, access to justice mechanisms and institutions (such as police stations and specialized courts)."[83] A key feature of access-to-justice programs built around legal empowerment is their proactivity in public outreach, that is, active practices in the community, so as to bring the justice system closer to the citizenry, rather than compelling the citizenry to come to the justice system.[84]

The impact of such programs appears to be significant. Reviewing "all available evidence" on 199 civil-society-led legal empowerment efforts worldwide, Goodwin and Maru find that 68 percent of these reported increases in the willingness to act or actual action among people in the targeted community, with most reporting both.[85] Seventy-three studies (37 percent) reported that interventions led to the successful acquisition of remedies, entitlements, or information for those reached by the program under evaluation. In a 2018 book, Vivek Maru and Varun Gauri provide a first-of-its-kind comparative analysis of community paralegals in six developing countries: Indonesia, Kenya, Liberia, Philippines, Sierra Leone, and South Africa. They offer quantitative and qualitative evidence to show that community paralegal services "increased people's understanding of law and government, increased their confidence to take action, and allowed them to achieve at least a partial solution to an injustice they would have otherwise had to bear."[86]

Beyond a Legal Services Model: Diverse and Inclusive Forms of Justice Provision

When considering access to justice disparities, the tendency of legal professionals is to view the issue in terms of a "crisis of unmet legal need." But as Rebecca Sandefur argues with reference to the United States civil justice crisis, this is a mischaracterization of the problem: "Justice is about just resolution, not legal services. . . . [T]here is a wider range of options. Solutions to the access-to-justice crisis require lawyers working with problem-solvers in other disciplines and with other members of the . . . public whom the justice system is meant to serve."[87] This echoes the perspective of many who work in developing countries, who contend that access to justice is a right that "concerns more than just access to courts: it concerns access to an effective remedy for a problem protected by the law." An access-to-justice policy "therefore implies the creation or strengthening of each body, state or community, centralized or decentralized, which may . . . be able to give a response, with impartiality and integrity, to the demands of people, especially to those who are the most disadvantaged."[88] This further dovetails with arguments from a legal pluralist perspective, which emphasize the need for alternatives to state justice institutions to better reflect and respond to the worldviews and logics of culturally distinct groups.[89] To this end, analysts advocate inviting "substantive participation [by previously excluded communities] in crafting the rules that will be applied to them, and in operating the system that will apply those rules."[90]

One reform initiative in this "alternatives to legal services" vein is the creation of multidimensional, multiple-entry justice centers that seek to provide people, especially those in the most vulnerable sectors, integrated services, anchored in a more horizontal approach to communication and interaction, that aim to prevent the escalation of conflicts in the community. For example, "justice houses" were developed in Colombia in the late 1990s and now number over a hundred across the country. They were designed to "remove barriers that restricted access to justice (grouping several institutions in a single building, placing justice houses in vulnerable areas)" and to "decentralize the supply of justice starting with the use of alternative methods of conflict resolution" in order to boost self-management of conflicts by citizens.[91] The first access-to-justice center in Argentina was established by the Ministry of Justice and Human Rights in the city of Buenos Aires in 2008 with the twin goals of "bringing justice services closer to the people who need them" and offering "a holistic response to justice-related problems by providing other services that people experiencing justice problems might need under the same roof." Today, ninety such centers are functioning around the country, combining legal, psychological, and social work services in creative, collective, and sustained ways.[92] Similar centers are operating in sub-Saharan Africa as well. In Uganda, for example, Justice Centers work to coordinate services with NGOs, and "evidence shows improved provision of services, better geographic outreach and fewer service gaps."[93] All such programs aim to "support alternative pathways to justice" and to "tailor services to justice needs."[94] In doing so, they invite and permit individuals to participate in the system as equal rights-bearers.

Sometimes, however, options outside the formal (state) justice system may be more effective in solving justice problems. This is because "for many groups with a distinct cultural identity," like Indigenous peoples or those of African descent in Latin America, "the goal is not to secure the same substantive notions of justice, but rather to pursue alternative ones altogether, ones that will more closely reflect their own normative framework. For indigenous groups and other communities bound by a common identity, this means not only finding ways to enhance agency within the formal system, but also expanding the reach of customary, indigenous legal systems."[95] A 2014 study by the UN Expert Mechanism on the Rights of Indigenous Peoples notes that informal justice institutions offer some advantages over state justice institutions in terms of access to justice because they "may reduce the need for travel if they are conducted in the local area, may cost less, may be less prone to corruption and discrimination and can be conducted by trusted people in a language that everyone understands and in a culturally accessible manner."[96] Generally speaking, informal justice institutions "are consent and justice oriented" and "aim at restoring social peace instead of enforcing abstract legislation."[97] For these and other reasons, they are often the preferred venue for those seeking justice in developing countries.[98] In some places, where the state justice system is absent or has broken down due to armed conflict, informal justice institutions are the only option.[99] Whether by choice or by default, then, in many countries, the vast majority of disputes are processed through customary justice forums.[100] (See Box 17.6.)

Box 17.6 Judge Claudia Escobar on Indigenous People in the Justice System in Guatemala

---

Approximately 40 percent of people in Guatemala are Indigenous, and most are settled in areas outside of the main cities. Indigenous people experience various barriers to the justice system, most notably the language barrier, but also legal formalism. The system is all-Spanish, and it is not always cognizant of Indigenous customs or traditions. Sometimes claims have to be presented in writing, with backing from a lawyer. The language barrier can be addressed through translators, which the law requires for non-Spanish-speakers. The customs can be trickier: Indigenous communities have their own ways of solving problems, and their perspective may be different from those of the traditional court system. There is certainly more than one way to solve a problem, and the legal system often fails to recognize that.

It is important neither to denigrate nor romanticize informal/customary justice institutions. They are frequently criticized for failing to adhere to international human rights standards (such as due process safeguards and prohibitions on cruel or inhumane punishments such as flogging or banishment), and they often reinforce patriarchal norms and practices that don't give women and children sufficient voice or consideration.[101] They are also "susceptible to elite capture and the quality of the justice is often dependent on the skills and moral values of the individual operator."[102] However, rather than target them for replacement by state justice institutions, which often suffer from similar flaws, an access-to-justice approach that takes seriously diversity and inclusion should seek to provide legal recognition to such informal and customary justice institutions, engage them in respectful and patient dialogue, and provide them opportunities for human rights training.[103]

In sum, in the quest to expand access to justice, it is important to remember that what people often seek are practical solutions and remedies that may not require a full-blown judicial intervention. Moreover, effective solutions should involve "full participation, decision-making and ownership by those often excluded or marginalized by the justice system," meaning a need to attend in tandem to formal and informal justice arrangements and processes.[104]

Conclusion

Expanding and equalizing access to justice is an urgent part of the development agenda. For too long, justice sector reforms in developing countries have been conceived and designed from the top down, and have focused too heavily on what goes on in or around the courtroom between the various operators of the system.[105] In this chapter, we have argued for a fresh approach to justice reform, designed to foster diversity and inclusion, and aimed at transforming justice systems to be more "of, by, and for the people."[106] This can be targeted through reforms in three main areas. First, formal justice system institutions should socially diversify their ranks, train legal professionals with an understanding of systemic inequities affecting the community they serve, and provide incentives that reward their professionals' commitment to a more sensitive and inclusive justice. Second, legal empowerment strategies should be introduced or prioritized to enable marginalized individuals to identify and claim rights, to know when, where, and how to seek legal remedies when their rights are violated, and to make proactive use of justice institutions when needed. Third, justice systems should incorporate alternative, multidimensional, and integrated forms for resolving conflicts and obtaining remedies such that individuals can access *justice*, and not simply formal legal services, in a way that better reflects the worldviews and needs of culturally distinct groups in society.

With this three-pronged approach, we aim to offer suggestions for practitioners that help close gaps in access to justice and rights. In designing specific forms and content of justice initiatives, practitioners should keep in mind three lessons that the examples we have discussed in this chapter provide. First, "situations vary from country to country, therefore there are no templates that identify generic entry points for access to justice programming. . . . The challenge is to learn from other experiences (in particular, those from developing countries that have overcome similar challenges) but also to provide customized solutions for particular situations."[107] Second, any access-to-justice initiatives should follow a horizontal approach, including targeted populations in the design, operation, and evaluation of any project. As Sepúlveda and Donald argue regarding poor communities, "People living in poverty have invaluable expertise, knowing better than anyone what barriers they face and what their justice needs are. The best legal empowerment measures . . . are bottom-up, informed by a deep and firsthand understanding of the social context."[108] Third, access-to-justice initiatives should aim at collaboration among diverse actors, including civil society movements, international organizations, and state institutions, in order to ensure coordinated and sustainable efforts to advance the "people-centered approach to justice." One model is that developed by The Hague Institute for Innovation of Law and Reos Partners to create "justice transformation labs." These labs "take a systemic, collaborative, and experimental approach to justice, combining evidence-based and stakeholder-driven approaches. These labs can be implemented at country level, in partnership with leading national stakeholders, or at sub-national or multi-local levels."[109]

Access to justice is both a fundamental right in itself and crucial to the protection of all other rights. Addressing disparities to close gaps in access to justice and rights thus requires policies that place previously excluded and marginalized sectors of society at the center of the efforts, so as to enable "development programmes to be shaped by perspectives of the people who are intended to benefit" and "make equality in law possible through . . . legal mechanisms that compensate for *de facto* inequalities."[110]

Notes

1. Rigoberta Menchu Tum is a Guatemalan political and human rights activist. In 1992, she won the Nobel Peace Prize "for her struggle for social justice and ethno-cultural reconciliation based on respect for the rights of indigenous peoples." From "Rigoberta Menchú Tum Reflects on Working Toward Peace," https://www.scu.edu/mcae/architects-of-peace/Menchu/essay.html.

2. In 2012, the UN issued its Declaration of the High-Level Meeting on the Rule of Law, which "emphasized the right of equal access to justice for all, including members of vulnerable groups, and reaffirmed the commitment of Member States to taking all necessary steps to provide fair, transparent, effective, non-discriminatory and accountable services that promote access to justice for all" (paras. 14 and 15). See UN General Assembly 2012; United Nations n.d. b. The United Nations Development Programme defines access to justice as the "ability of people from disadvantaged groups to prevent and overcome human poverty by seeking and obtaining a remedy, through the justice system, for grievances in accordance with human rights principles and standards" (Teehankee 2003). See also United Nations n.d. a. For the text of international human rights provisions on access to justice, see Box 17.1.

3. Francioni 2007.

4. Task Force on Justice 2019. These include an estimated 4.5 billion people who lack legal identity, land or housing titles, and formal work arrangements, which are the basis for protecting assets and accessing economic opportunities or public services; 1.5 billion people who face obstacles to obtaining justice for civil, administrative, or criminal justice problems; and 253 million people who are stateless, who are victims of modern slavery, or who live in states that do not provide basic security. See World Justice Project 2019a.

5. Based on survey data, the Task Force on Justice deems the most common types of justice problems to be violence and crime, land tenure problems, unresolved family problems, money issues, debts or consumer rights, access to public services, and legal issues related to work or business (2019, 15, 58–59). The World Justice Project has found that, in the face of such problems, most people do not turn to lawyers and courts: "Less than a third (29%) of people who experience a legal problem sought any form of advice to help them better understand or resolve their problem, and those who did seek assistance preferred to turn to family members or friends. Even fewer (17%) took their problem to an authority or third party to mediate or adjudicate, with most preferring to negotiate directly with the other party." See World Justice Project 2019b.

6. This is a phenomenon not restricted to developing countries. See Pleasence and Balmer 2018; Finoh and Sankofa 2019.

7. Tyler 2009; Kirk and Papachristos 2011; Marien and Hooghe 2011; Nivette 2016.

8. See, for example, Inter-American Commission on Human Rights 2015; Human Rights Watch 2017; Amnesty International 2019; Luengo-Cabrera and Butler n.d.

9. Task Force on Justice 2019, 13.

10. Mounk 2018.

11. Task Force on Justice 2019, 52–53; Sandefur 2019.

12. Task Force on Justice 2019, 52–53. According to Article 1 of the UN Convention on the Rights of the Child, "child" refers to every human being below the age of eighteen years unless, under the law applicable to the child, majority is attained earlier.

13. Jung Thapa 2015; United Nations n.d. c.

14. Sieder, Contreras, and Flores 2012.

15. IOM 2019.

16. Brinks 2009, 6.

17. This is by no means unique to such initiatives; indeed, numerous analysts have criticized the lack of assessment in orthodox rule of law programming (see, e.g., Hammergren 2007; Golub 2009b).

18. Othman 2009, 350.

19. Task Force on Justice 2019.

20. Golub 2009b, 377.

21. Unfortunately, in many countries, corruption and submission to formal or de facto powers persist in the justice system, and politicians have no interest in transforming this situation because it helps them maintain impunity. Pásara 2014, 21–22.

22. UNODC 2002, "Value 1: Independence: Principle," "Application 1.3." Our emphasis.

23. Inter-American Court of Human Rights, Case of *Reverón Trujillo v. Venezuela*. Preliminary Exception, Merits, Reparations and Costs. Judgment of June 30, 2009. Series C No. 197, paras. 147 and 148; Inter-American Court of Human Rights, Case of *Herrera Ulloa v. Costa Rica*. Preliminary Exceptions, Merits, Reparations and Costs. Judgment of July 2, 2004. Series C No. 107, para. 171.

24. Gargarella 2002.

25. Gargarella 2002, 8.

26. For example, worldwide, women constitute only 27 percent of judges, 25 percent of prosecutors, and less than 10 percent of police See IDLO 2018, 39.

27. Omatsu 1997, 1; Ifill 1997, 95; Beiner 2017.

28. Mansbridge 1999.

29. Gilligan 1982.

30. Some studies have found statistically significant differences in the way that individual male and female judges rule in sexual discrimination cases (Songer, Davis, and Haire 1994; Boyd

et al. 2010; Chew 2011; Haire and Moyer 2015) or in the decisions of Black compared to White and Hispanic judges in employment discrimination cases (Chew and Kelley 2012), but most studies find limited to no evidence of such a difference in other kinds of cases (see Schanzenbach 2005). The lack of difference is often attributed to the constraints that law itself places on all judges (limiting their interpretive discretion) as well as on social pressure for women and minorities to conform to established institutional perspectives and practices (see Hunter 2015).

31. Farhang and Wawro 2004; Peresie 2005; Boyd et al. 2010; Cox and Miles 2008; Kastellec 2013.
32. Boux 2016. For other examples of how women lawyers and judges can make a difference in the justice experience for women and girls, see IDLO 2018, 18.
33. Goodin 2008, 249 (citing Rawls 1971, 358–359); Milligan 2006, 1206; Beiner 1999, 113; Page 2008.
34. Associated Press 2016.
35. Chen 2003; Ifill 2000. See also Lambda Legal n.d.
36. Othman 2009, 361–362.
37. Carlton 2003, ix; Peffley and Hurwitz 2010; Weinberg and Nielsen 2011, 313.
38. Hale 2014. In this spirit, see OAS General Assembly Resolution 2887 of 2016, which encourages states, "in selecting judges of the Inter-American Court of Human Rights and commissioners of the Inter-American Commission on Human Rights, to nominate and elect persons that would ensure a membership that provides balance in terms of gender, representation of the different regions, population groups, and legal systems of the Hemisphere, while guaranteeing the requirements of independence, impartiality, and recognized competence in the field of human rights." AG/RES.2887 (XL VI-O/16), http://www.oas.org/en/sla/dil/docs/ag-res_2887_xlvi-o-16.pdf.
39. Scherer and Curry 2010; Badas and Stauffer 2018; Clayton, O'Brien, and Piscopo 2019.
40. IDLO 2018, 27.
41. Muñoz et al. 2017.
42. See, for example, Lawless and Fox 2005; Mohr 2014.
43. Malleson 2009, 387–389.
44. Kenney 2012, 27.
45. IDLO 2018, 36.
46. Paul and Smith 2008, 453. On this phenomenon more generally, see Biernat and Vescio 2002.
47. Malleson 2006, 391–393; Thornton 2007.
48. Malleson 2006.
49. "The propensity for 'in-group' bias by male gatekeepers, and the male-centered definition of what constitutes relevant 'legal expertise' for promotion can mean that women may be unconsciously or consciously bypassed for promotion or assumption to positions of power within the judiciary" (IDLO 2018, 36). On this phenomenon in political candidate recruitment, see Norris and Lovenduski 1995.
50. IDLO 2018, 36.
51. De Sousa Santos 2014, cap. 4.
52. Charn 2003; Tyler and Sevier 2013.
53. Turenne 2015, 13. A wide range of resources and programs used in the U.S. state judicial systems are available at National Center for State Courts n.d. There is a need for empirical studies on the effects of such programs on judicial behavior as well as on the perception of citizens affected by them, directly or indirectly.
54. See, e.g., Dobbin and Kalev 2018.
55. Brinks 2018, 7–8.
56. For US examples, see Podkopacz 2005. See also Institute for the Advancement of the American Legal System 2016.

57. Rottman and Tyler 2014, 1050.
58. Ghai and Cottrell 2009, 5.
59. Brinks 2009, 22.
60. Maru and Gauri 2018, 5, 3.
61. Maranlou 2015, 142.
62. Alsop, Bertelsen, and Holland 2006, 11.
63. UNDP 2008.
64. Maranlou 2015, 149 (citing Anderson 2003).
65. Sarat 1977, 449 (citing Carlin, Messinger, and Howard 1967, 62–63).
66. Ramos 2015.
67. Bennett et al. 2017.
68. O'Donnell 2016.
69. Task Force on Justice 2019, 12.
70. O'Donnell 2016; Maru et al. 2020.
71. Buvinic and O'Donnell 2016.
72. Sepúlveda and Donald 2015, 247.
73. Sepúlveda and Donald 2015, 247 (citing UNHCR 2013); Goodwin and Maru 2017, 172.
74. See e.g., Harbers 2020; Buvinic and O'Donnell 2016.
75. O'Donnell 2016; Eken 2010.
76. Maru et al. 2020.
77. Maru et al. 2020.
78. Vapnek, Boaz, and Turku 2016, 44.
79. USAID n.d.
80. See BBC Media Action n.d.
81. See Ahluwalia and Jackson 2017.
82. See Themis n.d., addressed briefly in De Sousa Santos 2014, 62–65.
83. Echegoyemberry et al. 2019, 192.
84. Brinks 2009, 22.
85. Goodwin and Maru 2017, 173.
86. Maru and Gauri 2018, 14.
87. Sandefur 2019, 54.
88. Ramírez, Otamendi, and Álvarez 2009, 556.
89. Brandt and Valdivia 2006.
90. Brinks 2009, 5.
91. Poder Judicial 2015, 62.
92. See NYU CIC 2019; Gobierno de Argentina n.d.
93. Lawson, Dubin, and Mwambene 2020; Dubin 2016.
94. Task Force on Justice 2019, 63.
95. Brinks 2018, 2.
96. UN Human Rights Council 2014.
97. Röder 2013.
98. See Danish Institute for Human Rights 2012.
99. Röder 2013.
100. For example, in places like Bangladesh, Burundi, Malawi, and Sierra Leone, it is estimated that over two-thirds of disputes are handled by customary justice forums. See Wojkowska 2006, 12.
101. Faúndez 2009, 107.
102. Wojkowska 2006, 6.
103. Faúndez 2009, 126–128.
104. Othman 2009, 349.

105. Golub 2009a; Task Force on Justice 2019.

106. Hilbink 2019.

107. Wojkowska 2006, 6.

108. Sepúlveda and Donald 2015, 254.

109. Bojer and Muller 2019.

110. Sudarshan 2009, 626; Ramírez, Otamendi, and Álvarez 2009, 557.

Bibliography

Ahluwalia, Kanwal, and Elanor Jackson. 2017. "How Can Media and Communication Address Violence Against Women and Girls?" *Media Action Insight Blog*, BBC. November 30. https://www.bbc.co.uk/blogs/mediaactioninsight/entries/8ac5922b-360f-4f7f-91f8-7b1148d4fd83.

Alsop, Ruth, Mette Bertelsen, and Jeremy Holland. 2006. *Empowerment in Practice: From Analysis to Implementation*. Washington, DC: World Bank.

Amnesty International. 2019. "Sri Lanka: Impunity Fuels Recurrence of Violence." May 18. https://www.amnesty.org/en/latest/news/2019/05/sri-lanka-impunity-fuels-recurrence-of-violence/.

Anderson, Michael. 2003. "Access to Justice and Legal Process: Making Legal Institutions Responsive to Poor People in LDCs." Working paper. Sussex Institute of Development Studies. https://opendocs.ids.ac.uk/opendocs/handle/20.500.12413/3969.

Associated Press. 2016. "Former Head of Guatemala's Congress Convicted of Bribery." AP News, October 28. https://apnews.com/e113408547844d5d9dcd145e21a89dbc/Former-head-of-Guatemala%27s-congress-convicted-of-bribery.

Badas, Alex, and Katelyn E. Stauffer. 2018. "Someone Like Me: Descriptive Representation and Support for Supreme Court Nominees." *Political Research Quarterly* 71, no. 1: 127–142. https://journals.sagepub.com/doi/10.1177/1065912917724006.

BBC Media Action. n.d. "Radio for Women's Rights." https://www.bbc.co.uk/mediaaction/where-we-work/africa/sierra-leone/womens-rights-radio-show.

Beiner, Theresa M. 2017. "Is There Really a Diversity Conundrum." *Wisconsin Law Review* 285, no. 2: 285–304. https://heinonline.org/HOL/LandingPage?handle=hein.journals/wlr2017&div=13&id=&page=.

Beiner, Theresa M. 1999. "What Will Diversity on the Bench Mean for Justice." *Michigan Journal of Gender and Law* 6, no. 1: 113–152. https://repository.law.umich.edu/mjgl/vol6/iss1/4/.

Bennett, Cudjoe, Manka Banda, Lior Miller, Joseph Ciza, William Clemmer, Mary Linehan, and Larry Sthreshley. 2017. "A Comprehensive Approach to Providing Services to Survivors of Sexual and Gender-Based Violence in Democratic Republic of Congo: Addressing More than Physical Trauma." *Development in Practice* 27, no. 5: 750–759. doi: 10.1080/09614524.2017.1329400.

Biernat, Monica, and Theresa K. Vescio. 2002. "She Swings, She Hits, She's Great, She's Benched: Implications of Gender-Based Shifting Standards for Judgment and Behavior." *Personality and Social Psychology Bulletin* 28, no. 1: 66–77. doi:10.1177/0146167202281006.

Bojer, Mille, and Sam Muller. 2019. "Closing the Global Justice Gap with Transformation Labs." Reos Partners. September 24. https://reospartners.com/closing-the-global-justice-gap-with-transformation-labs/.

Boux, Holly. 2016. "Sexual Assault Jurisprudence: Rape Myth Usage in State Appellate Courts." PhD dissertation, Georgetown University. https://repository.library.georgetown.edu/handle/10822/1040722.

Boyd, Christina L., et al. 2010. "Untangling the Causal Effects of Sex on Judging." *American Journal of Political Science* 54, no. 2: 389–411. https://web.law.columbia.edu/sites/default/files/microsites/law-theory-workshop/files/sex_paper.pdf.

Brandt, Hans-Jürgen, and Rocío Franco Valdivia. 2006. *Justicia Comunitaria en los Andes: Perú y Ecuador—El Tratamiento de Conflictos: Un estudio de actas en 133 comunidades indígenas y campesinas en Ecuador y Perú. Vol. I*. Lima, Perú: Instituto de Defensa Legal. https://www. academia.edu/33607402/Justicia_comunitaria_en_los_Andes_Per%C3%BA_y_Ecuador_El_ Tratamiento_de_Conflictos_Un_estudio_de_actas_en_133_comunidades.

Brinks, Daniel. 2018. "Access to What? Legal Agency and Access to Justice for Indigenous Peoples in Latin America." *Journal of Development Studies* 55, no. 3: 348–365. https://www. academia.edu/33607402/Justicia_comunitaria_en_los_Andes_Per%C3%BA_y_Ecuador_El_ Tratamiento_de_Conflictos_Un_estudio_de_actas_en_133_comunidades.

Brinks, Daniel M. 2009. "From Legal Poverty to Legal Agency: Establishing the Rule of Law in Latin America." March 1. https://repositories.lib.utexas.edu/handle/2152/22487.

Buvinic, Mayra, and Megan O'Donnell. 2016. "Identification and Gender Equality: A Two-Way Street." Center for Global Development. January 4. https://www.cgdev.org/blog/identification- gender-equality-two-way-street.

Carlin, Jerome, Sheldon L. Messinger, and Jan Howard. 1967. *Civil justice and the poor: issues for psychological research*. New York: Russell Sage Foundation, 1967. https://www.russellsage.org/ civil-justice-and-poor.

Carlton, Alfred P. Jr. 2003. *Justice in Jeopardy: Report on the American Bar Association Commission on the 21st Century Judiciary*. Chicago: American Bar Association. https://www.opensociety foundations.org/publications/justice-jeopardy-report-american-bar-assocation-commiss ion-21st-century-judiciary.

Charn, Jeanne. 2003. "Service and Learning: Reflections on Three Decades of the Lawyering Process at Harvard Law School." *Clinical Law Review* 10, no. 1: 75–114. https://heinonline.org/ HOL/LandingPage?handle=hein.journals/clinic10&div=8&id=&page=.

Chen, Edward M. 2003. "The Judiciary, Diversity, and Justice for All." *California Law Review* 91, no. 4: 1109–1124. https://lawcat.berkeley.edu/record/1118776/files/fulltext.pdf.

Chew, K. 2011. "Judges' Gender and Employment Discrimination Cases: Emerging Evidence- Based Empirical Conclusions." *Journal of Gender, Race, and Justice* 14, no. 2: 359–374. https:// scholarship.law.pitt.edu/cgi/viewcontent.cgi?article=1385&context=fac_articles.

Chew, Pat K., and Robert E. Kelley. 2012. "The Realism of Race in Judicial Decision Making: An Empirical Analysis of Plaintiffs' Race and Judges' Race." *Harvard Journal of Racial and Ethnic Justice* 28: 92–115. https://harvardblackletter.org/wp-content/uploads/sites/8/2012/11/HBK1 021.pdf.

Clayton, Amanda, Diana Z. O'Brien, and Jennifer M. Piscopo. 2018. "All Male Panels? Representation and Democratic Legitimacy." *American Journal of Political Science* 63, no. 1: 113–129. https://doi.org/10.1111/ajps.12391.

Cox, Adam B., and Thomas J. Miles. 2008. "Judging the Voting Rights Act." *Columbia Law Review* 108, no. 1. https://chicagounbound.uchicago.edu/cgi/viewcontent.cgi?article=1291&context= law_and_economics.

Danish Institute for Human Rights. 2012. "Informal Justice Systems: Charting a Course for Human Rights-based Engagement." UNDP, UNICEF, and UN Women. https://www.unwo men.org/-/media/headquarters/attachments/sections/library/publications/2013/1/infor mal-justice-systems-charting-a-course-for-human-rights-based-engagement.pdf?la= en&vs=5500.

De Sousa Santos, Boaventura. 2014. *Para Uma Revoluçao Democrática de Justiça*. Coimbra: Ediçoes Almedina.

Dobbin, Frank, and Alexandra Kalev. 2018. "Why Doesn't Diversity Training Work? The Challenge for Industry and Academia." *Anthropology Now* 10, no. 2: 48–55. https://scholar. harvard.edu/dobbin/publications/why-diversity-training-doesn%E2%80%99t-work-challe nge-industry-and-academia.

Dubin, Adam. 2016. "Innovations in Access to Justice for Africa´s Poorest: Lessons Learned, Insights Gained." Speech at Crawford School of Public Policy, Australian National University, February 10 and 11. https://1library.co/document/zx245gvq-innovations-access-justice-afr ica-poorest-lessons-learned-insights.html.

Echegoyemberry, N., S. Pilo, L. Bercovich, and M. Almela. 2019. *Empoderamiento jurídico y abogacía comunitaria en Latinoamérica: experiencias de acceso a la justicia desde la comunidad*.

Washington, DC: Namati. https://namati.org/resources/emp-juridico-abog-comunitaria-latam/.

Eken, Michele. 2010. "Kenya's Controversial Digital ID Scheme Faces Pushback." Open Society Justice Initiative. December 19. https://www.justiceinitiative.org/voices/kenyas-controversial-digital-id-scheme-faces-push-back.

Farhang, Sean, and Gregory Wawro. 2004. "Institutional Dynamics on the Us Court of Appeals: Minority Representation under Panel Decision Making." *Journal of Law, Economics, and Organization* 20, no. 2: 299–330. https://gspp.berkeley.edu/assets/uploads/research/pdf/article_5.pdf.

Faúndez, Julio. 2009. "Community, Justice Institutions, and Judicialization: Lessons from Rural Peru." In *Justice for the Poor: Perspectives on Accelerating Access*, edited by Ayesha Kadwani Dias and Gita Honwana Welch, 106–129. New York: Oxford University Press. https://link.springer.com/chapter/10.1007%2F978-1-137-10887-6_8.

Finoh, Maya, and Jasmine Sankofa. 2019. "The Legal System Has Failed Black Girls, Women, and Non-Binary Survivors of Violence." ACLU. January 28. https://www.aclu.org/blog/racial-justice/race-and-criminal-justice/legal-system-has-failed-black-girls-women-and-non.

Francioni, F. 2007. *Access to Justice as a Human Right*. New York: Oxford University Press.

Gargarella, Roberto. 2002. "Too Far Removed from the People: Access to Justice for the Poor—The Case of Latin America." Chr. Michelsen Institute Workshop, United Nations Development Programme, Oslo Governance Centre. https://gsdrc.org/document-library/too-far-removed-from-the-people-access-to-justice-for-the-poor-the-case-of-latin-america/.

Ghai, Yash, and Jill Cottrell. 2009. *Marginalized Communities and Access to Justice*. New York: Routledge.

Gobierno de Argentina. n.d. "Centros de Acceso a Justicia." https://www.argentina.gob.ar/justicia/afianzar/caj.

Gilligan, Carol. 1982. *In a Different Voice*. Cambridge, MA: Harvard University Press.

Golub, Stephen. 2009a. "Focusing on Legal Empowerment: The UNDP LEAD Project in Indonesia." In *Justice for the Poor: Perspectives on Accelerating Access*, edited by Ayesha Kadwani Dias and Gita Honwana Welch, 373–413. New York: Oxford University Press.

Golub, Stephen. 2009b. "Make Justice the Organizing Principle of the Rule of Law Field." *Hague Journal on the Rule of Law* 1, no. 1: 61–66. doi:10.1017/S187640450900061X.

Goodin, Robert E. 2008. *Innovating Democracy: Democratic Theory and Practice After the Deliberative Turn*. Oxford: Oxford University Press.

Goodwin, Laura, and Vivek Maru. 2017. "What Do We Know About Legal Empowerment? Mapping the Evidence." *Hague Journal on the Rule of Law* 9: 157–194. https://doi.org/10.1007/s40803-016-0047-5.

Haire, Susan B., and Laura P. Moyer. 2015. *Diversity Matters: Judicial Policy Making in the U.S. Courts of Appeals*. Charlottesville: University of Virginia Press.

Hale, Brenda. 2014. "Women in the Judiciary." The Fiona Woolf Lecture for the Women Lawyers' Division of the Law Society. June 27. https://www.supremecourt.uk/docs/speech-140627.pdf.

Hammergren, Linn. 2007. *Envisioning Reform: Conceptual and Practical Obstacles to Improving Judicial Performance in Latin America*. University Park: Pennsylvania State University Press.

Harbers, Imke. 2020. "Legal Identity for All? Gender Identity in the Timing of Birth Registration in Mexico." *World Development* 128: 1–11. https://ideas.repec.org/a/eee/wdevel/v128y2020ics0305750x19304279.html.

Hilbink, Lisa. 2019. "Judges, Citizens, and a Democratic Rule of Law: Building Institutional Trustworthiness to Recover Public Trust." *Latin American Legal Studies* 5: 1–36. http://lals.uai.cl/index.php/rld/article/view/50.

Human Rights Watch. 2017. "'One Day I'll Kill You': Impunity in Domestic Violence Cases in the Brazilian State of Roraima." June 21. https://www.hrw.org/report/2017/06/21/one-day-ill-kill-you/impunity-domestic-violence-cases-brazilian-state-roraima.

Hunter, Rosemary. 2015. More Than Just a Different Face? Judicial Diversity and Decision-Making, *Current Legal Problems* 68, no. 1: 119–141, https://doi.org/10.1093/clp/cuv001.

IDLO. 2018. "Women Delivering Justice: Contributions, Barriers, Pathways." International Development Law Organization, Rome. https://www.idlo.int/publications/women-delivering-justice-contributions-barriers-pathways.

Ifill, Sherrilyn A. 2000. "Racial Diversity on the Bench: Beyond Role Models and Public Confidence." *Wahington and Lee Law Review* 57, no. 2: 405–495. https://scholarlycommons.law.wlu.edu/cgi/viewcontent.cgi?article=1380&context=wlulr.

Ifill, Sherrilyn A. 1997. "Judging the Judges: Racial Diversity, Impartiality and Representation on State Trial Courts." *Boston College Law Review* 39, no. 1: 95–149. https://lawdigitalcommons.bc.edu/bclr/vol39/iss1/3/.

Institute for the Advancement of the American Legal System. 2016. "Transparent Courthouse Revisited: An Updated Blueprint for Judicial Performance Evaluation." https://iaals.du.edu/sites/default/files/documents/publications/transparent_courthouse_revisited.pdf.

Inter-American Commission on Human Rights. 2015. "Situation of Human Rights in Honduras." Organization of American States, Washington, DC. December 31. http://www.oas.org/en/iachr/reports/pdfs/Honduras-en-2015.pdf.

IOM. 2019. "Access to Justice: A Migrant's Right." International Migration Law Unit, International Organization for Migration. June. https://www.iom.int/sites/default/files/our_work/ICP/IML/iml-infonote-access-to-justice.pdf.

Jung Thapa, Saurav. 2015. "Gender-Based Violence: Lesbian and Transgender Women Face the Highest Risk but Get the Least Attention." *Voices* (blog), World Bank. https://blogs.worldbank.org/voices/gender-based-violence-lesbian-and-transgender-women-face-highest-risk-get-least-attention.

Kastellec, Jonathan P. 2013. "Racial Diversity and Judicial Influence on Appellate Courts." *American Journal of Political Science* 57, no. 1: 167–183. https://www.jstor.org/stable/23496550.

Kenney, Sally. 2012. *Gender and Justice: Why Women in the Judiciary Really Matter.* New York: Routledge.

Kirk, David S., and Mauri Matsuda. 2011. "Legal Cynicism, Collective Efficacy, and the Ecology of Arrest." *Criminology* 49, no. 2: 443–472. https://doi.org/10.1111/j.1745-9125.2011.00226.x.

Kirk, David S., and Andrew V. Papachristos. 2011. "Cultural Mechanisms and the Persistence of Neighborhood Violence." *American Journal of Sociology* 116, no. 4: 1190–1233. https://www.journals.uchicago.edu/doi/10.1086/655754.

Lambda Legal. n.d. "The Stunning Lack of Diversity on the State Court Bench." https://www.lambdalegal.org/node/42701.

Lawless, J. L., and R. L. Fox. 2005. *It Takes a Candidate: Why Women Don't Run for Office.* New York: Cambridge University Press.

Lawson, David, Adam Dubin, and Lea Mwambene. 2020. *Gender, Poverty and Access to Justice: Policy Implémentation in Sub-Saharan Africa.* New York: Routledge.

Luengo-Cabrera, Jose, and Tessa Butler. n.d. "Impunity in Mexico: A Rising Concern." Justice in Mexico. https://justiceinmexico.org/impunity-mexico-rising-concern/.

Malleson, Kate. 2009. "Diversity in the Judiciary: The Case for Positive Action." *Journal of Law and Society* 36, no. 3: 376–402. https://www.jstor.org/stable/25621979.

Malleson, Kate. 2006. "Rethinking the Merit Principle in Judicial Selection." *Journal of Law and Society* 33, no. 1: 126–140. https://www.jstor.org/stable/3557206.

Mansbridge, Jane. 1999. "Should Blacks Represent Blacks and Women Represent Women? A Contingent 'Yes.'" *Journal of Politics* 61, no. 3: 628–657. https://wappp.hks.harvard.edu/publications/should-blacks-represent-blacks-and-women-represent-women-contingent-%E2%80%9Cyes%E2%80%9D.

Maranlou, Sahar. 2015. *Access to Justice in Iran: Women, Perceptions, and Reality.* New York: Cambridge University Press.

Marien, Sofie, and Marc Hooghe. 2011. "Does Political Trust Matter? An Empirical Investigation into the Relation Between Political Trust and Support for Law Compliance." *European Journal for Political Research* 50, no. 2: 267–291. https://ejpr.onlinelibrary.wiley.com/doi/abs/10.1111/j.1475-6765.2010.01930.x.

Maru, Vivek, and Varun Gauri, eds. 2018. *Community Paralegals and the Pursuit of Justice.* New York: Cambridge University Press. https://www.cambridge.org/core/services/aop-cambri dge-core/content/view/219EB6294721B11BB25B1C8A3A2ACE29/9781107159716AR.pdf/ Community_Paralegals_and_the_Pursuit_of_Justice.pdf?event-type=FTLA.

Maru, Vivek, Laura Goodwin, Aisha Khagai, and Mustafa Mahmoud. 2020. "Digital IDs Make Systemic Bias Worse." *Wired.* February 5. https://www.wired.com/story/opinion-digital-ids-make-systemic-bias-worse/.

Milligan, Joy. 2006. "Pluralism in America: Why Judicial Diversity Improves Legal Decisions About Political Morality." *NYU Law Review* 81, no. 3: 1206–1247. https://www.nyulawreview. org/wp-content/uploads/2018/08/NYULawReview-81-3-Milligan.pdf.

Mohr, Tara Sophia. 2014. "Why Women Don't Apply for Jobs Unless They're 100% Qualified." *Harvard Business Review.* August 25. https://hbr.org/2014/08/why-women-dont-apply-for-jobs-unless-theyre-100-qualified.

Mounk, Yascha. 2018. *The People vs. Democracy: Why Our Freedom Is in Danger and How to Save It.* Cambridge, MA: Harvard University Press.

Muñoz, S. M., V. Basile, J. Gonzalez, D. Birmingham, A. Aragon, L. Jennings, and G. Gloeckner. 2017. "(Counter)narratives and Complexities: Critical Perspectives from a University Cluster Hire Focused on Diversity, Equity, and Inclusion." *Journal of Critical Thought and Praxis* 6, no. 2: 1–21. doi: 10.31274/jctp-180810-71.

National Center for State Courts. n.d. "Gender and Racial Fairness." https://www.ncsc.org/Top ics/Access-and-Fairness/Gender-and-Racial-Fairness/Resource-Guide.aspx.

New York City Housing Court. n.d. "Court Navigator Program." https://www.nycourts.gov/cou rts/nyc/housing/rap_participating.shtml.

Nivette, Amy. 2016. "Institutional Ineffectiveness, Illegitimacy, and Public Support for Vigilantism in Latin America." *Criminology* 54, no. 1: 142–175. https://onlinelibrary.wiley.com/doi/abs/ 10.1111/1745-9125.12099.

Norris, P. and J. Lovenduski. 1995. *Political Recruitment: Gender, Race, and Class in the British Parliament.* New York: Cambridge University Press.

NYU CIC. 2019. "The Argentinians Who Bring Justice to the People Who Need It Most." Medium. March 1. https://medium.com/sdg16plus/the-argentinians-who-bring-justice-to-the-people-who-need-it-most-efee671c0043.

O'Donnell, Megan. 2016. "Why Registration and ID Are Gender Equality Issues." Center for Global Development. July 11. https://www.cgdev.org/blog/why-registration-and-id-are-gen der-equality-issues.

Omatsu, Maryka. 1997. "The Fiction of Judicial Impartiality." *Canadian Journal of Women and the Law* 9, no. 1: 1–16. https://heinonline.org/HOL/LandingPage?handle=hein.journals/cajw ol9&div=8&id=&page=.

Page, Scott E. 2008. *The Difference: How the Power of Diversity Creates Better Groups, Firms, Schools, and Societies.* New ed. Princeton, NJ: Princeton University Press.

Pásara, Luis. 2014. *Una Reforma Imposible—La Justicia Latinoamericana en el banquillo. (An Impossible Reform—Latin American Justice on the stand).* Lima: Editorial PUCP.

Paul, David, and Jessi L. Smith. 2008. "Subtle Sexism? Examining Vote Preferences When Women Run Against Men for the Presidency." *Journal of Women, Politics and Policy* 29, no. 4: 451–476. https://www.tandfonline.com/doi/full/10.1080/15544770802092576.

Peffley, Mark, and Jon Hurwitz. 2010. *Justice in America: The Separate Realities of Blacks and Whites.* New York: Cambridge University Press.

Peresie, J. L. 2005. "Female Judges Matter: Gender and Collegial Decisionmaking in the Federal Appellate Courts." *Yale Law Journal* 114, no. 7: 1759–1790. https://digitalcommons.law.yale. edu/ylj/vol114/iss7/5/.

Pleasence, Pascoe, and Nigel J. Balmer. 2018. "Measuring the Accessibility and Equality of Civil Justice." *Hague Journal on the Rule of Law* 10, no. 2: 255–294. https://link.springer.com/article/ 10.1007/s40803-018-0079-0.

Poder Judicial. 2015. *Juntos Construyamos Centros de Justicia Ciudadanos.* Santiago: Poder Judicial, República de Chile.

Podkopacz, M. 2005. "Report on the Judicial Development Survey." Fourth Judicial District of the State of Minnesota. May. https://www.mncourts.gov/Documents/4/Public/Research/Judicial_ Development_Survey_%282005%29.pdf

Ramos, M. 2015. "Algunas consideraciones teóricas y prácticas sobre el acceso a la justicia." In *El acceso a la justicia en América Latina: Retos y Desafíos*, edited by H. Ahrens et al. San José, Costa Rica: Universidad para la Paz. https://namati.org/resources/el-acceso-a-la-justicia-en-america-latina-retos-y-desafios/.

Rawls, John. 1971. *A Theory of Justice*. Cambridge, MA: Harvard University Press.

Röder, Tilmann J. 2013. "Informal Justice Systems: Challenges and Perspectives." Max Planck Institute for Comparative Public Law and International Law. https://worldjusticeproject.org/ sites/default/files/informal_justice_systems_roder.pdf.

Rottman, David, and Tom Tyler. 2014. "Thinking About Judges and Judicial Performance: Perspective of the Public and Court Users." *Oñati Socio-Legal Series* 4, no. 5: 1046–1070. https://papers.ssrn.com/sol3/papers.cfm?abstract_id=2541450.

Sandefur, Rebecca L. 2019. "Access to What?" *Dædalus*, Winter. https://www.amacad.org/publ ication/access-what.

Sandefur, R. L., and T. Clarke. 2016. "Roles Beyond Lawyers: Summary, Recommendations and Research Report of an Evaluation of the New York City Court Navigators Program and Its Three Pilot Projects." American Bar Foundation, National Center for State Courts, and Public Welfare Foundation. https://papers.ssrn.com/sol3/papers.cfm?abstract_id=2949038.

Sarat, Austin. 1977. "Studying American Legal Culture: An Assessment of Survey Evidence." *Law and Society Review* 11, no. 3: 427–488. https://doi.org/10.2307/3053128.

Schanzenbach, Max. 2005. "Racial and Sex Disparities in Prison Sentences: The Effect of District-Level Judicial Demographics." *Journal of Legal Studies* 34, no. 1: 57–92. https://www.journals. uchicago.edu/doi/abs/10.1086/425597?journalCode=jls.

Scherer, Nancy, and Brett Curry. 2010. "Does Descriptive Race Representation Enhance Institutional Legitimacy? The Case of the U.S. Courts." *The Journal of Politics* 72, no. 1: 90–104. https://citeseerx.ist.psu.edu/viewdoc/download?doi=10.1.1.333.6739&rep=rep1&type=pdf.

Sepúlveda Carmona, Magdalena, and Kate Donald. 2015. "Beyond Legal Empowerment: Improving Access to Justice from the Human Rights Perspective." *The International Journal of Human Rights* 19, no. 3: 242–259. https://www.tandfonline.com/doi/abs/10.1080/13642 987.2015.1029340?journalCode=fjhr20.

Sieder, Rachel, Hebert Contreras, and Carlos Yuri Flores. 2012. *Dos Justicias: Coordinación interlegal e intercultural en Guatemala*. Guatemala City: F & G Editores.

Songer, Donald R., Sue Davis, and Susan Haire. 1994. "A Reappraisal of Diversification in the Federal Courts: Gender Effects in the Courts of Appeals." *The Journal of Politics* 56, no. 2: 435–439. https://scholarcommons.sc.edu/cgi/viewcontent.cgi?article=1063&context=poli_facpub.

Task Force on Justice. 2019. "Justice for All—The Report of the Task Force on Justice: Conference Version." Center on International Cooperation, New York. http://www.justice.sdg16.plus/.

Themis. n.d. "Promotoras legais populares." Themis: Género Justiça Direitos Humanos. http://the mis.org.br/fazemos/promotoras-legais-populares.

Teehankee, Julio C. 2003. "Background Paper on Access to Justice Indicators in the Asia-Pacific Region." La Salle Institute of Governance and United Nations Development Programme. https://www.un.org/ruleoflaw/files/Access2JusticeIndicators.pdf.

Thornton, Margaret. 2007. "Otherness on the Bench: How Merit Is Gendered." *Sydney Law Review* 29, no. 3: 391–413. https://www.researchgate.net/publication/228194393_Otherness_ on_the_Bench_How_Merit_Is_Gendered.

Turenne, Sophie ed. 2015. *Fair Reflection of Society in Judicial Systems: A Comparative Study*. New York: Springer.

Tyler, Tom. 2009. "Legitimacy and Criminal Justice: The Benefits of Self-Regulation." *Ohio State Journal of Criminal Law* 7, no. 1: 307–359. https://digitalcommons.law.yale.edu/cgi/viewcont ent.cgi?referer=&httpsredir=1&article=4026&context=fss_papers#:~:text=First%2C%20leg itimacy%20is%20important%20with,the%20case%20of%20voluntary%20cooperation.

Tyler, Tom R., and Justin Sevier. 2013. "How Do the Courts Create Popular Legitimacy? The Role of Establishing the Truth, Punishing Justly and/or Acting Through Just Procedures." *Albany Law Review* 77, no. 3: 1095–1137. https://digitalcommons.law.yale.edu/fss_papers/4991/.

UN General Assembly. 2012. "Resolution 67/1: Declaration of the High-Level Meeting of the General Assembly on the Rule of Law at the National and International Levels." A/RES/67/1. November 30. https://www.un.org/ruleoflaw/files/A-RES-67-1.pdf.

UN Human Rights Council. 2014. "Access to Justice in the Promotion and Protection of the Rights of Indigenous Peoples: Restorative Justice, Indigenous Juridical Systems and Access to Justice for Indigenous Women, Children and Youth, and Persons with Disabilities." August. https://undocs.org/A/HRC/27/65.

UNDP. 2008. "Making the Law Work for Everyone." Commission on Legal Empowerment of the Poor, United Nations Development Programme. https://www.un.org/ruleoflaw/files/Making_the_Law_Work_for_Everyone.pdf.

UNHCR. 2020. "Guatemala: UN Expert Concerned by Process to Appoint Judges." Press release, February 18. https://www.ohchr.org/EN/NewsEvents/Pages/DisplayNews.aspx?NewsID=25573&LangID=E.

UNHCR. 2013. "Birth Registration." Child Protection Issue Brief. UN High Commissioner for Refugees, Geneva. https://www.refworld.org/pdfid/523fe9214.pdf.

United Nations. n.d. a. "Sustainable Development Goal 16." https://sustainabledevelopment.un.org/sdg16.

United Nations. n.d. b. "Access to Justice." United Nations and the Rule of Law. https://www.un.org/ruleoflaw/thematic-areas/access-to-justice-and-rule-of-law-institutions/access-to-justice/.

United Nations. n.d. c. "Vulnerable People." https://www.un.org/en/letsfightracism/women.shtml.

UNODC. 2002. "The Bangalore Principles of Judicial Conduct." UN Office on Drugs and Crime. https://www.unodc.org/pdf/crime/corruption/judicial_group/Bangalore_principles.pdf.

USAID. n.d. "National electronic court information system 'E-SUD.'" [In Uzbek.] http://v3.esud.uz/#.

Vapnek, Jessica, Peter Boaz, and Helga Turku. 2016. "Improving Access to Justice in Developing and Post-Conflict Countries: Practical Examples from the Field." *Duke Forum for Law and Social Change* 8: 27–44. https://scholarship.law.duke.edu/dflsc/vol8/iss1/2/.

Weinberg, Jill D., and Laura Beth Nielsen. 2011. "Examining Empathy: Discrimination, Experience, and Judicial Decisionmaking." *Southern California Law Review* 85: 313–352. http://www.americanbarfoundation.org/publications/375.

Wiggan, J., and C. Talbot. 2006. "The Benefits of Welfare Rights Advice: A Review of the Literature." National Association of Welfare Rights Advisers, London. https://citeseerx.ist.psu.edu/viewdoc/download?doi=10.1.1.502.198&rep=rep1&type=pdf#:~:text=Literature%20suggests%20welfare%20rights%20advice,significant%20financial%20gains%20for%20clients.&text=Some%20evidence%20that%20it%20may,is%20not%20conclusive%20on%20this.

Wojkowska, Ewa. 2006. "Doing Justice: How Informal Justice Systems Can Contribute." United Nations Development Programme, Oslo. https://www.un.org/ruleoflaw/files/UNDP%20DoingJusticeEwaWojkowska130307.pdf.

Women's Justice Initiative. n.d. "Nuestros Programas." http://womens-justice.org/es/our-work/our-programs/.

World Justice Project. 2019a. "Measuring the Justice Gap." https://worldjusticeproject.org/our-work/research-and-data/access-justice/measuring-justice-gap.

World Justice Project. 2019b. "Global Insights on Access to Justice." https://worldjusticeproject.org/our-work/research-and-data/global-insights-access-justice-2019.

18

Enabling Civil Society and Social Movements

Shaazka Beyerle and Sayed Ikram Afzali

If you don't listen to the voices of those who suffered the most, then who are you negotiating for?

—Ruth Ojiambo Ochieng, Ugandan civic leader

Introduction

Civil society organizations (CSOs), informal groups, communities, and regular citizens foster social cohesion and enable inclusion through organizing, advocacy, and nonviolent action. They often also seek inclusion—civic voice, power, and participation in decision-making—to mitigate or end violent conflict, to build peace, and to improve people's lives and citizen-state relations. This chapter examines inclusion through this dual lens. It explores the role of active civil society and the impact of organized nonviolent action in mobilization toward and realization of inclusive, citizen-oriented peace and development. Further, the chapter explores the implications and recommendations for those seeking to enable work by civil society, particularly in fragile contexts. In sum, the chapter explains why attention to and inclusion of local actors and stakeholders in peacebuilding and development are essential to durable gains in societies around the world (see Box 18.1).

Box 18.1 Three Key Terms

Civil society: "The arena—outside of the family, the state, and the market—which is created by individual and collective actions, organizations and institutions to advance shared interests. This formulation includes non-governmental organizations [NGOs], private voluntary organizations, people's movements, community-based organizations, trade unions, charities, social and sports clubs, cooperatives, environmental groups, professional associations, consumer organizations, faith based organizations and the not for profit media."[1]

Civil society organizations (CSOs): The "multitude of associations around which society voluntarily organizes itself and which represent a wide range of interests and ties."[2]

Nongovernmental organizations (NGOs): A subset of CSOs at the local, national, or international level. NGOs are usually organized around specific concerns or issues, have a task orientation, and are driven by people with a common interest. They also carry out services and humanitarian activities, represent public concerns to state and non-state elites, educate people about their rights, encourage citizen engagement and nonviolent action, monitor government and non-state actor policies and practices, including those of corporations and multilateral institutions. NGOs often conduct research and provide analysis and policy recommendations.[3] While the terms "CSO" and "NGO" are frequently used interchangeably, CSOs are commonly considered to be closer to the grassroots, while NGOs are often perceived as being more technocratic, elitist, and removed from citizens.

Why Civil Society Inclusion?

Civil society inclusion is essential to conflict resolution and equitable development. Civic entities—both formal and informal—play complementary and critical roles in peacebuilding and in fostering socioeconomic advancement. CSOs can increase accountability among parties in violent conflict, which can boost peace process credibility in the eyes of the public. The direct participation of civil society groups in peace negotiations and decision-making has been found to improve the likelihood that the underlying causes of the violent conflict are addressed. Additionally, civil society inclusion in peace negotiations is linked to increased durability of peace agreements.

In 2018, the World Bank and the United Nations published the groundbreaking joint study *Pathways for Peace: Inclusive Approaches to Preventing Violent Conflict* to improve how "domestic development processes interact with security, diplomatic, justice, and human rights efforts to prevent conflicts from becoming violent." It identified civil society, including social/collective mobilization (aka "social movements"), as a central actor in the conflict and peace landscape. Box 18.1 summarizes key excerpts from the report.

Pathways for Peace pointed to the importance of civil society, including social movements, in mobilizing coalitions for action and peace, and in addressing grievances that spur and prolong violent conflict, such as inequality, exclusion, and injustice.[4] A Nordic Trust Fund-supported World Bank report similarly found that "even in fragile contexts and highly corrupt environments social organizations can be effective. Indeed, especially in these environments, grassroots movements may be essential to gaining legitimacy, building trust, and partnering with the state" (see Box 18.2).[5]

Box 18.2 How Civil Society Contributes to Conflict Prevention and Resolution, Peacebuilding and Development: Takeaways from the United Nations/World Bank Pathways for Peace Report

---

Civil society actors can promote confidence and build trust, which encourages cooperation among members of society and creates incentives for collective action. . . . This ability to build bottom-up trust gives civil society an instrumental role in forming coalitions for peace.

Civil society and community-based actors, in particular, are central to the resolution and prevention of conflict. Civic associations, such as neighborhood or community organizations, often contribute to cohesion that helps to buffer against risk of violence, especially when they build relationships across different social groups.[6]

Civil society groups also play an important role in promoting social norms that discourage violence—for example, by increasing awareness of the costs of violent conflict and showcasing opportunities that can come from engagement across rival groups.[7]

Civil society organizations play a crucial part in mediating the state-society relationship by maintaining space for dialogue and expression of dissent.[8] CSOs, in many cases, play a role in holding the state accountable, which becomes increasingly important in high-risk situations, when the space for dialogue often narrows.[9]

Civil society may directly mediate conflict, work through local peace committees, or participate in national peace processes.[10] They can also work indirectly, by helping to shift norms and behaviors to increase commitment to peace.[11]

Once violence takes hold, civil society actors can help to prevent further escalation. Over the longer term, they can help to build more responsive state institutions, contributing to sustaining peaceful pathways.[12]

In part, the success and influence of civil society may derive from the use of non-violent action. Erica Chenoweth and Maria Stephan found that from 1900 to 2014, violent struggles achieved their goals in only 27 percent of cases, while peaceful campaigns succeeded 50 percent of the time (see Figure 18.1).[13] Equally significant was the conclusion that nonviolent campaigns had a 46 percent success rate against repressive opponents, compared with only 20 percent for violent campaigns. Further, the probability of a civil war erupting within ten years of the end of the conflict was 43 percent for violent campaigns and 28 percent for nonviolent campaigns. Moreover, nonviolent action enhanced democratic outcomes and processes.[14]

The question then becomes, how does active civil society peacefully exert pressure, derive leverage, and encourage peace and development, and what are the elements of its successes?

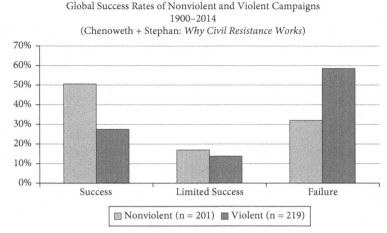

Figure 18.1 Global Success Rates of Nonviolent and Violent Campaigns, 1900–2014
Credit line: Slide courtesy of Maria Stephan, Senior Advisor to the Horizons Project (PartnersGlobal Institute and Humanity United).

Approaches to Inclusive Citizen-Driven Change, Peacebuilding, and Development

Underpinning the growing interest in citizen engagement and nonviolent action is recognition that regular people—mobilized through social movements, campaigns, and civil society entities—have power.[15] Through collective nonviolent action, citizens can assert social, economic, political, and psychological pressure on elites to overcome marginalization, solve shared problems, and push for change. Nonviolent civic initiatives have contributed to equitable development; improving public service delivery; preventing or rectifying graft and mismanagement; pressuring elites for policy, fiscal, and legislative changes; supporting honest officials and democratic state institutions; and shifting policies around global financial corruption.[16]

People power can bring a strategic advantage by adding extra-institutional pressure to push for change when state and non-state power-holders are indifferent to people's problems and demands, beholden to special interests, and corrupt and/or unaccountable, or when institutional channels are weak, blocked, or ineffective.[17] Contemporary movements such as Black Lives Matter for racial justice and #MeToo against sexual harassment and gender-based violence are reverberating around the world, pushing to change systems of exclusion and abuse.

In part, the success and power of nonviolent action may lie in its potential to advance inclusion. Active civil society—including social movements, community-led civic initiatives, and engaged citizens at the micro or macro levels—is associated with at least four forms of inclusion:

1. *Practicing inclusion.* Research indicates that nonviolent action has a tendency "to create large, inclusive, and diverse movements composed of broad segments of society."[18] This is primarily due to the nature of social movements and community-based initiatives, which are built upon three elements: shared grievances and goals; voluntary participation; and unity among a variety of formal and informal civil society entities, citizens, and even state actors and international supporters.

2. *Cultivating inclusion.* Social movements and CSOs connected to the grassroots foster a sense of collective responsibility to tackle problems, collective ownership of the civic effort, and collective identity among participants. While intangible, these feelings can motivate inclusive behavior by fostering commitment, cooperation, and coordination, helping overcome fear and apathy, and encouraging participation.[19] As well, nonviolent action initiatives can often help to spread norms and skills related to inclusion and peaceful dispute resolution, which are essential to cultivating cooperative relations both between citizens and between citizens and the state in fragile and post-violent-conflict settings.

3. *Advancing inclusion.* People-power initiatives can give voice to groups and citizens who are socially and economically marginalized or excluded from governance and decision-making affecting their lives, including during peace negotiations and post-conflict rehabilitation and development. This includes supporting local ownership of development initiatives and citizen-state engagement, which in turn contributes to restoring the social contract. Box 18.3 summarizes findings from the Secure Livelihoods Research Consortium, a multiyear research initiative on state-building, public services, and livelihood recovery in fragile situations and settings of violent conflict.

4. *Legitimizing through inclusion.* Local ownership of development, peacebuilding, and anti-corruption initiatives adds legitimacy to shared citizen grievances and demands that can be critical to overcoming obstacles and resistance from state and non-state elites and mitigating pushback or repression. (See Box 18.3.)[20]

How does civic action play out on the ground to promote stability, improve governance, and foster inclusion? The next section presents cases where CSOs and local nonviolent action contributed to conflict transformation and development.

Box 18.3 Findings from the Secure Livelihoods Research Consortium (SLRC), 2011–2016

The SLRC conducted quantitative and qualitative research across eight countries that experienced fragility and violent conflict (Afghanistan, Democratic Republic of the Congo, Nepal, Pakistan, Sierra Leone, South Sudan, Sri Lanka, and Uganda). Among the findings were that citizens' perceptions of and attitudes regarding the state, particularly at the local level, improve through inclusion and engagement—that is, when they are consulted, when they feel heard, and, most critically, when they directly participate in development and state-building activities. The authors conclude that "it is as important to concentrate on how services are delivered—meaning whether people are consulted about service delivery or participate in decision-making, whether accountability mechanisms exist, whether people view the processes as fair—as on what is delivered."[21] In other words, in contexts affected by violent conflict, citizen participation in the development process and elite engagement with local organizations and community-based initiatives are essential for durable progress.

Highlights from Around the World

Civil Society Action for Civilian Protection

Communities in many parts of the world have engaged in extraordinary unarmed resistance to protect themselves. In places such as Mexico and Colombia they have established zones of peace during war.[22] Nonviolent intervention has also been used to contribute to peacekeeping, peacemaking, and peacebuilding. Trained, unarmed civilian peacekeeping forces provide protection, create safe spaces for dialogue among conflict parties and even communities, and provide a link between local peace workers and the international community. Nonviolent Peaceforce and Peace Brigades International have engaged in these ways.[23]

Nonviolent Mobilization for Peacebuilding: Sub-Saharan Africa

Women's leadership and participation in peace processes and conflict resolution have been found to be "instrumental in shifting toward peaceful pathways in many countries."[24] But when women and civil society are excluded from these processes, they often engage in nonviolent action to be heard. Through active CSOs, women-led campaigns have pushed warring parties to negotiate and agree to accords, include the voices and demands of women, monitor peacebuilding and recovery efforts, and support democratic transitions. Chapter 3 of this volume highlights the 2003 Women of Liberia Mass Action for Peace movement, in which Christian and Muslim women forged ties and engaged in creative nonviolent resistance to end a horrific civil war and usher in democracy after over two decades of brutal dictatorships.

In neighboring Sierra Leone, which endured nearly three decades of military dictatorship and an equally brutal civil war, civic leader Zainab Hauwa Bangura founded WOMEN (Women Organised for a Morally Enlightened Nation) in 1994, which rallied marginalized market women, religious and traditional leaders, women's groups, and other civil society entities (including professional organizations, labor unions, and teachers' unions), and later the nation at large, through a general strike to pressure the regime for democratic elections. Subsequently, she created the Campaign for Good Governance to consolidate democratic governance, foster peacebuilding and reconciliation, address human rights violations and corruption, and advance women's empowerment.[25]

Nonviolent action campaigns were also instrumental in bringing the concerns and priorities of women and children into Somali peace negotiations. In 2000, at the first Somali peace and reconciliation conference, women were excluded because only representatives of the five warring clans (all men) were included. Asha Haja Elmi, a civic leader and cofounder of Save Somali Women and Children, a cross-clan network, launched a campaign combining tactics of protest and dialogue. Consequently, women participated in the deliberations as the "sixth clan," resulting in the transitional national government and a quota for women's representation in the parliament. They also put forward an extensive set of community concerns, thereby "broadening the conception of what it means to build peace beyond the mere brokering of power."[26]

More recently, in 2006 during the Juba negotiations between the Ugandan government and the Lord's Resistance Army (LRA) armed group, the Ugandan Women's Coalition for Peacebuilding refused to give up when women affected by the conflict were excluded from the talks.[27] Through their contacts with community-based organizations, volunteers in the conflict area videotaped more than two thousand women describing their experiences and demands relating to the negotiation agenda. In conjunction with other innovative nonviolent tactics and engagement with the United Nations Development Fund for Women (UNIFEM), they pressured those involved in the talks to view the video. The video functioned as a form of mass mobilization and became an essential tool for incorporating women's psychosocial and economic concerns into the agreement. Though the LRA backed out of the deal, women's demands were integrated into the Uganda Government Framework on Peace and Recovery Development Plan. The women's coalition subsequently launched a new monitoring campaign, again driven by volunteers, to track its implementation, include local women's priorities for local projects, and rectify problems at the grassroots. Work continues to the present.[28]

Local Mobilization for State-Building and Anti-Corruption: Afghanistan

Despite more than two decades of international military intervention and support for state-building, Afghanistan suffers from fragility, violent conflict, and corruption. International tolerance of corruption has fundamentally undermined reconstruction efforts in Afghanistan. Between 2002 and 2019, the United States alone spent almost $133 billion for reconstruction.[29] According to former United States ambassador Ryan Crocker, "the ultimate point of failure for our efforts . . . wasn't an insurgency."[30] Rather, it was the "weight of endemic corruption" that prolonged the war in Afghanistan and prevented the reconstruction of a stable state.[31] Capture of institutions by corrupt political elites resulted in their being used for the elites' personal and group interests to the detriment of ordinary citizens. Regular people suffered immensely due to graft in the justice, security, and service delivery institutions. According to a recent survey, a large majority of Afghans have been negatively affected by corruption; as a result, three-quarters of respondents did not trust public services, government, and development actors, including donors and non-governmental organizations.[32] Disregard of corruption on the part of national and international elites and the general exclusion of citizens from the state-building process resulted in state failure to deliver on the social contract. This, in turn, increased the gap between the citizens and the state, creating a trust deficit that insurgents, terrorists, and criminal networks have exploited to weaken successive governments and to capture territory and state institutions. Even prior to the withdrawal of American troops from the country, the catastrophic collapse of the Afghan government and Taliban takeover in August 2020, the latter already controlled large swathes of territory in many instances were overseeing service delivery (primarily in health and education). They have been using the citizen-state void to present themselves as so-called protectors of the public interest—a de facto alternative to the corrupt state.

Community-based monitoring (CBM) is an initiative pioneered by Integrity Watch Afghanistan, an Afghan civil society organization. It promotes integrity in public services (including infrastructure, education, health, justice, and extractives) by involving citizens and communities in monitoring service providers and holding the government accountable. The program started in 2007 in direct response to growing public complaints about the low quality of aid projects funded by international donors. Since then, more than 1,300 community-level projects, such as schools, health clinics, irrigation systems, and roads, have been monitored by communities. This process involves engaging with elites such as local officials, contractors, and sometimes even international actors to disrupt the status quo, in which citizens are excluded from the process and corruption is rife.[33]

CBM starts with Integrity Watch mobilizing local communities to select and monitor construction projects in their area through community-led surveys and the election of volunteer representatives. These monitors receive training on the basics of construction projects (such as simple testing of construction materials and checking the quality of masonry work) and social skills (for example, communication, advocacy, and power mapping at the local and provincial levels). Monitors visit the projects each week, provide feedback to the contractors, report back to their communities in open forums, and provide monitoring data to Integrity Watch. In addition, community outreach events are organized to inform the community of their rights, including access to information. These steps allow the entire community to be included in the process and to take action when needed. The majority of problems have been resolved at the local level. But when contractors are not responsive, community representatives raise their concerns with provincial officials and other stakeholders, including donors, through sectoral monitoring groups that have been established and coordinated by Integrity Watch. These groups are groundbreaking in that they bring together formerly marginalized locals with state officials, donor representatives, and contractors to actively address and resolve problems based on citizen-derived documentation. In some instances, community members increased pressure through such nonviolent tactics as petitions, letter-writing, and on occasion sit-ins. Overall, the model bolsters collective problem-solving and helps mend the social fabric in traumatized contexts.

The initial aim of the CBM model was to improve the quality of construction projects and aid effectiveness. A randomized control trial carried out by researchers at the University of California, San Diego concluded:

> Our experiment spans five Afghan provinces and four years of road quality measurement using our own trained technical teams. We find that trained monitors cause dramatic improvements in road quality, producing roads that are better able to endure difficult Afghan winters. Our two-level randomization design shows these effects are not concentrated near trained villages, but spill over to the entire road.[34]

As of September 2019, the CBM model had improved the quality of 1,266 construction projects by resolving 78 percent of the problems identified; it also enabled citizens' inclusion in the governance and development process. The CBM model has helped citizens become active agents and partners in development, rather than voiceless and passive receivers of aid. Thus, the model has helped transform power relations. On the one hand, regular people, who were once seen as mere beneficiaries, are becoming protagonists and rights holders making claims on the state. On the other hand, government officials accustomed to being in the driver's seat without any accountability are starting to earn legitimacy through responsiveness to the demands of citizens. In fact, the CBM model is helping restore citizen trust in the state through engagement and collaboration for improved public services and corruption prevention.

CBM has been expanded to education (local schools) and justice (courtrooms), and a spin-off initiative is building youth participation; 151 women and 381 men have been elected as monitors in these sectors (it is less common for women to serve as construction monitors). Thus far, 479 schools have been monitored and 60 percent of the identified problems have been addressed.

The CBM initiative has also had a broader impact on social accountability. After facing hurdles accessing information about construction projects in the early years due to the lack of a legal framework, Integrity Watch successfully advocated with other CSOs and the media for what is today Afghanistan's Access to Information Law, considered to be the best in the world according to the Centre for Law and Democracy.[35] In turn, discussions of law and advocacy have permeated public discourse; citizens, including journalists, are now asking for information on a wide range of issues such as corruption, management of state resources, and government decision-makings. CBM has helped create a virtuous accountability circle, and it is providing a mechanism for citizen engagement and inclusion in many different sectors on a wide range of issues.

Through CBM, Integrity Watch Afghanistan is wielding power, amplifying citizen voices, practicing inclusion on the ground, countering social marginalization, collectively solving problems, and engaging with elites. Just as important are the intangible outcomes: community resilience and positive citizen-state relations are being nurtured, all of which are essential for a renewed social contract. While Afghanistan's future trajectory is uncertain, what is clear is that the knowledge, capacities, citizen agency and grassroots problem-solving engendered by Integrity Watch Afghanistan's community-based monitoring (CBM) have not vanished and the lessons remain highly pertinent. In late 2021 efforts are underway to continue CBM initiatives, initially for the delivery of public health services in the midst of the Covid-19 pandemic crisis.

Lessons and Recommendations

Building an active, resilient civil society and advancing inclusive development go hand in hand with efforts to foster enhanced citizen-state engagement and rule of law. How can the international community reinforce these interlinked goals? We conclude with six recommendations.

Adopt a Systems Approach

Fragility, violent conflict, and corruption are interactive and can have direct and indirect relationships and outcomes. Rather than address them separately, a systems approach is necessary to understand relationships, interactions, and possibilities for change.[36] Conflict transformation and development actors should consider how their policies and practices function and interact with positive and negative factors within a given fragile or violent-conflict-affected context.[37] In contrast to tactical interventions devoid of context and designed or driven by external actors, approaches built upon systems analysis integrate top-down (elite-driven) and bottom-up (civil society) strategies in a more holistic manner. Implicit in this approach is recognition that change is a process involving multiple strategies, actors, and incremental gains (see Box 18.4).

Box 18.4 What Is Systems Thinking?

Based on a definition by Danny Burns, systems are complex webs of relationships between people, processes, state and non-state entities, and the context in which they are situated. The focus is on understanding the relationships between or among actors and actions within a system and how they impact each other.[38]

Understand Power Dynamics

When mapping power relations and shifts in a given context, international peacebuilders and development practitioners should take into consideration informal as well as formal power systems. While formal systems may exist on paper, they may be weak and corrupt. Hence, in the short term, they may not provide reliable institutional channels for reform, justice, and change. There are often parallel informal systems, including but not limited to people power, that are also important in post-violent-conflict and other fragile contexts.

Promote Inclusion Through Unity Between National and Subnational Civil Society Groups

Civil society is stronger, more effective, and more inclusive when formal organizations are directly or indirectly connected to the grassroots, including social movements and community-based groups. International peacebuilding and development practitioners can enable such connections by supporting opportunities for dialogue, coalition-building, strategizing, cooperation, and even joint action. National CSOs can mobilize citizens, partner with grassroots groups, or serve as strategic allies for local initiatives. Such collaboration is essential for promoting effective, durable development, particularly in fragile contexts where the state may be weak and/or corrupt. The Ugandan Women's Coalition for Peacebuilding and UN regional officials played such roles during negotiations with the Lord's Resistance Army. In 2014, Integrity Watch was part of a national civil society effort pushing for the enactment of the improved Access to Information Law, and subsequent campaigns by the Oversight Commission on Access to Information. The impact is visible on the ground: before the legislation, community access to information in Integrity Watch's CBM infrastructure initiative was 80 percent, and currently it is 98 percent.

Support Local Empowerment and Community-Based Civic Initiatives

Meaningful inclusion involves fostering an enabling environment for civil society and social movements to play an active role in conflict resolution, development, and responsive, democratic governments. More generally, this consists of encouraging platforms "for inclusion, participation, and voice to citizens and involving them directly in the provision of services can significantly improve citizens' perceptions of the state."[39] International actors can contribute by investing in local groups that foster citizen agency. The Listening Project, a six-year initiative gathering six thousand views in twenty societies about international assistance (including humanitarian programs, development, peacebuilding, human rights, and environmental issues) found that respondents wanted more ownership and opportunities to play an active role in their own development. "When a community is not engaged," said an Afghan aid worker, "the problem is more than just lack of sustainability. These projects are more easily destroyed by violence."[40]

External actors can also directly or indirectly bolster capacities and confidence, provide technical training and expertise, broker engagement and dialogue with elites, access information, and integrate civil society expertise into policies and implementation. In Afghanistan, access to information in conjunction with nonviolent action and engagement with elites has proved to be a powerful combination. Monitors interviewed in the aforementioned University of California study affirmed that Integrity Watch's intervention made it possible to gain access to project contracts, allowing them to compare the specifications with actual work. It also found that "the [CBM] program was effective due to the combination of the technical training and the newly created channels of accountability, helping to reconcile mixed findings in past literature where programs often provided only one of these."[41]

Civil society and international actors can specifically help foster an enabling environment for social movements and community-based initiatives through building community-organizing skills, synergizing nonviolent action and peacebuilding, fostering peer-to-peer exchanges within a country/territory or across borders, increasing media exposure, and offering solidarity. Finally, flexible financial support to pilot, sustain, and expand community-led efforts can be useful in some contexts. Short-term projects are not conducive to sustainable outcomes at the community level. For instance, Integrity Watch was able to initially test the CBM model thanks to core support from Making Integrity Work (TIRI) and the Norwegian Agency for Development Cooperation (NORAD). Later, core support from the Swedish International Development Agency was crucial for the program to organically scale up the number of communities and to add new sectors.

Take a Back Seat to Locally Led Initiatives

Inclusion of citizen voices and demands in peacebuilding, reconstruction, and development is advanced when grassroots initiatives are strongly community-led and community-driven. A Civicus/Open Forum for CSO Development study found that across numerous countries and different contexts, CSOs reported that donors do not pay enough attention to local priorities and systems.[42] Rather than occupying the driver's seat, international actors should build on such organic structures and bottom-up solutions.[43] Community-based monitoring draws upon the resources and opportunities within locales rather than marshaling outside means, which are often very costly, such as renumerated third-party monitoring by professional engineers. Like other forms of nonviolent action, CBM relies largely on volunteers instead of paid staff. Research shows that non-monetary "social incentives" such as recognition can more effectively encourage behaviors benefitting the community as a whole.[44] In addition, the CBM model has emphasized the inclusion of the larger community instead of engaging with individual citizens. Research has also found that social networks can influence individual behavior. Therefore, programs channeled through communities are more effective than those that target individuals.[45] This form of inclusion is effective in reducing cost and influencing behaviors for resilience and social change in fragile contexts.

Include Civil Society and Social Movement Voices in the Policy Arena

It's essential that formal civil society organizations genuinely elevate social movements and local voices at the national policymaking level. Not only do grassroots perspectives and proposed solutions matter, but they can bring a collective source of legitimacy and power to the policy sphere. For example, Integrity Watch has launched "Integrity Dialogues," covering local municipalities and education, health, and justice sectors; these dialogues bring citizens and civil society organizations together with officials to address problems and make improvements through citizen engagement.[46] Just as important, civil society and social movement actors should be included in peacebuilding and development negotiations, as well as in policymaking forums and mechanisms at the international level. For example, as part of its vision for an inclusive approach to peacebuilding, the United States Institute of Peace (USIP) launched the Youth Advisory Council. It "enables USIP staff to engage youth as partners, experts, and practitioners while elevating youth voices and experience to the international level."[47]

Conclusion

Inclusion through an active civil society facilitated by nonviolent civic initiatives, campaigns, and social movements can help bridge the gap between citizens and the state and can improve trust in fragile contexts. Experience from around the world demonstrates that community engagement can take various forms, which can transform conflict, improve stability, and contribute to good governance, development, and human rights. Peacebuilding, governance, and development initiatives can only achieve progress in tandem; international practitioners should take into consideration the role that grassroots civic initiatives can play and provide an enabling environment for active civil society capacity development and efficacy, particularly in fragile contexts.

Notes

1. Mati, Silva, and Anderson 2010.
2. Atwood 2012, 7.
3. See the website of the Civil Society Unit, United Nations, https://outreach.un.org/ngorelati ons/content/about-us-0, accessed November 15, 2019.
4. World Bank and United Nations 2018.
5. Beyerle et al. 2017, ix.
6. Aslam 2017; Varshney 2002.
7. Barnes 2009.
8. Marc et al. 2012.
9. Chenoweth and Stephan 2011.
10. Nilsson 2012, 258; Wanis-St. John and Kew 2008.
11. Barnes 2009.
12. Dahl, Gates, and Nygård 2017.
13. Chenoweth and Stephan 2011. New data extending the research to 2014 was provided to the authors by Dr. Stephan.
14. Pinckney 2018.
15. *Citizen engagement* refers to two-way interactions between people and elites (both state and non-state) in which the people can provide input and influence decisions affecting socioeconomic development, peace processes, governance, accountability, land/resources management, etc. *Nonviolent action* is "a way for ordinary people to exert power collectively without the threat or use of violence" to challenge oppression and injustice, and gain social, political and economic change. It involves strategizing, planning, organization, communications, and tactical selection and sequencing. Interchangeable terms are people power, nonviolent resistance, and civil resistance. While it is an extra-institutional phenomenon, it is often combined with the strategic use of institutional tools and mechanisms. See Bloch and Schirch 2019, 8. *Social movements* are "fluid groups of people, organizations, coalitions and networks that use nonviolent collective action to advance change-oriented goals" and involve some degree of organizing and unity-building. They can include multiple campaigns, sometimes conducted at the same time or sequentially. See Bloch and Schirch 2019, 19; Stephan, Lakhani, and Naviwala 2015. *Campaigns* are planned civic initiatives involving sequenced nonviolent action tactics to gain change-oriented goals. Campaigns usually have an identifiable

beginning, middle, and end. See Bloch and Schirch 2019, 19. On social movements generally, see Bhonagiri 2016; Karbowska and Chen 2018; Lemma 2018; Masters and Osborn 2010; World Bank 2017.

16. See Ackerman and Beyerle 2014; Beyerle 2014; Beyerle et al. 2017; Beyerle and O'Regan 2019; Coelho and von Lieres 2010; Dey 2019; Fox 2015; Fox and Aceron 2016; Gaventa and Gregory 2010; Halloran and Flores 2015.
17. Beyerle 2014.
18. Bethke and Pinckney 2019, 7.
19. Beyerle 2014.
20. Beyerle 2014.
21. Sturge et al. 2017, ix.
22. Kaplan 2017.
23. See the websites for these two organizations at https://www.nonviolentpeaceforce.org/ and https://www.peacebrigades.org/.
24. UN Women 2015, 116.
25. World Movement for Democracy n.d.; Zainab Hauwa Bangura personal communication to Shaazka Beyerle, October 2004 and October 2019.
26. George-Williams 2006, 94.
27. The Ugandan Women's Coalition for Peacebuilding consists of approximately twenty-one national civil society organizations, which in turn are connected to community-based organizations with close ties to locals.
28. Ruth Ojiambo Ochieng interview by Shaazka Beyerle, August 29–30, 2019, Washington, DC.
29. SIGAR 2019, 41.
30. SIGAR 2016, 10.
31. SIGAR 2016, 10.
32. McDevit and Adib 2018, 3.
33. Beyerle 2014.
34. Berman et al. 2017, 1.
35. FreedomInfo 2014; Centre for Law and Democracy n.d.
36. Grady et al. 2017.
37. Burns 2014.
38. Burns 2014, 1.
39. World Bank and United Nations 2018, 160.
40. Anderson, Brown, and Jean 2012, 128.
41. Berman et al. 2017, 1.
42. Poskitt and Dufranc 2011.
43. Beyerle et al. 2017.
44. World Bank 2015, 51–55.
45. World Bank 2015.
46. Ehsany 2019.
47. United States Institute of Peace website, accessed September 1, 2019, https://www.usip.org/programs/youth-advisory-council.

Bibliography

Ackerman, Peter, and Shaazka Beyerle. 2014. "Lessons from Civil Resistance for the Battle Against Financial Corruption." *Diogenes* 61, nos. 3–4: 82–96.
Anderson, Mary, Dayna Brown, and Isabella Jean. 2012. *Time to Listen: Hearing People on the Receiving End of International Aid*. Cambridge, MA: CDA Collaborative Learning Projects.

Aslam, Ghazhia. 2017. "Civic Associations and Conflict Prevention: Potential, Challenges, and Opportunities—A Review of the Literature." Background paper for the United Nations–World Bank Flagship Study "Pathways for Peace: Inclusive Approaches to Preventing Violent Conflict."

Atwood, J. Brian. 2012. "Partnering with Civil Society: 12 Lessons from DAC Peer Reviews." OECD.

Barnes, Catherine. 2009. "Civil Society and Peacebuilding: Mapping Functions in Working for Peace." *International Spectator* 44, no. 1: 131–47.

Berman, Eli, Michael Callen, Luke N. Condra, Mitch Downey, Tarek Ghani, and Mohammad Isaqzadeh. 2017. "Community Monitors vs. Leakage: Experimental Evidence from Afghanistan." https://lukecondra.files.wordpress.com/2017/07/iwa_14june2017.pdf.

Bethke, Felix S., and Jonathan Pinckney. 2019. "Non-Violent Resistance and the Quality of Democracy." *Conflict Management and Peace Science* 38, no. 5: 503–523.

Beyerle, Shaazka M. 2014. *Curtailing Corruption: People Power for Accountability and Justice.* Boulder, CO: Lynne Rienner.

Beyerle, Shaazka, David Bulman, Marco Larizza, and Berenike Schott. 2017. *Citizens as Drivers of Change: How Citizens Practice Human Rights to Engage with the State and Promote Transparency and Accountability.* Washington, DC: World Bank. https://openknowledge.worldbank.org/handle/10986/27653.

Beyerle, Shaazka, and Davin O'Regan. 2019. "Overcoming Hurdles to Citizen Activism for Fiscal Governance." Fiscal Futures Blog Series, Transparency and Accountability Initiative, April. https://www.internationalbudget.org/2019/04/fiscal-futures-citizen-activism-for-fiscal-governance/.

Bhonagiri, Aditi. 2016. "Social Movements: Topic Guide." GSRDC, University of Birmingham, August. http://www.gsdrc.org/wp-content/uploads/2017/03/SocialMovements.pdf.

Bloch, Nadine, and Lisa Schirch. 2019. *Synergizing Nonviolent Action and Peacebuilding: An Action Guide.* Washington, DC: United States Institute of Peace. https://www.usip.org/publications/2019/04/snap-synergizing-nonviolent-action-and-peacebuilding.

Burns, Danny. 2014. "Assessing Impact in Dynamic and Complex Environments: Systemic Action Research and Participatory Systemic Inquiry." Centre for Development Impact Practice Paper No. 8, Institute for Development Studies, September. https://opendocs.ids.ac.uk/opendocs/handle/20.500.12413/4387.

Centre for Law and Democracy n.d. "Global Right to Information Rating: Afghanistan." Accessed August 28, 2019. https://www.rti-rating.org/country-data/Afghanistan/.

Chenoweth, Erica, and Maria J. Stephan. 2011. *Why Civil Resistance Works: The Strategic Logic of Nonviolent Conflict.* Columbia Studies in Terrorism and Irregular Warfare. New York: Columbia University Press.

Coelho, Vera S. P., and Bettina von Lieres. 2010. "Mobilizing for Democracy: Citizen Engagement and the Politics of Public Participation." In *Mobilizing for Democracy: Citizen Action and the Politics of Public Participation*, edited by Vera Coelho and Bettina von Lieres, 1–20. London: Zed Books.

Dahl, Marianne, Scott Gates, and Havard Mokliev Nygård. 2017. "Securing the Peace." Background paper for the United Nations–World Bank Flagship Study "Pathways for Peace: Inclusive Approaches to Preventing Violent Conflict," World Bank.

Dey, Nikhil. 2019. "When the People Demand Transparency for Accountability." Fiscal Futures Blog Series, Transparency and Accountability Initiative, April. https://www.internationalbudget.org/2019/04/fiscal-futures-when-the-people-demand-transparency-for-accountability/.

Ehsany, Rasool. 2019. "Integrity Dialogues Bring Citizens and Justice Institutions Together in Northern Afghanistan." Integrity Watch, July 4.

Fox, Jonathan. 2015. "Social Accountability: What Does the Evidence Really Say?" *World Development* 72: 346–361.

Fox, Jonathan, and Joy Aceron. 2016. "Doing Accountability Differently: A Proposal for the Vertical Integration of Civil Society Monitoring and Advocacy." U4 Anti-Corruption Resource Center, Chr. Michelsen Institute, Bergen, Norway. https://www.u4.no/publications/doing-acc

ountability-differently-a-proposal-for-the-vertical-integration-of-civil-society-monitoring-and-advocacy.

FreedomInfo. 2014. "Afghan President Signs Access to Information Law." December 9. http://www.freedominfo.org/2014/12/afghan-president-signs-access-information-law/.

Gaventa, John, and Barrett Gregory. 2010. "So What Difference Does It Make? Mapping the Outcomes of Citizen Engagement." Working Paper, Institute of Development Studies, University of Sussex. https://gsdrc.org/document-library/so-what-difference-does-it-make-mapping-the-outcomes-of-citizen-engagement/.

George-Williams, Desmond, University for Peace, and Africa Programme. 2006. *"Bite Not One Another": Selected Accounts of Nonviolent Struggle in Africa*. Addis Ababa: University for Peace, Africa Programme. https://novact.org/wp-content/uploads/2012/09/Bite-not-One-Another-Selected-Accounts-of-Nonviolent-Struggle-in-Africa-Desmond-George-Williams.pdf.

Grady, Heather, Kelly Diggins, Joanne Schneider, and Naamah Paley Rose. 2017. "Scaling Solutions Toward Shifting Systems." *Rockefeller Philanthropy* Advisors, September. https://www.rockpa.org/wp-content/uploads/2017/09/05-18_RockPA-ScalingSolutions-WEB.pdf.

Halloran, Brendan, and Walter Flores. 2015. "Mobilizing Accountability: Citizens, Movements and the State." *Transparency and Accountability* Initiative, London. http://www.transparency-initiative.org/archive/wp-content/uploads/2015/05/Movements-and-Accountability-Final.pdf.

Kaplan, Oliver Ross. 2017. *Resisting War: How Communities Protect Themselves*. Cambridge: Cambridge University Press.

Karbowska, Natalia, and PeiYao Chen. 2018. "Takeaways from 'Stronger Together: New Frontiers in Funders Supporting Social Movements.'" Human Rights Funders Network, June 13. https://www.hrfn.org/resources/takeaways-from-stronger-together-new-frontiers-in-funders-supporting-social-movements/.

Lemma, Solomé. 2018. "Twenty-Five Ways Funders Can Support Social Movements." *Inside Philanthropy*, May. https://www.insidephilanthropy.com/home/2018/5/10/25-powerful-ways-funders-can-support-social-movements.

Marc, Alexandre, Alys Willman, Ghazia Aslam, Michelle Rebosio, and Kanishka Balasuriya. 2012. *Societal Dynamics and Fragility: Engaging Societies in Responding to Fragile Situations*. New Frontiers of Social Policy. Washington, DC: World Bank. https://openknowledge.worldbank.org/handle/10986/12222?showrfull&locale-attribute=fr.

Masters, Barbara, and Torie Osborn. 2010. "Social Movements and Philanthropy: How Foundations Can Support Movement Building." *The Foundation Review* 2, no. 2: 12–27.

Mati, Jacob, Federico Silva, and Tracy Anderson. 2010. "Assessing and Strengthening Civil Society Worldwide." Civicus, Johannesburg, April 17. https://www.civicus.org/images/Assessing_and_Strenghtening_CS_Worldwide_2008-2010.pdf.

McDevit, Andrew, and Ezatullah Adib. 2018. "National Corruption Survey 2018: Afghan's Perceptions and Experiences of Corruption." *Integrity Watch Afghanistan*. https://iwaweb.org/wp-content/uploads/2014/12/NCS__2018__English__WEB.pdf.

Nilsson, Desirée. 2012. "Anchoring the Peace: Civil Society Actors in Peace Accords and Durable Peace." *International Interactions* 38, no. 2: 243–266.

Pinckney, Jonathan. 2018. *When Civil Resistance Succeeds: Lessons for Building Democracy After Popular Nonviolent Uprisings*. Washington, DC: International Center on Nonviolent Conflict Press.

Poskitt, Adele, and Mathilde Dufranc. 2011. "Civil Society Organizations in Situations of Conflict." Open Forum for CSO Development Effectiveness, Civicus. https://www.civicus.org/view/media/cso_conflict_complete_report.pdf.

SIGAR (Special Inspector General for Afghanistan Reconstruction). 2016. "Corruption in Conflict: Lessons from the U.S. Experience in Afghanistan." September. https://www.sigar.mil/pdf/lessonslearned/SIGAR-16-58-LL.pdf.

SIGAR (Special Inspector General for Afghanistan Reconstruction). 2019. "Quarterly Report to the United States Congress." July. https://www.sigar.mil/pdf/quarterlyreports/2019-07-30qr.pdf.

Stephan, Maria J., Sadaf Lakhani, and Nadia Naviwala. 2015. *Aid to Civil Society: A Movement Mindset*. Washington, DC: United States Institute of Peace. https://www.usip.org/publications/2015/02/aid-civil-society-movement-mindset.

Sturge, Georgina, Richard Mallett, Jessica Hagen-Zanker, and Rachel Slater. 2017. "Tracking Livelihoods, Service Delivery, and Governance: Panel Survey Findings from the Secure Livelihoods Research Consortium." Secure Livelihoods Research Consortium. https://securelivelihoods.org/publication/tracking-livelihoods-service-delivery-and-governance-panel-survey-findings-from-the-secure-livelihoods-research-consortium/.

UN Women. 2015. *Preventing Conflict, Transforming Justice, Securing the Peace: Global Study on the Implementation of United Nations Security Council Resolution 1325*. New York: UN Women. http://www.peacewomen.org/sites/default/files/UNW-GLOBAL-STUDY-1325-2015%20(1).pdf.

Varshney, Ashutosh. 2002. *Ethnic Conflict and Civic Life: Hindus and Muslims in India*. New Haven, CT: Yale University Press.

Wanis-St. John, Anthony, and Darren Kew. 2008. "Civil Society and Peace Negotiations: Confronting Exclusion." *International Negotiation* 13: 11–36.

World Bank. 2015. *World Development Report 2015: Mind, Society, and Behavior*. Washington, DC: World Bank.

World Bank. 2017. *World Development Report 2017: Governance and the Law*. Washington, DC: World Bank. https://www.worldbank.org/en/publication/wdr2015.

World Bank and United Nations. 2018. *Pathways for Peace: Inclusive Approaches to Preventing Violent Conflict*. Washington, DC: World Bank. https://openknowledge.worldbank.org/handle/10986/28337.

World Movement for Democracy. n.d. "Former Chair—Zainab Bangura (Sierra Leone)." Accessed August 28, 2019. https://www.movedemocracy.org/person/zainab-hawa-bangura-sierra-leone.

19

Altering the Narrative and the Narrators to Overcome Norms and Stereotypes

Ann Towns, Wazhma Frogh, and Amelia Cotton Corl

The first problem for all of us, men and women, is not to learn, but to unlearn. We are filled with popular wisdom of several centuries just past, and we are terrified to give it up.

—Gloria Steinem[1]

Introduction

Why is attention to norms and narrators so important in the promotion of diversity and inclusion? Marginalization plays out in society at individual and collective levels, where those with authority and power direct people to enforce policies and carry out practices. Dominant actors have a vested interest in continuing systems of inequality to strengthen their position in the hierarchy of the geographic or cultural context in which they operate. Those powerful actors create concrete policies and practices, but also shape the culture that dictates how marginalized individuals are treated in our communities. Only by meaningfully addressing these actors and their behaviors can systemic change effectively take root.

In this chapter, we define and deconstruct the creation of narratives that reinforce and perpetuate marginalization. We begin by defining the term "norm" and exploring how norms are transmitted and changed. A discussion of "framing" follows, further contextualizing how norms form the foundation of our individual and collective behavior. We pivot to a discussion of "narrators"— who they are and how they work. Then we take a deep dive into norm change in Afghanistan, with insider insights from a leading global activist. The chapter closes with a framework to guide the creation of context-specific tools and approaches, enabling the reader to translate an awareness of norms to a plan for transformative change.

Understanding Norms

What Are Norms?

An important part of understanding change in the social world necessitates comprehending what social norms are, how they work, and how they change. Indeed, the concept of "norms"—which we use equivalently to "social norms"—is very helpful for describing and explaining a range of human relations and behaviors. Simply put, norms are social standards of behavior for actors of a given identity.[2] They are inherently social, in the sense that they exist and are shared among groups of people as common belief systems rather than simply existing as subjective beliefs inside individual people's heads. Norms are so central to society that it is no exaggeration to claim that "society *means* that norms regulate human conduct."[3] In other words, all societies are based on norms, and knowing norms helps members of society know how to behave as expected and considered appropriate by others. In familiar contexts, we know how to dress for a job interview, how to address a doctor at the hospital, or how to appear knowledgeable in a classroom. Norms can serve various functions, some of them rational and others seemingly more arbitrary. Regardless, the power and efficacy of norms stem from their support among relevant actors.[4] Once a particular norm loses social support, it weakens or ceases to exist and is replaced by another norm. The nineteenth-century European norm that women wear skirts and men wear pants has been replaced by norms supporting women (but not men) wearing either skirts or pants.

As suggested by these definitions, norms are closely linked with identity and social roles. Norms always point out what is expected of individuals *with specified identities or roles*, whether related to gender, occupation, age, nationality, family role, and so on. So, to understand how norms work, we have to engage with questions of identity and social roles. Norms communicate what the relations are between behavior and identity or social role.[5] Norms help people establish and understand what is appropriate for a particular kind of human, whether teacher, mother, ballerina, or elder. To know norms is to know how to go on as a certain kind of actor, which generally involves a great deal of tacit knowledge and an understanding of systems and patterns of behavior.[6] To know norms is also to know how to be interpreted differently—how one would have to behave to be treated as, say, a student rather than a teacher in a classroom. Among other things, this might involve sitting at the desks facing the front of the room (rather than standing at the front of the room and facing the desks), speaking only after raising one's hand and being called on to speak, or asking questions rather than lecturing. Knowing norms can also help actors to avoid being grouped together with stigmatized roles and identities. For instance, in the first half of the twentieth century, some Latin American women's suffrage activists drew on racist ideas about civilization and enlightenment to argue that only literate women should be allowed to vote, which would mean suffrage would not be extended to Indigenous people. Literate women were much more "advanced" than Indigenous people, they contended, and were thus supposedly educated enough to handle the vote.[7] Getting to engage in or avoid certain behaviors can be of great importance in expressing identity. When there is great pride in or attachment to an identity, there may be particular resistance to changing norms associated with that identity. Campaigns by British missionaries to end female genital cutting in Kenya in the 1920s—in a context of growing African resistance to British colonialism—failed miserably. This was partly because female genital cutting became interpreted as a mark of national identity; the campaign was resisted as a colonial campaign intended to change national norms.[8]

Norms are fundamentally also about *social value* and thus *social hierarchies*. They express what kinds of behavior are valued and valuable for specific actors in particular contexts. Actors that meet expectations and engage in behavior that is valued are recognized as "normal" and escape social sanctions. For instance, where norms of heterosexuality are strong, marrying someone of the opposite sex is considered normal and the couple does not have to deal with the stigma entailed in forming a same-sex relationship. Since heterosexuality is the norm, there is a "coming out" for homosexual individuals and couples, absent for those who are presumed to be straight (i.e., "normal"). Engaging in appropriate behavior is often also important to maintaining high social standing among peers. Indeed, norm conformity is its own source of social standing, which may or may not overlap with economic wealth, willingness to use force, or other sources of authority.[9] For instance, following religious norms in contexts where religiosity is valued garners respect, regardless of one's economic resources. Similarly, conforming to norms of being a "cultured" or "intellectual" person where this form of culture is valued may also provide a person esteem, regardless of economic class.[10] Norm conformity thus carries social rewards, as those who conform are seen as normal, at a minimum, and often also respectable. Therefore, attempts to change a norm must take into consideration people who not only value that norm but derive social status from conforming. In addition, conforming to normative expectations may be a way for social "inferiors" to pay respect to authority figures, such as elders, parents, religious leaders, or teachers.[11]

Engaging in transgressive behavior, on the other hand, can lead to social penalties and stigma.[12] As German social theorist Ralph Dahrendorf pointed out in the 1960s, social norms always involve tacit or overt sanctioning of behavior.[13] The social penalties for nonconformity range from minor to life-threatening. Arriving too dressed up to a London dinner among friends may be slightly embarrassing and may result in some snickers, whereas two men who kiss in public in the US state of Alabama may put themselves at risk of physical violence for violating heterosexuality norms. Importantly, norms help establish what are "good" and "bad" behaviors, what is desirable and undesirable, and what is "normal" and "abnormal" for a particular kind of actor. Indeed, conforming to norms carries social rewards and disregarding norms can lead to ridicule, shunning, violence, or other social penalties. Inequalities between those who conform and those who do not (or those who do so poorly) are built into the very fabric of society and are an inescapable effect of the existence of norms. Attempts to change norms must take such inequalities into account. Norm transgressions can be costly and dangerous, both to those who benefit and to those who are already stigmatized in a given normative order. And, as can be seen from the case of Afghanistan discussed later in this chapter, those who are stigmatized and may want normative change can face particularly harsh penalties for attempting to bring about transformations.

All societies, all communities, all social groups, and all social relations rest on norms. But this does not mean that norms function as holistic and intact value systems that are universally accepted and abided by. Norms may exist in tension or conflict within a group. Social groups or some of the individuals therein may face multiple norms from an array of contexts. With globalization and the considerable international flows of people and ideas, communities that remain untouched by outside influence are exceptional. People migrate, often bringing ideas and norms to the communities in which they settle. They often maintain ties with their communities of origin, which can be a conduit for transmitting norms from the place of resettlement to the community of origin. The global grasp of capitalism has reached virtually every part of the globe, bringing with it norms of the consumer culture and the market. Close to 60 percent of the world's population uses the internet regularly, a medium that enables access to norms and ideas beyond one's immediate community.[14] Even in tight-knit communities with high levels of norm conformity, there may be individuals who cannot comply or who do not want to comply with social expectations. They may have a different view of the desirability of dominant norms, even if they feel like they have to try to comply. Norms are almost always at least potentially contested, and it takes work to reproduce and stabilize norm-following behavior.[15]

The fact that norm compliance is not ensured can be good news for those who seek to empower marginalized groups, as the contested nature of norms can be used strategically to bring about change. It is crucial to get a sense of whether a norm is overtly or covertly contested and to identify actors who might be willing participants in normative change, as we will discuss shortly.

Norms may also be inherited or inferred by imitation, as humans are social beings who pick up cues about acceptable behavior from others. The behavior, dress, and appearance of high-status groups or individuals, such as the very wealthy, may be emulated by others. The inordinate online popularity of wealthy socialites such as Paris Hilton or the participants in the Real Housewives franchise has helped transmit certain gender norms of the very wealthy to both men and women. For those seeking change, it is important to be cognizant of whether existing norms are transmitted through active socialization efforts, or inadvertently and indirectly.

Norms, Narratives and Framing

Norms are not free-floating. They are part of established relationships of power, and often express economic inequalities. Norms are also part of dominant narratives about the history, future, or functions of a society, community or social group. A *narrative* is a story, a way of selecting and putting together disparate facts and weaving these into a coherent account with a beginning and an end.[16] Narratives are crucial for giving individuals and collectives a sense of purpose and place in the world.[17] Narratives help give broader meaning to norms, placing them in a story about what is valued; the origins, order, and future direction of a social group; who are its respected protagonists and despised antagonists; and what kinds of practices distinguish a group from others. In most communities and social groups, there are shared narratives with similar themes, norms, heroes, villains, victims, and historical sequences. What is more, many communities provide their particular spin on one or several common contemporary basic narratives: narratives of economic development, scientific rationality, liberal justice, ethnocultural tradition, and religious doctrine/tradition/justice. (See Box 19.1.)

Box 19.1 Contrasting "Protest Movements" in the United States, 2020–2021

In 2020 and 2021 in the United States, vastly contrasting narratives surrounded "protests" by the left and right ends of the political spectrum. The contrasting views were on full display in the media, splashed across headlines. They revealed the power of narratives to drive beliefs and behavior, including racist and polarizing attitudes and action.[18]

In May 2020, the murder of George Floyd, an African American man, by Minneapolis police during an arrest stemming from an allegedly counterfeit $20 bill sparked global movement for racial justice. Black Lives Matter mobilized hundreds of thousands of people and drove headlines for months. Vastly different narratives were fed to different political communities nationwide. Reports in the press even noted, "The more liberal [news] outlets often minimized property damage and some of those things [associated with the Black Lives Matter marches]. But to a very great degree, an asymmetrical degree, Fox News, Sinclair, conservative outlets stressed the idea that Antifa was stoking these protests as opposed to a broad-ranging sense of injustice. They said incidents and accusations against police were overblown. And there was all this kind of spin, information, misinformation, all of which tended to affect how people understood what took place."[19] Content analysis of reporting supported reports of differences in the coverage of protests by different media outlets.[20]

This event—and media coverage of it—was contrasted just seven months later by coverage of the storming of the US Capitol following the 2020 presidential election. Similarly divergent narratives were visible and commented upon in the media: "The January 6, 2021 incident at the U.S. Capitol was widely covered by the news media—however, the type of language used to describe it varied greatly from publication to publication."[21] Differences in coverage were noted at the time: "The nation watched yesterday as pro-Trump extremists stormed the Capitol. And what you saw and your understanding of the events may depend on where you tuned in—one of the broadcast networks, a cable news network or one of the emerging far-right cable channels."[22]

Both Black Lives Matter mobilization and the march on the Capitol were framed as different forms of "protest." But they laid bare how different narratives reach different subpopulations and showed how narratives shape attitudes regarding efforts to promote inclusion and equity. Danielle Kilgo notes, "[We] found that narratives about the women's march and anti-Trump protests gave voice to protesters and significantly explored their grievances. On the other end of the spectrum, protests about anti-black racism and indigenous people's rights received the least legitimizing coverage."[23]

Crucially, narratives are always biased and reflect a particular perspective. They necessarily include and validate some actors, norms, and events while discrediting and silencing others. No narrative can be all-encompassing. Political scientists Molly Patterson and Kristen Renwick Monroe underscore that common and widely circulating narratives can be challenged and reinterpreted by actors who do not recognize their place in the story, or who find the narrative unfair or incorrect.[24] For instance, in the United States, dominant narratives about the United States as "the land of the free" and a beacon of freedom and individual rights have been contested for decades. African American civil rights advocates, Native American activists, feminists, and others have challenged this narrative in different ways. Each claim that the "land of the free" narrative has placed men of European origin at the center, portraying Native populations as antagonists and ignoring the genocidal campaigns against them; remaining silent on the subordination of women; and downplaying the enslavement and reinforcing oppression of African Americans. If the narrative about the United States were to place any of these other groups at the center as protagonists, the story of the United States would look quite different, with a different beginning, sequences, and main points about victims, heroes, and villains.

Those interested in changing norms need to understand not only the specific norms but also the shared narratives that give the norms meaning. To change norms is also to alter narratives, and there are more and less effective ways of approaching transformation. Scholars interested in the deliberate change of norms have long used the concept of "framing" to understand how advocates for change successfully connect norms with broader narratives.[25] A *frame* is a schema of interpretation, a way to narrate and make sense of a behavior and to portray it as desirable or undesirable, good or bad. How a behavior is framed affects how actors behave—whether they endorse or reject a norm and related practice. Social movements and other advocates for change are well aware of this fact, and they often make strategic decisions about how best to package and present change. Effective frames for normative change tap into dominant narratives and values. If economic development is central among target actors, then framing the empowerment of marginalized groups in terms of economic gains is more likely to be successful. (See Box 19.2.) If scientific rationality is central, then framing the case for empowerment of the marginalized as the scientific and rational thing to do is more likely to be effective. If religious doctrine is central, then framing women's empowerment in religious terms, as the will of God, is more likely to be successful. And so on.

Box 19.2 The Economic Frame Supporting Diversity and Inclusion

Supporting the economic argument for diversity and inclusion, recent studies have demonstrated how increasing the diversity of teams yields tangible financial benefits.[26] This research documents how in the United States there is a linear relationship between racial and ethnic diversity and better financial performance: for every 10 percent increase in racial and ethnic diversity on the senior executive team, earnings before interest and taxes (EBIT) rise 0.8 percent.[27] In addition, they found that in the United Kingdom, greater gender diversity on the senior executive team corresponded to the highest performance increase: for every 10 percent increase in gender diversity, EBIT rose by 3.5 percent.[28]

An even more comprehensive study—of more than twenty-two thousand firms across ninety-one countries—affirmed not just the value of female representation in the leadership team but the value of a pipeline to build leadership capacity over time.[29] This study found that women on corporate boards and in "C-suite" positions have a positive impact on firm performance. The authors emphasized the noticeable effect of female CEOs and said that it is not just getting women to the top that matters; rather, creating a pipeline of female managers working at every level of the organization is what yields benefits.

Actors for change need to be strategic, and they need to adapt their message to be persuasive. For instance, women's movements around the world have often had to frame their demands in terms of the common good or economic gain that results from empowering women, even though the activists themselves were clearly often personally driven by a sense of injustice and likely wished that arguments about justice for women had been effective.[30] Indeed, efficiency and expediency arguments are often necessary to bring about change. However, framing normative change in ways that tap into dominant identities and narratives is also crucial. In a context in which non-Western cultural tradition is important, framing empowerment in terms of the superiority of liberal, Western progress—as is surprisingly often done—is counterproductive and foolish. A much better approach would be to find ways to situate empowerment within dominant narratives about non-Western cultural tradition. This can be done by finding examples of empowerment in non-Western history, or by finding cases of empowerment in respected non-Western communities, to frame empowerment as not only compatible with non-Western cultural tradition but perhaps also necessary for those cultures' survival. Some Muslim women's rights activists have grafted their calls for equality onto narratives about the elevated status of women in premodern Islamic tradition.[31] Other Muslim feminists have tried to use the reintroduction of premodern sharia mandates as a frame for the empowerment of women.

Who Controls the Message

What Do We Mean by Narrators?

When striving to advance diversity and inclusion, we work with a wide array of individuals and groups within the normative contexts. Increasingly, people are connected and online, sharing information and opinions at unprecedented speeds across the world. *The "narrators" are any actors shaping messages about events, people, and information in public spaces.* These narrators develop and perpetuate specific meaning and representation to their followers, to those who oppose them, and to the broader population. Look no further than the U.S. evening news to see that reporting on local crime—reinforcing gender norms as well as racial and ethnic stereotypes—profoundly shapes public opinion about the most urgent problems (crimes perpetrated by Black men and other men of color) and the path to their resolution ("law and order" policies and minimum mandatory sentencing).[32] Without question, the prolific study of the influence of the media on public opinion tells us that prime-time television narrators are especially powerful in shaping how citizens form opinions.[33]

But the media—film and television—are by no means the sole narrators in our modern, interconnected world. Actors create and disseminate messages virtually and personally, but the same principle holds true as in the earliest social movements: *those empowered and able to deliver a public message shape the perception of cultural norms and traditions.*

Scholars have often used the term "dominant actors" or "strategic actors" to describe those who lead the narrative at any given time.[34] These actors can reshape the way the past is recalled—labeled "collective memory"—or the way the present or future will be interpreted.[35]

What Narrators Do to Shape the Message

As described earlier, scholars of social movements have used the concept of "framing" to understand the construction of meaning in a wide variety of contexts. These scholars are building on the work of sociologist Erving Goffman, who originated framing theory, to understand not only how narrators frame, or shape, the message, but also how these approaches are used to bring about collective action.[36]

Narrators typically engage in three types of framing activities:

- *Diagnostic framing*, which involves identifying the problem, and attributing its causes
- *Prognostic framing*, where the narrator articulates a proposed solution to the problem
- *Motivational framing*, where the narrator issues the "call to arms" or describes the rationale for engaging

Within these framing processes, the element of storytelling is critical, enabling narrators to be compelling and engaging.[37] Together, framing activities are meant to drive individuals and groups to action.[38]

With an understanding of these component parts, we can view the descriptions of marginalized groups and broader interpretations of inequality with a more critical eye.

While some narrators are intentional in articulating and reinforcing marginalization, many others are unintentionally serving as narrators, describing marginalized groups in ways that are born of and perpetuate unconscious or implicit bias. Whether a narrator weaves conscious or unconscious bias into framing activities, the next stage unfolds in dissemination.

The Impact of Narrators on Marginalization

Framing activities illustrate how narrators wield power in the creation and dissemination of their ideas. Inherent in the continuation of many norms we see the embeddedness of stigma and marginalization, and in the case study on Afghanistan, even danger.

Dominant actors—those with power in a given context—have a vested interest in continuing systems of inequality. Their control over the message is a function of power and hierarchy within a given geographic or cultural context. Power and hierarchy are common themes that run through the following examples, where we see how narratives are used to perpetuate marginalization by those in power.

Minority groups occupy positions of less power and lower status than majority peers across the globe. Consider the case of Roma women in the Czech Republic, where Roma constitute the largest minority in the country, but stereotypes and prejudice—the instruments of marginalization—are pervasive. These attitudes shape the cultural norms and behaviors of those who control access to employment and health services.[39] Roma women face obstacles driven by the intersectionality of their marginalization—as both women and Roma—from those who see their engagement and employment as a threat to their position in society. Roma women have a harder time finding work, and they are discharged earlier from the hospital following childbirth because of their ethnicity. Norms and narratives have consequences for these women's well-being; they translate to devastating impacts for marginalized groups.[40]

While global attitudes toward female employment are changing, findings from a recent study of more than 150,000 respondents across 142 countries revealed that

> worldwide, the majority of women would prefer to be working, *and men agree.* A total of 70% of women and a similar 66% of men would prefer that women work at paid jobs. This total notably includes a majority of women who are not currently in the workforce.... But more importantly, this is true in almost all regions worldwide, including several regions where women's labor force participation is traditionally low, such as the Arab States.[41]

In addition, this study found evidence contrary to the norms advanced by men regarding women's work and their contribution.

> Worldwide, the majority of employed women say what they earn is at least a significant source of their household's income. More than one in four women say they provide the main income for their households, but men are still more likely to say they provide the main source of income. This pattern holds in every part of the world except for Eastern Asia.

The disconnect between perception and reality reflects a common path for normative change. Opportunities emerge for changing actions and behaviors, while narratives remain entrenched. The deep roots of norms around women's work affect not only men's attitudes but women's as well.

Additional research reveals how entrenched gender norms impact female employment in Jordan, which has the lowest rate of female labor force participation in the world (of countries not in active conflict). Findings indicate that even women's *estimates* of the extent of men's disapproval are low. While 35 percent of women believe their male counterparts disapprove of them working in mixed-gender environments, 60 percent of men admit they disapprove.[42] Additionally, while 42 percent of women believe their male counterparts disapprove of married women returning after 5:00 P.M., in reality 70 percent of men disapprove.[43] Powerful norms around women's roles—and married women's roles, specifically—continue to be strongly held. This disapproval hinges on male control of the household and views that reinforce women's economic marginalization. Perpetuation of the status quo holds as a result of dominant actors. In this case, men's position remains consistent and powerful.

What we can see from these examples about women in the paid labor market is that narratives and narrators matter a great deal in the lived experiences of marginalized groups. Sometimes norms are misrepresented, and sometimes they are misperceived. And at times norms can be miscast as too backward or too progressive. Diversity, inclusion, and evolving gender norms face challenges as the balance of power changes in the country and in the home. But where can we turn to check the pulse of larger trends in norms?

Public opinion polling—at least those polls with empirical rigor—can be a valuable source of evidence for those prioritizing diversity and inclusion around the world. This data can also illuminate where norms are or are not changing regardless of what the dominant actors say. Objective and comprehensive methods can reveal important changes not reflected in the dominant narratives. Recent analysis from the Pew Research Center is illustrative.[44] (See Figure 19.1.)

As we see in Figure 19.1, measuring progress toward equality—a useful data point for decreasing marginalization—should be examined through the lens of who surrenders power at the expense of equality. When assessing and evaluating norms within a society, it can be critical to question and examine standard assumptions regarding attitudes and norms. It can be easy to miss evolution in societal norms, as well as vast disparities in perspectives regarding what is "appropriate" or permissible.

Each of these examples demonstrates why attention to the intersection of power, hierarchy, and marginalization is crucial for meaningful and sustainable transformation of norms. Understanding the powerful relationships between norms, narrators, and narratives provides those advocating for diversity and inclusion of marginalized groups with concrete and actionable evidence. (See Box 19.3.)

Extended Case Study: Women's Rights in Afghanistan (2001–2021)

This in-depth case study by prominent Afghan leader Wazhma Frogh provides first-person reflections on the ways in which narratives about culture can be weaponized to perpetuate marginalization, inequality, and violence. (See Box 19.4.) It provides important lessons for how to effectively counter actors opposed to equity and inclusion.

The Context

Afghanistan came into the limelight globally following the 9/11 attacks in the United States, but it faced war and conflict for decades. The Taliban regime came to power in

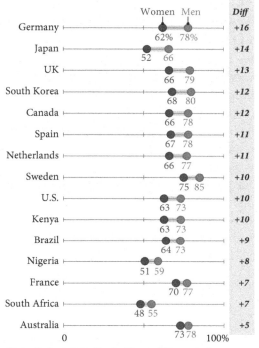

In many countries, men are more likely than women to say gender equality has increased in their country

% who say gender equality has increased over the past 20 years in (survey country)

Note: Only statistically significant differences shown.
Source: Spring 2018 Global Attitudes Survey. Q9.
PRW RESEARCH CENTER

Figure 19.1 In Many Countries, Men Are More Likely than Women to Say Gender Equality Has Increased in Their Country

Credit line: In many countries, men are more likely than women to say gender equality has increased in their country, in "A Changing World: Global Views On Diversity, Gender Equality, Family Life and the Importance of Religion." Pew Research Center, Washington, D.C. (2019) https://www.pewresearch.org/global/2019/04/22/a-changing-world-global-views-on-diversity-gender-equality-family-life-and-the-importance-of-religion/.

the 1990s following decades of turmoil and conflict; they enforced the strictest Islamist rules and treated citizens brutally, especially women, until being toppled in 2001 by a US-led international coalition. Post-2001–2021 marked a new chapter in the life of Afghans, especially women. Emerging following Taliban oppression with the scars of civil war, Afghan women who learned basic coping skills as refugees in Pakistan and Iran mobilized. In 2004, for the first time, Afghan women succeeded in getting gender equality enshrined in the constitution. A 25 percent quota in the national legislative assembly brought scores of women into political leadership. Millions of women who had had almost no rights under Taliban rule returned to school and work.

Box 19.3 Narrators, Narratives, and Misinformation in the First Year of the COVID-19 Pandemic

In 2020, COVID-19 began its ravaging tour across the globe. Massive misinformation regarding everything from the origin of the virus to the symptoms, treatment, and efficacy of the vaccine is just now being unpacked in the literature.[45] In the United States, the promulgation of false and misleading information was unprecedented in scale, partly as a result of the powerful narrators advancing falsehoods.[46] In discussing the threat, Dr. Kasisomayajula Viswanath, professor of health communication at the Harvard T. H. Chan School of Public Health, noted, "Most of the time . . . misinformation around diseases is not in the spotlight. But what has made misinformation and disinformation about COVID-19 so bad is that it was picked up and spread by political figures, including President Donald Trump. That greatly amplified it and it brought misinformation and disinformation into the mainstream."[47] The continued perpetuation of falsehoods by influential narrators and political figures has had significant implications for the spread of disease and vaccine hesitancy, which continues to be significantly higher among supporters of the former president and his allies.[48]

Box 19.4 Wazhma Frogh

Coauthor Wazhma Frogh was seventeen years old when she realized the challenges faced by refugee women and children in camps in Peshawar, Pakistan. Through community engagement, community mobilization, and grassroots empowerment efforts, Wazhma has enabled local voices to influence national legislation, policies, and programs in Afghanistan. In particular, she has worked with local women leaders to initiate local conflict resolution efforts that impact peace and security at the national level.

Twenty years of international engagement created opportunities for Afghans to connect with the world. Thousands of young Afghan women studied in the United States, the United Kingdom, and other European countries. Those who returned took part in rebuilding their war-torn communities. By the time the Taliban reassumed power in August 2021 women comprised some 30–40 percent of the Afghanistan civil service, with many in the lead as ministers, deputies, ambassadors, and general directors. The number of women in the police, judiciary, and law enforcement agencies had doubled and tripled between 2016 and 2019.

All this progress was always fragile and vulnerable. The Taliban attack women and fight women leaders and politicians as a tool of war. But society at large also remains conservative with regard to women's freedoms. Outside cities and urban areas, local practices often oppress and suppress women and girls, and an informal code of conduct rules women's lives. The country's Independent Human Rights Commission reports that 80 percent of arranged marriages are forced on young girls, and children as young as ten are married off. Domestic violence claims many women's lives, and the rate of self-immolation among women continues to rise. Any conversation about Afghan women's rights starts by citing "culture, norms, and traditions"; this essentially means that patriarchy and masculine power rule women's lives, since men have the social, political, and economic power at the family, community, and social levels. Men use their power to define and attribute their way of life to norms and cultural practices.

Culture and Norms in Afghanistan

Understanding the term "culture" in Afghanistan is very complex. As a result of war and conflict over the past forty years, the dynamics of the Afghan culture have not been fully analyzed. However, the norms, values, thoughts, and perceptions that are considered part of the culture have been evolving and changing shape.

In Afghanistan, local norms are primarily determined by the powerful men of the community. This includes the religious leader, the tribal leader, and the political leader, who often possess weapons and maintain armed men around them to enforce those norms. For example, conflict between two young local men can often turn deadly, given the access to weapons. When this happens, the local response is frequently to try to address the dispute within the community, rather than going to the police. So the Jirga (tribal court) of elders decides that the murderer's family will give a virgin daughter for marriage to a man in the family of the deceased. In many instances, the girl is a child six to eighteen years old. This practice, which is called *baad*, is enforced by local tribal and political leaders, religious clerics, and powerful armed men. In some parts of Afghanistan, this is a norm that continues today. The practice is illegal, but in the absence of a local government presence and a responsive justice system, it persists. For years, activists have targeted *baad*, facing resistance from local authority figures, who justify such norms as "culture." But there is significant hypocrisy for the powerful; if a similar incident takes place in the family of a powerful figure, not only does the man get away with the crime, there is also no normative pressure on the man's father to give away his daughter in exchange for a murder committed by his son. It is a powerful demonstration of the fact that frequently it is only less powerful communities and individuals who bear the brunt of cultural norms.

Religion is an important driver of cultural norms in Afghanistan. Powerful actors use religion to perpetuate and enforce norms, even when they contradict Islam explicitly. This approach is an unflaggingly successful weapon employed by religious clerics and even by mullahs, who lack any professional training and knowledge of religion but who have learned religious teachings from their fathers and other elders. These powerful individuals—who have millions of listeners—preach in narratives that reinforce norms limiting women's access to education, work, and public life. Their Friday sermons are attended by millions of men who listen to and accept their way of life. Since men are dominant within the household, when they bring those views from the mosque to the family, these narratives are valued and enforced among the young men, girls, and women, who accept what is dictated by the head of the family. To date, there has not been any form of resistance or countering of these mullahs because they have a very strong network and they are unified. Additionally, there are more than two hundred thousand mullahs across Afghanistan, many of them with official entitlements, meaning that anyone who dares to counter them risks facing death. In 2015, for example, Farkhunda, a twenty-five-year-old female student of religious studies, confronted a mullah in a shrine in downtown Kabul; thousands of men attacked her, tortured her, and killed her in public, provoked by the mullah. Her family had to flee Afghanistan, as they too faced threats. Farkhunda's fate is commonly cited to silence women when they speak up.

More recently, local armed groups (including the Taliban) actively engaging in conflict have had a major role in changing norms in most parts of Afghanistan, both urban and rural, given their activity in cities and across the provinces. These armed groups make decisions that are imposed on communities, and they perpetrate violence and abuse to terrorize locals. As a result, norms that used to govern the lives of rural communities have changed drastically over the past twenty years. Tribal leaders and informal dispute resolution mechanisms (Jirgas and people's councils) used to define and redefine norms locally, but these structures have either eroded or been overtaken by insurgents. The central narrators have evolved as communities have evolved. Earlier in my career, the central narrators adhered to traditional norms and the players came from traditional roles—tribal leaders, community leaders, or religious leaders. These actors were not involved in most politics, because there was a government presence. Governance structures included Jirgas, which decided community matters, both civil and criminal. As the insurgency became more pervasive in most of the country, the central narratives and practices came from gunmen, war commanders, and armed groups. They framed their actions using cultural justifications to favor one group over another, ultimately defining how communities manage affairs on a daily basis.

Evolving Norms for Women

Though some norms defining how women are identified, expected to behave, and to appear at the local and national levels continue to remain very much the same, the levels of awareness, education, and mobility among women have improved significantly since 2001, which is affecting how women are perceived at all levels. For example, when WPSO started advocating for quotas for women in the National Assembly, designating two seats for women from each province, it was unclear if even one woman would be included, as no women held local political office. But when the quota was approved, the campaigns began. Millions of women mobilized around the country, and sixty-eight women went to parliament.

I vividly remember that community members in a southern province in 2005 wouldn't even sit to talk face-to-face with a woman who came to represent them in the parliament. Over time, she became their biggest champion, and scores of tribal leaders accompanied her in her third term in the parliament. This is tangible evidence of change related to shifting norms, and it happened because community members were able to see that she delivered for them and continued to be their champion. By 2020, being a female politician was no longer new in Afghanistan. Communities were used to seeing it, and female politicians came from rural, more conservative areas as well.

The Taliban's leaders and combatants on the ground have an ancient understanding of religion and how it should be enforced. They interpret religious texts in the most rigid ways and consider their way of life as the norm that should be practiced in communities. Afghanistan has come a long way in two decades, and the increased exposure and opportunities inside and outside have enabled people to see norms and traditions critically, particularly younger men and women who have access to information technology and who connect with peers in the region and globally; they oppose the Taliban form of life.

On August 15, 2021, when the Taliban walked into Afghanistan's presidential palace, it marked the end of 20 years of US-led engagement and nascent Afghan democracy. A peace deal with the United States in February 2021 and a withdrawal of NATO and US troops enabled the Taliban to take over Afghanistan in just over two months. Since the Taliban's return to Kabul, women have been banned from work, disappeared from local media, prohibited from engaging in sports, business or work outside the home.[49] Girls are not able to go to school beyond grade six. There is a wave of resistance brewing locally involving women's groups, young girls and some male allies, who take to the streets in small numbers, defiant.[50] It remains to be seen how Afghan women and girls will fare longer-term, however, there is no doubt that the Afghan society is a changed one.

The Women and Peace Studies Association Approach

When the Afghan government decided to talk to the Taliban in 2010, women's groups and activists mobilized around the country and advocated to participate in the process. Cultural norms were used to justify exclusion: women were not fighting on the ground, they were not in the government forces, and even the very limited number of women in the army and the police were not allowed to go into combat because that goes against cultural norms. Adherence to cultural norms fueled resistance and opposition to women's direct engagement. To address these powerful narratives, WPSO (see Box 19.5) traveled the country, mobilized local women groups, and documented how women played a role in local peacebuilding efforts; it helped us get some space in this process. However, decision-making continued to exclude women. When the president consulted political and faction leaders on matters of national interest, not a single woman was found in those meetings. And where women are excluded from the power structures at the community level, they are consequently marginalized in national structures too. But when women resisted these norms by seeking opportunities for participation and leadership, they were viewed as violating cultural norms that are perceived as sacred by communities. In the most extreme cases, this was deadly for women.

One of my greatest tools for addressing powerful narrators and norms involves playing an insider and outsider simultaneously. While I understand the challenges and realities of the country as an Afghan, I am cognizant of my limitations as an urban, Western-educated Afghan woman. Early on, I would engage with community members, mullahs, tribal leaders, and politicians directly, which put my team and me at risk. To address these risks, though it wasn't easy, I cultivated a network of supporters and women leaders who share my vision. It took more than five years, but it enabled me to work more effectively with troubleshooters by my side. The network of local women leaders was not created but formed on its own as we

---

Box 19.5 The Women and Peace Studies Organization—Afghanistan

The Women and Peace Studies Organization (WPSO-Afghanistan), a national civil society initiative led by women, is focused on elevating women's perspectives and roles within local communities to advance peace. WPSO works with women peacebuilders, especially younger influential leaders at the local level, enhancing their capacity to resolve local conflicts and connecting them with national processes so that their impact is magnified. WPSO also uses research and advocacy to promote the vision that inclusion leads to sustainable peace and harmony in Afghanistan.

Since 2012, WPSO has worked in over twenty provinces to establish local-level platforms that engage up to two hundred local peacebuilders, including female teachers, female nurses, women in local government, and elder women who have a voice in resolving family- and village-level conflicts. Beyond women in local peacebuilding, WPSO-Afghanistan focuses on security sector reform, trains female police, does targeted recruitment of women for the police force, and works with the Ministry of Interior to advocate for improved and safer working environments for female police.

continued interacting, engaging, training, and mentoring each other. In addition to women leaders, allies include male political leaders who believe in women's rights but cannot declare public support; mullahs and religious scholars with contemporary and more open interpretations of religion; and so many young men who do not conform to the norms of the patriarchy in their societies. While they may not risk publicly denouncing violence against women, they facilitate my access to the community and defuse tensions when extremists and conservatives are critical of our efforts.

Religious allies in particular have had an evolving role with our organization. If they serve as explicit allies, they come under immense scrutiny and face threats to their own lives. In one instance, a religious council that was supportive of my efforts eventually yielded to the pressures of local warlords who led the council and returned to an antagonistic position regarding women's groups.

The importance of male allies cannot be denied. We would not have access to any community without allies ranging from provincial governors to police chiefs, local politicians, and other influential figures. But less overt collaboration is most effective, as it minimizes the risk of media or public backlash. Often allies have achieved political and social influence by taking very conservative positions, and partnering with our organization could turn their constituencies against them.

Managing the network of allies is complex and time-intensive, but sustaining network continuity is key. This does not necessarily mean having them as direct beneficiaries of funded projects; it means intentionally maintaining a meaningful connection that is valuable to them, in order to keep the relationship and the communication channel active. Each week, my team is intentional about checking on members and informing them of training, meetings, and conferences inside and outside Afghanistan. By ensuring that network members are able to use our connections nationally to voice their concerns, we reinforce that this is not a one-sided relationship.

In recent years, the most pervasive and complex issues facing communities where we have worked—such as violent extremism—have been dealt with directly by these women leaders. We contribute to their mobilization, but we are not at the forefront anymore. This is the empowerment we sought. Our contribution was the tools, the facilities, and resources; but the brains, power, and momentum are the women's own. We have been able to prevent some forced and child marriages with the support of these local allies and networks. Women, including younger women, have been able to find a platform and voice, and connecting them with the national-level processes has given them credibility. Many of the women I started working with twenty years ago are in local and national political positions now as members of Provincial Councils and the National Assembly. To me, this speaks to changes in norms. We created and nurtured space to question and critically look at norms that weren't actually indigenous, but were enforced by those who wanted to continue to rule by keeping communities in darkness.

Over twenty years of work, my biggest lesson learned is that what we consider norms and culture are very fluid. People change when they see their lives getting better. Women mobilized, took up space, and spoke up for themselves because they thought the norms held them back. But this cannot happen without creating platforms, empowering local communities, and being patient with change. Though the future in Afghanistan is uncertain, the power to foster the evolution of norms is clear.

Building Practice from Theory: Key Takeaways for Addressing Norms

Throughout this chapter, we have introduced the theories that underlie norms and their importance. We affirmed that norms are social standards of behavior for actors of a given identity, emphasizing how norms are about social value and social hierarchies.[51] We provided examples of how norm transgressions are particularly enforced on marginalized groups. Building on this basic understanding, we highlighted the ways in which norms are transmitted and changed—through active socialization, or inadvertently and indirectly. We situated norms within the structures of narratives and framing, revealing how they are both partial and perspectival. Delving into frames—the schemas of interpretation—we explored how powerful actors known as narrators control the message in a given context. Going stepwise through the framing activities of narrators—diagnostic, prognostic, and motivational—we revealed the ways in which these narrators can perpetuate and reinforce marginalization. Finally, this theoretical foundation was illustrated in an in-depth case study from a leading activist in the field. Understanding the evolution of gender norms in Afghanistan provides a valuable set of reflections as to how this work plays out in a dynamic and evolving context.

The Importance of Examining Norms

Before exploring the tools and approaches for *changing* norms, we must emphasize the inherent value of *examining* norms. The theories and examples shared throughout this chapter are meant to convey several key points regarding how norms shape our existence. One important feature is that the exercise brings greater sensitivity to the existence and importance of norms. They are like the air we breathe, ever-present and often invisible.

When efforts to examine norms are undertaken by individuals and groups, we see that people have improved capacity to navigate existing norms, such as in the case of women in Afghanistan. In addition, we see that examination of norms enables people to engage critically and question assumptions when blanket statements are made about norms or culture as if they are static, one-dimensional, or universally shared within communities and societies. We observe numerous examples of this across the globe related to gender norms in domestic and professional roles.

Examining norms can also lay the foundation for changing them or enabling them to evolve. What follows are tools for deploying a critical eye toward norms that shape perceptions of ourselves and others within a given context. These tools include ideas for structuring examination, as well as for engaging in norm transformation.

Critical Observation

In any sector in any country worldwide, gathering information about relevant norms and the drivers of continuity is important. It may challenge assumptions about marginalized populations and will likely reveal potential barriers to changing norms.

Engaging productively requires engaging with local actors and local networks, identifying the norms that reinforce marginalization, and learning from local actors whether norms are overtly or covertly contested. It's critical to remember that norm transgressions can be dangerous, and that those who have the most to gain from change may be most at risk. Consider whether people affected by a norm know that alternatives to this norm exist.[52] Unless there is awareness of alternatives, change is inconceivable, as the norm is taken for granted.

Reflectiveness is critical. It can be essential to question assumptions about the instruments of marginalization, the process of inclusion, and the objective of advocacy. Communicating and correcting misassumptions, seeking objectivity in evidence, and collecting quantitative data (such as public opinion polling) may capture broad-based support that runs counter to dominant narratives.

Analyze Norms by Mapping the Narrators and the Narratives

A map of powerful actors (narrators) and the ways they frame and mobilize around these issues (narratives) can help to develop a comprehensive understanding of how and why marginalization persists. It can be useful to identify the authoritative voices on the issue, the narratives they advance, and the communication channels they use. Consider who is identified as the "problem," or those who are silenced by not being mentioned at all (*diagnostic framing*). Consider who is identified as part of the "solution," and again who is silenced (*prognostic framing*). Reflect on how actors are mobilizing constituents to take action or to bring about change (*motivational framing*).

Create Your Frames

For those who seek to effect change, like Wazhma Frogh, the creation and mobilization of frames are critical. Begin with a clear definition of the change you seek, and create your diagnostic, prognostic, and motivational frames in parallel. Remember that effective frames for normative change successfully tap into dominant narratives and values. If economic development is central, then framing the empowerment of marginalized groups in terms of the economic gains from empowerment is more likely to be effective. If scientific rationality is central, then framing empowerment as the scientific and rational thing to do is more likely to be effective. If religious doctrine is central, then framing the empowerment in religious terms is more likely to succeed, and so on.

In addition, actors for change need to be strategic, and often need to adapt their message to be persuasive. Consider whether economic efficiency frames and material leverage tactics are possible and effective—many actors find economics persuasive. Existing norms are often anchored in, supportive of, and expressive of economic status and economic relations. Unless the international community is shunned, change can sometimes be incentivized, if there is access to funding.[53]

Consider the value of framing claims for change around valued and dominant narratives and identities. Reworking existing narratives and identities can sometimes be more effective than trying to replace them entirely. Existing norms often express and manifest valued identities. Rather than trying to replace these identities, it may be better to graft new norms onto these identities. Change needs to be locally appropriate, so validate tactics with local networks and trained advocates.[54]

Mobilize to Change Norms

Mobilization should be driven by three key factors: (1) the motivational frame, (2) the capacity of local actors, and (3) the degree of resistance from dominant actors. The following should be carefully weighed in creating a mobilization strategy:

- *Do international actors help the cause?* Assessing whether international actors—including local chapters of international NGOs—are assets depends upon how international actors are regarded by local people. If they are considered a threat to national or local "tradition," as is currently the case among anti-gender-equality advocates in Hungary, for instance, then showcasing the involvement of the international community is counterproductive. However, where local or national actors care about their relations to the international community, transnational advocacy networks that connect local actors with international organizations and foreign governments can be very effective.[55]

- *Do marginalized individuals and groups support change?* Those seemingly disempowered by existing norms and narratives may be more inclined to support change, but don't make assumptions. For example, there is no reason to assume all women will rush to support claims about women's empowerment. Women are not a monolithic group (nor are any social groups)—some may be empowered by existing norms, others may find existing norms and their own subordination just and appropriate, and some may be too fearful and marginalized to dare endorse change. Additionally, while those with the most status in a social group are often best positioned to bring about change, they may have the most to lose from norm change, and it can be difficult to bring them along.

- *Individual leaders and change—whom to target?* Influential actors can include traditional leaders, religious authorities, local or national political officials, admired pop culture figures, or military heroes. If these individuals can be persuaded to promote norm change, it's very helpful—when norm leaders "are particularly influential individuals," others are more likely to follow.[56] "Recruiting influential locals to one's cause will tend to have an outsize impact on the community, to the extent that many community members value their opinion and look to them for guidance."[57] Of course, this can be a double-edged sword, as nonpolitical influential actors stepping into change movements can be controversial. For example, US celebrity Kim Kardashian is an advocate for prison reform and has contributed to visibility of the issue, but some people will never take the issue seriously simply as a result of her involvement.

Conclusion

Whether seeking to be an informed observer, a grassroots activist, or a policymaker, understanding the norms and narrators who shape messaging and behaviors will be critical to elevating the voices and needs of marginalized groups. Equipped with an understanding of how issues are framed and the tools to change the narrative, any individual or group can meaningfully and substantively raise awareness and contribute to transformative change.

Notes

1. Steinem 1971.
2. Jepperson, Wendt, and Katzenstein 1996.
3. Dahrendorf 1968, 173.
4. Berger and Luckmann 1966.
5. Towns 2010.
6. Giddens 1979, 67.
7. Towns 2010.
8. Keck and Sikkink, 69–70.
9. Bourdieu 1986.
10. Bourdieu 1986.
11. Shell-Duncan et al. 2018.
12. Goffmann 1963; Towns 2010, 2012; Adler-Nissen 2015.
13. Dahrendorf 1968, 167.
14. Kemp 2019.
15. Towns 2010; Wiener 2018.
16. Patterson and Monroe 1998.
17. Patterson and Monroe 1998.
18. Lane et al. 2020.

19. Folkenflik 2021.
20. Zaina et al. 2020.
21. Bhutada 2021.
22. Deggans and Folkenflik 2021.
23. Kilgo 2020. Also see Kilgo and Harlow 2019.
24. See Patterson and Monroe 1998.
25. Keck and Sikkink 1998; Chong and Druckman 2007.
26. Hunt, Layton, and Prince 2015; Peterson 2016.
27. Hunt, Layton, and Prince 2015.
28. Hunt, Layton, and Prince 2015.
29. Peterson 2016.
30. Towns 2010; Kraditor 1971.
31. Mir-Hosseini 2006.
32. Sacco 1995.
33. Baum and Potter 2008; Gamson and Modigliani 1989; McCombs 2004.
34. "Dominant actors": Cuc et al. 2006; Lee and Myers 2004. "Strategic actors": Hensmans 2003.
35. Halbwachs and Coser 1992.
36. Benford and Snow 2000; Gamson, Fireman, and Rytina 1982; Snow et al. 1986.
37. Kent 2015.
38. Benford and Snow 2000, 618.
39. Lidová, Kajanová, and Tovt 2015.
40. Lidová, Kajanová, and Tovt 2015.
41. Gallup and ILO 2017, 6.
42. Felicio and Gauri 2018.
43. Felicio and Gauri 2018.
44. Poushter and Fetterolf 2019.
45. Shahi, Dirkson, and Majchrzak 2021; Au, Bright, and Howard 2020.
46. Brennen et al. 2020.
47. Sweeny 2021.
48. Ivory, Leatherby, and Gebeloff 2021.
49. Barr, 2021.
50. Weeda, 2021.
51. Jepperson, Wendt, and Katzenstein 1996.
52. Cloward 2016, 135.
53. Cloward 2016, 146.
54. Familiarize yourself with resources such as the Solutions Journalism Network and the Frameworks Institute, which can provide evidence and inspiration for certain frames for specific issues.
55. Keck and Sikkink 1998.
56. Cloward 2016, 175ff., 190ff.
57. Cloward 2016, 251.

Bibliography

Adler-Nissen, Rebecca. 2015. "Stigma Management in International Relations: Transgressive Identities, Norms and Order in International Society." *International Organization* 68, no. 1: 143–176.
Au, Hubert, Jonathan Bright, and Philip N. Howard. 2020. "Social Media Junk News on George Floyd Protests." COMPROP Coronavirus Misinformation Weekly Briefing, June 8. Oxford

Internet Institute. https://demtech.oii.ox.ac.uk/wp-content/uploads/sites/93/2020/06/ComP rop-Coronavirus-Misinformation-Weekly-Briefing-08-06-2020.pdf.

Barr, Heather. 2021. "List of Taliban Policies Violating Women's Rights in Afghanistan." Human Rights Watch. September 29. https://www.hrw.org/news/2021/09/29/list-taliban-policies-violating-womens-rights-afghanistan.

Baum, Matthew A., and Philip B. K. Potter. 2008. "The Relationships Between Mass Media, Public Opinion, and Foreign Policy: Toward a Theoretical Synthesis." *Annual Review of Political Science* 11, no. 1: 39–65. https://doi.org/10.1146/annurev.polisci.11.

Benford, Robert D., and David A. Snow. 2000. "Framing Processes and Social Movements: An Overview and Assessment." *Annual Review of Sociology* 26: 611–639.

Berger, Peter, and Thomas Luckmann. 1966. *The Social Construction of Reality.* New York: Doubleday.

Bhutada, Govind. 2021. "How News Media Is Describing the Incident at the U.S. Capitol." *Visual Capitalist* (blog). January 16. https://www.visualcapitalist.com/how-news-media-is-describ ing-the-incident-at-the-u-s-capitol/.

Bourdieu, Pierre. 1986. "The Forms of Capital." In *Handbook of Theory and Research for the Sociology of Education*, edited by John Richardson, 241–258. Westport, CT: Greenwood.

Brennen, J. Scott, Felix M. Simon, Philip N. Howard, and Rasmus Kleis Nielsen. 2020. "Types, Sources, and Claims of COVID-19 Misinformation." Fact sheet. Reuters Institute for the Study of Journalism. April. http://www.primaonline.it/wp-content/uploads/2020/04/COVID-19_ reuters.pdf.

Cialdini, Robert B., and Melanie R. Trost. 1998. "Social Influence: Social Norms, Conformity and Compliance." In *The Handbook of Social Psychology*, edited by Daniel Todd Gilbert, Susan T. Fiske, and Gardner Lindzey, 151–192. New York: McGraw-Hill.

Chong, Dennis, and Jamie Druckman. 2007. "Framing Theory." *Annual Review of Political Science* 10: 103–126.

Cloward, Karisa. 2016. *When Norms Collide: Local Responses to Activism Against Female Genital Mutilation and Early Marriage.* Oxford: Oxford University Press.

Cuc, Alexandru, Yasuhiro Ozuru, David Manier, and William Hirst. 2006. "On the Formation of Collective Memories: The Role of a Dominant Narrator." *Memory and Cognition* 34, no. 4: 752–762. https://doi.org/10.3758/BF03193423.

Dahrendorf, Ralf. 1968. *Essays in the Theory of Society.* Stanford: Stanford University Press.

Deggans, Eric, and David Folkenflik. 2021. "A Look at How Different U.S. Media Outlets Covered the Pro-Trump Riot on Capitol Hill." NPR, January 7. https://www.npr.org/2021/01/07/954562 181/a-look-at-how-different-u-s-media-outlets-covered-the-pro-trump-riot-on-capitol-.

Eidevald, Christian. 2009. "Det finns inga tjejbestämmare—Att förstå kön i förskolans vardagsrutiner och lek." Dissertation, School of Education and Communication, Jönköping University. https://www.diva-portal.org/smash/get/diva2:158528/FULLTEXT01.pd.

Felicio, Mariana T., and Varun Gauri. 2018. "Hashemite Kingdom of Jordan: Understanding How Gender Norms in MNA Impact Female Employment Outcomes." Report no. ACS25170. World Bank. June. http://documents1.worldbank.org/curated/en/859411541448063088/pdf/ ACS25170-PUBLIC-FULL-REPORT-Jordan-Social-Norms-June-1-2018-with-titlepg.pdf.

Folkenflik, David. 2021. "How Media Coverage of the George Floyd Story Plays into His Accused Killer's Trial." NPR, March 10. https://www.npr.org/2021/03/10/975769781/how-media-cover age-of-the-george-floyd-story-plays-into-his-accused-killers-tria.

Gallup and ILO. 2017. *Towards a Better Future for Women and Work: Voices of Women and Men.* Washington, DC: Gallup Organization and the International Labour Organization. https:// www.ilo.org/wcmsp5/groups/public/---dgreports/---dcomm/---publ/documents/publicat ion/wcms_546256.pdf.

Gamson, William A., Bruce Fireman, and Steven Rytina. 1982. *Encounters with Unjust Authority.* Dorsey Series in Sociology. Homewood, IL: Dorsey Press.

Gamson, William A., and Andre Modigliani. 1989. "Media Discourse and Public Opinion on Nuclear Power: A Constructionist Approach." *American Journal of Sociology* 95, no. 1: 1–37. http://www.jstor.org/stable/2780405.

Giddens, Anthony. 1979. *Central Problems in Social Theory: Action, Structure and Contradiction in Social Analysis.* London: Palgrave.

Goffmann, Erving. 1963. *Stigma: Notes on the Management of Spoiled Identity.* New York: Simon & Schuster.

Halbwachs, Maurice, and Lewis A. Coser. 1992. *On Collective Memory. The Heritage of Sociology.* Chicago: University of Chicago Press.

Hensmans, Manuel. 2003. "Social Movement Organizations: A Metaphor for Strategic Actors in Institutional Fields." *Organization Studies* 24, no. 3: 355–381. https://doi.org/10.1177/0170840603024003908.

Hunt, Vivian, Dennis Layton, and Sara Prince. 2015. "Why Diversity Matters." McKinsey. January. https://www.mckinsey.com/business-functions/organization/our-insights/why-diversity-matters.

Ivory, Danielle, Lauren Leatherby, and Robert Gebeloff. 2021. "Least Vaccinated U.S. Counties Have Something in Common: Trump Voters." *The New York Times*, April 17. https://www.nytimes.com/interactive/2021/04/17/us/vaccine-hesitancy-politics.html.

Jepperson, R. L., A. Wendt, and P. J. Katzenstein, eds. 1996. *The Culture of National Security: Norms and Identity in World Politics.* New York: Columbia University Press.

Keck, Margaret, and Kathryn Sikkink. 1998. *Activists Beyond Borders: Advocacy Networks in International Politics.* Ithaca, NY: Cornell University Press.

Kemp, Simon. 2019. "Digital 2019: Global Internet Use Accelerates." We Are Social. January 30. https://wearesocial.com/blog/2019/01/digital-2019-global-internet-use-accelerates.

Kent, Michael L. 2015. "The Power of Storytelling in Public Relations: Introducing the 20 Master Plots." *Public Relations Review* 41, no. 4: 480–489.

Kilgo, Danielle K. 2020. "What Do We Want? Unbiased Reporting! When Do We Want It? During Protests!" The Conversation. January 16. http://theconversation.com/what-do-we-want-unbiased-reporting-when-do-we-want-it-during-protests-120123.

Kilgo, Danielle K., and Summer Harlow. 2019. "Protests, Media Coverage, and a Hierarchy of Social Struggle." *Small Group Research* 24, no. 4: 320–338. https://doi-org.proxy.library.georgetown.edu/10.1177/1046496491223003.

Kraditor, Aileen. 1971. *The Ideas of the Woman Suffrage Movement, 1890–1920.* New York: Anchor Books.

Lane, Kimberly, Yaschica Williams, Andrea N. Hunt, and Amber Paulk. 2020. "The Framing of Race: Trayvon Martin and the Black Lives Matter Movement." *Journal of Black Studies* 51, no. 8: 790–812. https://doi-org.proxy.library.georgetown.edu/10.1177/0021934720946802.

Lee, Jiunn Chieh, and Michael D. Myers. 2004. "Dominant Actors, Political Agendas, and Strategic Shifts over Time: A Critical Ethnography of an Enterprise Systems Implementation." *The Journal of Strategic Information Systems* 13, no. 4: 355–374. https://doi.org/10.1016/j.jsis.2004.11.005.

Lidová, Lenka, Alena Kajanová, and Šárka Tovt. 2015. "How Can Prejudices and Stereotypes Affect Everyday Life of Roma Women?" *Journal of Nursing, Social Studies, Public Health and Rehabilitation* 1–2: 40–45. http://casopis-zsfju.zsf.jcu.cz/journal-of-nursing-social-studies-public-health-and-rehabilitation/administrace/clankyfile/20150625075023234025.pdf.

McCombs, Maxwell E. 2004. *Setting the Agenda: The Mass Media and Public Opinion.* Cambridge, UK: Blackwell.

Mir-Hosseini, Ziba. 2006. "Muslim Women's Quest for Equality: Between Islamic Law and Feminism." *Critical Inquiry* 32, no. 4: 629–645.

Patterson, Molly, and Kristen Renwick Monroe. 1998. "Narrative in Political Science." *Annual Review of Political Science* 1: 315–331.

Peterson, Randall S. 2016. "Four Steps to Leading Diverse Teams Effectively." *London Business School Review* 27, no. 3: 40–43. https://doi.org/https://doi.org/10.1111/2057-1615.12140.

Poushter, Jacob, and Janell Fetterolf. 2019. "A Changing World: Global Views on Diversity, Gender Equality, Family Life and the Importance of Religion." Global Attitudes Project, Pew Research Center. April 22. https://www.pewresearch.org/global/2019/04/22/a-changing-world-global-views-on-diversity-gender-equality-family-life-and-the-importance-of-religion/.

Sacco, Vincent F. 1995. "Media Constructions of Crime." *The Annals of the American Academy of Political and Social Science* 539, no. 1: 141–154. https://doi.org/10.1177/000271629553 9001011.

Shahi, Gautam Kishore, Anne Dirkson, and Tim A. Majchrzak. 2021. "An Exploratory Study of COVID-19 Misinformation on Twitter." *Online Social Networks and Media* 22: 100104. https://doi.org/10.1016/j.osnem.2020.100104.

Shell-Duncan, B., A. Moreau, K. Wander, and S. Smith. 2018. "The Role of Older Women in Contesting Norms Associated with Female Genital Mutilation/Cutting in Senegambia." *PLoS One* 13, no. 7: 1–19.

Snow, David A., E. Burke Rochford, Steven K. Worden, and Robert D. Benford. 1986. "Frame Alignment Processes, Micromobilization, and Movement Participation." *American Sociological Review* 51, no. 4: 464–481.

Steinem, Gloria. 1971. "A New Egalitarian Lifestyle." *The New York Times*, August 26. https://www.nytimes.com/1971/08/26/archives/a-new-egalitarian-life-style.html.

Sweeny, Chris. 2021. "Fighting the Spread of COVID-19 Misinformation." Harvard T. H. Chan School of Public Health. February 9. https://www.hsph.harvard.edu/news/features/fighting-the-spread-of-covid-19-misinformation/.

Towns, Ann E. 2012. "Norms and Social Hierarchies: Understanding Policy Diffusion 'from Below.'" *International Organization* 66, no. 2: 179–209.

Towns, Ann E. 2010. *Women and States: Norms and Hierarchies in International Society.* Cambridge: Cambridge University Press.

Utbildningsdepartementet. 2004. *Den könade förskolan—Om betydelsen av jämställdhet och genus i förskolans pedagogiska arbete. Delbetänkande av Delegationen för jämställdhet i förskolan.* Stockholm: SOU.

Weeda, Mehran. 2021. "Afghanistan: Women Are at the Forefront of Protests against the Taliban." *The Conversation*, September 13. https://theconversation.com/afghanistan-women-are-at-the-forefront-of-protests-against-the-taliban-167669.

Wiener, Antje. 2018. *Contestation and Constitution of Norms in Global International Relations.* Cambridge: Cambridge University Press.

Zaina, H., J. El Baba, A. Al Alami, A. Noor, and H. Hassouna. 2020. "Comparative Content Analysis of the Coverage of Black Lives Matter Protests by CNN and OAN from May 26 2016 to November 8 2020." *KIU Interdisciplinary Journal of Humanities and Social Sciences* 1, no. 3: 12–24. https://kijhus.kiu.ac.ug/assets/articles/1607427957_comparative-content-analysis-of-the-coverage-of-black-lives-matter-protests-by-cnn-and-oan-from-may-26-2016-to-november-8-2020.pdf.

SECTION V
CONCLUSION

20

Shaping a Future That Embraces Equity and Inclusion

The Agenda for Progress

Carla Koppell With contributions by Yvette Burton

The arc of the moral universe is long, but it bends towards justice.
—Reverend Martin Luther King Jr.[1]

The failure to embrace diversity and advance inclusion has created fissures that are tearing at the seams of societies around the world. Daily newspaper headlines and contemporary trends reveal the lack of equity and inclusion to be vital concerns globally. Greater focus is long overdue. Properly prioritizing inclusion and equity always has been moral, ethical, and fair; today, it is essential to continued stability and prosperity.

This volume considers proven ways to leverage and celebrate diversity and foster inclusion. The chapters speak to theory and practice. The multinational group of authors offer best practices and lessons learned from around the world; they embody and symbolize the diverse, global community committed to advancing inclusion and equity.

This concluding chapter discusses the road forward. Drawing on the book as a whole to advance conclusions that are cross-cutting, it begins with a granular discussion of how programs, research, and advocacy can do better. The text then considers larger, more transformational changes that are advised. The book concludes discussing the magnitude of potential gains, and the challenge ahead.

Critical Next Steps for Progress

Emerging from the text is an unmistakable conclusion: there is a lot of room for progress. The world is rife with inequality, marginalization, and discrimination. Equally apparent is the lack of attention to fostering—and, in some quarters, interest in offering —greater inclusion.

The book as a whole reveals that current structures, systems, and organizations could do a great deal to help advance inclusion without radical transformation. Concurrently, progress could be driven by advocacy that builds on lessons from the ongoing movements highlighted in Section II. Focusing on progress in specific ways would enable substantial improvement.

Among the highest priorities is the urgent need for *strengthened data and analysis*. Problems can't be addressed if they cannot be seen. Too often, disparities are invisible because data isn't collected or analyzed to reveal who is ahead and who is falling behind. This book reveals throughout why more granular data is critical to addressing disparities and to spurring people to action and advocacy for vulnerable and marginalized groups.

Examples continually arise. Disaggregated data was critically important and valuable to recognizing that Blacks, Hispanics, and Native Americans in the United States suffered far higher infection and mortality rates during the COVID-19 pandemic.[2] Data was also used to try to prioritize greater equity in vaccine distribution, and it revealed how women and people of diverse backgrounds faced greater economic challenges in pandemic recovery.[3] Dissemination of granular information strengthened the foundation for effective response in the short term, and for addressing underlying disparities in the longer term. The visibility of the inequality also rallied people to action and helped steer more effective planning for response and recovery.

Yet data and statistics spotlighting disparities often remain stubbornly unavailable. Efforts to advance gender equality and women's and girls' empowerment are aided tremendously by data revealing the cost of women's disempowerment and the yawning disparities between men's and women's well-being. (Discussions of gender inequality were most frequent across this book because they are substantially better documented by data.) For virtually every other marginalized group, data is spotty at a global level, and absent in many countries and communities. The same is true for data on subgroups, such as women of different ethnic or racial backgrounds, and data at subnational levels. This makes progress far more difficult. It becomes harder to make the case for inclusion to skeptics, and to design and evaluate the effectiveness of interventions intended to reach across subcommunities.

Quantitative and qualitative assessments of the added value from focusing on inclusion and addressing inequality are even less common, but those too are very important. As discussed in Chapter 9, the movement for more inclusive peacebuilding is boosted by research revealing that peace processes are more likely to succeed and endure when civil society and women are included. Similarly, Chapter 15 demonstrates that a focus on empowerment in development is enhanced by evaluative evidence showing that the gains are greater when inclusion and equality are advanced. A child nutrition project in Bangladesh, implemented by CARE, paired work to advance women's empowerment with a series of other interventions; the project evaluation showed that the focus on women's empowerment enhanced the impact of other interventions on children's nutritional well-being while also elevating women's voice and influence.[4] That conclusion was clear only because CARE invested in an evaluation that teased out the impacts of different interventions and various combinations of interventions. Unfortunately, few assessments specify how focusing on inclusion enhances the broader impact of projects and programs.

Better use of global benchmarks and indices that reflect collective well-being also unmasks disparities. One example: the standard global measure of countries' progress is per capita GDP. But that average calculation obscures vast disparities in income and well-being among groups within countries. It also reduces well-being to a simplistic general calculation of goods and services across the economy. Embracing alternatives, such as the Inclusive Wealth Index, gives greater insight into society and the inequalities that persist.[5] Economists including Thandika Mkandawire, Branko Milanović, Dennis Snower, and Thomas Piketty have all considered how better to approach global understanding and appreciation of societal well-being and wealth in light of, and in order to tackle, persistent and growing inequalities.[6]

The evolution by the United Nations from the Millenium Development Goals (2000–2015) to the Sustainable Development Goals (2015–2030) is a hopeful sign; commitments to inclusion are woven throughout the SDGs, with marginalized and vulnerable groups specifically recognized and indicators of progress to shared prosperity embedded in the metrics. Hopefully, the SDGs mark recognition that more fulsome assessments of national (and individual) well-being are essential.

A greater focus on outcomes and results also drives inclusion. Today, programs often measure success based on inputs, such as dollars invested, or outputs, like training sessions completed. Peace negotiations focus on accords signed. Shifting the focus to evaluations of outcomes and impact increases the pressure to foster inclusion and to make investments in programs that truly make change. For example, measuring the success of development programs by the resulting increase in beneficiary income or employment status obligates program implementers to confirm meaningful program results. Further, it creates an incentive to look for program participants who benefit most, because they reflect well on projects. It also helps drive inclusion, given the evidence that inclusiveness delivers results for development.

Similarly, when durable peace and security are used to measure successful peace negotiations, it pushes mediators to focus on peace accord implementation and the quality of the post-conflict process, as called for in Chapter 10. There is less inclination to continue focusing predominantly on getting combatants to sign accords that have little hope of enduring. Additionally, it removes the incentive to generate verbal commitments to peace that are abandoned shortly thereafter.

Increased attentiveness to and management of technology and its impacts is also essential. Technology can be a vehicle for development, for social justice, and for greater mutual understanding among diverse groups around the world. Mobile phones provide access to banking and financial services, as well as education.[7] Improved seed varieties reduce vulnerability to droughts and pests.[8] Debit cards and mobile money facilitate humanitarian relief distribution. The #MeToo and

#BlackLivesMatter movements raise global awareness of and solidarity around, respectively, the need to fight gender-based violence and advance women's rights, and the need to confront racism.[9]

But while technology has enormous potential to deliver for everyone, today its benefits are often overshadowed by its costs. Unequal access is creating societies with haves and have-nots. For instance, the OECD reports that "some 327 million fewer women than men have a smartphone and can access the mobile Internet." And COVID-19 exacerbated existing inequalities. In Africa, the poorest children had difficulty accessing online education; less than 1 percent of these households have access to the internet and/or computers, while over 20 percent of the wealthiest families have a computer and/or internet access.[10] As noted in Chapter 1, digital communications platforms are also often sources of divisiveness and misinformation. Further, they can be tools of state repression.[11] And misuse and abuse of new channels of communication undermine systems of governance and drive polarization.

To flip back the narrative so that technology is harnessed for good, a concerted global effort is needed. Malign actors need to be removed. Resources need to be dedicated to ensuring universal access to advanced technology. Communication channels need to be regulated to ensure they disseminate reliable information, build bridges, and foster mutual understanding. In essence, the global community needs to ensure that technology helps advance progress by building social capital, fostering social inclusion, and closing disparities in power, wealth, and influence among different subpopulations.

Engaging the broader range of local stakeholders is key. Reading across this volume, it becomes clear that there are concrete benefits to engaging with a broader range of people in countries and communities. As Chapter 18 explains, those who work and lead locally in different segments of economies and societies can problem-solve in creative, unique ways. This is true in conflict resolution, post-conflict reconstruction, environmental management, development, and advocacy. In the absence of broad engagement, peacebuilding and development efforts are stymied.

Equally important, local people often better understand their local contexts. The case study of Afghanistan in Chapter 19 is illustrative. Domestic experts are uniquely situated to help navigate and transform local norms and cultures. Though some local people perpetuate antiquated ideas, others are vanguards of change, brave and committed to progress. Leveraging their knowledge and personal investment in peace and prosperity is essential to the sustainability of interventions. An Overseas Development Institute analysis confirmed that foreign-funded civil society organizations tend to be costlier and to have less durable impact.[12]

Unfortunately, the vast majority of funds for development and peacebuilding are invested through foreign organizations led and staffed mostly by foreign experts. A very small proportion flows to local organizations or local governments. In fact, "of the $4.1 billion that US foundations gave overseas between 2011 and 2015, just 12% went directly to local organizations based in the country where programming occurred."[13] A far smaller percentage of that funding goes to local organizations led by women or representatives of other marginalized groups.[14] That funding may also be less flexible, and support short-term projects rather than long-term efforts.[15] Moreover, requirements for local engagement, local subcontracting, and local participation are usually limited. Across the board, interventions are substantially enriched when local organizations and local experts are engaged and involved and when local knowledge is valued. It also results in more sustainable investments.

Designing programs that address exclusion and inequality even as they promote development and address conflict accelerates change. Today, many interventions are designed with a single, primary focus—to promote economic, political, or social well-being; to prevent, resolve, or rebuild following conflict; or to address exclusion and inequality. Experts are prepared to work in one domain or another. But, as discussed in Chapter 2, it's fairly clear that maximal benefit accrues from attending to multiple objectives—that is, from tackling exclusion while addressing conflict and development.

Promoting equity and inclusion as part of development and peacebuilding efforts enhances the likelihood of enhanced impact and offers broader societal benefits. Efforts to halt the spread of transmissible diseases fail if they cannot reach all afflicted subpopulations. As outlined throughout the book, whole populations suffer from the economic marginalization of women, LGBTQI populations, Indigenous peoples, and others. Additionally, inclusion in one effort also often delivers benefits later. For example, as touched on in Chapter 3, a flagging disarmament, demobilization, and reintegration effort in Liberia was facilitated because women were engaged in the peace talks; had they been shut out during negotiations, it would have been far more difficult to leverage their skills and networks when implementing the accord.

Similarly advantageous is an enhanced focus on conflict prevention while advancing development. As Chapter 1 explains, the countries that are less developed are increasingly the same ones that are fragile or conflict-affected. It is, therefore, ever more important to address drivers of conflict, including grievance or marginalization. Explicitly considering how investments impact social cohesion, as well as wealth and resource distribution, helps development investments contribute to stability and security. Similarly, it reduces the risk that interventions inadvertently increase inequalities or inflame divisions within societies.

Big-Picture Observations and Needs

The discrete steps just enumerated deliver important incremental progress. But true transformation requires bigger changes. Several of the chapters allude to the larger challenges that deserve more attention, given their import and long-term implications.

First of all, the international affairs profession needs to look inward. This book calls for promoting development, addressing conflict, and fostering good governance by engaging a wider range of participants and delivering for a broader mix of beneficiaries. Yet, with the exception of brief explorations in Chapter 11 of the security sector and in Chapter 16 of the justice sector, as well as Chapter 13 on humanitarian assistance, authors don't consider the lack of diversity within international relations itself, as well as within the subfields of development, conflict resolution, and peacebuilding.

The reality today is that international affairs does not leverage the full range of voices and perspectives when promoting peace and prosperity globally. Men from the majority subpopulations in countries comprise the largest share of senior leaders of foreign ministries, donor assistance agencies, and many non-governmental organizations and private firms addressing development and violent conflict. For example, a 2020 US Government Accountability Office report found that the proportion of African Americans and women within the US Department of State civil service actually decreased from 34 to 26 percent and from 61 to 54 percent, respectively, over the last fifteen years.[16] Release of that report just preceded and has fed into a critical reevaluation of race issues in the American international affairs field (see Box 20.1).

Box 20.1 Diversity in International Affairs: Reflections on the United States
Yvette Burton

By definition, the United States' journey toward "a more perfect union" centers on becoming one community of belonging. The United States' foreign policy mission assumes a clear understanding of the dynamics of diversity in American policy, cross-sector partnerships, learned lessons about inclusion-driven aspirations, and shared objectives:

> The U.S. Department of State leads America's foreign policy through diplomacy, advocacy, and assistance by advancing the interests of the American people, their safety and economic prosperity.[17]

Yet the degree to which America is able to connect diverse communities in mutual interest is proportional to its ability to join those diverse countries in common global purpose. When leaders limit their consideration of civil rights in America to its local implications, they promulgate unintended socially constructed values and principles; codification of irresponsible attitudes and behaviors; and a distorted global baseline of what is expected from all nations. Further, leaders and organizations have limited understanding of diverse contexts and perspectives, positioning them poorly to predict and react to civil unrest and global affairs.

For centuries, race has been a central organizing element of world politics. However, international relations agencies and scholarship do not appreciate that racial diversity, inclusion, and equity are critical to understanding the world. Not understanding these connections is corrosive of the field's integrity. The anti-Japanese racist posture underlying US engagement in World War II fostered the broader anti-Asian sentiment that shaped the North Atlantic Treaty Organization. The racial lens of the Cold War shaped the US approach to Africa, Asia, Central America, the Caribbean, and South America. Today, the murder of George Floyd is widely viewed as a step toward a more democratic United States. Black Lives Matter is the Arab Spring for America, an "American Spring." This is a moment of opportunity in international affairs as well.

International institutions have the unique ability to transform the landscape of state interests. This shift of intent is not achievable without access to diverse insights stemming from a diverse workforce and leadership practices. In the private sector, organizations and companies have established global policies and practices that demonstrate the value of inclusion to performance. Diversity, equity, and inclusion are presented as a mature framework for enabling organizations to seize a broad set of opportunities. The emphasis is on the organization's ability to harness the richness in the diversity of its human capital. This stands in contrast to most international affairs institutions, where employee efforts at self-help are sometimes framed as working against the goals and mission of the enterprise.

During times of great uncertainty, the world looks to the United States as a north star of values and purpose. The international affairs community's commitment to building a safer and more democratic world begins with people. Traditionally underrepresented and marginalized groups can help magnify US influence in the pursuit of equality and justice throughout global society. International relations institutions must cultivate inclusiveness and empower all people to grow personally and professionally. To effectively advance US foreign policy objectives, boundary-spanning partnerships and a systems view are mission critical.

Diversity within organizations offers concrete benefits for operations. Private companies with diverse corporate boardrooms are more profitable. Heterogeneous problem-solving teams get better results.[18] Diverse leadership teams benefit organizations, particularly as the workforce becomes more diverse.[19] Nonetheless, diversity and inclusion are not prioritized in international programs, in part because the teams designing, implementing, and evaluating those programs often aren't diverse.

An emphasis on inclusion in international affairs is long overdue. Such a focus would enable better modeling of the inclusion and equality sought through international law and program interventions. The practice would benefit from the broader range of perspectives brought by a more varied workforce. The emphasis on diversity and inclusion in addressing conflict and development would also increase. Most fundamentally, organizations working to promote peace and prosperity globally would better reflect the world in which we live.

Even as we think about the sector itself, *critical reflection on historical narratives is needed,* as those narratives shape opinions and perspectives regarding the community of nations. Chapter 8 discusses how portrayals of history are shaped and framed by perspectives and preconceived notions that are one-sided or false. Frequently, experts and professionals are unaware of these biases, which are perpetuated by versions of history that gloss over (or write out) the ways discrimination and marginalization have shaped storylines.

For example, throughout history racism has influenced foreign policy decision-making and international relations theory.[20] Anti-Asian bias shaped US engagement in World War II, and it influences global immigration, refugee, and counterterrorism policy today. Yet there is limited discussion of how biases drive policy, sidelining a recurring theme of international affairs policymaking.

Similarly, the international affairs community has defined "developing" and "developed" countries, with "developed countries" typically characterized as nations generally more capable of delivering for their populations. But these generalizations no longer apply. In 2020, aid-assisted countries such as Jordan, and Bosnia and Herzegovina had longer life expectancies than Denmark and the United States.[21] "Developed countries" such as Italy, Spain, United States, and the United Kingdom had COVID-19 case fatality rates exceeding those of many "developing countries," including Ghana, Ethiopia, Nepal, and Bangladesh.[22]

Narratives, sometimes patronizing and discriminatory, also shape perspectives regarding international engagement overall. Symbolic in this regard is the evolution of the name of the journal *Foreign Affairs,* which launched in 1910 as *The Journal of Race Development* and featured articles such as "The Point of View Towards Primitive Races." Central to analyses at the time was the view that there were "civilized" and "uncivilized" people; this perspective informed vibrant debates over how "higher races" should treat "lower races."[23]

Development assistance is similarly burdened by its history. Long presented as beneficent charity to lesser peoples, foreign aid has not evolved with the changing status of nations and growing global interdependence, with the incredible human capacity within "developing countries," or with the wealth, resources, and influence of "emerging economies." Nor is there general appreciation or understanding of the critical benefits that accrue to the global community and to donors from investments that ensure global environmental protection; prevent the spread of disease; provide markets, partners, and resources to enhance global trade; or build alliances and relationships around the world.

Only by reassessing and dismissing false, biasing conceptualizations of the international landscape and acknowledging the racist, sexist narratives that often prevail can a more accurate vision of cooperation and collaboration emerge.

Beyond narratives, *essential reflections on the structures and institutions that govern international relations* are needed. While this book is premised on the idea that equity and inclusion can be advanced in essential ways working with and through existing institutions, there are those who believe that may not be possible. Vitalis, Seth, Andrews, and Acharya, among others, question and examine whether and how systems and organizations born of colonialism, Eurocentrism, sexism, and racism can truly advance equity, inclusion, and justice.[24]

At a minimum, it is clear that *global governance needs to adapt.* The world has evolved profoundly since many global governance institutions were put in place following World War II. In the ashes of war, multilateral organizations were structured to provide a forum for discussion among member nation-states, particularly the most powerful and wealthiest in the postwar period.

Fast forward more than seventy-five years and the world has changed. The constellation of global players is different. The United Nations had 51 member states when it was founded in 1945; today there are 193 member states.[25] But changes in power and influence haven't led to altered UN leadership structures. Newer countries and emerging economies have limited scope for being heard and expanding their influence.

Additionally, nongovernmental actors—notwithstanding their importance or impact on world events—have few platforms to engage meaningfully in formal international settings. Existing structures marginalize the voices of anyone who is not part of formal national governments around the world: civil society groups; people underrepresented in formal government, including women, youth, people with disabilities, and Indigenous peoples; and ethnic, linguistic, and religious minorities. Chapter 7 discusses this in greatest detail with regard to Indigenous peoples, but it is a recurrent theme throughout the book. Somewhat ironically, it is often these people whom the international legal instruments advancing human rights (described throughout Section II, and in Chapter 2 and Chapter 17) are designed to advance and protect; these groups continue to be seriously marginalized in global governance and decision-making.

Recognize It's Hard

The strongest foundation for progress comes from large-scale reflection and transformation. But that will take time, a great deal of advocacy, and a lot of goodwill. Contemporary events reveal that few leaders are inclined to share wealth, power, and influence, much less cede them. That should not deter progress. But it presents a substantial impediment.

Supporting the growing global consensus that greater inclusion and equality are needed is ever stronger evidence of their benefits; as a result, there are more supporters for advancing these laudable goals. There is also increasing pushback. Some leaders are trying to hide the evidence. Others have started to question the fact base, sowing seeds of doubt regarding the mounting research that elevating collective well-being is important and valuable. Still others are trying to roll back rules and policies that were put in place to advance inclusion and equality. All of this is happening because some groups and individuals don't want to share power and wealth. They are willing to sacrifice the long-term well-being of many for the short-term benefit of a few.

Simultaneously, there is growing global understanding that inclusion and equity are smart, ethical goals. Numerous movements globally, particularly among young people, provide a tremendous foundation to build on. Yet even among allies there are challenges. Recognizing and honoring the differences among people and within communities can be fraught. Unintended insults are common.[26] Resentment of those who benefit from privilege sometimes sparks division, even among like-minded people. Rather than fostering an embrace of difference and uniqueness, recognition of each individual's multiple identities can result in ever greater fragmentation, and create barriers rather than bridges. Additionally, in a world of constrained resources, the allocation of limited funds and opportunities can lead to divisive competition; it is challenging to determine who are most deserving, who should be prioritized, and the criteria that should be used to address inequity and to rectify past wrongs.

Transforming unequal societies requires a willingness to address biases that have been baked into organizations and structures over centuries. Further, it requires an openness to critically examining and unwinding narratives that introduce and perpetuate exclusion and inequality. And it requires doing so without creating further alienation and polarization. Perhaps most fundamentally, advancing inclusion and equality will require sharing wealth, power, and opportunity among a broader share of the world's population.

The Road Ahead

A global embrace of diversity requires work, as does a comprehensive push for inclusion that results in greater equality. That said, there are many clear ways to pursue progress. Creating and sustaining momentum will be fundamental.

One key will be recruiting ever more allies. Today, many people are not focused on—or aware of—the disparities that exist. Similarly, they are not cognizant of how we all benefit from greater diversity or more fulsome inclusion. There is an enormous need to educate people and raise awareness. The best approaches to persuasion will vary. Some people will be convinced by appealing to their morality and sympathy, providing insight into the harm being done to marginalized and vulnerable people around the world. Others will be persuaded by a pragmatic case that brings forward the evidence of the forgone benefits resulting from exclusion and isolation. Still others will need to be compelled to comply with legal mandates to act in the best interests of whole communities. Critical will be broad-based engagement with people across government and civil society, as well as those working locally, nationally, and globally.

We can meet today's greatest challenges—such as climate change and global health pandemics—only by working as one global community. Further, we will triumph only by mobilizing and harnessing the intellect, skills, and goodwill of all the world's citizens. The charge today is to create a global ecosystem where all people—regardless of identity, status, or residence—can contribute to and benefit from the fruits of their labor. Only by advancing inclusion and equality can we channel that untapped power into collective problem solving for global good.

Notes

1. Martin Luther King Jr., recipient of the 1964 Nobel Peace Prize, "Remaining Awake Through a Great Revolution," speech given at the National Cathedral, March 31, 1968.
2. Wilder 2020.
3. Ogedegbe and Inouye 2021; Flores et al. 2021; Madgavkar et al. 2020.
4. Nosbach, Champion, and ul Mutahara 2014.
5. United Nations University 2013.
6. Mkandawire 2001; Milanovic 2016; Snower 2019; Piketty and Goldhammer 2015.
7. Silver et al. 2020; World Bank 2017.
8. FAO 2014.
9. Hillstrom 2019.
10. World Bank 2020.
11. Frantz, Kendall-Taylor, and Wright 2020.
12. Glennie et al. 2012.
13. Peace Direct and Kantowitz 2020.
14. CARE 2021.
15. Peace Direct and Kantowitz 2020.
16. US Government Accountability Office 2020.
17. U.S. Department of State, n.d. Accessed on October 3, 2021.
18. Gupta 2019.
19. Hunt et al. 2020.
20. Zvobgo and Loken 2020; Anievas, Manchanda, and Shilliam 2015.
21. Geoba 2020.
22. Johns Hopkins University of Medicine 2020.
23. Hall 1910.
24. Vitalis 2015; Seth 2011; Andrews 2021; Acharya 2018.
25. United Nations n.d.

26. A "microaggression" is "a comment or action that subtly and often unconsciously or unintentionally expresses a prejudiced attitude toward a member of a marginalized group (such as a racial minority)" (Merriam-Webster n.d.). "Unconscious bias" refers to the "social stereotypes about certain groups of people that individuals form outside their own conscious awareness" (UCSF 2020).

Bibliography

Acharya, Amitav. 2018. *Constructing Global Order: Agency and Change in World Politics.* Cambridge: Cambridge University Press.

Andrews, Kehinde. 2021. *The New Age of Empire: How Racism and Colonialism Still Rule the World.* New York: Bold Type Books.

Anievas, Alexander, Nivi Manchanda, and Robbie Shilliam. 2015. *Race and Racism in International Relations: Confronting the Global Colour Line.* Milton Park: Routledge.

CARE. 2021. "Time for a Better Bargain: How the Aid System Shortchanges Women and Girls." February. https://www.care.org/wp-content/uploads/2021/03/She-Leads-in-Crisis-Report_4.7.21_updated.pdf.

FAO. 2014. "Appropriate Seed Varieties for Small-Scale Farmers." Food and Agricultural Organization of the United Nations. http://www.fao.org/3/a-i3768e.pdf.

Flores, L. E., et al. 2021. "Assessment of the Inclusion of Racial/Ethnic Minority, Female, and Older Individuals in Vaccine Clinical Trials." *JAMA Network Open* 4, no. 2: e2037640. doi: 10.1001/jamanetworkopen.2020.37640.

Frantz, Erica, Andrea Kendall-Taylor, and Joseph Wright. 2020. "Digital Repression in Autocracies." Varieties of Democracy Institute. March 2020. https://www.v-dem.net/media/filer_public/18/d8/18d8fc9b-3ff3-44d6-a328-799dc0132043/digital-repression17mar.pdf.

Geoba. 2020. "The World Population Top 100+ by Country (2020)." Geoba Gazetteer. http://www.geoba.se/population.php?pc=world.

Glennie, Jonathan, Ahmed Ali, Maia King, Alastair McKechnie, and Gideon Rabinowitz. 2012. "Localizing Aid: Can Using Local Actors Strengthen Them?" Overseas Development Institute. https://odi.org/en/publications/localising-aid-can-using-local-actors-strengthen-them/.

Gupta, P. 2019. "Top Management Team Heterogeneity, Corporate Social Responsibility Disclosure and Financial Performance." *American Journal of Industrial and Business Management* 9: 1076–1093. doi: 10.4236/ajibm.2019.94074.

Hall, G. Stanley. 1910. "The Point of View Toward Primitive Races." *The Journal of Race Development* 1, no. 1: 5–11. doi: 10.2307/29737843.

Hillstrom, Laurie Collier. 2019. *The #MeToo Movement.* Santa Barbara, CA: ABC-CLIO.

Hunt, Vivian, Lareina Yee, Sara Prince, and Sundiatu Dixon-Fyle. 2020. "Delivering Through Diversity." McKinsey & Company. January 17. https://www.mckinsey.com/business-functions/organization/our-insights/delivering-through-diversity.

Johns Hopkins University of Medicine. 2020. "Mortality Analyses: Mortality in the Most Affected Countries." Johns Hopkins Coronavirus Resource Center. https://coronavirus.jhu.edu/data/mortality.

Madgavkar, Anu, Olivia White, Mekala Krishnan, Deepa Mahajan, and Xavier Azcue. 2020. "COVID-19 and Gender Equality: Countering the Regressive Effects." McKinsey & Company. July 17. https://www.mckinsey.com/featured-insights/future-of-work/covid-19-and-gender-equality-countering-the-regressive-effects.

Merriam-Webster. n.d. "Microaggression." Accessed October 12, 2020. https://www.merriam-webster.com/dictionary/microaggression.

Milanovic, Branko. 2016. *Global Inequality: A New Approach for the Age of Globalization.* Cambridge, MA: Harvard University Press.

Mkandawire, Thandika. 2001. "Social Policy in a Development Context." United Nations Research Institute for Social Development. Programme Paper Number 7. https://www.unrisd.

org/80256B3C005BCCF9/httpNetITFramePDF?ReadForm&parentunid=C83739F8E9A9A
A0980256B5E003C5225&parentdoctype=paper&netitpath=80256B3C005BCCF9/(httpA
uxPages)/C83739F8E9A9AA0980256B5E003C5225/$file/mkandaw1.pdf.

Nosbach, Marc, Heather Champion, and Mariam ul Mutahara. 2014. "Women's
Empowerment: The Journey So Far: The Experience of the SHOUHARDO Program in
Bangladesh." CARE and US Agency for International Development. https://care.org/wp-cont
ent/uploads/2020/05/SHOUHARDO20Women27s20Empowerment20Report.pdf.

Ogedegbe, Gbenga, and Sharon K. Inouye. 2021. "Injustice in Health: Now Is the Time to Change
the Story." Editorial. *Annals of Internal Medicine*. July. https://doi.org/10.7326/M21-1279.

Peace Direct and Riva Kantowitz. 2020. "Radical Flexibility: Strategic Funding for the Age of
Local Activism." Peace Insight. https://www.peaceinsight.org/reports/peacefund.

Seth, Sanjay. 2011. "Postcolonial Theory and the Critique of International Relations." *Millennium*
40, no. 1: 167–183. https://doi.org/10.1177/0305829811412325.

Silver, Laura, Aaron Smith, Courtney Johnson, Jingjing Jiang, Monica Anderson, and Lee Rainie.
2020. "Mobile Connectivity in Emerging Economies." Internet, Science & Tech, Pew Research
Center. September 11.

Snower, Dennis J. 2019. "Toward Human-Centered Capitalism." Brookings Brief. November.
https://www.brookings.edu/wp-content/uploads/2019/11/Toward-human-centered-capitali
sm_20191106.pdf.

UCSF. 2020. "Unconscious Bias." Office of Diversity and Outreach, University of California, San
Francisco. https://diversity.ucsf.edu/resources/unconscious-bias.

United Nations. n.d. "Growth in United Nations Membership." https://www.un.org/en/about-us/
growth-in-un-membership.

United Nations University. 2013. "Towards Building a Sustainable Society: What Is the Inclusive
Wealth Index?" UNU Office of Communications. January 1. https://unu.edu/events/archive/
lecture/what-is-the-inclusive-wealth-index.html.

US Department of State. 2021. "About." Accessed October 2, 2021. https://www.state.gov/about/.

US Government Accountability Office. 2020. "State Department: Additional Steps Are Needed
to Identify Potential Barriers to Diversity." January 27. https://www.gao.gov/reports/GAO-
20-237/.

Vitalis, Robert. 2015. *White World Order, Black Power Politics: The Birth of American International
Relations*. Ithaca, NY: Cornell University Press. http://www.jstor.org/stable/10.7591/j.ctt
20fw654.

Wilder, Julius M. 2020. "The Disproportionate Impact of COVID-19 on Racial and Ethnic
Minorities in the United States." *Clinical Infectious Diseases* 72, no. 4: 707–709. https://doi.org/
10.1093/cid/ciaa959.

World Bank. 2020. "Digital Technologies in Education." https://www.worldbank.org/en/topic/
edutech.

World Bank. 2017. "Global Findex: Access to Mobile Phones and the Internet Around the World."
Global Findex. https://globalfindex.worldbank.org/.

Zvobgo, Kelebogile, and Meredith Loken. 2020. "Why Race Matters in International Relations."
Foreign Policy. June 19. https://foreignpolicy.com/2020/06/19/why-race-matters-internatio
nal-relations-ir/.

Index

For the benefit of digital users, indexed terms that span two pages (e.g., 52–53) may, on occasion, appear on only one of those pages.

Tables, figures, and boxes are indicated by *t*, *f*, and *b* following the page number